9.27.01

Literature and
Its Times

VOLUME 3

Growth of Empires to the
Great Depression
(1890-1930s)

Literature and Its Times

Profiles of 300 Notable Literary Works and
the Historical Events that Influenced Them

Joyce Moss • George Wilson

GALE

DETROIT   NEW YORK   TORONTO   LONDON

Literature and Its Times

Profiles of 300 Notable Literary Works and the Historical Events that Influenced Them

VOLUME 3

Growth of Empires to the Great Depression (1890-1930s)

JOYCE MOSS • GEORGE WILSON

STAFF

Jeff Hill and Lawrence J. Trudeau, *Production Editors*
Susan Trosky, *Permissions Manager*
Kimberly F. Smilay, *Permissions Specialist*

Mary Beth Trimper, *Production Director*
Evi Seoud, *Production Manager*
Shanna Heilveil, *Production Assistant*

Cynthia Baldwin, *Product Design Manager*
Mary Claire Krzewinski, *Senior Art Director*

Barbara J. Yarrow, *Graphic Services Supervisor*
Randy Bassett, *Image Database Supervisor*
Robert Duncan, *Scanner Operator*
Pamela Hayes, *Photography Coordinator*

∞™The paper used in this publication meets the minimum requirements of American National Standard for Information Sciences—Permanence Paper for Printed Library Materials, ANSI Z39.48-1984.

ISBN 0-7876-0606-5 (Set)
ISBN 0-7876-0609-X (Volume 3)

Printed in the United States of America
10 9 8 7 6 5 4 3

Library of Congress Cataloging-in-Publication Data

Literature and its times : profiles of 300 notable literary works and the historical events that influenced them / [edited by Joyce Moss and George Wilson].
       p.   cm.
   Includes bibliographical references and index.
   Contents: v. 1. Ancient times to the American and French Revolutions, (pre-history-1790s) -- v. 2. Civil wars to frontier societies (1800-1880s) -- v. 3. Growth of empires to the Great Depression (1890-1930s) -- v. 4. World War II to the affluent fifties (1940-1950s) -- v. 5. Civil rights movements to future times (1960-2000).
   ISBN 0-7876-0607-3 (vol. 1 : alk. paper). -- ISBN 0-7876-0608-1 (vol. 2 : alk. paper). -- ISBN 0-7876-0609-X (vol. 3 : alk. paper). -- ISBN 0-7876-0610-3 (vol. 4 : alk. paper). -- ISBN 0-7876-0611-1 (vol. 5 : alk. paper)
   1. Literature and history. 2. History in literature. 3. Literature--History and criticism.
I. Moss, Joyce, 1951-   . II. Wilson, George, 1920-   .
PN50.L574 1997
809'.93358--dc21

                                                      97-34339
                                                      CIP

Contents

Preface. vii

Acknowledgments xi

Introduction xiii

Chronology of Relevant Events xv

Contents by Title xxvii

Contents by Author xxix

Photo Credits. xxxi

Entries.   1

Index. 433

Preface

"Even a great writer can be bound by the prejudices of his time . . . we cannot place Shakespeare in a sealed container. He belonged to his time," notes Alexander Leggatt in his essay "*The Merchant of Venice*: A Modern Perspective" (William Shakespeare, *The Merchant of Venice* [New York: Washington Square Press, 1992], 217). This reasoning, applicable to any work and its author, explains why *Literature and Its Times* fixes a wide range of novels, short stories, biographies, speeches, poems, and plays in the context of their particular historical periods.

In the process, the relationship between fact and fantasy or invention becomes increasingly clear. The function of literature is not necessarily to represent history accurately. Many writers aim rather to spin a satisfying tale or perhaps to convey a certain vision or message. Nevertheless, the images created by a powerful literary work—be it the Greek poem *Iliad*, the Spanish novel *The Adventures of Don Quixote,* or the American play *The Crucible*—leave impressions that are commonly taken to be historical. This is true from works that depict earlier eras to ones that portray more modern occurrences, such as the world wars or race relations. The fourteenth-century poem *Inferno* from the *Divine Comedy* by Dante Alighieri is probably the most powerful example. So vividly does *Inferno* describe Hell that for more than two centuries people took its description as truth, going so far as to map Hell according to the details of the poem.

In taking literature as fact, then, one risks acquiring a mistaken or an unverified notion of history. Yet, by the same token, history can be very well informed by literary works. An author may portray events in a way that for the first time aptly captures the fears and challenges of a period, enabling readers to better understand it and their own place in the historical continuum. This is easily illustrated by tracing novels that feature women's issues, from Nathaniel Hawthorne's *The Scarlet Letter* (1640s setting) to Leo Tolstoy's *Anna Karenina* (1870s) to Alice Walker's *The Color Purple* (1920s–40s) and Amy Tan's *The Joy Luck Club* (1940s–80s).

Placing a given work in historical context involves pinpointing conditions in the society in which it was written as well as set. Stephen Crane's *Red Badge of Courage* is set in the early 1860s. Published three decades later, it was written in a different social context and, in this case, in response to a literary trend of Crane's own era. Only by gaining insight into this era as well as the one in which the work takes place can it be fully appreciated; *Literature and Its Times* therefore addresses the author's time frame too.

The task of reconstructing the historical contexts of a work can be problematic. There are stories—the tales of England's King Arthur, for example—that defy any attempt to fit them neatly into a particular time. Living in a later era, their authors, consciously or not, mixed events that actually belong to two or more different periods. In some cases, this is an innocent mistake by a writer who did not have the benefit of accurate sources. In other cases, fidelity to the actual events of the time is of little concern to the writer; his or her main interest is the fictional world to be portrayed. In still other cases, the mixture of times is intentional. Happily, present-day knowledge makes it possible for this series to begin unweaving the historical mixture in these types of works.

Literature and Its Times relates history to literature on a case-by-case basis, intending to help readers respond fully to a work and to assist them in distinguishing fact from invention in the work. The series engages in this mission with a warm appreciation for the beauty of literature independent of historical facts, but also with the belief that ultimate regard is shown for a literary work and its author by positioning it in the context of pertinent events.

Selection of Literary Works

Literature and Its Times includes novels, short stories, plays, poems, biographies, essays, speeches, and documents. The works chosen for inclusion have been carefully selected on the basis of how frequently they are studied and how closely they are tied to pivotal historical events. Reflected in the selection are works not only by classic and still widely read authors but also by noteworthy ethnic and female authors. To finalize the selection, the complete list of titles was submitted to a panel of librarians, secondary teachers, and college professors. Please see "Acknowledgments" for a specific listing of these reviewers.

Format and Arrangement of Entries

The five volumes of *Literature and Its Times* are arranged chronologically from ancient times to the present. The set of entries within each volume is arranged alphabetically by title. As the series progresses, the range of years covered in each successive volume grows narrower due to the increasing number of works published in more recent times.

Each entry is organized according to the following sections.

1. **Introduction**—identifying information in three parts:

   The literary work—describes the genre, the time and place of the work, and the year(s) it was first performed or published;

   Synopsis—summarizes the storyline or contents;

   Introductory paragraph—introduces the literary work in relation to the author's life.

2. ***Events in History at the Time the Literary Work Takes Place***—describes social and political events that relate to the plot or contents of the literary work and that occurred during the period the story takes place. Subsections vary depending on the literary work. The section takes a deductive approach, starting with events in history and telescoping inward to events in the literary work.

3. ***The Literary Work in Focus***—describes in brief the plot or contents of the work. Generally this summary is followed by a subsection on one or more elements in the work that illuminate real events or attitudes of the period. The subsection takes an inductive approach, starting with the literary work and broadening outward to events in history. It is usually followed by a third subsection detailing the sources used by the author to create the work.

4. ***Events in History at the Time the Literary Work Was Written***—describes social, political, and/or literary events in the author's lifetime that relate to the plot or contents of the work. When relevant, the section includes events in the author's life. Also discussed in the section are the initial reviews or reception accorded to the literary work.

5. ***For More Information***—provides a list of all sources that have been cited in the entry as well as sources for further reading about the different issues or personalities featured in the entry.

If a literary work is set and written in the same time period, sections 2 and 4 of the entry on that work ("Events in History at the Time the Literary Work Takes Place" and "Events in History at the Time the Literary Work Was Written") are combined into the single section "Events in History at the Time of the Literary Work."

Additional Features

Whenever possible, primary source material is provided through quotations in the text and material in sidebars. There are also sidebars with historical details that amplify issues raised in the main text and with anecdotes that give readers a fuller understanding of the temporal context. Timelines appear in various entries to summarize intricate periods of history. To enrich and further clarify information, historically noteworthy illustrations have been included in the series. Maps as well as photographs provide visual images of potentially unfamiliar settings.

Comments and Suggestions

Your comments on this series and suggestions for future editions are welcome. Please write: Editors, *Literature and Its Times,* Gale Research, Inc., 835 Penobscot Building, Detroit, Michigan 48226-4094; or call toll-free: 1-800-877-4253.

Acknowledgments

For their careful review of entries in *Literature and Its Times*, the following professors and lecturers from the University of California at Los Angeles (UCLA) deserve the deepest appreciation:

English Department

Robert Aguirre
Martha Banta
Lynn Batten
A. R. Braunmuller
Daphne Brooks
King-Kok Cheung
Michael Colacurcio
Ed Condren
Jack Kolb
Jinqui Ling
Chris Mott
Michael North
Barbara Packer
David Rodes
Karen Rowe

Comparative Literature Department

Eric Gans
Kathryn King
Mary Kay Norseng
Ross Shideler

Slavic Languages and Literature Department

Micheal Heim
Peter Hodgson

Gratitude is also extended to professors from other institutions for their valuable review of selected entries, and to history department chairman Robert Sumpter for his guidance and reviews:

Rabbi Stanley Chyet, Hebrew Union College
Agnes Moreland Jackson, Pitzer College, English and Black Studies
Michael McGaha, Pomona College, Romance Languages and Literatures— Spanish Section
Robert Sumpter, Mira Costa High School, History Department

A host of contributers assisted in collecting and composing data for the entries in *Literature and Its Times*. Their painstaking hours of research and composition are deeply appreciated.

Diane R. Ahrens
Eric A. Besner
Suzanne C. Borghei
Luke Bresky
Anne Brooks
Corey Brettschneider
Thomas Cooper
Patricia Carroll
Terence Davis
Mark Druskoff
Shelby Fulmer
Betsy Hedberg-Keramidas

Acknowledgments

Ryan Hilbert
Lisa Gabbert
Anne Kim
Amy Merritt
Michael Le Sieur
Barbara A. Lozano
Michele Mednick
Michelle Miller
Larry Mowrey
Evan Porter
Edward R. OþNeill
David Riemer
Monica Riordan
Jane E. Roddy
George Ross
Rita Schepergerdes
Roberta Seid
Shira Tarrant
Benjamin Trefny
Pete Trujillo
Lorraine B. Valestuk
Colin Wells
Sandra Wade-Grusky
Allison Weisz
Jeannie Wilkinson
Denise Wilson
Brandon Wilson
Antoine Wilson

A special thank you is extended to Lorraine B. Valestuk, Ph.D., for her refinement of data and to Cheryl Steets, Ph.D., for her deft copy editing. Anne Leach indexed the volumes with proficiency and literary sensitivity. The editors also thank Larry Trudeau and Jeff Hill of Gale Research for their careful editorial management.

Lastly the editors express gratitude to those who guided the final selection of literary works included in the series:

Neil Anstead, Director of Humanities,
   Los Angeles Unified School District
William Balcolm, Librarian,
   Villa Park Public Library, Villa Park, IL
Marth Banta, Professor,
   University of California at Los Angeles
Carol Clark, Head Librarian,
   Robert E. Lee High School, Springfield, VA
Chris García, Head Librarian,
   Beverly Hills Children's Library, Beverly Hills, CA
Nancy Guidry, Young Adult Librarian,
   Santa Monica Public Library, Santa Monica, CA
Kenneth M. Holmes, Ph.D.,
   Educational Consultant,
   Educational Concepts Unlimited, Bellville, IL
Carol Jago, Mentor Teacher,
   English Department, Santa Monica Public High School, Santa Monica, CA
Jim Merrill, Instructor,
   Oxnard Community College, Oxnard, CA
Mary Purucker, Head Librarian,
   Santa Monica High School, Santa Monica, CA
Karen Rowe, Professor,
   University of California at Los Angeles
Hilda K. Weisburg, Librarian,
   Sayreville War Memorial High School, Parlin, NJ
Dr. Brooke Workman, Teacher,
   West High School, Iowa City, IA
Richard Yarborough, Professor,
   University of California at Los Angeles

Introduction to Volume 3

Volume 3 of *Literature and Its Times* opens with literary works that examine the ideas of empire and community in post-Victorian Europe, and it ends just as the nations of the world are about to dispute territorial claims across the globe in World War II. Spanning times in which war, revolution, and economic depression were ravaging nations, the volume's works question the political, social, racial, and religious bonds that link members of a society to one another.

Turn-of-the-century progress in the social sciences—sociology, psychology, and anthropology—changed forever the way people thought about themselves and their cultures. Comparative anthropology, for example, gradually led writers to re-evaluate the colonialism that arranged cultures hierarchically, with European society at the pinnacle of civilization. In literature, works like Isak Dinesen's *Out of Africa* and E. M. Forster's *A Passage to India* suggest that colonized cultures have a sophistication and beauty of their own, and that European incursions into foreign lands are not necessarily to the benefit of all concerned. H. G. Wells's science fiction tale *The War of the Worlds* may be read as a revenge fantasy of sorts, in which Martian invaders subject earth's colonizing nations to some of the cruelties these nations visited upon other peoples. In psychology, as the theories of Sigmund Freud and Carl Jung gained currency, writers began to examine the intricacies of individual motivation and personality. Robert Louis Stevenson's *The Strange Case of Doctor Jekyll and Mr. Hyde* offers one such exploration of a person's inner life; John Steinbeck's *Of Mice and Men* features a mentally disabled character; and Eugene O'Neill's *Long Day's Journey into Night* examines the psychological dynamics of individuals in the context of a family unit. Less directly psychological but related to these works are thriller tales of the period, such as the detective fiction of Dashiell Hammett (*The Maltese Falcon*) and the mystery writing of Daphne du Maurier (*Rebecca*).

Sociology meanwhile documented the growth of urban communities with squalid living conditions. In the United States, the conditions under which so many immigrants—and African American migrants—lived became the focus of a new philosophy of social change known as "progressivism." In response primarily to the dismal working and living conditions brought on by rapid industrialization of cities in the North, social activists sought to institute labor policies, including child labor laws, minimum wage levels, unions, antitrust legislation, and other provisions that would safeguard the weakest and poorest members of society. Writers of the time proved to be among the most effective of social protesters. For example, the great novel of the Progressive Era, Upton Sinclair's *The Jungle,* exposes the Chicago meat-packing industry for the dishonest and exploitative enterprise that it was in the early part of the century, and the novel became directly responsible for the institution of the 1906 Pure Food and Drug Act.

The streets of Northern cities in early twentieth-century America teemed with newcomers from Europe and the South, people in search of employment, a better standard of living, and freedom from past social constraints. With their presence came strong tensions, as the various ethnic populations negotiated barriers of race, nationality, and language in the effort to live together. European immigrants developed ethnic enclaves. Betty Smith's *A Tree Grows in Brooklyn* focuses on an Irish community in New York, for example. African Americans likewise established communities of their own in the North, where they gradually developed a political voice as well as a distinctive artistic culture, creating works like Richard Wright's *Black Boy* and Langston Hughes's *Not without Laughter*. Both in the North and the South, America's black population soon came to the bitter realization that the dream of a new post-Civil War society, in which they lived as free and equal citizens with white Americans, would not readily materialize. Harper Lee's *To Kill a Mockingbird* gives ample proof of the racial resentments that still smoldered in the American South well into the 1930s. In the Southwest, another ethnic group, Mexican migrants, meanwhile encountered dilemmas of their own, as portrayed in the biography *Barrio Boy* by Ernesto Galarza.

Americans were not alone in experiencing social upheaval. Russia felt the effects of the collapsing aristocratic order, reflected in Anton Chekhov's *The Cherry Orchard*. In Ireland, James Joyce wrote fiction (*Dubliners* and *Portrait of the Artist as a Young Man*) that questions cultural, political, and religious ways. Along with such challenges came a new liberalism about the role of women, a breaking away from their restriction to the domestic sphere. This transformation has been reflected, and to some degree aided, by writings that touch on the lives of women around the globe—from Virginia Woolf's *A Room of One's Own* (England) to Laura Esquivel's *Like Water for Chocolate* (Mexico) to Isaac Bashevis Singer's "Yentl, the Yeshiva Boy" (Poland). In the United States, such writings feature various regions—for example, the South (Kate Chopin's *The Awakening*) and the Midwest (Willa Cather's *O Pioneers!*)—as well as various ethnic groups—African Americans (Zora Neale Hurston's *Their Eyes Were Watching God* and Alice Walker's *The Color Purple*), Caucasians (Edith Wharton's *The House of Mirth*), and Chinese Americans (Amy Tan's *The Kitchen God's Wife*).

Rival colonial ambitions of European nations contributed to the outbreak of World War I, in which Great Britain battled Germany for European supremacy. Erich Maria Remarque's *All Quiet on the Western Front* tells the grim story of trench warfare from the German point of view, while Ernest Hemingway's *A Farewell to Arms* displays similar abhorrence of the carnage of the war as seen through an American's eyes. The aftermath of the "Great War" proved to be a disillusioning time, as people returned to an unchanged world in which the old class system and many of the same economic players once again prospered. T. S. Eliot's poem *The Waste Land* examines the despair of the English, trapped by poverty and dehumanizing technology, while D. H. Lawrence's short story "The Rocking-Horse Winner" builds on English economic tribulations as well. Claude McKay's *Home to Harlem* portrays another type of postwar dehumanization, as black soldiers who risked their lives for America returned home to discrimination and race riots in its crowded urban centers.

Conditions worsened for everyone in subsequent years as the Great Depression descended on Europe and North America. This economic collapse made capitalism look like a failure, and it resulted in people's adopting a more positive attitude to communism. A growing number of Americans went on to develop left-leaning political views, inspired most directly by the recent revolutionary upheaval in Russia. In America, government suspicion of socialism and especially communism led to crackdowns against the political left, which affected writers such as Lillian Hellman (*The Little Foxes*), who came under attack for her portrayal of white industrialists as greedy, immoral, antilabor manipulators. The fiction of other writers (Richard Wright's *Native Son*) meanwhile reflected the effect of communists on the disenchanted in America.

Setting the tone for the nation, President Franklin Delano Roosevelt resolved that capitalism would indeed survive, as shown by his First Inaugural Address. Most Americans had little chance to sit around debating politics, however—the Depression had turned life into an everyday struggle for existence, as families scrabbled for adequate food and shelter. John Steinbeck's *The Grapes of Wrath* chronicles the despair experienced by a family who moves from Oklahoma to California in a failed attempt to find a better life and a compassionate community. On a lighter note, Truman Capote's "A Christmas Memory," while it does not conceal the poverty in which its characters live, nonetheless dwells on the close personal ties bred of a time of hardship.

Chronology of Relevant Events

1890–1930s

CHANGING EMPIRES

The turn of the twentieth century saw developments worldwide in the colonization of one people by another. Africa became a chessboard whose pieces fell under the control of various European players. The British consolidated their power there, and were joined as colonizers of Africa by the French, the Belgians and the Germans. Meanwhile, British colonial rule in India gradually weakened and tensions increased between England and Ireland. In Eastern Europe, mass discontent manifested itself in a number of pogroms that drove local Jews from the areas in which they had established their businesses and homes.

	Historical Events	Literary Works Set in the Period
1880	1880s–90s French start acquiring colonies in North Africa and Asia	
	1880–1920s Irish Cultural Revival begins, tries to re-establish Irish language and celebrate Irish literature, arts, and history	
	1884–1902 2.5 million square miles of new territory is added to British Empire	
1890	1890 Jewish expulsion from Western Gubernais (Lithuania, Ukraine, Byelorussia); divorce scandal of Charles Parnell ends his leadership of the Home Rule Party in Ireland	
		1894–1905 *Dubliners* by James Joyce
	1895 British government sets up East Africa Protectorate in present-day Kenya	
	1895–98 H. G. Wells combines science and social criticism in novels credited with helping to launch the science fiction genre	
1900		1900s *A Portrait of the Artist as a Young Man* by James Joyce
		1900 *Kim* by Rudyard Kipling

Historical Events	Literary Works Set in the Period
1901 British finish Uganda Railroad to Lake Victoria, headwaters of the Nile River	
1902 Joseph Chamberlain offers persecuted Jewish populations in Russia and Poland 5,000 acres of land in British East Africa as a homeland; they decline in 1905	
1903 Orville and Wilbur Wright take first successful airplane flight	
1904 Russia and Japan are at war; Japanese victories shake European power structure and lead to uprisings in Russia	
1905 Movement of Sinn Fein (Irish nationalists) is founded; Russia becomes constitutional monarchy; Polish nationalist unrest	1905 *Fiddler on the Roof* by Joseph Stein
1910	
1911 France cedes part of the African Congo to Germany	
1914 World War I comes to the British and German African colonies	1914–31 *Out of Africa* by Isak Dinesen
1916 Easter Rebellion is mounted in Dublin by Sinn Fein; Sinn Fein becomes strong political force committed to violence if necessary for Ireland to achieve independence from Britain	
1917 Balfour Declaration suggests Palestine as homeland for European Jews	
1919 Mohandas Gandhi first appears as Indian nationalist leader in wake of Amritsar riots in which 379 Indians are killed by British forces	
1920 1920 Home Rule Bill divides Ireland into two regions, each with its own parliament; Russian/Polish war; Britain establishes most of Kenya as Crown colony	1920s *A Passage to India* by E. M. Forster
1922 Gandhi is jailed in India for civil disobedience	
1925 Republic of Ireland is declared; British presence in India begins to fade	
1930	
1940	1940s *The Little Prince* by Antoine de Saint-Exupéry

THE SPREAD OF SCIENCE AND SOCIOLOGY

The late Victorian and early Edwardian periods of English history were dominated by a variety of discourses that promised to regulate and explain society according to specific scientific principles. Although the forty-year-old discussion of Darwinism was still potent, psychology was the new favorite discipline. As the work of Sigmund Freud and Carl Jung became more widely known, psychology took hold of scholarly and popular imagination the world over. In the physical sciences, new breakthroughs in atomic theory, agriculture, and medicine promised to bring great benefits to humanity.

1890	1885–1906 *Of Human Bondage* by W. Somerset Maugham
	late 1800s *The Strange Case of Dr. Jekyll and Mr. Hyde* by Robert Louis Stevenson
	late 1800s *The War of the Worlds* by H. G. Wells
1898 Marie Curie and Pierre Curie discover radium	
1899 William James publishes *Talks to Teachers on Psychology*	

Historical Events	Literary Works Set in the Period
1900 early 1900s Mental retardation is perceived as one of the most significant social problems, sterilization is advised for its victims	early 1900s *Of Mice and Men* by John Steinbeck
	early 1900s *Pygmalion* by George Bernard Shaw
1900 Max Planck develops quantum theory; Niels Bohr develops theory of atomic structure; Sigmund Freud publishes *The Interpretation of Dreams*	
1905 Albert Einstein publishes his theory of relativity	
1910	
1912 Carl Jung publishes *Psychology of the Unconscious*; Emil Durkheim, pioneer of modern sociology, publishes *The Elementary Forms of Religious Life*; serum therapy is discovered as cure for pneumonia; Piltdown Man is "discovered"—purported to be 50,000 years old, it is ultimately proved a fraud with skull of human, jaw of ape	1912 *Long Day's Journey into Night* by Eugene O'Neill
1916 F. W. Mott advances theory of shell-shock	
1917 Freud publishes *Introduction to Psychoanalysis*	
1920	
1925 Scopes Trial in Dayton, Tennessee, argues evolutionary theory	
1930	1930s *Rebecca* by Daphne du Maurier
1933 Fortified milk first appears on shelves	
	1937–39 *All Creatures Great and Small* by James Herriot
1938 Ngaio Marsh publishes detective novel *Artists in Crime*, one of several by her to bring respect to the genre	
1939 Mechanical dairy machines first appear in England; Alcoholics Anonymous is founded in the United States	
1940	

PROGRESS AND PROGRESSIVISM

In the early decades of the century, American industry soared as new products (notably the automobile) and new technologies (like the assembly line) changed the nation's way of life forever. Along with the flow of people from Europe and the American South to factories in the American North came a need to monitor living and working conditions. The term "progressivism" applies to the appearance of a number of social reform movements within the United States at the turn of the twentieth century. Largely a Protestant phenomenon, progressivism initiated changes in industry, public services, welfare, health (mental and physical), environmental protection, and American foreign policy. The attitudes behind the movement led ultimately to America's entry into the First World War, which President Woodrow Wilson saw as a fight for democracy throughout the world.

1890 1890 The publication of Jacob Riis's *How the Other Half Lives,* a photojournalistic examination of poverty in American cities, spurs reform in New York City and elsewhere	

Historical Events	Literary Works Set in the Period
1892 Ellis Island immigrant reception center opens in New York City's harbor; Pinkerton Strike against Carnegie Steel Company in Pennsylvania sets union organization back	
1900 1900s Frank Lloyd Wright designs new houses and offices that reflect his socialist leanings, aiming for beauty and convenience at both home and work	
1901 Theodore Roosevelt becomes U.S. president upon assassination of William McKinley; Socialist Party of America is founded	1901–13 *Our Town* by Thornton Wilder 1901–19 *A Tree Grows in Brooklyn* by Betty Smith
1903 Women's Trade Union League is formed; Ford Motor Company is founded	
1904 "Muckraker" journalist Lincoln Steffens publishes *The Shame of the Cities,* about corruption in St. Louis, Missouri	
1906 Pure Food and Drug Act is passed	1906 *Cold Sassy Tree* by Olive Ann Burns 1906 *The Jungle* by Upton Sinclair 1906–15 *Ragtime* by E. L. Doctorow
1908 Ford's Model T is first produced (a total of 10,607 produced at $850 each); child labor laws are introduced	
1908–17 Ashcan school of art focuses on urban scenes	
1909 William Taft is elected president	
1910 1910 Jane Addams publishes *Twenty Years at Hull House,* recounting her life as a social worker among immigrants in Chicago	
1911 National Progressive Republican League is founded	
1912 Federal workers begin eight-hour work day; Industrial Workers of the World (IWW) strike in Lawrence, Massachusetts; "Bull Moose" Progressive Party is founded	1912 *The Red Pony* by John Steinbeck
1913 First assembly line is set up by Henry Ford; Charles Beard publishes *An Economic Interpretation of the Constitution of the United States,* drawing attention to the economic forces that influenced the framers of the American Constitution; 16th Amendment gives Congress power to collect income tax	
1916 Railroad workers begin eight-hour work day; Ford produces 730,041 cars at $360 each	1916 *A Death in the Family* by James Agee
1920 1920 Census shows for the first time that more Americans live in urban than in rural areas	

Historical Events	Literary Works Set in the Period

THE NEW SOUTH

The Civil War, which had supposedly given American blacks their freedom as well as their civil rights, was forty years in the past, but the promise of a "new South" had failed to materialize. "Jim Crow" laws enforced racial segregation in every possible venue, from phone booths to hospitals, and black Americans were prevented by various local laws and policies from exercising their right to vote. In the 1890s, farmers of all races weathered financial setbacks, while the rise of industry in the South concentrated wealth and power in the hands of a new class of white businessmen.

	Historical Events	Literary Works Set in the Period
1890	1893–97 Economic depression hits the United States	1890–1920 "A Worn Path" by Eudora Welty
	1894 Boll weevil destroys Southern cotton crop, forcing the South to diversify its economic base; industrialization begins in earnest	
	1896 In *Plessy v. Ferguson,* U.S. Supreme Court rules "separate but equal" treatment for blacks is constitutional, setting the stage for extensive racial segregation in the South	1896–1905 *Noon Wine* by Katherine Anne Porter
	1897 Walter Hines Page, a Southern publisher, delivers famous "The Forgotten Man" speech in Greensboro, N.C., calling for an end to class barriers among white Southerners	
	1899 Booker T. Washington publishes *The Future of the American Negro*	
1900	1900 Texas farmers produce 2.5 million bales of cotton; income from farming is on the rise	1900s *Sounder* by William H. Armstrong
		1900 *The Little Foxes* by Lillian Hellman
		1900–37 *Their Eyes Were Watching God* by Zora Neale Hurston
	1903 W. E. B. Du Bois publishes *The Souls of Black Folk*	
	1906 Antiblack race riots in Atlanta, Georgia	
		1908–37 *Black Boy* by Richard Wright
1910	1910 Industrialization of Southern cotton industry makes textiles primary Southern industry	
	1913 Spartansburg, N.C., sheriff is tried in court for stopping a lynching (he is acquitted)	
	1917 In *Buchanan v. Warley,* Supreme Court rules that zoning codes based on race are unconstitutional	
1920	1920s George Washington Carver, black agricultural inventor and professor at Tuskegee Institute in Alabama, tours white college campuses	1920s–40 *The Color Purple* by Alice Walker
	1924 Ku Klux Klan membership reaches 4.5 million	
1930	1930s Southern Women for the Prevention of Lynching is founded to stop mob violence against black Americans	1930s *To Kill a Mockingbird* by Harper Lee
	1931 *Scottsboro* case begins as nine African American men are charged with the rape of two white women; the evidence is weak, but the group are convicted within two weeks by all-white jury and sentenced to electric chair; none of them are actually executed, but they serve long prison terms	
	1932 William Faulkner's *Light in August* is published	
	1939 The film *Gone with the Wind* opens	

Historical Events	Literary Works Set in the Period

GREAT MIGRATION AND HARLEM RENAISSANCE

Although Southern blacks had begun to leave the South in droves after the Civil War, the largest number of them—almost half a million—moved north during World War I to fill job openings in factories and to escape the "Jim Crow" inequities of the South. Northerners, however, showed hardly more racial tolerance than Southerners, and violence ensued across the North. Meanwhile, the establishment of black communities in major cities like Chicago and New York fostered the growth of distinctive music and literature. The Harlem Renaissance (1920s–mid 1930s), which brought African American writers, artists, musicians, and politicians to national prominence, helped shape a distinctive black American identity and forever changed American culture.

1900

1908 Race riot in Springfield, Illinois, Lincoln's hometown, leaves three African Americans dead

1909 National Association for the Advancement of Colored People (NAACP) is founded in New York City by white and black intellectuals

1900s *Not without Laughter* by Langston Hughes

1908–37 *Black Boy* by Richard Wright

1910

1914–19 500,000 people move from the rural South to cities of the North and Midwest

1915 D. W. Griffith's film *Birth of a Nation* opens; NAACP wins Supreme Court case against "grandfather clause," which some Southern states used to prevent blacks from voting

1917 Race riots in East St. Louis, Illinois, kill 39 African Americans

1919 "Red Summer"—race riots in Chicago and Washington, D.C., are among 20 such riots across country; Marcus Garvey starts "Black Star" shipping line to encourage travel and trade between black Americans and Africans; black World War I veterans parade down New York City's Fifth Avenue, to great applause

1919 *Home to Harlem* by Claude McKay

1920 1920–30 Harlem Renaissance flourishes in New York City

1921 "Shuffle Along," starring Josephine Baker, draws crowds of theatergoers to Harlem

1927 Duke Ellington plays at Harlem's Cotton Club

1928 Chicago's black community sends Oscar DePriest to Washington as congressman

1929 Great Depression effectively ends Harlem Renaissance

1930

1930s *Native Son* by Richard Wright

1932 Wallace Thurman publishes *Infants of the Spring,* satirizing the Harlem Renaissance; Sterling Brown publishes *Southern Road,* a book of black dialect poetry

GROWTH OF SOCIALISM AND REVOLUTION

Capitalism grew apace in the United States, encouraged by a turn-of-the-twentieth-century gold rush in the Yukon region of Canada. Disparity between the rich and the poor grew too, spurred by worldwide industrialization. With the rise of industrial capitalism in the West, and the continuing history of class oppression in Europe and Asia, socialism and communism, with their attention to workers' rights and anti-imperialist racial equality, gained new currency. From Russia and China to Mexico and America, socialist and communist movements and revolutions put new leaders in power, challenged the traditional ways of ordering society, and established new forms of community.

Historical Events	Literary Works Set in the Period
1896 Five-year Klondike gold rush begins in Canada's Yukon Territory	
1898–1901 Boxer Rebellion in China (nationalist, antiforeigner movement)	1898 *The Call of the Wild* by Jack London
1900	1900s *The Good Earth* by Pearl S. Buck
1901 Socialist Revolutionary Party emerges in Russia; Eugene Debs founds Socialist Party in America	
	1904 *The Cherry Orchard* by Anton Chekhov
1905 Czar Nicholas gives Russians a constitution after revolution threatens in Russia; Emma Goldman founds *Mother Earth,* a journal of radical socialism and avant-garde art in America	1905–25 *Barrio Boy* by Ernesto Galarza
1910 1910 Ten-year Mexican Revolution and Civil War erupts	1910 *Like Water for Chocolate* by Laura Esquivel
	1911–49 *The Kitchen God's Wife* by Amy Tan
1912 Eugene Debs wins one million votes as American Socialist party presidential candidate	
	1913 *The Old Gringo* by Carlos Fuentes
1916 Americans mount expedition against Mexican guerilla Pancho Villa over seizure of American cattle	
1917 Russian Revolution occurs	
1919 U.S. Communist Labor Party is founded; American radical John Reed publishes *Ten Days That Shook the World,* a sympathetic personal account of the Bolshevik Revolution; U.S. Attorney General rounds up 6,000 Americans believed to have communist sympathies	
1920 1920 Trial of Italian anarchists Nicola Sacco and Bartolomeo Vanzetti, on bank robbery and murder charges, begins in Boston	
1921 Russian Bolsheviks under Lenin defeat "White Russians"	
1927 Sacco and Vanzetti are executed	
1927–49 Chinese Civil War between Guomindang and Communists	

Historical Events	Literary Works Set in the Period
1930	
1931 "John Reed" societies spring up across United States	
1933–39 Stalin rids Communist Party of his "enemies" in Russia	
1938 U.S. House Committee on Un-American Activities is founded	

WORLD WAR I AND ITS AFTERMATH

The most terrible bloodbath Europe had known to date, World War I was, in part, an attempt to settle rival British and German claims to the control of world-wide colonies. America broke its long tradition of isolation from European affairs, joining the war against Germany and her allies in 1917. Killing 8 million military people and 6 million others, and leaving another 20 million homeless, wounded, or sick, World War I produced an emotional legacy of widespread hopelessness and loss of faith in technology and government.

Historical Events	Literary Works Set in the Period
1914 Archduke Franz Ferdinand of Austria-Hungary is assassinated by Bosnian nationalists armed by Serbs; World War I ensues; Germany enters war on side of Austria-Hungary	1914–18 *All Quiet on the Western Front* by Erich Maria Remarque
1914 Woodrow Wilson issues declaration of American neutrality	1914–18 *The Road from Home* by David Kherdian
1914 The Allied powers of Russia, France, and Great Britain sign Treaty of London, each promising not to make a separate peace with Germany/Austria-Hungary	1914–31 *Out of Africa* by Isak Dinesen
1915 1915 German submarine sinks British ship *Lusitania*, killing 125 Americans on board	
1916 Battles of Verdun, the Somme, and Jutland	
1917 On April 6, U.S. Congress declares war on Germany and Austria-Hungary; Italian Army is defeated at Battle of Caporetto	
1917 Bolshevik Revolution in Russia	1917? *A Farewell to Arms* by Ernest Hemingway
1918 On November 11, armistice ends World War I in the West	
1919 Worker's Party, the future Nazi (National Socialist German Workers') Party, is founded in Germany	
1920 1920 Nineteenth Amendment gives American women the vote; League of Nations is founded in Geneva, Switzerland (America does not join, despite Woodrow Wilson's efforts)	1920s *The Waste Land* by T. S. Eliot
	1920s "A Child's Christmas in Wales" by Dylan Thomas
	1920 "The Rocking-Horse Winner" by D. H. Lawrence
1921 "Lost Generation" of American writers and artists, including Ernest Hemingway, F. Scott Fitzgerald, William Carlos Williams, and Ezra Pound, depart for Europe	
1922 Czech writer Karel Čapek stages his play *R.U.R.*, about the dehumanizing effects of technology, coins the term "robot"	
1925 1925 Adolf Hitler publishes *Mein Kampf*	

Historical Events	Literary Works Set in the Period

TWENTIETH-CENTURY FEMINISM—ENGLAND AND AMERICA

Although women in England and America had agitated for suffrage before World War I and made strides in the fight for sexual equality, they then put their political aspirations aside until the fate of Europe was decided. After the armistice, they were "rewarded" for their wartime independence and support for the troops. Consideration of their war efforts hastened the passage of women's suffrage—within a year of the peace treaty that ended the "Great War," both American and British women were given the right to vote.

Historical Events	Literary Works Set in the Period
1848 First women's rights meeting in America at Seneca Falls, New York	
1869 Two woman suffrage groups are founded in New York and Boston	
1873 Woman's Christian Temperance Union crusades for prohibition and woman suffrage	
1873–97 Association for the Advancement of Women sponsors a three-day conference in a different American city each year	
1890s Wyoming, Colorado, Idaho, and Utah grant women in their states the vote	late 1800s *The Awakening* by Kate Chopin
	late 1800s "Yentl, the Yeshiva Boy" by Isaac Bashevis Singer
1896 National Association of Afro-American Women and Colored Woman's League merge to form National Association of Colored Women	
1903 Emmeline, Sylvia, and Christabel Pankhurst found Women's Social and Political Union in England; Woman's Trade Union League is formed in America	
	1905 *The House of Mirth* by Edith Wharton
1911 Women around the world protest as Marie Curie, who is awarded the Nobel Prize for the second time, is refused admission to French Academy of Science because she is a woman	
1913 Alice Paul founds National Woman's Party; 5,000 suffragettes parade down Washington's Pennsylvania Avenue; 40 women are hospitalized in ensuing riot	1913 *O Pioneers!* by Willa Cather
1914 Margaret Sanger is indicted for distributing information on birth control; "Perils of Pauline" film serial starring Pearl White features resourceful, athletic heroine	
1915 Carrie Chapman Catt becomes head of National Woman Suffrage Association, determines to abandon state-by-state suffrage agitation and takes the movement to the national stage; Jane Addams and 80 women go to the Hague to protest World War I	
1916 Margaret Sanger opens birth control clinic in Brooklyn, the first in America, publishing information in Yiddish, English, and Italian	
1917 Jeanette Rankin of Montana becomes first U.S. Congresswoman	

1850

1870

1890

1910

Historical Events	Literary Works Set in the Period
1918 British women over the age of 30 are given the vote	
1919 On June 4, Nineteenth Amendment gives American women the vote	
1921 First Miss America pageant in Atlantic City	
1923 National Woman's Party in America proposes Equal Rights Amendment	
1925 Wyoming's Nellie Tayloe Ross becomes first female governor	late 1920s *A Room of One's Own* by Virginia Woolf
1932 Amelia Earhart becomes first woman to fly solo across Atlantic Ocean	

1930

PROHIBITION

Passed in 1919, the Eighteenth Amendment, also called the Prohibition Amendment, made it illegal for Americans to sell, make, or transport alcoholic beverages. It was enforced by the Volstead Act, which defined alcoholic beverages as those containing more than 0.5 percent alcohol. At first, the act seemed to have a beneficial effect—family violence decreased, jails were emptier, and the number of people plagued by alcoholism dropped. Soon, however, the importation of bootleg liquor from Canada and Mexico became the major occupation of organized crime, whose members wreaked havoc on law and order in American cities. It became fashionable, even glamorous, for ordinary citizens to break the law by drinking alcohol in "speakeasies." In 1933 the passage of the Twenty-first Amendment ended Prohibition.

Historical Events	Literary Works Set in the Period
1890 Women's Christian Temperance Union has 150,000 members	
1895 National Anti-Saloon League is founded in Washington, D.C.	
1916–28 Price of whiskey rises 520%	
1919 In January, the Eighteenth Amendment, forbidding the manufacture, transport, and sale of alcoholic beverages, is passed into law in America; in October, Congress passes Volstead Act to enforce it	
1920 F. Scott Fitzgerald publishes *This Side of Paradise,* helps usher in glamorous "Jazz Age"	1920–22 *Babbitt* by Sinclair Lewis
1922 Association against the Prohibition Amendment supports first candidate; it continues fight against "dry" candidates in polls until repeal of Prohibition	1922 *The Great Gatsby* by F. Scott Fitzgerald
1928 Herbert Hoover is elected president, partly on Prohibition platform	1928 *Dandelion Wine* by Ray Bradbury
1929 Al Capone's bootleg liquor empire brings him $20 million annually; President Hoover orders investigation into viability of Volstead Act	late 1920s *The Maltese Falcon* by Dashiell Hammett
1933 In February, Twenty-first Amendment repeals the Eighteenth and ends Prohibition	

1890

1910

1930

THE GREAT DEPRESSION AND THE NEW DEAL

The 1920s were an affluent decade, a time of growth and prosperity in industry and communications. New appliances increased leisure time in the United States, and radio, movies, advertising, and mass-market magazines gave rise to a new class of personalities—the national celebrities. But suddenly the hopefulness of the decade came to an abrupt halt. In 1929 the famous stock market crash on Wall Street dragged mainstream America into the depression that afflicted Europe as well as America, and had already been plaguing agricultural communities for some years. Rural areas continued to suffer, their farmers flocking to cities in search of work. In 1932 the newly elected Franklin Delano Roosevelt promised the United States a "New Deal"—a plan to end the depression and return economic and social prosperity to the nation.

Year	Historical Events	Literary Works Set in the Period
		1910–1940s *Bound for Glory* by Woody Guthrie
1920	1920s Sports and movie stars first become national celebrities in America; economic prosperity is enjoyed in urban centers; agricultural depression is suffered by America's farmers	1920s *A Day No Pigs Would Die* by Robert Newton Peck
1925		
	1929 On October 29, "Black Monday," stock market crash ushers in a decade of economic depression; 700 banks fail across United States; radio becomes a form of popular entertainment with introduction of *Amos 'n' Andy* show	
1930		1930s "A Christmas Memory" by Truman Capote
		1930s *The Heart Is a Lonely Hunter* by Carson McCullers
	1932 Franklin Delano Roosevelt is elected president; unemployment reaches 25 percent, with 13 million Americans out of work, one million homeless, and 65 percent living in poverty	1932 *Roll of Thunder, Hear My Cry* by Mildred Taylor
	1933 National Industrial Recovery Act creates Public Works Administration, which establishes and improves national infrastructure (highways, public housing, and dams), putting unemployed people to work; Labor Relations Board is established	
	1933–34 "Century of Progress" exhibition in Chicago	1933 First Inaugural Address by Franklin Delano Roosevelt
1935	1935 Social Security Act guarantees welfare benefits, unemployment insurance, and old-age pension	mid–late 1930s "The Secret Life of Walter Mitty" by James Thurber
	1936 Farm Security Administration builds camps in California for migrant workers; Hoover Dam is completed	
	1938 Fair Labor Standards Act sets workday hours and minimum wage; Orson Welles presents radio adaptation of novel *The War of the Worlds* that alarms listeners	
	1939 9.5 million Americans still unemployed	
1940	1939–40 "World of Tomorrow" is theme of New York City's World's Fair	

Contents by Title

All Creatures Great and Small
  James Herriot 1

All Quiet on the Western Front
  Erich Maria Remarque 8

Awakening, The
  Kate Chopin 15

Babbitt
  Sinclair Lewis 21

Barrio Boy
  Ernesto Galarza 28

Black Boy
  Richard Wright 36

Bound for Glory
  Woody Guthrie 44

Call of the Wild, The
  Jack London 51

Cherry Orchard, The
  Anton Chekhov 57

"Child's Christmas in Wales, A"
  Dylan Thomas 63

"Christmas Memory, A"
  Truman Capote 68

Cold Sassy Tree
  Olive Ann Burns 75

Color Purple, The
  Alice Walker 80

Dandelion Wine
  Ray Bradbury 88

Day No Pigs Would Die, A
  Robert Newton Peck 94

Death in the Family, A
  James Agee 100

Dubliners
  James Joyce 106

Farewell to Arms, A
  Ernest Hemingway 112

Fiddler on the Roof
  Joseph Stein 119

First Inaugural Address
  Franklin D. Roosevelt 125

Good Earth, The
  Pearl S. Buck 131

Grapes of Wrath, The
  John Steinbeck 138

Great Gatsby, The
  F. Scott Fitzgerald 146

Heart Is a Lonely Hunter, The
  Carson McCullers 153

Home to Harlem
  Claude McKay 159

House of Mirth, The
  Edith Wharton 166

Contents by Title

Jungle, The
Upton Sinclair 174

Kim
Rudyard Kipling 181

Kitchen God's Wife, The
Amy Tan 189

Like Water for Chocolate
Laura Esquivel 196

Little Foxes, The
Lillian Hellman 203

Little Prince, The
Antoine de Saint-Exupéry 211

Long Day's Journey into Night
Eugene O'Neill 218

Maltese Falcon, The
Dashiell Hammett 225

"Most Dangerous Game, The"
Richard Connell 231

Native Son
Richard Wright 236

Noon Wine
Katherine Anne Porter 243

Not without Laughter
Langston Hughes 249

O Pioneers!
Willa Cather 257

Of Human Bondage
W. Somerset Maugham 264

Of Mice and Men
John Steinbeck 269

Old Gringo, The
Carlos Fuentes 277

Our Town
Thornton Wilder 284

Out of Africa
Isak Dinesen 290

Passage to India, A
E. M. Forster 297

Portrait of the Artist as a Young Man, A
James Joyce 305

Pygmalion
George Bernard Shaw 312

Ragtime
E. L. Doctorow 319

Rebecca
Daphne du Maurier 326

Red Pony, The
John Steinbeck 334

Road from Home, The
David Kherdian 338

"Rocking-Horse Winner, The"
D. H. Lawrence 344

Roll of Thunder, Hear My Cry
Mildred Taylor 350

Room of One's Own, A
Virginia Woolf 356

"Secret Life of Walter Mitty, The"
James Thurber 364

Sounder
William H. Armstrong 370

Strange Case of Dr. Jekyll and Mr. Hyde, The
Robert Louis Stevenson 377

Their Eyes Were Watching God
Zora Neale Hurston 383

To Kill a Mockingbird
Harper Lee 390

Tree Grows in Brooklyn, A
Betty Smith 397

War of the Worlds, The
H. G. Wells 404

Waste Land, The
T. S. Eliot 411

"Worn Path, A"
Eudora Welty 418

"Yentl, the Yeshiva Boy"
Isaac Bashevis Singer 425

Contents by Author

Agee, James
    A Death in the Family 100

Armstrong, William H.
    Sounder 370

Bradbury, Ray
    Dandelion Wine 88

Buck, Pearl S.
    The Good Earth 131

Burns, Olive Ann
    Cold Sassy Tree 75

Capote, Truman
    "A Christmas Memory" 68

Cather, Willa
    O Pioneers! 257

Chekhov, Anton
    The Cherry Orchard 57

Chopin, Kate
    The Awakening 15

Connell, Richard
    "The Most Dangerous Game" 231

Dinesen, Isak
    Out of Africa 290

Doctorow, E. L.
    Ragtime 319

du Maurier, Daphne
    Rebecca 326

Eliot, T. S.
    The Waste Land 411

Esquivel, Laura
    Like Water for Chocolate 196

Fitzgerald, F. Scott
    The Great Gatsby 146

Forster, E. M.
    A Passage to India 297

Fuentes, Carlos
    The Old Gringo 277

Galarza, Ernesto
    Barrio Boy 28

Guthrie, Woody
    Bound for Glory 44

Hammett, Dashiell
    The Maltese Falcon 225

Hellman, Lillian
    The Little Foxes 203

Hemingway, Ernest
    A Farewell to Arms 112

Herriot, James
    All Creatures Great and Small 1

Hughes, Langston
    Not without Laughter 249

Hurston, Zora Neale
    Their Eyes Were Watching God 383

Contents by Author

Joyce, James
Dubliners 106
A Portrait of the Artist as
a Young Man 305

Kherdian, David
The Road from Home 338

Kipling, Rudyard
Kim. 181

Lawrence, D. H.
"The Rocking-Horse Winner" 344

Lee, Harper
To Kill a Mockingbird 390

Lewis, Sinclair
Babbitt. 21

London, Jack
The Call of the Wild 51

Maugham, W. Somerset
Of Human Bondage 264

McCullers, Carson
The Heart Is a Lonely Hunter 153

McKay, Claude
Home to Harlem 159

O'Neill, Eugene
Long Day's Journey into Night 218

Peck, Robert Newton
A Day No Pigs Would Die 94

Porter, Katherine Anne
Noon Wine 243

Remarque, Erich Maria
All Quiet on the Western Front 8

Roosevelt, Franklin D.
First Inaugural Address 125

Saint-Exupéry, Antoine de
The Little Prince 211

Shaw, George Bernard
Pygmalion 312

Sinclair, Upton
The Jungle 174

Singer, Isaac Bashevis
"Yentl, the Yeshiva Boy" 425

Smith, Betty
A Tree Grows in Brooklyn 397

Stein, Joseph
Fiddler on the Roof 119

Steinbeck, John
The Grapes of Wrath 138
Of Mice and Men 269
The Red Pony 334

Stevenson, Robert Louis
The Strange Case of Dr. Jekyll
and Mr. Hyde 377

Tan, Amy
The Kitchen God's Wife 189

Taylor, Mildred
Roll of Thunder, Hear My Cry 350

Thomas, Dylan
"A Child's Christmas in Wales" 63

Thurber, James
"The Secret Life of Walter Mitty" 364

Walker, Alice
The Color Purple 80

Wells, H. G.
The War of the Worlds 404

Welty, Eudora
"A Worn Path" 418

Wharton, Edith
The House of Mirth 166

Wilder, Thornton
Our Town. 284

Woolf, Virginia
A Room of One's Own. 356

Wright, Richard
Black Boy 36
Native Son 236

Photo Credits

James Wight (James Herriot), photograph. Matrix International. Reproduced by permission. —James Wight (James Herriot) with lamb, photograph. Matrix International. Reproduced by permission. —Richard Thomas and Ernest Borgnine in a scene from the 1979 television adaptation of *All Quiet on the Western Front* by Erich Maria Remarque, photograph. The Kobal Collection. Reproduced by permission. —Erich Maria Remarque, © Jerry Bauer. Reproduced by permission. —Kate Chopin, photograph. —Warren G. Harding, photograph. The Library of Congress. —Mary Nolan (flapper) in a scene from the film *Shanghai Lady,* photograph. Corbis-Bettmann. Reproduced by permission. —Porfirio Díaz, photograph. The Library of Congress —César Chávez, photograph. AP/Wide World Photos. Reproduced by permission. —Segregation sign, "Negro Waiting Room." AP/Wide World Photos. Reproduced by permission. —Segregation sign at a Jackson, Mississippi, railroad station, photograph. AP/Wide World Photos. Reproduced by permission. —Soup kitchen, photograph. AP/Wide World Photos. Reproduced by permission. —Hobo colony, photograph. AP/Wide World Photos. Reproduced by permission. —Dog team and sled, photograph. University of Washington Libraries. —Marshall and Louis Bond with their dog Jack, photograph. Huntington Library. —Anton Chekhov, photograph. The Library of Congress. —David Lloyd George, photograph. Library of Congress. —Dylan Thomas, photograph.

AP/Wide World Photos. Reproduced by permission. —Illicit still, photograph. Corbis-Bettmann. Reproduced by permission. —Rosa Parks being fingerprinted by police officer, Montgomery, Alabama, photograph. AP/Wide World Photos. Reproduced by permission. —Spinner at frame, photograph. Corbis-Bettmann. Reproduced by permission. —Alice Walker, photograph. AP/Wide World Photos. Reproduced by permission. —Whoopi Goldberg and Margaret Avery in a scene from the 1985 film adaptation of *The Color Purple* by Alice Walker, photograph. The Kobal Collection. Reproduced by permission. —Ray Bradbury, photograph. Archive Photos, Inc. Reproduced by permission. —Robert Newton Peck, photograph.

James Agee, photograph. The Bettmann Archive/Newsphotos, Inc. Reproduced by permission. —James Joyce, photograph. AP/Wide World Photos. Reproduced by permission. —Ernest and Hadley Hemingway, photograph. —Ernest Hemingway with lion, photograph. The Granger Collection, New York. Reproduced by permission. —Unemployed lining up outside a relief kitchen in New York City, photograph. AP/Wide World Photos. Reproduced by permission. —Franklin Delano Roosevelt, photograph. UPI/Corbis-Bettmann. Reproduced by permission. —Paul Muni and Luise Ranier in a scene from the 1937 film adaptation of *The Good Earth* by Pearl S. Buck, photograph. Archive Photos, Inc. Reproduced by permission. —Pearl S. Buck, photograph. AP/Wide World Photos. Reproduced by permission. —Dust Bowl, photograph. AP/Wide World Photos, Inc. Reproduced by permission. —Migrant family, photograph. AP/Wide World Photos, Inc. Reproduced by permission. —Robert Redford and Mia Farrow in a scene from the 1974 film adaptation of *The Great Gatsby* by F. Scott Fitzgerald, photograph. The Kobal Collection. Reproduced by permission. —Zelda Fitzgerald, photograph. —Female workers examining textiles for imperfections, 1912, Boston, Massachusetts, photograph. Corbis-Bettmann. Reproduced by permission. —Claude McKay, photograph. The Granger Collection. Reproduced by permission. —James Reese Europe, photograph. Corbis-Bettmann. Reproduced by permission. —Edith Wharton, photograph. —Stairway in the Ogden Mills house at Staatsburg, New York, photograph. Beinecke Rare Book and Manuscript Library. Reproduced by permission. —Packinghouse worker, photograph. —Upton Sinclair, photograph. —Map of northern India, illustration. —Rudyard Kipling, photograph. —Chiang Kai-Chek, photograph. AP/Wide World Photos, Inc. Reproduced by permission. —Amy Tan, photograph. AP/Wide World Photos. Reproduced by permission. —Emiliano Zapata, photograph. The Granger Collection, New York. Reproduced by permission. —Laura Esquivel, photograph. © Jerry Bauer. Reproduced by permission.

Scene from the 1939 production of *The Little Foxes* by Lillian Hellman, photograph. The New York Public Library. Reproduced by permission. —Joseph McCarthy and Roy Cohn, photograph by Walter Bennett. Time-Life Syndications. Reproduced by permission. —Antoine de Saint-Exupéry, photograph. —Charles de Gaulle, photograph. AP/Wide World Photos, Inc. Reproduced by permission. —Eugene O'Neill, photograph. AP/Wide World Photos, Inc. Reproduced by permission. —Humphrey Bogart in a scene from the 1941 film adaptation of *The Maltese Falcon* by Dashiell Hammett, photograph. Springer/Corbis-Bettmann. Reproduced by permission. —Elijah Muhammad, photograph. AP/Wide World Photos, Inc. Reproduced by permission. —Richard Wright, photograph. AP/Wide World Photos. Reproduced by permission. —Katherine Anne Porter, photograph. © Jerry Bauer. Reproduced by permission. —Langston Hughes, photograph. The Bettmann Archive/Newsphotos, Inc. Reproduced by permission. —Bessie Smith, photograph. AP/Wide World Photos. Reproduced by permission.

—Log cabin, photograph. Corbis-Bettmann. Reproduced by permission. —Willa Cather, photograph. UPI/Corbis-Bettmann. Reproduced by permission. —W. Somerset Maugham, photograph. AP/Wide World Photos, Inc. Reproduced by permission. —Los Gatos ranch, photograph. Steinbeck Research Center at San Jose State University. Reproduced by permission. —John Steinbeck, photograph. AP/Wide World Photos, Inc. Reproduced by permission. —Francisco Villa, photograph. AP/Wide World Photos, Inc. Reproduced by permission. —Carlos Fuentes, photograph. AP/Wide World Photos. Reproduced by permission. —Scene from the 1938 production of *Our Town* by Thornton Wilder, photograph. Billy Rose Theatre Collection/The New York Public Library at Lincoln Center, Astor, Lenox, and Tilden Foundations. Reproduced by permission. —Thornton Wilder, photograph. Billy Rose Theatre Collection. Reproduced by permission. —Karen Blixen (Isak Dinesen), photograph. Corbis-Bettmann. Reproduced by permission. —Karen Blixen (Isak Dinesen), photograph. Corbis-Bettmann. Reproduced by permission.

Mohandas Gandhi, photograph. AP/Wide World Photos, Inc. Reproduced by permission. —E. M. Forster, photograph. AP/Wide World Photos, Inc. Reproduced by permission. —James Joyce, photograph. Culver Pictures Inc. Reproduced by permission. —Dormitory at Clongowes Wood School, photograph. —George Bernard Shaw, photograph. The Library of Congress. Reproduced by permission. —Audrey Hepburn in a scene from *My Fair Lady,* photograph. AP/Wide World Photos, Inc. Reproduced by permission. —E. L. Doctorow, photograph. © Jerry Bauer. Reproduced by permission. —Malcolm X, photograph. AP/Wide World Photos, Inc. Reproduced by permission. —Joan Fontaine and Laurence Olivier in the 1940 film adaptation of *Rebecca* by Daphne du Maurier, photograph. Springer/Corbis-Bettmann. Reproduced by permission. —Joan Fontaine and Judith Anderson in the 1940 film adaptation of *Rebecca* by Daphne du Maurier, photograph. Springer/Corbis-Bettmann. Reproduced by permission. —John Steinbeck, photograph. AP/Wide World Photos, Inc. Reproduced by permission. —Hanging of Armenian doctors, photograph. —David Kherdian, photograph. Reproduced by permission. —D. H. Lawrence, photograph by Nicholas Muray. The Granger Collection, New York. —Fannie Lou Hamer, photograph. AP/Wide World Photos. Reproduced by permission. —Virginia and Leonard Woolf,

All Creatures Great and Small

by
James Herriot

James Alfred Wight worked as a country veterinarian in Yorkshire for almost thirty years before his wife convinced him to record his experiences in a book. Written under the pen name James Herriot, the result was a wealth of tales that reveal the author's love for the country, animals, and extraordinary people who inhabit rural England. Emotional as well as informational, *All Creatures Great and Small* illustrates the love and respect a man feels for his livelihood.

> ## THE LITERARY WORK
> A novel set in England's Yorkshire Mountains between 1937 and 1939; published in 1972.
>
> ## SYNOPSIS
> A newly graduated veterinarian learns the trade in the northern English mountains and valleys of Yorkshire.

Events in History at the Time the Novel Takes Place

The life of a country veterinarian. In rural England a veterinarian has the responsibility of caring for all the animals in an entire agricultural community. The community can range from a section of one large town to many small towns miles apart, and always includes the out-of-the-way farms off the main roads. Not only do country veterinarians tend the large livestock on farms, they also care for smaller animals like dogs and cats. As depicted in *All Creatures Great and Small,* many veterinarians keep small animal surgeries at their offices. Here they perform some operations; however, farm calls comprise most of their duties.

The job can be extremely taxing because of the unlimited hours a country veterinarian must maintain, but there are benefits, too. Herriot recalls an old teacher discussing the career. "If you become a veterinary surgeon you will never grow rich but you will have a life of endless interest and variety" (Herriot, *All Creatures Great and Small,* p. 134).

Yorkshire. The Dales are the highlands of Yorkshire. Hilly country dotted with farms and small towns, the area is one of the last remaining areas of natural splendor in industrialized England. These northern highlands sit in uncrowded countryside filled with pastures, fields, and clean air permeated by the scents of innumerable flowers. Herriot found such surroundings quite pleasing, and shared his love of Yorkshire with his readers.

Yorkshire is a diverse blend of lands and lifestyles. The "north riding," an area of highlands and valleys, features many small communities, a few large ones, and miles of open country. Between the great expanses of farmland lie a sprinkling of towns. It is in one of the smaller towns, Thirsk, that the author made his start in the country veterinary business, and he bases many of his stories on this town. A characteristic feature of Thirsk is its bustling marketplace, set on cobblestone streets that were laid down generations ago. Other towns of the Dales include Richmond, Leeds, Leyburn, Middleham, and Sowerby. The whole region is the site of many historic churches.

Farms. Dating back to the Norse settlers of the ninth century, traditional Yorkshire farms changed little over the years. The house was generally connected to the barn, allowing the farmer a chance to tend to his stock without facing the sometimes harsh elements. There was usually a dairy, a cooling room for cheeses, and a loft for beef, ham, and pickled meats within the house to allow easy access to provisions at all times. A farmer's life was very isolated, and almost every activity revolved directly around his livestock and crops. Farms had to be self-sufficient in maintaining their supply of food since deliveries were infrequent and centers of commerce far.

The farms of the 1930s were not highly specialized in one agricultural area as are modern ones. Instead farmers of the region raised a blend of livestock and crops to ensure that their enterprise would yield a steady profit throughout every year. Hence it was common to find a variety of livestock—sheep, dairy and beef cattle, pigs, hens, geese, and goats—within the yard of a typical farm.

THE MILK LORRY

In the 1920s and 1930s, a truck called a "milk lorry" collected full churns (large jugs) of milk from farms. The lorries then transported the milk to butter and cheese factories, and to market places for immediate sale. Today, the lorries have been replaced by tanker trucks that use pipelines to move the milk from the farms into the trucks.

Cows and the dairy. Farmers of the Dales often felt sentimental about their cows: feeding them well, allowing them free range on nice days and warm shelter on cool nights, and sometimes even naming them were common practices. Mentioned in *All Creatures Great and Small* are a few such names—Daisy, Mabel, and even Kipperlugs. This habit of naming the livestock shows the respect some farmers had for their livelihood, and the genuine love they felt for the animals, whom they viewed almost as partners in business.

Types of cows found in the Dales vary in breed. The Hereford, which fattens easily on a regular grass diet, is the most numerous beef breed. A red-bodied cow, the Hereford has a

white belly and head. The black-and-white Friesian, weighing nearly half a ton or more, is the most commonly found dairy cow. Other cows in Yorkshire include the Dairy Shorthorn, used both for milking and beef, the gentle Jersey cow, and the Guernsey. The amount of milk produced varies with the type of cow. Friesians average about three gallons daily but may yield as much as six gallons. The cow's milking cycle is not continuous. "A cow may be expected to milk for nine months after the birth of her calf. She is then dry for three months until the next calf is born—that at least is the ideal sequence" (Mossman, p. 117).

Safety was always a major concern in the consumption of milk. Bacteria could easily multiply during the transition between farm and home, and diseases such as tuberculosis and typhoid were commonly transferred by milk at one time. The eradication of bovine tuberculosis began in 1922, when herds were subjected to a tuberculin test. A premium was paid on milk certified to be free of the disease. The Ministry of Agriculture regulated the inspections using local veterinarians. Any cows testing positive had to be slaughtered.

Horses. Before tractors and other mechanical advancements were introduced to Yorkshire, horses provided most of the power for the execution of heavy tasks. The time of the novel marks a transition period in British agriculture, an era when the horse was beginning to be replaced. Horses would nevertheless remain a sentimental favorite for many farmers. Even today they can be found throughout Yorkshire's Dales.

The largest of England's horses, the Shire, can weigh more than a ton and can stand six feet high at the shoulder. In 1066 it was introduced to England by William the Conqueror as transport for knights. The Cleveland Bay is considered the native horse of Yorkshire. Not as heavy as the Shire or another type, the Clydesdale, it is been able to perform the same amount of work without as much exertion, making it cheaper to keep.

The deep affection some farmers feel for their animals is reflected in the actions of an old horseman named John Skipton in *All Creatures Great and Small*. After receiving over fifteen years of work from two favorite horses, he allows them a beautiful private pasture in a remote section of woods in which they are to live out their lives. For the next twelve years, he travels over the hills every day to visit them, bringing along treats to brighten their lives. What some in the Dales see

1950s. Farmers' awareness of life outside of rural Yorkshire dramatically increased with the arrival of motion pictures as well. Movie theaters in towns brought people out from their farms to enjoy a bit of spectator entertainment.

The pub. Not simply a place providing an evening's entertainment, the English pub served food as well as drinks and provided rooms in which patrons could spend the night on occasion. The countryside pub was much more similar to a customer's home than to a common bar today. In fact, there were no bars at all in the traditional English country pub. Instead, big rooms resembling expansive kitchens decked with tables, chairs, and tall stools provided a warm atmosphere. Patrons generally relaxed around a large stove or fireplace and discussed regional events.

Patronized by a mostly male clientele, many of the original pubs brewed their own ales and stouts and offered them to customers along with some of the better bottled beers in the country. After brewing beers in the cellars of the establishments, landlords would invite favored drinkers to the basement to enjoy private tasting sessions.

The Novel in Focus

The plot. The story begins with an anecdote describing a difficult calf-birthing and the snide suggestions of a disagreeable farmer. The anecdote is a typical incident from *All Creatures Great and Small,* a memoir that recaps the early years in the life of country veterinarian James Herriot.

After the first chapter, the novel unfolds chronologically following Herriot's graduation from Glasgow University as an M.R.C.V.S (Member of the Royal College of Veterinary Surgeons) and his subsequent search for a job in a saturated market. Faced with the prospect of working for no pay or taking a job in an unrelated field, Herriot responds to the advertisement for a veterinarian's assistant in Darrowby, a small town in the Yorkshire Dales. There he meets Siegfried Farnon, a brilliant and devoted veterinarian who has a special talent for forgetting things.

Quickly befriending his charming but absent-minded employer, Herriot is immediately faced with solving the maladies typical of English farm animals. Using fields and barns as his operating rooms, he meets the farmers who help form the foundation of British society. It is from the lives of these characters that the stories are mainly

James Herriot

as the eccentricity of an old farmer, Herriot portrays as a sign of respect and love.

Horse trading was a common activity in the area during the 1930s. Specializing in the horse trade, gypsy families made frequent appearances in north Yorkshire on their way to horse shows. The families would arrive in horse-drawn carriages and set up camp in wooded clearings for short periods of time, usually no longer than a week.

Entertainment. Dalesfolk relied upon their own creativity for entertainment, though because maintaining the farms involved so much work there was little time for indulging in leisure activities. Making crafts, playing card games, and reading were some of the home-centered pursuits that people did enjoy.

In the 1930s, however, life changed forever in Yorkshire as the phenomenon of radio reached the small towns. Many farms purchased radios, whose programs kept them informed of news outside of their immediate pastures. In fact, the radio, called a "wireless," became the main source of outside information to reach the farms. The early wireless was a bulky object requiring heavy glass-encased batteries that could only be recharged at the local hardware or grocery store. The radio's popularity would grow considerably after electricity reached the area in the 1940s and spun, as the young vet travels among the farms in a car without brakes—because his boss repeatedly forgets to fix them. He meets people and animals of all shapes and sizes throughout his travels. One of the people is his employer's carefree brother, Tristan, a romantic and directionless young man who proves to be a grand drinking partner and matchmaker for Herriot. One of the animals is Tricki Woo, a spoiled Pekingese dog whose taste for sweets leaves him looking like "a bloated sausage with a leg at each corner" (*All Creatures Great and Small,* p. 205).

THE GREAT YORKSHIRE SHOW

Since 1838 the Great Yorkshire Show has been the annual grand event showcasing Yorkshire's best livestock. Originally hosted by a range of towns around the area, its home is now Harrowgate, where the festival takes place for three days every July. Along with contests for the animals, the event highlights farming and rural life in Yorkshire. Herriot gives the following description: "In avenue after avenue, the latest machines and equipment are displayed. Sheep are sheared, horses shod and goats milked in demonstrations of farm work. In the main show ring, the heavy horses parade, glittering and jangling in their finery, packs of hounds are shown, and one of the biggest draws is the show-jumping competition" (Herriot, *The Best of James Herriot,* p. 470). The Show is Yorkshire's largest annual event.

Life's adventures unfold both at the office and throughout the countryside. Efforts at bringing order to the business lead to the hiring of Miss Harbottle, a secretary specializing in organization. Her testy relationship with the forgetful Siegfried soon proves comical as she strives for order and he for freedom.

The element of humor is highlighted by Siegfried's scheme to provide fresh food. He proposes the purchase of chickens and swine to cultivate in the backyard. The plan is soon foiled by the escape of the livestock, which run amok through the marketplace despite the efforts of his outnumbered and overmatched brother.

In the field treating the countryside's sick animals, Herriot encounters both tragedy and miracles. He treats pigs named Queenie and dogs named Mr. Heinz and makes the necessary visits to keep healthy the cows and horses that form

the backbone of the thriving agricultural economy in Britain. It is on these rounds that James meets a young woman named Helen. After a series of dates that prove remarkably inauspicious, the two find themselves falling in love. The story of the fledgling country vet culminates with his marriage to Helen in the Dales and their subsequent honeymoon. He and his new wife prove their devotion to their country and their work by spending the days after their marriage on a farm giving tuberculin tests. Herriot's newly established life seems complete.

Over time, Herriot comes to regard Yorkshire as his home and refers back to what might have been with no regrets. He describes the "high clean-blown land where the scent of grass or trees is never far away" with an obvious love, and leaves readers with no doubt that he truly believes his life has made him a "privileged person" (*All Creatures Great and Small,* p. 247).

Accents. Out of the pages of *All Creatures Great and Small* comes a mix of dialects. Placed directly between England and Scotland, Yorkshire possesses a wide range of accents throughout its many valleys and mountains. The language is not simply muddled by the mixture of the two countries; it is inherently different because of its peculiar mix of Norse and Celtic roots. The area therefore features a great number of English variations for which translations are often required.

The countryside inspires unique dialects because of the isolation of the farms. Otherwise unheard accents were sometimes retained by farmers whose most frequent contact with the world at large could be the country vet. The voices of the region are as varied as the characters who speak them in a land that has been farmed for over a thousand years. "Just a young pig, isn't she?" Herriot asks an observing farmer in the pages of his novel. The farmer affirms this with "Aye, nobbut a gilt," the term *gilt* standing for a female pig who is grown but has not yet given birth (*All Creatures Great and Small,* p. 131).

A specialized vocabulary was developed by the farmers of the area, from which a few examples follow: Hills are generally referred to as "dales" by people in reference to the highlands. The valleys below are known as "vales." Barns are called "field-houses" or "cow-houses" in Swaledale, but residents of Wharfedale and Craven prefer "laithes." As shown in *All Creatures Great and Small,* nearly everything in Yorkshire possesses a variety of names, depending on who

Herriot examines a lamb for infectious disease.

is describing it. Even towns possess multiple names. The author's home town is called Tresche, Tresch, Treusig, Thrysk, and Uisge, aside from simply Thirsk. Each area has furthermore developed a personalized form of speech so that some of the various towns, and even some farms, may have their own distinctive accent and some unique phrases to describe common occurrences of the area. In Yorkshire, for example, people speak of a light-milking cow as "operating on three-cylinders."

Sources. The author of *All Creatures Great and Small,* whose real name was James Alfred Wight, was a country veterinarian by profession, but he had a penchant for storytelling and a hidden desire to write. After twenty-eight years of hearing stories about daily veterinary adventures, Joan Danbury Wight told her husband that fifty-year-old vets never became authors. Taking it as a challenge, he bought some paper and retold the events of his younger life. The author took on the pen name James Herriot out of respect for the anonymity of the country veterinarian's profession. Soon afterward, *All Creatures Great and Small* became an instant classic.

It is an autobiographical work, focused in Yorkshire's invented little town of Darrowby, which is, according to Herriot, "a bit of Thirsk,

something of Richmond, Leyburn and Middleham and a fair chunk of my own imagination" (Herriot, *James Herriot's Yorkshire,* p. 22). The book follows the author's own story, from his Glasgow University graduation with an M.R.C.V.S. membership to his marriage a few years later. The character Siegfried Farnon was based on the author's real-life elder partner. Any characters mentioned, animal or human, were based upon memories of the author's early career.

The name of the book was derived from a hymn by Mrs. Cecil Alexander, which ran: "All Things Bright and Beautiful, All Creatures Great and Small, All Things Wise and Wonderful, The Lord God Made Them All." Herriot also named three other books written about his younger days after the hymn.

Events in History at the Time the Novel Was Written

Farms. The most striking difference between the Yorkshire farmland of the 1930s and that of the 1970s was the disappearance of the small farm. The advent of large business and the increasingly mechanized techniques applied in farming to stimulate productivity created a vastly different world. Horses were replaced by tractors, hand-milking was replaced by machines, and in Herriot's view, a bit of the personality of the people was lost:

> I think [the farmers] have altered most of all; the hard-bitten old characters with their idiosyncrasies and their black-magic cures who formed such a fertile source for my writing are very hard to find now. They have been largely replaced by the new breed of highly knowledgeable young men whose skill has made British agriculture so efficient, but who are not as interesting as their fore-fathers.
>
> (Herriot, *The Best of James Herriot*, p. 22)

Agricultural technology. Technological advances have largely changed the farming industry, decreasing the amount of labor needed and increasing the yield of crops and livestock.

THE UNSTEADY MARRIAGE OF BUSINESS AND FARMING

Because agriculture must obey the laws of nature, and business often only follows the laws of productivity, the match of the two has not always been ideal and has sometimes been humorous. This anecdote about lambing, or the birth of baby sheep, demonstrates the lack of understanding business sometimes had about agriculture. "There is a story of a London-based company which acquired an Australian sheep station. The price of wool rose sharply and a cable was sent from [the] head office saying 'Start Shearing.' The reply was immediate, 'Cannot shear. Lambing.' Management, in an attempt to adjust the birthing process to their own convenience, cabled again, 'Stop Lambing. Start Shearing'" (Mossman, p. 70).

A mechanical milker was introduced to northern England in 1939 at the Great Yorkshire Show, held at the time in Halifax. The original contraption was powered by an oil-fueled engine. Though electricity did not reach the Dales until the 1940s and 1950s, and despite the relative slowness of the first machine (which took about eight minutes to milk a cow, the same time as a person) it was the first step toward mechanizing the dairy farmer's tasks. Quickly improved upon, the machine became popular.

The most visible, and audible, development in farming, however, was the tractor. Though the tractor had been invented earlier, it took quite a while before it became a fixture in Yorkshire. Economic slumps in the 1930s and 1940s, along with an abundance of cheap labor, made their use superfluous. There were

about 55,000 tractors on English farms in 1939. A subsequent need to produce a large quantity of food during World War II, coupled with the shortage of labor, caused a quadrupling in the number of tractors in use by 1945. The advent of the tractor brought an enormous increase in the productivity of British agriculture and helped spark the replacement of much manual labor by machines.

Reception. "When I first started to write at the advanced age of fifty," wrote Herriot, "I thought it would stop at one book and nobody would ever discover the identity of the obscure veterinary surgeon who had scribbled his experiences in snatched moments of spare time" (Herriot, *James Herriot's Yorkshire*, p. 22). Despite his modest expectations, Herriot's first book went on to sell 50 million copies in twenty countries.

The reception of *All Creatures Great and Small* was almost universally positive. A main reason for the book's popularity was its tenderheartedness and the simple honesty of the stories told. "What the world needs now, and does every so often, is a warm, G-rated, down-home, and unadrenalized prize of a book that sneaks onto the bestseller lists for no apparent reason other than a certain floppy-eared puppy appeal" (Doerner, p. 88). This gentleness in Herriot's writing allowed readers an easy familiarity with his book's stories. Each new story, explained one critic, was like meeting an old friend again and feeling as if no time had been spent apart (Gillebaard, p. 4).

Negative reviews mentioned the moralistic quality of Herriot's tales, the repetitiveness of some of his stories, and his use of abrupt plot shifts. Perhaps reflecting an urban reaction to rural life, some reviewers faulted the monotony of farm life and the veterinarian's tendency toward "Disneyization, i.e., rule by lovable animals" (Lingeman, p. 13).

By and large, however, the public loved the stories of the country vet, and *All Creatures Great and Small* was an immediate bestseller. The author himself felt like it was almost too much of a success. Though he was grateful to fans who wanted his autograph, he said on at least one occasion that he much preferred his privacy.

For More Information

Doerner, William R. "How Now, Brown Cow?" *Time* (February 19, 1973): 88.

Gillebaard, Lola D. *Los Angeles Times Book Review* (June 7, 1981): 4.

Herriot, James. *All Creatures Great and Small.* New York: St. Martin's, 1972.

Herriot, James. *The Best of James Herriot: Favourite Memories of a Country Vet.* New York: St. Martin's, 1982.

Herriot, James. *James Herriot's Yorkshire.* New York: St. Martin's, 1979.

Lingeman, Richard R. "Animal Doctor." *New York Times Book Review* (September 18, 1977): 13.

Mossman, Keith. *The Shell Book of Rural Britain.* Oxford: Alden, 1978.

Whiteman, Robin. *In the North of England: The Yorkshire Moors and Dales.* New York: Rizzoli, 1991.

All Quiet on the Western Front

by
Erich Maria Remarque

Erich Maria Remarque, the son of a book-binder, was born in Germany in 1898. A bright and perceptive student with strong interests in music, art, and literature, Remarque decided to pursue a teaching career. But in 1916, before he could complete his training, Remarque was drafted into the German army along with other fellow students. He served in a sapper unit, which was responsible for fortifying positions behind the front, until he was wounded by an artillery attack in July 1917. His experiences at the front and the antiwar sentiment that they produced in him form the central core of his most famous novel, *All Quiet on the Western Front*.

Events in History at the Time the Novel Takes Place

The outbreak of war. In reaction to Austria's harsh attempts to control Serbian commerce, on June 28, 1914, Archduke Franz Ferdinand of Austria-Hungary was assassinated by a Serbian nationalist in Sarajevo. As the Austrian government plotted a suitable retribution against the Serbs, the effect on Russia was taken into consideration. Because Russia was closely allied with Serbia, Austrian officials worried that the slightest aggression against the Serbs would result in Russian involvement. As a precaution, Austria sought support from Germany, its most powerful ally. Kaiser Wilhelm II immediately vouched for Germany's assistance, telling the Austrian powers that his nation would support whatever action the Austrian government might take.

THE LITERARY WORK

A novel set during World War I on Germany's western front; published in 1929.

SYNOPSIS

A young infantry soldier describes the horrible realities of World War I's trench warfare and the drastic consequences of the war upon his generation.

On July 23, 1914, the Austrian empire presented an ultimatum to the Serbs, demanding that they suppress Serbian nationalist activity by punishing activists, prosecuting terrorists, squashing anti-Austrian propaganda, and even allowing Austrian officials to intrude into Serbian military affairs. Two hours before the expiration of the forty-eight-hour deadline on the ultimatum, Serbia responded. Its response fell short of complete acceptance of the terms and so was rejected by the Austrian authorities. As war between Austria and Serbia loomed on the horizon, both sides experienced a massive groundswell of optimism and patriotism regarding the impending conflict.

Austria declared war on Serbia and immediately began shelling Serbian defenses. As these aggressions began, the Russian army started mobilizing to aid the Serbs, and it was soon clear that Russia was going to become thoroughly involved in the war. Two days later the German army began to mobilize and entered the war to support Austria. Germany was jubilant about the prospect of war and believed that its entrance into the conflict was perfectly justified. On August 1, 1914, Germany's Kaiser spoke to a crowd of thousands, telling them, "A fateful hour has fallen upon Germany. Envious people on all sides are compelling us to resort to a just defense . . . war will demand enormous sacrifices in blood and treasure but we shall show our foes what it means to provoke Germany" (Kaiser Wilhelm II in Moyer, p. 72).

Germany's strategy for the war began with a heavy assault on France, which was an ally of the Russians. To facilitate this assault, the German troops marched through Belgium. Great Britain, Belgium's ally, immediately sent an ultimatum to the German army to withdraw from Belgian soil. When the ultimatum went unanswered, Britain declared war on Germany. During one week of political and military machinations, Germany found itself facing Russian, French, and British enemies who outnumbered their own army 10 million to 6 million.

War in the trenches. As Germany engaged the French and British armies in the West, it became clear that a decisive victory was not an immediate possibility. Both sides in the conflict settled themselves into trenches and dugouts in preparation for a war of attrition. New weapons such as the machine gun and more efficient artillery made the trenches a necessity. Soldiers on open ground would be decimated by the newfangled instruments of death. Opposing trenches were typically several hundred yards apart. The middle ground, which was laced with barbed wire, soon became known as "no man's land." Constant firefights and artillery barrages removed all foliage from this area and made it nearly impossible to cross.

Daring raids across this deadly no man's land became one of the chief pursuits of infantrymen in the trenches. During these raids, supported by fire from their own side, soldiers would cross the treacherous ground and penetrate enemy barbed wire with the help of either well-placed artillery attacks or special rifle attachments that gathered several strands of wire together and then fired a bullet, severing them. Upon reaching the enemy lines, soldiers would first throw a volley of hand grenades into the trenches and then attack the surprised defenders with bayonets. While these raids did not typically result in major casualties to defenders, they devastated enemy morale and bolstered the confidence of the attackers. In *All*

Quiet on the Western Front, Paul Baumer participates in such a raid. Caught in no-man's land by shellfire, Baumer takes shelter in a shallow hole. When a French soldier also seeks shelter there, Baumer stabs him and feels tormented by guilt as he watches the young man die. This scene illustrates the traumatic nature of the raids.

A soldier's life in the trenches. The round of duty along the western front differed little for soldiers on either side of the conflict. Most of the night would be spent at hard labor, repairing the trench walls, laying barbed wire, and packing sandbags. After the dawn stand-to, when every man would line up on the firing step against the possibility of a morning attack, the rest of the day would generally be spent in sleep or idleness, occasionally interrupted by sentry duty or another stand-to when enemy activity was suspected. Despite the sometimes lengthy periods of calm along the front, life in the trenches was filled

---

THE WESTERN FRONT

The western front was a 475-mile-long battle-line between the Germans and the Allied forces. Along this line of fighting were 900,000 German troops and 1.2 million Allied soldiers, or roughly 1,900 and 2,500 men per mile of front. Overall, the western front was not a continuous trench, but rather a string of unconnected trenches and fortifications.

---

with constant dangers. In addition to artillery attacks and surprise raids, soldiers suffered afflictions brought on by a daily existence in wet and unsanitary conditions. The lack of fresh foods and the soggy environment in the trenches resulted in "trench foot," an affliction that turned the feet green, swollen, and painful. Another ailment suffered by soldiers in the trenches was the debilitating, though not fatal, trench fever, transmitted by the lice that infested everyone after a day or two in the line. Typically the first stop after being granted a relief or a leave from duty was the delousing station, and then the baths. In *All Quiet on the Western Front,* Baumer and his comrades take several trips to the delousing stations during their service on the front.

The influence of the older generation. Central to *All Quiet on the Western Front* is the attack on members of Germany's older generation for imposing their false ideals of war on their children.

Richard Thomas and Ernest Borgnine in a 1979 television adaptation of *All Quiet on the Western Front.*

The older generation's notions of patriotism and their assumptions that war was indeed a valorous pursuit played a crucial role in the conflict. The chief sources of this pro-war ideology were the older men of the nation: professors, publicists, politicians, and even pastors. As the war began, these figures intensified the rhetoric, providing all the right reasons why killing the young men of France and Britain was a worthy and noble endeavor. One Protestant clergyman spoke of the war as "the magnificent preserver and rejuvenator" (Moyer, p. 9). He went on to say that the war would bring an "end to deceit, hypocrisy, self-aggrandizement, and immorality" and would bring about "a revival of trust, honesty, decency, and obedience" (Moyer, p. 9). Government authorities in Germany did everything in their power to encourage young men to enlist, even granting students special dispensation to complete final examinations early so as to be able to join up sooner. As the war broke out, more than a million young men volunteered for service.

In the novel, Remarque uses the character of the schoolteacher Kantorek to develop the novel's attack against the older generation. Kantorek's constant encouraging of the young men to enlist—"Won't you join up, Comrades?" he urges (Remarque, *All Quiet on the Western Front,* p. 11)—prompts Baumer's entire class to volunteer for service. As the plot unfolds, with each successive death of Baumer's classmates, the novel further condemns the attitudes and influences of the older generation. In the novel, Baumer himself denounces the pressure they ex-

THE HUMAN COST OF THE WAR			
Country	Killed or Died	Wounded & Missing	Prisoners	Total Casualties
Russia	1,700,000	4,950,000	2,500,000	9,150,000
British Empire	908,371	2,090,212	191,652	3,190,235
France	1,357,800	4,266,000	537,000	6,160,000
Italy	650,000	947,000	600,000	2,197,000
United States	116,516	204,002	4,500	323,018
Serbia	45,000	133,148	152,958	331,106
Germany	1,773,700	4,216,058	1,152,800	7,142,558
Austria-Hungary	1,200,000	3,620,000	2,200,000	7,020,000

erted. "For us lads of eighteen," he observes, "they ought to have been mediators and guides to the world of maturity, the world of work, of duty, of culture, of progress—to the future" (*All Quiet on the Western Front*, p. 12). Baumer continues, "The idea of authority, which they represented, was associated in our minds with a greater insight and a more humane wisdom. But the first death we saw shattered this belief" (*All Quiet on the Western Front*, p. 12). In a final condemnation of this older generation, Baumer says, "While they continued to write and talk, we saw the wounded and dying. While they taught that duty to one's country is the greatest thing, we already knew that death-throes are stronger" (*All Quiet on the Western Front*, p. 13). Though Remarque, who was drafted into military service, had not been inspired to enlist by the urgings of Germany's middle-aged middle class, he still resented their false influence and betrayal of the young men in his generation.

On the home front. While their young men suffered on the western front, German civilians at home made their own sacrifices. As the war continued, a failure in the potato harvest in December of 1916 forecasted additional sacrifices on the horizon. In place of their usual seven-pound-per-week ration of potatoes for each person, German citizens would now receive five pounds of potatoes and two pounds of turnips, a food previously used only as animal fodder. To make matters worse, the list of rationed foods continued to grow. Diminishing grain supplies led to a severe cutback in the bread production. The ration for butter and other fat foods dropped to

two ounces per person per week. Milk was also scarce, and fruits and vegetables disappeared from the German diet completely. With the poorer diet came new health problems—stomach, skin, and digestive disorders became common. These difficult conditions are illustrated in *All Quiet on the Western Front* when Baumer returns home on leave. During the stay, Baumer uses his soldier's ration card to provide nourishing food for his family members, who have been completely deprived because of the increasing shortages.

The Novel in Focus

The plot. Influenced by their patriotic teacher, Kantorek, Paul Baumer and his German classmates have volunteered for military service on the western front. Their first disillusionment occurs during boot camp, where the vicious drill-sergeant Himmelstoss subjects them to seemingly endless torment and harassment.

At the front, they experience firsthand the gruesome realities of the war; in one of the early chapters they visit Kemmerich, one of their classmates whose leg has been amputated after suffering a wound in battle. As Kemmerich lies dying, another of Baumer's comrades, Müller, asks if he can have Kemmerich's boots, a request that illustrates the cold practicality of warfare. Before Kemmerich dies, he tells Baumer to give the boots to Müller.

Between battles, Baumer and his friends smoke cigarettes, relax, and forage for food in the surrounding countryside. The group forms a close bond of friendship despite the grueling conditions in the trenches.

As the number of casualties grows, Baumer's company is reduced from 150 men to 80, and younger men are brought to the front. With the new men comes Himmelstoss, the despised boot camp sergeant. Himmelstoss continues his abusive behavior toward Baumer and his comrades, and the men plot revenge. Disguised in hoods, they find Himmelstoss away from the camp, pounce on him, and beat him.

After being granted a leave, Baumer returns home to visit his mother, who is sick with cancer. His stay proves less than pleasant. Unable to adjust even temporarily to a tranquil life back home, Baumer becomes anxious to rejoin his comrades. He readily returns to the trenches after a tearful parting with his mother.

In the trenches, the men cope with the discomforts of rats, lice, and deprivation. During a patrol into no man's land, Baumer takes cover in a shallow hole. When a French soldier also dives into the hole for cover, Baumer reflexively stabs him. Unable to make himself finish the Frenchman off, Baumer is tormented by guilt as he watches the young soldier die and realizes the senselessness of the war.

During an attack Baumer is wounded by a shell and is taken to convalesce in a military hospital. The horrible wounds and deaths of many of the soldiers around him again reinforce his realization of the horrible human cost of the war.

When Baumer is released from the hospital, he returns again to the front. In his absence casualties have continued to mount. He is the only survivor among the students from Kantorek's class. The final chapter of the novel reports that Paul Baumer fell to his death on a day in which the army record consisted of a simple statement: all quiet on the western front.

Remarque's antiwar sentiment. The novel's most potent and recurring focal point is of a sense of disillusionment with the institution of war. As Baumer spends a greater stretch of time at the front, he realizes with increasing clarity the hypocrisy of this war and the horrible realities of combat that the war propaganda of the older generation failed to mention. Listening to the conversations of his comrades, Baumer senses their disillusionment with the war and their feelings of betrayal by the older generation. In one conversation between the men, the soldier Albert asks his friends, "But what I would like to know, is whether there would not

Erich Maria Remarque

have been a war if the Kaiser had said no?" (*All Quiet on the Western Front,* p. 203). The soldiers have realized by this point that the petty politics of Europe's leaders have resulted in their personal involvement in the war. As the conversation continues, the soldier Kropp poses a basic question: "It's queer, when one thinks about it, we are here to protect our fatherland. And the French are over there to protect their fatherland. Now who's in the right?" (*All Quiet on the Western Front,* p. 203). When Kropp states that war is caused by one side offending the other, the soldier Tjaden replies, "Then I haven't any business here at all, I don't feel myself offended" (*All Quiet on the Western Front,* p. 204). Their conversation underscores the pointlessness of the conflict and the thousands of lives needlessly ended in its battles.

An even more poignant attack against war appears when Baumer stabs the French soldier in no man's land. Baumer regrets the stabbing and tries to talk to the man as he lies dying. "Comrade," Baumer says, "I did not want to kill you. If you jumped in here again, I would not do it. . . . But you were only an idea to me before, an abstraction that lived in my mind and called forth its appropriate response" (*All Quiet on the West-*

ern Front, p. 223). Baumer continues talking to the man:

> For the first time I see that you are a man like me . . . now I see your wife and your face and our fellowship. . . . Why do they never tell us that you are poor devils like us, that your mothers are just as anxious as ours, and that we have the same fear of death. . . ?
>
> (All Quiet on the Western Front, p. 223)

This scene more than any other condemns the war and its useless pitting of innocent against innocent.

It was the powerful effectiveness of scenes such as these that made Nazi leaders of the 1930s condemn Remarque's novel, and their disapproval would eventually lead to the revocation of his German citizenship during the Third Reich's reign.

Sources. Many elements of All Quiet on the Western Front come directly from Remarque's own experiences on the front. Remarque, like the novel's narrator, Baumer, was a student when the war broke out. Remarque was drafted, and his duties in the sapper unit to which he was assigned included fortifying positions behind the front by laying barbed wire and building gun emplacements, bunkers, and dugouts, all within range of enemy gunfire. There are several episodes in the novel in which Baumer and his comrades are sent with shovels to repair damaged fortifications. These scenes, no doubt, are modeled after Remarque's own experiences in a sapper unit. Also based on Remarque's real-life experience is Baumer's wound and convalescence in a military hospital in Duisburg. After recovering, Remarque was sent back into service, but unlike Baumer, he did not return to the front or die in action. Peace was declared just before Remarque returned to the conflict.

Many aspects of Baumer's personal life are also based on Remarque—for example, Remarque's mother, like his character's, was dying from cancer during his service at the front. However, the reason why each was granted a leave differs— whereas Baumer returns home to visit his sick mother, Remarque went back home to attend his mother's funeral.

Events in History at the Time the Novel Was Written

Germany's lost generation. Remarque was one among the many younger Germans who felt that their lives had been permanently damaged by the war. In 1928, while writing All Quiet on the Western Front, he had been working a series of odd jobs that brought a meager income and little satisfaction. Like others, he blamed his inability to find a fulfilling career or sustained happiness on the war and the crucial coming-of-age period that it had stolen from him. Numerous passages in the novel highlight these feelings and comment on the development of the "lost generation," a term also applied to the post-World War I generation of Allied lands. This group of youths felt robbed of time and hope by the war. During one conversation between the soldiers, Albert complains about the future awaiting him after the war, "That's just it. Kat and Detering and Haie can go back to their jobs because they had them already. Himmelstoss too. But we never had any. How will we ever get used to one after this, here?" (All Quiet on the Western Front, p. 86). As the conversation ends, Baumer continues in this vein in his narration: "We agree that it's the same for everyone; not only for us here, but everywhere, for everyone who is of our age; for some more, and to others less. It is the common fate of our generation" (All Quiet on the Western Front, p. 87). Perhaps the most powerful statement about the fate of this lost generation is found in Remarque's preface to the novel, in which he writes:

> This book is to be neither an accusation nor a confession, and least of all an adventure, for death is not an adventure to those who stand face to face with it. It will try simply to tell of a generation of men who, even though they may have escaped shells, were destroyed by the war.
>
> (Remarque, preface)

Reception of the novel and the rise of the Nazis. After its publication in its original German in 1929, All Quiet on the Western Front was interpreted worldwide as a manifesto for pacifism and antimilitarism. An American film version of the novel, released in 1930, reinforced this concept. The book, the film, and the author himself all became the subject of heated political debate in Germany at a time when Hitler's Nazi party was rising to power. In response to the novel, the Nazi party unleashed propaganda in an attempt to defame Remarque by claiming that he was a French Jew, and that his real name was Kramer. More serious than simple defamations was the Nazis' attempt to imprison Remarque when they came to full power in 1933. Fortunately, Remarque had just left for Switzerland to begin a new book.

Remarque's works were among those publicly burned in Berlin in front of the Opera House on

May 11, 1933. Both students and Nazi speakers denounced the authors whose writings they burned. As flames consumed Remarque's works, a speaker shouted to the crowd, "Against literary betrayal of the soldiers of the World War, for the education of the nation in the spirit of truthfulness. I consign to the flames the works of Erich Maria Remarque" (Wagener, p. 6).

In the opinion of numerous scholars, Remarque might have avoided the public burnings of his books and subsequent exile had he submitted to a specific request of the Nazis. Joseph Goebbels, Germany's propaganda minister during the Third Reich, offered to leave him and his works unmolested if he would simply attribute all responsibility for the film *All Quiet on the Western Front* to his Jewish publisher. Remarque refused.

Though Remarque was safely out of Germany, the Nazis were still able to exact revenge on the famous writer. On December 16, 1943, Remarque's sister Elfriede was accused of making defeatist remarks and beheaded with an axe. Roland Freisler, the judge of the People's Court that presided over her trial, told her that "be- cause her brother was beyond the control of the court she would have to atone for his guilt" (Wagener, p. 7).

Though it cost him his German citizenship and the life of his sister, *All Quiet on the Western Front* was Remarque's greatest literary achievement. To this day, the poignant depiction of Paul Baumer, who lives and dies in the trenches of World War I, remains one of the most powerful testaments against war.

For More Information

Moyer, Laurence. *Victory Must Be Ours: Germany in the Great War, 1914-1918.* New York: Hippocrene, 1995.

Remarque, Erich Maria. *All Quiet on the Western Front.* 1929. Reprint. New York: Ballantine, 1982.

Wagener, Hans. *Understanding Erich Maria Remarque.* Columbia: University of South Carolina Press, 1991.

Young, Brigadier Peter. *The Marshall Cavendish Illustrated Encyclopedia of World War I.* New York: Marshall Cavendish, 1984.

The Awakening

by
Kate Chopin

THE LITERARY WORK

A novella set on Grand Isle in the Gulf of Mexico and in New Orleans during the late 1800s; published in 1899.

SYNOPSIS

Inspired by an unconsummated love affair, a woman seeks to break the constraints of her gender.

Kate Chopin was born as Katherine O'Flaherty on February 8, 1851, in St. Louis, Missouri. In 1870 she married into the Creole family of Oscar Chopin and afterward lived in New Orleans, Louisiana. Kate Chopin came to know intimately the social eccentricities of this tight-knit ethnic group. Chopin's *The Awakening* explores the cultural realm of the Creole community, focusing also on the changing position of women at the turn of the century. Although Chopin professed no political connections with feminism, her story presents, through the person of Edna Pontellier, an independent and feminist character.

Events in History at the Time of the Novella

The Creoles. The term *creole* applies to the Louisiana-born descendants of the original French or Spanish settlers. Concentrated predominantly in New Orleans, the Creoles originally inhabited the "downtown" or northern half of the city above Canal Street known as the Vieux Carré. Although Spanish in its physical appearance, the spirit of the Vieux Carré was decidedly French. Fond of entertainment and in possession of a pronounced *joie de vivre* ("joy of life"), Creole culture pursued its leisure-time activities with enthusiasm. In the 1800s such endeavors might find a Creole gentleman at a cock-fighting pit, gambling house, cabaret, or one of the area's many cafés. Chopin's society in *The Awakening* consists of well-to-do Creoles who feel themselves separate from Anglo-Americans. Members of a close-knit community, these Creoles generally maintained strict social boundaries that would bend little for outsiders. Writes Chopin, "Mrs. Pontellier, though she had married a Creole, was not thoroughly at home in the society of Creoles. . . . They all knew each other, and felt like one large family, among whom existed the most amicable relations" (Chopin, *The Awakening*, p. 11).

Creole gentlemen ruled their households and expected from their wives the utmost devotion. In return, the husbands provided a generous environment. Although society deemed it acceptable for Creole men to engage in extramarital affairs, they always took meals and attended social engagements with their wives. A contemporary of Chopin's states that "Creole women, as a rule, are good housekeepers, are economical and industrious. When one pauses to think that these women were reared as princesses, with slaves at their command, one realizes that noble blood has made noble women" (Shaffter in Chopin, p.

120). The Creole wife usually presided over a large family, and households of ten children were not uncommon during the 1800s. These children provided a focal point for their mothers' lives. Edna, however, does not accept this role. Mr. Pontellier frequently rebukes his wife for a perceived neglect of the family. He asks Edna, "If it [is] not a mother's place to look after children, whose on earth [is] it?" (*The Awakening*, p. 7). As was the case with other refined women of this era, the female Creole strove to perfect her accomplishments and talents. She excelled at singing, painting, music, and conversation. As one writer explains, "Women's rights, for them [Creole women], are the right to love and be loved, and to name the babies rather than the next president or city officials" (Shaffter in Chopin, p. 121). In such a social climate it is little wonder that Mr. Pontellier consults a physician about his wife's "odd" behavior. He remarks that "she's got some sort of notion in her head concerning the eternal rights of women" (*The Awakening*, p. 67), and he cannot fathom her dissatisfaction. Ultimately, Edna Pontellier realizes that she cannot fit into the mold that her husband and his society fashioned for her.

Women's political and social movements. Most biographers of Kate Chopin note that the author shied away from political and ideological associations. Nonetheless, she does create, through the person of Edna Pontellier, an uncommonly independent female voice. While Mrs. Pontellier may not be intended to champion women's rights, the novella in which she appears was set and written at a time of transition in the women's rights movement.

In 1848 the world witnessed its first women's political convention at Seneca Falls, New York. Headed by Lucretia Coffin Mott and Elizabeth Cady Stanton, the two-day gathering addressed women's issues before sixty-eight women and thirty-two men. Organizers drafted a Declaration of Sentiments that included, among other issues, a call for women being granted the right to vote. For the first time in history, women publicly challenged the notion of "separate spheres" (the division of labor and interests between the male "public sphere" and the female "private sphere"). The Seneca Falls Convention is considered the first attempt to establish women's rights as an organized movement.

Over the next forty years, the suffrage movement (to allow women the right to vote) gained momentum and became the premier cause of women's rights advocates. Its supporters divided into two factions, the National American Woman's Suffrage Association and the American Woman Suffrage Association. While both struggled to gain the vote for women, they differed on tactics. The second group avoided other controversial issues, such as divorce rights, believing they would hurt the struggle for the vote by upsetting male decision makers. There was disagreement too over whether to campaign for the vote on the federal level or on a state-by-state basis. In 1890 the two factions finally united to form the National American Suffrage Association, which for the time being abandoned the federal route and the issue of divorce rights. Instead the focus narrowed to gaining the vote for women in various states.

Women cited their domestic experience as well as their supposed moral superiority as reasons why they should be entitled to vote. The female had long been regarded as the moral arbiter within the home. Women now used this status to argue that they should be allowed to do for their states what they did for their families. But progress was slow; not until 1920 would all women in the United States be able to vote, thanks to the passage of the Nineteenth Amendment to the U.S. Constitution. Meanwhile, many women were denied basic rights, especially in the South. In Louisiana, where *The Awakening* takes place, a married woman did not even legally own the clothes she wore.

There was, despite such obstacles, a widespread movement to found women's clubs for self-improvement. In her novella, Chopin makes mention of the women's clubs that sprang up during the mid- to late 1800s. These clubs were formed not only as forums within which women could informally educate themselves but also as venues for the discussion of political issues. Disregarded by many males, the clubs nonetheless provided an important grassroots effort in furthering women's rights. When Mr. Pontellier consults the doctor about Edna's sudden independent streak, Doctor Mandelet asks, "Has she been associating of late with a circle of pseudo-intellectual women—superior spiritual beings?" (*The Awakening*, p. 66). His scorn clearly implies that he does not believe in the intellectual capacities of these clubwomen. Yet some of their clubs grew to wield great influence in solving social ills. By 1890 the grassroots women's groups were widespread enough to organize themselves into the General Federation of Women's Clubs. Clearly the clubs were helping to shape women into a potent political force.

Louisiana women. New Orleans, where Chopin lived for a time and where *The Awakening* is set, was actually the home of the first women's club in the American South. In 1884, the "Woman's Club" of New Orleans was founded as a support group for the city's working women. Within a year, the club opened its ranks to all women, and membership soared. The club had a mixed political and social agenda; its members set out to obtain equal pay for equal work, to promote the intellectual growth of women, and to improve the community.

The New Orleans Woman's Club quickly attached itself to the national women's rights movement, after which it drew into its fold even more of the city's women. With their membership dues, the women rented and then bought a succession of clubhouses in ever more prosperous neighborhoods. The club became socially acceptable, even desirable. Not only did it sponsor community outreach programs—distributing food and clothing to disaster victims, for example—but it also hosted lectures, concerts, classes, and plays.

The Woman's Club spawned other women's societies in the city, the state, and throughout the South. Devoted to the study of geography, literature, politics, or sociological questions, these societies helped educate Southern women in various ways. Louisiana's first suffrage association—the Portia Club—was founded in 1892 as an offshoot of the original New Orleans Woman's Club.

Dorothy Dix and women's issues. Beginning in 1895, Dorothy Dix, whose real name was Elizabeth Gilmer, published an advice column for women in the New Orleans paper *The Daily Picayune*. As the first column of its kind, "Dorothy Dix Speaks" gave voice to the growing female involvement in public issues. Dix's column could not have been launched at a more opportune time.

In her January 23, 1898, article entitled "The American Wife," Dix discusses the role of women in the household. She states that the American wife is forced to "be a paragon of domesticity, an ornament in society, a wonder in finance and a light in the literary circle to which she belongs" (Dix in Chopin, p. 129). In managing the household affairs, a woman must take complete responsibility, because most men do not wish to be bothered about domestic particulars. Chopin echoes these sentiments in her novella. Rebuking his wife for neglect of the children, Mr. Pontellier says that he "had his hands full with his

Kate Chopin

brokerage business. He could not be in two places at once; making a living for his family on the street, and staying at home to see that no harm befell them" (*The Awakening*, p. 7). With such pressures upon women, Dix notes in another column, their thoughts of suicide come as little surprise. Dix states that if suicide is ever justifiable, women have far more reason to take their own lives than men. Chiefly, "woman's whole life is one long lesson in patience and submission. She must always give in" (Dix in Chopin, p. 134). In the novella, unable to submit and be patient any longer, Edna Pontellier swims out to sea, possibly to drown. On her way, she thinks of Léonce and the children. "They were a part of her life. But they need not have thought that they could possess her, body and soul" (*The Awakening*, p. 114). Coincidentally, Dix's column on suicide appeared during the same year as *The Awakening*.

Quadroons. New Orleans of the mid- to late 1800s relied on its own code of racial segregation. Persons with African blood occupied the bottom of the social ladder. This category was further broken down according to the degree of African ancestry. People with 1/16th, 1/8th, or 1/4th black blood were the highest on this scale and referred to as octoroons; the term quadroon refers specifically to a person with 1/4 black ancestry. After them, in descending social order, came the mulattos (1/2 black), griffes (3/4 black), and sacatras (7/8 black). The Pontellier family, like many Creole households of the late 1800s, employs a quadroon as a nurse for the children.

Regarded as great beauties, quadroon women often became mistresses of Creole men. Although the quadroon in Chopin's novella is not having an affair with Mr. Pontellier, such an arrangement would not have been out of the ordinary. Because Louisiana in the 1800s was populated by far fewer white women than white men, interracial affairs were common. An 1807 law (which remained on the books until 1972) outlawed marriages of mixed races; as an alternative, Louisiana society turned to the practice of *plaçage*. Under this arrangement, a man would formally settle an illicit dowry of sorts with a quadroon's family. He would furnish her with a house and a comfortable living in exchange for her sexual and social services. While such women did gain a certain status in Creole society, they and other quadroons remained lower than their white counterparts and received less than equal treatment. The quadroon nurse in *The Awakening* follows after the Pontellier children "at the respectful distance which they [the Pontelliers] required her to observe" (*The Awakening*, p. 13).

Victorian women and sexuality. Prior to the late nineteenth century, people believed that women were inherently less lustful than men. This opinion prevailed especially in Protestant, middle-class households. Between the 1790s and the 1830s, America witnessed a rise in evangelical religion. These churches taught their parishioners that sexual intercourse served only as a means of child production. The act itself was a sin, not to be enjoyed. In Protestant circles, public opinion advocated female chastity and sexual control to promote human virtue. Reinforcing this opinion was an idea spread in manuals of the day that women's "superior delicacy" meant they harbored less sexual desire than men (Gregory in Cott, p. 166). Girls who grew up with such notions often continued to hold these beliefs in their adult lives.

The novel's Edna Pontellier has grown up among Protestants in Kentucky blue-grass country. "She was an American woman, with a small infusion of French, which seemed to have been lost in dilution" (*The Awakening*, p. 6). Coming from this environment, she expresses shock at the Creole women's casual references to sex and sexuality. Her own Protestant upbringing had taught her that polite conversation did not include such talk and that a "good" woman possessed no inclination toward physical love. Only when her feelings are awakened by a lover does Edna realize the absence of passion in her own life.

The Novella in Focus

The plot. The novel opens as Edna Pontellier takes a summer holiday on Grand Isle in the Gulf of Mexico. Prior to this, Edna has led a typical domestic life for a woman of her elevated economic and social status. As the wife of a prominent New Orleans financier, Mrs. Pontellier troubles herself with little besides the care of her household and the maintenance of her social engagements. While not a blood member of the Creole milieu in which she lives, Mrs. Pontellier fits in comfortably with these acquaintances of her husband. She discovers a special kinship with one younger man in particular, Robert Lebrun.

In the Creole circles of her day men did not harbor jealousies toward their wives' male acquaintances, since a woman's betrayal of her husband was considered unthinkable. No one takes notice, therefore, when Mrs. Pontellier and Robert begin spending an inordinate amount of time together. From bathing in the sea to special boating trips, the two remain inseparable for the duration of the summer. Robert's sudden departure for Mexico not only shocks Edna, but it leaves her quite alone. Unable to relate to her husband and his obsession with money and social appearances, Edna no longer displays the conventional behavior expected of a wife and mother.

The end of the summer brings the Pontellier family back to New Orleans, along with most other upper-class New Orleans' Creoles. Instead of taking up her former household responsibilities, however, Edna is unable to forget the freedoms that summer on Grand Isle offered. She begins seeking new assertions of her independence at home, refusing social calls, asserting her will against that of her husband, and even ignoring her father's commands. Although concerned about the sanity of his wife, Mr. Pontellier attributes her change of habits to female caprice. When Mr. Pontellier leaves for New York on a business trip, Edna decides to remain in New Orleans without him.

Temporarily left alone, Edna, who has always enjoyed painting as a hobby, begins to explore her artistic talents more intensively. She earns a meager income of her own and gains a defiant independence. In an effort to ease her romantic longing for Robert, Edna makes the acquaintance of another male devotee, a noted seductive cad named Alcée Arobin. With his help, she moves from her prominent New Orleans mansion on Esplanade Street into a smaller residence. Soon Robert Lebrun returns from abroad.

With some trepidation Robert expresses his affection for Edna, stating that he left the country only to avoid troubling her marriage. Unfortunately, their reunion is short-lived. Convinced that the relationship could never be a happy one, Robert leaves again—this time for good. Knowing "there was no human being whom she wanted near her except Robert," Edna swims slowly out to sea, perhaps to drown (*The Awakening,* p. 113).

The ideal Southern woman. The character Adèle Ratignolle serves as a foil to Edna Pontellier. Complacent in manner, devoted to her husband and children, Madame Ratignolle embodies the quintessential well-bred Creole woman of New Orleans. In her subservience and dedicated maternity, she contrasts with virtually every major characteristic of Mrs. Pontellier. Writes Chopin, "There are no words to describe her [Madame Ratignolle] save the old ones that have served so often to picture the bygone heroine of romance and the fair lady of our dreams" (*The Awakening,* p. 10). In comparing Madame Ratignolle to a "bygone heroine" Chopin seems to suggest that she has many of the characteristics that society valued in women in the pre-Civil War South. Growing up on lush plantations, women who conformed to these values strove toward pure, refined elegance and grace. One writer remarks that "nowhere else in America have hospitality and social intercourse among the better classes been so cultivated or have constituted so large a part of life as in what is called the old South" (Tillett in Chopin, p. 122). Among other qualities, physical beauty, neatness, grace, and an unwavering devotion to family and friends comprised the attributes of the ideal woman.

Much of this idealistic persona was destroyed by the Civil War and in the postbellum period of Reconstruction that followed. Many formerly wealthy women were forced into financial hardship after the war and lost their slave laborers. As a result, some of these Southern women became less devoted to refined behavior, although others, like Adéle Ratignolle, managed to preserve the ideal attributes. Chopin writes, "There was nothing subtle or hidden about her charms;

her beauty was all there, flaming and apparent" (*The Awakening,* p. 10). Madame Ratignolle expresses an appropriate degree of shock when Edna Pontellier confesses that she would not sacrifice herself for her children. Although willing to die for them, Edna does not wish to consume herself in motherhood. Madame Ratignolle, on the other hand, craves just such an existence of devoted motherhood.

Southern custom admired helplessness in women. In fact, in some instances, competent, able-bodied women would rely on the charity of friends rather than seek a means through which to support themselves. When ill, Madame Ratignolle demands the presence of her friends and family. Because her husband leaves her bedside for a moment, she asks, "Where is Alphonse? Is it possible I am to be abandoned like this—neglected by everyone?" (*The Awakening,* p. 108). She does not even wish to face the rigors of a bad cold without her husband at her side. In contrast, Edna abandons her husband and children in favor of death. Not by any means the ideal Southern woman of the past, Edna Pontellier better represents an emerging, more independent, attitude that women in the South as well as other regions were beginning to display at the turn of the century.

Sources. Kate Chopin draws heavily from her own personal history in the composition of her novella. The situation and setting for the book come entirely from the pages of Chopin's own life. Like her main character, Chopin married into a wealthy Creole family and moved with her husband to New Orleans. The Chopins also maintained a summer residence on Grand Isle. Oscar Chopin, like Léonce Pontellier, worked as a broker and maintained an office on Carondelet Street, New Orleans' version of Wall Street. (Actually he was a cotton factor—an agent, a banker, and a broker all under one roof.) The author also showed the same defiant independence that she gives to her character. She liked to stroll alone throughout New Orleans, smoking cigarettes, a prohibited way to walk for women of her social standing. In *The Awakening,* Edna remarks, "I always feel so sorry for women who don't like to walk; they miss so much—so many rare little glimpses of life" (*The Awakening,* p. 105). Long walks are a way in which Edna asserts her independence, as Chopin did in real life.

Unlike her character, however, Kate Chopin became involved in Oscar Chopin's business. A very odd situation for the times, Oscar consulted his wife in business affairs, and she often accompanied him on visits to the cotton mills that he represented. The Chopins, in fact, enjoyed a much more egalitarian marriage than did the Pontelliers. However, just as rumors circulated about Edna Pontellier's character, New Orleans gossips told vicious tales of Kate's flirting. When Oscar died, "some of the wives felt that their husbands' sympathy for the young widow prompted them to be a little more solicitous in helping her . . . than was necessary" (Toth, p. 164). Whether the Chopin marriage was happy or not has given Chopin biographers some cause for debate. But the author and her husband do not appear to have experienced the severe marital problems that face Edna and Oscar Pontellier in Chopin's novella.

Chopin uses events from her own life even for small details. Edna seeks the friendship of an older woman and accomplished pianist, Mademoiselle Reisz. Moved by her music, Edna finds the strength to become an artist in her own right. As a young girl, Kate Chopin took piano lessons from her great-grandmother, Madame Charleville. The older woman became an important mentor for the young Chopin, teaching her French and relating tales of her strong matrilineal heritage and of pioneering days in the Louisiana Purchase region. Throughout her life, Kate maintained her musical studies and her belief in the strength of women. In fact, Chopin's first published short story, "Wiser Than a God," tells the tale of a pianist who loves her craft more than a young suitor.

Reception of the novella. Published in 1899, Chopin's novella originally encountered criticism and hostility. The *Public Opinion* writes, "If the author had secured our sympathy for this unpleasant person [Edna] it would not have been a small victory, but we are well satisfied when Mrs. Pontellier deliberately swims out to her death in the waters of the gulf" (*Public Opinion* in Chopin, p. 151). In a similar vein the Chicago *Times-Herald* notes, "It was not necessary for a writer of so great refinement and poetic grace to enter the overworked field of sex fiction" (*Times-Herald* in Chopin, p. 149). So intense was the public outcry against the book that it was removed from library shelves in Chopin's hometown of St. Louis, Missouri, and its publication resulted in her being refused membership in the St. Louis Fine Arts Club. After going out of print, it remained so for over fifty years until the feminist movement rediscovered *The Awakening* as an insightful piece of feminist literature.

For More Information

Chopin, Kate. *The Awakening.* Edited by Margaret Culley. New York: W. W. Norton, 1976.

Cott, Nancy F., and Elizabeth H. Pleck. *A Heritage of Her Own: Toward A New Social History of American Women.* New York: Simon & Schuster, 1979.

Gil, Carlos B., ed. *The Age of Porfirio Díaz.* Albuquerque: University of New Mexico Press, 1977.

Lindig, Carmen. *The Path from the Parlor: Louisiana Women, 1879-1920.* Lafayette: The Center for Louisiana Studies, 1986.

Toth, Emily. *Kate Chopin.* New York: William Morrow, 1990.

Ware, Susan, ed. *Modern American Women.* Belmont, Calif.: Wadsworth, 1989.

Babbitt

by

Sinclair Lewis

Born and raised in Sauk Centre, Minnesota, Harold Sinclair Lewis (1885-1951) suffered a relatively awkward childhood. His mother died when "Harry" was five, and the orange-haired, gangly youth was less popular than his older brothers, remaining something of an outsider both at his hometown school and at Yale. His first novel, *Our Mr. Wren*, appeared six years after he received his Yale degree in 1908, and was followed by his best-known works, which were written during and about the rapidly changing America of the 1920s. The success of *Main Street* (1920), a novel that depicted the ways of a little midwestern town rather like Sauk Centre, earned him widespread acclaim. *Babbitt,* his next effort, succeeded even more impressively; largely on its strength, Lewis became the first American to win the Nobel Prize in Literature, in 1930.

Events in History at the Time of the Novel

Postwar politics. Surprisingly, perhaps, for a novel that opens in the spring of 1920, *Babbitt* seldom refers directly to the first world war. An armistice was declared on November 11, 1918, and the Treaty of Versailles, which set down the terms of peace, was signed the next spring. In the war's aftermath, the country entered a period of drastic social, technological, and economic transformation; in politics, on the other hand, conservatism dominated the American scene during the 1920s, often taking the form of reaction against new developments that were perceived as threatening. In the novel, when Babbitt talks politics with his neighbors, it is generally agreed that the nation needs a probusiness ad-

> ### THE LITERARY WORK
>
> A novel set from 1920 to 1922 in Zenith, an imaginary midwestern American city; published in 1922.
>
> ### SYNOPSIS
>
> Tracing two years in the life of George Babbitt, a self-proclaimed "representative business man," Lewis offers a sharp satire of America's prosperous white middle-class.

ministration. This attitude affected the outcome of the presidential election of 1920, in which voters chose the Republican, Warren Harding. While his Democratic predecessor, Woodrow Wilson, envisioned a continuation of America's political and financial commitments in war-weary Europe, Harding offered a comparatively easy and profitable return to peacetime industry and commerce. Harding promised, in campaigning for office, a return to normalcy.

Reaction. Yet just what was this "normalcy" to which Americans wished to return? It would prove to be a rather conservative one in some ways. Wartime propaganda had successfully inspired the nation with a sense of its patriotic duty to hate and combat an insidious foreign enemy, and many sought new enemies to replace the German kaiser and his agents when the war ended. This resulted in official attacks against the American Left. Alarmed by the successful revolution of the Bolsheviks in Russia (1917) and by an increasingly organized and recognized labor movement at home, the American business community and its supporters condemned communism, socialism, and labor unionism as barely distinguishable parts of a dangerous conspiracy involving dirty, ungrateful immigrants and their dupes. In 1919, faced with high inflation and increasing resistance in their efforts to bargain with employers, over a million workers took part in labor union strikes of one form or another. Repeatedly, these strikes failed as the public and the judiciary supported corporate interests against "the radicals." At the height of the crisis, Attorney General A. Mitchell Palmer ordered a series of notoriously unconstitutional raids on communist meetings, making wholesale arrests without warrant. Although massive New Year's Day raids on communist headquarters across the country yielded no evidence of any violent plot—despite the jailing of six thousand men and the seizure of all materials and documents found—fears of Bolshevism continued to haunt the popular imagination well into the 1920s.

Organized intolerance thrived in other forms. Zealous patriots formed various independent groups in order to keep a vigilant eye on "Reds," or communists, and their sympathizers. Perhaps the most extreme of these groups, the Ku Klux Klan (KKK), enjoyed a massive revival throughout the country at this time; its members persecuted as "un-American" black, Jewish, and, depending on the locale, Catholic, Asian, and other minorities, not excluding whites judged to be politically or morally undesirable.

In accordance with the times, the mushrooming growth of the KKK (a few hundred members strong in 1919, but an estimated 4.5 million in 1924) owed much to salesmanship; for every $10 membership a Klansman, or "Kleagle," managed to sell, he could pocket four dollars. By encouraging its members actively to solicit other joiners, the Klan merely followed the example set by many of the more respectable brotherhoods, organizations, and clubs that also prospered during the 1920s—service clubs such as the Boosters and the Rotarians, and fraternal orders such as the Elks, the Knights of Pythias, and the endless college fraternities. The novel's Babbitt—a Booster, an Elk, an active Republican, a Chamber of Commerce member, an Athletic Club member, a Sunday school committee member, a real-estate brokers' association member, and a member of the antisocialist "Good Citizens' League"—embodies this craze for belonging. The question of who or what Babbitt would be without the official identities these associations confer is one the novel returns to repeatedly.

President Warren G. Harding

Prohibition. The Eighteenth Amendment, which forbade the manufacture, transport, and sale of alcoholic beverages, passed into law in 1919, and took effect on January 16th, 1920; it was repealed in 1933. Called the Prohibition Amendment, it enjoyed widespread support from women. Also supporting the amendment were rural voters (Prohibition came to be regarded as the revenge of rural America on an increasingly urbanized nation), and a good number of drinkers who, possibly inspired by a spirit of self-discipline left over from the war, appear to have thought that they could quit anytime. However, the postwar peace brought with it a celebratory mood of self-indulgence that had to be reckoned with in the nation.

Although *Babbitt* was written well before the heyday of bootleggers like Al Capone, whose career was made possible by Prohibition, some of the weaknesses of this legislation were already obvious by 1922—for example, the tremendous difficulties of enforcement and the illicit glamour that drinking gained from illegalization. Sophisticates or would-be sophisticates, whether they came from major cities or towns anxious to become major cities, all hastened to dissociate themselves from the hick-town "Puritan" aura that clung to the advocates of "dryness." This impulse comes into play in the novel when Babbitt, carousing at a sleazy burlesque show in Monarch, where he is attending a realtors' convention, insists drunkenly that his hometown is just as disreputable: "Snothin you can't find in Zenith. Believe me, we got more houses and hootch-parlors an' all kinds o' dives than any burg in the state" (Lewis, *Babbitt*, p. 175). Many ordinary citizens (thirsty, but otherwise beyond reproach) took to patronizing the "dives" where alcohol remained available.

Modern morals. In the same years that saw the failure of Prohibition, American culture went through other changes that disturbed moral traditionalists, especially in regard to courtship and sex. Women in particular showed the effects of this shift, not just in their daring new fashions (higher hemlines, higher heels, short hairstyles, and sleeveless, open-throated evening gowns), but in the cigarettes they now enjoyed and the alcohol they now imbibed. Additionally, the women showed more daring in taking part in new dance styles that involved much more physical contact and—as parents worried—while sitting in the cars that more and more young people were driving. Lewis's novel calls attention to these new customs by comparing Babbitt's memory of his engagement to Myra (in which the first kiss was trustingly accepted as implying a marriage proposal) to the more carnal understanding between Babbitt's son and Eunice Littlefield.

This relaxation of the moral code—which did not affect the younger generation alone—sprang from other causes in addition to the unsupervised privacy offered by cars, the drinking habits altered by Prohibition, and the temptation sparked by immodest clothes. First, thanks to America's participation in the war, over 2 million American soldiers had been sent to Europe, where many of them encountered a more tolerant attitude toward sex. Secondly, conventional American ideas on this topic were shaken by the popularization of Sigmund Freud's psychological theories, which were interpreted (or misinterpreted) as an argument against sexual taboos. Finally, moral conservatives complained that the popular new motion pictures, with their passionate kissing scenes, were encouraging lewd behavior. While this last observation might make fears of a moral breakdown seem ridiculous from a more modern perspective, the change in moral standards could hardly be denied; even those who took part in it sometimes observed it with

concern. Lewis's novel raises some moral questions about the extramarital affairs of the characters Babbitt and Paul Riesling that were timely concerns during the era.

Car culture. Americans fell in love with the automobile in the 1920s; the number of cars on the road nearly quadrupled between 1919 and 1929, reaching well over 23 million. Mass production techniques pioneered by Henry Ford just after the turn of the century had continued to improve, and combined with successful mass marketing, yielded a phenomenal growth in ownership. By 1921, though, Ford's reliable but primitive Model T was losing ground to faster, more comfortable, and more stylish competitors. With advances in paint technology, cars became available in dazzling colors; high-pressure "balloon" tires enhanced the handling and the ride; and roads improved to smooth the way for these gorgeous new machines. Those with old-fashioned tastes, like Babbitt, might hang on stubbornly to their old, open-air roadsters, but the future plainly belonged to the covered sedan, as Babbitt's son points out to his father at one point in the novel.

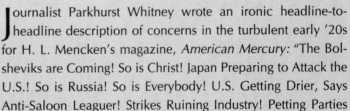

SOUND THE ALARM!

Journalist Parkhurst Whitney wrote an ironic headline-to-headline description of concerns in the turbulent early '20s for H. L. Mencken's magazine, *American Mercury:* "The Bolsheviks are Coming! So is Christ! Japan Preparing to Attack the U.S.! So is Russia! So is Everybody! U.S. Getting Drier, Says Anti-Saloon Leaguer! Strikes Ruining Industry! Petting Parties Ruin Younger Generation! . . . Anglo-Saxon Supremacy Menaced by Inferior Race . . . Rotary Speaker Says Business is Service!" (Whitney in Smith, p. 36).

Cars began to take on a special symbolic value during the 1920s, a mysterious importance they would retain in future decades. They stood for the wonders of technology and industry; Ford was hailed as a hero, the genius of the modern era. Repeatedly, Lewis's novel pokes fun at the car-worship indulged in by his hero: "To George F. Babbitt, as to most prosperous citizens of Zenith, his motor car was poetry and tragedy, love and heroism. The office was his pirate ship but the car his perilous excursion ashore" (*Babbitt*, p. 24).

An example of the daring new women of the Prohibition Era.

Boomtowns. American agriculture suffered terribly when the high wartime demand for food crops decreased in 1920. Overproduction brought down the price of wheat and other foodstuffs, which brought down rural real estate values as a result. Many farmers went bankrupt, unable to keep up mortgage payments that had been based on the inflated land values of the war era. As a result, millions left the countryside for the more prosperous cities and towns, creating a boom in the urban and, above all, suburban real estate business. Developers bought and subdivided rural properties at the edges of urban centers at a record rate, quickly erecting houses of all styles: colonial, Tudor, or, for more exotic tastes, Venetian (complete with canals) and Spanish-Alhambra.

Speculators did their best to anticipate the developers' moves, sometimes unethically, with the help of information from friends in public office or in industry. In Lewis's novel, a corrupt deal between the Babbitt-Thompson Realty Company and the Zenith Street Traction Company (a streetcar company) offers a fair illustration of how the land market could be exploited. By a secret agreement, Babbitt-Thompson and the officers of the Traction Company cooperate on land deals when, for example, a new repair garage is to be built in a suburban town. The streetcar company officers illegally inform the Babbitt-Thompson real estate firm of the plan for the new garage before the plan is made public. The Babbitt-Thompson realtors quietly and cheaply buy up land in the suburb; since the law only permits realtors to act as brokers in such purchases, they pretend to act on behalf of a wealthy, well-connected politician who, for 10 percent of the take, also distributes bribes to a few key friends in public office who might otherwise uncover and blow the whistle on the scam. The property, in high demand because it is needed for the repair garage, then gets sold to the streetcar company at inflated prices. The streetcar company's officers pretend to be horrified at such gouging, knowing all along that once Babbitt-Thompson secretly rewards them for their cooperation, the streetcar company's loss will have become their personal gain.

Broadly, this scam suggests just how well business and government could get along together. Although it only came to light in 1923, the Teapot Dome scandal confirms Lewis's depiction of current government corruption; in the spring of 1922, Albert Fall, Harding's Secretary of the Interior, leased federal oil-reserve lands to private oil companies, secretly and without competitive bidding, in return for bribes.

The Novel in Focus

The plot. Though his review praised *Babbitt* enthusiastically, H. L. Mencken said that the novel had "no plot whatever" (*Babbitt*, p. 20). Certainly the early chapters support this claim to the extent that they describe George Babbitt's comfortable daily life without giving many hints of a noteworthy event or chain of events that might affect it. The reader learns about Babbitt's suburban neighborhood, Floral Heights; his house, with its many convenient electric sockets; his kindly, unglamorous wife, Myra; and his children—Rona (stuffy), Ted (fashion-conscious), and Tinka (the baby). Also introduced are the real estate office that Babbitt and his father-in-law own, the local socialites whom he envies, and, somewhat ominously, the "fairy child" who visits him in his dreams.

The central plot line emerges more clearly in the fifth chapter: Babbitt confesses to vague feelings of discontent when he lunches at the Athletic Club with his dearest friend, the discontented and unhappily married Paul Riesling. Solid and complacent as he seems, Babbitt shares some of Riesling's unease: "I belong to the church, I play enough golf to keep in trim, and I only associate with good, decent fellows. And yet, even so, I don't know that I'm entirely satisfied" (*Babbitt*, p. 61). Ultimately, Lewis's novel examines the nature and the consequences of Babbitt's restlessness.

The consequences weigh heavily because in Zenith, U.S.A., "normalcy" is so much the rule that even such hesitant complaints as Babbitt's run the risk of social condemnation. As a "Regular Guy" who ordinarily enjoys the stodgy banter of the club's lunchtime gang, Babbitt knows it is "very bad form" to dine with his old friend in private (*Babbitt*, p. 60)—all the more so, in view of his social-climbing ambitions. Soon enough, this friendship sets him at odds with the community. After Paul goes to jail for shooting his wife, Zilla, Babbitt goes through a crisis. He drinks to excess; he defends the right to strike and other "liberal" views, he declines to join the "Good Citizens' League," he has an affair, and he begins to lead a double life. At last, alarmed by Myra's appendicitis, he repents and returns to the paths of duty and conformity. In the final chapter, Babbitt's rebellion against conventional morality and politics is behind him, but he decides (for better or worse) to condone his son's hasty elopement with the girl next door.

The training ground. As indicated above, Lewis's career as a fiction writer became successful only after he published *Main Street,* but he had been writing (some fiction, but also poems, reviews, editorials, and articles) since 1903, his first year as a student at Yale. At different points he held jobs as copy editor at the San Francisco *Evening Bulletin;* journalist-editor for the Waterloo, Minnesota, *Daily Courier;* assistant editor for *Adventure Magazine* and *Transatlantic Tales;* syndicated book reviewer for the Publishers' Newspaper Syndicate; and advertising manager for the George H. Doran publishing company. On these jobs Lewis developed a sharp eye for the unintentionally funny moments in the everyday literature of newspapers, advertising, and popular speeches.

"YOU'VE GOT A TREAT COMING"

Lewis was never known for his modesty or tact. As George Jean Nathan, *The Smart Set*'s theater editor, tells the story, he and his friend H. L. Mencken ran into Lewis for the first time at a cocktail party in New York. The novelist had just finished *Main Street,* but the novel was still at the printer. Although he was at that point nothing more than a drunken stranger to the two editors, Lewis threw his arms around their shoulders, bellowing: "I'm so far ahead of most of the men you two think are good that I'll be gottdamned if it doesn't make me sick to think of it! Just wait till you read the gottdamned thing. You've got a treat coming . . . and don't you boys make any mistake about *that!*" (Lewis in Schorer, p. 284).

In *Babbitt,* the hero's own promotional letters and speeches overflow with moments of this sort, and his friends Howard Littlefield (a Ph.D. in economics who works as an advertising consultant) and Cholmondley "Chum" Frink (syndicated newspaper poet, inspirational lecturer, advertising agent) are authors as well. At a dinner party, Frink discusses a "literary problem" with Babbitt and some other guests—namely, the wording of an ad for the Zeeco automobile. Awkwardly, he admits his inferiority to a greater man: "Do you know the fellow who's really *the* American Genius? The fellow who you don't know his name and I don't either, but his work ought to be preserved so's future generations can

judge our American thought and originality today? Why, the fellow that writes the Prince Albert Tobacco ads!" (*Babbitt,* p. 120). Of course, Lewis's novel itself preserves dozens of slogans and sales pitches in the form of barely exaggerated parodies of ads during that era—for example, the ad that impresses Frink so deeply: "Prince Albert is john-on-the-job—always joy'usly more-*ish* in flavor; always delightfully cool and fragrant! For a fact, you never hooked such double-decked, copper-riveted, two-fisted smoke enjoyment!" (*Babbitt,* p. 120). Lewis took delight in mimicking the advertisers' elaborate fantasies of fulfillment and, in so doing, he captured an important early phase in twentieth-century consumer-culture.

Sources. In regard to real-life models, Lewis can hardly have chosen the name for Babbitt's wife without thinking of Myra Hendryx, the girl he worshipped from a distance as a teenager in Sauk Centre. Babbitt's father-in-law is his business partner; likewise, Lewis worked briefly (and not very happily) at the Sauk Centre *Herald* for C. F. Hendryx, Myra's father.

Literary influences can be identified too. *Babbitt* belongs to a fairly well-established American tradition of businessman-novels; some of the more important authors to contribute to this tradition—authors whose work Lewis knew well—were W. D. Howells (*The Rise of Silas Lapham, The Quality of Mercy*) and Theodore Dreiser (*The Financier*). From Upton Sinclair, best known for *The Jungle,* an investigative novel that exposed the abuses of the Chicago meat-packing business, Lewis learned the power of realistic social criticism. Also, as a regional novel set in the Midwest, *Babbitt* owes a debt to Sherwood Anderson's *Winesburg, Ohio.*

If anyone had an impact on Lewis's satirical side, it was the magazine editor, H. L. Mencken, who ran *The Smart Set* from 1914 to 1923 (and, from 1924-1933, the widely read *American Mercury*). *The Smart Set* featured a regular section devoted to ridiculous "clippings" (collected in the same spirit as the ones that appear in *Babbitt*) taken mostly from small-town newspapers. Mencken once lamented that the United States was "the first great empire in the history of the world to ground its whole national philosophy on business" (Mencken in Bode, p. 168), and he always expressed a hearty contempt for the self-satisfied ignorance that—in his opinion—the thriving herd of middle-class Americans constantly displayed. Lewis first met Mencken in 1920 and was understandably delighted when the critic, whom he had admired for some time, praised *Main Street* in the pages of *The Smart Set.* A year later, Mencken wrote to inquire about Lewis's next novel (*Babbitt*), Lewis replied, "I think you'll like it—I hope to Christ you do" (Lewis in Bode, p. 186).

Reviews. Mencken liked *Babbitt,* as he wrote in a review that probably helped the novel's sales. *Babbitt's* great strength, Mencken claimed, was its faithful depiction of a typical citizen: "I know of no novel that more accurately presents the real America" (Mencken, p. 22). Sherwood Anderson's review in *The New Republic* runs counter to this assessment, finding that Lewis had missed something crucial in his depiction of America's towns and cities: "Here is a man writing who, wanting passionately to love the life around him, cannot bring himself to do so, and who, wanting perhaps to see beauty descend upon our lives like a rainstorm, has become blind to the minor beauties our lives hold" (Anderson, pp. 27-8). "There's a lot more to America," concurred Robert Littell in another *New Republic* review (Littell in Knight and James, p. 318). The question of whether *Babbitt* is too one-sidedly harsh could not help but arise in the reviews. Certainly the novel offended some readers, as satires typically do. A review in the Greensboro *Daily News* anticipated the negative responses, then went on to pronounce its own judgment on Lewis's work

> His book will be reviled from one end of this land to the other. It will be hated, spat upon, possibly burned. . . . But it will be read. And it ought to be read . . . because it attacks shams and hypocrisies and poltrooneries and dishonesties."
>
> (G. W. J. in Knight and James, p. 318)

For More Information

Anderson, Sherwood. "Sinclair Lewis." In *Sinclair Lewis: a Collection of Critical Essays.* Edited by Mark Schorer. Englewood Cliffs, N.J.: Prentice-Hall, 1962.

Bode, Carl. *Mencken.* Carbondale: Southern Illinois University Press, 1969.

Knight, Marion A., and Mertice M. James. *Book Review Digest.* Vol. 18. New York: H. W. Wilson, 1923.

Lewis, Sinclair. *Babbitt.* New York: Harcourt, Brace, 1922.

Mencken, Henry Louis. "Portrait of an American Citizen." In *Sinclair Lewis: A Collection of Critical Essays.* Edited by Mark Schorer. Englewood Cliffs, N.J.: Prentice-Hall, 1962.

Schorer, Mark. *Sinclair Lewis: An American Life.* New York: McGraw-Hill, 1961.

Smith, Page. *Redeeming the Time: A People's History of the 1920s and the New Deal.* New York: Penguin, 1987.

Barrio Boy

by
Ernesto Galarza

Ernesto Galarza was born in the small town of Jalcocotán, Mexico, in 1905. While he was still a small boy, challenges to the thirty-year reign of Mexican dictator Porfirio Díaz resulted in widespread revolt. Fearing separation from Ernesto's young uncles through forced military or mining service, the family fled northward. The family—uncles José and Gustavo, mother Henriqueta and son Ernesto—rode the newly opened Southern Pacific Mexican Railroad to Mazatlán, Mexico; the border community Nogales; Tucson, Arizona; and Sacramento, California. More than forty years later, Galarza was persuaded to record his memories of his acculturation experiences, ending with his enrollment in a Sacramento high school.

Events in History at the Time the Autobiography Takes Place

Politics. Porfirio Díaz had become president of Mexico in 1876. Except for four years (1880-1884) during which he gave the reins of government to his friend Manuel Gonzáles, Díaz had ruled autocratically and continuously through 1905, the year Galarza's autobiography begins. The president-dictator was to rule for another five years thereafter.

Díaz had recognized the need for Mexico to improve its economic base and had done much to encourage foreign investments, particularly in mining and in the railroad system needed to bring the mined materials to market. By 1905 mining of silver, copper, and coal had become

THE LITERARY WORK

An autobiography set in Mexico, Arizona, and California between 1905 and about 1925; published in 1971.

SYNOPSIS

Ernesto Galarza recalls the travels of his family from a small mountain village of west central Mexico to Sacramento, California, at the start of the Mexican Revolution.

Mexico's major industries. Still, small isolated villages were home to much of Mexico's population throughout the mountain ranges that enclosed the country.

The villages and the *rurales*. Díaz's plans for Mexico's development had little effect on these small communities. No special roadways connected them to the larger towns. Most of them existed without electricity or sewage systems and took their water from nearby streams. Residents built one-room homes out of the rock and soil in the area, covered them with tile roofs, and walled off an area behind the house to keep out the wilderness beyond and protect the family animals. A typical village consisted of a few houses lining both sides of a single dirt road and, of course, some sort of common ground, a square or plaza. In such small villages there were often no church buildings and no schools. By 1910 education had become universal and mandatory in

Mexico, but there was no provision for it in the mountain villages.

Occasionally the residents would walk or ride to the nearest town to petition the government for help, particularly in establishing schools. More often, contact with the government was through the *rurales,* soldiers of the national government who would ride horseback through the villages to demand taxes, to take rations for themselves, or to look for young men to conscript for work in the mines. Except for avoiding the rurales, the typical village resident had little to do with the national government and received little attention from it.

Revolution. During Díaz's era, a few Mexicans favored by the government grew increasingly wealthy, and the division between rich and poor grew ever more distinct. By the time of Galarza's birth, the Mexican plantation or *hacienda* system was fully developed. Millions of landless Mexicans worked at the whims of hacienda managers. They were harshly treated and very poorly paid.

By 1910 Francisco Madero had become the leader of an antigovernment movement that called for government and land reform. Forces loyal to Díaz clashed with Madero's followers, the Maderistas, and with other rebels. Within a year, Díaz was overthrown and Madero became president of Mexico for a short time. He was immediately opposed by several generals. The revolution would continue for another decade with various rebel leaders vying for the leadership. Suddenly, young male villagers were needed not only for mine work, but to fight on one of the sides of a civil war in which they had little to gain.

As tensions rose and landowners panicked, Mexicans throughout the rural areas began a massive migration, "A la capital o al norte" (to the capital city [Mexico City] or to the north) (Galarza, *Barrio Boy,* p. 28). In February of 1910, from Ciudad Juarez (the city of Juarez) alone, 2,380 Mexican peasants legally crossed the border into the United States. The promises of land and the ousting of Porfirio Díaz failed to stem this tide. Between 1911, when the family of Galarza began its own migration, and 1921, nearly a quarter of a million Mexicans joined in the flight to the United States.

Fleeing Mexican peasants first gathered in centers where transportation was available—the larger towns and cities. Located along the western ridges of the Sierra Madre Mountains, these towns were themselves not large. In 1911 the city of Tepic, the first stop for the Galarza family,

Porfirio Díaz

counted just over 10,000 residents. The largest community on the path, Mazatlán, was just twice that size.

Most of the traveling villagers had little money. They found housing in the poorer parts of the larger communities and earned cash however possible until they were able to take the next step on their journey. Men living in these "barrios," areas occupied by migrants from closely connected communities, hired themselves out as day laborers on the developing railroad. Women sewed and provided other services for the more affluent townspeople. Galarza's mother, Henriqueta, for example, had gained an old foot pedal sewing machine, an Ajax, in her divorce settlement. The Ajax accompanied the Galarza family on the first legs of their journey, allowing Henriqueta to help with the family finances.

California farm labor. By the end of the nineteenth century, many impoverished Mexicans had found opportunity in the fields of Texas. Later, as the revolution gained headway, the dislocated villagers on the west side of Mexico's mountain ranges saw hope in the valleys of California. Both Texas and California had long depended on immigrant labor to work the fields, build railroads, and to provide services in the developing cities. America initially encouraged Mexican laborers to immigrate, seeing them as less of a threat than the growing Asian labor force. Contractors—Mexican labor recruiters—replaced the hacienda managers as the source of jobs. The pattern of employment and attitudes toward immigrants had been established by the time the Galarza family left Mexico. Carey McWilliams describes the unwritten policy in *Factories in the Fields*:

> The practice has been to use a race for a purpose and then to kick it out, in preference for some weaker racial unit. In each instance, the shift in racial units has been accompanied by a determined effort to drive the offending [undesired] race from the scene.
>
> (McWilliams, p. 130)

NUMBER OF UNITED STATES IMMIGRANTS FROM MEXICO	
1890-1900	971
1900-1910	49,000
1910-1920	250,000
1920-1930	459,287

(Adapted from Galarza, *Barrio Boy,* 1964, p. 28)

Among the first laborers in the American West were Chinese immigrants, but by the 1890s they had become too numerous and too solidly established as excellent workers for the comfort of many whites. Viewed as a threat to the white population, the Chinese were beaten, robbed, and otherwise encouraged to leave. They were in time replaced by Japanese workers in the fields, who, in turn, grew in number and effectiveness. By 1910 the Japanese had become worrisome, too; they organized to hire their own field bosses and contractors, which only added to the distrust. When the Mexican Revolution began, Japanese immigration was being discouraged. The door consequently opened wider for Mexican laborers as well as for workers from Europe and India.

At first, Mexican laborers were welcomed without restraint in Texas and California. As the numbers of immigrants rose, however, both federal and state governments attempted to control the migration. Regulations were enacted to limit the business of contract farm labor, to place per-person taxes on workers brought in by contractors, and to demand that permanent immigrants pass literacy tests conducted in English. Nevertheless, between 1900 and 1940 as many as one million Mexicans left their native land to work in the United States.

Sacramento. Sections of the existing towns throughout the farm areas of the American Southwest soon had populations of migrant workers that exceeded in size the towns they had come from in Mexico. Sacramento, for example, with a population of about 50,000 in 1910, included about 10,000 Mexican, Indian, and European immigrants. It was a small but growing city, destined to reach a population of 65,000 by the end of the first quarter of the 1900s. Sacramento was dominated by the capitol building and its churches—which, along with its Mexican-based name may have been the only elements recognizable by the Mexican immigrants. Most of these Mexican immigrants found low-cost and substandard housing near the Sacramento River in what was known properly as lower Sacramento, a name warranted by the area's condition, although it was not much different in elevation than the rest of the city.

Field workers. Some, but not by any means all, of Sacramento's Mexican residents earned their way as field laborers on the nearby farms. Here they found conditions similar to those in Mexico, where farm hands had been recruited, bossed, and sometimes harassed by managers of the large haciendas. On the haciendas peasants had been paid miserable wages, and they had been left to find their own shelter once the crops were harvested. In California, the farm laborers found giant farms organized on the hacienda pattern. The earlier large Spanish land grants in California had been taken over by American occupiers, and the hacienda boss had been replaced by independent contractors. These intermediaries between workers and landowners hired, fired, and neglected the workers in ways that resembled their mistreatment in Mexico. The major differences between the giant farms of California and the landholdings of Mexico were the absence of revolution and the abundant demand for seasonal laborers. Wages remained dismal, although better than Mexico's hacienda pay. Mexicans working California farms could earn large wages by Mexico's standards; some made as much as 60¢ a day.

The Autobiography in Focus

The contents. Galarza's autobiography begins with his birth in 1905, chronicling the young boy's life until about 1920, when he enters high school in Sacramento. (The dates are estimated since Galarza provides none). The story is divided into three basic parts—early life in a small Mexican village, migration to California, and life in the "barrio" of lower Sacramento. More specifically in his introduction, Galarza describes five sections: Mexican village life, his family's uprooted wanderings in response to revolution, flight, life in the Sacramento barrio, and living on the outskirts of the barrio (Barrio Boy, p. 2).

Galarza introduces readers to his first home, established when two uncles and his mother move to Jalcocotán leaving his Lutheran father in a larger town (Miramar) and carrying mother Henriqueta's only property from the breakup of the marriage, an old Ajax sewing machine. They live in one of a handful of similar homes built along a wide dirt street that parallels a mountain stream. It is a place where a young boy's chief occupations are keeping out of the way of hardworking elders, running constant errands for every adult in the village, and watching the animals—a burro, dog, and chickens—at work and play. Jalco, as the town is nicknamed, numbers among the many forest villages in which a boy's chief sources of education are the stories of his mother, observations of the adult men at work, and the few travelers that pass through the village. Galarza recalls the pre-dawn departures of his uncles going to work in nearby fields and the monotony of diet among the villagers. His account also describes the sense of community among the residents, none of whom are wealthy or even financially secure. Galarza graphically illustrates the size of the community:

> Whatever happened in Jalcocotán had to happen on our street because there was no other place for it to happen. Two men, drunk with tequila, fought with machetes on the upper edge of the village until they were separated and led away by neighbors. A hundred faces peered around doorways watching the fight. When someone died people joined the funeral procession as it passed by their doors.
>
> (Barrio Boy, p. 11)

The bulk of the narrative documents the family flight to escape conscription of the two uncles—a flight along the west coast of Mexico from Tepic to Mazatlán and then to Nogales, the last stop before the U.S. border. Along the route, there were many new sights to excite the young Ernesto, novelties such as electric lights (in a festival at Tepic), town markets, locomotives (which he had only heard of from his uncles who worked

on the tracks), and the great contrast between the homes of the wealthy landowners and the poor in every city.

Another first for Ernesto is his participation as a gang member in a city barrio in Mazatlán. He also discovers the tediousness of railroad travel and its primitive accommodations; much of the trip is made in open flatbed cars. More importantly, the seven- or eight-year-old begins his education, learning to read the shop signs in Tepic and Mazatlán and enduring study sessions at home directed by his mother.

Finally in Sacramento, Ernesto struggles to understand the many American dialects he encounters there. He attends formal school for the first time, and takes his first job to add to the family income, becoming a *pozolera*, a soup stirrer in an open restaurant. It is a job not unlike one he might have had in Mexico. As he grows older, the family prospers enough to move just outside the barrio. Ernesto remembers his mother's death in this new house, and tells of the peace he and his uncle found upon moving back to an apartment in the more culturally comfortable barrio. Here Ernesto grows old enough to attend high school and to begin taking jobs in the nearby fields.

Acculturation. The Galarzas had to adjust to a continually changing environment in more than just the physical sense as they moved from one society to the other. The flight to California was triggered and encouraged by the constant threat of the Mexican revolution. After Madero had forced Díaz's resignation from the presidency, several contenders for the office arose. Though Madero was elected president of Mexico, his rule was challenged by Emilio Zapata, Bernardo Reyes, Pascual Orozco, and Felix Días. Travelers escaping the war often did not know who the political opponents were, only whom they themselves supported. When the moment came to flee from the revolution, there was little time to prepare for a new society.

The family also experienced shifting conditions on their way to Sacramento. Back in their own village everyone had been poor, but even in nearby Tepic they had to adjust to the wide difference between the few rich and many poor. Tepic had its own barrio in which residents from several nearby villages found a common ground—poverty—and tried to keep some semblance of their new subcommunity by establishing "turf," which the young men protected with rocks.

Galarza's youth allowed him to finally abandon his village upbringing and adapt to American society with what seems from his story to be relative ease. The depth of change is suggested by the boy's discovery of indoor toilets in a hotel in Nogales.

> I was left alone in the room for M-E-N. I examined it with great care—the smooth enamel bowl with water in the bottom, the wooden lid with a large hole that looked like a horse collar, the small brown box up near the ceiling, the chain hanging from it. Pressed for time I finally decided it was safe enough to try. I buttoned up and looked at the sign, remembering what the clerk had said, making it sound very important. I grabbed the chain with both hands and pulled. A small torrent of water gushed into the bowel, swirling and disappearing down the drain with a deep, sonorous gargle. I waited a few minutes and pulled the chain again.
>
> That night I got up several times to go to the toilet, until I was ordered to go to sleep.
>
> (*Barrio Boy*, p. 185)

Galarza's mother had some of her own adjustments—like discovering the availability of food and new ways to gather and prepare it. In the village, "she stirred the ashes in the *pretil* [a brick counter serving as a stove], blew on the coals, and presently was laying tortillas on the *comal*. She placed a pot of beans in one corner of the fire pit and took down from the shelf some cheese wrapped in a napkin" (*Barrio Boy,* p. 113). In Sacramento, the immigrants found that Americans put everything in cans and boxes. Galarza lists Dutch Cleanser, corn flakes, Karo syrup, and butter as items new to the villagers from Mexico.

The village of Galarza's birth had operated on a largely self-directed basis, with neighbors coming together to make common decisions and to help one another. In Sacramento, Mexican immigrants along with other newcomers to the city were gathered in the area between Fifth Street and the river adjacent to the Japanese shop community between L and N Streets. Galarza points out a major adjustment to living in a noncooperative community—"the Americans had by no means given it [the barrio] up to us" (*Barrio Boy*, p. 199). The people in control, from bartenders to rent collectors, insurance salesmen, riverboat officers, landladies, police officers, and teachers were all gringos, or whites. The Mexican *colonias* (immigrants) learned with difficulty to address these people in positions of power in a new language, mastering such introductory English phrases as "hau-Mochee" (How much?), "hua-ti-nees, plees" (What time is it, please?) and "tanks you" (Thank you)—all pronounced as the vari-ous immigrants interpreted the many English dialects they heard.

Sources. Galarza recounts his experience light-heartedly and with a sense of pleasure in his original culture and in the family's accomplishments in accepting and being accepted in the larger California society. It is a tale with which he had grown quite familiar before the creation of the book. Ernesto Galarza told the stories in *Barrio Boy* many times in the fifty years before the autobiography was written. In 1928 he married Mae Taylor, and the couple had two daughters. As the girls grew up, Galarza began to tell his stories to them. All the members of the family encouraged Ernesto to shape them into a book. By 1971, he had been active in trying to define and defend the rights of farm workers and had written nearly a dozen books.

Multiculturalism and civil rights became prominent issues for debate in the 1960s, and accounts of Americans who had survived the cultural clashes to become leading spokespersons for equality were popular book subjects. Galarza's *Spiders in the House* had been published by the University of Notre Dame Press, and when this publisher arranged a grant under which Galarza's autobiography could be written, the author/activist was happy to gather the memories that had entertained his daughters into the book *Barrio Boy*.

Events in History at the Time the Autobiography Was Written

Farm labor and the government. By the time Galarza's autobiography was written, events had occurred that served to both confuse and aid the Mexican immigrants to the United States. Railroads had expanded, increasing the market for farm goods and the need for farm hands. During the 1920s, Mexican workers, whether helping out seasonally and returning to Mexico or establishing permanent U.S. residency, were welcomed.

The Great Depression changed this tolerant attitude. With about one-third of the labor force in the United States out of work by 1933, jobs became a precious commodity. The thousands of non-Mexicans who became idle made the imported workers less essential. The Depression had also severely decreased consumer spending, resulting in a loss of marketability for agricultural commodities in general. In response, President Franklin Roosevelt began federal programs to pay farmers to destroy some crops, such as cotton, early in the 1930s. The reduced harvest

César Chávez

shrank the number of farm labor jobs and, accompanied by the increase in job-seeking Americans, made the import of Mexican farm workers very unpopular. Terrible weather conditions throughout the Plains states exacerbated the problem. As fierce dust storms destroyed small farms, white farm owners transformed themselves into migrant workers. These new migrants competed with Mexicans for desperately needed jobs, and this competition fueled the fire of antagonism toward the Mexican laborer.

Labor unions. At the same time, activists were attempting to organize the migrant farm workers into a group represented by a labor union. Ernesto Galarza, having graduated from Occidental College and earned his master's degree at Stanford University (he would later earn a doctorate at Columbia University), became active in union work, first speaking for the Mexican workers through the Pan American Union and then working in California with the United Farm Workers and the National Agricultural Workers' Union.

World War II. The wartime demand for soldiers and factory workers drained the nation of laborers, restoring the Mexican farm workers' welcome status in California. This time the welcome was endorsed by the federal government, which organized farm owners and contractors to import and provide for thousands of farm workers. The temporary measure instituted in 1942, called the Bracero Program, provided needed farm workers and endured until 1964.

The conditions of the Bracero Program made Mexican workers particularly attractive. They were brought to the fields when needed and returned to Mexico when the work was done. Mostly young men, they migrated alone, leaving their families in the growing cities on the Mexican side of the border. Thus, the contractors and farm owners did not have to deal with helping families move or provide much in the way of benefits and housing. While eagerly recruited, the Mexican farm hands were often treated shabbily.

Ernesto Galarza and other Mexican leaders renewed the battle for better farm labor treatment, now directing their attention to abolishing or reforming the Bracero Program. Galarza particularly took up the Bracero cause, championing Mexican immigrants, whom he characterized as "folks with plenty of nothing" (Galarza, *Merchants of Labor,* p. 17). New vigor for the cause came in the 1960s. César Chávez came to Oxnard, California, to develop a Community Service Organization that would aid farm workers in times of legal and medical need. He remained to direct a powerful farm labor union. Gathered under a flag bearing a black eagle, the National Farm Workers Association took aggressive action to aid the migrant farm workers and to improve the living conditions in the city barrios. In the years just before *Barrio Boy* was published, Chávez led strikes against exorbitant rent increases in public housing in Tulare County, against contract-breaking low wages among flower workers in MacFarland, and against the grape growers. Galarza himself had led such labor actions on a smaller level since 1951, the year he organized a strike among tomato workers.

Barrio Boy was just one of the books Galarza wrote to reveal the plight of the Mexican farm worker and migrant laborer in general. He had begun with *Strangers in Our Fields,* a report of the Joint United States-Mexico Trade Union of 1956. Galarza followed that with *Merchants of Labor: The Mexican Bracero Story* (1964) and *Mexican-Americans in the Southwest: A Report of the Ford Foundation* (1966), before writing *Spiders in the House and Workers in the Field* (1970) and *Barrio Boy* (1971).

Reception and recognition. *Barrio Boy* was just one of many books published in this era of multicultural consciousness, the arts teaming with legislative action and new organizations in an effort to publicize and correct racial and economic injustices. Galarza contributed greatly to this mass of literature, following *Barrio Boy* with four other volumes for adults and a dozen books for children. In this body of new literature, *Barrio Boy* became a classic in the newly formed ethnic studies programs of the universities.

For his many years of service and his prolific writings, Ernesto Galarza has been recognized as a leader among Mexican writers. He was named an Officer of the Order of the Condors from the Republic of Bolivia, was awarded an honorary doctorate from Occidental College (1971), received a community service award from Santa Clara County, and was presented with a Chicano Studies Diploma from Stanford University.

For More Information

Altman, Linda Jacobs. *Migrant Farm Workers: The Temporary People.* New York: Franklin Watts, 1994.

Brenner, Anita. *The Wind Swept Mexico.* New York: Harper, 1943.

Galarza, Ernesto. *Barrio Boy*. South Bend, Ind.: University of Notre Dame Press, 1971.

Galarza, Ernesto. *Merchants of Labor: The Mexican Bracero Story*. Santa Barbara, Calif.: McNally & Loftin, 1964.

Galarza, Ernesto. *Spiders in the House and Workers in the Field*. South Bend, Ind.: University of Notre Dame Press, 1970.

McWilliams, Carey. *Factories in the Fields*. 3rd ed. Santa Barbara, Calif.: Peregrine, 1971.

Shorris, Earl. *Latinos: A Biography of the People*. New York: W. W. Norton, 1992.

Black Boy

by
Richard Wright

Born in 1908, Richard Wright grew to adulthood in the American South at a time when legalized racial segregation and discrimination were firmly entrenched there. He experienced firsthand the severe economic, social, and psychological limitations placed on blacks in the United States during the era. Wright continued to encounter racial prejudice even after he moved north to Chicago in 1927. In *Black Boy*, he describes his struggle against these obstacles on the path to his becoming a well-known author.

THE LITERARY WORK

An autobiography set in Mississippi, Arkansas, Tennessee, and Chicago, from 1908 to 1937; first part published in 1945, second part in 1977.

SYNOPSIS

A black author describes his experiences growing up in both the South and North.

Events in History at the Time the Autobiography Takes Place

Southern race relations. More than thirty years after the Civil War had ended and given slaves their freedom, many Southern whites continued to deem blacks an inferior and, to them, a threatening race. This perception is reflected in works by Southern scholars of the early twentieth century, including *The Negro a Beast, or, In the Image of God* and *The Negro, A Menace to American Civilization.* It was an attitude that governed interracial relations in the South while Richard Wright was growing up.

During this period, many members of white society exercised their prejudices toward blacks under a complex system of racial etiquette. Southern culture demanded that blacks act and be treated in a manner appropriate to their status. Black people of all ages were called by their first names and nicknames, or simply "boy," "girl," or "nigger." Most whites, on the other

hand, expected blacks to greet them with a formal "Mr.," "Mrs.," "sir," or "ma'am." Similar deference was expected in all situations. Blacks were expected to wait in any line until all whites were served first, and to yield the right of way to whites when walking or driving. When blacks entered a white home, they customarily entered only through the back door. For a black man to laugh at, contradict, or express anger toward a white man could prove unwise. It was also dangerous for a black person to assert or even hint that a white person was lying. Furthermore, blacks who demonstrated intellectual curiosity or superior intelligence were discouraged from education. For example, Richard Wright states in *Black Boy* that his local library prohibited blacks from borrowing books. His white coworkers expected him to be ignorant, so he felt compelled to hide from them the books that he read.

Blacks who did not follow these rules of interracial etiquette with an outward cheerfulness were accused of being "uppity." They risked retribution from whites who wanted to ensure that blacks "stayed in their place." A reputation for being "uppity" could lead to difficulties in securing a job, as it did for Richard Wright in *Black Boy*. White employers didn't want to hire a black person who wouldn't act in a subservient manner. Furthermore, breaking this entrenched code of social conduct could have physically dangerous repercussions. Whites tortured, beat, or killed many blacks in the South to punish them for imagined social infractions such as not calling them "sir." Between 1889 and 1931, it is estimated that over three thousand people were lynched in the South; 85 percent of these were black. The early twentieth century was an oppressive and sometimes terrifying time for blacks in the South.

Jim Crow. Blacks in the early twentieth-century South were constrained not just socially but legally as well by "Jim Crow" laws. Southern state and local government bodies strived hard to make it difficult for blacks to exercise their right to vote. The authorities introduced poll taxes—a fee that had to be paid in order to vote in elections. This type of tax made it expensive for Southern blacks—most of whom were dismally impoverished—to vote. Some places also required them to demonstrate their ability to read and interpret passages from the Constitution. Local white election officials administered the tests and determined who passed. No matter how well a black person tested, it was easy and common for white officials to arbitrarily decide he or she was too illiterate to vote. Many localities likewise enacted a "grandfather clause" declaring that only those whose ancestors had been eligible to vote in 1860 could legally register to vote. The ancestors of the vast majority of blacks had still been slaves in 1860. This "grandfather clause" therefore disenfranchised most blacks of voting age for many years. Those blacks who overcame these legal barriers were frequently terrorized by whites when they attempted to participate in the electoral process.

Besides disenfranchising blacks, by the early twentieth century all Southern states had passed laws institutionalizing the separation of the races. Public places were segregated, including churches, schools, libraries, phones, restrooms, beaches, water fountains, parks, auditoriums, buses, sports and recreation facilities, hospitals, the military, orphanages, prisons, asylums, and courthouses. There were separate white and black funeral homes, morgues, and cemeteries.

Blacks ate in their own restaurants, lived in separate boarding houses, and attended different theaters. Richard Wright grew up in a time when segregation touched nearly every aspect of Southern life.

Poverty. In the early twentieth-century South, about a third of all whites and a majority of blacks belonged to a low-income stratum. Tenant farmers of both races in rural areas struggled every year against constantly mounting debt. Unskilled laborers in towns and cities, like Richard Wright's mother, searched for permanent jobs that would provide sufficient income to live on. Earning enough money to pay rent and feed a family could often prove difficult. In *Black Boy*, Wright describes the feeling of hunger that gnawed at him constantly in his childhood even when his mother was employed full-time. For families like his, financial security was rare.

The children of poor families were expected to care for themselves independently from an early age because both parents worked full-time to make ends meet. By the age of fifteen, most boys in poor families had begun to work to supplement their family's income. Wright states in his autobiography that most of his high-school classmates worked mornings, evenings, and weekends. The author himself worked at several jobs before he graduated high school.

Poverty also affected Southern whites in similar ways. Whites who aspired to bettering themselves, however, didn't face the numerous obstacles that blacks did. A white person was more likely to be hired for a job than a black one. Employment opportunities outside the manual labor sector—such as clerks, bookkeepers, and stenographers—were closed to blacks. They were more likely to be given the unskilled jobs that no one else wanted, and they were discouraged from trying to aspire to anything better. It was also standard practice to pay blacks a lower wage than whites for the same type of work.

Blacks who managed to achieve economic success despite these obstacles were often condemned or terrorized by whites who wanted to keep blacks in an inferior economic position commensurate with their low social status. In 1925, for example, a black physician and his fiancée were beaten and seriously wounded by gunfire when whites forced them off the road near Meridian, Mississippi. The National Association for the Advancement of Colored People (NAACP) investigated and attributed the attack to jealousy among local whites because of the doctor's new car and home. Richard Wright

A segregated waiting room.

states in *Black Boy* that his uncle was murdered by whites jealous of the man's successful saloon business. The murderers were never arrested. In the early twentieth century South, not even financial success could ensure security for black people.

Black life in the North. A steady stream of blacks began to migrate from the South to the North after the end of the Civil War. Later, during Richard Wright's youth, 1.5 million blacks moved north between 1910 and 1930. It was believed that racism was less prevalent outside the South. One Greenville, Mississippi, man wrote, "I want to get my family out of this cursed south land; down here a negro man is not good as a white man's dog" (Grossman, p. 3). One Alabaman wrote to the Chicago *Defender*, a widely circulated black newspaper, in 1917: "i am in the darkness of the south and i am trying to get out. . . . i am counted no more then a dog help me please help me o. . . . i mean business i work if i can get a good job" (Alvarez, p. 86). Most who moved to northern cities like Chicago and New York were also looking for better-paying jobs, since wages there were generally higher than they were in the South. Overall, the North was seen by Southern blacks as a land of opportunity.

But urban blacks were largely excluded from white-collar jobs as well. Meanwhile, at the blue-collar or manual-labor level, Northern white laborers felt their jobs and economic opportunities threatened by the growing number of blacks competing with them for positions. They therefore struggled to prevent blacks from gaining union membership and the better training and jobs that went along with such membership.

Northern blacks also faced residential discrimination from whites who didn't want to live in a racially mixed neighborhood. This was accomplished both by real estate practices and intimidation. Real estate agents tended to turn black customers away from white neighborhoods, and blacks who still managed to move into white communities often encountered violence. For example, Dr. Ossian Sweet, a European-educated physician, moved his family into a white neighborhood in Detroit. The house was soon surrounded by a hostile crowd of white neighbors. One of the occupants opened fire, killing one white. Charges of first-degree murder were brought against all eleven blacks in the house. Overall, middle- and lower-class blacks became increasingly restricted to a single, primarily run-down section of the average northern city.

Communism. The American Communist Party emerged after the Russian Revolution of 1917. Communists believed that all of history was leading up to the inevitable overthrow of the capitalist system by the working class. They further believed that the workers of the world were responsible for the wealth their labor created. Therefore they, rather than the owning class, should have control over that wealth.

THE SCOTTSBORO CASE

In March of 1931, a year in which *Black Boy* is set, nine black teens were traveling by train in the South. After two white women accused them of rape, the police took them off the train in northern Alabama (in a small town near Scottsboro) and arrested them. During the trial, overwhelming medical and other evidence made it clear that the women hadn't been raped at all. Nevertheless, a white jury in Alabama quickly convicted all nine of the "Scottsboro boys" and sentenced eight to death. The American Communist Party launched a protest movement against the convictions. International Labor Defense, an organization associated with the Party, got involved in the legal appeal process and began to publicize the case. The series of trials that followed attracted national attention as they continued through the 1930s. The white Southern jurists on the case never acquitted any of the defendants. But charges were eventually dropped against four of the defendants and the remaining five were given sentences that ranged from twenty years to life in prison. Four of them gained early paroles and one escaped.

Through the 1920s, the American Communist Party remained a tiny sect outside of mainstream culture. After reaching a peak of 40,000 in 1919, its membership fell to 7,545 in 1930. With the onset of the Great Depression, however, many Americans grew disillusioned with capitalism. The economic crisis seemed to bear out the communist belief that capitalism was flawed and in the process of complete disintegration. Communism became a more attractive alternative, claiming about 100,000 members by the mid-1930s. Many intellectuals and artists like Richard Wright, critical of the status quo, joined or voiced support for the goals of the American Communist Party. Thousands of young people with no visible prospects of employment in industry or in the professional or academic world joined the American Communist Party as well.

The Party was one of the few political organizations in the United States to take a firm stand in favor of racial justice. Communists believed that capitalism exploited and oppressed working-class blacks more ruthlessly than any other group. Racism hurt all workers because it allowed wealthy white capitalists to profit from lower-wage black labor and extract even greater wealth from the system. The working class was also divided by the prejudice that created conflict between black and white sectors, who in reality shared the same economic interests. Communists wanted to unite black and white workers together for greater strength. They demanded the abolition of race discrimination and full social and political equality for blacks.

H. L. MENCKEN

H. L. Mencken was one of the most influential magazine editors in the United States in the 1920s, at the time when Richard Wright discovered his writings. An ardent individualist, Mencken attacked anything that limited personal freedoms, and his caustic blasts of Southern culture enraged many. He wrote, for example, the following for the *Chicago Tribune* in the late 1920s: "Fundamentalism, Ku Kluxry, revivals, lynchings, hog wallow politics—these are the things that always occur to a northerner when he thinks of the south. . . . All over this great and puissant nation, of course, frauds and fanatics flourish, but nowhere else are they taken so seriously as in the late Confederacy" (Mencken, pp. 249-50).

The Autobiography in Focus

The contents. Richard Wright grew up in a poor Southern family. Early in his youth, his family moved to a two-room apartment in Memphis, Tennessee. Even though his father was employed full-time, Wright experienced continuous hunger. The situation worsened when his father deserted the family to live with another woman; his mother then took a job as a cook for a white family. Wright and his brother were home alone most of the day. Before long, his mother became quite ill. Temporarily unable to support her sons, she placed them in an orphanage. Unhappy there, Wright tried to run away.

Eventually his mother recovered and moved the family to live with her sister in Elaine, Arkansas. Wright's uncle owned a successful saloon there, catering to the many black workers in the area. For the first time in his life, the boy's constant hunger was satisfied. His comfort was short-lived, however. One day whites who were apparently jealous of his uncle's business success killed him. The family fled in terror to West Helena, Arkansas.

Wright's aunt eventually moved away. Soon after, his mother again fell too ill to work. Wright, though only ten years old, took various odd jobs in the neighborhood to contribute to the family's income. Paying rent continued to be a problem, especially after Wright's mother suffered a stroke of paralysis and became bedridden. The family moved in with Wright's grandmother.

Though the environment in which he grew up never provided much encouragement, Wright began to write stories. One of them was published in a local black newspaper, the *Southern Register*. Wright began to dream of moving north to Chicago and becoming a writer.

As he grew older, Wright's awareness of the pervasive nature of white racism in the South increased. For example, he was once assaulted by a white youth for not addressing him as "sir." Wright always found it difficult to restrain his personality in the way that white Southern culture demanded. After losing a string of jobs in a brief period of time, he realized that his ability to hold a job in the South depended upon learning to hide his true feelings. Even hiding them, however, didn't guarantee success. Wright left a job with an optical company. The interest he had shown in learning the trade enabled him to better his position there, but his white coworkers then used intimidation and threats to drive him from the job.

Wright moved to Memphis in 1925 and found a job in another optical company. While reading the Memphis *Commercial Appeal,* he discovered an article that attacked H. L. Mencken for criticizing the South. Wright was intrigued to find someone else dissatisfied with the world in which he lived. He wanted to read Mencken's works, but blacks were not allowed to check books out of the local library. He secretly borrowed the card of a coworker he trusted and used a forged note to convince the librarian he was only borrowing books for a white person. Reading Mencken instilled in Wright a desire to use writing to fight the injustices of his world. He continued to read voraciously. Meanwhile, he finally saved up enough money to move to Chicago.

Originally published separately, the second part of *Black Boy* begins with Wright's arrival in

Chicago. He observed that racial prejudice was not so violent there as it had been in the South. He found various short-term jobs as a porter, dishwasher, and postal clerk. With the onset of the Great Depression, however, employment opportunities disappeared. So many others were looking for work that it became extremely difficult to find a job. He applied for relief at the local Department of Public Welfare. The Department assigned him a position as an orderly in a medical research institute in a hospital. There he noticed that the lowest jobs, those of orderly and janitor, were all held by blacks, while the nurses and doctors were all white.

During this time, a coworker from a previous job urged Wright to attend a meeting of the John Reed Club, a cultural organization affiliated with the Communist Party. He was surprised by the courteous treatment and lack of racial bias exhibited by the white members of the club. Attracted by the idea of uniting kindred oppressed peoples around the world, Wright became involved in the Communist Party. His writing was published in various pieces of the Party's literature. Eventually, the Party decided that members like Wright should spend more time politically organizing and less on artistic endeavors. Wright therefore decided to separate from the Party, though he still agreed with its principles. The Party labeled him a traitor, and members drove him away from a Communist May Day celebration. The book ends with Wright turning his focus to writing as a means of expressing his vision of the world.

The black experience of racism. The racism directed at blacks in the southern United States during the early twentieth century became the focus of Richard Wright's *Black Boy*. He believed that racial prejudice severely limited blacks in the South, preventing them from enjoying the full spectrum of human existence, and he wrote his autobiography to illustrate this. Southern culture actively discouraged blacks from aspiring to higher political, social, and economic status. Being black in the South meant not only facing a job market that routinely discriminated against anyone who was black, it also meant being forced to sublimate one's personality just to survive.

In *Black Boy,* Wright paints a vivid picture of the psychological consequences of racism. He writes that a friend told him to always exercise severe self-restraint in front of white people for his own safety. But "it was utterly impossible for me to calculate, to scheme, to act, to plot all the time. I would remember to dissemble for short periods, then I would forget and act straight and human again" (Wright, *Black Boy,* p. 218).

Blacks who expressed rebellion against the racist actions of whites risked their lives. Survival depended upon a passive response. This inability to fight back often led to feelings of helplessness, despair, and impotence. In *Black Boy,* for example, after Wright's uncle was killed by whites, "There was no funeral. . . . There was no period of mourning. . . . There were only silence, quiet weeping, whispers, and fear. . . . Aunt Maggie was not even allowed to see his body nor was she able to claim any of his assets" (*Black Boy,* p. 64).

Later Wright worked in a white-owned clothing store that catered to poor blacks. There, "the boss, his son, and the clerk treated the Negros with open contempt, pushing, kicking, or slapping them. . . . I kept on edge, trying to stifle my feelings and never quite succeeding" (*Black Boy,* p. 212). Once, at the same job, he saw his supervisors drag a frightened black woman to the back of the store under the indifferent gaze of a white policeman. He heard her piercing screams. When the bloody, crying woman later stumbled out of the store, the policeman accused her of drunkenness and arrested her. Wright states that he was shocked but "they would not beat me if I knew enough to keep my mouth shut" (*Black Boy,* p. 213).

Sources. In 1943 Richard Wright accepted an invitation to speak to the sociology students of Fisk University, a prominent black school in Nashville. He told them about his life as a black American author. The students' enthusiastic response helped inspire him to write a book about his own life. After the speech, he returned home and devoted himself to the project for the next eight months. The finished manuscript chronicled his life from childhood through his break with Communism in the late 1930s. His publisher believed that the book-buying public would be most interested in Wright's years living in the South. He therefore suggested that only the first part, ending with his 1927 departure for Chicago, be released. Wright agreed. *Black Boy: A Recollection of Childhood and Youth* was published in 1945. His Chicago memories were published under the title of *American Hunger* in 1977.

Events in History at the Time the Autobiography Was Written

World War II. The United States entered the Second World War in December of 1941. U.S. troops were ostensibly fighting to protect what

The segregated railroad station in Jackson, Mississippi, 1955.

President Roosevelt called the four freedoms of American democracy: freedom of speech and expression, freedom of worship, freedom from want, and freedom from fear. However, these freedoms had not yet been attained by many Americans—particularly blacks.

Racial discrimination was common to military life. Until 1943, no black was allowed to enlist in the U.S. Marine Corps or in the army air forces. Blacks in the rest of the armed forces were trained in segregated camps and fought in separate units. Just as in civilian life, blacks in the military were regularly limited to the most menial assignments. American defense industries also discriminated against their black employees during the 1940s.

The hypocrisy of racism in a democratic society fighting for freedom became evident to increasing numbers of Americans during World War II. More became involved in the fight for civil rights at home. A. Philip Randolph, president of a black union called the Brotherhood of Sleeping Car Porters, began to insist that the government require defense contractors to integrate their work forces. In fact, he planned a march in Washington, D.C., to gather support. President Roosevelt convinced him to cancel the march, promising in return to establish a Fair Employment Practices Commission (FEPC) to investigate racial discrimination in war industries. The

FEPC's enforcement powers were limited, but its creation was a symbolic victory for the civil rights movement of the 1940s. Civilian protests were also launched by the Congress of Racial Equality (CORE). This group of black and white Chicagoans organized frequent sit-ins and demonstrations protesting discrimination in public places like theaters and restaurants; CORE groups soon became active in other cities as well. The system of racial prejudice that Richard Wright described in *Black Boy* was still quite prominent in the 1940s, but more individuals were beginning to get involved in the fight for civil rights.

Civil rights movement—the 1970s. Written at the same time as the first part of *Black Boy* but set in the North, the second part was published thirty-two years later in 1977. By this time the contemporary civil rights movement had scored some victories—the 1964 Civil Rights Act had, for example, outlawed racial discrimination in voting, hiring practices, and public accommodations. Racism did persist, however, and reared its troublesome head in the North during this era. In 1965 civil rights leader Martin Luther King, Jr., moved to Chicago, where the second part of *Black Boy* is set. "I've been in demonstrations all across the south," said King, "but I can say that I have never seen—even in Mississippi and Alabama—mobs as hostile and hate-filled as I've seen in Chicago" (King in Weisbrot, p. 182). King's campaign turned civil rights into a nationwide rather than just a Southern cause but did little to change ghetto life. Frustrated, new black leaders in the 1960s began calling for black power—specifically the control over such institutional bodies as law enforcement, schools, and other public services. A share in power, not just integration, had become a primary goal for these blacks.

The federal government, nevertheless, continued to promote integration in public education. Busing became a divisive issue during this era; judicial authorities ordered cross-town busing of blacks and whites to each other's public schools in an effort to eradicate segregation. White Northerners rebelled against this decree. In 1974 five thousand Bostonians staged an antibusing march, and parents shifted nearly 20,000 white students from Boston's public schools to private ones. By 1976, a year before the second part of *Black Boy* appeared, blacks constituted a majority in Boston's public schools. The city had, in effect, resegregated itself, a pattern adopted to a greater or lesser extent in many other cities across the nation.

Reviews. *Black Boy* was first published in March 1945. It immediately became a Book-of-the-Month Club selection and remained on the best-seller list through November of that year. Wright received hundreds of fan letters from blacks and whites about his work, and it received high praise from many critics.

Not everyone was enthusiastic, however. Its vivid depiction of racism made the book highly controversial. Many stores and libraries, particularly those in the South, refused to carry it, and newspapers like Mississippi's *Natchez Democrat* would not print ads for the book. By 1977, when the second part was published under the title *American Hunger,* the 1940s edition had gained wider acceptance. Though critics praised it as a moving and revealing account, the 1977 publication earned less acclaim than the first part of the autobiography.

For More Information

Alvarez, Joseph A. *From Reconstruction to Revolution: The Blacks' Struggle for Equality.* New York: Atheneum, 1972.

Grossman, James R. *Land of Hope: Chicago, Black Southerners, and the Great Migration.* Chicago: University of Chicago, 1989.

McMillen, Neil R. *Dark Journey: Black Mississippians in the Age of Jim Crow.* Urbana: University of Illinois, 1989.

Mencken, H. L. *The Bathtub Hoax and Other Blasts and Bravos from the* Chicago Tribune. New York: Alfred A. Knopf, 1958.

Solomon, Mark I. *Red and Black: Communism and Afro-Americans, 1929-1935.* New York: Garland, 1988.

Weisbrot, Robert. *Freedom Bound: A History of America's Civil Rights Movement.* New York: W. W. Norton, 1990.

Wright, Richard. *Black Boy.* 1945. Reprint. New York: HarperCollins, 1993.

Bound for Glory

by
Woody Guthrie

Woody Guthrie was born into an upper-class family in Okemah, Oklahoma, in 1912. Musically gifted, he experienced many hardships during his childhood, including an increasingly poverty-stricken household and the breakup of his family. During the Great Depression, Guthrie set out on his own for California. He spent time in the state's migrant camps, composing songs and riding trains from one place to the next. A left-wing political activist, he eventually became an acclaimed folksinger. *Bound for Glory* details his experiences on the road to fame and also brings alive the historical realities of the era.

> ## THE LITERARY WORK
>
> An autobiography set in Oklahoma, Texas, California, New York, and on the open road from the 1910s to the 1940s; published in 1943.
>
> ## SYNOPSIS
>
> *Bound for Glory* details the life of the well-known folksinger Woody Guthrie. As an "Okie," an Oklahoma Dust Bowl refugee, Guthrie spent a large portion of his life playing music and riding trains and boxcars back and forth across the country.

Events in History at the Time of the Autobiography

From the "Red Scare" to the Great Depression. Ushering in the 1920s was a "red scare" in America—a fear of a communist revolution in the country. This scare followed on the heels of the 1917 communist takeover of Russia and the 1919 founding of two American communist parties. Uniting into one party in 1921, the American communists remained small, but there was heated reaction to them from many Americans.

Although widespread fear of a communist revolution similar to Russia's subsided somewhat in the 1920s, society's antiradical stance remained strong. There was widespread opposition to the growth of labor unions in the nation, which were viewed at first as un-American collectives. Business leaders set out to crush the unions, and

achieved some success. In 1921 they rid the nation's meat-packing plants of labor unions, and in 1922 judges prohibited a strike in the railway industry. The labor movement flagged for a time, then revived. Membership grew, and the movement split into two divisions in 1935—the American Federation of Labor (AFL) and the workers who would form the Congress of Industrial Organizations (CIO). The latter faction proceeded to try unionizing industries whose employees had not yet organized, but from the shipping docks of the West to the textile mills of the East, employers fought back. Workers were beaten, gassed, and even murdered to prevent them from instituting union organizations in the companies where they worked.

A soup kitchen for the poor during the Great Depression.

At the same time, the 1920s brought a rising number of consumer products to the nation. Output in the automobile and construction industries soared, and electricity in homes became commonplace, bringing radio into the average household. America's first radio station, KDKA of Pittsburgh, began broadcasting in 1920; by 1923 the United States boasted over three hundred stations. The radio stations, as well as record companies, began searching for talent to fill this new market. Meanwhile, the overall production of consumer items continued apace until the end of the 1920s, when economic collapse descended on the nation.

Beginning in 1929, a devastating downswing in business known as the Great Depression left millions jobless, hungry, and homeless. Consumption flagged, businesses went bankrupt, and basic needs went unmet. Without food, people stood in breadlines for government handouts. The jobless rate climbed from 1.5 million in 1929 to 12.1 million in just three years, and more than a million homeless roamed the nation in search of work. There were feelings of anger, despair, and desperation. Lynch mobs reappeared during this era, hanging suspects without due process of the law. Their targets were usually blacks, as in the post-Civil War era when racial strife had also been inflamed by economic difficulties.

Introducing the "New Deal," President Franklin Delano Roosevelt took office in 1933 and offered the nation innovative programs to put the jobless to work and to reduce misery. Many responded positively. "Roosevelt is the only president we ever had," said one worker, "that thought the Constitution belonged to the poor man too" (Bailyn, p. 739). But the Communist Party, which gained momentum at this time, disagreed. In its view, the New Deal was not radical enough. Party membership increased from 7,650 in 1930 to 75,000 in 1938. Though still small, the party influenced a cross-section of Americans beyond its hard-core members—mostly workers but also Woody Guthrie and other nonconformists of the troubled 1930s.

Oil booms. In *Bound for Glory,* Woody Guthrie describes his life in several oil boom towns located in Oklahoma and Texas. Oil prices rose dramatically as the automobile industry expanded. This price increase spawned new exploratory searches for oil in Oklahoma and nearby states, which quickened growth in the area. From 1925 to 1931, the counties that would make up the future Dust Bowl region were vigorously developed.

Once oil was found, old communities would rapidly expand and new ones would suddenly appear in a manner similar to the gold rush areas of earlier times:

> The discovery of a new pool of oil by an enterprising wildcatter would ignite a frenzy of excitement and a furious scramble to lease the most promising lands. . . . This rush of humanity would stimulate the frantic construction of hotels, cafes, pool halls, and other establishments designed to meet the needs of the workers.
>
> (Franks, Lambert, and Tyson, p. 5)

Pipelines were constructed to transport the oil from these towns to larger metropolitan areas such as Denver, Colorado. Streets were paved, highways expanded, and water and sewer systems developed. Some communities even held festivals in order to celebrate the oil deposits that surrounded them.

Because of oil discoveries, many communities in Oklahoma and Texas actually experienced economic growth from 1929 to 1931, the preliminary years of the Great Depression. In general, however, when the oil deposits dried up, these thriving communities faded as quickly as they had grown. Men such as Guthrie's father often lost as much money as they earned. After the boom, towns like *Bound for Glory*'s Okemah boarded up their cafés and hotels.

The Dust Bowl. Throughout the 1930s, the southern portion of the Great Plains suffered under severe weather patterns. Technically, the term "Dust Bowl"—first used by a reporter named Robert Geiger who wrote for a paper called *The Evening Star*—refers to particular counties in Colorado, Kansas, New Mexico, Texas, Oklahoma, and Nebraska. The phrase is associated with the severe drought, wind erosion, economic depression, and subsequent migration from that area during this time. Harvests failed year after year as farmers found their crops pummeled by hail, drought, freezing temperatures, floods, and even plagues of rabbits and grasshoppers.

One of the most famous sights of the Dust Bowl were "rollers," or severe dust storms. Rollers were huge clouds of dust that blocked out the sun, making visibility impossible. These storms dumped several feet of dust onto farms and stripped the land of its topsoil. In 1933 the town of Goodwell, Oklahoma, recorded 70 days of severe dust storms while Texhoma, Oklahoma, reported 139. Some of the storms destroyed houses, property, and lives as well as crops. The air grew so heavy with dust that many people died of dust pneumonia. During a dust storm in Pampa, Texas—fearing, it seems, for his life—Guthrie wrote the song "So Long, It's Been Good to Know You." These severe dust storms, along with economic factors, prompted many people living in the Dust Bowl area, as well as in Arkansas and Missouri, to leave their homes and migrate west in search of a better life. Whole families moved together, becoming known as "Dust Bowl refugees," or, more negatively, "Okies."

Riding the rails. In 1933 the Great Depression reached its severest depths. A portion of the one million homeless had by this time become a transient group that moved from place to place in search of work. Guthrie spent years living among these transients, absorbing the particulars of the lifestyle. Some of these people viewed themselves as part of a long hobo tradition that had its roots in the previous century:

> They developed an elaborate mythology and customs to make it more palatable. They took names like Denver Fly and Mobile Mac, Poison Face Time and Dick the Stabber. They told long, improbable tales around the campfire . . . about legendary hoboes, good towns and bad. . . . They made up songs about life on the bum: some dripping with overripe romanticism, but others with a rough honesty that cut through the myths.
>
> (Klein, p. 44)

As described in Guthrie's autobiography, the towns through which these transients passed were often hostile. The average community saw them as a threat and took measures to prevent the homeless from settling in the area. Many of them ate at soup kitchens or, like Guthrie himself, were forced to beg for food. They lived in roadside camps called "hobo jungles" or on skid row, a district of cheap hotels, saloons, and employment agencies frequented by society's underclass.

Moving from one place to another was an essential part of transient life. Some people traveled in order to find work, while others simply considered rootlessness an integral part of the hobo tradition. Many of the transients "flipped" trains, the term used for hopping on and off the cars without paying.

Transients most often rode on freight cars and placed themselves almost anywhere on board the railway vehicles. They rode inside cars, underneath them, on top, in the front, and on the sides. Of course, flipping trains was quite dangerous and people often died in the process. Boxcar

A "hobo jungle," 1931.

doors opened without warning, sometimes hurling inhabitants out the door. Cargo shifted, crushing those beneath it. The most courageous transients rode the rods, propping themselves along the four-foot bar underneath the train, inches away from the tracks.

Folksingers and songs of the 1930s and 1940s. Folksingers like Guthrie became very popular during the 1930s and '40s for a number of reasons. Both the radio and phonograph industries had expanded during the 1920s, and by the close of the decade they had begun to promote Texas cowboy songs, hobo and train tunes, and country blues to a growing nation of music consumers.

As the Okies migrated into California during the 1930s, their musical interests encouraged this turn in the entertainment industry. Music took a prominent place in the social activities of the migrants. Guitars, fiddles, harmonicas, and banjos were a common form of entertainment at their campsites.

Many Okies sought employment as musicians when their search for other types of work in California failed. In his autobiography Guthrie does not mention that his cousin Jack was a talented musician in California. Jack, whose stage name was "Oklahoma," concocted a radio program called "The Oklahoma and Woody Show," thus providing Guthrie with one of his first encounters with the entertainment industry. His popularity grew, and later in the decade he received more than a thousand fan letters a month as the sole "hillbilly" singer on the Los Angeles radio station KFVD. Many of these letters were from Okies themselves, who enjoyed Guthrie's music, anecdotes, and cornpone philosophy. Despite the fact that he was well read, Guthrie learned to cultivate an image as a naive, poor, rural person to appeal to his audience. This image of him permeates *Bound for Glory*.

Guthrie, however, did not gain his greatest fame in California. He left the state at the end of the decade for New York, where the folksong movement was extremely politically oriented. Urban left-wing political activists viewed folksingers and their songs as a means of spreading ideology. The communist and other leftist movements, which had gained popularity during the 1930s, actively sought out singers like Guthrie to spread their ideals to the middle class. Folksongs were sung at political rallies and union meetings. *Bound for Glory* does not detail Guthrie's involvement in left-wing politics, but he sang at communist fund-raisers and even had his own editorial column for six months in a communist paper, *The People's World*. The left-wing activists hailed Guthrie as an Okie troubadour who represented a class of oppressed people. He went on to spend the early 1940s writing protest songs with Pete Seeger and the Almanacs, a musical group dedicated to raising social consciousness through song.

The songs that Guthrie wrote or cowrote were often topical and dealt with issues of immediate importance. "This Land Is Your Land," one of Guthrie's most well-known tunes, for example, parodies Irving Berlin's "God Bless America." Guthrie's version declares that all people own the land, not just the rich and powerful. "A sign was painted said: Private Property," says one verse of the song. "But . . . God Blessed America for me" (Guthrie in Klein, p. 141).

Guthrie himself actively promoted the perceived relationship of folksong to political ideology when he notes, "As long as we've got wrecks, disasters, cyclones, hurricanes, explosions, lynchings, trade union troubles, high prices and low pay, as long as we've got cops in uniform battling with union pickets on strike, folksongs and folk ballads are on their way in" (Guthrie in Botkin, p. 60).

The Autobiography in Focus

The contents. *Bound for Glory* is the autobiographical account of Woody Guthrie's life, beginning with his boyhood and ending during the war years. The autobiography starts in the 1940s on a train "bound for glory," then flashes back to Guthrie's beginnings. Sprinkled through the work are incidents that bring up social issues of the day, such as the prejudice expressed by the racial epithet "nigger."

Guthrie chronicles his boyhood in Okemah, Oklahoma, a small farming community of about a thousand inhabitants. As a toddler he lives in a big seven-room house. His father works hard to provide the family with material goods and a comfortable lifestyle, and Guthrie spends his own days the same way other boys do. He gets into many fights, even participating in gang warfare. As he grows up, he develops a reputation as a tough kid. People place bets on his fighting abilities, encouraging the winner of any fist fight to take on Guthrie. "Betcha cain't lick ol' Woody!" they often taunt (Guthrie, *Bound for Glory*, p. 136).

A series of hardships strikes the Guthrie family during the singer's childhood. Their beautiful, seven-room house mysteriously burns to the ground. The family moves into a smaller, stone house, but the adjustment adversely affects the health of Guthrie's mother, who is afflicted with Huntington's chorea, a disease of the central nervous system. His father meanwhile encounters financial difficulties, and then a cyclone hits town and rips the roof off the new house. The Guthries move across town.

Okemah grows into an oil boom town. The population swells and Guthrie's father once again makes a great deal of money by buying and selling land. Dance halls, saloons, and gambling houses spring up overnight. Life, it seems, has become good again.

Yet trouble strikes once again. According to *Bound for Glory,* their old kerosene stove blows up while his sister, Clara, irons on it. The flames burn her so badly that she dies, after which Guthrie's mother deteriorates further.

The Guthries leave town for a while but cannot find work. They return to Okemah exactly one year later, moving into a dirty house in the shabby part of town. Okemah is no longer a boom community. Many people have left, stores are boarded up, and both work and money appear to be scarce.

Fortunately, Guthrie's father and his brother, Roy, find good jobs selling auto licenses. Too young for a real job, Guthrie decides to plant a garden and sell the produce. One day, as he and his mother sit outside near the house, they notice smoke drifting out from between the wooden chinks. As his father enters the house to find the source of the smoke, the oil stove explodes. Severely burnt, Guthrie's father goes to western Texas to recuperate. His mother is sent to an insane asylum, and he and his brother are left to fend for themselves.

Guthrie chooses to live in the ramshackle gang fort that he helped build with his friends. He earns money by scrounging through garbage heaps, finding bits and pieces of scraps to sell to the junk man. He also works at odd jobs such as washing spittoons and shining shoes.

Years later, Guthrie's father writes from Texas that his burns have finally healed and he is again working in the land business. Seventeen years old at the time, Guthrie joins him in Pampa, Texas. Pampa is another oil boom town, so work proves easy to find. Here Guthrie holds a variety of odd jobs; one of them is selling alcohol illegally.

Guthrie, now in his twenties, receives a letter from his aunt Laura in Sonora, California, encouraging him to leave dusty Texas and move to her state. Following her advice, he leaves for California, becoming adept at riding railroad trains without paying, evading the police, and begging for food.

During his train rides, Guthrie meets many homeless people. Most are seeking jobs, riding the train to a place that might offer them employment. They fight against one another but also share food, drink, and cigarettes. They swap stories and evade the police and train guards who try to keep the homeless from riding for free. Sometimes sneaking inside boxcars, sometimes on top, they endure choking dust, freezing rain, and unbearable wind or heat.

After many adventures, Guthrie reaches his aunt's house. Dirty and ragged, he knocks on her door. A butler answers, and suddenly Guthrie realizes he does not want the easy, soft, life of the rich. So Guthrie excuses himself and again takes to the open road.

Guthrie rides the rails with other men, playing songs on his guitar and looking for work. He arrives at migrant labor camps that are filled with people waiting for jobs.

Composing songs for the people he encounters, Guthrie sometimes earns money by playing in the saloons.

> I'd play my guitar and sing the longest, oldest, and saddest songs and ballads I knew; I'd nod and smile and say thank you every time somebody dropped a penny or a nickel into my cigar box.
>
> (*Bound for Glory*, p. 327)

He travels and plays his guitar through forty-two states, living on the tips he made. Guthrie becomes famous during his travels; he performs on the radio and makes records. The autobiography documents how, despite his fame, he chooses to remain poor and to continue the way of life that inspires his songs. In one of the final chapters, he describes a fateful decision. Guthrie has been invited to audition for a job at the Rainbow Room in New York City. The bosses become excited when they hear him sing, and start telling him what he will have to wear and how he must sing in order to please their audience. Guthrie walks out. Instead of taking the job, he finds a friend, jumps on a barge, and leaves. A short while later the book ends where it began, on a train bound for glory.

Migration west. Many Okies ended up picking fruit as migrant workers in California. Historically, migrant workers in this state were isolated from the local community and subject to severe discrimination. In 1935 they were excluded from the retirement and unemployment protec-

tion of a newly established Social Security system set up as part of FDR's New Deal. In 1938 they were excluded from the wage and hours regulations of the Fair Labor Standards Act. Such discrimination often left the migrant workers poverty-stricken. The Okie migrants resided in huge, unsanitary squatter or labor camps, with whole families living in cars, trucks, or shacks. Sometimes they were stranded in the orchards without work, or even enough money for gas to leave the area. Many quickly found themselves in debt to a farm's store, which charged exorbitant prices for food and supplies. Guthrie describes the living conditions of such camps in *Bound for Glory*:

> The camp was bigger than the town itself. People had dragged old car fenders up from the dumps, wired them from the limbs of oak trees a few feet off of the ground and this was a roof for some of them. Others had taken old canvas sacks or wagon sheets, stretched the canvas over little limbs cut so the fores braced each other, and that was a house for those folks. . . . Lots of people, families mostly, had some bedclothes with them, and I could see the old stinky, gummy quilts and blankets hung up like tents, . . . there was scatterings of cardboard shacks, where the people had lugged cartons, cases, packing boxes out from town and tacked them into a house.
>
> (*Bound for Glory*, p. 329)

A MELODY FOR THE OKIES, "DO RE MI"

~

Many of Guthrie's songs chronicle the experience of the Okies in California and the state's negative reception of the newcomers.

> Now, the police at the port of entry say
> "You're number fourteen thousand for today."
> Oh if you ain't got the do re mi, folks,
> If you ain't got the do re mi,
> Why, you'd better go back to beautiful Texas,
> Oklahoma, Kansas, Georgia, Tennessee.
> (Guthrie quoted in Gregory, p. 232)

The injustices that gave rise to such conditions prompted Guthrie and other radicals to make an attempt at politically organizing farm laborers to fight for their basic rights. Yet the Okies were only partially willing to listen. While they came from a strongly Democratic background and responded to appeals on behalf of the common man, many were less willing to agree with the radicals' ideas about racial equality. The Okies, moreover, distrusted the radicals and therefore proved difficult to organize into a cohesive, leftist political entity.

Sources. *Bound for Glory* is Guthrie's account of his life, based loosely on his own experiences as a child, folksinger, migrant worker, and transient. More concerned with political and social issues of his day than with other matters, he omitted some personal details and fabricated others. According to biographer Joe Klein, for example, Clara did not die because the old kerosene stove exploded while she ironed on it, as *Bound for Glory* claims. In fact, writes the biographer, in a fit of rage because her mother kept her home from school to do housework, Clara set her dress on fire, intending to burn it only slightly to frighten her mother. To Clara's surprise, the dress exploded into flames that consumed much of her skin, without which she soon froze to death.

Reviews. Guthrie was commissioned to write his autobiography and paid an advance of $500 for it by E. P. Dutton, a publishing house. Originally entitled *Boomchasers*, *Bound for Glory* left out so many critical parts of Guthrie's life that some considered it a piece of fiction. Other readers recognized the book's failures but responded positively to its humor and style despite its defects. Critical reception to *Bound for Glory* was generally favorable. Reviewers often mentioned in passing aspects of the book regarded as flaws—the fabrications, attempts to use dialect, and clumsy illustrations—but generally commended the writing. One critic for the *New Yorker* even predicted:

> Some day people are going to wake up to the fact that Woody Guthrie and the ten thousand songs that leap and tumble off the strings of his music box are a national possession, like Yellowstone or Yosemite, and part of the best stuff this country has to show the world.
>
> (Fadiman in Klein, p. 259)

The book, however, caused Guthrie some personal trouble. One chapter graphically describes his cousin, Warren Tanner, sadistically killing kittens. Upset by the portrayal, Tanner sued Guthrie for libel.

Guthrie's romantic life is practically nonexistent in his autobiography. It says that he lived in Pampa in a small shack. In reality, he shared that shack with his wife Mary and their children. As he traveled, he often left Mary behind to care for the kids, and eventually they split permanently. He later married a woman named Marjorie Greenblatt, who became instrumental in helping him edit his autobiography.

Guthrie only vaguely hints at his political activities and the relationship of his songs to political protest. From the 1920s to the 1940s, left-wing political ideology was a strong force in the United States. Communist activists openly sought folksingers as representatives of "the people," and Guthrie fit this bill. He, in fact, entered into a long-term relationship with left-wing politics and the Communist Party, whose ideas also appealed to other musicians of his day.

For More Information

Bailyn, Bernard, et al., eds. *The Great Republic: A History of the American People.* Lexington, Mass.: D. C. Heath, 1985.

Botkin, Benjamin A. "The Folklore Scene." *New York Folklore Quarterly* 22, no. 1, pp. 59-61.

Franks, Kenny, Paul Lambert, and Carl Tyson. *Early Oklahoma Oil.* College Station: Texas A & M University Press, 1981.

Gregory, James N. *American Exodus.* New York: Oxford University Press, 1989.

Guthrie, Woody. *Bound for Glory.* 1943. Reprint, New York: E. P. Dutton, 1968.

Klein, Joe. *Woody Guthrie: A Life.* New York: Alfred A. Knopf, 1980.

Reuss, Richard. "American Folklore and Left-Wing Politics, 1927-1957." Ph.D. diss., Indiana University, 1971.

Wormser, Richard. *Hoboes: Wandering in America, 1870-1940.* New York: Walker, 1994.

The Call of the Wild

by
Jack London

John Griffith London, the illegitimate son of a freelance philosopher and self-proclaimed Professor of Astrology father and an emotionally distant spiritualist mother, was born January 12, 1876, in San Francisco, California. The boy, later known as Jack, spent much of his childhood working odd jobs to help support his family. After traveling abroad on a seal-hunting ship and tramping across much of the United States, Jack briefly attended the University of California at Berkeley. When news of the gold rush in the Yukon reached him, he packed his bags and left California with thousands of other would-be prospectors to test his mettle in the frozen north. After spending the winter and the spring of 1898 in the Yukon, London had not found an ounce of gold and was suffering the effects of scurvy, a disease brought about by dietary deficiencies. Realizing he was beaten, London returned to California without gold, but with a wealth of experiences and impressions from the Klondike that would soon be captured in the stories and novels for which he became famous. The most successful of these Klondike tales is *The Call of the Wild*, a novel that propelled London to the forefront of American fiction.

Events in History at the Time of the Novel

The Depression and Coxey's Army. In the America of Jack London's youth, a small group of powerful men controlled the banks, railroads, public utilities, and most of the basic industries. Depressions struck the American economy from

---

THE LITERARY WORK

A novel set in the Yukon region of Canada in 1898 during the Klondike gold rush; published in 1903.

SYNOPSIS

Buck, a pampered dog living on a California ranch, is kidnapped and taken to the Yukon, where he becomes a sled dog and eventually reverts to the most basic animal savagery.

1873 to 1878, 1883 to 1885, and 1893 to 1897. Between 1881 and 1906, some 30,000 strikes and lockouts occurred, affecting 200,000 businesses and over 9.5 million workers. The financial panic of 1893 prompted one of the worst depressions the nation had yet experienced. From these desperate financial conditions sprang such groups as the Nationalists, the Christian Socialists, and the Populists, all of which organized themselves to protest economic conditions. Jacob S. Coxey's solution to the depression was monetary inflation and a plan of federal work relief on public roads. When his plan went unheeded by Congress, Coxey decided to "send a petition to Washington with boots on" (Coxey in Johnston, p. 11).

On March 25, 1894, Coxey and his army of unemployed workers left Massillon, Ohio, for Washington, D.C. During the same month, similar armies organized themselves in Los Angeles and San Francisco. Charles T. Kelly, a printer by trade, became the spokesman for one branch of the San Francisco army. At the behest of local authorities, Kelly's Army left the Bay Area for Sacramento—Jack London, seeing the mass of disgruntled workers as an opportunity for escape, freedom, and adventure, set out after the army, eventually joining a contingent from Reno, Nevada, who themselves were trying to catch up with Kelly's band.

During one episode along the way, London and several other "soldiers" gorged themselves on a supply of food intended for equal distribution among the group. London justified this theft by saying, "This was hard on the army, I allow, but the ten of us were individualists. We had initiative and enterprise. We ardently believed that the grub was to the man who got there first and the Vienna [coffee boiled in milk] to the strong" (London in Johnston, p. 14).

THE LEADER OF THE TEAM

In a sled team, a good leader dog was crucial. During the winter of 1897-1898, when dogs were selling for $200 in Dawson, lead dogs were commanding $300 each. A well-trained dog relieved the driver of half the work involved in driving the team. The qualities required in a good lead dog were intelligence, discipline, and responsiveness. It was the lead dog's responsibility to keep to the trail and hold the harness taut. Leaders were generally of the native breeds, with some exceptions. Jeremiah Lynch, a former United States senator, believed that the Scottish collie made the best leader. In *The Call of the Wild*, Buck kills the native lead dog, Spitz, and assumes the position of leader himself.

Though London abandoned the march just after crossing the Mississippi River, this trek with Coxey's radicals had a profound influence on his life, paving the way for his eventual advocacy of communism. In fact, it was as London "tramped" his way back to California that he first read Karl Marx and Friedrich Engels's *Communist Manifesto,* a book which would dramatically affect his future writings. Also, London's enjoyment of the freedom of the march and his subsequent "tramping" would inspire him to head for the promise of gold in the frozen Klondike just a few years later.

Gold rush on the Klondike. On August 16, 1896, gold was discovered on Bonanza Creek, a tiny branch of the Klondike River in the Yukon territory in northwest Canada. Some fifty miles to the west of the creek sat the U.S.-Canada border of Alaska, which numerous gold prospectors would cross. As news of the discovery spread throughout the territory, countless prospectors in the United States and Canada abandoned their diggings in other areas and headed for the Klondike. In July of 1897, two gold-laden ships brought evidence of the newly discovered wealth to the west coast: the *Portland* arrived in Seattle, and the *Excelsior* arrived in San Francisco. Jack London was living across the San Francisco Bay in Oakland at the time.

Almost immediately, a stream of men headed north, determined to win their share of the Klondike's wealth. Three factors combined to create the massive response to the gold rush: the existence of vast amounts of gold, the publicity given to the discovery in the press of the time, and the tremendous evolution of transportation systems since the era of the fur trade. While some men did find gold in the frozen north, most fortunes were made by those who provided supplies or services to the thousands of would-be prospectors.

The miners soon realized that little mining could be undertaken during the Klondike's brutal winters, during which they were forced to take whatever shelter they could find, spending exorbitant prices for lodging, food, and other supplies. After one season in the rugged Klondike, most miners headed south, even poorer than before. Of the 250,000 men who sought gold in the Klondike, only 50,000 actually reached the region's interior; only 1,000 returned richer than they were when they started. London, like so many others, was beaten by the Klondike and returned with empty pockets, broken health, and a severe case of scurvy. Fortunately he also brought with him a wealth of material, which he would soon incorporate in the novel that launched his career as one of America's greatest writers.

Dogs in the Klondike. The gold rush created a need for a reliable, weatherproof transportation system in the Klondike, a need that could be met by only one available resource: dogs. As a result, dogs became synonymous with winter transportation between 1897 and 1900, and proved useful in the summer too. Dogs hauled equipment, delivered mail, and labored in the mines themselves. During the summers, the dogs were used as pack animals; during the winters they pulled sleds. By 1899 there were ap-

Dog team and sled, similar to the one Buck led.

proximately four thousand dogs in the mining town of Dawson. Most of the animals were privately owned, but transportation companies owned some as well. During the summer months gold was brought into Dawson from the mines by dog trains consisting of fifteen to twenty dogs, each carrying a thirty-pound pack. A fifteen-dog train could haul $122,400 worth of gold. During the summer, the dog trains operated twenty-four hours a day, six days a week. During the winter, dog punchers, as the drivers of the dog teams were called, worked eight hours a day, averaging twenty miles with a load of twelve hundred pounds.

Various breeds of dog were used for freighting in the Yukon. The most sought-after were the native breeds—the husky, the malamute, and the "Siwash," or Indian dog. Though they were often bad-tempered, giving rise to vicious dog fights, these native dogs were well suited to the task and to the environment, being strong in the back and legs as well as having thick outer and inner coats of hair, and paws that were well furred between the pads and toes. Native dogs also showed an incredible talent for scavenging, a skill that was crucial for survival in the frozen Yukon. During the gold rush, however, the importing of non-native dogs for sale became a brisk business. In fact, the number of outside

dogs far exceeded the number of native breeds in use at this time. These outside dogs did not have the strength and adaptability of the native dogs, but some, like the St. Bernard and the mastiff, were unsurpassed at short-distance hauling.

On the trail, dogs were fed dried salmon, each dog receiving two pounds of fish each day. They were fed once a day, and always at night. This was done to encourage them to make better time on the trail, as dogs tended to become lazy after feeding.

Under optimum conditions, a team of five native dogs could pull a sled with a 1,000-pound load a distance of fifteen to twenty-five miles in a single day. Generally, the sled was loaded at the ratio of 160 pounds to each dog. With their heavy fur, over-sweating was a constant problem when dogs pulled heavy loads. To remedy this condition, the driver stopped frequently and let the dogs cool off by rolling in the snow. Another problem the dogs faced was injury from ice crystals forming between the pads of their feet. When a driver saw a dog limping, he would stop and thaw the pads by putting them in his mouth and drying them with a cloth. In *The Call of the Wild,* when Buck's feet are injured by the cold and roughness of the ice, he is given small moccasins to keep his feet warm.

The Novel in Focus

The plot. Buck, a massive dog, half Saint Bernard, half Scotch shepherd, leads a life of luxury on Judge Miller's ranch in the Santa Clara Valley in California. Because of the current gold rush in the Yukon territory, strong dogs have become a premium commodity. Manuel, the gardener's helper, kidnaps Buck and sells him to dog-traders. Along his journey, Buck adapts quickly to the "law of club and fang," realizing that his animal strength is no match for the brutality of his human trainers. Two French-Canadian government couriers, Perrault and François, eventually buy Buck and take him into the Yukon as a sled-dog.

Buck learns that to survive the harsh conditions and the savagery of the dog-pack, he must be cunning and ruthless. His civilized morals disappear as survival becomes the driving force of his existence. Buck comes into conflict with Spitz, another dog on the team. When the two dogs fight to the death, Buck triumphs, leaving the mortally wounded Spitz to be devoured by the raging dog pack. In the wild conditions, Buck begins to dream of an ancient past and senses the primal call of the wild, urging him to throw off all vestiges of civilization and revel in pure animal savagery.

Buck is traded to another team, this one pulling a mail sled for the postal service. After several exhausting months of this, he is sold to an inexperienced trio of prospectors, Hal, Charles, and Mercedes. First they feed the dogs too much, and then as the food runs out on their long journey, they feed them too little. Mercedes adds to the exhaustion of the dogs by riding on the sleigh. When the dogs stop pulling because of complete fatigue, Hal whips them mercilessly. John Thornton, a prospector camped nearby, stops Hal and takes Buck away from the inept threesome. Hal, Charles, and Mercedes move on, only to be killed when the ice gives way behind them, pulling humans, dogs, and sled into "a yawning hole."

For the first time, Buck has in Thornton a master he can love. Buck proves this love on several occasions. In two circumstances he saves Thornton's life, once by attacking Black Burton during a barroom brawl, and another time by pulling Thornton out of a series of dangerous rapids. In another act of devotion, Buck wins Thornton a $1,600 bet by single-handedly pulling a thousand pounds on a sled. Thornton and his two partners, Hans and Pete, use the money to support an expedition to find a lost mine. They finally find it and begin mining. Buck runs free through the forests as the men dig for gold, continually testing himself against the harsh environment.

When Buck returns to camp and discovers that Yeehat Indians have surprised and killed his owner and the two other men, he loses his last connection to mankind and civilization and reverts back to his wild nature. In a fury, he kills several of the Indians and becomes legendary among the Indians as a Ghost Dog and an evil spirit. Buck fights against and then joins a wolf pack and creates a superior strain of animal by mating with a wolf. The novel ends as Buck becomes totally absorbed into the natural world.

The individual vs. the pack. In the midst of America's troubled financial climate, London became interested in schools of thought that offered some explanation for the difficult economic conditions. One of the first scholars whose works he read was German philosopher Friedrich Nietzsche, whose concept of the supreme "Übermensch" (superman) thrilled London's sense of rugged individualism. Yet through his experience with Coxey's Army and interactions with Oakland communists, as well as his readings of the *Communist Manifesto,* London was forced to consider the needs of the masses. Buck's struggles in *The Call of the Wild* mirror London's own difficulties in finding a compromise between his drastically contrasting belief systems.

Buck fights his way to the top of the pack, becoming the leader of the sled-dog team after he conquers Spitz in a brutal fight. Despite his aggressively individualistic tendencies, Buck also realizes that the sled team can only function if all of the dogs ignore their individual needs and work to serve simply as one small part of a greater whole. London, struggling to support his family through a long series of grueling employments, came to appreciate the ideas of men such as Eugene V. Debs, the great union organizer, who wanted to shift control of government and industry from capitalist entrepreneurs to workers, making them the ruling class of the United States and the world.

As biographer Carolyn Johnston notes, London's beliefs became a contradictory blend of individualism and socialist concepts, as he "believed that superior individuals could bring about the redemption of workers by initiating socialism, thus changing the environment which had produced inferiority" (Johnston, p. 49). Johnston continues to support the similarities be-

Marshall and Louis Bond with their dog Jack (center), the inspiration for Buck.

tween London and his canine counterpart Buck when she writes:

> The image of the wolf symbolized his dilemma: how to rise out of the working class and still join with it in hastening the revolution. He wanted to be a self-sufficient lone wolf, raging against the forces of nature and ruthlessly fighting for survival. At the same time he was the wolf in the pack, needing comradeship in order to survive as he had during his escapades as a seal hunter. Of course, London preferred to be the leader of the pack.
>
> (Johnston, p. 14)

In the final sentence of the novel, considered by many critics to be the finest sentence of the work, London captures perfectly the dual elements of his sociopolitical agenda as he describes Buck's life with the wolf pack:

> When the long winter nights come on and the wolves follow their meat into the lower valleys, he may be seen running at the head of the pack through the pale moonlight or glimmering borealis, leaping gigantic above his fellows, his great throat a-bellow, as he sings a song of the younger world, which is the song of the pack.
>
> (London, *The Call of the Wild,* p. 101)

Sources. When Jack London boarded the *Umatilla,* a ship bound for the Klondike, on July 25, 1897, he dreamed of making a quick fortune in gold that would guarantee his rapid rise from the working class. After a physically exhausting tour of the gold-rush country, London failed to recover a single ounce of the precious metal. What London did find, however, was of even greater value. Despite his failure as a prospector, London immediately recognized the Klondike's potential as a source of material for his fiction. Long winter nights spent telling stories with other would-be prospectors supplied London with a wealth of ideas. Many details that he would incorporate into his future writings, especially those involving the Klondike's dangerously frigid conditions or the particulars of traversing the treacherous northern wilderness, came directly from London's own experiences. London himself had run the trail into Dawson on which Buck gets one of his first lessons with the sled-team.

One of the questions most frequently asked by readers of the novel concerned the source material for Buck. After much controversy over the issue, with one Dawson woman claiming her dog was the model for the novel's hero, London finally settled the issue by announcing that Buck was actually a dog owned by Judge Marshall Bond, a rancher in the Santa Clara Valley. The real-life Buck was taken to the Klondike by the judge's son Louis. For the detailed traits of the other dogs in the story, London relied on material from Egerton R. Young's book, *My Dogs of the Northland*. With vivid depictions of the sled dogs and vibrant descriptions of the majestic atmosphere of the Klondike, inspired by his own experiences, London created a novel that would establish him as one of America's most popular writers.

LONDON'S FINANCIAL MOTIVATIONS

Throughout his literary career, London stated that his chief motivation for writing was not out of a love or interest in literature, but rather for the sake of money alone. In an interview with Emanuel Haldeman-Julius, London describes his feelings: "The only reason I write is because I am well-paid for my labor—that's what I call it—labor. I get lots of money for my books and stories. I tell you I would be glad to dig ditches for twice as many hours as I devote to writing if only I could get as much money. To me, writing is an easy way to make a fine living" (London in Poupard, p. 256).

The critics. When the Macmillan Company bought the rights to *The Call of the Wild* in 1903, they determined to heavily promote Jack London's third novel. Thousands of dollars were spent on deluxe bindings, beautiful illustrations, and marketing efforts. This extra treatment paid off, and *The Call of the Wild* became one of the best-selling novels of the time. London received $2,700 for the rights to *The Call of the Wild*, an incredible sum, considering that Stephen Crane received only $90 a decade earlier for the rights to *The Red Badge of Courage*.

In addition to bringing London financial gain, *The Call of The Wild* was critically successful as well. A reviewer in *Current Literature* magazine wrote, "This is by far the best piece of work which has come from the pen of this gifted author. . . . The book rises above mere story telling, and possesses elements of the best in literature—scope, vitality, and fullness" (*Current Literature* in Perry, p. 130). Another critic, Carl Sandburg, saw something deeper in the novel: "*The Call of the Wild* is the greatest dog-story ever written and is at the same time a study of one of the most curious and profound motives that play hide-and-seek in the human soul" (Sandburg in Poupard, p. 254). Sandburg goes on to describe this motive, "The more civilized we become the deeper is the fear that back in the barbarism is something of the beauty and joy of life we have not brought along with us" (Sandburg in Poupard, p. 254). One of Macmillan's editors, George Jean Nathan, like Sandburg, saw the novel as a "dog-story" and felt that this choice of subject matter was a major factor in the novel's success. Nathan wrote, "In the many years of my incumbency as a magazine editor, it was a general, and occasionally embarrassing, fact that any half-way good dog story usually attracted wider attention among the readers" (Nathan in Perry, pp. 130-31). And this particular dog story, *The Call of the Wild*, did more than attract attention. It, in fact, catapulted Jack London from his position as an unrecognized author of short stories and magazine articles to the front rank of American novelists.

For More Information

Bennett, Gordon. *Yukon Transportation: A History*. Ottawa: National Historic Parks and Sites Branch, 1978.

Johnston, Carolyn. *Jack London—An American Radical?* Westport, Conn.: Greenwood, 1984.

London, Jack. *The Call of the Wild*. New York: Bantam, 1981.

Perry, John. *Jack London: An American Myth*. Chicago: Nelson-Hall, 1981.

Poupard, Dennis, ed. *Twentieth-Century Literary Criticism*. Vol. 9. Detroit: Gale Research, 1983.

Sinclair, Andrew. *Jack: A Biography of Jack London*. New York: Harper & Row, 1977.

The Cherry Orchard

by
Anton Chekhov

The son of a grocer, Anton Pavlovich Chekhov was born into a family of modest means in Taganrog, Russia, in 1860. Anton's father, Pavel, made some unsound business dealings, and in 1875 he went bankrupt and fled to Moscow, leaving his family behind. Anton Chekhov eventually moved to Moscow too, where he began writing as a career in order to support his family. Living in Moscow, Chekhov became one of Russia's foremost short story writers and dramatists. He later moved to Yalta, completing *The Cherry Orchard,* the last of his four major plays, less than a year before he died of tuberculosis in 1904.

Events in History at the Time of the Play

The decline of the nobility. Over the course of the nineteenth century, the power of Russia's noble families eroded. Many of the families had incurred overwhelming debts. Landowners such as the play's Mrs. Ranevsky went bankrupt by not making productive use of their property or securing enough alternate income.

The financially pressed property owners, or gentry, presided over an unpaid work force of serfs, who were usually obligated to make debt-payments to the owners. Many serfs could not survive without supplementing what they harvested from a portion of the estate. They did so through craft production and occasional wage work in a factory or on another manor lord's property.

The serfs were freed in 1861 by Czar Alexander II. Their initial euphoria was outstripped only by the numbing realization that in actuality, lit-

tle had changed. The options open to them were either agricultural wage work under similar conditions to the ones that had prevailed before emancipation or equally exploitive factory jobs in the burgeoning industrial sector.

As capitalism began to flourish in the 1880s and 1890s, however, freed serfs became increasingly aware of their power as a work force and considered going on strike. At the same time, a handful of hard-working, bright entrepreneurs like Lopakhin in *The Cherry Orchard* found loopholes by which they might make a fortune and purchase the land on which their families had toiled for generations. At the other end of the spectrum, the gentry class who owned the land were unaccustomed to hard work, and often resisted change until it was too late.

Land ownership. Overwhelmed by mortgages and loans past due, the landed gentry lost millions of acres of property between 1877 and 1905. The Nobles' Land Bank was established in 1885 to cope with the crisis, its purpose "to make more easily accessible to the hereditary nobility the means of preserving for their posterity the estates in their possession" (Robinson, p. 131). With this goal in mind, the bank lent large sums at lower rates than those charged by the official Peasants' Land Bank on loans to peasants.

By 1904 over one third of their mortgaged estates were pledged to the Nobles' Land Bank. Occasionally banks and private institutions demanded that properties be auctioned off in order to settle the account. In Chekhov's play Mrs. Ranevsky receives ample warning that her estate will be auctioned off in this fashion, but neither she nor her family is willing to take the drastic measures necessary to save their property. Instead of compromising its grandeur, they prefer to lose it altogether.

Although the Russian Orthodox Church and imperial state remained major landowners, mer-

---

CHEKHOV'S DISTRUST OF THE INTELLIGENTSIA

I don't trust our intelligentsia, hypocritical, bogus, hysterical, uneducated and lazy as it is.... I believe in individuals, I see salvation in isolated personalities scattered here and there throughout Russia; whether they're intellectuals or peasants they are our strength, few of them though there are.

(Chekhov in Hingley, p. 308)

---

chants and peasants now had the opportunity and sometimes the funds to purchase this available land, which they did. "Great God in heaven, the cherry orchard's mine!" exclaims Lopakhin, almost unable to believe what has happened (Chekhov, *The Cherry Orchard*, p. 282). Dispossessed gentlefolk were left with two options: to risk destitution by squandering the remainder of the money from the sale, or to follow Lopakhin's capitalist example.

The intelligentsia. The rise of a new class of secular intellectuals, later called the intelligentsia, took place during the first half of the nineteenth century. Initially the members of this unofficial group were mostly aristocrats who engaged passionately in discussions of ethical and political questions. Later their ranks were swelled by anyone with a similar outlook and level of education, regardless of social class. The sons of provincial priests formed a subgroup that was particularly attracted to the intelligentsia.

The quality valued most by these intellectuals was a love of truth, a concept that for them com-

bined knowledge with justice. They met regularly in small groups and published radical journals that were often banned, since this search for justice and their alienation from the authorities led them to question the practices of the ruling autocracy.

Part of their search for truth manifested itself as a love of science, and in *The Cherry Orchard* Trofimov complains that many pseudo-intellectuals only talk about science instead of using it to benefit the average Russian. When the University of St. Petersburg closed because of student riots in 1861, a leading intellectual urged the students: "Into the people, to the people (*v narod! k narodu*)—there is your destination, banished men of science" (Billington, p. 391). The impulse to take the fruits of learning to the ordinary people was already being put into practice in the novel Sunday-school movement, which flourished between 1859 and 1862 and provided free part-time instruction for the poor, who could not afford to attend the costly secular schools that were the primary source of education in Russia at the time.

The ambitious populist movement that brought about these and other changes in imperial Russia suffered a serious blow in the last two decades of the nineteenth century, following the 1881 assassination of Alexander II. The new czar introduced censorship and repression harsh even by Russian standards, and the utopian expectations of the 1870s faded. They were replaced by so-called "small deeds," and Chekhov, like the perpetual student Trofimov in his play, denounced the intellectuals who had given up without admitting it.

Under the reign of Czar Alexander III, the murdered monarch's son, people who continued to agitate for an improvement in working conditions were frequently arrested or sentenced to forced labor. In fact, the censor ordered Chekhov to rewrite references in *The Cherry Orchard* to bad working conditions and the disillusionment that followed the emancipation of the serfs. The play, however, still contains a veiled allusion to Trofimov's time at forced labor; it appears in Mrs. Ranevsky's surprise at how much Trofimov has aged and in his comment to Anya:

> I'm young and I'm still a student, but I've had my share of hardship. . . . And I've been landed in some pretty queer places. I've seen a thing or two in my time, I can tell you.
> (*The Cherry Orchard*, p. 270)

Only one year after the premiere of *The Cherry Orchard*, the repressive conditions incited hundreds of thousands of Russian workers and their

Anton Chekhov

families to begin openly agitating in the form of strikes, demonstrations, and the eventual revolutions of the early twentieth century.

The revolution of 1905. Despite emancipation and the selling of property by the nobility, most peasants were still unable to feed and care for themselves decently because of a lack of land. Revolutionist agitators had been working for decades to incite the rural population to demand their rights, but the job was not easy since the imperial police were adept at terrorizing the already miserable peasants. Agitators met with sympathy but also with realistic responses like the following:

> If everyone agreed to rise at the same time, if you went around and talked to all the people, then it could be done. We tried several times to rise. We demanded our rights to the land. It was useless. Soldiers were sent down and the people were punished and ruined [*The response of a Ukrainian community to Katerina Breshkovskaia, an agitator and later a leader of the Socialist Revolutionaries*].
>
> (Riha, pp. 347-48)

On the 9th of January, 1905, also known as "Bloody Sunday," an orderly crowd of peasants approached St. Petersburg's Winter Palace, singing patriotic and religious hymns. Hoping to petition the czar for a modicum of human rights, representation in government, and an improvement in working conditions, the protesters drew the fire of his troops instead, and several hundred were killed. That month more than 400,000 factory workers went on strike. Two prominent groups of followers of Karl Marx, the Social Democrats and the Socialist Revolutionaries, seized this opportunity to advocate the overthrow of the autocracy. Resistance continued until the government made two important concessions in the fall of that year.

In one of the concessions, the government pledged to guarantee inviolability of person and liberty of conscience, speech and assembly; in addition, no law could be made without the consent of the new parliament, called the Duma, although the czar reserved an unqualified veto power. In the second major concession to reform, the Peasants' Land Bank would increase assistance to villagers wishing to purchase land, and most of the peasants' remaining debt-payments were canceled.

These concessions were followed by a general relaxation of the movement, signaling that many participants acted out of economic need rather than a single-minded desire to overthrow the autocracy. But the Duma was dissolved several times in an ongoing struggle between protesters and the government, which finally culminated in the Russian Revolution of 1917.

The Play in Focus

The plot. One cold May morning, genteel Mrs. Ranevsky returns home from Paris to her estate in Russia. She had left her home five years earlier, grief-stricken at the deaths of her husband and young son. Now, however, she is glad to walk through the familiar rooms, to be reunited with the members of her household, and to gaze out over the glorious, blossoming cherry orchard.

The Ranevsky family, their friends, and their servants are preoccupied with ordinary concerns, ranging from marriage proposals and deaths to proper winter clothing. In addition, the principal characters wonder how to pay the arrears on the mortgaged estate. If a solution is not found, the property will be sold at auction in August.

Several unlikely possibilities are suggested: the maid will win the lottery, one of the daughters will marry a rich man, someone will leave them money suddenly, a wealthy aunt will be persuaded to help them. Lopakhin, a merchant known to the family, insists that their only recourse is to cut down the orchard immediately and divide up the property for rental to vacationers—a solution Mrs. Ranevsky and her brother feel is too vulgar to be considered seriously. As the deadline approaches, when they think about the problem at all, the family vaguely hopes that an answer will materialize.

On the day of the auction, the Ranevsky household hosts a grand ball, which it cannot afford. Occasionally, Mrs. Ranevsky wonders aloud whether the estate has been sold or not, and finally the answer comes: Lopakhin has bought it. She weeps bitterly.

Two months later, their things packed or set aside for sale, the family prepares to leave. As they are saying their goodbyes, an axe can be heard chopping down a tree in the distance. Sorry for the tactlessness of the workmen, Lopakhin hurries out to stop them until the family leaves. Although saddened, Mrs. Ranevsky and her brother credit their overall good spirits to the sale of the orchard, which freed them from some of their worries.

Once everyone has left, the sound of the axe resounds again in the orchard. The elderly manservant Firs emerges and curls up on the sofa, drained of life. The eerie, far-away sound of a string breaking—heard earlier in the play—is also heard again. Silence follows—only to be broken by the sound of the axe cutting into a cherry tree in the distance.

PRONUNCIATION GUIDE

Mrs. Lyuba Ranevsky	Mrs. Lyuba RaÑEvsky
Leonid Gayev	Lee-oh-NEED GUYev
Yermolay Lopakhin	YeermoLYE LoPAhin
Pyotr Trofimov	Pyotr TroFEEmov
Boris Simeonov-Pishchik	Boris SeemYOHnov PEEshik
Semyon Yepikhodov	SeemYOHn YepiHOdov
Dunyasha	DoonYAsha (short "oo")
Firs	FEERS

The sale of an orchard. It is a common criticism that "nothing happens" in a Chekhov play. And indeed, what is so dramatic about the sale of an orchard, when not even the auction takes place onstage? What the audience does see is a society in transition, and perhaps the answer lies there.

By 1904 the social order had been stood on its head, with the result that an insolent valet like the play's Yasha can serve alongside a devoted, lifelong manservant like Firs. Thus in Chekhov's play Lopakhin, a merchant and former serf, can buy an estate, and Mrs. Ranevsky's brother, Gayev, will take a job at the bank. The characters in this jumbled social milieu might feel that in the transition itself, a great deal is happening.

But is this transition a purely economic one? The student Trofimov offers a possibility that goes deeper:

> Just think, Anya. Your grandfather, your great-grandfather and all your ancestors owned serfs, they owned human souls. Don't you see that from every cherry-tree in the orchard, from every leaf and every trunk, men and women are gazing at you? Don't you hear their voices? Owning living souls, that's what has changed you all so completely, those who went before and those alive today, so that your mother, you yourself, your uncle—you don't realize that you're actually living on credit. You're living on other people, the very people you won't even let inside your own front door.
>
> (*The Cherry Orchard*, p. 269)

Here Chekhov plays on the Russian landowner's custom of referring to serfs as souls, despite the fact that the landowner often treated them worse than animals. And yet Trofimov sounds as if he means what he is saying quite literally. His description implies a unique type of disregard: the act of owning another person's soul, absorbing it into one's property, and not even realizing it.

These implications cast the sale of the orchard and the transition of this society in a new light. The cherry blossoms may be lovely, but the orchard, because of the suffering it represents for all concerned, *must* go, and it must go according to the rules of the new social order. With typically Chekhovian humor and gentleness, the action of the play resolves into the characters' acceptance of these facts.

Sources, composition, and translation. *The Cherry Orchard* started to take shape in Chekhov's mind as early as the beginning of 1901. However, the playwright did not settle down to work until the spring and summer of 1903. In the meantime, he had been distracted by ill health, good fishing, and the editing of earlier works for his publisher.

The loss of the fictional Mrs. Ranevsky's estate recalls the foreclosure on the Chekhov family home in 1876. The difference, of course, is that the sprawling estate has belonged to Ranevsky's aristocratic family for generations, whereas the merchant-class Chekhovs were never able to fully pay off what they owed to possess completely even a modest house. In fact, the loss of a family home underlies other works by Chekhov too, such as *Platonov* (c. 1880) and *The Belated Blossom* (1880-82). These minor works, which antedate *The Cherry Orchard* by more than twenty years, have sometimes been seen as sensational, heavy-handed precursors to it.

Chekhov conceived of the play as a four-act comedy with elements of farce, intending it for the Moscow Art Theater. One of the Theater's most famous actors and producers was Konstantin Stanislavsky. In his memoir *My Life in Art*, the actor-producer explained that several of the play's characters were inspired by people whom Chekhov observed in the summer of 1902 while staying at the estate of Stanislavsky's mother. Inspiration for some characters has also been attributed to people whom Chekhov met earlier, in mid-1888. In any event, Chekhov wrote and revised the parts with specific actors from the Moscow Art Theater in mind. One of them was his wife, Olga Knipper, who played Mrs. Ranevsky, though he originally wrote the role of Varya for her.

Soon after completing the play, Chekhov rewrote two short passages banned by the censor. One referred to contemporary workers' living conditions. The other hinted at the demoralization resulting from freeing the serfs in 1861.

Repeated requests for permission to translate his works were channeled to Chekhov through his wife, but he refused them, suspecting foreigners could not appreciate Russian literature. How, he wondered, could the play make sense in countries with "no billiards, no Lopakhins, no students like Trofimov"? (Hingley, p. 305). Chekhov was probably joking about the billiards at least, even if Gayev is constantly calling out billiard shots. ("In off on the right into the corner. Screw shot into the middle" [*The Cherry Orchard*, p. 251].) Even so, when it came to would-be translators, he advised his wife:

> Tell them you know nothing, tell them I don't answer your questions and all that. I can't stop them, can I? So let them translate away; no sense will come of it anyway.
>
> (Hingley, p. 300)

Production and reviews. From his home in Yalta, Chekhov followed up the manuscript he sent of *The Cherry Orchard* to the Moscow Art Theater with advice on casting and interpretation. The actor-producer Stanislavsky promptly

annoyed Chekhov with a telegram fawning over the new play:

> JUST READ PLAY SHAKEN CANNOT COME TO SENSES IN UNPRECEDENTED ECSTASY ... SINCERELY CONGRATULATE AUTHOR GENIUS.
>
> (Hingley, p. 300)

Unfortunately Chekhov and Stanislavsky could not agree on the fundamental nature of the play. What the playwright insisted was a comedy, the director could see only as a tragedy. Chekhov tried to make himself as clear as possible, explaining, for example, that the recurring stage direction "*through her tears*" was only an indication of the character's mood, not a call for damp eyes. He was outraged at an inaccurate description of the plot and setting, which was widely circulated as publicity. He was so frustrated, in fact, that he burned all the copies of the manuscript except the one far away in Moscow.

Gravely ill by this time, Chekhov nevertheless made the trip to the former capital, where he attended rehearsals almost daily. He deliberately stayed away from the premiere on January 17, 1904. It was, as it turned out, the day his colleagues had chosen to surprise him with a celebration of his twenty-fifth year as a writer (they were, in fact, at least a year premature). A messenger sent after Act 2 reported thunderous applause and begged Chekhov to come to the theater. He complied. There the play ground to a halt between Acts 3 and 4. In a grand display of the clichés Chekhov abhorred, at least ten speeches were made, congratulatory telegrams read, and gifts bestowed. Coughing and weak, Chekhov made the best of it. He smiled wryly when addressed as "dear and most honoured author," an echo of Gayev's sentimental line in Act 1: "dear and most honoured book-case" (Hingley, p. 304).

Following the festive, successful opening night, the play did well at the Moscow Art Theater and toured Russia's cities. "It's a success, can you imagine?" a pleased Chekhov wrote to his wife late in February (Chekhov, *Anton Chekhov's Life and Thought*, p. 467). He and his wife traveled to a German spa in the hope of improving his health, but his plans for another play and a short story were cut short by his death the following July.

For More Information

Billington, James H. *The Icon and the Axe: An Interpretive History of Russian Culture*. New York: Alfred A. Knopf, 1966.

Chekhov, Anton. *The Cherry Orchard*. In *Five Plays*. Translated by Ronald Hingley. *The World's Classics*. Oxford: Oxford University Press, 1980.

Chekhov, Anton. *Anton Chekhov's Life and Thought*. Translated by Michael Henry Heim in collaboration with Simon Karlinsky. Evanston, Ill.: Northwestern, 1996.

Hingley, Ronald. *A New Life of Anton Chekhov*. London: Oxford University Press, 1976.

Riha, Thomas, ed. *Imperial Russia, 1700-1917, Volume 2: Readings in Russian Civilization*. 2nd ed., rev. Chicago: University of Chicago Press, 1969.

Robinson, Gerold Tanquary. *Rural Russia under the Old Regime: A History of the Landlord-Peasant World and a Prologue to the Peasant Revolution of 1917*. Berkeley: University of California Press, 1969.

Stanislavsky, Konstantin. *My Life in Art*. Translated by J. J. Robbins. New York: Meridian, 1955.

"A Child's Christmas in Wales"

by

Dylan Thomas

Welsh poet Dylan Thomas was born in 1914, the year that World War I began, in Swansea, on Wales's southern coast. Like his other autobiographical writings, "A Child's Christmas in Wales" is packed with details that vividly illustrate what life was like for a child growing up in Wales between the world wars. The seaside town was a small world of its own—beyond which from the child's point of view lay a bigger world of mystery and excitement.

Events in History at the Time the Short Story Takes Place

Economic and political background. Wales's vital role in the economic and political life of Great Britain forms the backdrop to Swansea's prosperity during the era in which Thomas grew up. In the economic sphere, Welsh coal mines had helped fuel the Industrial Revolution of the eighteenth and nineteenth centuries, bringing fortune both to Wales itself and to Britain as a whole. Welsh foundries, producers of iron and tin among other metals, also contributed to the prosperity, as did more traditional products such as wool and slate, a hard gray rock used in roofing. A shipping industry grew around these exports, giving bustle and purpose to Swansea and other port cities. For a young boy, the vessels linked Swansea to the mysterious outside world. As Thomas writes in another autobiographical piece, they were "ships steaming away into wonder and India, magic and China, countries bright with oranges and loud with lions" (Thomas, "Reminiscences of Childhood," p. 3).

THE LITERARY WORK

A short story set in Swansea, Wales, in the early to mid-1920s; published in *Harper's Bazaar* in 1950 and in Thomas's collection of autobiographical sketches, *Quite Early One Morning*, in 1954.

SYNOPSIS

The narrator remembers his childhood Christmases in a busy Welsh port town.

In political life, Britain's only Welsh prime minister, David Lloyd George, had recently steered the nation through the dark days of World War I. Pride in Lloyd George's leadership gave the Welsh a boost in their traditional rivalry with the English. Throughout history, the Welsh have been dominated by their powerful English neighbors, who finally conquered them in the twelfth and thirteenth centuries. Much of Welsh legend is based on resisting the English. In "A Child's Christmas in Wales," Thomas evokes such legends, referring to a distant past when "we chased . . . the English and the bears" (Thomas, "A Child's Christmas in Wales," p. 15).

Poverty. Wales's prosperity gradually began to decline in the years of Thomas's boyhood, mostly because oil was replacing coal as industry's most common fuel. In general, rural North Wales, with its coal mines and sheep farms, was (and is) poorer than the more urban, industrial, and populous South Wales. But even a busy

Prime Minister David Lloyd George

southern seaport like Swansea had impoverished neighborhoods. Near the end of "A Child's Christmas in Wales," Thomas writes of walking through "the poor streets, where only a few children fumbled with bare red fingers in the wheel-rutted snow and catcalled after us" ("A Child's Christmas in Wales," p. 20). The situation for the poor worsened as unemployment grew when coal mines shut down in the 1920s. By contrast, Thomas's own family was financially comfortable in the 1920s; his father, who taught literature at Swansea Grammar School, had a secure job.

Cultural revival. Along with the prosperity it enjoyed, Wales had undergone a revival of its traditional Celtic culture in the nineteenth century. Poetry played the central role in this revival—the biggest cultural event of the year was the *eisteddfod,* a national poetry and music festival that spanned several days. The festival, still held in the modern era, comes to a climax with a poetry contest, in which a panel of judges crowns the victorious bard, or poet. His poetry must meet the highest standards—and it must be in Welsh. Though usage of the language has declined (today it is spoken by about one in five of the Welsh people), it remains an important symbolic element of the Welsh national character.

Nowhere is this Welshness more strongly expressed, assert various authorities, than in Welsh poetry. In fact, Dylan Thomas was often criticized for writing his poetry in English. As a national icon, the poet in Wales plays a role similar to that of the cowboy in America. Reputed to have mystical powers and linked to the mysterious druids (religious figures from ancient times), bards are the national heroes of Welsh culture.

Anglo-Welsh poets. Thomas began his own poetic career in the 1930s, joining what became an entire generation of other young Welsh poets who were also writing in English. He would become the most famous of these so-called Anglo-Welsh poets, many of whom were friends of his. Like "A Child's Christmas in Wales," his other writings tend to focus on the inner world. He uses descriptions of the outer world mostly to illustrate the feelings and impressions created in the individual. This approach leaves limited room for treating political or social issues. Others (though by no means all) in the Anglo-Welsh group wrote more directly of such topical issues. Their poems represent concerns that make up an important part of the larger context in which "A Child's Christmas in Wales" is set. As Thomas puts it in a 1946 essay about them:

> They wrote, not of the truths and beauties of the natural world, but of the lies and ugliness of the unnatural system of society under which they worked—or, more often during the nineteen-twenties and thirties, under which they were not allowed to work. They spoke of the Wales they knew: the coaltips, the dole-queues [welfare lines], the stubborn bankrupt villages, the children, scrutting for coal on the slagheaps.
>
> (Thomas, "Welsh Poets," p. 69)

While "A Child's Christmas in Wales" is a fond and light-hearted recollection of childhood, this darker vision remains just below the surface. Thomas, indeed, hints at it with his brief but vivid mention of the "poor streets," where children with "bare red fingers" have a very different Christmas from the cosy middle-class holiday of his own memories ("A Child's Christmas in Wales," p. 20).

The Short Story in Focus

The contents. "A Child's Christmas in Wales" does not have a plot in the usual sense. Instead the descriptive passages fall into a structure of three parts. The story opens with the narrator remembering not one particular Christmas, but all the Christmases of his boyhood. His memories of them are rolled up together like a snowball going downhill. The narrator picks one memory at random, recalling the Christmas Eve that his friend Jim's house caught on fire. The fire is quickly put out, and after recounting this amusing episode the narrator breaks off.

In the second section, the narrator imagines a conversation with a young boy, who asks questions about life in the now-distant time of the narrator's own boyhood. The young boy asks about the postman, whom the narrator depicts as a Santa Claus-like figure, with rosy cheeks and a bag slung over one shoulder. He also asks about presents. In response, the narrator divides the gifts into Useful Presents (mostly woolen mittens, scarves and other items of clothing, and books with no pictures) and Useless Presents (candy, toys, and a coloring book). He then moves on to the family scene: food and drink is set out, mistletoe is hung, cats lounge in front of the fire. The festive house features many relatives—uncles smoking cigars and talking, and aunts sitting quietly.

In the third and final section, we have just the narrator's voice again. He recalls some sights, sounds, and smells of the town on a Christmas Day. Returning home, he further describes the household. After a turkey dinner, the uncles might nap by the fire while the aunts help to clean up. The narrator describes how he sat and played with a present, or perhaps went out to find some friends and play in the snow or walk down to the seashore. Returning for afternoon tea, he might venture back out into the early darkness to go caroling with friends. Once, he remembers, they sang the Christmas carols in front of a dark and spooky house. Hearing a whispery voice from inside, they all ran away. At home, the family sang songs as well, until the boy went to bed.

Inner world, outer world. Like "A Child's Christmas in Wales," Thomas's other autobiographical stories and his poetry both show his fascination with childhood. In particular, Thomas explores the feelings and perceptions special to childhood, often (as in "A Child's Christmas in Wales") from the nostalgic point of view of an adult. He shows the reader the outer world (home, Swansea, Wales, and society in general) through the lens of a child's inner world—but the lens is held up to the eye of an adult, the narrator.

This perspective allows the story "A Child's Christmas in Wales" to not only expose but also comment on behavior and customs. For example, Thomas gently pokes fun at the uncles and

aunts, whose behavior on Christmas morning fits in with the social standards of the day. The uncles smoke cigars and chat, while the aunts sit timidly by:

> Some few large men sat in the front parlors, without their collars, Uncles almost certainly, trying their new cigars, holding them out judiciously at arm's length, returning them to their mouths, coughing, then holding them out again as though waiting for the explosion; and some few small aunts, not wanted in the kitchen, nor anywhere else for that matter, sat on the very edges of their chairs, poised and brittle, afraid to break, like faded cups and saucers.
> ("A Child's Christmas in Wales," p. 18)

THE POWER OF MUSIC IN WELSH CULTURE

The famous choirs of the South Wales valleys . . . used to be as much social as artistic phenomena—vehicles of mass feeling, or religious certainty, or universal taste. . . . When the Victorian miners' leader William Abraham found himself faced with an unruly crowd, he had only to raise his hands and strike up a hymn, "and hardly had he reached the second line," a wondrous Scottish observer recorded, "than he had the vast audience dropping into their respective parts, and accompanying him like a great trained choir" (Morris, p. 138).

While both uncles and aunts are figures of fun, the picture also reveals much about the different roles of men and women in British society at the time. In the child's memories the uncles remain nameless, but the aunts develop into fleshed-out characters. In developing them, Thomas's story illustrates social attitudes about women. With humor, for example, the story reveals attitudes about women and drinking, which was seen as a man's activity.

> Auntie Bessie, who had already been frightened, twice, by a clock-work mouse, whimpered at the sideboard and had some elderberry wine. The dog was sick. Auntie Dosie had to have three aspirins, but Auntie Hannah, who liked port [a kind of wine], stood in the middle of the snow-bound back yard, singing like a big-bosomed thrush.
> ("A Child's Christmas in Wales," p. 19)

The story reveals that Auntie Hannah is bold enough to drink openly, once she offers the excuse of its being a holiday. Auntie Bessie, on the other hand, uses her pretended fear of a wind-up mouse as a reason for having some elderberry wine. The reader can guess that as a boy the narrator accepted the excuses, but later sees through them. Similarly the boy makes no connection between Auntie Hannah's liking port and her standing out in the snow belting out a song, though presumably the narrator does. The uncles' drinking, by contrast, is not even mentioned, though we may be certain that it was going on—men would commonly drink port or brandy, for example, while smoking their cigars.

Sources. Like most of Thomas's stories, "A Child's Christmas in Wales" is loosely based on the author's own childhood memories. The house is the Thomases' house at 5 Cwmdonkin Drive in Swansea. Both of Thomas's parents had a number of siblings, and one of the uncles in the story is perhaps his father's brother Arthur, who lived near Swansea and worked for the railroad. The other uncles and the aunts are probably based on some of his mother's brothers and sisters. She had seven in all, including a sister named Theodosia. Called Dosie for short, she probably served as the model for the Auntie Dosie who needs aspirin.

Dylan Thomas

SWANSEA AND THE WORLD OUTSIDE

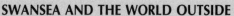

In another autobiographical piece, "Reminiscences of Childhood," Thomas explains how some well-known aspects of Welsh culture and history left their impressions on him as a youngster:

> This sea-town was my world: outside a strange Wales, coal-pitted, mountained, river-run, full, so far as I knew, of choirs and football teams and sheep and storybook tall hats and red flannel petticoats, moved about its business which was none of mine.

> Beyond that unknown Wales with its wild names like peals of bells in the darkness, and its mountain men clothed in the skins of animals perhaps and always singing, lay England which was London. . . . It was a country to which only young men travelled (Thomas, "Reminiscences of Childhood," p. 3).

In his autobiographical stories, Thomas generally uses a near-even mix of real names and made-up ones that either disguise real people or represent a mix of several people. Auntie Hannah and Auntie Bessie seem to have been created in this last way. Auntie Hannah may have been

partly inspired by his mother's sister Elizabeth Ann (like Auntie Hannah, a singer), whom he called Aunt Polly.

Lastly, the most direct sources for Thomas's story were the World War II radio broadcast and the postwar magazine article described below.

Events in History at the Time the Short Story Was Written

Postwar recovery. Though they date from the period shortly after World War I, the memories that make up "A Child's Christmas in Wales" were shaped and recorded just after World War II. Between these two world wars, from 1918 to 1939, Wales saw a steady erosion of its earlier prosperity. With the end of World War II in 1945, however, a period of recovery began for both Wales and Great Britain as a whole, continuing through Thomas's death in 1953. During the Second World War, Thomas had helped support his family by working in radio and film. After the war, he would continue writing and broadcasting many more radio pieces, including plays, stories, and essays as well as poetry. At times, he was performing a broadcast nearly every week.

Thomas's rich, melodic voice made the readings very popular. Best known in the literary world as a poet, to the public Thomas became famous for his dramatic readings on the radio. People were eager to forget about the troubles of war and economic hardship, and the humor and cosy nostalgia of many of the pieces struck a chord.

In the final months of the war the BBC (British Broadcasting Corporation) approached him about doing a holiday broadcast called "Memories of Christmas." One of the earliest of his autobiographical broadcasts, this would later become part of "A Child's Christmas in Wales."

Reception. In 1947 Thomas published another short piece about Christmas, this time in the magazine *Picture Post.* Called "Conversation about Christmas," it was a dialogue about the holiday between two speakers, "Small Boy" and "Self." Then, in 1950, he combined that short piece with the earlier "Memories of Christmas" and published the resulting work in the magazine *Harper's Bazaar.* He called it "A Child's Memories of Christmas in Wales." He was paid $300 for it, a welcome sum since he was always short of cash. None of these pieces received much attention.

Two years later, however, Thomas was in New York, where he had arranged to make a phonograph recording of his poetry. At the last minute, he decided he wanted to read the story from *Harper's Bazaar* as well. On the record it received its present title, "A Child's Christmas in Wales," which it kept when published with other works in *Quite Early One Morning* (1954). Though the record sold slowly at first, since Thomas's death in 1953 it has become his most famous recording. Its popularity has ensured that the story itself is still widely read. It is especially beloved in America, where Thomas enjoyed several successful reading tours before his death. Many finely illustrated children's versions can now be found.

For More Information

Ackerman, John. *Dylan Thomas: His Life and Work.* London: Macmillan, 1991.

Morgan, Kenneth O. *Rebirth of a Nation: Wales 1880-1980.* New York: Oxford University Press, 1981.

Morris, Jan. *The Matter of Wales.* New York: Oxford University Press, 1984.

Thomas, Dylan. "A Child's Christmas in Wales." In *Quite Early One Morning.* New York: New Directions, 1954.

Thomas, Dylan. "Reminiscences of Childhood." In *Quite Early One Morning.* New York: New Directions, 1954.

Thomas, Dylan. "Welsh Poets." In *Quite Early One Morning.* New York: New Directions, 1954.

"A Christmas Memory"

by
Truman Capote

Truman Capote, virtually abandoned by his mother as a child, was raised during the Depression of the 1930s by distant cousins in a small Alabama town called Monroeville. He spent the bulk of his time with his favorite cousin, Sook Faulk. Sook exerted a formidable influence on Capote, and her eccentric mannerisms and childlike innocence inspired many of his short stories. Capote's "A Christmas Memory," a short story so renowned that it has been published individually, pays homage to the pleasure and excitement Sook's holiday rituals brought her young cousin.

Events in History at the Time the Short Story Takes Place

The South during the Depression. In "A Christmas Memory" the Great Depression has taken its toll; Buddy and his friend fantasize about giving each other the expensive presents that they are too poor to buy. The Depression was precipitated by the stock market crash of October 29, 1929, also referred to as "Black Monday." Two weeks after the crash, the value of stocks declined by more than 37 percent. Soon afterward, banks all over the country collapsed like dominoes. Industry slowed to a standstill, and by 1933, about a third of the American work force was unemployed. In the South many mills and factories, which local townspeople depended on for jobs, closed down. Alabama was particularly hard hit, experiencing the largest decline in total nonfarm employment of all Southern states during the 1930s.

The tremendous poverty of many Southerners forced them to become creative in devising means of survival. As an example, for medicinal purposes they schooled themselves in both Native American and their own ancestral homeopathy, gaining a broad knowledge of herbs, barks, and roots that had healing powers. White Southerners, particularly poor whites, made liberal use of Indian medicine, some of them becoming highly proficient in the curative value of plants. In the short story, Buddy's friend knows many old Indian cures. Southern woods and swamps contained enough medicinal plants to fill a pharmacy, and there existed an herb, root, or bark to alleviate practically any illness or injury:

> Powdered alum stopped bleeding. Black elderberries cured constipation, and the flowers and bark, when made into a salve using lard, healed scalds and burns. A tea made from rhubarb stopped diarrhea. A poultice made from sheep sorel cured cancer. Alder-bark tea was good for chills. Wormwood tea cured cholera, red clover leaf took care of pimples,

calamus root stopped cramps, papawroot tea cured gonorrhea.

(Flynt, p. 219)

When a holiday or special occasion required presents for friends or relatives, they baked homemade treats or crafted their gifts out of natural substances—like bark and straw—and throwaway objects found around the house. "They could not afford furniture or utensils. So they carved goblets and plates, made pottery and glazed it, built furniture from vines or wood . . . and designed toys from peach seeds, mountain laurel or pine bark" (Flynt, p. 211).

FDR and the New Deal. In the story Buddy's prized possession is a letter on White House stationery thanking him for the fruitcake that he sent to President Franklin Delano Roosevelt. Roosevelt, a Democrat, was elected in 1932 on the strength of his determination to end the Depression. Roosevelt called his solution "The New Deal," a plan that provided jobs through agencies such as the Works Progress Administration (WPA) and federal monetary relief to the states to help the unemployed. Despite Roosevelt's innovative efforts, however, it was not the New Deal but industrial mobilization for World War II that ended the Depression.

Prohibition: the "dry" years. In "A Christmas Memory," the holiday fruitcake recipe includes a forbidden ingredient—whiskey. As Buddy explains in the story, state laws prohibited the sale of alcohol throughout the country. The passage in 1919 of the Eighteenth Amendment to the Constitution had made the manufacture, sale, and transportation (but not the use) of alcoholic beverages illegal, instituting the Prohibition period, which lasted until 1933.

The Eighteenth Amendment was the culmination of years of successful campaigning by the Anti-Saloon League, also referred to as "the Drys." Anti-alcohol sentiment grew during World War I, particularly against beer, since no red-blooded patriot wanted to drink alcohol brewed by German foes. Support for Prohibition was also connected to an increasing discomfort with urbanization in America. After the war, opportunity in urban, industrialized areas lured many Americans away from the rural heartland. The Anti-Saloon League's strongest supporters came from the rural South. To many of these religious-minded country folk, drinking was associated with urban immorality. They conceived of the typical American city as a hotbed of sin, symbolized by the dark, sleazy, back-room bar.

Though passage of the Eighteenth Amendment may have been a success for the Drys, Prohibition itself was not. The fact that the Eighteenth Amendment refused to go so far as to prohibit the *use* of alcohol suggested that the majority of Americans were ambivalent about its regulation. This ambivalence led to uneven enforcement of the law. Prohibition failed to keep alcohol out of people's hands; it simply forced them to work a little harder to get it. By 1928 gangsters who ran their "bootlegging" operations out of underground bars called "speakeasies" were reaping huge profits by selling liquor, and the country became disillusioned with Prohibition. After his election in 1932, Franklin Roosevelt spearheaded the passage of the Twenty-first Amendment repealing national Prohibition. Some states, however, held out and did not repeal their own prohibition laws until much later.

SOUTHERN CHRISTMAS TRADITIONS

American Christmas folk customs vary depending on the region in which they have originated. The common practices of lighting the Yule log, baking the fruitcake, and singing carols all hark back to England. Many uniquely Southern traditions derived from the Yuletide customs brought to the new world by some of the first colonists to the region, who were descendants of the English Cavaliers. Unlike the Puritan settlers, who prohibited Christmas festivities in New England until 1681, the Cavaliers merrily celebrated the season by singing, dancing, ringing bells, feasting, and lavishly decorating their homes. In the antebellum South, the celebration began weeks before Christmas day itself, just as it does in the postbellum years of the story.

Christmas memory. Even before Prohibition, a considerable number of Southerners earned a living by producing "moonshine" whiskey, which was made from corn and brewed in home stills. Southern states had passed local laws outlawing liquor before the Eighteenth Amendment, and when it was repealed in 1933, every Southern state, including Alabama, retained some form of official restraint on the manufacture and sale of liquor. At the same time the South saw the collapse in the 1920s and 1930s of industries on which many citizens depended for jobs and income, such as the mountain lumber and coal industries. A number of Southerners from these

Discovery of an illegal still during Prohibition.

industries and on failing farms turned to moonshining and bootlegging for survival. Usually operating out of their own homes, as HaHa Jones does in the story, men became the primary makers and consumers of whiskey, although women as well as men often sold it. In the early 1930s, Virginia, the Carolinas, Georgia, and Alabama were the states with the greatest number of illegal stills—makeshift devices for vaporizing and condensing liquid from fermented produce into alcohol. Altogether the South held some 14,321 stills in 1931, 67.1 percent of the nation's total (Kirby, p. 211). After the repeal of the antiliquor amendment, the number of Southern stills lessened, but the region still claimed a large share. Meanwhile, sheriffs and other government agents continued to hunt down moonshiners and bootleggers, the search often ending in bloodshed. During the Depression, these private battles took on a symbolic, public importance as rebellious moonshiners struggled to maintain what had become an independent way of life in the rural South and to preserve one of their few sources of income in a hunger-driven decade.

The Short Story in Focus

The plot. The narrator, known only as Buddy, is a young student recalling a childhood Christmas memory. In the flashback, he is seven years old and lives with relatives in a house in the rural South. Buddy's parents are conspicuously absent; his cousin, a woman in her sixties whom he calls his "friend," is the closest thing to a mother he has.

Buddy's friend excitedly leads him in a series of traditional Christmas rituals, beginning on the cold November morning when she announces that it's fruitcake weather. The ceremonial preparation of the fruitcakes assumes great importance. Buddy and his cousin spend an entire day foraging in the woods for pecans and scraping together every penny for their "Fruitcake Fund" to purchase the necessary ingredients. But the most difficult task is obtaining the whiskey to add to the recipe.

The sale of alcohol is illegal, so Buddy and his friend are forced to travel to a disreputable dive owned by an Indian named HaHa Jones. HaHa's name is a misnomer; he is a large man with a giant scar on his face who, according to legend, never laughs—until the day the elderly hunchbacked woman and the delicate boy appear at his doorstep requesting a quart of his best whiskey. "Which one of you is a drinkin' man?" he asks gleefully. When Buddy hands HaHa their money, he refuses it:

> "Tell you what," he proposes, pouring the money back into our bead purse, "just send me one of them fruitcakes instead."

"Well," my friend remarks on our way home, "There's a lovely man. We'll put an extra cup of raisins in his cake."

(Capote, "A Christmas Memory," p. 25)

A few days later, the fruitcakes are baked and shipped to friends, casual acquaintances, and famous people whom they have never met; even President Roosevelt receives his annual cake. The two cooks then dip into the leftover whiskey, and Buddy's friend dreams about Eleanor Roosevelt serving the fruitcake at a White House dinner party. When relatives appear in the evening and find Buddy tipsy, they chastise his friend. She retreats to her room in distress, but Buddy comforts her with the promise that tomorrow they will find a wonderful Christmas tree.

The next morning they venture into the woods and cut down a majestic tree that they decorate with homemade ornaments and odds and ends found in the attic. Since they can't afford to buy presents for their relatives, they spend the rest of the day creating gifts. Their poverty stings only when Buddy wishes he could give his friend a knife, a radio, and the chocolate-covered cherries she craves. His friend desperately wants to surprise Buddy with a brand new bicycle. Instead they construct elaborate kites for each other out of paper and old magazine photographs, just as they have done every year.

They spend Christmas day happily watching their homemade kites soar in the breeze. It is a perfect holiday that the contented pair relish, blissfully ignorant that unforeseen circumstances and the passing of time will soon separate them forever. "Those Who Know Best" (the adults in charge) send Buddy to military school. In his absence his friend continues to bake her fruitcakes alone until one November morning, "she cannot rouse herself to exclaim 'Oh my, it's fruitcake weather!'" ("A Christmas Memory," p. 45).

From the fictional to the real. In the story Buddy lives with a number of relatives but shares a special kinship only with the character he identifies as "his friend."

Other people inhabit the house, relatives; and though they have power over us, and frequently make us cry, we are not, on the whole, too much aware of them. We are each other's best friend. She calls me Buddy, in memory of a boy who was formerly her best friend. The other Buddy died in the 1880's, when she was still a child. She is still a child.

("A Christmas Memory," p. 13)

The friend is based on Sook Faulk, Capote's beloved elderly cousin and surrogate mother.

Buddy's friend in the story exhibits many of Sook's peculiar personality traits and superstitions. For example, she is so fearful of the number thirteen that she spends the thirteenth of every month in bed. Buddy's description of his friend lends insight into Sook's simple lifestyle:

[S]he has never: eaten in a restaurant, traveled more than five miles from home . . . read anything except funny papers and the Bible, worn cosmetics, cursed, wished someone harm, told a lie on purpose, let a hungry dog go hungry. Here are a few thing she has done, does do: killed with a hoe the biggest rattlesnake ever seen in this county . . . dip snuff . . . tame hummingbirds . . . talk to herself, take walks in the rain, grow the prettiest japonicas in town, know the recipe for every sort of old-time Indian cure.

("A Christmas Memory," pp. 19-20)

DIPPING SNUFF

In "A Christmas Memory" Buddy makes a point of mentioning "dipping snuff," the process of inhaling or chewing tobacco, as one of the things his cousin does. For pre-colonial Southern Indian tribes, tobacco's medicinal purposes made it a sacred crop. When Columbus arrived on North American shores, the welcoming natives presented him with golden tobacco leaves, and, not knowing what they were, he threw them away. Eventually, the American colonists learned the native techniques of inhaling tobacco's powder and chewing or smoking the coarser sections of the plant. Approximately 90 percent of the tobacco produced in the United States came to be grown in the South, and the recreational practice of using the raw plant for dipping snuff appears to have been a uniquely Southern habit.

Sook could only be drawn outside the safe boundaries of home for two important annual rituals—the Christmas fruitcake preparation, and a trip to the woods to find herbs. Sook's sole income came from an herbal remedy for dropsy, a common disease of the time that caused excess water in the tissues. According to a biography of Capote, Sook obtained the recipe from an Indian medicine man and collected pocket money by selling the medication for $2 a jar.

The epilogue in the Random House edition of "A Christmas Memory" claims that Sook Faulk died in 1938 while Capote was in military school, but biographer Gerald Clarke states that she died in 1946. If she died in 1946, it is possible that Truman spent at least one more Christmas with Sook on his occasional trips back home during the early 1940s. After her death, Capote memorialized her in many of his short stories, including "A Christmas Memory."

Sources. Capote believed in merging fiction and nonfiction together in his writing, the two "coming into a conjunction like two big rivers" (Grobel, p. 89). Most of his short stories were drawn from his childhood experiences in Monroeville, Alabama.

IN A FOREST OF LINGERIE ADS

Some of the best fiction produced during the 1940s and 1950s appeared in women's magazines—where "fine fiction found a nest in a forest of lingerie ads" (Clarke, p. 81). "A Christmas Memory" first appeared in *Mademoiselle* magazine in 1956, thanks to the efforts of George Davis, the editor who first published Truman Capote's stories. Davis, an aspiring author sidelined by writer's block, worked for both *Mademoiselle* and *Harper's Bazaar*. During his stints as fiction editor, he boldly showcased many talents, including Capote, along with the work of Virginia Woolf, W. H. Auden, and Carson McCullers.

"A Christmas Memory" focuses primarily on the experiences of Truman and Sook. Truman Capote's real mother, Lillie Mae Persons, was unhappy in her marriage and so left her son with relatives in Alabama. Although Truman's estranged parents made sporadic attempts to involve themselves in Truman's childhood, he never felt close to either of them. Sookie, as he affectionately called her, took him under her wing and won the affection that a child normally reserves for his parents. Innocent and guileless, Sook ranked low in the family's pecking order. One Capote biographer referred to her as "so childlike, she was thought to be retarded by many people," going on to explain that "in fact she was merely so shy and unworldly as sometimes to appear simpleminded" (Clarke, p. 16). The young Capote was meanwhile thought to be a delicate child with feminine features; worried that he was a "sissy," his mother later sent him to military school in an attempt to graft more masculine traits on the boy (Clarke, p. 42).

Capote and Sook were lonely outsiders and kindred spirits.

The two were constant companions from 1930 until 1932, when Capote's mother returned to Alabama to collect her son. Remarried to a man she adored and now living in New York City, Lillie Mae decided she was finally ready to be a mother, so she spirited Truman away to New York, leaving Sook emotionally crushed.

Making brief appearances in the story are a few minor characters also based on people in Capote's life. According to Capote's aunt, an Apache Indian named Victorio from whom Sook purchased her contraband alcohol inspired the character of HaHa Jones. The relatives in the story who chastise Buddy's friend for giving him alcohol are based on the unmarried cousins with whom young Capote lived. Jennie Faulk, a successful, iron-willed businesswoman, was the sole breadwinner of the household, and everyone deferred to her. Jennie's parents were white sharecroppers, and she was determined to escape the backbreaking work of picking cotton that employed so many Southerners. Remembering the bloody hands and knees she had suffered as a child picking cotton, Jenny shared the aspirations of many a disgruntled sharecropper who moved to the city at the turn of the century seeking better pay in factory or mill jobs. Instead of entering a mill, however, she discovered that she had a talent for making hats. She started her own millinery business, which enabled her to support her sisters Callie and Sook, and her brother Bud. Capote's biographer Gerald Clarke describes their residence as "a strange household he entered in Monroeville, unique to the South, peculiar to the time: three quarrelsome sisters in late middle age, their reclusive older brother, and an atmosphere heavy with small secrets and ancient resentments" (Clarke, p. 15). Despite their differences, the Faulks always believed in the responsibilities and loyalties that familial bonds required. Thus, they felt no qualms about taking young Capote into their fold when his mother deposited him on their doorstep.

Events in History at the Time the Short Story Was Written

The new South. By the 1940s, the decade in which "A Christmas Memory" was written, the arm of industrial wartime mobilization had stretched into the South. Sharecroppers and farmers—displaced by the new factories, plants,

Rosa Parks is arrested on February 22, 1956, for her participation in the Montgomery bus boycott.

and military bases that the government constructed throughout the region—found higher-paying positions as unskilled laborers in the war industry. The South's industrial boom was furthered by the outbreak of the Korean War in 1950. By the 1950s, production work had replaced farming as the predominant occupation in the area, and the total farm population had declined 25 percent.

In 1956, the year in which the short story was published, Congress passed an act funding the construction of an elaborate system of highways linking the entire nation. This National System of Interstate and Defense Highways replaced the South's difficult muddy, dusty roads with easy-to-navigate freeways that linked many Southern backwoods to a growing metropolis. Along with rapid industrialization, this sophisticated highway network led to an increase in urbanization, and the South grew far more cosmopolitan throughout the 1950s and 1960s than it had been in the time recalled by Capote's short story.

Southern society, like its economy, experienced dramatic changes during this era. Capote's home state of Alabama, churning with turmoil, was the scene of many significant historical events. In 1955 the first organized, nonviolent civil rights protest occurred in the form of a public bus boycott in Montgomery, Alabama, after Rosa Parks, a black woman, refused to give up her seat to a white man on a public bus. Lasting 381 days, the boycott ended in success in 1956 when the Supreme Court ruled that segregation on busses was unconstitutional. The federal government and civil rights activists were beginning to force the South into a new, more progressive era.

Reviews. "A Christmas Memory" prompted William Goyen in the *New York Times Book Review* to call Capote "that old Valentine maker" with a talent for "catching the off-beat nature of people" (Goyen, p. 5). Katherine Gauss-Jackson, writing in *Harper's Magazine* (December 1966), favorably compared the story to Dylan Thomas's classic "A Child's Christmas in Wales." It became generally accepted as one of Capote's finest short stories.

Truman Capote himself considered "A Christmas Memory" his most perfect work. His frequent public readings of the story left no dry eyes in the audience. The last words Capote spoke on his deathbed in 1984 were, "It's me—it's Buddy," as if he were summoning Sook. Perhaps the greatest testimony to the power of the story was the place of honor it received at his burial—his good friend Joanne Carson read "A Christmas Memory" at his funeral.

For More Information

Capote, Truman. *A Christmas Memory.* New York: Random House, 1956.

Clarke, Gerald. *Capote: A Biography.* New York: Simon & Schuster, 1988.

Flynt, Wayne. *Poor but Proud: Alabama's Poor Whites.* Tuscaloosa: University of Alabama Press, 1989.

Goyen, William. "That Old Valentine Maker." *New York Times Book Review* (November 2, 1958): 5.

Grobel, Lawrence. *Conversations with Capote.* New York: NAL Books, 1985.

Kirby, Jack Temple. *Rural Worlds Lost: The American South, 1920-1960.* Baton Rouge: Louisiana State University Press, 1987.

Cold Sassy Tree

by
Olive Ann Burns

Olive Ann Burns was born in 1924 and grew up in Banks County, a rural area of Georgia. She attended school in the nearby town of Commerce, which served as the model for the fictional town of Cold Sassy. When she was a child, Burns's father told her stories about his childhood in Georgia and specifically recounted the story of his grandfather, who, after his wife died, married a much younger woman. These characters served as the models for Grandpa Blakeslee and Miss Love Simpson in *Cold Sassy Tree*. In real life, their union caused an uproar in the small Southern town at a time when traditional notions of proper behavior bumped up against societal changes.

THE LITERARY WORK

A novel set in the fictional town of Cold Sassy, Georgia, in 1906; published in 1984.

SYNOPSIS

A boy's recently widowed grandfather marries and, as a result, sets off a scandal in the tiny town of Cold Sassy, Georgia.

Events in History at the Time the Novel Takes Place

The Progressive Era. The election of Teddy Roosevelt as U.S. president in 1900 marked the beginning of a period known as the Progressive Era, which lasted until the United States entered World War I in 1917. The Progressive Era started as a response to the panic of the 1890s, an economic depression in which many people lost their jobs and both urban and rural living conditions deteriorated. During this era, middle-class social workers, ministers, intellectuals, and writers voiced their concerns over the social conditions of American society and encouraged the government to enact laws to reform these shortcomings. Middle-class women, in particular, played a large role in the reform movements of the Progressive Era. Progressive Era leaders hoped to improve the conditions of society through their efforts to end alcohol consumption, enact child labor laws, improve schools, and gain the right to vote for women.

One of the most significant legal actions taken during this period was the prohibition of alcohol. Progressive Era reformers believed that a ban on alcohol would reform society by removing the negative effects of alcohol consumption. In 1913 the Anti-Saloon League endorsed an amendment to the Constitution banning alcohol, an amendment that Congress adopted six years later in 1919. Many states, however, enforced prohibition laws prior to this amendment, becoming "dry" states much earlier. In 1907 Georgia passed a prohibition law, and before the passage of that law, 125 of the 145 counties in Georgia had already taken legal action on a local basis, declaring themselves dry. In *Cold Sassy Tree,* Grandpa Blakeslee ignores the prohibition law in his county, as demonstrated by his secret trips to the still in the closet at his daughter's house, where he drinks his alcohol.

The Progressive Era was also a time when people worked to forbid the widespread employment of children in factories, citing the dangerous conditions and long hours as reasons for such a ban. The typical employer, in fact, liked to hire children because he could pay them less money than adult men or women.

In *Cold Sassy Tree*, a girl named Lightfoot, who is a friend of the main character, Will, works in a mill in order to earn money after both of her parents die. Lightfoot rarely attends school because she has to work to give money to her aunt, who raises her.

NATIONAL CHILD LABOR LEGISLATION

Progressive reformers worked to enact nationwide legislation to ban the employment of young children. The New York-based National Child Labor Committee coordinated a child labor reform movement, and between 1905 and 1907 two-thirds of the states had passed some form of child labor legislation. The committee also supported a nationwide bill in 1906 to prevent the employment of children in mines and factories. Although the law was defeated, Congress did establish a children's bureau in the Department of Labor in order to investigate child workers.

The large number of women involved in the reform movements of the Progressive Era eventually caused a resurrection of the question of why American women were not allowed to vote. They began once again to push for women's suffrage by organizing meetings and appealing to the federal and local governments for the vote. Although the political movement for women's suffrage originated in the mid-nineteenth century, it gained national attention during the first two decades of the twentieth century. One of the characters in *Cold Sassy Tree*, Miss Love, has attended suffrage meetings and worked to obtain the vote for women. Such efforts were not immediately fruitful, however. It took nearly twenty years for the suffrage movement to achieve success when American women finally gained the right to vote on June 4, 1919, with the passage of the Nineteenth Amendment.

Industrialization. Before the Civil War, the South was a predominantly agricultural region particularly dependent on cotton exports. In the aftermath of the Civil War, however, the South turned its attention to the development of industry. While railroads were limited to the North and Northwest prior to the Civil War, they extended into the South in the postbellum period.

On the heels of railroads came the building of factories whose owners would now be able to transport their goods on the trains. Textiles—spun or woven materials—were the most prominent goods produced by factories in the South. These textile factories enjoyed great success and, by 1920, the Southern factories owned about one-half of the active cotton spindles in the country. The number of mills in the South rose from 161 in 1880 to 239 in 1890, and to 400 in 1900.

Mill work proved difficult. It required laborers to work in dim factories, their bodies bent over for long periods, checking the spindles. Mill workers were often described as pale, hunched over, and generally unhealthy. They often caught lung diseases because of the lint-filled air they breathed in the factories. Pitied, the mill workers occupied a lower position on the social ladder than other Southerners.

Mill work in the South was often a family affair, including the children. In 1900, as many as 30 percent of Southern textile workers were under the age of sixteen. *Cold Sassy Tree* features two mill children, Lightfoot and Hosie Roach, a boy the main character fights with at school. Children who worked in the mill often dropped out of school after two or three years so that they could work longer hours to earn extra money for their families.

Southern way of life. Southerners shared certain preferences and biases particular to their region of the nation. Many Southerners hated anything connected with the Northern states, a hatred that stemmed from the Confederate defeat in the Civil War. In *Cold Sassy Tree*, Grandpa Blakeslee leads the Fourth of July Confederate parade each year and tries to never visit Yankee states like New York. Interestingly, though, he marries Miss Love, a Yankee from Maryland. The anti-North bias carried over into politics during this period. Many Southerners hated the Republican party because of its role in the Civil War. The South showed a strong commitment to the Democratic party in its voting. In the novel, Will reflects this commitment in his excitement at hearing the Democratic president, Theodore Roosevelt, speak.

Southerners also had strong religious beliefs. Will's family is Southern Presbyterian and follows many rules stemming from this faith. Expected, for example, to observe the Sabbath, Will

A child worker in a Southern cotton mill, 1908.

is not allowed to read the comics on Sunday. Southerners also followed rituals such as mourning for a long period following the death of a loved one. The Blakeslee family mourns for weeks following Grandma Blakeslee's death. This emphasis on mourning helps explain why the town is so surprised when Grandpa Blakeslee decides to marry so soon after the death of his wife.

Modern appliances in Southern towns. The early part of the twentieth century was a time of great technological change. One of the most significant inventions was the telephone, invented in 1876. By 1899 there were already a million telephones in use in America. In *Cold Sassy Tree*, Will says that his own house has a phone but that Grandfather Blakeslee still refuses to buy one, a reflection of the fact that some Americans continued to resist using this innovation in 1906.

In addition to the telephone, households were modernized in other ways during this period. Indoor plumbing replaced the outdoor toilets, or "privies," of the nineteenth century. In *Cold Sassy Tree*, Will's family has two indoor bathrooms. Grandpa Blakeslee, however, refuses to build an indoor bathroom, preferring instead to rely on the outhouse.

Perhaps the most dramatic example of technology's impact on life was the automobile. The first automobile was manufactured in 1895, but it was the founding of the Ford Motor Company in 1903 that led to the mass production of a reliable car easily affordable to the average American. The first Model T appeared in 1908 and sold for $850. Motor vehicle registration began to sky-rocket, jumping from 8,000 in 1900 to 78,800 in 1905. People living in rural towns such as Cold Sassy were often some of the first to purchase cars so that they could drive from one isolated area to another. In cities, on the other hand, people had access to trains and street cars. The increased use of the automobile sparked some basic changes, not the least of which was the construction of a system of roads enabling drivers easier access routes.

The Novel in Focus

The plot. Will Tweedy is fourteen years old and lives with his parents in a small town in Georgia named Cold Sassy, so named because of the sassafras trees that western pioneers looked for in this cold region between the mountains and Augusta, Georgia. At the outset of the novel, Will's grandmother dies, leaving her husband, Grandpa Blakeslee, a widower. Three weeks after Granny Blakeslee's death, Grandpa Blakeslee tells his two daughters—Loma and Mary Willis (Mary is Will's mother)—that he is going to marry a young woman in town named Love Simpson. They feel that their father's marriage is inappropriate so soon after his wife's death. Grandpa Blakeslee explains that he wants someone to help him take care of the home and prepare his meals. According to Grandpa Blakeslee, there is no reason to wait after his wife's death because "she's dead as she'll ever be" (Burns, *Cold Sassy Tree*, p. 8). The family is afraid that people will think that Grandpa had loved Miss Love and had wanted to marry her before Grandma died, which would disgrace them all.

In spite of these fears, Grandpa Blakeslee elopes with the "Yankee" Love Simpson, and she moves into his house. Slowly Miss Love starts to influence Grandpa's life. She suggests that he cut his beard, and she rearranges the furniture in the house. The relationship is morally upright—they sleep in separate rooms. Miss Love and Grandpa have made an agreement: she will stay in his house and take care of him, and in return when he dies, she will inherit the house. Neither of them believes this is a marriage for love.

MILL TOWNS

Southern mill owners purchased property surrounding the mills, where they constructed houses for their workers to live. Crude cabins, the structures were rundown, poorly built, and overcrowded. Mill owners also opened schools in their town in order to educate the children who worked in the factories. In *Cold Sassy Tree,* the nearby town of Cold Sassy allowed the mill children to attend the town school after the mill school shut down.

The couple decide to go to New York City to make a purchase for the store that Grandpa Blakeslee owns. On their trip, they unexpectedly fall in love. They return with news about a new car-selling business, which Miss Love has convinced Grandpa Blakeslee to begin, as well as the news that Miss Love is pregnant. Soon after their return, Grandpa grows sick and dies. His daughters inherit the store, and Miss Love inherits the house. She decides to stay in Cold Sassy in order to raise her child there.

Meanwhile, fourteen-year-old Will Tweedy, the narrator of the story, has done some maturing of his own. He has been a confidant to his grandfather and continues to be one to Miss

Love until the end of the novel. The teenager also survives two rather momentous events in his young life—being run over by a train and kissing a girl for the first time. The girl, Lightfoot, comes from nearby Mill Town. Described with warmth and a dash of humor, the unexpected kiss is interrupted by someone who catches the pair in the act.

The Southern family. Reflected in *Cold Sassy Tree* are the strong ties of the Southern family. All of the members of the Blakeslee family live within walking distance of one another and see each other often. Grandpa Blakeslee stops by his daughter's house every morning and then goes to work with his son-in-law at the store. Also, in order to keep the business within the family, Grandpa wills his store to his daughters. Typically the father made the decisions in a Southern family, and the children did not question those decisions. When Grandpa Blakeslee informs his daughters that he plans to marry Miss Love, they disapprove but do not share their opinion with him because he is the father. Similarly, Will does not question his father's right to punish him for misbehaving. Another characteristic of the Southern family was a strong sense of honor. There were certain ways to behave and certain behaviors to avoid in order to preserve the good reputation of the family. The Blakeslees fear that the entire family's name will be tarnished by Grandpa Blakeslee's marriage to Miss Love.

Sources. Burns based the family in *Cold Sassy Tree* on the stories that her father told her about his family. Her great-grandfather, like Grandpa Blakeslee, married a younger woman soon after his wife died. Affecting the dialogue in her novel was Burns's own personal experience. She spent her entire life in the South, attending college in North Carolina and working as a journalist there as well. When she fell ill with cancer, Burns turned her attention to novel writing.

Events in History at the Time the Novel Was Written

The South in the early 1980s. In some ways, the South of the early 1980s still resembled the South of the early 1900s. The region was still predominantly Democratic in its voting preferences, and religion remained a strong force there. Textile mills still employed many workers, and one early 1980s study showed that women workers in at least one Southern mill (Firestone Textiles of Gastonia) had changed little. None of these female mill workers graduated from high school (Dillman, p. 179); on the other hand, they showed a strong sense of connection to their own town and family.

In other ways, the South in general and Georgia in particular did undergo dramatic changes over the seventy-five year period. For example, in 1980 one-quarter of the eligible voters in Georgia were black. At the turn of the century, black men had often been dissuaded from voting by poll taxes, literacy tests, and other such deterrents. The black voters of 1980 in Georgia, like the state's larger population, generally supported the Democratic party. Over the years, though, the Republican Party had gained ground in the state. By the 1980s Democrats generally prevailed in Georgia's local elections, while the Republicans tended to win the national contests. There were some changes in women's behavior too. In the early 1980s some of Georgia's females worked hard to pass the Equal Rights Amendment, which would have made gender discrimination illegal. However, they were unable to secure enough votes and it failed to pass. In 1983, however, the Georgia legislature did overturn a legal code that held that the father was the head of the family and that the wife was subject to him.

Reception. Response to *Cold Sassy Tree* was mostly positive. Readers and critics praised Burns's depiction of her Southern characters and her portrayal of Southern life and vernacular. The *New York Times Book Review* took issue with the use of dialect in the novel, complaining that "Will says 'would of' endlessly" (Mooney, p. 227). But even this review admits that "the author effectively conveys the world view of an adolescent boy" and that her writing evokes an admirable portrait of the grandfather and his new wife. A review in the *Library Journal,* moreover, praises the novel's use of dialect, saying that Burns "deftly captures the language of rural Georgia in her first novel" (Mooney, p. 227).

Burns began work on the sequel to *Cold Sassy Tree* entitled *Leaving Cold Sassy Tree,* which was to take up the story of Will as a twenty-five-year-old who faced the prospect of fighting in World War I as well as marrying a young school teacher. While working on the sequel, however, Burns died of heart failure on July 4, 1990.

For More Information

Burns, Olive Ann. *Cold Sassy Tree*. Boston: G. K. Hall, 1985.

Cobb, James C. *Industrialization and Southern Society, 1877-1984.* Lexington: University Press of Kentucky, 1984.

Dillman, Caroline Matheny, ed. *Southern Women.* Waleska, Ga.: Hemisphere, 1988.

Grantham, Dewey W. *Southern Progressivism: The Reconciliation of Progress and Tradition.* Knoxville: University of Tennessee Press, 1983.

Hearden, Patrick J. *Independence and Empire: The New South's Cotton Mill Campaign, 1865-1901.* DeKalb: Northern Illinois University Press, 1982.

Ling, Peter J. *America and the Automobile: Technology, Reform, and Social Change.* Manchester: Manchester University Press, 1990.

Mooney, Martha T. *Book Review Digest.* Vol. 81. New York: H. W. Wilson, 1986.

The Color Purple

by
Alice Walker

Born in 1944, novelist and poet Alice Walker grew up in the rural South, which provides the setting for much of her fiction. Active as a student in the civil rights movement of the 1960s, she began publishing novels in the 1970s that explored themes of racial and sexual conflict and identity. Her third novel, *The Color Purple* (1982), continued in this vein, enjoying huge critical and commercial success and making Walker an influential if controversial figure on the contemporary literary scene.

THE LITERARY WORK

A novel set in the American South in the 1920s to 1940s; published in 1982.

SYNOPSIS

Celie, a young black girl, overcomes the abuses of sexism and racism to grow into a strong, independent woman.

Events in History at the Time the Novel Takes Place

Black men and women in the rural South. The South in the early twentieth century remained largely rural and agricultural. Poverty was widespread, and sharecropping had replaced slavery as the central source of black labor, upon which Southern agriculture still relied. Beginning in 1915, many blacks broke away from sharecropping to seek a better life in the industrial cities of the North, participating in an ongoing exodus from the South called the Great Migration. Many more, however, stayed behind, struggling under the twin burdens of extreme poverty and entrenched discrimination.

For those who stayed, both men and women, life remained hard. The women faced not only racial discrimination but also sexual oppression, which made their existence there generally arduous, painful, and sometimes dangerous. Both sexes struggled to define their family roles within the only context available, that of white society. But "traditional" white family roles often proved inappropriate, or difficult to apply, in the situations in which blacks found themselves. For instance, white society demanded that men act as family authority figures. Yet black men found their self-respect challenged and undercut by racism every day in subtle and not-so-subtle ways. Without a stable sense of self-respect, authority proved elusive and the result was sometimes behavior that verged on tyranny. In *The Color Purple,* Celie's father and husband both illustrate this psychological phenomenon. Her father (later revealed as her stepfather) mistreats her and her sister, raping Celie repeatedly and fathering her two children before selling her to her husband, who also abuses her mentally and physically. Such behavior, though by no means universal, was not an isolated phenomenon. The black woman fell victim to abuses by both white assailants and black ones.

> The sexual assault of black women was so prevalent . . . after slavery ended that outraged black women and men wrote articles . . . pleading with the American public to take action against the white and black male offenders.
>
> (Hooks, p. 57)

Where it existed, this behavior had roots in a cultural attitude that devalued black women—an attitude shared not only by whites but by many black men. "I believe that as a general thing we hold our girls too cheaply," observed black female activist Fannie Barrier Williams. "We have all too many colored men who hold the degrading opinions of ignorant white men, that all colored girls are alike—that is, in being of low worth and easy virtue" (Williams in Giddings, p. 114).

Jim Crow society. By the 1920s the post-Civil War period of Reconstruction lay almost half a century in the past, along with the hard-won progress in civil rights it had brought to newly freed African Americans in the South as well as elsewhere. Aided by a reactionary Supreme Court, the Southern backlash against Reconstruction had solidified into the "Jim Crow" regime of enforced segregation between blacks and whites and white domination. Based on the principle of white supremacy, and named for an antebellum black minstrel character, Jim Crow laws created separate societies for blacks and whites. From theaters to drinking fountains, and from schools to cemeteries, blacks were faced with signs that turned them away ("Whites only") or equated them with animals ("No colored or dogs"). Such restrictions constantly reminded blacks of their inferior status in white eyes.

Aside from creating separate societies for whites and blacks, Jim Crow laws ensured that when blacks and whites did mix, they would do so on terms that guaranteed white dominance. When women began to wear bobbed hairstyles that led them to patronize barber shops, for example, a popular trade for Southern blacks, the city of Atlanta, Georgia, passed a law forbidding black barbers to practice their profession on women or on children younger than fourteen. The laws themselves were less important, however, than the attitudes they represented and supported. In fact, the laws were only one tool by which whites kept blacks "in their place." So effective were these tools that the white power structure usually did not even need to invoke the laws. In the novel, this situation is illustrated by the misadventures of Celie's friend Sofia, an independent and strong-willed black woman who runs afoul of the system. Celie admires Sofia for standing up to black men who try to bully her. When Sofia stands up to white bullying, however, she is arrested, severely beaten, and sentenced to twelve years in jail.

Miscegenation. Through the centuries of slavery and into the Jim Crow era, racial domination had a sexual aspect. It fostered in the minds of white slavemasters the idea that a female slave should be sexually accessible to her white master at any time. This situation was at least partly responsible for the social devaluation of black women. Even after slavery, white dominance in the South meant that in some situations black women still remained subject to the sexual whims of white men. Miscegenation—literally "mixed birth"—became common, though the sexual abuse behind it remained nonetheless horrifying for black women through the generations. By the twentieth century most American blacks had at least some white blood, and conversely many whites had at least some black blood. The implications of having mixed blood were vastly different in Southern white society and black society. Within black society, the racial mixture often provided a framework for a social hierarchy based on hue, one in which light skin was seen as more desirable than dark.

HISTORIAN PAULA GIDDINGS ON MISCEGENATION

Because of historical circumstances as much as attitude, fair complexions were associated with the upper classes. Blacks with White forebears usually had more educational and economic opportunities, were more easily accepted, and thus made up a disproportionate number of achievers. Of the 131 men and 8 women listed in W. E. B. Dubois's *Who's Who of Colored Americans,* published in 1916, for example, 124 of the men and all of the women were of mixed heritage.

(Giddings, p. 186)

In *The Color Purple,* Celie's friend Squeak visits her white uncle, the warden, to get Sofia transferred from jail to a lighter punishment. Two aspects of this complicated episode are especially revealing. First, Squeak uses reverse psychology to manipulate her uncle, lying to him that Sofia

Alice Walker

is happy where she is and that the lighter duties—serving as a white woman's maid—would be harder on her. Thus, Sofia's friends, who have concocted the plan, make no attempt to use the blood relationship. Instead, they plan on the warden ignoring Squeak's "request" and doing the opposite of what she supposedly wants. Second, the warden's behavior—he takes advantage of Squeak's visit to rape her—shows how little the blood relationship means to him. As a black woman, even his niece, she represents nothing more to him than a chance for a casual sexual encounter. Thus, for both black and white in the novel, mixed heritage does nothing to bring the races closer; rather it offers each an opportunity to exploit the other.

Lynching. The violence implicit in much of miscegenation's history found more overt expression in lynching, which flourished in the South from the 1880s to the 1930s. Legally defined as mob murder by three or more persons, as used by whites against blacks, lynching usually amounted to assassination, usually by hanging, on the pretext of a perceived or manufactured "offense." Like Jim Crow laws, lynching arose as a white reaction against black freedom, a way for Southern whites to reassert control over the black population. It peaked in the 1890s, when close to 100 blacks were lynched each year in the South, with 160 being lynched in the peak year—1892. Lynching had a sexual aspect, for a common excuse was the alleged rape of a white woman by a black man. As black antilynching crusader Ida B. Wells pointed out, a rape charge could be provoked by consensual relations between a black man and a white woman, or by nothing more than eye contact that a white perceived as a threat. It could furthermore serve as a manufactured excuse for getting rid of a black man who was prospering financially, or one whose attitude was not submissive enough to please local whites.

Lynching also often had an economic aspect, for whites commonly used it against blacks who competed against them in business. The lynching in Memphis in 1892 of Ida B. Wells's friends Thomas Moss, Calvin McDowell, and Henry Stewart fell into this category, for they had opened a grocery store that took black customers away from a white-owned store across the street. It was this case that started Wells, a black woman journalist living in Memphis at the time, on the antilynching crusade that would make her famous. In the novel Celie's father is lynched under similar circumstances in the early 1900s, after he

built a prosperous business that cut into the profits of nearby white-owned establishments.

Black religion. African Americans at the beginning of the twentieth century were mostly Methodist or Baptist. These had been the only two sizable denominations in the South to come out against slavery, and blacks had begun forming their own Methodist and Baptist congregations as early as 1773. The first large black church was established in 1816, when a number of black religious leaders met in Philadelphia to found the African Methodist Episcopal Church (AME), which still plays a leading role in the black religious community.

LYNCHING IN THE 1920S TO 1940S

Although the lynching referred to in *The Color Purple* takes place at the beginning of the 1900s, shortly after Ida B. Wells began her antilynching crusade, this type of mob violence against especially blacks persisted during the era in which the novel takes place. The total number of lives claimed tapered off from 233 recorded lynchings in the 1920s to 111 in the 1930s to 30 in the 1940s, and there were efforts to pass the Dyer Anti-Lynching Bill in Congress, which among other penalties would have made anyone who participated in a mob murder guilty of a felony. Although the bill passed in the U.S. House of Representatives in 1937, it died in the Senate under the pressure of Southern speechifying.

The black religious experience in America (as elsewhere in the West) has been deeply influenced by elements carried over from African culture and religion. African religions tended to be heavily participatory, and their musical, incantatory style was transported over as slaves and free blacks took up Christianity. For example, black churches have featured singing, along with stirring sermons in which the preacher is answered and encouraged at key points by the congregation. In *The Color Purple,* Celie addresses many of the letters in the novel to God, though her conception of God evolves as the novel progresses. Her sister Nettie, who becomes a Christian missionary in Africa, contributes to this evolution by introducing African religious ideas.

There isn't any way, writes Celie to her sister, to read the Bible and not think that God is white.

Whoopi Goldberg as Celie and Margaret Avery as Shug Avery in the film adaptation of *The Color Purple.*

Some years later, in a letter that resumes their conversations about God, Nettie replies that God is different to her now after all her years in Africa—more spirit that ever before and more an inner than outer reality. Not being tied to what God looks like, she assures Celie, is liberating. It frees a person.

Africa. By the 1920s European colonial rule was well-established throughout the African continent. Colonial tensions between the European powers had contributed to the outbreak of World War I, and with the defeat of Germany in 1918, France and Britain divided its colonies among them. European political rule had the economic aim of exploiting Africa's vast natural resources; this material interest was buttressed by claims of bringing "civilization" to the "savage" Africans. Often "civilization" required killing large numbers of blacks who resisted it. Particularly resistant, for example, were the Igbo people of Nigeria, who rose up against the British again and again in the early 1900s. The British nevertheless persisted, deciding, for instance, who should be local governor instead of letting the Igbo villagers decide in their own customary way. As demonstrated by this example, once in place "civilization" worked to facilitate white political and economic domination. Walker illustrates this process in the novel through the life of Nettie,

Celie's sister, who witnesses the exploitation of the villagers among whom she lives.

The Novel in Focus

The plot. The novel consists entirely of letters, first from Celie to God, later between Celie and her sister Nettie. Through these letters, which form a sort of diary, the events of Celie's life and the lives of those close to her unfold to the reader. Fourteen-year-old Celie writes to God because her stepfather Alphonso (whom she believes to be her father) has ordered her to "tell nobody but God" that he is raping her repeatedly (Walker, *The Color Purple*, p. 1). Fearing that her beloved younger sister Nettie will be next, Celie continues to submit, and gives birth to two children by Alphonso. Her children, a boy and a girl, are sent away.

After their mother's death, a man the novel calls Mr. ———, a widower with children, asks Alphonso for Nettie's hand in marriage, but Alphonso offers Celie instead, along with a cow. Mr. ——— agrees, and Celie goes to live with her new husband, effectively becoming his property. Mr. ——— beats her and forces her to work in the fields picking cotton. Nettie comes to stay briefly with them, but when she refuses to sleep with Mr. ———, he sends her away. Unbeknownst to Celie, Nettie goes to work in town for the black missionary couple, Samuel and Corrine, who have adopted Celie's two children.

Mr. ———'s girlfriend, a glamorous singer called Shug Avery, moves in and befriends Celie. Shug—short for Sugar—provides the first warmth and companionship in Celie's life since Nettie's departure. Far from resenting Shug's presence, Celie loves her, and Shug herself becomes less responsive to Mr. ——— after witnessing his abuse of Celie. One day, Shug realizes that Mr. ———, or Albert, has been hiding the letters that Nettie has written to Celie over the years. The letters are located, and Celie learns from them that her sister has gone to Africa as a missionary with Samuel and Corrine. Always submissive in the past, Celie is now enraged and wants to kill Albert, but Shug dissuades her. Instead, Shug encourages her to sew, and Celie begins making comfortable, loose-fitting pants, which she gives to her friends.

From Nettie's letters, which continue to arrive, Celie learns that her own two children, Olivia and Adam, have grown up to resemble their mother. After Corrine dies, Nettie marries Samuel and tells him that she is really the children's aunt. When the village in which they live is destroyed to make way for a rubber plantation, they plan to return by ship to America.

Samuel has revealed to Nettie that Alphonso was not her real father, but had married her mother after her father was lynched. When Alphonso dies, Celie claims the house that rightfully belongs to her, and she and Shug move in. There she runs a prosperous pants-making business. Albert, who has grown up emotionally through the passing years, lives with them. The novel ends with the safe return of Nettie, Samuel, Olivia, Adam, and Adam's African wife, Tashi.

Celie's voice. The novel's setting remains indeterminate, though it is clearly somewhere in the countryside of the deep South. Celie's letters, written in black dialect, reflect this rural environment; by contrast, Nettie, who has gone to school, writes in standard English. The novel uses Celie's simple but expressive language to illuminate her character, as in the following passage, which Celie records soon after coming to live with Mr. ———:

> He beat me like he beat the children. Cept he don't never hardly beat them. He say, Celie, git the belt. The children be outside the room peeking through the cracks. It all I can do not to cry. I make myself wood. I say to myself, Celie, you a tree. That's how come I know trees fear man.
>
> (*The Color Purple*, p. 23)

As Celie grows from a submissive but survival-oriented girl into a strong, independent woman, her language becomes a badge of honor to her, a reminder of her identity and of the hardships she has survived. Even after she has established a successful business, she resists efforts by well-meaning friends to change the way she speaks. "Look like to me only a fool would want you to talk in a way that feel peculiar to your mind," she writes to Nettie (*The Color Purple*, p. 223). Just as she rejects others' ideas of how she should talk, so does Celie learn to reject others' expectations of how she should live and behave. Her independent voice reflects her independent character, and ultimately it is this independence that brings her happiness and fulfillment.

Other characters in the novel, too, find happiness only to the degree that they follow Celie's example in refusing to conform to social norms. Mr. ———'s son, Harpo, for example, tries to control his wife, Sofia, by beating her, because he thinks that is how a man should behave. His marriage falls apart when Sofia first fights back and then leaves. Years later, they get back together because Harpo no longer tries to control Sofia. Instead, he looks after the house, while she works, an arrangement that comes naturally to both, but which he had earlier felt would undermine his manhood.

The destructiveness of gender expectations occupies a central place in the novel, and it is on this topic that Celie's voice proves most powerful. Abused by men, Celie experiences interpersonal love with Shug, though she is forced to accept that Shug has other needs as well. Even Mr. ———, who like his son Harpo has grown over the course of the novel, ends up helping Celie sew pants—for women to wear, as well as men.

Sources. Alice Walker grew up in rural Georgia, in an area where most blacks still worked at sharecropping, like the characters in *The Color Purple*. Blinded in her right eye at age eight, she had a scar on her eye that was not removed until she was a teenager. She spent much of the intervening period alone, writing poetry, a pastime that perhaps helped inspire her creation of Celie, a girl who feels ugly and who also takes comfort from loneliness in writing.

The novel itself is loosely based on Walker's own family history—what she later called "the imagined and vastly rearranged lives of my mother and father and grandparents before I was born" (Walker, *The Same River Twice*, p. 25). Walker borrowed the name of her own maternal grandmother, Nettie, for Celie's beloved sister in the novel, while this same grandmother's strength in the face of abuse clearly inspired much of Celie's own character. Walker's grandfather provided the basis for the character of Mr. ———, who despite his cruelty is ultimately portrayed as being worthy of love.

Events in History at the Time the Novel Was Written

South Africa. By the mid-1970s, the colonial era in Africa was over. White-controlled regimes had largely given way to black-run governments, the most notable exception being the Republic of South Africa, whose then-white government maintained the system of strict racial segregation called apartheid. Having prevailed in the civil rights struggles of the 1960s, many African Americans now took a special interest in South Africa. Alice Walker, a veteran of sit-ins and other antisegregation protests in the deep South, numbered among these African Americans. Her awareness of South Africa's racial injustice went hand-in-hand with a growing awareness of racial injustice elsewhere in the world—and the economic exploitation often accompanying it.

In her book *The Same River Twice* (1996), Walker discusses the changes that *The Color Purple*'s success (and the success of the movie version) made in her life. Included in *The Same River Twice* is a magazine article called "Erasing a 'Black Spot'" from 1983, as the film version of *The Color Purple* was going into production. The article describes the "relocation" of blacks to certain sections of South Africa by its government. Walker sent the article to Quincy Jones, the film's producer, together with a note revealing its relevance to her description of colonial Africa in *The Color Purple*.

> Some of the most important scenes in "West Africa" are the ones about the building of the road, the starting of the rubber plantation and the destruction of the Olinka village. . . . Indigenous people's traditional housing in Central America, Africa and the U.S. is destroyed and replaced by the most rudimentary hovels, as the people gradually become mere workers on land now owned by people who live elsewhere. The article . . . on South Africa illustrates this. The "housing units" (really toilets) are forced on the people with an attitude that even this is more than they deserve. "Erasing a 'Black Spot'" could have come

straight from The Color Purple.
> (Walker, *The Same River Twice*, p. 56ff)

Race and gender issues. Along with the black civil rights movement, the 1960s also brought demands for equal treatment for women. Women's rights advocates continued their struggle into the 1970s and 1980s. Black women as a group rarely participated in the feminist movement of the era, though a number of individuals did. Their absence has been explained by Bell Hooks in *Ain't I a Woman: Black Women and Feminism*. In the 1950s society encouraged black women, as it did all women, to assume a more passive, subordinate role to the men in their lives. There was a concerted effort to reverse the advances that had been made during World War II, when women joined the work force to fill job vacancies and became more independent of men. After the war men, black and white alike, wanted to see women back in the home, and role models in magazines and television helped the men spread this message with success. Black as well as white mothers taught their daughters, who came of age in the 1970s, that a man should be the most important element in their lives, not a job or their own self-development. A woman's primary purpose, the ideal, was for her to be a man's helpmate, an old notion from the Victorian times of the 1800s, only now for the first time black women too were being sold this idea. They were being led to believe that the woman's place was indeed in the home, and many in the 1970s accepted this role. Aside from the general pressure placed on all women to do so, black women had racial reasons to submit to this pressure. Many black women believed that racial liberation and progress could be realized only through the growth of a strong, male-dominated black society. This, they reasoned, should take first priority over the struggle for equal rights for women.

Other black women suggest that their experience, as well as their struggle for rights, was different from white women's. Walker herself claims that the word *womanist* is more fitting for the black female's struggle than feminist.

> Womanist. . . . A Black feminist or feminist of color. . . . Usually referring to outrageous, audacious, courageous or willful behavior. Wanting to know more and in greater depth than is considered "good" for one. . . . Acting grown up.
> (Walker in Grant, p. xlix)

A womanist is further described as a female who has managed to develop survival strategies, while in a state of being oppressed because she is black and female, to preserve her family and her people. The term furthermore "means being and acting out who you are and interpreting reality for yourselves. In other words, Black women speak out for themselves" (Grant, p. 1).

Reception. *The Color Purple* quickly became a bestseller upon its release in 1982, winning its author wide critical acclaim along with that year's Pulitzer Prize for Fiction and the American Book Award for Fiction. Many critics praised its use of dialect as the medium through which Celie's character is defined and developed. The book also provoked controversy, however, especially for its portrayal of black men, which some (especially black men) saw as unfairly harsh. Though a few critics objected to what they saw as deficiencies of plotting, most saw such problems as less important than the power and individuality of the novel's language and the strength of its characterizations. "Plot, setting, tone, and style," wrote Dorothy Randall-Tsuruta in *The Black Scholar* (Summer 1983), "are elements usurped by the excellent characterization"; the novel, the reviewer concluded, is a masterful mix of "period speech and behavior" (Randall-Tsuruta, pp. 54-5).

For More Information

Giddings, Paula. *When and Where I Enter: The Impact of Black Women on Race and Power in America.* 1984. Reprint. New York: Bantam, 1985.

Grant, Jacquelyn. "Womanist Theology: Black Woman's Experience as a Source for Doing Theology." In *Encyclopedia of African American Religions.* New York: Garland, 1993.

Hooks, Bell. *Ain't I a Woman: Black Women and Feminism.* Boston: South End, 1981.

Kirby, Jack Temple. *Rural Worlds Lost: The American South, 1920-1960.* Baton Rouge: Louisiana State University Press, 1987.

Randall-Tsuruta, Dorothy. Review of *The Color Purple. The Black Scholar* 14 (Summer 1983): 54-5.

Walker, Alice. *The Color Purple.* 1982. Reprint. New York: Pocket, 1985.

Walker, Alice. *The Same River Twice: Honoring the Difficult.* New York: Scribner, 1996.

Dandelion Wine

by
Ray Bradbury

Ray Bradbury was born in Waukegan, Illinois, in 1920. Although he had moved to Los Angeles, California, by the time he was twelve years old, he retained vivid memories of life in his small Midwestern birthplace. By focusing on Waukegan's nearly rural atmosphere and ignoring the bustling activities of the lakeport town, Bradbury used it as inspiration for the fictional community of Green River, where his novel *Dandelion Wine* is set.

THE LITERARY WORK

A novel set in rural Illinois in 1928; published in 1975.

SYNOPSIS

Twelve-year-old Douglas Spaulding spends a summer coming of age in Green River, a town patterned after Waukegan, Illinois.

Events in History at the Time the Novel Takes Place

The 1920s. World War I had occupied America's attention since 1914 and, though the fighting ended in 1918, the war would not reach its final conclusion for the United States until the Treaty of Berlin was ratified in 1921. Three hundred thousand American soldiers returned from Europe to swell the ranks of industrial workers and consumers. Following a short period of adjustment, America began to apply its wartime industrial activity to the creation of consumer goods. In the decade following 1920, American manufacturing would increase by two-thirds and American lives would change dramatically.

The automobile ushered in an age of technological progress. Before the war, motor vehicles had begun to gain popularity, but early production and pricing had made the family automobile a luxury item. Led by auto pioneer Henry Ford, the manufacturers began to develop mass production techniques, and after the war these as-sembly-line practices lowered the cost of automobiles to such an extent that they became affordable to most working families. By 1924 the average worker could purchase a Ford Model T for only $200. Soon a consumer could even buy the pieces of a Ford in a kit and assemble the automobile at home to reduce the price even further. There was a phenomenal growth in the number of vehicles produced and purchased during these years. In the decade between 1920 and 1930, the number of automobiles in the United States swelled from 9 million to 26.5 million.

The rapid increase in automobiles stimulated the construction industry and the growth of cities. The American public demanded better roads so that they could make full use of their new vehicles. (Even before this decade of affluence, Waukegan had modernized its town to include paved streets.) Auto manufacturers led the way in the construction of new assembly factories, which, in turn, drew huge numbers of workers away from farms and small towns to cities in which these factories were located. Urban life had great appeal during these years, and a new method of making purchases became a popular feature of it. Installment buying became a mark of the successful city dweller. By 1926 three-fourths of all cars were purchased on time—buyers would take home the finished automobile but pay for it over a period of months.

A second stimulus to the economy was electricity. Before the war only one in five American homes enjoyed this source of power. By the mid-1920s this number had increased to two out of every three homes. The new source of power encouraged the growth of factories to produce for the home "luxury" items, that is, items that ran on electricity. Manufacturers produced refrigerators, which began to replace the old iceboxes that literally stored ice to keep foods cool, and toasters and automatic washing machines became commonplace.

For entertainment, Americans turned to movies and the recently developed medium of radio. Around 1900, the motion picture arts had evolved from the simple, hand-cranked nickelodeon into the silent movies shown in theaters; the first American film with a plot, *Great Train Robbery,* made its debut in 1903. By 1925 Warner Brothers was experimenting with "talkies." Americans embraced the movies as a leisure-time diversion and flocked to the theaters in record numbers. By the end of the decade, the motion picture industry claimed an audience of 80 million people a year and an annual income of $2 billion. In addition, the 1920s saw the debut of radio. Amateurs had been experimenting with radio for more than a decade before the first broadcast was sent out in 1920 from station KDKA in Pittsburgh. Other cities followed Pittsburgh's example, and within two years there were 564 broadcast stations in the United States.

Bigness and standardization became the marks of quality and success during this period in American history. There had once been nearly a hundred small auto-makers, most using traditional building methods where a group of workers completed many different tasks. The assembly line production techniques pioneered by Henry Ford allowed his company improve upon such traditional methods. Ford increased output to the point where a new car rolled off the assembly line every ten seconds; such efficiency lowered costs and eventually resulted in the elimination of many of Ford's competitors. By 1930, 83 percent of all American cars came from just three automobile manufacturers—Ford, General Motors, and Chrysler. In 1926 and 1927, radio followed the trend toward bigness and standardization. The National Broadcasting Company and Columbia Broadcasting System began organizing networks of stations and financing network programming by selling advertising time slots on the radio.

Along with all these changes came new developments in American values. Consumerism now seemed a rampant part of American culture, as reflected by an incident involving Henry Ford himself. "One day someone brought to us a slogan which read: 'Buy a Ford and save the Difference.' I crossed out save and inserted 'spend'—'Buy a Ford and Spend the Difference.' It is the wiser thing to do" (Ford in Bailyn, p. 721). Although church membership increased in the 1920s, many churches adjusted their tone to reflect new priorities in society. Sermons dealt less with hellfire and damnation and became more soothing. Dress took on a looser style for women, one that did away with corsets and long skirts. It was the era of the flapper, with her bobbed hair, short skirt, and casually held cigarette. As both men and women broke from traditional values, smoking rose by 250 percent in the nation.

Americans responded to the new advertising and concentration on consumption by buying in great quantities, and abandoning to some degree the traditions of thrift and conservation, relics of a Puritan past. Most, however, did not abandon old values altogether. They lived instead by their peculiar mix of local standards. As one historian notes, "In rural communities and city neighborhoods, people judged one another by . . . standards that applied specifically to their own localities" (Bailyn, p. 721). But the focus on consumerism became widespread. By the late 1920s, there were signs that Americans had overextended their production capacities and their credit. A few banks around the nation began to close, and jobs became harder to find. The "progressive" decade would come crashing down with the collapse of the stock market in late 1929—a year after the stories in *Dandelion Wine* take place.

Waukegan, Illinois. Located just thirty-five miles north of Chicago, the town of Waukegan had begun as a fort, and by 1928 had grown to be a pleasant, modern community with a population of 22,000. The streets were well paved and often tree-shaded. A popular summer resort, the town had superior bathing facilities on Lake

Ray Bradbury

Michigan. Year-round, Waukegan was the home of many Chicago businessmen. Its main set of buildings consisted of the county courthouse, public library, YMCA, high school, and Masonic Temple. It also had a fine harbor, which carried on a brisk trade in farm and dairy products. Along the lakefront the town had its share of industry: iron works, a sugar refinery, a brewery, and various consumer-goods factories.

The small town quickly dissolved eastward and northward into suburbs with scattered homes among vacant fields and expanses of farm and dairy land. It is this part of Waukegan after which the town of Green River in *Dandelion Wine* is patterned. Only in a preface to the book's 1975 edition does the author acknowledge the presence of the industrial harbor section of Waukegan:

> But of course, I had noticed them and, genetic enchanter that I was, was fascinated by their beauty. Trains and box cars and the smell of coal and fire are not ugly to children. Ugliness is a concept that we happen on later and become self-conscious about . . . if your boy is a poet, horse manure can only mean flowers to him; which is, of course, what horse manure has always been about.
>
> (Bradbury, *Dandelion Wine*, p. x)

In Waukegan, as in Green River, there was a downtown business district with a few stores and a theater where the residents could enjoy films starring such contemporary sensations as Charlie Chaplin. Silent pictures had been around for about three decades, and pictures accompanied by sound were just coming to town, having been invented three years earlier. The 10¢ Saturday matinee enjoyed with a 5¢ bag of candy was a popular diversion.

The Novel in Focus

The plot. *Dandelion Wine* is the story of twelve-year-old Douglas Spaulding growing up in a large house shared with his brother, parents, grandparents, and a great-grandmother. The sights, sounds, and smells of the rich farmland around them play a large role in their decidedly un-urban lifestyle. The thread connecting the segments of the story is the widening difference between the tranquil old-style semirural life and the encroaching technological society.

In the segments into which the book is divided, Douglas enjoys the daring but protected pleasure of sleeping outdoors in his grandparents' cupola. He wanders in the fields, whose smells and sights bring him to the realization that he, himself, is part of this living mass. Douglas joins his grandfather in collecting dandelions from which the old man presses nectar and prepares homemade dandelion wine—which, at the appropriate time, Douglas is allowed to taste.

Douglas momentarily joins the consumer-driven age when he tries to buy a pair of sneakers without enough money. He is unsuccessful, but this does not disturb his enjoyment of the peaceful life in Green River. A deal is finally struck with the store owner, enabling Douglas to acquire the sneakers.

Douglas enjoys growing up with time to arrive at his own decisions about important elements in life—the role of parents, the importance of dandelions, the living historical sources embodied by the older generation. This atmosphere is broken only by the excitement aroused by occasional thrusts of technology. The town's new trolley comes Douglas's way, but collapses before it is in use for very long. The community inventor is encouraged to create a Happiness Machine, which turns out to bring sadness instead and finally is allowed to burn up. The dandelions and dandelion wine are threatened by the development of a new grass that does not allow weeds to grow (and which Grandfather wisely decides not to plant). A murder takes place in the ravine between the rural section of town and the industrial section, suggesting a connection between the violence and the intrusion of industrial society into the rural setting. Wealthy neighbors buy an electric car and use it to ride around on the sidewalks—until it stops, similarly showing the fragility of technology.

However, Bradbury's work is not just a protest of dehumanizing technology, as one explanation points out:

> Bradbury is not writing about the gadgets of conquest; his real concern is the soul and moral imagination.
>
> (Kirk, pp. 18-19)

Technology. There is no television in Green River. Public television had not yet been invented in 1928, but the town inventor, Leo Auffmann, is asked to build a "Happiness Machine." His wife, Lena, does not think it necessary, but Leo wants to be a good neighbor.

> [Lena:] "That machine . . . we don't need it."
> [Leo:] "No, . . . but sometimes you got to build for others. I been figuring, what to put in it. Motion pictures? Radios? Stereoscopic viewers? All those in one place so any man can run his hand over it and smile and say, 'Yes sir, that's happiness.'"
>
> (*Dandelion Wine*, p. 55)

In the end, Leo invents a giant orange box with all the modern technology of 1928 loaded in it. A participant in the great adventure sits in the large box and experiences sights and sounds of places the person has always wondered about but never visited. But the machine creates beautiful visions that remain unfulfilled and leave the viewer empty once out of the box. Lena tries it, then when the electrical parts short and start a fire, delays calling the fire department until the box is well consumed.

There are other examples of the unreliability of new industrial technology and modernization. Douglas becomes almost fatally ill with an ailment that the town doctor cannot cure with his modern remedies. Mr. Jonas, the town eccentric, is more successful; out of the junk he collects and redistributes, Jonas finds a treatment that cures the boy. Then, when Douglas's grandmother changes her kitchen habits for up-to-date tools and methods, her marvelous cooking suddenly becomes inedible. Through one event after another, the book reflects concern for the dehumanizing effect of technology.

In sharp contrast to the technological failures, *Dandelion Wine* presents a romantic picture of rural life: fireflies and katydids, the smell of wild plants, berries and dandelions to harvest, Grandmother's cooking of savory and filling dishes, neighbors who support you and whom you support, and the agonies of losing friends and loved ones. The novel is a story of community, a community rapidly disappearing under the pressure of technology.

Sources. Two sources can be identified for *Dandelion Wine:* Bradbury's own experiences as a child growing up in Waukegan and his later experiences in writing science fiction, always with a suspicion of technological advances and with an undying faith in the abilities of humans to overcome all obstacles. Certainly the rapid and little-regulated growth of television in the thirty years after World War II must have served as a stimulus for creating the idea of the Happiness Machine.

Events in History at the Time the Novel Was Written

The 1950s. The first story that would be included in *Dandelion Wine* appeared in magazines in 1946—the last in 1957. The decade between these dates was a period in many ways similar to the 1920s. The United States had emerged on the winning side of another world war and business at home was thriving. Production of automobiles for consumers, interrupted by military needs, resumed explosively. In 1940 there had been just over 32 million cars on American roads. By 1949 this number had increased to over 44 million. The mileage of paved roads had meanwhile extended to 1.6 million miles—one mile for each square mile of land in the United States.

The automobile industry collected 9 million workers into factories in major cities, resulting in construction of suburban residences and reducing the populations of small rural towns. For a number of reasons, including the growth of labor unions in the United States, many workers saw their standard of living improve to the degree that they soon made up a growing middle class. In conjunction with this improved standard of living, the 1950s, like the 1920s setting of *Dandelion Wine,* became a consumer-centered society. Refrigeration, fast foods, and an array of new products designed to bring ease to tasks at home, especially in food preparation, began to change the traditional kitchen, once the heart of the family community.

The G.I. Bill, which was passed in 1944, encouraged many returning soldiers to go back to school. Meanwhile, the number of farm workers dropped by one third in the 1950s. But the invention of Henry Ford's Fordson tractor had spawned a wide variety of large and powerful farm tools. The result was that while the number of farm workers declined, farm productivity rose by one third. Of course, the average farm family could neither afford the new equipment nor compete without it. Standardization made new inroads into American society as large corporations increasingly displaced the family farm in the agricultural sector.

PARALLELS BETWEEN THE 1920S AND 1950S

1920s	1950s
• Post-World War I decade	• Post-World War II decade
• Period of prosperity	• Period of prosperity
• Consumer-driven generation	• Consumer-driven generation
• Spread of radio	• Spread of television
• Establishment of standardized products	• Increase in standardization
• Appearance of novels such as *The Great Gatsby* by F. Scott Fitzgerald, stressing the dehumanizing effects of the era	• Appearance of novels such as *Catcher in the Rye* by J. D. Salinger, stressing the threat the era posed to a person's feelings of individuality

---

Wartime factories shifted their energies to the manufacture of consumer goods when peacetime returned. At the same time, production of weapons to compete in a cold war with the Soviet Union and in real battles in the Far East continued, causing American industry to expand to an all-time high. American manufacturers were investing $10 billion a year in new equipment, construction, and marketing.

In the 1950s, as in the 1920s, bigness was a mark of success. American corporations expanded into multinational giants. Yet the number of poor in America also grew. This decade saw not only farm workers being excluded from the technological explosion but also blacks, the elderly, and poor urban whites.

Just as in the 1920s radio had spread through the nation, in the 1950s a new mass medium captured the attention of the nation—television.

The first commercial television broadcast made its debut in 1930. But by 1940 there were only half a dozen regularly broadcasting stations in as many cities in the United States; television receivers were not even sold to the American public until 1939. Their production was cut off entirely when the country entered World War II in 1941. The television industry boomed in the postwar period; by the mid-1950s there were nearly 500 stations and 40 million home television receivers in America. Variety shows, situation comedies, and other types of programs quickly became standardized as the radio networks established themselves in television. In the 1950s most television viewers were locked into the offerings of three major networks—NBC (National Broadcasting Company), CBS (Columbia Broadcasting System), and the relatively new ABC (American Broadcasting Corporation). Like Leo Auffmann's "Happiness Machine" in Bradbury's novel, some people found television to be a box that promised much but in the end left participants empty of any truly meaningful experience.

Reception. Though it is classified as a novel, *Dandelion Wine* was assembled from a collection of Bradbury short stories written over the period of time between 1946 to 1957. In 1975 Bradbury added an introduction and the novel was published by Alfred A. Knopf. The immediate and continuing popularity of *Dandelion Wine* is revealed in its publishing record—nine printings between 1975 and 1989. Although *Dandelion Wine* received a generally positive reception from critics, they often disagreed about Bradbury's central themes. Russell Kirk noted that Bradbury is more concerned with "the soul and the moral imagination" (Bryfonski, p. 68), while Willis McNelly sees his focus as the conflict "ultimately between human vitality and the machine" (Bryfonski, p. 70). A. James Stupple notes that Bradbury treats the dilemma created by the dual attractions of past and future, stasis and change, in his other writings as well, although in *Dandelion Wine,* Bradbury "appears far less certain about the relative values of the past and stasis" (Bryfonski, p. 70). Stupple continues: "Perhaps in this regard Bradbury can be seen as representative of a whole generation of middle class Americans who have found themselves alternatively attracted to the security of an idealized, timeless, and static past… and the exciting, yet threatening and disruptive future world of progress and change, especially technological change" (Bryfonski, p. 70).

For More Information

Bailyn, Bernard. *The Great Republic: A History of the American People.* Vol. 2. Lexington, Mass.: D.C. Heath, 1985.

Bradbury, Ray. *Dandelion Wine.* 1975. Reprint. New York: Alfred A. Knopf, 1989.

Bradford, Tim. "Dandelion Wine." *Chicago Review* 22 (1971): 2-3.

Bryfonski, Dedria, ed. *Contemporary Literary Criticism.* Vol. 10. Detroit: Gale Research, 1979.

Kirk, Russell. *The World of Ray Bradbury.* New York: Arlington House, 1969.

Mankiewicz, Frank, and Joel Swerdlow. *Remote Control: Television and the Manipulation of American Life.* New York: Times Books, 1978.

A Day No Pigs Would Die

by
Robert Newton Peck

Robert Newton Peck grew up in a Shaker family on a Vermont farm during the 1930s and 1940s. His father supplemented the family income by working as a pig slaughterer. Peck himself continued to farm in his adult life, viewing his writing as a sideline. Drawing on his own experience as an adolescent and later as an independent farmer, Peck wrote a novel about a boy approaching his teenage years in the sparse context of a Shaker family. Although Peck himself was not born until 1928, he sets *A Day No Pigs Would Die* in the era of Calvin Coolidge, who was president of the United States between 1923 and 1928.

Events in History at the Time the Novel Takes Place

The 1920s. The decade that followed the end of World War I proved to be enormously prosperous for the United States. There was a brief business depression from 1920 to 1922, then a wondrous upswing that would last until 1929. The standard of living rose for the majority of Americans, and industrial production almost doubled over the decade. Automobile manufacturing experienced phenomenal growth, and the revolutionary and affordable invention captured the imagination of Americans of all stripes, including the Shakers. Besides using cars for work and for pleasure, the Shakers embraced the newly invented radio as well.

Farmers, in general, however, benefited from all this new technology at a far slower pace than

THE LITERARY WORK

A young-adult novel set on a Vermont farm in the 1920s; published in 1972.

SYNOPSIS

An adolescent struggles to abide by Shaker ways, which demand no frills—not even the use of store-bought clothes. The lifestyle demands that everyone and everything be useful, even the boy's pet pig.

city folk, who in 1920 for the first time made up more than half the population in the nation. Only one farmhouse out of every ten, for example, had electricity on its premises during the decade. And while many urban dwellers reveled in their relative prosperity, farmers—for the first time a minority in the country—continued to experience hard times even after 1922. The price of hogs, for instance, a commodity that would have affected the farmer Haven Peck in the novel since he also worked as a pig slaughterer—dropped by 50 percent in 1921. As the decade progressed, many farmers, unable to keep up with payments for money owed, lost their land altogether while others just barely managed to scrape by. Haven, who reminds his son in the novel that it won't be long before the family finishes making payments for their farm—appears to belong to this last group. The most profitable farming, on the other hand, was done by those who used costly farm innovations, such as mechanized harvesting devices and newly developed chemical fertilizers that helped earn huge profits.

The Shakers. Shakerism—variously considered to be a religious movement, an experiment in socialism, or both—has its roots in England and perhaps France as well. In England there was a small group of religious enthusiasts led by two tailors, James and Jane Wardley, who became known as the Shaking Quakers or Shakers because of the trembling or shaking of their bodies during worship. They are thought to have been influenced both by the Quakers and by the French Prophets, a group whose followers frequently began to shake and shout, falling into a trancelike condition. By the early 1770s a young Englishwoman named Ann Lee (1736-1784) had become deeply involved in Wardley's society.

Until this point, Lee, a blacksmith's daughter, had apparently lived a life filled with sorrow—exposure as a child to mill work in the early English sweatshops and a juvenile marriage that resulted in four children, who all died at birth or in early childhood. After the death of her last child in 1766, Ann became a powerful leader of the Shaker movement, adding to its religious emotionalism and austerity in lifestyles. She called on followers to forsake the institution of marriage, and she advocated celibacy.

> I am married to the Lord Jesus Christ. He is my head and my husband, and I have no other! I have walked hand in hand, with him in heaven. . . . I am Ann the Word.
>
> (Lee in Andrews, *The People Called Shakers,* p. 12)

> You must forsake the marriage of the flesh or you cannot be married to the Lamb, nor have any share in the resurrection of Christ.
>
> (Lee in Andrews, *The People Called Shakers,* p. 20)

In 1772, then thirty-six years old, Ann brought a group of eight followers to America, where they struggled to establish a self-sufficient community at Niskeyuna, near Albany, New York. There the Shakers built a single large house with separate floors for men and women. It was to be the pattern for future Shaker communities, which were always constructed around segregated, communal buildings and dependent on agriculture.

Beliefs of the American Shakers. The Shakers believed in living by the voice of God in one's heart. Furthermore, they held to the notion that Christ had appeared on earth first through Jesus and then through Ann Lee. According to her teachings they espoused celibacy, or abstinence from sexual relations, and also embraced the concept of communal goods, education, and hard labor. The religion of Christ, Ann Lee had counseled, meant doing constant battle against idleness and lust. Property was to be held in common, which meant joint ownership of goods for full members of the senior order. Full membership, however, was not mandatory to belong to the hierarchy of Shaker orders.

- Highest was the third or senior order—consisting of full members who surrendered all their worldly goods to the order, making them common property. These Shakers renounced natural family ties to join the church family, which may have included as many as 150 members.
- In the middle were Shakers who retained ownership of some or all of their property but surrendered the use of it as well as their own services or labor to the order. In return, they received food, lodging, clothing, and medical care.
- Lowest in the hierarchy were those who adopted Shaker beliefs but chose to stay in their own homes with their natural families and to hold on to their own property. They looked to the organized Shakers for religious leadership but remained independent in other ways, maintaining their ties to their children, spouses, and worldly goods.

The family in *A Day No Pigs Would Die* would have been among the several thousand Shakers in the lowest hierarchal order.

Growth and decline. Religious leaders thought of the orders as stepping stones up the hierarchy, although there was movement in and out of each order, and some people always remained in the order they joined. The Shaker movement on the whole grew as the decades passed, with societies appearing in one state after another. As is evident from the chart below, though, there was never one in Vermont, where *A Day No Pigs Would Die* is set.

State	Number of Shaker Societies
Massachusetts	5
Ohio	4
New York	3
Maine	3
Connecticut	1
New Hampshire	2
Florida	1
Kentucky	2
Indiana	1
Georgia	Unknown

(Adapted from Desroche, p. 134)

Estimates place the number of Shakers living in their own communities at about 6,000 around 1850. The advocacy of celibacy, though, resulted in an aging community with few new members. So as the nineteenth century progressed, Shakerism claimed fewer members, even though the number of communities rose and Shaker-controlled land grew to around 49,335 acres.

Despite this decline, the Shakers managed to build a reputation for hard work done with excellence. Producing their own food, clothing, and furniture, they soon developed businesses that brought money into the communities. Shakers sold herbs and seeds through catalogs and in small shops, and their pharmaceutical plants became popular. Among the innovations they have been credited with are the flat broom, clothespins, circular saw, and washing machine. Shaker furniture, another achievement, became a desirable commodity to people outside the communities. Built simply and ruggedly, the Shaker chairs and long trestle tables, often painted a dark red, provided income for the communities. In addition, some Shakers established mills and blacksmith shops. These enterprises grew so swiftly that each Shaker community was for a time obliged to hire outside help in their shops. By the 1900s, though, the movement had declined to such an extent that the Shakers themselves found it necessary to take jobs outside their own community. This explains why Rob's father in *A Day No Pigs Would Die* must leave his farm every day to work for a man who slaughters pigs.

SHAKERS IN THE TWENTIETH CENTURY

Year	Number of Shakers
1906	516
1916	367
1926	192
1936	92

(Adapted from Desroche, p. 138)

The Shaker lifestyle. According to Ann Lee, the godly way was for a man to lead the family—in the case of either a husband-wife family or a church family. Only when the man was not present could a woman take the lead. (Ann Lee justified her lead position because Jesus Christ, the male figure, was not physically present.) Thus, when Haven Peck dies in the novel, his twelve-year-old son must take charge of the family.

Shakers lived under a code called the Millennial Laws—for a long period unwritten, but known to every believer. These "laws" affected every aspect of life. Men and women could not work together in pairs or speak to each other. Women could not speak in church. Everything must be in its proper place. Only the elders of the community could approve transactions with or visits to outsiders. Absolutely nothing was to be done on the Sabbath to make the day more enjoyable. Plain dress was demanded and made by the seamstresses within the community (or, in the case of independent families, by the women of the house). Furniture, too, should be plain, built for function rather than appearance, and not overly concerned with comfort.

The Shakers believed that everyone should work. In fact, people living in Shaker communities rose at 4:30 in the morning and ended the day with an 8:00 o'clock evening dedication session in which they gathered in their communal rooms and stood in a posture of contrition and humility before their God. Between these hours, every aspect of communal life was organized. Shakers living outside the organized communities, as is the case in the novel, practiced much of this daily behavior.

Plainness carried Shakers to the grave. Coffins were simple, undecorated wooden affairs. Graves were frequently dug among the orchard trees and left unmarked. A person's deeds were considered his or her gravestone—the place of the body did not need to be remembered. Furthermore, death was not a threat to be feared since immortality followed. This helps explain why in the novel Haven Peck faces his own impending death with such a matter-of-fact demeanor.

The Novel in Focus

The plot. Robert, a twelve-year-old boy living as a Shaker on a Vermont farm, encounters a neighbor's cow suffering through a difficult birthing. The boy helps in delivering twin calves and then rescues the mother cow from suffocating to death because of a large goiter, an enlargement of the thyroid gland in the neck. In the process, Rob's arm is severely chewed up and readers are introduced to the austere life of the Shakers as his mother tends to the wounds by stitching up the bitten arm with her sewing needle and thread.

Robert Newton Peck

In gratitude, the neighboring farmer, a Baptist named Mr. Tanner, presents Rob with a baby pig. After some negotiations between Rob's father and Mr. Tanner (because Shakers do not accept gifts for such volunteered help), Rob gets to keep the pig.

Rob tends his pet pig until it is nearly fully grown. By that time, Mr. Tanner's two calves are also nearly matured. He decides to enter them in the county fair, hiring Rob to show the calves. Pinky, the pig, is also entered in the fair and wins a blue ribbon for being the best-behaved pig there.

Meanwhile, Shaker ways have raised many questions in Rob's mind. A neighbor, a boy with whom Rob attended school, sports a brand new, store-bought, and very colorful jacket; Rob does not understand why he cannot have one too. But the family still has to scrimp and save to pay off the purchase of the farm. Besides, Shaker ways call for all believers to wear very plain clothes, ones that are, moreover, handmade by the women of the family. Rob questions the Shaker code:

> The only thing I'd wanted was a bicycle.... [B]oth Mama and Papa would have looked at a bicycle as a work of the Devil. A frill. And in a

Shaker household, there wasn't anything as evil as a frill. Seemed to me the world was full of them.
>
> (Peck, *A Day No Pigs Would Die*, p. 23)

Neither does Rob understand why he cannot go to see the local baseball team play on Sunday afternoon. After all, the viewers just sat there and watched; it wasn't like they went to the park to play. But the Shaker ways demand that true followers not engage in any activity just for enjoyment on the Sabbath, not even a walk along a shady road.

On the Shaker farm, everyone and everything has to be productive. So, when Pinky grows to adulthood, there are only two choices: the pig can become a brood pig and regularly produce litters, or it can serve as food for the family. Pinky turns out to be unable to bear offspring. When Haven Peck, Rob's father, cannot find a deer to supply winter meat, Rob, now thirteen, is called upon to help his father kill the pet pig, which he does. It is a task the father knows well how to execute since he is helping to pay off the farm by working as a pig slaughterer. But keenly sensitive to how emotionally difficult it sometimes is to do "what's got to be done," he takes it upon himself to help his son grow up in this way (*A Day No Pigs Would Die*, p. 139).

Rob and his father feel deep love for each other, but there is little display of emotion in the household. Rob never sees his father smile, and only once sees him weep—the day Pinky is slaughtered. Rob himself barely breaks the somber tradition the day his father dies. Rob arranges for a plain pine casket to be placed on the long kitchen table. The father is laid out in the casket and a few nearby believers, including the men of the slaughterhouse where his father had worked, take time off to come to the funeral. Tradition calls for the oldest surviving male to give the brief funeral dedication, which Rob does. He has already dug a grave in the orchard for the coffin. There is no marker at the grave, since a Shaker's deeds are viewed as his or her monument. As Rob steps into the role of man of the household, he reflects on his father's greatness, and on the neighboring Tanners and the pig slaughterers, who have stopped work to pay their last respects on this day when no pigs would die.

Shaker attitudes toward outsiders. In the loose community of the story, the Shakers lived among people of other religions but were careful not to become beholden to neighbors of different faiths. If Rob's family had lived in a

Shaker commune, distance from other people would have been kept by the rule demanding that anyone speaking or doing business with an outsider must have the consent of the commune's elders. Rob describes the Shaker attitude when Aunt Matty, a Baptist, comes to visit. She attempts to teach the boy grammar and allows that he would get better than a "D" in the subject if he were a Baptist.

> That was it! That there was the time my heart almost stopped. . . . Baptists were a strange lot. They put you in water to see how holy you were. Then they ducked you under the water three times. Didn't matter a whit if you could swim or no. If you didn't come up, you got dead and your mortal soul went to Hell. But if you did come up, it was even worse. You had to be a Baptist.
>
> (*A Day No Pigs Would Die*, p. 64)

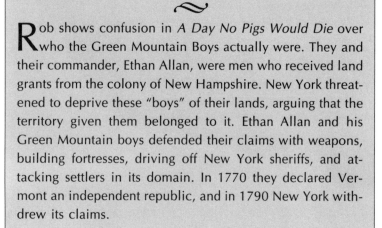

THE GREEN MOUNTAIN BOYS—WHO THEY REALLY WERE

Rob shows confusion in *A Day No Pigs Would Die* over who the Green Mountain Boys actually were. They and their commander, Ethan Allan, were men who received land grants from the colony of New Hampshire. New York threatened to deprive these "boys" of their lands, arguing that the territory given them belonged to it. Ethan Allan and his Green Mountain boys defended their claims with weapons, building fortresses, driving off New York sheriffs, and attacking settlers in its domain. In 1770 they declared Vermont an independent republic, and in 1790 New York withdrew its claims.

As the story proceeds, Rob is astounded to come to the realization that his father considers his Baptist neighbor, Mr. Tanner, a better farmer than himself and that the three people his father had most respect for outside his own family were Baptists. In the end Rob decides to claim a friendship with Mr. Tanner, while, in the Shaker tradition, not becoming beholden to him.

Sources. *A Day No Pigs Would Die* is drawn from the author's own experiences. He was raised in the Shaker tradition on a farm in Vermont. His father, to whom the book is dedicated, killed pigs for a living. In 1972, as the book was published, Robert Newton Peck still thought of himself as a farmer first, then as a writer.

Events in History at the Time the Novel Was Written

Shakers in the 1970s. By 1975, only a handful of Shakers remained—there were two surviving communities, at Canterbury, New Hampshire, and Sabbathday Lake, Maine. The carefully built-up business in pharmaceutical herbs and in sturdy furniture had virtually disappeared. Only the Shaker tradition that had led to an almost excessive accumulation of land enabled the few to survive. As membership in communes declined and conditions became untenable, the remaining members sold their property and merged with another commune. Sometimes, the old buildings were simply abandoned as members moved to join a stronger unit.

Outsider interest in the Shakers declined swiftly in the 1920s, when the novel takes place, but it had revived by the time of its writing in the 1970s, in part because of the efforts of some individuals. The number of Shakers was diminishing so rapidly that Edward Deming Andrews and his wife, Faith Andrews, committed themselves to preserving vestiges of the movement. They collected examples of Shaker handwork and began to interview the few remaining practitioners. From these interviews came a number of pamphlets and books about Shaker life and traditions. The results of the Andrews' efforts included the establishment of "Shaker rooms" at the Henry Francis du Pont Winterthur Museum in Delaware, home to the country's foremost collection of period furnishings, and the 1975 dedication of a Shaker library there. Along with the Andrews' individual efforts, the protests of the era gave rise to a new regard for the Shakers as an alternative to mainstream society.

America in the early 1970s. Shakerism, had it remained a strong movement, would have found some common ground with American social trends in 1970. Antiwar movements dominated the news. Many Americans were opposed to their own government's participation in a futile, and some thought baseless, war in Vietnam. Opposition to armed conflict regardless of its causes had long been a basic principle of the "Shaking Quakers."

Shaker experiments in communal life, which rested on equality of labor and the rewards of work, were coming to a close by 1970. In 1972, the year *A Day No Pigs Would Die* was published, few Americans were concerned with a dying socialist movement. Members of the Republican Party, then in power, were discovered to have burglarized Democratic Party headquarters, and the news was filled with detailed accounts of the "Watergate" break-in and subsequent cover-up. The case would bring about the resignation of President Richard Nixon in 1974. Americans became a more disillusioned group, many developing a great distrust of government that grew into a distrust of all large and organized institutions. As a result, while the Shaker movement was fading, membership in all organized religions began a steep decline.

Experiments in communal living, however, had not subsided. At the beginning of the 1900s, there were few new attempts to create socialist utopias, but between the 1930s and the 1960s the United States saw nearly six hundred such experiments within its borders. Student rebellions, drug experimentation, and general disillusionment with the nation resulted in a renewal of the communal spirit, doubling of the number of communal arrangements in the 1960s and 1970s. Few of these communities were religiously oriented, although religious communities proved twice as likely to survive as nonreligious ones. The new self-sustaining communities bore such descriptive names as Drop City, New Buffalo, and Mahogany. Collectively, they represented variations in commitment to total communal life, as had the individuals and groups in the Shaker movement.

In reaction to all this activity, the two remaining Shaker societies closed their doors, so to speak, refusing to take in any new members. As one Shaker historian notes, the communes of the 1960s and 1970s often involved a sexual looseness and drug experimentation by young people who seemed unwilling to accept the discipline necessary for Shaker life, factors that boded ill for the maintenance of Shaker ways (Stein, p. 387).

Reception. *A Day No Pigs Would Die* received a mixed reception. Reviewers were struck by this first novel of Peck's, which dared to feature the brutality of daily farm life. They denounced the book for its vivid images of coarse farm experiences, but also lauded the novel for its simple story line. Reviews ran the gamut of emotions.

> I found this book sometimes sickening, often entrancing. . . . I could feel the author digging me in the ribs demanding my tears or my laughter.
> (*Christian Science Monitor,* in Samudeo, p. 1010)

> Enjoyable light reading.
> (*Library Journal,* in Samudeo, p. 1010)

> All in all, more an exercise than a real evocation.
> (*Saturday Review of Literature,* in Samudeo, p. 1010)

Shakers pointed out the purely fictional nature of elements in the story, such as mention of a Shaker congregation or meeting in the town of Learning, Vermont. At least some Shakers preferred to regard it as a story about a boy in rural Vermont, which it unarguably is.

For More Information

Andrews, Edward Deming and Faith Andrews. *Fruits of the Shaker Tree of Life.* Stockbridge, Mass.: Berkshire Traveller, 1975.

Andrews, Edward Deming. *The People Called Shakers.* New York: Dover, 1963.

Desroche, Henri. *The American Shakers.* Translated and edited by John K. Savacool. Amherst, Mass.: University of Massachusetts Press, 1971.

Peck, Robert Newton. *A Day No Pigs Would Die.* New York: Alfred A. Knopf, 1973.

Roberts, Ron E. *The New Communes: Coming Together in America.* Englewood Cliffs, N.J.: Prentice-Hall, 1971.

Samudeo, Josephine, ed. *Book Review Digest.* Vol. 69, New York: H. W. Wilson, 1973.

Stein, Stephen J. *The Shaker Experience in America: A History of the United Society of Believers.* New Haven, Conn.: Yale University Press, 1991.

A Death in the Family

by

James Agee

Poet, journalist, film critic, screenwriter, and novelist, James Agee died in 1955 at the age of only forty-nine. He had almost completed his autobiographical novel *A Death in the Family* after working on it for nearly two decades. Agee had written its ending but not yet finished revising the text by the time of his death. Set in Knoxville, Tennessee, where Agee himself grew up, the novel recreates his childhood experience of his own father's death, providing a closeup view of life in a small American city in the period just before the nation's entry into World War I.

Events in History at the Time the Novel Takes Place

Changing times. The first two decades of the twentieth century ushered in innovative notions that would soon take a central place in American life. While they had begun taking shape earlier, only in the early twentieth century did many of them begin reaching forms recognizable today. The opening pages of *A Death in the Family* touch on two of the most distinctive of them, mass production and mass culture. These forces would help shape the twentieth century into an era that many historians, mindful of America's role in world affairs and its own way of life, have described as the "American" century. *A Death in the Family* briefly alludes to America's emerging role as a world power. Other developments are explored more fully as the novel progresses: tensions between city and countryside in an in-

THE LITERARY WORK

A novel set in Tennessee around 1916; published in 1958.

SYNOPSIS

A young boy struggles to understand and accept his father's death.

creasingly urban society, and between secular and religious lifestyles in an age of growing skepticism. Behind these issues lay the backdrop of racial tension, as both blacks and whites in the South lived with the legacy that slavery had left on racial relations in the region.

Mass production. No single feature characterizes the modern world better than mass production, the use of standardized parts and techniques to make large numbers of inexpensive and identical consumer items. Quintessentially American, this method of manufacturing in fact had its roots in the American Revolution, when firearms were in such short supply that cheap and rapid ways of making them had to be devised. (When English firearms manufacturers adopted such techniques in 1855, they called them "the American method.") Pioneered by Eli Whitney and others, by the end of the nineteenth century mass production had become firmly established in American industry.

Mass production, however, reached its definitive expression only in 1913, when Henry

Ford introduced the assembly line in the manufacture of automobiles. The popular Model T Ford—cheaply and rapidly put together by a line of workers, each installing a single, standardized part—became the first mass-produced car. By the late 1920s, 5 million cars would have been made in this way. In *A Death in the Family,* six-year-old Rufus's father, Jay Follet, has bought one of these early Fords and is killed in a nighttime accident when it veers off the road. The novel's central event—Jay's death—thus hinges on this symbol of innovation, which Jay had purchased over his wife Mary's objections. "*Progress,*" Mary's own father bitterly utters in a discussion about the car after news of the accident. "We mustn't—stand—in the way—of Progress" (Agee, *A Death in the Family,* p. 141). Many Americans shared this ambivalent attitude toward the car—perceiving it to be foul-smelling, noisy, and dangerously fast as it began to replace the horse-drawn carriage on America's streets and roads.

Mass culture. While mass production began to offer goods for the material side of modern life, mass culture started to define its nonmaterial side. Electric printing presses came into use during the nineteenth century, allowing books, magazines, and newspapers to reach much larger audiences than before. By the early decades of the twentieth century, electronic media such as film and radio (and later television) were offering a truly standardized form of entertainment to the American public.

Edwin Porter's silent early masterpiece *The Great Train Robbery* appeared in 1903, and its success hinted at a huge popular market for movies. The American film industry was firmly established within a decade, and from 1913 to 1917 movie pioneers Cecil B. De Mille and D. W. Griffith made the first feature-length films. Most popular, however, were the short comedy films of the first *bona fide* movie star, Charlie Chaplin. In 1916, Chaplin's was the most widely recognized face in America. Six-year-old James Agee certainly recognized it, for one of his favorite pastimes was to sneak out to a Charlie Chaplin movie with his father—just as Rufus and his father are doing as *A Death in the Family* opens.

America's role in the world. While such innovations were changing American life at home, the country's international position was also undergoing a transformation. The Spanish-American War in 1898 marked the beginning of the United States's dominant role among the world's pow-

James Agee

ers. In that war, the U.S. first supported Cuba against its colonial ruler, Spain, then soon became involved in fighting over other more distant Spanish colonies, such as the Philippine Islands in the Pacific Ocean. Victory over Spain brought American rule to the Philippines and other former Spanish possessions, constituting a virtual American empire overseas.

American expansionism continued under President Theodore Roosevelt, notably in Central America. There, for example, the United States helped Panama break away from Colombia and then won concessions to build and control the Panama Canal. James Agee's father worked for the U.S. Post Office in Panama for several years after the canal's opening in 1904, a period briefly—if humorously—recalled in *A Death in the Family.*

Rural-urban split. During the century's first two decades the nation's cities were growing ever more populous; the 1920 U.S. Census showed that for the first time more Americans lived in urban areas than rural. A number of factors contributed to this shift. First, heavy immigration led to the rise of large ethnic neighborhoods in cities such as New York and Chicago, where immigrants tended to settle. Second, many smaller towns and cities saw little or no growth, as people there began moving to larger cities in increasing numbers.

Mass production and mass culture also encouraged the growth of the cities. Mass production is "capital intensive," meaning that it requires a large initial investment into equipment such as machinery. It also relies on a heavy volume of production in order to realize profit. Mass production thus meant large factories, and large factories needed to be close to large labor pools, which could be found in cities. Factories attracted city newcomers looking for work—both those from the countryside and those from other countries. Meanwhile, movies and other media made the attractions of urban life increasingly visible, often portraying cities as glamorous and exciting places.

THE SCOPES TRIAL

In broad terms, city life encouraged a secular outlook while rural life provided a base of support for more fundamentalist forces in society. Nowhere would these growing tensions be better illustrated than in rural Dayton, Tennessee, about sixty miles southeast of Knoxville, in 1925. The arrest and trial of school teacher John Scopes for teaching Darwin's theory of evolution to his class, in violation of a Tennessee law passed earlier that year, grew into a public spectacle. Large city newspaper reporters, most notably H. L. Mencken of the Baltimore *Sun*, portrayed the small town as hopelessly backward to the paper's city readers. Mencken and others ridiculed the law's fundamentalist supporters, especially famous orator William Jennings Bryan, who volunteered to prosecute Scopes in court.

These changes exacerbated tensions between rural and urban values and lifestyles, tensions that often had overtones of class divisions. As people in cities and large towns increasingly began to consider themselves sophisticated, they became disdainful of those living in rural areas. In *A Death in the Family*, Mary's middle-class, town-based gentility contrasts sharply with Jay's family background among the mountain farms of rural eastern Tennessee. Mary's family accepts Jay only reluctantly, considering his social background to be inferior. Such tensions as portrayed in the novel reflect actual tensions that existed between the families of Agee's parents.

Tensions over religious belief. Conflicts also arose between those who held certain religious beliefs and the growing numbers of nonbelievers in society. Various factors had contributed to an increasingly secular outlook among Americans. The introduction of the scientific theory of evolution, for example, marked by the publication of Charles Darwin's *On the Origin of Species* in 1859, conflicted with the belief in the literal truth of the Bible, on which many traditional religious groups insisted. Also, the growth of cities, whose populations tended to be more sophisticated than rural dwellers—or at least to view themselves as such—contributed to the development of skepticism. Even some fundamentalists began to adopt more moderate views.

Rufus's family provides an exception to this evolving state of affairs in that Mary, Rufus's middle-class and town-raised mother, has strong religious beliefs, while Jay and his mountain family do not. Mary's extreme piety contrasts, however, with the agnosticism of her father (Rufus's grandfather). In real life, Agee's maternal grandfather shared the agnosticism of his fictional counterpart, an attitude gaining ground in towns and cities of the time.

Racial issues in Tennessee. By 1916 racial segregation had been institutionalized for decades by the South's Jim Crow laws. In the North, a trickle of black migrants from the South was rapidly turning into the northbound stream that would be called the Great Migration (1915-1930). The bulk of these immigrants would come from states in the Deep South, such as Georgia and Mississippi. Tennessee, by contrast—the last state to secede from the Union and the first to rejoin it after the Civil War—had always been a border state between North and South. Its geographic and political position, however, had resulted not in a general moderation of racial attitudes, but instead in an uncommonly dramatic polarization of the two extremes. Illustrating these extremes, Tennessee was the birthplace both of the nation's first antislavery journal, *The Emancipator* (in 1819), and of the Ku Klux Klan (in 1865). As Tennessee historian Wilma Dykeman observes, "Emancipators and klansmen each found a following in Tennessee" (Dykeman, p. 20).

Six-year-old Rufus, however, knows nothing of racial conflict, embarrassing the black woman his mother employs by innocently asking her about her skin. Later, older boys tease him by chanting that Rufus is a "nigger's name" (*A Death in the Family*, p. 217). When he asks his mother what they mean, she tells him that he should be proud of his name:

> Some colored people take it too, but that is perfectly all right and nothing for them to be ashamed of or for white people to be ashamed of who take it. . . . And Rufus: don't ever speak that word "nigger."
>
> (*A Death in the Family*, p. 219)

Agee's own middle name was Rufus, which is what he was called as a child. In fact, he was teased in this same way about his name by older boys.

The Novel in Focus

The plot. The novel begins with a prologue, told in the first person, entitled "Knoxville: Summer 1915," in which the adult narrator recalls a childhood summer in the small Tennessee city. Switching to third-person, the story opens with six-year-old Rufus Follet and his father, Jay Follet, going downtown to a Charlie Chaplin movie after dinner. Rufus's mother, Mary, half-jokingly objects, describing Chaplin as a "vulgar" and "nasty" comedian (*A Death in the Family*, p. 11). After the movie, Rufus and his father stop in a bar, where Jay Follet has a couple of quick drinks and shows off his son. They walk on together through the quiet evening and stop to sit on a rock on a hill overlooking the city.

Late that night, Jay and Mary receive a phone call from Jay's brother Ralph, who is at the Follet family home in the mountain country outside of Knoxville. Ralph asks Jay to drive out right away, as their father has suddenly been taken seriously ill. Ralph has clearly been drinking; both Jay and Mary suspect that he has exaggerated the gravity of the illness. They realize, however, that Jay has no choice but to go anyway, in case the situation is as bad as Ralph claims. Despite the hour, Mary makes Jay a large breakfast before he drives off. He will try to be back by the next day, before the children go to sleep, he says.

While his father is away, Mary's Aunt Hannah takes Rufus shopping, buying him a cap that he likes. Jay, meanwhile, has found that his suspicions were correct, and that Ralph had exaggerated their father's illness. He prepares to return.

Later that evening, Mary gets a call from a man who tells her that Jay has had an accident and asks her to send a male relative to the site. Flustered, she lets him hang up without asking for more details about Jay and calls her brother Andrew, who drives out to the accident site. Aunt Hannah comes over to sit up with Mary. After a long wait, Andrew returns with the news that

Jay's car had gone off the road at high speed on his way home, and that he was killed instantly. Mary's parents come over, and her family sits up with her as they grieve together. Toward the end of the vigil, the exhausted family believes for a moment that they feel Jay's presence with them in the house.

Rufus awakes the next morning eager to show his father the new cap, but is surprised to find his father not home and his mother lying in bed looking ill. Mary tells him to wake his younger sister Catherine, for there is something she has to tell them both. He does so, and Mary says that their father will not be coming home at all. When Rufus asks why, she explains that he was badly hurt, so that God put him to sleep and took him to heaven. Rufus asks if his father is dead, and Mary answers yes. Pondering this, Rufus helps Catherine dress, and they go downstairs to breakfast with Aunt Hannah.

Aunt Hannah explains the manner of Jay's death more fully, describing how he was thrown from the car after it went off the road. Later Rufus attempts to impress the boys who have teased him by sharing details of the accident, which has made the local paper. Afterwards, however, he is deeply ashamed for using his father's death in this way. Preoccupied with vague feelings of guilt, Rufus continues to try to grasp the event as the family prepares for the funeral. Mary is visited by a priest, who tells her that Jay cannot receive a full Episcopalian burial because he was not baptized (Mary is a devout Episcopalian). Before the funeral takes place, Rufus views his father's body.

Rufus and Catherine are then put in the care of a family friend so that the adults can attend the funeral. The friend, however, takes the children to a spot where they watch the procession from a distance. In the novel's final scene, Uncle Andrew takes Rufus for a walk. Describing the funeral, he tells Rufus how a butterfly first settled on the casket as it was lowered into the ground, then flew straight up into the sky as the casket touched down at the bottom of the grave.

The family and the individual. *A Death in the Family* repeatedly shows its characters as essentially alone, and yet sustained in their loneliness by family love and support. This is true of each character, though in different ways. Much of Agee's artistry lies in the subtlety with which he keeps each character's essential solitude in the reader's mind even while illuminating the complex relationships that sustain the family. This subtlety and complexity are what give the novel its true-to-life feel, lending its events and personalities a relevance to the reader's own experiences. As one critic comments, through the novel's "preciseness . . . Agee captures . . . a suggestion of what all families experience as they are buffeted by living" (Kramer, p. 155).

In the opening scene, Rufus senses loneliness in his father, though his parents' marriage is a happy, loving one. In some paradoxical way, Rufus perceives, the loving family actually exacerbates the loneliness even while comforting it:

> He felt that although his father loved their home and all of them, he was more lonely than the contentment of all this family love could help; that it even increased his loneliness, or made it hard for him not to be lonely. He felt that sitting out here, he was not lonely; or if he was, that he felt on good terms with the loneliness; that he was a homesick man, and that here on the rock, though he might be more homesick than ever, he was well.
>
> (*A Death in the Family*, p. 19)

FICTIONAL CHARACTER	REAL-LIFE PERSON
Mary Follet	Laura Tyler Agee
Jay Follet	Hugh James Agee (called Jay)
Ralph Follet, Jay's brother	Frank Agee
Hannah Lynch, Mary's aunt	Jessie Tyler
Joel Lynch, Mary's father	Joel Tyler
Catherine Lynch, Mary's mother	Emma Tyler
Catherine Follet, Rufus's sister	Emma Agee

Rufus's own loneliness has so far been a child's—that is, his parents' loving presence has been enough to comfort him. With the death of his father, however, Rufus is initiated into the loneliness of an adult, a "homesickness" that remains even when one has returned "home." The idea of home will be a recurrent one in the novel, signifying not so much a place as a state that has been lost and can never be recaptured. His father's death cuts Rufus off from "home" in this sense; thus, he roams the house looking for comfort in concrete signs of his father's existence, even wiping the inside of his father's ashtray with his finger. "There was nothing like enough to keep in his pocket or wrap up in a paper. He

looked at his finger for a moment and licked it; his tongue tasted of darkness" (*A Death in the Family*, p. 281).

In real life, the author, Agee, would experience loneliness after his own father's death. He was still part of a family, albeit a smaller one, yet he is said to have felt a prolonged sense of loneliness when his mother moved her two children to the grounds of St. Andrews, an Episcopalian boarding school for boys—mostly the sons of farmers. While Agee was consigned to a dormitory, his mother and sister moved into a cottage, at which he was free to gaze but to which he was almost never permitted to go.

Composition and sources. When Agee died in 1955, he had written the novel's ending, but it was unclear to his editors how much revision he had intended for its main body. The handwritten manuscript was just over three hundred pages, of which about two hundred pages made up the main narrative of the events surrounding Jay's death. The remaining one-third consisted of material relating certain experiences that Rufus had before his father's death. Some of these passages illustrate his relationship with his father; some of the others show him being teased by older boys. Uncertain about how Agee intended to integrate this material, his editors put it in two italicized sections after part 1 and part 2. They also included what became the novel's prologue, "Knoxville: Summer 1915," originally written as a short story in 1935 and published in the magazine *Partisan Review* in 1938. "It was not a part of the manuscript Agee originally left," they wrote, "but the editors would certainly have urged him to include it in the final draft" (Frontispiece to *A Death in the Family*).

Virtually all of the characters in the novel are based on characters in Agee's own family. Some, like Rufus's maternal grandfather Joel, have the same first names of their real-life counterparts. Other names, like that of his mother, Mary, are made up (Agee's mother was named Laura). The only major character who seems completely invented is Jay's 103-year-old great-great-grandmother, whom the Follets visit and who, though unable to speak, seems to recognize Rufus as Jay's boy.

Events in History at the Time the Novel Was Written

Great Depression. Agee began sketches for an autobiographical novel in the mid-1930s, though he did not begin work on *A Death in the Family* in earnest until the 1940s. After completing "Knoxville: Summer 1915" in 1935, he collaborated with photographer Walker Evans on a book documenting the lives of rural Alabama sharecroppers during the Great Depression of the 1930s. Called *Let Us Now Praise Famous Men,* it has become a classic of documentary journalism. Agee was fascinated by these poverty-stricken country farmers, whose lives were so similar to those of his Agee ancestors in the Tennessee mountain country. His experiences living with sharecropper families while writing the book influenced him profoundly, and may have helped inspire the scene in which Rufus and his Follet relatives visit Jay's great-great-grandmother in her remote mountain cabin.

Postwar politics. A number of factors combined to push Agee toward writing a novel that explored in a subjective and artistic way the most important event of his childhood: his father's death. As in any such literary work, the author's own psychological motivations were of principal importance. Still, some external considerations seem to have been at work as well—chief among them Agee's frustration with the atmosphere of anticommunist repression that dominated postwar American politics. Agee and a number of his left-wing friends (whose political outlook he shared) had long worked as writers for Time, Inc., where their views had been tolerated by conservative publisher Henry Luce. The relative political tolerance of the 1930s, however, had come to an end, and Agee felt increasingly uncomfortable working for Luce in the late 1940s. He made plans to leave Time soon after beginning *A Death in the Fam-ily,* which he saw as the free exploration of his artistic impulses denied him by the restraints of journalism.

Reception. On its publication in 1957, *A Death in the Family* was immediately recognized as a masterpiece, winning posthumous fame (and a Pulitzer Prize) for its author. Critics especially praised its poetic language, noting Agee's earlier career as a poet (most finding the novel superior to the author's poetry). *A Death in the Family* has been compared to such works as D. H. Lawrence's *Sons and Lovers* (1913), and Thomas Wolfe's *Look Homeward, Angel* (1929) in its detailed and loving observation of family relationships. Leading critic Alfred Kazin called it "an utterly individual and original book . . . the work of a writer whose power with English words can make you gasp" (Kazin in James, p. 8).

A play adaptation of the book, called *All the Way Home* (from the novel's last line), was produced in 1960 and became a hit on Broadway, also winning a Pulitzer Prize. A film version of the novel, also called *All the Way Home,* was made in 1963, with Robert Preston as Jay Follet.

For More Information

Agee, James. *A Death in the Family.* New York: McDowell, Obolensky, 1957.

Bergreen, Lawrence. *James Agee: A Life.* New York: Dutton, 1984.

Dykeman, Wilma. *Tennessee: A Bicentennial History.* New York: Norton, 1975.

James, Mertice M., and Dorothy Brown. *Book Review Digest.* 53rd ed. New York: H. W. Wilson, 1958.

Kramer, Victor A. *James Agee.* Boston: Twayne, 1975.

Dubliners

by
James Joyce

James Augustine Joyce, who revolutionized English literature with his shocking language and literary style, was born February 2, 1882, in a Dublin suburb. The oldest son in a Catholic family of ten children, Joyce was educated largely by the Jesuits. At sixteen, the young man considered entering the priesthood but realized that celibacy was not for him. Shortly thereafter he made an abrupt about-face and rejected the church entirely, although it dominated his imagination for the rest of his life. He rebelled against his Catholic upbringing and against the domestic politics of his native land, leaving Dublin for the European continent in 1904 and never returning. Joyce's fiction, including *Dubliners,* dismantles and critiques middle-class Irish Catholic society, questioning marriage, faith, and nationalism.

Events in History at the Time of the Short Stories

Ireland and England. Even though Joyce claimed to be disgusted by its cultural paralysis and its political ineptitude, Ireland, and specifically his hometown of Dublin, dominated his literary imagination throughout his life. To understand his insistence upon depicting the stagnation and hopelessness of the country—which he certainly exaggerated to some degree—it is crucial to be aware of the historical legacy of the Irish. Ireland had known many centuries of economic and cultural impoverishment, political suppression, and religious conflict from the Middle Ages until Joyce's day, and these hardships were especially harsh for Irish Catholics. Though his fiction is set in contem-

---

THE LITERARY WORK

A collection of fifteen short stories set in Dublin, Ireland, between 1894 and 1905; begun in 1904 and published in Dublin in 1914.

SYNOPSIS

Joyce's semi-autobiographical collection of short stories speaks of the despair and, in the author's view, the cultural paralysis of the Irish people as they struggle with economic and cultural depression at the turn of the twentieth century.

---

porary times, the social situation of which Joyce complains had its roots deep in Irish history.

To one degree or another, the Irish had been considered subjects of the English throne since the twelfth-century reign of the English regent Henry II. At the time, a Norman named Richard Fitz Gilbert de Claire, or "Strongbow," had set himself up as a ruler in Ireland through an opportune marriage and political savvy, but King Henry quickly nipped such political ambitions in the bud by sailing to Ireland and demanding loyalty. Henry received it. English control of Irish life reached its peak seven centuries later, with the 1800 Act of Union, which abolished the Irish Parliament and made Ireland part of Great Britain, like Scotland and Wales. As a result, Ireland was governed directly from London, though it was nominally a separate nation. Under the Act of Union, Ireland would send 100 members to the House of Commons in London, and 32 men to the House of Lords. At the time, the House of Commons (the political body of the elected members of Parliament) had 658 members—Ireland, in effect, would be governed by a Parliament in which it had less than 1/6 of the members. Combined with the prejudiced antipathy of the British toward the Irish—whom many British considered inferior—this state of affairs rankled Irish people of various religions and classes.

The troubled relationship between Ireland and England was made infinitely worse in the mid-nineteenth century by what the Irish regarded as the indifferent attitude displayed by the British during the Potato Famine of 1845. Ireland's poor subsisted almost entirely on a diet of potatoes, and when a blight wiped out the entire national crop one year, Ireland was devastated. The famine is estimated to have killed one million Irish between 1845 and 1851, and to have driven another million to emigrate. This emigration continued, though more slowly, well into Joyce's day; by 1901, the country claimed less than one-half the population that it had had in 1841. The response of the government in London appeared casual and ineffective in coping with the human disaster in Ireland. Behind many of the late nineteenth-century cultural revival movements that arose in Ireland in Joyce's youth was the collective remembrance of this treatment. While he would ultimately reject nationalist movements that merely criticized the English (and the English language) without looking too closely at Irish weaknesses, the young Joyce did dabble in several nationalist groups, including *Sinn Fein* ("Ourselves Alone"), which developed in later years into the political arm of the Irish Republican Army (IRA).

Joyce's Dublin. Ireland in Joyce's day was still an overwhelmingly agricultural society, with two major urban centers at Belfast and Dublin. The latter was the largest Irish city, with a growing population of 375,000, and its greatest employer the Guinness brewery. The next two most successful business enterprises in the city consisted of whiskey and biscuit production. There was, in effect, no heavy industry.

Dublin is an ancient city. Founded by the Vikings in 842, Dublin's name in Scandinavian means "dark pool." After London, it is commonly regarded as the second metropolis of the British Empire. But it also has a strong history as a Catholic city; in fact, medieval Christian monks from Ireland were responsible for bringing Christianity to much of Britain. With its heritage as a Viking capital, a Christian capital, and a British

capital, Dublin possessed a former greatness that made its stagnation that much more intolerable to Joyce. In *Dubliners* as in all his fiction, he was obsessed with the details of the locale, with representing precisely the exact spread of the land, the actual names of streets and businesses, the minutia of everyday business transactions and customs. He once speculated that it would be possible for later generations to almost perfectly reconstruct turn-of-the-century Dublin from reading his works. In letters sent from Europe to his younger brother Stanislaus, Joyce, trying to give *Dubliners'* individual stories an exact realism, asked such questions as:

> "The Sisters": Can a priest be buried in a habit?
> "Ivy Day in the Committee Room": Can a municipal election take place in October?
> "A Painful Case": Are the police at Sydney Parade of the *D* division?
>
> (Joyce in Beja, p. 36)

Such scrupulous attention to detail and the use of real names and places actually alarmed Joyce's potential publishers, who feared libel suits. To the contrary, many businesses and places from Joyce's Dublin that survived into the present invariably use their inclusion in his fiction to their commercial advantage.

MIRROR, MIRROR

Joyce had a difficult time trying to get *Dubliners* published. Various editors demanded changes in style, in content, in tone. Outraged and obstinate, Joyce fired off letters in his own defense, one of which includes his justification for the unpleasant imagery and language that permeates the stories: "It is not my fault that the odour of ashpits and old weeds and offal hangs round my stories. I seriously believe that you will retard the course of civilization in Ireland by preventing the Irish people from having one good look at themselves in my nicely polished looking-glass" (Joyce, *Letters I,* 63-4).

Irish Catholics. Joyce struggled with his theological attractions to and repulsions from the Roman Catholic Church throughout his life, and his fiction readily portrays this. But Catholicism was not merely a religion in Ireland; because the privileged classes in Dublin were nonnative British Protestants, Catholicism—the traditional religion of the vast majority of the Irish—became associ-

James Joyce

ated with grassroots Irish cultural and political identity. There were Irish Protestants in the land too, and they clashed with their English counterparts on nonreligious issues, but for the Catholic majority in Ireland it was religion that defined their plight.

The factional strife that continues to plague Ireland to the present day has its roots in medieval politics and Renaissance religious wars in Europe. Situated so close to England, Ireland almost inevitably became drawn into the political ambitions of its aggressive neighbor. The tight hold kept on the Irish by the English monarchy constricted during the Protestant Reformation of the fifteenth and sixteenth centuries, when, for various reasons related to conflict between the monarch and pope, England outlawed the Catholic religion. To ensure that the traditionally Catholic Irish did not side with England's Catholic enemies of France and Spain, England began a long process of land appropriation and resettlement that resulted in the Irish Catholics losing their land and homes to new English and Scottish Protestant settlers sent there by the English crown. Through a very complicated series of legislative acts, the Irish Catholics found themselves powerless and impoverished; at various stages, they lost the right to vote, own property, hold government positions or, as late as 1849, be educated in Irish history, literature, and language.

By Joyce's era, the Irish Catholic lot had improved somewhat—they could once again vote, own land, and run for most government offices—but the writer could not forgive the Catholic Church for what he saw as its complicity in the religious and cultural oppression suffered by its faithful. Throughout the long years of gradual political and social disenfranchisement suffered by the Irish Catholics, the church had, with a few notable exceptions (including Father Thomas Burke, who is mentioned in Joyce's short story "Grace"), counselled acceptance of the situation and as an institution avoided entering the political arena itself. There were critics other than Joyce who wondered what the use was of a church that did nothing to lessen the spiritual or physical suffering of its congregants, instead advocating servile obedience to a Protestant regent. Nonetheless, Joyce's criticism of the Catholic Church is certainly somewhat extreme. The Catholics who had emerged from the famine years with land or resources counted themselves lucky and were reluctant to rock the political boat. Their fathers and grandfathers had been distinctly less fortunate than they, and the smallest economic and political liberties by then allowed must have seemed immense good fortune to Joyce's contemporaries.

Cultural "revival." The character Gabriel Conroy in the short story "The Dead" bristles at being labeled a "West Briton"; the term was used derisively among certain nationalist Irish to denote someone who sided with the English politically and culturally. At the turn of the century, cultural revival movements, based mostly in Dublin, were gathering strength in their attempt to combat the lack of cultural awareness and pride among the Irish. Because for generations the powerful upper classes in Ireland had been Protestant English and Scots, Irish culture had become associated with impoverishment and defeat, and was either abandoned or neglected by the Irish. In the story when Gabriel protests, "if it comes to that, you know, Irish is not my language" (Joyce, *Dubliners,* p. 169), he is telling the truth—few Irish people could speak or read Irish, for it was neither taught in schools nor used socially except in the most remote parts of the country. In 1851 only 25 percent of the population could speak Irish; by 1911 that figure had dwindled to 12 percent.

The problem of cultural decline had been addressed in scholarly articles for a century before the 1893 founding of the Gaelic League by a Protestant named Douglas Hyde. The Gaelic League sought to revive the Irish language as the national tongue, to teach and publish Gaelic literature of the past and to encourage new writers to write in Gaelic. The idea won widespread approval, and within ten years some of its goals were being met: Irish language and literature were being taught regularly (though not uniformly) in centers of learning at every level, from primary school to university. Joyce's story "A Mother" alludes to the "language movement"—although in this story it seems to amount to little more than members of a social club fond of "saying goodbye to one another in Irish" (*Dubliners*, p. 123). In the long run the measures to reinstitute Gaelic as the primary language of Ireland were not very successful. English would continue to supplant the Irish tongue to a large degree, although some patriotic Irish still prize their ability to speak Gaelic and continue to do so among family and friends.

The Irish cultural revival of Joyce's era took on other forms. The Gaelic Athletic Association, for example, founded in 1884, strove to boost the popularity of "hurling"—an Irish game approximating a hybrid between lacrosse and field hockey—while discouraging such English sports as polo and cricket. Some dismissed the efforts made by such organizations as the Gaelic Athletic Association, which may or may not have made up the game of "Irish football" to replace English football. In the critics' eyes, these efforts amounted to so much "green spray paint" applied over English customs and rituals to make them seem authentically Irish.

The most famous manifestation of the Gaelic revival is the literary movement referred to as "the Irish literary revival." The literature associated with this movement tends to be characterized by heavy use of Irish mythology and the frequent appearance of the peasant character, as well as by experimentation with an Irish-English linguistic blend. The movement was led by such writers as W. B. Yeats, George Russell, and Lady Gregory. Joyce, too, is often counted among their number, although he would no doubt be less than pleased to be so considered. He felt that the focus on mythology continued the Irish habit of looking to the past, rather than the future. "Ancient Ireland is dead just as ancient Egypt is dead" (Joyce in Deane, p. 40), he states, intending to replace the poets and legends of old with a new kind of writer and a new set of tales. Rather than flattering Irish culture, they would shame and goad it into revitalization.

Parnell. The most overtly political of the *Dubliners* stories, "Ivy Day in the Committee Room" describes a forlorn collection of political strategists who have gathered together on October 6, 1902, the eleventh anniversary of Charles Parnell's death; the story was written in the summer of 1905. What happened to Parnell at the hands of the Irish irked Joyce throughout his literary career and turns up time and again in his writings in a scene of betrayal all too characteristic of Irish politicians.

Parnell, a Protestant landlord, became the leader of the Irish Home Rule movement in 1879. The "Home Rulers" struggled for greater powers of self-rule than the 1800 Act of Union permitted Ireland. Specifically, they aimed to restore an independent parliament to Ireland, one that was not merely part of a larger legislative body of Great Britain. Parnell's vigor and determination made him a hero among Irishmen of all denominations, but the English were, understandably, not impressed with his political antics. In "Ivy Day," Mr. Henchy reminisces fondly:

> He was the only man that could keep that bag of cats [the British Parliament] in order. "Down ye dogs! Lie down, ye curs!" That's the way he treated them.
>
> (*Dubliners*, p. 118)

But it was not the English who ultimately brought down the great leader. Parnell was named as co-respondent in the divorce of William and Katherine O'Shea. Though separated, the O'Sheas were still married; in an age when divorce was difficult and even scandalous, Mrs. O'Shea had for a long time simply been living with Parnell. In 1889 Captain O'Shea finally sued for divorce, and the revelation that Parnell was an adulterer discredited him so completely that he was ousted from the leadership of the Home Rule party one year later. So heated had been the reaction in Ireland to his role in the scandal that it had ruined his career. Parnell died at age forty-five in 1891, probably due to complications from fatigue.

James Joyce wrote often about Parnell, whom he considered to have been betrayed by his fellow Irishmen and by Catholics in particular. The ultra-conservative Catholic Church, whose laws forbid divorce among its flock, became Parnell's worst domestic enemy in the O'Shea scandal. The religious authorities punished Parnell's Catholic allies in the Home Rule movement by refusing them church rites. The "lost leader," whom Joyce clearly regarded as Ireland's brightest hope for self-rule, reappears in Joyce's later fiction, *Portrait of the Artist as a Young Man, Ulysses,* and *Finnegans Wake,* as well as in his social criticism. This last group includes, prominently, an Italian essay from 1912, entitled "L'Ombra di Parnell" ("The Shade of Parnell"). In the essay, Joyce sarcastically congratulates his Irish compatriots: "They did not throw him to the English wolves; they tore him to pieces themselves" (Joyce in Bolt, p. 4).

The Short Stories in Focus

The plot. *Dubliners* fifteen stories are broken into four groups—childhood ("The Sisters," "An Encounter," "Araby"), young adulthood ("Eveline," "After the Race," "Two Gallants," "The Boarding House"), mature life ("A Little Cloud," "Counterparts," "Clay," "A Painful Case"), and public life ("Ivy Day in the Committee Room," "A Mother," "Grace"); and one additional story, his most famous, "The Dead," stands alone.

ON SECOND THOUGHT

Sometimes, thinking of Ireland it seems to me that I have been unnecessarily harsh. I have reproduced (in *Dubliners* at least) none of the attraction of the city (Joyce in Beja, p. 320).

In a letter to his brother Stanislaus, James Joyce indicated that these works were heavily autobiographical, dealing with his childhood, with people that he knew, with the very streets of Dublin that he walked every day. Although the stories are distinct and stand alone, they are intertwined to such an extent that some critics point out that *Dubliners* sometimes resembles a novel, with characters from one story appearing in the periphery of another.

Joyce intended that the fifteen stories of *Dubliners* all contribute to the general theme of paralysis—cultural, religious, and political—that he saw as characteristic of life in Ireland's capital city. For example, the character Eveline, in the story of that name, cannot bring herself to escape her abusive father and bleak future through sailing away with her love; the boy in "Araby" falls prey to a romantic idea of an Oriental fair and is disillusioned; Maria in "Clay"

is literally blindfolded and cannot put her life and habits in context. In "The Dead," the self-important Gabriel Conroy discovers in a devastating revelation that his wife had had a youthful romance that has haunted her memory ever since. The haunting conclusion of "The Dead" captures the frozen emotional landscape in which all the characters of *Dubliners* live their lives:

> Yes, the papers were right: snow was general all over Ireland. It was falling on every part of the dark central plain, on the treeless hills, falling softly upon the Bog of Allen and, farther westward, softly falling into the dark mutinous Shannon waves. It was falling, too, on every part of the lonely churchyard on the hill where Michael Furey lay buried. It lay thickly drifted on the crooked crosses and headstones, on the spears of the little gate, on the barren thorns. His soul swooned slowly as he heard the snow falling faintly through the universe and faintly falling, like the descent of their last end, upon all the living and the dead.
>
> (*Dubliners,* p. 298)

Publish or perish. In 1905 the London publisher Grant Richards received the manuscript of Joyce's *Dubliners,* and agreed two months later to publish the collection. Little did Joyce know that the struggle to publish *Dubliners* would occupy him for the next ten years. By April, complications with the printer had arisen. According to the law of the time, printers were legally responsible for whatever literary material they printed, and even though Joyce was willing to take a few risks with risqué language and imagery, or with politically unpopular sentiments, his printer was not. After a series of negotiations with an unwilling Joyce, Richards decided he could not publish the collection after all, and *Dubliners* was shipped to various other publishers, with no success.

Finally, in 1909, Joyce offered *Dubliners* to George Roberts of the Irish publishing house Maunsel & Co. Roberts accepted the work, promising that it would be published within fifty-four weeks. He too, however, balked at issuing the stories as they were, on the grounds that certain stories were too sexually explicit, too true-to-life (as mentioned, Joyce used the names and places of real businesses in Dublin), or too politically inflammatory (Joyce suggests in "Ivy Day" that the English king Edward VII was a womanizer who drank too much). Roberts waffled for years and finally in 1912 destroyed the sheets, or ready-to-print copies, of *Dubliners,* and went so far as to demand that

Joyce repay Maunsel & Co. for their expenses in so doing.

At long last, in 1913, Grant Richards reconsidered his earlier position and published *Dubliners* in 1914.

A man of style. Although Joyce was to revolutionize English literature through his adoption of a "stream of consciousness" technique, *Dubliners* is written in a direct, straightforward style, which some have linked to the Realist literary movement growing in America and Europe at the time. Realism offered "a slice of life" in a quasi-scientific way devoid of most cause-and-effect commentary; Joyce's remark that *Dubliners* was to hold a mirror before the Irish places him in this movement, as does his attention to everyday, colloquial patterns of speech. But Joyce always strove to go beyond the mere recounting of facts, and it is his regular use of symbols, symbols created out of everyday objects (like snow, fire, a blindfold) and familiar names (like Gabriel), that most strongly characterizes his work.

Sources. In his scathing attacks on the Catholic establishment in Dublin, Joyce was inspired by perhaps the greatest of Catholic writers, and the greatest of church critics, the Italian poet Dante. Dante's *Divine Comedy*, a three-volume epic poem about heaven, hell, and purgatory, openly criticizes corrupt churchmen and the poisonous politics of Dante's beloved city, Florence. One of *Dubliners*' stories, "Grace," is heavily influenced by the *Divine Comedy*, structurally and in terms of plot. Tom Kernan wakes from a nasty fall in a men's washroom—Joyce's version of Dante's Inferno, or Hell; he is then cajoled into making a religious retreat with three friends, a sort of Purgatorio; and finally, ends up in church, a heavily satiric version of Heaven. In a characteristically Joycean gesture, however, the priest, Father Purdon, is a well-fed mishandler of the Bible; his sermon caters to the spiritual ease of the wealthy.

Reviews. Once *Dubliners* was finally published, the reviews were generally positive, if lukewarm. The *Times Literary Supplement* suggested, for example, that "*Dubliners* may be recommended to the large class of readers to whom the drab makes an appeal, for it is admirably written" (Bolt, p. 39). Despite the publisher's fears, the book did not result in lawsuits, outrage, or scandal, although mention was made repeatedly of the collection's "morbidity," "sordidness," and "unpleasantness" (Bolt, p. 39).

For More Information

Beja, Morris. *James Joyce: A Literary Life*. Columbus: University of Ohio Press, 1992.

Bolt, Sydney. *A Preface to James Joyce*. 2nd ed. Burnt Mill, Essex: Longman House, 1992.

Deane, Seamus. "Joyce the Irishman." *The Cambridge Companion to James Joyce*. Edited by Derek Attridge. Cambridge: Cambridge University Press, 1990.

Joyce, James. *James Joyce's* Dubliners: *An Annotated Edition*. Edited by John Wyse Jackson and Bernard McGinley. London: Sinclair-Stevenson, 1993.

Joyce, James. *Letters*. Vol. 1. Edited by Stuart Gilbert. New York: Viking, 1957.

Joyce, Stanislaus. *My Brother's Keeper: James Joyce's Early Years*. Edited by Richard Ellmann. New York: Faber, 1958.

Manganiello, Dominic. *Joyce's Politics*. Routledge: London, 1980.

Parrinder, Patrick. "Dubliners." In *James Joyce: Modern Critical Views*. Edited by Harold Bloom. New York: Chelsea House, 1986.

A Farewell to Arms

by
Ernest Hemingway

Ernest Hemingway was born in Oak Park, Illinois, on July 21, 1899. After a brief stint as a reporter for the *Kansas City Star,* Hemingway joined a volunteer American Red Cross unit as a driver in World War I. He served in Italy and was seriously wounded during an Austrian attack. Shortly after the war, Hemingway lived in Paris, where he became a key figure of what is sometimes called the "Lost Generation." The term refers generally to the post-World War I generation, whose members felt disillusioned with the war and its consequences; more specifically, the term refers to a group of leading writers and artists of the period. This was the time in which Hemingway began work on *A Farewell to Arms,* a novel that epitomized his disillusionment with the war.

THE LITERARY WORK

A novel set in Italy during World War I; published in 1929.

SYNOPSIS

An American military officer in the ambulance service becomes romantically involved with a British nurse. The officer deserts the Italian army and flees to Switzerland with the nurse, who is pregnant with his child. The nurse and child die during childbirth, and the officer concludes that trusting in the possibility of happiness is a mistake.

Events in History at the Time the Novel Takes Place

World War I. The outbreak of World War I, or the "Great War," began with a territorial dispute between the vast empire of Austria-Hungary and the nation of Serbia. After the Balkan Wars of 1912-1913, Serbian nationalists took on the cause of the South Slavs of the Austria-Hungarian empire, deciding that it was time for these people to be liberated. These Serbian nationalists believed that their aims could be furthered with the assassination of the Austrian archduke Franz Ferdinand. On June 28, 1914, the archduke and his wife Sophie were shot dead by a young Serbian radical while touring Sarajevo.

The leaders of Austria-Hungary saw the murder as a good opportunity to launch aggressions against Serbia and to increase the empire's prestige and power in the Balkans. With promises of German support, Austria-Hungary declared war on Serbia. Subsequently Russia, committed to protecting fellow Slavs in Serbia, mobilized its troops against Austria-Hungary. When France also began to mobilize for war on the side of Serbia, Germany declared war on both France and Russia. German troops invaded Belgium to secure a position for an assault on France, and Great Britain, committed to Belgium's defense, then declared war against Germany.

On September 5, 1914, Russia, France, and Great Britain, also known as the Allied Powers, concluded the Treaty of London, each promising not to make a separate peace with the Central Powers of Germany and Austria-Hungary. The outbreak of the war was generally greeted with confidence and satisfaction by the people of Europe, who were inspired by a surging patriotism. Most Europeans felt that the conflict would run its course much more quickly than previous wars because of recent developments in weapons and strategy. But as the armies entrenched themselves on the both the western front, where the Central Powers faced the French and British, and the eastern front where the Central Powers faced the Russians, prolonged battles ensued. Participants and citizenry alike realized that the initial hopes for a rapid resolution would not be realized.

Technological advancements in World War I. The development of new and improved weapons around the turn of the twentieth century greatly influenced the course of World War I. The most powerful advancements were the machine gun and the rapid-fire artillery gun. The modern machine gun, developed in the 1880s and '90s, was a reliable belt-fed gun capable of firing 600 bullets per minute with a range of more than 1,000 yards. Newly developed field artillery benefited from the introduction of improved loading mechanisms and brakes. Without brakes, a mounted gun moved out of position during firing and had to be re-aimed after each round. The new brakes meant that the guns did not need to be repositioned and so increased the rate of fire and the accuracy of the artillery. Yet another invention that profoundly changed the face of war was not itself a weapon. This device, invented to control cattle of the western United States, was barbed wire, and it became a key factor in the shaping of World War I battlefields.

With these innovations came trench warfare, the predominant method of battle in World War I. Armies positioned themselves in elaborate trench networks defended by barbed wire, machine guns, and heavy artillery. Usually supported by artillery fire, infantry forces assaulted the trenches of the opposing army in an attempt to gain ground. This new style of trench fighting was characterized by short attacks made under barrages of artillery; suicide assaults against machine gun positions; elaborate tunnel mining; brutal night skirmishes in "no man's land," the open area between the opposing trenches; and moving walls of artillery fire that, in some battles, could send eighteen shells into each square yard of battlefront. Understandably this warfare was incredibly deadly. In a single day of fighting

during the Battle of the Somme, for example, the British army suffered 57,470 casualties.

Italy's role in World War I. Since 1882 Italy had been allied with Germany and Austria-Hungary through the Triple Alliance. Because this treaty was only a defensive pact, and Austria-Hungary and Germany were the aggressors in World War I, Italy was not obliged to enter the war on their side. Even though the Italian government refused to become involved, it demanded that Italy should still profit from the conflict. If Austria-Hungary improved its position in the Balkans, the Italians wanted the Trentino, a piece of Austrian-held land that some Italians had desired for years. When Austria was slow to meet this request, Italy demanded the immediate surrender of the border region of South Tyrol and several islands in the Adriatic Sea. By the time Germany persuaded the Austrians to agree to these demands, Italy had begun negotiations with the other side. Having no stake in the European territory themselves, Allied Forces leaders of Russia, England, and France immediately promised Italy the desired land from Austria as well as aid in expanding the Italian territories in Northern Africa if Italy would join them in the fight against the Central Powers. Italy agreed to join the Allies in the secret Treaty of London on April 26, 1915, and immediately began mobilization efforts. Italy's ostensible role in the conflict was to divert the Austrian forces in order to keep them from aiding the German army on the western and eastern fronts.

KEY PARTICIPANTS IN WORLD WAR I	
Allied Forces	*Central Powers*
France	Germany
Great Britain	Austria-Hungary
Russia	Turkey
United States	Bulgaria
Italy	

Italy was poorly prepared for war, however, and made little progress against the Austrians during the first year of the conflict. Both sides traded victories and defeats during the almost nonstop battles of the Isonzo, a strategically important river in Italy. During 1916 alone, Italy suffered 500,000 casualties in the course of this fighting. It is during one of these battles that Hemingway's Frederick Henry is wounded in *A Farewell to Arms*.

The ambulance service in World War I. With the development of the technologically advanced weaponry that was determining the course of the war came the need for better emergency medical services. In the early nineteenth century, ambulance service had been defined as the "hospital establishments moving with armies in the field, and organized for providing early surgical assistance to the wounded after battles" (Haller, p. 1). By the twentieth century, the term *ambulance* had also come to mean the actual vehicles that carried the wounded, this definition deriving from British and American misuse of the term.

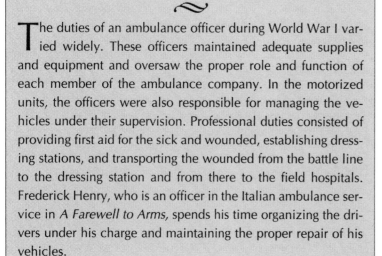

AMBULANCE OFFICERS

The duties of an ambulance officer during World War I varied widely. These officers maintained adequate supplies and equipment and oversaw the proper role and function of each member of the ambulance company. In the motorized units, the officers were also responsible for managing the vehicles under their supervision. Professional duties consisted of providing first aid for the sick and wounded, establishing dressing stations, and transporting the wounded from the battle line to the dressing station and from there to the field hospitals. Frederick Henry, who is an officer in the Italian ambulance service in *A Farewell to Arms*, spends his time organizing the drivers under his charge and maintaining the proper repair of his vehicles.

The immediate and effective evacuation of the wounded not only avoided the permanent loss of many soldiers' battlefield services, but also helped the morale of those who remained fighting. Prior to successful ambulance use, the prospect of being abandoned on the battlefield made soldiers less willing to fight; it also meant that able-bodied soldiers would not have to leave the firing line to assist the wounded to safety. Ambulances also became crucial in the medical severity of a wound. The prompt evacuation of stricken soldiers could mean the difference between a minor injury and a wound that became fatal because of infection or delayed treatment.

On the eve of World War I, ambulances of the British and American armies were a mixture of horse-drawn and machine-powered vehicles. Motorized vehicles were put to use as ambulances almost from their inception. Yet even with the benefit of motorized vehicles, the resources of medical personnel were sorely tested during the war. The drastic rise in casualties that came as a result of the innovations in weapons technology more than compensated for improved evacuation procedures. During the Battle of the Somme, personnel worked three days just to clear the wounded and dead from the battlefield.

Despite the humanitarian function of the ambulance service, it was not uncommon for its personnel to face the same violence experienced by the soldiers. Despite precautions, such as the use of the Red Cross flag while on the field, stretcher parties and ambulance crews took hostile fire—and during major battles sustained heavy casualties. In many circumstances it became common for the medical personnel to remove their white arm-bands and uniforms, which made them easy targets for enemy guns. In *A Farewell to Arms*, Frederick Henry is wounded by artillery fire while serving as an ambulance officer during one of the battles by the Isonzo River. This episode in the novel is modeled after Hemingway's own injury suffered on the Fossalta di Piave front in 1918.

The Novel in Focus

The plot. Frederick Henry is an American serving as a volunteer ambulance officer in Italy during World War I. The Italians are fighting the Austrians in an attempt to hinder their aid to the German army on the western and eastern fronts. Henry's ambulance unit is stationed in Gorizia, a northern Italian town that had previously been held by the Austrian forces. When Henry earns a leave during a break in the fighting, he spends his time drinking and carousing with his roommate, Rinaldi, an Italian army surgeon.

Rinaldi tells Henry about the beautiful English nurses at the hospital and mentions one Miss Barkley in particular. Henry meets Catherine Barkley in the hospital with Rinaldi and finds her indeed very beautiful. During their first meeting, Catherine tells Henry about her fiancé, who was killed in the Battle of the Somme. At first, Henry is not in love with Catherine, but he does desire an affair with her. But despite his initial intentions not to become romantically involved, Henry realizes that he is lonely without Catherine and tries to spend more time with her.

During one of the Italian forces' battles with the Austrians, Henry is wounded by an explosion from a mortar round and one of his drivers is killed. Rinaldi visits Henry in the field hospital and encourages him to petition for a medal. Henry is sent to the American hospital in Milan, and Catherine arranges to be transferred there as well. At this point, Catherine and Henry truly fall in love and spend every free moment together. This is made easier by Catherine's assignment as the night nurse in Henry's ward. As their physical intimacy continues, Henry worries about the immorality of their relations. Catherine is not in the least concerned with these considerations. When she informs Henry that she is pregnant, she asks him if he feels trapped. He replies that men always feel trapped.

After his recovery Henry is sent back to the front and finds that the war is going poorly. He is constantly confronted by visions of death and has several realizations about the destruction and pointlessness of war. When the Germans and Austrians begin their drive into Italy, the Italian troops are forced to retreat from the city of Caporetto. As the retreat becomes more chaotic, Henry shoots an Italian sergeant who refuses his order to help dig out an ambulance stuck in the mud. One of Henry's drivers, afraid of being killed, surrenders to the German army. Henry is confronted by Italian military police, who accuse him of treason for retreating from the enemy. Realizing that all retreating officers are being sent to a firing squad, Henry runs away. He then takes off his uniform and deserts.

Henry reunites with Catherine in the small Italian town of Stresa. With Henry out of military service, they are finally able to enjoy a few moments of happiness. During this tranquil time, Henry fishes at the lake and befriends the elderly and distinguished Count Greffi. Feeling he and Catherine must leave Italy, Henry plans their escape to Switzerland, just across the lake from Stresa. During a heavy storm, Henry borrows a boat and rows all night to reach the Swiss border.

Happy in neutral Switzerland, Henry and Catherine discuss marriage, but Catherine asserts she wishes to wait until after the baby is born. Henry takes Catherine to the hospital when she goes into labor. The doctor announces that they must perform a Caesarean section to save the mother and child, and Henry agrees. Despite the emergency operation, both the baby and Catherine die. Henry realizes the risks of falling in love

and determines not to put faith in anything but himself.

Antiwar sentiment in *A Farewell to Arms*. One of the most powerful and pervasive elements in *A Farewell to Arms* is its constant condemnation of war and the false idealism that flourishes during wartime. The condemnation begins early in the novel when Frederick Henry has not yet made his own realizations about the futility and senselessness of the war. In Chapter 9, Henry discusses the war with his ambulance crew, who "were all mechanics and hated the war" (Hemingway, *A Farewell to Arms*, p. 48). One of the

---

WAR WOUNDS

With the use of more advanced weapons in World War I, the nature of injuries suffered by soldiers changed dramatically. In the recent Boer War (1899-1902) and Russo-Japanese War (1904-1905), most wounds had been inflicted by rifle bullets, and complications from these wounds were minimal. Unlike rifle bullets, the shrapnel, trench mortars, bombs, and hand grenades used during the trench warfare of World War I caused dreadful gashes and tears that required major surgery. Further complications arose from these wounds because soldiers lived in wet trenches and terrain that was often muddied, and thus microorganisms easily infected the wounds. Though a thorough dressing and cleansing of the wound could help prevent infections, no dressing was fully effective until the wounded were removed from the hostile germ-laden trench environment. When Frederick Henry is wounded in *A Farewell to Arms*, he is immediately treated with an antitetanus shot and his wounds are dressed with antiseptic. Hemingway's own wound was treated with an antitetanus shot, along with a dose of morphine. The wound had been caused by an Austrian trench mortar, which was essentially a five-gallon can filled with explosives and scrap metal.

---

drivers, Manera, expresses the sentiment that, "If everybody would not attack the war would be over" (*A Farewell to Arms*, p. 49). Henry, still full of idealism about the war, disagrees with this attitude and tells the drivers, "It would only be worse if we stopped fighting" (*A Farewell to Arms*, p. 48). Another driver, Passini, challenges Henry and says, "War is not won by victory. . . . Why don't we stop fighting? If they come down into Italy they will get tired and go away. They have

their own country. But no, instead there is war"
(*A Farewell to Arms,* pp. 50-1).

It is not until the retreat from Caporetto that
Henry comes full circle and discovers what he
perceives to be the true nature of war. During
the retreat Henry thinks about the war and talks
about the idealism that supports it:

> I was always embarrassed by the words *sacred,
> glorious,* and *sacrifice* and the expression *in vain.*
> We had heard them, sometimes standing in the
> rain almost out of earshot, so that only the
> shouted words came through, and had read
> them, on proclamations that were slapped up
> by billposters over other proclamations, now for
> a long time, and I had seen nothing sacred, and
> the other things that were glorious had no glory
> and the sacrifices were like the stockyards at
> Chicago if nothing was done with the meat
> except to bury it.
>
> (*A Farewell to Arms,* pp. 184-85)

At this point, Henry is thoroughly disgusted
and disillusioned with the war, and has come to
reject his earlier ideals. By showing this transformation in Henry and the events and conditions
that brought this change, the novel presents a
gradual and effective condemnation of wartime
idealism. During the time that Hemingway was
writing the novel, such sentiments of disillusionment with the war were commonly expressed by
the "Lost Generation," a group of writers and
artists of whom Hemingway was a leading figure.

Sources. Many of the situations and characters
in *A Farewell to Arms* came from Hemingway's
own experience with the war in Italy. Not long
after high school Hemingway volunteered as a
Red Cross ambulance driver in 1917. Just like
Frederick Henry, Hemingway was commissioned
as a second lieutenant in the Ambulance Corps.
Several other aspects of Hemingway's war ordeal
became part of Henry's experience in the novel.
Henry was posted in northern Italy and, like
Hemingway, received a wound from a mortar
round. Even the details of the wound to the leg
are based exactly on the novelist's own injury.

Henry recovers from his wound in a Milan
hospital, where he continues his affair with
Catherine. Hemingway also convalesced in Milan and, like his character Henry, fell in love with
his nurse, an American named Agnes von
Kurowsky, who was reciprocal in her affections.
Like Catherine in the novel, she volunteered for
the night shift to spend time with him. Unlike
Catherine, who becomes completely devoted to
Henry, Agnes jilted Hemingway and became engaged to an Italian nobleman.

Hemingway with his first wife, Hadley, who served as
one of the sources for Catherine Barkley in *A Farewell
to Arms.*

Henry's closet full of empty cognac bottles
and his bout of jaundice during his recovery
were also based on Hemingway's experiences in
the Milan hospital. The character of Count Greffi is based on the real-life Count Greppi, an
aged diplomat whom Hemingway met during a
trip to Stresa in September of 1918. One difference in Hemingway's experience is that he
did not actually arrive in Italy until the year after the battle at Caporetto, the climax in the
novel; he was still in high school during the famous retreat.

Events in History at the Time the Novel Was Written

Hemingway and the "Lost Generation." Several twentieth-century American writers came to
terms with their feelings for America and developed their own artistic abilities in Paris. The
French capital welcomed many young artists
who, in the 1920s, were little appreciated in the
United States. Other grounds for the growing
number of exiled artists in Paris included the effects of the war, which had brought many Amer-

Ernest Hemingway

icans to Europe for humanitarian reasons; a new and inexpensive steamship fare, called Tourist Third, that brought artists and students to Europe by the thousands; and the favorable exchange rate, which made life in Europe wonderfully inexpensive for American travelers. American artists could live fashionably in Paris, spending their free time drinking in cafés; by contrast, their compatriots on American soil were legally prevented from drinking alcohol because of the Prohibition (1922-1933).

This "Lost Generation" of American artists, as they came to be known, coalesced around their common feelings of disillusionment about the war. The label "Lost Generation" originated, in fact, in relation to the war. A French hotel owner was speaking to the writer Gertrude Stein about a mechanic repairing her car. The war, observed the hotel owner, had robbed young men like the mechanic of a proper education in their formative years, leaving them a lost generation. Stein, remembering the expression, applied it to Hemingway and his circle. Then he quoted the expression in his novel *The Sun Also Rises* (1926), and "the words became the label for an entire literary generation" (Hendrickson, p. 329). The label extended to writers like F.

Scott Fitzgerald and e. e. cummings, Americans who, like Hemingway, felt alienated from the pre-world war values of their nation. "For meaning," explains one historian of the Paris literary set, "Hemingway and his generation turned to art, that is, to its order and beauty, to the preservation of the word. Style was to be a barrier against chaos and the loss of faith" (Fitch, p. 163).

Hemingway's *A Farewell to Arms* epitomizes the disillusionment of the Lost Generation with its stark portrayal of war and its attack on the idealism that fueled the incredible bloodshed of World War I. Henry voices this perspective: "There were many words that you could not stand to hear and finally only the names of places had dignity. . . . Abstract words such as *glory, honor, courage,* or *hallow* were obscene beside the concrete names of villages, the number of roads, the names of rivers, the numbers of regiments and the dates" (*A Farewell to Arms,* p. 185).

A Farewell to Arms and the critics. *Scribner's* magazine paid Hemingway an unprecedented $16,000 for the serial rights to *A Farewell to Arms.* The June 1929 issue of *Scribner's* was banned in Boston because of its so-called immoral episodes and objectionable language, but the publicity of the banning merely aroused public interest in the novel and increased the already substantial sales of the book. The release of *A Farewell to Arms* in 1929 cemented Hemingway's reputation as one of America's greatest young writers.

Malcolm Cowley, a great admirer of Hemingway, remarked on the tenderness and seriousness of the novel, comparing it to Hemingway's earlier work: "The emotions as a whole are more colored by thought; perhaps they are weaker and certainly they are becoming more complicated. They seem to demand expression in a subtler and richer prose" (Cowley in Meyers, p. 220).

Philip Young praises Hemingway's style in his review of *A Farewell to Arms:* "[A Farewell to Arms] is a beautifully written book. The prose is hard and clean, the people come to life instantly and ring true. The novel is built with scrupulous care" (Young in Bryfonski, p. 274). Young also comments on the structure and themes of the novel: "[T]he action is tied into a perfect and permanent knot by the skill with which the two themes are brought together. As the unintentionally ambiguous title suggests, the two themes are of course love and war" (Young in Bryfonski, p. 274).

For More Information

Bryfonski, Dedria. *Contemporary Literary Criticism.* Vol. 13. Detroit: Gale Research, 1980.

Fitch, Noel Riley. *Sylvia Beach and the Lost Generation: A History of Literary Paris in the Twenties and Thirties.* New York: W. W. Norton, 1983.

Haller, John S., Jr. *From Farmcarts to Fords: A History of the Military Ambulance, 1790-1925.* Carbondale: Southern Illinois University Press, 1992.

Hemingway, Ernest. *A Farewell to Arms.* New York: Simon & Schuster, 1995.

Hendrickson, Robert. *The Facts on File Encyclopedia of Word and Phrase Origins.* New York: Facts on File, 1987.

Meyers, Jeffrey. *Hemingway: A Biography.* New York: Harper & Row, 1985.

Stokesbury, James L. *A Short History of World War I.* New York: William Morrow, 1981.

Fiddler on the Roof

Text by
Joseph Stein

In the early 1960s, writer Joseph Stein teamed up in America with composer Jerry Bock and poet Sheldon Harnick to create the musical *Fiddler on the Roof*. Stein, who would compose the text for the play, had already written several radio and television dramas, and Bock and Harnick had collaborated on songs for other musicals. Although Harold Prince, their manager, worried that a play about Jewish life in a small Russian town would appeal to only a small faction of the American public, *Fiddler on the Roof* proved to be highly successful.

THE LITERARY WORK

A musical play set in a Jewish community in Russia in 1905; first performed in 1964.

SYNOPSIS

Tevye, a poor milkman, is distressed to learn that three of his five daughters want to marry against his wishes. Each marriage challenges Tevye to reconsider the traditions by which he lives.

Events in History at the Time the Play Takes Place

Traditional Jewish marriage. In the Jewish villages of Russia and Eastern Europe, marriages were arranged by a matchmaker, or *shadkhen*. The shadkhen matched partners based on their wealth and education and sought the approval of neither the prospective bride nor groom, but rather of the young people's parents. The eldest daughter in a family usually had to marry before her sisters. Because brides were expected to provide a dowry (money or goods), poor girls rarely hoped for anything more than a poor husband. Even a poor bride was expected to give at least a pair of pillows, a white tablecloth, candlesticks, bedding, and tableware. A poor boy, however, could win the daughter and dowry of a rich man if he distinguished himself as a scholar. Marriage for love was an exception.

Threats to the survival of Jewish traditions in Russia. A fiercely religious people, Russian Orthodox Christians barely tolerated Jews within their country. Wild rumors like the infamous blood libel (the totally unfounded contention that Jews used the blood of Christians to bake matzo, the unleavened Passover bread) spread fear and suspicion among the Russians, especially the peasantry. The czars decreed strict laws limiting the number of Jews who might enter Russia and confining them to specific areas in the empire's western provinces.

Russia's military conquests in the eighteenth century brought millions of Jews under its administration. To cope with these Jews living within the borders of their growing state, the Russians created what was called the Pale of Settlement. The Pale was a narrow strip running along the western border of the empire, from the Black Sea in the south to the Baltic Sea in the north. Unlike Jews in other parts of Europe, who enjoyed a certain degree of self-rule, the Jews in the Pale shared towns and villages with other groups (Poles, Ukrainians, Lithuanians), all of whom were subject to the same laws. A number of the laws, which changed slightly under different czars, saddled the Jews in these towns and villages with extraordinary taxes while also prohibiting them from buying or leasing land, selling liquor, working on Christian holidays or settling outside the Pale.

Confining Jews to the periphery of the empire did not satisfy the czars. They undertook efforts to convert, expel, or destroy the Jews. In 1898, when questioned by the Council of the Jewish Colonization Association in Paris as to the future of the persecuted Jews in Russia, Constantine Pobyedonostzev, chief executive of the empire's Orthodox Church, replied "one-third will die out, one-third will leave the country, and one-third will be completely dissolved in the surrounding population" (Dubnow, v. 3, p. 10).

Assimilation. The first radical step toward the forced conversion of the Jews in Russia was the Edict of 1827, which conscripted able-bodied Jewish males into the Russian army for six years more than the customary period of twenty-five years for non-Jews. The additional six years, from age twelve to eighteen, were, in large part, devoted to the effort of converting Jewish boys to Christianity.

A list of supplementary clauses added that Jewish minors, unlike Christian children, would, at the age of twelve, be placed in "preparatory establishments for military training" (Dubnow, v. 2, p. 19). As these years of training did not count as part of the twenty-five years of active service, under the laws boys would have to leave their homes for as long as thirty-seven years.

The Jewish boys were usually dispatched to the Eastern provinces, like Siberia, far from any Jewish community. Here their re-education began. Rather than speaking their native Yiddish, which was the first language of 96.5 percent of all the Jews in Russia, they suddenly had to speak Russian. Priests attempted to convince the young Jews to convert to Christianity, and if they failed to do so, Russian soldiers devised other methods of persuasion. They fed the boys salted fish, for example, then denied them water until they agreed to be baptized. Or the soldiers might force the children to kneel by their beds in the evening until they agreed to convert. Obstinate children who still refused were beaten or flogged. Many died from the privations and abuse before the edict was repealed in 1855.

The establishment of secular schools, furthered in 1864 by the Public Schools Statute, was a less drastic means of encouraging assimilation among Jews. Following the examples set in western Europe, where the enlightenment movement had persuaded Jews to adopt secular education, the Russians founded nonreligious schools to replace the traditional Jewish ones. To encourage participation, the government reduced the term of military service for graduates of the new schools.

The government's efforts to secularize Jewish education harmonized with the aims of the *Haskalah,* or Jewish enlightenment, which began in Germany in the seventeenth century. The *maskilim* ("lovers of enlightenment") maintained that a secular education, and particularly the study of local languages, should supplement Torah study. They encouraged acculturation, renouncing traditional Jewish customs such as the growing of earlocks, or *payot.* The Haskalah resulted in a division within the Jewish community between the conservative Jewish orthodoxy and Jewish liberals who favored change. Although these liberals challenged some Jewish traditions, they nevertheless fought the intimidation of Jews by the czar.

Pogroms. Though Czar Alexander II introduced many liberal reforms during his reign (1855-1881), such as repealing the Edict of 1827 and emancipating the Russian serfs, he never went so far as to introduce a constitution. On March 1, 1881, a group of revolutionary terrorists assassinated the comparatively progressive czar, ushering in the reactionary reign of Alexander III, which historians consider "the beginning of the end for Jews in Russia" (Halberstam-Rubin, p. 26).

The assassination offered Alexander III, a zealous champion of the Orthodox Church, an excuse to revive oppressive policies. Although only one of the gang responsible for Alexander II's death was Jewish (a Jewish woman, Hesia Helfman, had sheltered the revolutionaries), newspapers insinuated Jewish complicity in the assassination. The political upheaval aroused violent anti-Semitism. Erupting in Elizabethgrad, Kiev, and several other cities were incidents of anti-Jewish plunder and assault as well as some devasting pogroms—massacres of the Jews, too often government-encouraged.

Authorities were slow to suppress the mob violence, which led many rioters to believe that the government endorsed their brutality, though this was not always the case. In one village a constable ordered the looting peasants to disperse. So convinced were they that the government approved of their actions that they demanded a written guarantee from the police saying they would not be held responsible for their failure to comply with imperial orders to "beat the Jews" (Dubnow, v. 2, p. 257). No such explicit orders existed, but clearly the rioters assumed they did.

In 1882 the government took peculiar measures to deal with the pogroms. To pacify troublesome gentiles, the "Temporary Rules" of May 3 ordered the eviction of Jews from rural areas of the Pale. At the same time the government warned that further pogroms would be promptly punished. Despite of the government's admonitions, however, pogroms still erupted.

Czar Nicholas II replaced Alexander III in 1894. Eager to unite the Russian people against rebel groups of the time, he appealed to the anti-Semitic tendencies inside the empire. By branding the rebel movement "the work of Jewish hands" (Dubnow, v. 3, p. 69), he sought not only to discredit the revolutionaries, but also to deflect the anger of the disgruntled peasants from the government to the Jews.

In 1905, to quell a surge in revolutionary activity, Nicholas II issued a manifesto bestowing civil liberties upon the Russian people. It resulted in a peaceful mood of optimism that was shattered by an outbreak of counter-revolutionary pogroms. The Jews suffered the brunt of the onslaught. Bloody pogroms led by the police claimed the lives of Jews in Odessa, Kiev, Elizabethgrad, Kishinev, and several other major cities. In a letter to his mother, Nicholas II presented his view of the violence. "The impertinence of the Socialists and revolutionaries," said Nicholas, "has angered the people once more; and because nine-tenths of the troublemakers are Jews, the people's anger turns against them. That's how the pogroms happened" (Nicholas II in Ro'i, p. 131).

Expulsion and emigration. The Temporary Rules of 1882 expelled 500,000 Jews from rural areas within the Pale of Settlement into its overcrowded towns. Jews were barred from several cities in the Pale, such as Kiev, and the two port cities of Sebastopol and Yalta. Outside the Pale, in 1891, 20,000 Jews were expelled from Moscow and 2,000 more were deported, many in chains, from St. Petersburg to the Pale. In 1910, as the threat of a communist revolution loomed on the horizon, expulsions of Jews from cities outside the Pale and villages within the Pale assumed "the character of an epidemic" (Dubnow, v. 3, p. 157).

Throughout the nineteenth century this upheaval, along with the menace of pogroms, drove Jews to flee Russia. The growing rate of emigration to the United States during the 1880s reflects the persecutions the Jews in Russia suffered under Alexander III. In 1881, 8,193 emigrants left Russia for the United States. In 1882 that number grew to 17,497, and by 1888 it was over 30,000.

Other emigrants fled Russia for the hallowed shores of Palestine. In 1882 the first "Lovers of Zion," emigrants inspired by a growing movement to re-establish Jewish independence, founded the colony Rishon le-Zion, near Jaffa. Emigrants from Russia and other parts of Europe followed, building colonies in Judea and Galilee. Within a few decades these settlements would multiply into the nation of Israel.

The Play in Focus

The plot. Yente, the Jewish matchmaker in an imaginary village in the Pale of Settlement called Anatevka, visits the home of Tevye the milkman one evening with a proposal. Tevye's wife, Golde, is pleased to hear that Lazar Wolf, the butcher, hopes to marry the eldest of her five daughters, Tzeitel. "Tevye wants a learned man," Golde warns the matchmaker, however, about her husband's opinion on the matter. "Fine," Yente replies, "so he won't marry him. Lazar wanted the daughter, not the father" (Stein, *Fiddler on the Roof*, p. 10).

Tevye returns from his rounds to hear news of evictions in a neighboring town. An edict from the authorities forced the Jews from their homes. As the elders mutter about this injustice a young man interrupts them, "You'll all chatter your way into the grave" (*Fiddler on the Roof*, p. 18). When asked by the others where he is from, the young man called Perchik responds "Kiev. I was a student in the university there." Perchik entreats Tevye to hire him as a tutor for his children. "I have five daughters," Tevye replies. When Perchik insists "girls should learn too," another man cries out, "a radical!" (*Fiddler on the Roof*, p. 21), but Tevye nevertheless agrees to hire Perchik.

Arriving home Tevye introduces his five daughters to their new teacher. Motel, a young tailor, has dropped by to visit Tzeitel and joins the family for dinner. Before the meal Golde tells Tevye he must go see the butcher, Lazar Wolf, but does not say why.

In a moment alone with Motel, Tzeitel informs him that Yente, the matchmaker, has passed by.

She fears that if Yente has found a match for her, she will be unable to marry Motel, whom she loves. She encourages Motel to "ask my father for my hand tonight. Now!" (*Fiddler on the Roof*, p. 25), but Motel is too timid.

Tevye meets the butcher Lazar at a local inn. When Lazar declares his intention to marry Tzeitel, Tevye agrees, reflecting "with a butcher, my daughter will surely never know hunger" (*Fiddler on the Roof*, p. 31). The Jews sing to celebrate the match. As they dance some Russians chime in and dance too. Although the Russians mean no harm, their antics unsettle the Jews.

Leaving the inn, Tevye runs into the local constable, who says he has some important news. He warns that there will be an "unofficial demonstration" against the Jews, "so that if an inspector comes through, he will see that we have done our duty" (*Fiddler on the Roof*, p. 36). This ill tiding dampens Tevye's spirits.

The next morning, after listening to Perchik explain a biblical story in terms of landowners and exploited workers, Hodel, one of Tevye's five daughters, exclaims, "I don't know if the rabbi would agree with your interpretation" (*Fiddler on the Roof*, p. 38). Perchik challenges her, insisting that, because she follows traditions, her mind is a rusty tool. "Do you know that in the city boys and girls can be affectionate without the permission of a matchmaker?" he says. "They hold hands together, they even dance together—new dances—like this" (*Fiddler on the Roof*, p. 39), he exclaims, taking Hodel's hands and dancing with her.

The same morning, Tevye awakes and finds Tzeitel. He informs her that she is to be married to Lazar Wolf. Tzeitel begs him to reconsider, insisting she cannot be happy with a man whom she does not love. Motel enters, out of breath. Having heard of Tevye's plans he has rushed over to propose to Tzeitel. The young couple proclaim their love for one another, and Tevye begrudgingly agrees to let them marry, even though he must break his promise to Lazar.

The next day the village gossips prattle on about Tzeitel's new engagement. Motel leaves Chava, another of Tevye's daughters, to mind the tailor's shop while he picks out clothes for his wedding. A Russian boy, Fyedka, enters and flirts with Chava. Although she is hesitant to respond to him, she does borrow a book he recommends.

A man named Mordcha plays the jester at Tzeitel's wedding. After a solemn moment in remembrance of the dead, Mordcha jokes about the hapless Lazar, "who has everything in the world, except a bride" (*Fiddler on the Roof*, p. 63). Lazar himself exclaims that he bears the couple no ill will and has even brought them gifts.

A squabble ensues between Lazar and the matchmaker Yente, both of whom defend the traditional marriage customs, and Tevye and Perchik, who both insist it is right for Tzeitel to marry the man she loves. Their raillery is cut short, however, by the arrival of the Russian constable and his men. The constable apologizes, "I see we came at a bad time, Tevye. I'm sorry, but the orders are for tonight" (*Fiddler on the Roof*, p. 68). He and his men turn over the tables, smash the dishes and windows, and hurl the wedding gifts to the floor.

Two months after Tzeitel's wedding, Perchik announces to Hodel that he must leave Anatevka for Kiev. But before he leaves, he wants to ask her a political question . . . about marriage. "This is a political question?" she rejoins, and he replies, "In a theoretical sense, yes. The relationship between a man and a woman known as marriage is based on mutual beliefs, a common attitude and philosophy towards society."

"And affection," Hodel adds. (*Fiddler on the Roof*, p. 75). She understands that Perchik is asking her to marry him, and gladly accepts, even though he will leave soon for Kiev. When Tevye enters they inform him of their plans. He replies that, although he allowed Tzeitel to marry Motel, he will not permit Hodel to marry a man who plans to abandon her before the wedding. Perchik insists, "We are not asking for your permission, only for your blessing" (*Fiddler on the Roof*, p. 78). Tevye is flabbergasted, but resigns himself to the match. "Love," he says, "it's a new style . . . very well, children, you have my blessing and my permission" (*Fiddler on the Roof*, p. 79). Later, in Kiev, Perchik is arrested and sent to Siberia. Hodel joins him.

Months after Hodel's departure, Chava approaches her father to tell him of her feelings for Fyedka, the young Russian. Appalled that she would even suggest marrying a non-Jew, Tevye exclaims, "never talk about this again" (*Fiddler on the Roof*, p. 92). Chava nevertheless marries Fyedka. When Golde mentions her name to Tevye, he shouts she is dead to him. They must forget her.

The constable appears again in the Jewish quarter to announce that a new edict decrees that they must abandon the village within three days. They may take what they can carry, but they must go. Tevye and Golde resolve to flee with their two youngest daughters to America, where a relative of theirs has settled. Tzeitel will stay in Warsaw until she and Motel earn enough money to join them. No one has heard from Chava, and Hodel wants to remain in Siberia, near Perchik. Yente the matchmaker announces her plans to go to Palestine, where she will continue to make matches and help the Jewish population grow. As Golde and Tevye load their belongings onto a rickety wagon, their youngest daughters dance around, singing about boats and trains and long journeys. "Behave yourself!" Golde orders. "We're not in America yet" (*Fiddler on the Roof*, p. 106).

Tradition and Tevye's daughters. Tevye explains that in Anatevka "every one of us is a fiddler on the roof, trying to scratch out a pleasant, simple tune without breaking his neck." "And how do we keep our balance?" he asks. "Tradition!" (*Fiddler on the Roof*, p. 1).

Yet as Tevye's three eldest daughters marry, each one of them defies tradition. Their decisions illustrate the forces that transformed Jewish life. While Tzeitel merely refuses the man chosen for her by the matchmaker, Hodel, influenced by Perchik's taunts and his "enlightened" attitudes, announces her decision to marry with or without her father's permission. Confronted with these changes, Tevye concedes "our old ways were once new" (*Fiddler on the Roof*, p. 79).

Tevye remains unwilling, however, to tolerate Chava's marriage to a non-Jew. To do so would be, in his eyes, turning his back on his faith and his people. Assimilation was a great temptation to the young, who, if they learned Russian and discarded Jewish habits, might find better jobs or suffer less derision. The older generations often had to struggle to ensure that their children would preserve the traditions. For Chava to marry a non-Jew at this period and place in history meant that her children would almost certainly not be raised as Jews; her offspring, who would otherwise be precious members of the Jewish community, would in short be lost to assimilation.

Sources. *Fiddler on the Roof* is based on short stories by Sholom Aleichem about Tevye the milkman and his daughters. Sholom Aleichem (a Hebrew salutation meaning "peace be with you") was the pen name for the famous Yiddish humorist Sholom Rabinowitz. Born in 1859 in the Ukrainian city of Pereyaslav, Aleichem studied at a Russian secular school before beginning his first job as a tutor. The success of his stories about Tevye the milkman enabled him to give up teaching and devote himself to writing. The pogroms of 1905 forced him to flee Russia with his family. He traveled throughout Europe and America before he died in 1916 in New York.

In Sholom Aleichem's first story about Tevye, a character modeled after a dairyman whom the author met in a resort town near Kiev, the daughters play no significant role. The plot for *Fiddler on the Roof* is taken from the third, fourth, and fifth stories, "Today's Children", "Hodl", and "Chava," which chronicle the conflicts between Tevye and his daughters.

The title "Fiddler on the Roof" was inspired by the paintings of Marc Chagall. A Jew born in 1887 in Russia, Chagall studied art both in St. Petersburg and Paris. He painted murals for the Yiddish Theater in Moscow and designed the scenery and costumes for some of Sholom Aleichem's plays. Several of his paintings depict a fiddler perched atop the rooftops of a Russian *shtetl,* or village settlement.

Events in History at the Time the Play Was Written

The 1960s. The 1960s in the United States was a period of social revolution. Stein selected the episodes and characters from Aleichem's short stories to create a fresh tale that "brought to the foreground an element implicit in the Tevye tales . . . the hostility, the violence, the injustice practiced by a ruling majority against a weak minority" (Stein in Richards, p. 242). In the midst of the civil rights movement, Stein tried to "point up the internal strength, the dignity, the humor of [the Jews in Russia] and, like the minorities today, their unique talent for survival" (Stein in Richards, p. 242).

Jews in the Soviet Union. After the communists assumed power in Russia following the 1917 Revolution, the Union of Soviet Socialist Republics, or Soviet Union, was formed. The country was originally headed by Vladimir Lenin, and, after his death, by Joseph Stalin. Lenin and Stalin continued the efforts of the czars to assimilate or even exterminate the Jews. Ultimately Yiddish schools were destroyed, many Yiddish language publications were banned, and Jewish cultural organizations were dissolved. During the infamous purges of the 1930s, tens of thousands of Jews, supposedly subversive fascists, were deported to Siberia or killed.

Russian peasants, who had been robbed of their land by the communist government, blamed Jews, whom they continued to perceive as wealthy landowners living at the expense of the workers. Some betrayed Jews in hiding to the Nazi authorities during World War II.

The death squads who followed German troops into the Soviet Union in the summer of 1941 received explicit orders to kill all Jews indiscriminately. The Jews who had survived the anti-Semitism of the czars and the oppression of Stalin suffered the first wave of the most extensive massacres in history. One million of the 3 million Soviet Jews were killed during World War II.

Many of the 2 million Jews who survived the Nazi invasion had fled into the Soviet interior. After the war they returned to find their land and homes occupied by Russians. When Israel was established in 1948, however, the Soviet government denied free emigration to Soviet Jews. Irritated by the appeals of Israeli diplomats, Soviet officials denounced Zionism as dangerous nationalism and accused Israel of conspiring with the United States to spread capitalist imperialism.

Stalin resumed his campaign to eliminate differences between classes and nationalities in the Soviet Union. The infamous Doctors' Plot was Stalin's plan to eliminate the Jewish question in the U.S.S.R. In the early 1950s several Jewish doctors were arrested on charges of malpractice leading to the deaths of party officials. *Pravda*, the Soviet newspaper, published headlines about a "plot" to undermine the government and listed scores of Jewish names. Stalin planned to try these doctors and use the convictions to unleash anti-Semitic pogroms. He had already ordered the construction of new barracks in Siberia to house deported Jews. The plans fizzled when Stalin fell ill and died in 1953.

Conflicts between the Soviet Union and Israel surged in the 1960s, as Western powers in the United Nations pressed for legislation allowing free emigration from any country. Under pressure to allow Soviet Jews to emigrate to Palestine or the United States, Soviet officials briefly relented. In 1966, two years after the initial performance on Broadway of *Fiddler on the Roof,* Soviet Prime Minister Aleksei Kosygin announced that the Soviet authorities would no longer prevent Soviet Jews from reuniting with their families abroad.

Reception. After its opening in 1964, *Fiddler on the Roof* won lavish praise from the press. John Chapman, a reviewer for the *New York Daily News,* called it "one of the great works of the American musical theater" (Chapman in Richards, p. 242). His colleague Howard Taubman added, "it catches the essence of a moment in history with sentiment and radiance" (Taubman in Richards, p. 242).

The play won the New York Drama Critics' Circle Award as best musical of 1964-65, the Page One Award of the American Newspaper Guild, and nine Antoinette Perry (Tony) Awards, including best musical of the year.

For More Information

Aleichem, Sholom. *Tevye the Dairyman and the Railroad Stories.* Translated by Hillel Halkin. New York: Schocken, 1987.

Burns, Stewart. *Social Movements of the 1960s.* Boston: Twayne, 1990.

Dubnow, S. M. *History of the Jews in Russia and Poland from the Earliest Times until the Present Day.* Translated by I. Friedlaender. 3 vols. Philadelphia: Jewish Publication Society of America, 1916-20.

Halberstam-Rubin, Anna. *Sholom Aleichem: The Writer as a Social Historian.* New York: Peter Lang, 1989.

Richards, Stanley. *Best Plays of the Sixties.* New York: Doubleday, 1970.

Ro'i, Yaacov. *Jews and Jewish Life in Russia and the Soviet Union.* Essex: Frank Cass, 1995.

Stein, Joseph. *Fiddler on the Roof.* New York: Crown, 1964.

Zborowski, Mark, and Elizabeth Herzog. *Life is with the People: The Jewish Little-Town of Eastern Europe.* New York: International Universities Press, 1952.

First Inaugural Address

by
Franklin D. Roosevelt

Born in Hyde Park, New York, in 1882, Franklin Delano Roosevelt (FDR) grew up in a family that enjoyed both wealth and political power. (President Theodore Roosevelt was a fifth cousin.) After beginning a promising political career of his own, FDR was stricken by polio in 1921. His condition left him unable to walk, but he nevertheless pursued an active political life. In 1932, as the Democratic nominee for president, FDR defeated Herbert Hoover, under whom the nation had plunged into the Great Depression. Taking office in a time of national crisis, Roosevelt saw that one of his first tasks was to restore American morale and faith in democratic government. He set out to achieve this aim in his first inaugural address.

Events in History at the Time of the Speech

The Great Depression. The Great Depression struck in 1929 and lasted until World War II. Its causes were complex, including the economic aftereffects of World War I, free-wheeling stock market speculation, and easy credit. Policies enacted by a series of Republican administrations exacerbated an already bad situation. Industrial production grew at a far more rapid rate than people's ability to buy consumer goods, and protectionist trade measures limited the foreign market for U.S. exports. Farm prices dropped sharply. Between 1914 and 1933, for example, the price of wheat declined from approximately 88¢ to 32¢ per bushel. At the same time, farmers' tax bur-

> **THE LITERARY WORK**
>
> A presidential inaugural speech delivered on March 4, 1933.
>
> **SYNOPSIS**
>
> Franklin D. Roosevelt rallied the spirit of the nation during a time of severe financial crisis, declaring that "the only thing we have to fear is fear itself."

dens doubled, and the cost of farming escalated. Farmers could no longer afford to buy the goods they needed to continue running their farms. Ultimately thousands of farmers lost their lands to insurance and banking institutions.

The stock market crash. On October 24, 1929, prices on the New York Stock Exchange dropped dramatically, triggering a dismal economic situation. Stockholders panicked and tried to sell their stock for whatever price they could get, but many stocks became worthless. Millions could not be sold at all. By mid-November people had lost a total of more than $26 billion in financial assets.

Fear swept through Wall Street. Frightened investors flocked to their banks to withdraw their money. In response, banks closed to protect their dwindling assets. Several banks failed entirely, and 9 million savings accounts vanished. Close to 700 banks failed in 1929, with some 2,300 more collapsing over the next two

A line for food: New York, 1934.

years. By the time Roosevelt took office, bank failures had eroded public confidence to such a degree that he felt compelled to address the issue directly in his inaugural speech. Such a direct reference on this ceremonial occasion was unusual, indicating the severity of the problem. The same day, March 4, 1933, in one of his first acts as president, Roosevelt declared an extended "bank holiday." All banks would remain closed until March 13 while Congress prepared for their reopening under stricter government supervision than before.

Poverty in America. The Great Depression deeply affected families and individuals across America. Unemployment, poverty, and hunger became a way of life for many as businesses and factories closed and workers were laid off. By 1932, the year before FDR took office, unemployment had risen to nearly 13 million, with nearly one in four people out of work. Nearly two-thirds of the people were living in poverty; meanwhile, a tiny fraction, one percent of the population, owned over a third of the nation's assets.

Roosevelt's predecessor, Herbert Hoover, had refused to institute government aid to the poor and unemployed, believing that aid programs would threaten America's ethic of rugged individualism. Instead, Hoover maintained that the

Depression, like an illness, simply had to run its course; only then would prosperity return. Meanwhile, bread lines and soup kitchens sprang up in every major city; hunger was so widespread that many soup kitchens ran out of food and had to turn people away. One Chicago reporter observed fifty men, women, and children fighting over the garbage left outside a restaurant.

Homelessness. By 1932 more than a million people were homeless. Roaming the country in search of work, they slept in flophouses, fields, caves, and parks. Communities of shacks arose; these became known as "Hoovervilles," named derisively after President Hoover. Even New York's Central Park was the site of a shantytown. In 1931 one rail company's officials discovered nearly 200,000 people hiding in its boxcars. Street corners filled with people selling apples or begging for money. "Brother, can you spare a dime?" asked Al Jolson in a popular song of the day (Jolson in Kirkendall, p. 10). An unprecedented despair spread throughout the nation; given this atmosphere of hopelessness, FDR's optimistic 1932 presidential campaign provided a welcome relief.

The election. Hoover's refusal to take action was perceived as cold, heartless, and stubborn, and his dour passiveness contrasted sharply with

Roosevelt's active, buoyant good cheer. An energetic campaigner, Roosevelt kept up a rigorous schedule, giving the lie to charges that his health was too frail for the job. The election's outcome was never seriously in doubt, so closely was Hoover identified with the national malaise. As commentator Joseph Alsop reported, "Poor Hoover . . . could hardly appear on the streets without being booed" (Alsop, p. 108). Meanwhile, Roosevelt's trademark grin and jaunty manner charmed crowds across the country. Roosevelt won by a landslide, receiving 472 electoral votes against Hoover's paltry total of 59.

Roosevelt's public image. While Roosevelt's image as an active, confident man was not an inaccurate reflection of his personality, at the same time that image was carefully and consciously controlled. The polio attack he had suffered in 1921 left him paralyzed from the waist down. He spent nearly all his time in a wheelchair. Roosevelt became the only national leader in American history with such a disability—and the only man to serve more than two terms as president, winning an unparalleled four elections.

In private, Roosevelt merely deemphasized his disability, rarely mentioning it even to those closest to him. In public, he struggled painfully to minimize it as much as possible. Wearing steel and leather leg braces that could be straightened and locked at the knee, and supported at the elbow by a strong companion, Roosevelt could "walk" short distances in a way that appeared almost natural. He could not stand up by himself, but with his braces locked and with the support of a podium, cane, or crutches he could remain standing for a short time. At his first inauguration, Roosevelt "walked" the thirty-seven paces to the podium—built with a special ramp instead of stairs—holding his son James's arm, then stood grasping the podium for support as he delivered his address. With such careful control of public moments, most Americans gained only a hazy idea of Roosevelt's condition. They supposed he was perhaps a bit lame if they thought about it at all.

Both before and after his election, Roosevelt enjoyed the tacit cooperation of the press in concealing the extent of his disability. Out of over 35,000 photos of FDR in the Presidential Library, only two show him in his wheelchair. Newsreels, the short films that featured the news in this age before television became popular, showed him only standing or seated, never being lifted, pushed, or carried from one position to another. In the thousands of political cartoons

of Roosevelt during his political career, he was never portrayed as disabled. Many cartoons, in fact, show him as vigorously active—running, jumping, even boxing, for example. After his election, Roosevelt held twice-weekly news conferences in which his informal, friendly manner won the affection of reporters. At the same time, he kept tight control over the information they were given.

FDR as public speaker. Roosevelt's superb oratorical skills had not come easily. At twenty-eight, when he had run for the New York State Senate, his wife, Eleanor, said that in speeches delivered then the words had rolled so slowly off his tongue and he had paused for so long that she worried that he would never go on (Freedman, p. 32). During his month-long campaign for state senate, FDR gave an average of ten speeches a day and quickly improved his speaking style. He soon began to open each speech with the warm phrase, "My friends"—a phrase he would later use to begin radio addresses during his presidency.

FDR GREETS THE PRESS

Beginning on March 8, 1933, Roosevelt met with the press twice a week and continued to do so for 998 times over the course of his next twelve years in office. Roosevelt loved to joke with reporters. Unlike prior presidents who required reporters to submit all their questions in writing, Roosevelt spoke with them directly, freely, and easily. This informal style made him very popular with the press.

Radio was America's most popular form of information and entertainment at the time of Roosevelt's inauguration. The first commercial radio stations appeared in 1920, and within a few years millions of households owned their own sets. The first president to take full advantage of the medium, Roosevelt had begun regular broadcasts while he was New York's governor. As president, Roosevelt broadcast his speeches to the American public to gain support for his policies.

Roosevelt's 1933 inaugural address was the first presidential inaugural speech ever broadcast on radio. A few days after taking office, he began his "fireside chats," a series of radio talks to everyday citizens. Millions of listeners tuned in regularly to hear Roosevelt's clear and reassuring explanations of the political issues facing the day.

The New Deal. In campaign speeches, Roosevelt had promised a "new deal" for America and for economic recovery. In his first inaugural address, he pledged "action, and action now" (Roosevelt, Inaugural Address, p. 12). What began as a promise soon grew into a patchwork of government programs and reforms. Though the Depression ended only with the stimulation to American industry produced by World War II defense spending, FDR's New Deal succeeded in restoring the nation's confidence and provided relief for its poorest citizens.

FOLKSONGS IN THE NEW DEAL ERA

Song lyrics from the early 1930s reflected the distinct experiences of a hopeful nation emerging from years of economic turmoil. Renowned folksinger Woody Guthrie described New Deal era songs as "the songs that the people sung when they heard the mighty good sounding promises of a reshuffle, an honest deck, and a brand new deal from the big shots" (Guthrie in Susman, p. 128).

Soon after his election, Roosevelt recruited a group of college professors and other intellectuals, known as the Brain Trust, to formulate the New Deal policies. Over the next few years FDR submitted a series of bills that easily passed through Congress. The New Deal would create federal agencies to aid farmers, homeowners, workers, and the unemployed. One of the first New Deal agencies, the National Labor Relations Board, was established in 1933 to enforce the National Labor Relations Act, which guaranteed the rights of workers to bargain as a collective group and to strike. Future programs would include the Social Security System, established in 1935 to prevent abject poverty during unemployment and old age.

To regulate the banks and businesses, the Roosevelt administration would create agencies such as the Securities Exchange Commission and the Federal Communications Commission. Minimum wage laws were to be instituted, and the tax system would be overhauled. The Works Progress Administration (WPA) would provide jobs to 8 million of the unemployed. Under its direction, workers would erect schools, parks

and bridges; bring electricity to rural areas; clean slums; plant forests; and repair roads. All these achievements, however, lay in the future as the untested and newly sworn-in president faced the inaugural crowd on March 4, 1933.

The Speech in Focus

The contents. Declaring that the American people could count on him for directness and honesty, Roosevelt opened his speech with an appeal for courage. This is the time, began Roosevelt, "to speak the truth, the whole truth, frankly and boldly" (Inaugural Address, p. 11). We need not be afraid of the country's condition, Roosevelt declared. This great nation will endure despite the uncertainties of the day. We need not shrink away from the challenge before us—"the only thing we have to fear is fear itself" (Inaugural Address, p. 11).

Taxes, income, and farm production were among the pressing concerns of the day. "Values have risen; our ability to pay has fallen . . . farmers find no markets for their produce; the savings of many years in thousands of families are gone" (Inaugural Address, p. 11). The most urgent task, said Roosevelt, was to put people back to work and restore the economy. Roosevelt pledged to regulate the business community while extending federal assistance to those in need.

Fortunately, Roosevelt declared, economic issues concern only material things. "Happiness lies not in the mere possession of money; it lies in the joy of achievement, in the thrill of creative effort" (Inaugural Address, p. 12). Foreshadowing the New Deal's job-oriented assistance programs, Roosevelt spoke of a moral reward in work that goes beyond "the mad chase for evanescent profits" (Inaugural Address, p. 12). The government itself should put people to work; at the same time it must provide cohesive, unifying management for the national economy. Above all, it must take charge. "There are many ways in which it [the economy] can be helped, but it can never be helped merely by talking about it. We must act and act quickly" (Inaugural Address, p. 13).

Stressing that such changes are allowed for within the flexible framework of the Constitution, Roosevelt affirmed his commitment to democratic principles. Yet, he warned, the "need for undelayed action may call for temporary departure from the normal balance" between branches of government (Inaugural Address, p.

Franklin D. Roosevelt

15). In a passage that drew cheers from the crowd, Roosevelt said that if he felt it were necessary, he would "ask Congress for . . . broad Executive power to wage a war against the emergency, as great a power that would be given to me if we were in fact invaded by a foreign foe" (Inaugural Address, p. 15).

Roosevelt's optimism. Roosevelt's happy, secure childhood, along with his own personality, combined to give him an invaluable gift: the absolute inner conviction that things would work out. On the occasion of his first inaugural address, Roosevelt sought above all to communicate this optimism to his audience—a deeply demoralized audience, whose faith in the future had been severely eroded, and whose fear of the future had ballooned out of all proportion.

Most of this first inaugural address is rhetorically straightforward and matter of fact in tone, even unmemorable. One phrase, however, stands out as the single quotation that most people know, remember, and forever associate with FDR: "the only thing we have to fear is fear itself" (Inaugural Address, p. 11). This stirring call to courage captures the paradox that both fear and courage feed on themselves. As Roosevelt well understood, both fear and faith have a capacity to

help fulfill the very expectations they arouse. Fear, Roosevelt sees, has power: it "paralyzes needed efforts to convert retreat into advance" (Inaugural Address, p. 11). Courage, or the faith to challenge fear, removes that paralysis.

Roosevelt's own physical condition had a bearing on his attitude to the connected traits of courage and optimism. Those who knew him said that in the years following his attack of polio, Roosevelt persisted tenaciously in the conviction that he would walk normally again. Even when it became clear that he would not, Roosevelt refused to accept the limitations that such a disability would normally have placed on his life. Though it was unthinkable for a man virtually confined to a wheelchair to entertain presidential aspirations, Roosevelt not only had them, but made them come true.

The optimism encapsulated so well in Roosevelt's first inaugural address endowed him with unique stature not only as a national leader, but as a world leader as well. The Depression was worldwide, and the economic threat to capitalism that it represented was matched by political threats to democracy itself. On the left, Soviet communism seemed to many in America and the world to offer a new and viable alternative to democratic capitalism's excesses. And on the right, fascism had arisen in Europe to offer another vision of state power, seducing many on that continent. Against this challenge to democracy Roosevelt stood virtually alone among world leaders. The English historian Sir Isaiah Berlin explains his uniqueness:

> The most insistent propaganda in those days declared that . . . democratic forces were played out, and that the choice now lay between two bleak extremes, communism and Fascism—the red and the black. To those who were not carried away by this patter, the only light left in the darkness was the administration of Roosevelt and the New Deal in the United States. At a time of weakness and mounting despair in the democratic world Roosevelt radiated confidence and strength. He was the leader of the democratic world, and upon him alone, of all the statesmen of the 1930s, no cloud rested.
>
> (Berlin, p. 24)

Roosevelt, Berlin continues, "was one of the few statesmen in the twentieth or any other century who seemed to have absolutely no fear at all of the future" (Berlin, p. 26). Berlin pinpoints the courage engendered by Roosevelt's optimism as the essential quality that gave him broad symbolic appeal: "He believed in his own strength and ability to manage, and succeed, whatever happened. . . . It was this, perhaps, more than any other quality, that drew men of very different outlooks to him" (Berlin, p. 26).

Sources. In composing his first inaugural address, Roosevelt drew on his own ideas and on the words of his close advisors Louis Howe and Raymond Moley. Moley wrote early drafts of the speech based on notes he had taken during conversations with the president-elect about FDR's wishes for its content.

The speech's most famous phrase ("the only thing we have to fear is fear itself") was probably inserted into one of these early drafts by Louis Howe. Until his death after a long illness in 1936, Howe was Roosevelt's long-time friend, campaign manager, and his closest advisor. While Howe said that he had seen the phrase in a newspaper ad, Eleanor Roosevelt disagreed with this explanation. She believed that the phrase was adapted from a famous sentence in the writings of the American transcendentalist author Henry David Thoreau. Mrs. Roosevelt said that a friend had given her a book of Thoreau's that she had left on FDR's bedside table the day before the inaugural ceremony. Thoreau's sentence reads "Nothing is so much to be feared as fear" (Thoreau, *Writings*, p. 468).

As published in Roosevelt's official papers, his inaugural speech opens with the rather ponderous sentence, "I am certain that my fellow Americans expect that on my induction into the Presidency I will address them with a candor and a decision which the present situation of our Nation impels." On the morning of Inauguration Day, as he looked the speech over, Roosevelt decided that he needed a shorter, simpler opening. "This is a day of consecration," he wrote at the top. Preparing to speak, he added one word to underscore the solemnity of the occasion, so that as delivered the speech opened with the sentence, "This is a day of national consecration."

Reception. Standing without a hat or overcoat in the cold wind, Roosevelt spoke for twenty minutes, during which the large inaugural crowd stood mostly silent. At the end of the speech, however, the steady applause lasted for long minutes. Millions more must have cheered at home after listening to the speech on radio. FDR's strong, confident voice and vigorous optimism succeeded almost within the twenty minutes of the speech in working a deep change in the national mood. And as Roosevelt had promised, the speech's impact was reinforced by immediate ac-

tion when he closed down the banks. Roosevelt's famous fireside chats and press conferences, begun within days of his taking office, also followed up the Inaugural Address's message of hope and courage.

Press and public alike generally welcomed the message. Some questioned Roosevelt's ability to make good on the promises of change and renewed prosperity. Edmund Wilson, the well-known critic, wrote that Roosevelt's words held "echoes of Woodrow Wilson's eloquence without Wilson's glow of life behind them" (Wilson in Davis, p. 32).

The most surprising reservations, though, were expressed by none other than Eleanor Roosevelt, the new First Lady. A strong supporter of democratic principles, Mrs. Roosevelt was deeply uncomfortable with the part of the speech in which her husband mentioned asking Congress for special powers to fight the Depression. Most disturbing of all, she said later that day, were the cheers, which were loudest at that part of the speech. Within two days, a group of thirteen powerful citizens, including Roosevelt's political mentor Al Smith and the influential journalist Walter Lippmann, had produced a signed demand that the new president be given exactly the sort of special powers he had mentioned in the address. During the coming administration, and indeed for the rest of her life, Eleanor Roosevelt devoted herself to protecting the rights that such powers would have threatened.

For More Information

Alsop, Joseph. *FDR: A Centenary Remembrance.* New York: Viking, 1982.

Berlin, Isaiah. *Personal Impressions.* New York: Penguin, 1982.

Davis, Kenneth S. *FDR: The New Deal Years 1933-1937.* New York: Random House, 1979.

Freedman, Russell. *Franklin Delano Roosevelt.* New York: Clarion, 1990.

Kirkendall, Richard S. *The United States, 1929-1945: Years of Crisis and Change.* New York: McGraw-Hill, 1974.

Roosevelt, Franklin Delano. Inaugural Address. In *The Public Papers and Addresses of Franklin D. Roosevelt. Volume 2: The Year of Crisis 1933.* New York: Random House, 1938.

Susman, Warren, ed. *Culture and Commitment, 1929-1945.* New York: George Braziller, 1973.

Thoreau, Henry David. *The Writings of Henry David Thoreau: The Walden Edition.* Edited by Bradford Torrey. Vol. 8. New York: Houghton-Mifflin, 1906.

The Good Earth

by

Pearl S. Buck

Pearl S. Buck was born in China in 1892, the daughter of American missionary parents. After growing up in rural Chinese communities, Buck was profoundly affected by the difficult cycle of life experienced by China's peasant farmers and their families. Her third novel, *The Good Earth,* was written in an attempt to show the rigors of Chinese country life and to draw attention to the plight of the majority of China's population. The novel's incredibly poignant depiction of this simple rural life made it an instant success and brought Buck acclaim as one of the world's finest authors.

THE LITERARY WORK

A novel set in China at the beginning of the twentieth century; published in 1931.

SYNOPSIS

A poor peasant farmer works patiently over the span of thirty years, gradually buying more land, raising a family, and becoming the most prosperous member of his community.

Events in History at the Time the Novel Takes Place

China's peasant farmers. Chinese civilization has always rested on an agrarian, peasant base. For centuries, between 80 and 90 percent of China's population has consisted of peasant farmers. The lives of these peasants are made up of difficult cycles of backbreaking labor tied always to the land. In relation to the vast population of China's fertile river valleys, the quantity of land has always been in short supply. China's agriculture is heavily dependent on controlling water, because of inadequate and unreliable rainfall in some regions, and because of the widespread rice cultivation that requires alternate flooding and draining of the fields. Wang Lung experiences the extremes of both of these problems in *The Good Earth;* first his crops die because of severe drought, and years later he is unable to plant his fields because rising flood waters have covered his land.

Because of these difficult conditions, survival in China's rural communities has always depended on the close cooperation of the group. Some scholars suggest that this need for cooperation has resulted in China's strong system of values, which governs all aspects of society. This value system emphasizes the importance of the group and subordinates the individual. In China, the family is the basic economic, political, and moral institution. At the turn of the twentieth century, the family, not the individual, owned property, paid taxes, and took responsibility for the legal or moral transgressions of one of its members. The family unit was therefore crucial to maintaining social discipline and order in peasant communities.

A family unit operated on the basis of a hierarchical structure. At its head was the grandfather or father of the family, who had absolute au-

Paul Muni as Wang Lung and Luise Ranier as O-lan in the 1937 film adaptation of *The Good Earth*.

thority over the other family members. He enjoyed complete control over his wife and could divorce her at will if she displeased or disobeyed him. Children owed their father filial piety, which meant that they had to obey him absolutely. If a child struck his father under any circumstances, he could be legally put to death. The young were furthermore subordinated to all elders as well as to the patriarch. Following this system, older siblings were treated much differently than younger ones.

The entire system is clearly illustrated in *The Good Earth* by Wang Lung's family. In the beginning of the story, even though Wang Lung's father has become old and decrepit and Wang Lung does all the work, it is the father who makes the decisions for the two, even choosing whom Wang Lung will marry. When Wang Lung takes over as the family's patriarch, all the authority becomes his and the family obeys him completely, but he is still subordinate to his uncle, even though the uncle is a lazy reprobate. When the uncle asks to borrow money, Wang Lung is convinced he will never pay it back but is compelled by the family hierarchy to lend it to him anyway.

The hierarchy of the family trickles down to the children in Wang Lung's family. In keeping with Chinese tradition, older children are ac-

corded many more privileges and respect than the younger ones. The first priority is to educate the eldest son, with little concern for the betterment of his younger brothers. Wang Lung's family follows this unbending hierarchy in *The Good Earth,* forming a strong enough unit to overcome drought, floods, and a swarm of locusts that threaten their food supply. Pearl S. Buck was strongly interested in the plight of China's peasants and stated several times that she wrote *The Good Earth* in an attempt to inform the world of the struggles they suffered. While depicting these struggles, her novel exposed in detail the lives of China's peasant society and provided the world with one of the first glimpses at the struggles of its many patient and untiring workers.

The status of Chinese women. Chinese women stood at the bottom of the social hierarchy. Women lacked all rights of property ownership and had no formal decision-making capacity within the family. The low status of women came primarily from the belief that they were temporary members or future deserters in their blood family, and strangers or intruders in their husbands' families. Because of the male-dominated family structure, women were always looked upon as outsiders. The only way for a woman to gain any status was for her to bear male children. This becomes evident in *The Good Earth* when Wang Lung displays significantly more appreciation for O-lan after she bears him two sons. Chinese brides were purchased for marriage with a bride-price that, in fact, symbolized the sale of her rights by her parents to her husband and in-laws. These bride-prices, paid by the prospective husband or his representative, detracted from women's status even further by treating the women as if they were possessions, creatures as easily bought and sold as farm animals. A well-known saying in China was, "A woman married is like a horse bought; you can either ride them or flog them" (Johnson, p. 12). Upon entering her husband's household, a Chinese woman had to endure not only the domination of her husband, but that of her mother-in-law as well. In *The Good Earth*, O-lan obeys Wang Lung completely, for Wang Lung's mother has died several years earlier. Another female enters the family, but with humiliating consequences for O-lan. She suffers the insult of Wang Lung bringing the concubine Lotus into the house.

Chinese superstition and religion. Many episodes in *The Good Earth* deal with the superstitions and concepts of religion held by Wang Lung and his peasant neighbors. In the early part of the novel, Wang Lung visits the village shrine often to burn incense and ask for good fortune from the two deities represented by clay statues inside. His family in particular takes pride in keeping the primitive statues clothed in paper robes and in maintaining their humble shrine. Wang Lung is never connected to any organized religion in the novel. This is perhaps because Chinese religion has tended to combine various aspects of different faiths, the main ones being Confucianism, Taoism, and Buddhism. The gods represented by the statues nevertheless play a major role in the fears and beliefs of the local farmers such as Wang Lung.

The farmers, for example, live in constant fear of the gods' wrath. When Wang Lung and O-lan become overly proud of their young son, they hide him under Wang Lung's coat and say out loud that he is sickly and weak so that the gods will not strike out at him as punishment for their pride. Later in the novel, Wang Lung defiantly speaks out against the deity in heaven when he sees that his lands are going to flood again; his overseer Ching, upset by the blasphemy, immediately says loudly, "Even so, he is greater than any one of us and do not talk so, my master" (Buck, *The Good Earth*, p. 274).

This system of fears and beliefs also places great value on luck. Wang Lung's family hopes for good luck from the small gods of the shrine, and the family members burn candles for luck and prosperity. When O-lan dies, Wang Lung consults a geomancer, essentially an astrologer, who predicts for him the luckiest date on which to bury O-lan. Even though the day is three months away, Wang Lung sets the funeral for the date deemed lucky by the geomancer.

Finally Buck's novel shows the reaction of the Chinese peasant population to Christianity. When Wang Lung and his family are living in the city, Wang Lung is given a flier by a foreigner. The flier depicts Christ hanging on the cross, but Wang Lung has no idea who the man is. When he shows the paper to his father, the old man says, "Surely this was a very evil man to be thus hung" (*The Good Earth*, p. 126). O-lan eventually uses the flier to line Wang Lung's shoes. The novel's author, who disapproved of missionary work even though she was the daughter of missionary parents, may be using this scene to show just how different Chinese culture was, and also to attack missionaries and other Christians who presumed to convert the Chinese from their own systems of belief to Christianity.

The Novel in Focus

The plot. The novel follows the life of Wang Lung, who enters the story as a young peasant farmer living in rural China with his aging father; his mother died six years earlier. Because his family is so poor, Wang Lung's only option for a wife is a slave girl from the House of Hwang in the city nearby. His father arranges the match, choosing a plain-looking kitchen slave, O-lan, assuming that such an unattractive girl must be a virgin, and that she will be a good worker because she knows she is not pretty.

Wang Lung is content with O-lan, who has a hearty body and works tirelessly both at home and in the fields. She bears him two sons, and labors at his side in the fields. With her help, Wang Lung begins to prosper and even puts aside enough money to purchase more land. He buys the land at a good price from the House of Hwang. Wang Lung begins to work the new land enthusiastically, feeling a bond between himself and the rich soil.

Despite his recent success, hard times fall upon Wang Lung and his neighbors when a drought strikes the land and the crops fail. Many peasants die from starvation and the survivors eat anything to survive, from stray dogs to tree bark and grass. Rumor has it that some of the villagers have even eaten the bodies of dead infants.

In order to survive, Wang Lung takes his family to the south, where he hopes to find better conditions in a big city. They live in a simple lean-to built from straw mats set against the city wall. The family begs for pennies while Wang Lung works pulling a ricksha, a man-powered passenger cart. Wang Lung notices the arrogance of the rich city people and the animosities the poor people feel toward the wealthy. When the fury of the poor erupts in rebellion and an outbreak of looting, Wang Lung and O-lan follow an angry mob into the house of a wealthy family, curious to see what will happen. A rich but frightened man is caught alone with Wang Lung. Thinking he will be killed, the man gives Wang Lung a handful of gold coins in exchange for his life. During the riot, O-lan, meanwhile remembers the tricks of her former masters and finds a small fortune in precious stones hidden behind a loose brick in the wall.

OPIUM ADDICTION IN CHINA

Opium was first imported to China in the seventh century by Arabian traders. European traders introduced opium smoking as medicine to the Chinese in the early 1600s. The Chinese government outlawed opium in 1729, but traders continued to exchange it for silk, porcelain, and other Chinese goods. In the late 1700s opium smoking became widespread among the Chinese. In *The Good Earth,* Wang Lung buys land at a reasonable price from the House of Hwang because of the old mistress's opium addiction. As the novel points out, "The old lady had not had her dole of opium to the full for many days and was like an old tigress in her hunger" (*The Good Earth,* p. 68). Wang Lung also entices his uncle and aunt to smoke opium because he knows they will become addicted and will waste away, becoming less able to cause problems in his house.

With their new wealth, the family leaves the city to return home. Wang Lung, hungry for extra land, buys more acreage from the House of Hwang, whose members have now fallen on hard times themselves because of their own weakness, idleness, and the mistress's opium addiction. His new land makes Wang Lung the largest landowner in the village, and he hires workers to till his fields.

When flood waters cover the majority of his fields, preventing him from working, Wang Lung seeks stimulation in one of the city's brothels. There, he falls in love with Lotus, a beautiful and petulant prostitute. Unable to be without her, Wang Lung buys her from the brothel and builds several rooms at his home to accommodate her. Lotus idles away each day in her rooms, eating rich foods and gossiping with the wife of Wang Lung's uncle and Cuckoo, a woman from the brothel who has become her servant and companion.

Now a prosperous landowner, Wang Lung refuses to have his sons work the land. Instead he sends them to be educated by a city schoolmaster. When Wang Lung catches his oldest son visiting with Lotus in her rooms, he beats them both and sends the son to a southern city to continue his education. Seeing that the second son is shrewd and businesslike, Wang Lung sends him as an apprentice to the grain market. Altogether O-lan bears her husband three sons and three daughters; only two of the daughters survive.

O-lan, exhausted from a life of childbearing and work, dies, and Wang Lung's father dies shortly after, leaving Wang Lung alone. In his old age he tires of Lotus, but falls in love with a gentle slave girl, only to find that his third son desires her also. The strong-willed young boy leaves home to become a soldier. The two older sons rival each other for status and plan how they will sell Wang Lung's precious land when he dies.

Women in China. An important aspect of *The Good Earth* is its depiction of the cruelties and injustices suffered by Chinese women. Buck's novel uses the character O-lan to illustrate the injustices. O-lan's parents sold her into slavery when she was ten years old because they needed the money and also because girls were considered useless by many parents who wanted only sons. When Wang Lung needs a wife, his father negotiates to buy O-lan for him from the House of Hwang, where she is a slave. A revealing discussion occurs when Wang Lung arrives to take her away from the Hwang family. The old mistress of the house promises that O-lan "will work well for you in the field and drawing water and all else that you wish" (*The Good Earth,* p. 18). From this discussion it is evident that the primary function of a Chinese wife is work. Wang Lung's excitement over his marriage stems completely from the work done by O-lan. She gathers wood for the fire, cooks all the food for the house, and finally when there is no more work in the house to do, she joins Wang Lung in the fields to labor there.

O-lan also bears Wang Lung's children. When she gives birth to Wang Lung's first son, he is pleased with her for bearing a boy, and happy because she immediately resumes her work in the fields after giving birth. He is also pleased when she gives birth to a second boy. However, when O-lan bears a daughter, there is no excitement, only disappointment. Just after giving birth, O-lan tells Wang Lung, "It is over once more. It is only a slave this time—not worth mentioning" (*The Good Earth,* p. 65). The novel describes Wang Lung's displeasure, "A sense of evil struck him. A girl! A girl was causing all this trouble in his uncle's house. Now a girl had been born in his house as well" (*The Good Earth,* p. 65). This scene exemplifies the Chinese belief in the inferiority of women and sets a precedent for the rest of the novel. When drought forces the family to leave for the south, O-lan is pregnant again. Just before they leave she gives birth. Wang Lung hears the child crying and is surprised when O-lan tells him that the baby girl is dead. When he takes his dead daughter into the field to bury her, he notices small bruises on her neck. O-lan has obviously killed the girl because its presence will only be a burden to the family in their desperate journey to the city.

The Good Earth also depicts the unjust practice of footbinding. Dating back almost one thousand years, footbinding was the painful and crippling custom of binding the feet of little girls so that their toes were forced back under their arches rather than allowed to grow out normally. It created tiny feet, thought beautiful by Chinese men who called them "lily feet." For several centuries, footbinding had been limited to women of the upper classes, but eventually it spread until by the nineteenth century over half of all Chinese women bound their feet. Though almost crippled by this process, Chinese women were expected to endure it to increase their appeal and beauty, and become more eligible for marriage. In the novel, when Wang Lung finds his young daughter crying and asks her why she cries, she tells him, "Because my mother binds a cloth about my feet more tightly every day and I cannot sleep at night" (*The Good Earth,* p. 251). O-lan has also told the daughter that her future husband will not

Pearl S. Buck

love her unless she keeps her feet small with constant binding.

The novel also portrays the lives of prostitutes through the character Lotus. Though Lotus lives a decadent lifestyle after Wang Lung buys her from the brothel in which she works, she still constitutes a clear example of the injustices suffered by Chinese women and the lack of options they have in life. Prostitutes were common in China in the early twentieth century. Typically they were women who had been sold into slavery as young girls and then sold to brothels for use as prostitutes. The author herself had been exposed to the unfair lives of China's peasant women, having witnessed firsthand the cruel practice of footbinding, and having worked at a shelter for prostitutes. These experiences undoubtedly influenced her writing of *The Good Earth,* prompting her to create characters and situations that realistically illustrate the extreme injustices suffered by Chinese women.

Sources. Pearl Buck's primary sources for *The Good Earth* can be traced back to her own experience in rural China. Born to American missionaries attempting to spread Presbyterian Christianity to the rural Chinese masses, Buck spent her childhood, adolescence, and much of her later life living in China. She sympathized with the downtrodden and impoverished rural farmers, and according to biographer Paul Doyle, "The impetus for her book was the anger she had felt because the common people of China were so often oppressed and abused" (Doyle, p. 30). Beyond this basic desire to illustrate the plight of the Chinese peasantry, Buck acknowledged that there was little more foundation for the novel, saying, "There was no plot or plan. Only the man and the woman and their children stood there before me" (Buck in Doyle, p. 30). These details, coupled with Buck's powerful narrative style, made the novel a major accomplishment in literature and provided a wealth of enlightening information on the condition of rural society in China—a significant achievement at a time when little was known in the West of the sprawling nation or its inhabitants.

Two years earlier Buck had written a short story called "The Revolutionist," which described a simple Chinese farmer named Wang Lung. This story was part of the foundation for *The Good Earth,* containing several scenes that became part of the novel, including Wang Lung's discovery of wealth after following looters into the house of a rich family, and his encounters with revolutionary preaching in the city. In all other respects, however, Buck's new novel developed into a completely different story.

Buck credits her narrative style to both the influence of the King James Bible, which she read and heard read frequently as the daughter of Presbyterian missionaries, and also to her reading of the classic Chinese sagas. Buck's fluency in Chinese provided many of the Chinese idioms in the story; Buck even stated that she thought the novel out in Chinese and then translated it into English as she wrote.

Buck's exposure to Chinese life provided her with material that translated into a novel with great depth of detail. Every aspect of peasant life is subtly introduced, from the peasants' superstitions to the precise formalities of Chinese weddings and funerals.

Events in History at the Time the Novel Was Written

Mao Zedong and Communism. As Pearl Buck was beginning her career as a writer in the late 1920s, Mao Zedong (also spelled Mao Tse-tung),

a student who became a revolutionary radical, was working to bring a communist government to China. Many of the feelings behind Mao's desires for a new government based on communism were the same feelings that had prompted Pearl Buck to write *The Good Earth.*

One of Mao's strongest beliefs was that women could play a valuable role in their communities and should not be forced to exist in a state of utter subservience or be deemed unimportant by their husbands and fathers. Mao proclaimed that the women's economic, political, and war mobilization activities in the turbulent 1920s had shown that women were a significant revolutionary force, a belief that contrasted sharply with the traditional image of women as useless in formal community affairs.

Mao also attacked the old system because it kept many of China's poorest men from ever marrying. The old system was a purchase marriage system, in which wealthy men could buy multiple wives, while the poorest men in society would be unable to marry at all. An example of the injustice of the old system can be seen in *The Good Earth* when because of his poverty Wang Lung has only one option for marriage—to take the unattractive slave girl O-lan as a wife. When Wang Lung asks for a wife, his father observes, "With weddings costing as they do in these evil days and every woman wanting gold rings and silk clothes before she will take a man, there remain only slaves to be had for the poor" (*The Good Earth*, p. 8).

Though Mao's central interests were directed toward creating a communist China, it is interesting that many of the issues he was most concerned with, including the role of women, and the old system's injustice to the peasant poor, also concerned Buck and were the primary forces that led her to write *The Good Earth.*

Reception of the novel. With its publication in 1931, *The Good Earth* turned into a literary phenomenon. The novel instantly became one of the most famous bestsellers in the history of American fiction, and it achieved wide popularity abroad. It was translated into thirty different languages; there were at least seven different Chinese translations alone. In addition to its public popularity, the novel won the Pulitzer Prize for Buck as well as the Howells Medal for Distinguished Fiction and became a major factor in her being the first woman awarded the Nobel Prize for Literature (1938).

The reviews in China varied. Filled with admiration, some Chinese congratulated the American author for writing such a realistic story.

Others, from the intellectual Chinese community, hated the book "because they didn't want foreigners to learn anything unpleasant about China . . . because some of them were dependent on foreigners . . . under their protection or pay" (Stirling, p. 109). Similarly, the Chinese in the United States, feeling that the novel dishonored their homeland, showed strong disapproval of it at first. This did not, however, deter the author. Deciding that she had done nothing more heinous than tell the truth as she saw it, Buck went on to write two more volumes—*Sons* (1932) and *A House Divided* (1935)—about the history of Wang Lung's children. Together with *The Good Earth* they would comprise the trilogy *House of Earth*.

For More Information

Block, Irvin. *The Lives of Pearl Buck: A Tale of China and America.* New York: Thomas Y. Crowell, 1973.

Bryfonski, Dedria, ed. *Twentieth Century Literary Criticism.* Vol. 18. Detroit: Gale Research, 1979.

Buck, Pearl S. *The Good Earth.* New York: Washington Square Press, 1994.

Doyle, Paul A. *Pearl S. Buck.* Boston: Twayne, 1980.

Grasso, June, Jay Corrin, and Michael Kort. *Modernization and Revolution in China.* London: M.E. Sharpe, 1991.

Johnson, Kay Ann. *Women, the Family and Peasant Revolution in China.* Chicago: University of Chicago Press, 1983.

Stirling, Nora B. *Pearl Buck: A Woman in Conflict.* Piscataway, N.J.: New Century, 1983.

The Grapes of Wrath

by

John Steinbeck

Born and raised in California, John Steinbeck portrays in many of his writings the beauty and agricultural promise that attracted thousands to that state during the Great Depression. He also examines the social tensions resulting from the rapid growth in this state. *The Grapes of Wrath* focuses on the plight of newcomers who, promised plentiful jobs as farm workers, instead find themselves competing desperately for few jobs at rock-bottom wages.

THE LITERARY WORK

A novel set in the Great Depression of the 1930s; published in 1939.

SYNOPSIS

After losing their Oklahoma farm, a family journeys to California, where they face hardship and injustice as migrant workers.

Events in History at the Time of the Novel

Great Depression. Most Americans think of the Great Depression as beginning with the stock market crash of 1929. For some, however, like dry farmers in the southern Plains states, it started earlier. Dry farming—agriculture without irrigation—had boomed in the region since the railroad arrived in the late 1800s. Wheat and corn were the favorite crops, and wheat prices soared with the outbreak of World War I in 1914. But farmers in Europe returned to their fields when the war ended in 1918, and American wheat exports dropped. Suddenly American farmers were getting much less for their crops. In the 1920s, an agricultural depression set in, contributing to the more serious economic downturn that followed.

Throughout the 1920s, farmers struggled to keep their farms going. Some had bought new land and equipment during the war years, thinking that the good prices and high demand were going to continue. Others had taken out mortgages on property. Many (like the fictional Joad family in *The Grapes of Wrath*) rented their land from a landlord, usually a bank that had taken the property when an earlier owner couldn't pay off a mortgage. Whether bound by loans, mortgages, or rent, many farmers in the 1920s faced mounting debts that were growing harder to pay. Just maintaining the payment schedule was worrisome and often difficult, and most hoped that better days were around the corner.

Instead, the whole economy took a nose dive beginning with the stock market crash in October 1929. The already low prices farmers were paid for their crops sank even lower as the entire nation plunged into economic depression. The landlords and banks, in trouble themselves, now pressed harder than ever for the money the farmers owed them.

Dust Bowl. At this critical point, nature, too, added to the farmers' troubles. From the early days of settlement through the 1920s, rain had

The Oklahoma Dust Bowl, 1936.

generally been plentiful in the Plains states. Beginning in 1931, however, six years of severe drought struck the region, quickly draining its groundwater supply. In addition, poor farming practices were taking a heavy toll on the land. Overgrazing by livestock, failure to rotate crops so that fields could recover, allowing animals to graze on the crop stubble instead of plowing it back under—these and other practices had robbed the soil of nutrients.

DUST BOWL DIARY

APRIL 25, 1934, WEDNESDAY:

Last weekend was the worst dust storm we ever had.... Many days this spring the air is just full of dirt coming, literally, for hundreds of miles. It sifts into everything. After we wash the dishes and put them away, so much dust sifts into the cupboards that we must wash them again before the next meal. Clothes in the closets are covered with dust.

(Low, *Dust Bowl Diary*, p. 95)

Without mountains or even many trees to provide cover, the Plains region has always been very windy. Now, in the hot, dry weather, the winds helped evaporate what little water was left in the soil. As the farmers tried to grow their crops in the poor, dry earth, it turned to dust. The winds picked up the dust, creating huge black clouds that darkened the sky for miles. A part of the natural ecosystem, such dust storms were not new to the Great Plains. During the 1930s, though, worsened by the farmers' abuse of the soil, they struck harder and more often than ever before. Fences, equipment, trucks, even whole buildings could be covered in a matter of hours. And when there were no storms, the constant winds piled the dust in deep drifts. Soon, the whole area—over 5 million square miles, from North Dakota to Texas, from Arkansas to New Mexico—became known as the Dust Bowl.

The worst storms in the Dust Bowl happened in a roughly four-hundred-mile-wide circle. Centered on the Oklahoma panhandle, this circle included parts of Oklahoma, Texas, Kansas, New Mexico and Colorado. But the dirt blizzards affected the whole eastern half of the nation as well. Bad storms in 1933 and 1934 dropped dust as far east as New York and Philadelphia. The worst of all came on Sunday, April 14, 1935, "Black Sunday," when thick, black clouds hid the sun over the Plains states. In hours, temperatures plunged fifty degrees in some places.

Okies. The harsh conditions of the Dust Bowl squeezed everybody, but they hit the small farmers hardest. Those who owed money on loans or mortgages couldn't pay when crops failed year after year. They lost their land to the banks. And the banks, which now owned more land than ever before, had to wring every penny of profit out of it. It was cheaper to have one man with a tractor visit many farms than to allow families of tenants to operate them. So the banks "tractored" the families off the land, as happens to the Joads in the novel's early pages. Often this meant literally driving a tractor through the home of the protesting family to make them leave.

Thus, thousands of families, already ground down by years of poverty and hardship, now found themselves homeless as well. For most, the future appeared bleak, but word spread that unlimited opportunity awaited in the far west, in the golden state of California. As Grampa Joad puts it, "'Course it'll be all different out there—plenty work, an' ever'thing nice an' green, an' little white houses an' oranges growing all around" (Steinbeck, *The Grapes of Wrath*, p. 141).

This tempting vision was reinforced by the appearance of numerous leaflets sent out to the stricken Plains region by California growers. The leaflets commonly stated that thousands of workers were needed at such-and-such a farm or orchard. Packing everything they could into their old cars or trucks, selling the rest at a loss, the homeless families began a great migration westward. Between half a million and a million people made the journey between 1933 and 1940, one of the biggest mass movements in U.S. history.

Like the Joads, nearly all took Route 66, which runs from Oklahoma City almost 2,000 miles straight west, through Texas, New Mexico, and Arizona to California. They optimistically called it the "Mother Road," but upon reaching California their joy died quickly. Instead of steady jobs, they found hostility and exploitation. Dirty from living in cars and tents, uneducated, and having their own seemingly peculiar ways and customs, they were despised and often attacked by local people. No longer were they farmers or landowners. Nor were they even seen as respectable citizens. Instead, since many came from Oklahoma, all were scornfully labeled "Okies," and the makeshift community camps they lived in were called "Okievilles."

Growers and migrants. The Okies had been farmers, familiar with the ways of the land, but they met an entirely new kind of agriculture in California. Instead of small family farms raising a variety of crops and animals, California agriculture was increasingly dominated by large, single-crop farms run by corporations. By 1935, 10 percent of the farms grew over 50 percent of the total crops produced in the state.

Work for these single-crop growers was pretty much limited to a short period at harvest time, when the crop had to be picked. These were the "jobs" promised in the leaflets, which the Okies thought were year-round, full-time positions. That assumption was wrong, for California agriculture needed migrant labor, workers for brief jobs who would then travel to the next job. While corn and wheat can be harvested by a single farmer with a tractor, California crops like fruits and cotton required large teams to pick them by hand quickly, before spoilage set in. The workers followed these crops, moving on to a new farm as its crop grew ready for picking. Outside of harvest time, there was no place in the economic system for them.

Exploitation. Earlier migrant workers in California had included Japanese, Chinese, Filipino, and Mexican immigrants. Whatever their origin, California's migrant workers were at the mercy of the growers. Outsiders, often homeless and desperate for work, migrants usually arrived in numbers greater than the available jobs. At no time was this surplus of workers greater than with the influx of Dust Bowl refugees.

The growers had hoped for such a surplus when they sent out the leaflets, which might advertise for perhaps 800 workers when there was work for only 500. Several thousand men might see the leaflets and respond. More workers meant lower wages—and thus higher profits for the grower. Early in their journey west, the Joads meet a ragged, dirty man who has returned from California and warns them. "The more fellas he gets, an' the hungrier, less he's gonna pay" (*The Grapes of Wrath*, p. 244). The man's wife and children have died of starvation and disease; by the end he is willing to work "jus' for a cup a flour an' a spoon a lard" (*The Grapes of Wrath*, p. 245).

Attempting to organize. Like other migrant workers before and after them, the Okies tried to organize labor unions that would help them stand up to the growers. Steinbeck portrays such attempts, and the growers' responses,

when the Joads find work at a peach orchard where, unknown to them, other migrants are on strike. As the Joads arrive, they are escorted by police past some shouting people and into the camp. Tom Joad, in some ways the novel's central character, sneaks out of the orchard to discover what is going on. He finds out that the men and women he'd seen earlier were striking workers. Tom comes across his old friend Jim Casy, now the strikers' leader. Their peaceful meeting is then broken up by two club-wielding policemen, one of whom kills Casy with a blow to the head.

THEIR BLOOD IS STRONG

John Steinbeck had already won recognition for his earlier novels *Tortilla Flat, In Dubious Battle,* and *Of Mice and Men.* Published in the 1930s, they had dealt with farming and labor issues in California during the Depression. In 1936 Steinbeck became concerned about the plight of the Okies, who by that time had been streaming into the state for several years. That fall, he began spending time among them, talking, hearing their stories, and observing their living conditions. He then wrote a series of newspaper articles for the San Francisco *News,* which were later collected in a book, *Their Blood Is Strong.* The book is often seen as a nonfiction forerunner of *The Grapes of Wrath,* which was written two years later, in 1938.

The episode shows how local institutions of power like the police worked on the side of the growers. Such incidents were not uncommon. In 1938, for example, a mob headed by a local sheriff burned down an Okie migrant camp in Kern County, a leading farming area where antimigrant feelings were especially strong. The penniless migrants, by contrast, had only their own unity on which to rely. But this unity was tenuous. With so many hungry, the growers could always find those desperate enough to work, even if it meant going against a strike. For example, the Joads are offered the same wage—five cents a box—that the strikers had demanded. Once the strike is broken, Casy tells Tom, the wage will go back down to two-and-a-half cents. The growers were willing to pay the higher wage for a short period in order to break the strike.

Federal camps. Upon taking office in 1933, President Franklin D. Roosevelt launched a com-

A family of migrant workers in the San Joaquin valley.

prehensive agenda of government programs to combat the Depression. Called the New Deal, these programs included new federal agencies designed to create employment opportunities and to improve the lot of workers and the unemployed. Among the many such agencies, the one that most directly touched the Okies' lives was the Farm Security Administration (FSA). Operating under the authority of the Department of Agriculture, in 1936 the FSA began building camps in California in which the homeless migrants could live. Ten such camps were finished by the following year, and Steinbeck visited several in his research for *The Grapes of Wrath*. In the novel the Joads stay at one, the Arvin Sanitary Camp, also called the Weedpatch Camp, in Kern County.

The FSA camps were meant not as permanent homes, but as models for the larger growers to use in building similar living quarters for the migrants. Far from luxurious or even comfortable, they provided only basic necessities: rough shelter, and "sanitary units" in which to shower, wash, use the toilet, and do laundry. The growers, however, generally failed to build actual living quarters for the migrant farm workers, so many of them ended up staying in the camps for longer periods than was originally intended.

The Novel in Focus

The plot. Tom Joad, about thirty, is hitchhiking home to his family's Oklahoma farm after being paroled from prison, where he was serving a sentence for killing a man (though he acted in self-defense). While on the road, Joad hooks up with a former preacher, Jim Casy, who also is returning to the area after a long absence.

On reaching the Joad farm, they find it and neighboring farms strangely deserted. Told that the family is with Tom's Uncle John, they find them at his place and soon learn that the Joads and other local families have been "tractored off" the land by the banks. The Joads are packing their truck to leave—like others, they have heard that sunshine and plentiful work are waiting in California. Before they leave, they go into town to sell their remaining farm equipment, horses, and furniture for the paltry sum of $18. It was far less than the goods were worth, but they had no choice.

It is agreed that Jim Casy will come with them, which makes thirteen in all: Grampa and Granma Joad, Uncle John, Pa and Ma Joad, Tom, his older brother Noah and teenage brother Al, their pregnant sister, Rose of Sharon, and her husband, and the youngest children, Ruthie and Winfield. After slaughtering their two remaining pigs and salting down the meat in barrels to preserve it, they set off early the next morning. At the last minute, Grampa refuses to leave the land and has to be drugged with a big dose of cough syrup. That night, as the Joads camp out with the Wilsons, another uprooted family whom they have befriended, Grampa dies of a stroke.

Traveling together, the two families reach California, but soon after they cross the border Mrs. Wilson falls ill and Mr. Wilson insists that the Joads go on by themselves. The trip has taken its toll on Granma Joad, who never recovered from her husband's death. As they cross the California desert at night, Granma dies. Ma Joad, who has been caring for her, hides her death from the others until the family is safely across the desert.

Their money nearly gone, the Joads reach a migrants' camp (an "Okieville") near Bakersfield, the major city at the southern end of California's fertile San Joaquin Valley. Men in the camp have been unable to find work. A man representing a grower arrives, however, and says that he'll be hiring many pickers shortly, further north in the valley.

He mentions the tempting wage of thirty cents an hour—but when Floyd, a new acquaintance of Tom's, tries to get the man to put it in writing, the man grows angry. He summons his companion, a deputy, and accuses Floyd of being a "red." The deputy harasses Floyd, then tries to arrest him. When Floyd hits him and runs, the deputy shoots and hits a nearby woman. As he is about to shoot again, Casy knocks him out. More deputies arrive. They arrest Casy, and the sheriff warns the migrants that they must leave.

Hearing of the federal camp at Weedpatch, the Joads go there and find a place in the crowded facility. There they find temporary respite from the harshness of life on the road, but work in the area is scarce and their money is running out. Leaving Weedpatch Camp, they head north and find a job picking peaches at an orchard where other workers are striking. The strike had come about when the grower had halved the workers' wages, to two-and-a-half cents a box. Casy, released from jail, is leading the strike. Tom is with him when the police raid the strikers and kill Casy; Tom, enraged, kills one of the policemen and goes into hiding. The family leaves the orchard, smuggling Tom out under a mattress.

They find work picking cotton, camping in an empty boxcar that the grower has provided as living quarters. While Tom hides in the bushes nearby, Ma brings him food. But when Ruthie brags that her brother killed a man, Ma

tells Tom that he must go before he is found. Tom says that he wants to try organizing other migrants, as Casy was doing when he was killed. Ma gives him a few of her hard-earned dollars before he departs.

Just as the cotton harvest is ending, heavy rains begin. During the rains, Rose of Sharon gives birth, but her baby is born dead. Soon the rains flood the boxcar floor and the family has to pile up their belongings and perch on the pile. Ma Joad insists that they get out of the wet boxcar. They wade through the torrent to the highway and find a barn. Inside are a boy and his father. The father is starving because he has given all his food to the boy, who begs the Joads for food to feed his father. The destitute Joads have nothing to offer—until Rose of Sharon gives the starving man milk from her breast, milk her body had produced for her dead child.

NEEDED AND HATED

The unique nature of California agriculture requires that these migrants exist, and requires that they move about. Peaches and grapes, hops and cotton cannot be harvested by a resident population of laborers.... Thus, in California we find a curious attitude toward a group that makes our agriculture successful. The migrants are needed, and they are hated. Arriving in a district, they find the dislike always meted out by the resident to the foreigner, the outlander.

(Steinbeck, *Their Blood Is Strong*, p. 1)

"I" and "we." *The Grapes of Wrath* addresses problems that concerned the whole nation in the period of the Depression: poverty, economic injustice, and the rights of workers against those of employers. In his approach to these issues, Steinbeck draws on a literary tradition with roots deep in American history, a tradition whose ideas go back to early American writers like Walt Whitman and Ralph Waldo Emerson. Steinbeck uses Jim Casy, the former preacher, to present these ideas, and then has Casy pass them on to Tom Joad.

Casy, the former preacher, quit preaching because his beliefs no longer fit in with those of the church. Yet he continues to consider himself a religious man. Instead of believing in a Holy Spirit separate from humanity, he has come to believe that somehow all of humanity together makes up the Holy Spirit. As he tells Tom, "Maybe that's the Holy Sperit—the human sperit—the wh le shebang. Maybe all men got one big soul ever'body's a part of" (*The Grapes of Wrath*, p. 31).

Putting financial profit ahead of this "one big soul" goes against Casy's new beliefs, which is why he becomes a labor organizer. By contrast, working for society's common good becomes in Casy's eyes a religious aim:

> I got thinkin' how we was holy when we was one thing, an' mankin' was holy when it was one thing. An' it got unholy when one mis'able little fella got the bit in his teeth and run off his own way, kickin' an' draggin' an' fightin'. Fella like that bust the holiness. But when they're all working together, not one fella for another fella, but one fella kind of harnessed to the whole shebang—that's right, that's holy.
>
> (*The Grapes of Wrath*, p. 105)

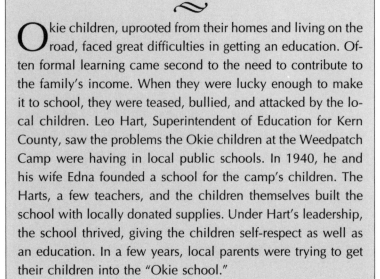

WEEDPATCH SCHOOL

Okie children, uprooted from their homes and living on the road, faced great difficulties in getting an education. Often formal learning came second to the need to contribute to the family's income. When they were lucky enough to make it to school, they were teased, bullied, and attacked by the local children. Leo Hart, Superintendent of Education for Kern County, saw the problems the Okie children at the Weedpatch Camp were having in local public schools. In 1940, he and his wife Edna founded a school for the camp's children. The Harts, a few teachers, and the children themselves built the school with locally donated supplies. Under Hart's leadership, the school thrived, giving the children self-respect as well as an education. In a few years, local parents were trying to get their children into the "Okie school."

Even employing others for your own profit ("one fella for another fella") goes against this view of what is "holy."

Such ideas clearly clash with the traditional American values of free enterprise and individualism. Charges of being a "red" (a socialist or communist) have been commonly leveled against labor organizers, playing on the nation's traditional distrust of socialist ideas to fight against the labor movement. For example, when Floyd tries to hold the employer to his promise, the man accuses him of "talkin' red, agitatin' trou-

ble" and then has him arrested (*The Grapes of Wrath*, p. 339). While Floyd was merely trying to obtain a written agreement, in some ways Casy's ideas do in fact have strong elements of socialism.

So did Steinbeck's, for *The Grapes of Wrath* is indeed a radical political document, a warning against the dangers of unrestrained capitalism. The wrath of the title refers to the anger of people who have lost even the basic necessities of survival. Their wrath threatens to overthrow those who possess society's wealth. "If you who own the things people must have could understand this," Steinbeck writes in a short descriptive chapter, "you might preserve yourself. . . . But that you cannot know. For the quality of owning freezes you forever into the 'I' and cuts you off forever from the 'we'" (*The Grapes of Wrath*, p. 195). Thus Steinbeck's novel attacks the very cornerstone of capitalism, the idea of ownership itself.

Sources. Steinbeck dedicated *The Grapes of Wrath* to his wife, Carol, and to Tom, who lived the novel. This Tom refers to Tom Collins, whom Steinbeck met in 1936. In August of that year, Steinbeck was visiting the federal camps for the migrants in California's Central Valley, doing research for his newspaper articles. Collins was in charge of Weedpatch Camp, which Steinbeck later featured in the novel. He was also the model for the sympathetic and understanding camp manager in the book, Jim Rawley. Through Collins's tireless efforts, and aided by the plentiful notes Collins kept, Steinbeck gained great insight into the migrants' world.

The character Jim Casy, too, has qualities in common with Tom Collins. Like Casy, Collins had a religious background, having trained as a priest. As a friend described him, "There was always something about Tom of the missionary. He had that . . . look in his eye, a way of smiling when you talked. You knew he had your better interests at heart" (Parini, p. 179). Also at Weedpatch was Sherm Easton, head of the camp's governing committee. According to a later manager of the camp, Easton and his family were the models for the Joads. Yet the Joads clearly sprang largely from Steinbeck's imagination, perhaps as mixtures of people he had met in his travels or seen elsewhere.

Reception. Steinbeck's attacks against capitalism provoked outrage, as did his portrayals of circumstances in both Oklahoma and California. A congressman from Oklahoma, for example, called the book "a lie, the black, infernal creation of a twisted, distorted mind" (Parini, p. 236). Growers in California claimed that it was unfair to them. School boards across the country banned it, claiming that it was obscene. It was not only banned but also publicly burned in Kern County, California, where much of it is set.

Yet within a few weeks of its publication, *The Grapes of Wrath* shot to the top of the bestseller lists and stayed there; it was 1939's top seller. Eleanor Roosevelt, the president's wife, praised it publicly and defended Steinbeck against his attackers. In 1940, the book won a Pulitzer Prize, and it is considered largely responsible for Steinbeck's 1962 Nobel Prize for Literature. Taking its place as a classic of American literature, it has since sold an estimated 15 million copies. An even wider audience has been introduced to the Joads through director John Ford's highly praised 1940 film adaptation.

The Grapes of Wrath, of course, also drew public attention to the plight of the migrants. Its suc-

cess gave Steinbeck a national voice, and he used it. It also won him several meetings with President Roosevelt. In the end, though, what put a halt to the Okies' nightmare of poverty was the same thing that ended the Depression as a whole: the nation's entry into World War II in 1941.

For More Information

Andryszewski, Tricia. *The Dust Bowl: Disaster on the Plains.* Brookfield, Conn.: Millbrook, 1993.

Low, Ann Marie. *Dust Bowl Diary.* Lincoln: University of Nebraska Press, 1984.

Parini, Jay. *John Steinbeck: A Biography.* New York: Henry Holt, 1995.

Stanley, Jerry. *Children of the Dust Bowl: The True Story of the School at Weedpatch Camp.* New York: Crown, 1992.

Steinbeck, John. *The Grapes of Wrath.* 1939. Reprint. New York: Penguin, 1976.

Steinbeck, John. *Their Blood is Strong.* San Francisco: Simon J. Lubin Society of California, 1938.

The Great Gatsby

by

F. Scott Fitzgerald

Born in Saint Paul, Minnesota, in 1896, Francis Scott Fitzgerald eventually settled in New York City. His writings frequently deal with the East Coast social circles and are best known for documenting the 1920s "jazz age" and the era of Prohibition. His novel *The Great Gatsby* deals with this period, and its literary and commercial success helped make him one of the most prominent literary figures of the time. From gangsters to Prohibition to contemporary social customs, Fitzgerald's work portrays a slice of New York during the 1920s.

Events in History at the Time of the Novel

New York in the 1920s. In the aftermath of the first world war, the United States experienced a rush of prosperity and optimism. Perhaps nowhere else did this social and economic change evidence itself more clearly than in New York City. Wall Street hosted the fervor of an unprecedented "bull"—or prosperous—market. People from all walks of life, from businessmen to teachers to clerks, began buying stocks "on margin." Instead of buying the stocks outright, they would deposit with a broker a percentage of money or other security as a provision against loss on the deal. In other words, without actually having enough money to back the stock, a person could own shares and speculate on the future of a corporation. These people were convinced of the unbridled prosperity of America's future—and with it—their own.

During this era, oil magnate John D. Rockefeller purchased a tract of land from Columbia University on which he began construction of an entertainment plaza that would be named Rockefeller Center. A rash of skyscrapers arose on the New York skyline. The old Waldorf-Astoria Hotel, a long-time monument of the elite New York social scene, fell to make room for a 102-story office building—at the time the tallest building in the world. Meanwhile, blocks away, construction began on the new Waldorf-Astoria, a magnificent 47-story structure that filled one square block. Attracted by all this construction, some of the wealthier New Yorkers left their old mansions for trendy penthouse apartments where they planted gardens on their terraces. Others moved out of their mansions into opulent hotels.

Afternoon hotel-room cocktail parties became the newest form of hospitality. The most infamous of these parties developed common attributes. Says one historian, "You might find your hostess installed in a five-room furnished suite at a luxurious hotel, its walls practically invisible under her aggregated Vermeers, Rembrandts, and Italian primitives" (Morris, p. 297). The parties arose with seemingly little or no effort. Guests would generally show up with one or two friends who had not received an invitation. People who became sick from alcohol overindulgence found themselves cordially led to bathrooms, and those who passed out were generally ignored. Often these cocktail parties began at or before 6:00 p.m., sometimes continuing into the next morning. The novel's narrator, Nick Carraway, attends such a gathering when he accompanies Mrs. Wilson and Tom Buchanan into New York City.

Women especially enjoyed the new freedoms of the 1920s. World War I had served as a liberating event in many ways. Through the National League for Women's Service, women took over jobs for the men who fought overseas. Following the war, many women were loathe to relinquish the feeling of financial independence their jobs had given them. Throughout New York City one found "flappers"—the young, trendy women flaunting short skirts, short hair cuts, feather boas, and jewelry. Conservative elements were shocked when the Waldorf-Astoria announced in the early 1920s that it would begin serving food to any woman unaccompanied by a man at any of its restaurants, and at any time of the day or night. Such a breach in protocol had been previously unknown. Jordan Baker, one of the characters in Fitzgerald's novel, is an athletic and independent female who represents the growing power of the female in America during this time.

Life under Prohibition. The era of Prohibition was the result of a century-long reform movement. Spurred by the Protestant churches during the 1880s and the 1890s, organizations such as the Women's Christian Temperance Movement and the National Prohibition Party lobbied for the restriction of alcohol sale and consumption. These organizers viewed alcohol as a dangerous drug that disrupted lives and families. They felt it the duty of the government to relieve the temptation of alcohol by banning it altogether.

In January of 1919, the United States Congress ratified the Eighteenth Amendment to the Constitution, outlawing "the manufacture, sale, or transportation of intoxicating liquors" on a national level. Nine months later, the Volstead Act passed, providing the means of enforcing such measures. Much to the dismay of Prohibitionists, however, the act had little effect on the alcohol-fueled hedonism of the American public.

The public reacted to Prohibition with a last night of binge drinking on January 15, 1920. For some time people had been stocking up on supplies of alcohol. But given the soaring prices, not even the wealthiest could afford to garner a lifetime reserve. New Yorkers crowded into their favorite bars, cafes, and restaurants in melancholy anticipation of the midnight hour, which would bring an end to their drinking. At the Waldorf-Astoria bar, one man sang "Auld Lang Syne" as a bartender wept. Few, however, foresaw the upcoming era of bootlegging, rumrunning, and speakeasies.

VOLSTEAD ACT

Passed in October 1919, the Volstead Act defined intoxicating liquor as drink that was more than 0.5 percent alcohol, determined penalties for selling liquor, called for injunctions against hotels, restaurants, and other establishments that sold liquor, and included a search and seizure clause.

A speakeasy was a place where the illegal alcoholic beverages were sold. One generally gained admission to a speakeasy through a sponsored membership by a trustworthy customer. Some provided membership cards, while others merely asked for passwords. This exchange of passwords at the door gave the "speakeasy" or "speak" its name. They existed everywhere and generally were easy to find. In fact, policemen were known to guide out of town visitors to the nearest speak, and sometimes even provide them with the password. At a typical speakeasy, a customer would wait for a light to come on above the door, a grill or small opening in the door would open, and the eye of the watchman would appear. If admitted, the customer might then entail pass through a series of locked doors, and at the final destination, the bartender provided a variety of watered-down scotches or gins.

Imbibers usually had little trouble obtaining alcohol without the benefit of a speakeasy. Rural distillers manufactured liquor, and "rumrunners" smuggled it into the city for resale. In the novel, Jay Gatsby has absolutely no difficulty in pro-

Robert Redford and Mia Farrow in the 1974 film adaptation of *The Great Gatsby*.

viding gallons of alcohol for his famous parties. Eventually the government realized that its Prohibition measures were pathetically ineffective. In 1933 Congress passed the Twenty-First Amendment, annulling Prohibition altogether.

Urban corruption. Ironically, the era of Prohibition fostered a huge underworld industry in many big cities, and New York was no exception. For years the city was under the control of the Irish politicians of Tammany Hall—a popular name for the small set of elected or appointed officials who dominated city politics. With the help of the local police force—again, mostly drawn from the Irish American community—the politicians of Tammany Hall virtually controlled New York law.

Charles Murphy headed Tammany Hall in 1922, the year the novel is set, and transformed it into a relatively incorrupt organization that supported major social legislation. He died just two years later, however, and by the time the novel was published, Tammany Hall had reverted to its previous ways. Authorities once again turned a profit on the dealings of the underworld, which in this decade included bootlegging, gambling, and prostitution. Police took money from shady operators engaged in these activities and, in return, "overlooked" the illegalities.

A major player in the Tammany Hall era went by the name of Arnold Rothstein (in the novel, he appears as Meyer Wolfsheim). Through campaign contributions to the politicians, Rothstein bought the protection of Tammany Hall. This assured him a virtual monopoly over prostitution and gambling in New York during the 1920s. He maintained his position until he was murdered in 1928.

A good friend of Rothstein's, Herman Rosenthal, suffered a similar fate. Fitzgerald refers to this incident in his novel. During a lunch with Gatsby and Nick, Wolfsheim remarks, "The old Metropole . . . I can't forget so long as I live the night they shot Rosy Rosenthal there" (Fitzgerald, *The Great Gatsby*, p. 74). While the author does not go into great detail about the events leading up to Rosenthal's murder, many readers at the time the novel was published would have remembered the incident. Through Rosenthal's various illegal activities, the mobster was a major force in New York corruption. To avoid trouble with the law, he regularly made "campaign contributions" to his political boss, Tim Sullivan. When Lieutenant Charles Becker, the head of police on New York's East Side, began laying claim to some of Rosenthal's payouts, Rosenthal complained to a reporter for the New York *World*. On July 13, 1912, the *World* published an exposé of the corruption of Tammany Hall and the New York police force. Two days later, Becker's men murdered Rosenthal on the steps of the Metropole. Unfortunately for Becker, Tammany Hall washed its hands of him. He and four of his men went to the electric chair for their part in the crime.

Other big-city criminals influenced Fitzgerald's novel as well. When Fitzgerald moved to Great Neck, Long Island, in the early 1920s, the trial of one of his neighbors was headline news. Edward Fuller had run a brokerage firm that filed for bankruptcy in June of 1922. He and his partner were convicted of gambling away millions of their customers' dollars. Fuller had risen to power on Wall Street through the aid of C. A. Stoneham. Owner of a racetrack, a casino, a newspaper, and the New York Giants, Stoneham's power stretched across the entire state. In an attempt to help Fuller out of his debt, Stoneham raided the Giants' cash box. Throughout the trial, incriminating papers disappeared, and witnesses were kidnapped. Fuller eventually served only twelve months of a lenient five-year sentence. The type of fatherly benevolence shown to Fuller by Stoneham surfaces in *The Great Gatsby*. As a young man, Gatsby learned his way around the law through the mentoring advice of Dan Cody, a miner, drinker, and gambler. Fitzgerald used this criminal character and others to create the aura of corruption and intrigue that pervades his novel.

The Black Sox Fix of 1919. The 1919 World Series was the center of a scandal that reverberated throughout the sports world. At the time, the Chicago White Sox led baseball in both talent and victories. Set to play the Cincinnati Reds in the World Series, the White Sox entered as the heavy favorites.

As a result of low game attendance during World War I, players' salaries had suffered cutbacks in the 1918 season. The owner of the White Sox, Charles Comiskey, had especially favored the cutbacks. Although he retained some of the best and biggest names in baseball, he paid them as poorly as the worst players in the league. The players complained and even threatened to strike, but Comiskey would not be persuaded to raise their pay. Three weeks prior to the start of the 1919 World Series, the White Sox first baseman, Arnold "Chick" Gandil, approached a bookmaker and gambler, Joseph Sullivan, with an offer to intentionally lose the series.

For some time Gandil had been formulating his plan. He had even managed to involve the Sox's star pitcher, Eddie Cicotte. Although Cicotte had to be won over through a great deal of persuasion, with his reluctant agreement, Gandil went into action. Six other players agreed to the fix. In addition to Gandil and Cicotte, they were Shoeless Joe Jackson (left fielder), George "Buck" Weaver (third baseman), Charles "Swede" Risberg (shortstop), Oscar "Happy" Felsch (center fielder), Fred McMullin (infielder), and Claude "Lefty" Williams (relief pitcher). The athletes fully expected their plan to succeed. Baseball in 1919—along with many other sports—was intimately connected to gambling. It was almost common knowledge that players sometimes "threw" games, or lost them on purpose.

Sullivan realized that on his own he would not be able to raise the $100,000 demanded up front by the eight White Sox players. He knew he would require the services of the "number one gambler-sportsman in America," Arnold Rothstein (Asinof, p. 24). Rothstein put up his own money to pay the players, and then began placing his own bets. Prior to the start of the series, rumors circulated about the legitimacy of the game. Losing the series five games to two, the Chicago White Sox caused one of the biggest sports upsets that the world had seen.

Casualties of the scandal mounted. In southside Chicago courts, there were an astounding number of civil cases for failure to pay alimony, bills, and mortgage payments. Each of the defendants claimed to have lost his life's savings by betting on the White Sox. This signaled authorities, and within months, the plot was exposed. For their part in the crime, the eight players were banned from baseball for life, and they earned the nickname the "Chicago Black Sox." The American public suffered disenchantment. In fact, the expression "Say it ain't so, Joe" refers to the public's disbelief that a well-known sports hero, Shoeless Joe Jackson, could have participated in the scandal.

THE COVER ARTWORK

With great expectations for Fitzgerald's work, the author's editor, Maxwell Perkins, commissioned a full-color illustrated jacket design from the Spanish artist Francis Cugat. Cugat had worked previously on movie posters and sets and was at the time employed as a designer in Hollywood. The Art Deco piece that he produced for the novel shows the outlined eyes of a woman looking out of a midnight blue sky above the carnival lights of Coney Island in Manhattan. The piece was finished seven months before the novel, and Fitzgerald may have used it to inspire his own imagery. He describes Daisy Buchanan as "the girl whose disembodied face floated along the dark cornices and blinding signs" of New York (*The Great Gatsby*, p. 85).

In the novel, Gatsby introduces Nick to Meyer Wolfsheim, telling Nick, "He's the man who fixed the World Series back in 1919" (*The Great Gatsby*, p. 78). Stunned, Nick thinks to himself, "It never occurred to me that one man could start to play with the faith of fifty million people—with the single-mindedness of a burglar blowing a safe" (*The Great Gatsby*, p. 78). Arnold Rothstein not only gambled with the faith of fifty million, but on this occasion he also won.

The Novel in Focus

The plot. Ironically, the title character of Fitzgerald's work does not appear until page fifty-two of the text. The author instead uses a minor, mostly unbiased narrator, Nick Carraway, to deliver his first-person tale. New to the upper-crust West Egg Village of Long Island, New York, Nick calls on his only friends in the area, his second cousin Daisy Buchanan and her husband Tom. He had known Daisy quite well when the two of them lived in the Middle West. Nick soon suspects that the Buchanans' marriage totters on the brink of failure. This impression is solidified the next afternoon when Tom takes Nick to meet his mistress, Myrtle Wilson, a woman married to a local mechanic. During their outing in New York City, Nick, Tom, and Mrs. Wilson enjoy an afternoon of drinking with friends. All but Mrs. Wilson hail from wealthy families and spend much of their time socializing.

The title character in the novel, Jay Gatsby, excels in the art of socializing, and he soon becomes important to both Nick and the Buchanans. With only a solid reputation for hosting lavish soirées, Gatsby remains a mystery to all who know him. No one quite knows how he amassed his fortune nor how he maintains this wealth, thus the rumors run rampant. Some accuse him of murder; others claim he's a bootlegger; Gatsby himself insists that he found his fortune with Dan Cody, a famous silver miner. The only fact concerning Gatsby that Nick learns for certain is that he is in love with Daisy Buchanan.

While growing up in Louisville, Kentucky, Daisy had been the town beauty and led the life of a socialite. Never in need of a date, she was held in high regard by the army officers at the nearby Camp Taylor. After one officer in particular, Jay Gatsby, captured her heart, Daisy had no further interest in the others. She remained with him until he shipped out to fight overseas in World War I. For some time after Gatsby's departure, Daisy seemed reluctant to see other suitors. In time, however, she began socializing and eventually became engaged to Tom Buchanan. On the eve of her wedding, Daisy received a letter from Gatsby that almost prevented the marriage. Although Daisy did walk down the aisle the following morning, it was not without hesitation. She nevertheless returned from her honeymoon a happy bride. The marital bliss, however, did not last, as Tom's infidelity prevented any true happiness.

Gatsby discloses his affections toward Daisy during a lunch engagement with Nick. Although he lives in the same area, he has shied away from approaching his former sweetheart. Gatsby implores Nick to set up a meeting, and the following afternoon Nick arranges a tea party for the three of them. After spending only a few short hours with Gatsby, Daisy's feelings of love are rekindled. The two begin to meet secretly.

Soon Tom becomes suspicious of his wife's affair. During a group outing to New York, Tom unleashes the rage of his jealousy. In a drunken fury, he accuses Gatsby of stealing his wife and insists that Daisy will not divorce him. Gatsby and Daisy depart together. Nick, Tom, and the others then follow in a different car, and turning a bend in the road, they come upon the scene of an accident. Apparently a car fitting the description of Tom's had just hit a female pedestrian and sped away. The dead victim was Myrtle Wilson.

For some time George Wilson had entertained his own suspicions concerning his wife's fidelity or lack thereof. After the accident, he mistakenly assumes that Gatsby was the object of her desires and locates him through Tom. As retribution for his wife's death, George confronts Gatsby at his home. Within a few minutes two shots ring out.

Both men are found dead by Nick and the household staff; it becomes apparent that George has shot Gatsby and then killed himself. Perhaps one of the most tragic events in the novel's conclusion occurs at Gatsby's funeral. For a man who had been the toast of New York's upper class, only one friend—Nick, the narrator—cares enough to show up at the grave and pay his last respects.

Gatsby, the accepted hoodlum. Perhaps one of the most unique aspects of Jay Gatsby's character is his unidentified connection with the underworld. A good friend to the notorious criminal Meyer Wolfsheim, Gatsby is tied to possibly shady dealings throughout the course of the novel. He repeatedly takes mysterious phone calls and steps aside for private, undisclosed conversations. Although Fitzgerald never reveals the sources of Gatsby's wealth, Gatsby's friends argue that he is possibly a bootlegger and that "one time he killed a man who had found out that he was nephew to von Hindenburg and second cousin to the devil" (*The Great Gatsby,* p. 65). Nonetheless, prominent citizens continue to associate with him.

Real-life personalities were highly esteemed for their alleged bootlegging under Prohibition,

and it was actually quite difficult for authorities to enforce the Volstead Act. Only 1,500 agents were assigned to the Prohibition task force, making it nearly impossible to patrol the 25,000 miles of coastlines and borders across which goods could be smuggled. At the onset of Prohibition, a bootlegging industry flourished from the start, and drinking became more in vogue than ever. Upper-class citizens gained prestige by offering outlawed alcohol to their house guests and by taking friends to popular speakeasies. According to one Fitzgerald biographer, "The bootlegger entered American folklore with as much public complicity as the outlaws of the Old West had enjoyed" (Le Vot, p. 129). The American public not only embraced customs that fell outside the arm of the law, but it also admired figures who lived without restraint. One such character is Gatsby, who flaunts the law with his business dealings and socializes with seemingly endless funds. Fitzgerald's novel, however, does not appear to champion this lifestyle, for Gatsby dies without a genuine friend.

HEARST'S INTERNATIONAL COVER

In May 1923, Fitzgerald and his wife Zelda appeared on the cover of *Hearst's International* magazine. At the time he was twenty-six, and she just twenty-three. The photo not only captures the couple, but the spirit of the times. With a budding literary career in progress, Fitzgerald was poised for great success. He had just signed a contract with his publisher, and the magazine cover photo signaled his entry into the Hearst realm of thirty-two newspapers, nine magazines, and a readership of 9 million.

Sources. F. Scott Fitzgerald set out to write a novel wholly representative of his era. It is little wonder then, that many characters and events in *The Great Gatsby* stem directly from real life. Fitzgerald's own biography shares details with the lives of his characters. Like Nick and Daisy, the author grew up in the Midwest. Fitzgerald lived in St. Paul, Minnesota, where he attended St. Paul's Academy during his high school years. Although his own family did not claim any great wealth, several of his academy friends, especially those with whom he took dancing lessons, did hail from wealthy backgrounds. They introduced him to a lifestyle that included parties, chauf-

Zelda Fitzgerald

feurs, and elite social circles. Like Nick, Fitzgerald did not have the means to become a part of these circles but was included as a gesture of friendship. In a move that paralleled that of his narrator's, Fitzgerald too left the Midwest and moved east. He attended college at Princeton University in New Jersey and lived most of his adult life in New York. While on the East Coast, Fitzgerald, like his characters, would become caught up in a whirlwind of endless parties.

In 1917, with the United States becoming involved in World War I, Fitzgerald enlisted as an army officer. While stationed for training at Camp Sheridan in Alabama, he met the love of his life, Zelda Sayre. Like Daisy, Zelda reigned as the princess of the Montgomery social scene. She had been voted "prettiest girl in class" during high school and was a favorite date among the young men at Alabama State University, Auburn University, and Camp Sheridan.

On October 26, 1918, Fitzgerald's unit left Montgomery for New York. From there they were scheduled to sail out to France. While they awaited departure, however, the war ended and an armistice was signed. The author's frustration

in not being able to participate in the Great War evidences itself in the character of Gatsby. Unlike Fitzgerald, Gatsby did fight overseas. He is even rumored to have been "a German spy during the war" (*The Great Gatsby,* p. 48).

Fitzgerald also drew on newsworthy personalities from his era. Already mentioned is the "czar" of the New York underworld Arnold Rothstein, transformed into the novel's character Meyer Wolfsheim. In real life, as in the fictional portrayal, this man was credited with the fixing the Chicago White Sox World Series of 1919.

Reception. After sending the manuscript of *The Great Gatsby* to Maxwell Perkins at Scribner's, his publisher, F. Scott Fitzgerald received this reply: "I think you have every kind of right to be proud of this book. It is an extraordinary book, suggestive of all sorts of thoughts and moods" (Perkins in Fitzgerald, p. 199). Unfortunately not all of the critics agreed. The novel's publication in April of 1925 was met with mixed reviews. The headline in the New York *World* read, "F. Scott Fitzgerald's Latest a Dud," while the *Brooklyn Eagle* stated that it could not find "one chemical trace of magic, life, irony, romance or mysticism in all of *The Great Gatsby*" (Fitzgerald, p. 202). Most critics, nevertheless, recognized it as the finest novel crafted by Fitzgerald to that point, and Gilbert Seldes of the *Dial* went so far as to maintain that it put Fitzgerald far ahead of all other young writers and most of the older ones in the United States. The initial sales of *The Great Gatsby* were, however, disappointing. It reached sales of only about 20,000 copies during his lifetime, which fell far short of the 75,000 the author expected.

For More Information

Allen, Oliver E. *The Tiger: The Rise and Fall of Tammany Hall.* Reading, Mass.: Addison-Wesley, 1993.

Asinof, Eliot. *Eight Men Out: The Black Sox and the 1919 World Series.* New York: Holt, Rhinehart and Winston, 1963.

Fitzgerald, Francis Scott. *The Great Gatsby.* New York: Simon and Schuster, 1925.

Le Vot, André. *F. Scott Fitzgerald.* New York: Doubleday, 1983.

Morris, Lloyd. *Incredible New York.* New York: Random House, 1951.

Timberlake, James H. *Prohibition and the Progressive Movement, 1900-1920.* Cambridge, Mass.: Harvard University Press, 1963.

The Heart Is a Lonely Hunter

by
Carson McCullers

Lula Carson Smith was born in Columbus, Georgia, in 1917 to Marguerite Waters Smith and Lamar Smith, owners of a jewelry shop. The girl's first dream was to be a concert pianist. She then resolved to become a writer and started to read all the great literature she could find. A special favorite of hers was Isak Dinesen's *Out of Africa,* (also covered in *Literature and Its Times*), a work McCullers first read in 1937, then reread annually thereafter. At age twenty-two, with only one short story in print, McCullers became an overnight celebrity when *The Heart Is a Lonely Hunter* appeared. The novel focuses on individuals who are outcasts in a 1930s Southern city because of racial, political, physical, and other prejudices.

Events in History at the Time the Novel Takes Place

Cotton mill towns in the 1930s. Bounded on one end by the stock market crash of October 29, 1929, and on the other by the bombing of Pearl Harbor on December 7, 1941, the 1930s saw the gravest economic depression the United States has ever faced. Although urban unemployment soared to a peak of 15 million in 1932, the worst afflicted in the country were the farmers. In 1932 farm incomes fell to less than half of the 1929 level. The result was that many farmers could no longer meet mortgage payments, and their farms were foreclosed and auctioned off. Between 1927 and 1932 the number of forced sales of Southern farms rose from 21 to

---

THE LITERARY WORK

A novel set in a Georgia cotton mill town in the 1930s; first published in 1940.

SYNOPSIS

Four lonely people are brought together by the fifth, a deaf-mute named John Singer, who catches their attention with his kindness and his ability to listen (through lip-reading) and understand.

---

46 per thousand. Despite the attempts of the American Cotton Cooperative Association to limit crop production, cotton prices continued to plummet, and textile mills poured out a surfeit of unwanted cloth onto the market. Between 1928 and 1932, the manufacturers' price fell below the margin needed to cover costs, and the mills suffered absolute losses.

Although McCullers describes the cotton mills in her novel as "big and flourishing," the men who work there nevertheless are "very poor," embodying the despair characteristic of the time period: "Often in the faces along the streets there was the desperate look of hunger and loneliness" (McCullers, *The Heart Is a Lonely Hunter,* p. 4).

Young women in the Depression. With the job market so bleak because of the Depression, many young people reacted by remaining in school for a longer period of time. High schools became a refuge in the 1930s—they were warm, free, and a place to go instead of work. In 1930 barely half of young people between the ages of fourteen and eighteen attended high school; by 1940 three-quarters attended. Peer culture, rather than parents, community, or church, influenced youth attitudes and set standards of behavior. Emphasis was placed on conformity. In a Southern mill town during the 1930s this meant reading the same comic strips, wearing the same clothes, or hanging out at the same corner drugstore. Popularity was crucial to social acceptance, and no one felt the pressure more acutely than adolescent girls. This is evident in the story when the female character Mick, a lover of sneakers and shorts with few friends, dons a dress and plans a party exclusively for her new schoolmates in an attempt to belong. She excludes the neighborhood kids, but her plan backfires.

Radio. Given the general climate of despair during the Depression years, popular culture became an important refuge. Radio came into its own in the 1930s (its second decade of existence), becoming the nation's most popular form of entertainment. By the end of the 1930s radio was an integral part of American life. Most homes had at least one receiver. Its influence as a leisure-time activity was so dramatic that by 1950, listening to the radio ranked second only to sleeping in the amount of time it consumed in the average person's life. Millions tuned in each week to *Amos 'n' Andy* and later to the *Eddie Cantor Show,* daytime dramas like *Ma Perkins,* serial dramas like *The Lone Ranger,* and President Franklin Delano Roosevelt's "Fireside Chats." Perhaps the most striking testament to the power of radio was the hysteria caused by Orson Welles's October 30, 1938, broadcast of an adaptation of H. G. Wells's novel, *The War of the Worlds,* (also covered in *Literature and Its Times*), in which millions of listeners actually believed that Martians had landed in New Jersey.

American blacks in the Depression. For many blacks, the Depression did not signal a significant change. "I've been in a depression ever since I've been in the world," said one black man in Chicago. "The Negro was born in the depression. It didn't mean much to him, the Great American Depression, as you call it. There was no such thing. It only became official when it hit the white man" (Turkel in Ware, p. 8). A similar point is made in Maya Angelou's memoir *I Know Why the Caged Bird Sings:* "The country had been in the throes of the Depression for two years before the Negroes . . . knew it. I think that everyone thought that the Depression, like everything else,

was for the white folks, so it had nothing to do with them" (Angelou, p. 41).

Still, for the first time, supporters of racial equality had, during the Depression, an ally in the White House—Eleanor Roosevelt. Throughout the 1930s she exerted continuing pressure on her husband and others in the government to fight discrimination against blacks. Her achievements were limited, however. Her husband, historians point out, had no choice but to balance the interests of the white Southern Democrats against those of the black community. Typical of his equivocal stance was his harsh condemnation of lynching combined with his refusal to support legislation that would make lynching illegal (Current, p. 773).

Black physicians in Georgia. Medicine is among the oldest professions among blacks in Georgia. During the antebellum plantation era the planters found it cheaper and more effective to keep their slaves healthy by using black healers rather than white ones. In spite of a lack of modern training, most black healers willingly accepted the role of physician. They were driven not only by their desire to help fellow blacks but also by the opportunity to raise their social status above that of the common working slave.

Immediately after the Civil War, the number of trained black physicians remained low. Few schools at that time would admit blacks to study a profession like medicine, and the ones that agreed to admit them did so on the understanding that they would emigrate to the African land of Liberia when their training was completed. Yet despite these obstacles, the number of black physicians in Georgia increased rapidly in the second half of the nineteenth century.

White physicians were often glad to give up their black patients because these patients were poor, and in order to properly serve them, the white physician had to enter into what many felt was an uncomfortably intimate relationship with the blacks. Many of the blacks who gained the education necessary to enter the professional class found their way to large cities, leaving the poorer rural blacks almost entirely without medical aid, except perhaps for the expensive and reluctant attentions of white doctors. Still, the medical profession grew in Georgia, and in 1933 a group of black physicians and other medical professionals opened a rural clinic at the Log Cabin Rural Community Center in Mayfield, Georgia.

Although black Georgians in the 1930s were still far behind whites in the degree of medical care they received, black physicians made a worthy contribution to improving the health of their community. Moreover, these medical men contributed to the cultural and social standing of the race.

The Novel in Focus

The plot. The story begins with two mutes—Spiros Antonapoulos, an overweight Greek who moves his hands only to say that he wants to eat, sleep, or drink, and John Singer, his thin and thoughtful companion. The two men have no friends and live together. But when a mild illness causes Antonapoulos to lose his sanity, he is taken away to an asylum, and Singer is left utterly alone.

No longer having a dinner companion, Singer decides to take all his meals at the New York Café. The owner of this café is Biff Brannon, a quiet, observant, and compassionate man. When a heavy-set alcoholic named Jake Blount comes to town and drinks for a week on credit, Biff tells him he can take his time settling the debt. Then Jake accosts Singer at a table and begins to talk. From the look on Singer's face, Jake feels that he has finally found someone who understands him. Later, when Jake discovers that Singer is a mute, it does little to shake his conviction that Singer understands him.

Unable to bear the empty apartment without his companion, Singer takes a room at the Kellys' boarding house. There he meets Mick, the Kellys' thirteen-year-old daughter. Mick is a precocious young tomboy, and ferociously independent. Her secret passion is classical music (Mozart, Beethoven, and others), which she can only hear by sneaking into the backyard of a large house and listening to the radio inside. Mick says little to her sisters and parents, electing instead to keep her thoughts to herself. But when she meets Singer, they strike up a friendship and she begins to confide in the mute. They soon become friends, and Singer buys her a radio of her own on which to listen to classical music.

The Kellys have a maid named Portia. Her father, Doctor Benedict Mady Copeland, is the only black doctor in town. He is also well read, particularly in philosophy, and although he has devoted his life to the betterment of black people, his pedantic and patronizing nature have driven a wedge between him and his family, forcing him into bookish isolation. When Singer happens to light Dr. Copeland's cigarette on the street, the doctor, a cynic when it comes to relations between the races, is struck by the gesture. It is the first time any white man has ever acted kindly

or respectfully toward him. When he tells Portia about a deaf-mute patient of his, she assures him that Singer will help.

Meanwhile, Mick has entered the Vocational High School. As a sort of rite of passage into womanhood, she plans a prom to which only her new high school peers are invited. For the occasion Mick discards her sneakers and shorts for an evening dress. After an awkward sequence in which the boys and girls refuse to leave their respective corners, Mick is approached by Harry Minowitz, a boy who lives next door. After a walk around the block with Harry, Mick returns to find that the party has been crashed by the neighborhood kids, and she calls it off.

Jake gets a job at a flying-jenny show (in other words, a merry-go-round show—at one time the merry-go-round was pulled by a jenny, a female donkey). When he tries to talk to some working men about their rights, they laugh at him. Jake also becomes one of the first to show an interest in Dr. Copeland's son Willie, who has been sentenced to hard labor for knifing a man. In prison camp Willie is mistreated, and he loses both feet to gangrene. Dr. Copeland tries to see the judge about the case, only to be beaten up outside the courthouse by angry whites and thrown in jail. Later Singer and Portia bail him out.

The Kellys, meanwhile, are having financial trouble. Singer is the only tenant in the boarding house who consistently pays his rent. Things

Early twentieth-century textile mill.

only grow worse when Mick's sister becomes ill and can no longer help support the family. Although Mick is told she is too young to work, she takes a job at a five-and-ten-cent store.

Singer makes two visits to the asylum to see Antonapoulos. On the first visit Singer uses sign language to tell his friend all about the events in town, but all Antonapoulos cares about is food. On Singer's second visit to the asylum, he discovers that Antonapoulos is dead. Singer feels desolate, and returning to town, goes up to his room and shoots himself in the chest.

Singer's death is a blow to his four companions. Jake Blount gets into a fight at work and flees town in fear of the police. Mick grows despondent. She works all day and has no time for music anymore. She feels betrayed by Singer's suicide. Dr. Copeland retreats back into his study. And Biff, unlike Singer, concludes that human suffering is something that simply must be endured, and sits alone once again at the New York Café.

Dr. Copeland and the educated black man in the South. Dr. Copeland is an anomaly in the Southern town in which *The Heart Is a Lonely Hunter* takes place. He received his education up north, and unlike many black professionals he returned to the rural community of his origin after completing his training. He spends his evening in a straight-backed chair in his kitchen reading the works of Spinoza and other philosophers, books that he does not fully comprehend: "He did not wholly understand the intricate play of ideas and the complex phrases, but as he read he sensed a strong, true purpose behind the words and he felt that he almost understood" (*The Heart Is a Lonely Hunter,* p. 60).

Dr. Copeland has dedicated his life to helping the black community. The town is filled with babies named Benedict Copeland or Benny Mae or Mayben—all in homage to the doctor who delivered them. But it is not enough for Copeland to offer medical advice. His mission is a larger one: to elevate his race. He scoffs at religion, and delivers more than babies, bringing along advice for the parents as well: "It is not more children we need but more chances for the ones already on the earth. Eugenic Parenthood for the Negro Race was what he would exhort them to" (*The Heart Is a Lonely Hunter,* p. 63). Copeland's education already sets him apart from the rest of the black community. Needless to say, his stern opinions and pedantic nature serve only to further separate him from the very people he wants so desperately to help.

Black doctors—especially in rural areas—were both leaders and outcasts in their communities. While not as wealthy as white doctors, they usually accumulated a larger per capita wealth than any other class of blacks, including those engaged in business. Their education and social standing and their efforts to promote higher standards of culture in their communities earned them tremendous respect. Yet these same factors alienated black doctors. They were marked as different. In the novel Dr. Copeland is indeed unconventional. He is a vegetarian and an atheist. His house does not resemble the miserable dwellings that surround it. He is critical of all blacks and of his family in particular. He regularly sees his daughter Portia, but when she ushers her brother Willie and husband Highboy into Dr. Copeland's house to make peace with her father, Dr. Copeland is frustrated by their lack of ambition and cannot help but lash out at them for their "misunderstanding, idleness and indifference" (*The Heart Is a Lonely Hunter,* p. 76).

Dr. Copeland's behavior reveals some of the pressures brought to bear on black men of his time who managed to raise their station in life. He becomes both a heroic and a tragic figure.

Sources. Like the unnamed setting in *The Heart Is a Lonely Hunter,* McCullers's hometown of Columbus, Georgia was a mill town. Directly across the river from Columbus was Phinx City, Alabama. Phinx, with its honky-tonks and coarser way of life, was known as "Sin City," and residents of Columbus were quick to point out that McCullers had doubtless gotten her ideas for what they called "all those wicked, dirty old stories" in "Sin City" (Carr, *The Lonely Hunter,* p. 18). But although McCullers did visit Phinx on occasion, there is little evidence to support this claim. In fact, it was not McCullers's habit to seek out experiences to use in her fiction, nor was it her practice to turn real people into thinly veiled fictional characters. She preferred instead to trust her imagination. Perhaps the best example of this is the case of Singer, the mute in *The Heart Is a Lonely Hunter.* McCullers had changed the character many times in her mind. When the right idea finally came to her, she said to her mother, "His name is John Singer, and he is a deaf-mute." When her mother, Marguerite Smith, asked how many deaf-mutes her daughter had known, McCullers replied, "I've never known one, but I know Singer" (Carr, *Understanding Carson McCullers,* p. 16). Later, when someone suggested she attend a "deaf and dumb convention" being held in a nearby town, McCullers declined, saying, "There is nothing those people could tell me. I have already written that

part of the novel" (Carr, *Understanding Carson McCullers,* p. 16).

This having been said, there are some noteworthy similarities between McCullers and her young female character Mick Kelly. Like Mick, McCullers was captivated by music, and took piano lessons as a child. Sick in bed at age fifteen, however, she was struck by an epiphany. "I've given up my dream of being a concert pianist," she told a friend. "But it's okay. I'm going to be a writer instead" (McCullers in Carr, *The Lonely Hunter,* p. 29). There are physical similarities too. Like Mick, McCullers was a tall and somewhat gangly girl, and she often felt different from her peers.

Physical deformities and handicaps in McCullers's fiction often serve as a sign of humanity's limitations, of its inability to fully give or receive love. An obvious example of this is the mute character Singer. McCullers herself was no stranger to physical discomfort. As a child she had suffered from pernicious anemia, pleurisy, and other respiratory ailments, and at fifteen she was stricken with rheumatic fever, incorrectly diagnosed and therefore improperly treated. Three strokes followed, and before she reached the age of thirty, the left half of her body was partially paralyzed and her mobility seriously impaired.

Reviews. Early reviews greeted *The Heart Is a Lonely Hunter* with great praise. The black novelist Richard Wright, writing for the *New Republic,* expressed his amazement at the "astonishing humanity that enables a white writer, for the first time in southern fiction, to handle Negro characters with as much ease and justice as those of her own race." He went on to say that the quality of the despair in the novel was "unique and natural . . . more natural and authentic than that of Faulkner" (Wright in Carr, *Understanding Carson McCullers,* p. 32). Rose Feld, in the *New York Times Book Review,* praised McCullers's "astonishing perception of humanity" (Feld in Carr, *Understanding Carson McCullers,* p. 33). Critics would over time come to regard *The Heart Is a Lonely Hunter* as one of the greatest twentieth-century novels published in the United States.

For More Information

Angelou, Maya. *I Know Why the Caged Bird Sings.* New York: Random House, 1969.

Best, Harry. *Deafness and the Deaf in the United States.* New York: MacMillan, 1943.

Carr, Virginia Spencer. *The Lonely Hunter: A Biography of Carson McCullers.* New York: Doubleday, 1975.

Carr, Virginia Spencer. *Understanding Carson McCullers.* Columbia: University of South Carolina Press, 1990.

Current, Richard N., et al., eds. *American History: A Survey, Sixth Edition.* New York: Alfred A. Knopf, 1983.

McCullers, Carson. *The Heart Is a Lonely Hunter.* New York: Houghton Mifflin, 1940.

Tindall, George Brown. *The Emergence of the New South: 1913-1945.* Baton Rouge: Louisiana State University Press, 1967.

Ware, Susan. *Holding Their Own: American Women in the 1930s.* Boston: Twayne, 1982.

Home to Harlem

by
Claude McKay

B orn in Jamaica in 1890, Claude McKay immigrated to America at the age of twenty-two to study scientific farming at Tuskegee Institute in Alabama. He transferred to Kansas State College before he left school altogether in 1914 and moved to New York. Settling in Harlem, McKay worked at menial jobs while writing poetry, as he had done before leaving Jamaica. He wrote colorfully about Harlem, describing its cabarets, jazz scene, and community life during the World War I era. In 1922 McKay left the United States, partly to escape "the suffocating ghetto of color consciousness" (Anderson, p. 221). He professed to have gained precious perspective on his experiences while abroad, which allowed him to do his best writing on Harlem. Written during this time, *Home to Harlem* draws on McKay's memories of the black American community.

THE LITERARY WORK

A novel set in Harlem, New York, around 1919; published in 1928.

SYNOPSIS

An African American soldier abandons his post in World War I and returns to his home in Harlem, New York.

Events in History at the Time the Novel Takes Place

Northern migration. In *Home to Harlem,* the main character, Jake, recounts the migration northward of his friend Zeddy, who originally lived in Petersburg, Virginia. Between 1916 and 1930, nearly one million African Americans made such a move, leaving their homes in the South to migrate to northern cities such as New York and Chicago. Those who became part of this "Great Migration," as it came to be called, believed that the North held better job opportunities and more political freedom. Many were soon disillusioned. White homeowners and landlords resisted black movements into their communities, and businesses showed a preference for white job-seekers. In New York City, black migrants streamed into an area named *Haarlem* (by its earliest Dutch settlers). This area, whose main thoroughfare was 125th Street, became one of the few places in which blacks could find housing.

In the 1910s African Americans became the dominant population in Harlem. Their population included a middle-class as well as a working-class sector. There were black doctors and intellectuals (such as the character Ray in *Home to Harlem*), and some fine houses, apartments, and churches in the neighborhood. Its black residents, remembered the African American leader A. Philip Randolph, exhibited a sense of urgency. They "were trying to do things, trying to achieve status for the race. You had the underworld, to be sure, but you had some good types of people. They set the tone of the community" (Randolph in Anderson, p. 117). By the early 1920s almost every black institution—from social service agencies to the major churches to black journals—had relocated to Harlem, turning it into a solidly black community.

Employment. With the beginning of World War I in 1914 came a rush of war manufacturing and many new job opportunities for blacks. When America entered the war in 1917, still more jobs were vacated as white laborers left to join the fight. For a while, blacks would not have to compete so fiercely with poor whites for jobs. But in the long run, America's entry into the war would do little to bring equality to its black citizens. There was racial violence even at the outset as America readied itself for war in 1917. A riot in St. Louis, Missouri, resulted in the deaths of forty blacks and half a dozen whites. And in Houston, Texas, thirteen black soldiers were convicted of killing seventeen whites who provoked them into a fight.

Blacks in World War I. When the United States entered World War I, the army recruited black Americans and placed them into segregated regiments headed by white commanders. At first, these units were not allowed to fight; the army instead restricted them to support tasks—loading and unloading cargo or stoking the fires on ships, for example. In *Home to Harlem,* Jake, a resident of Harlem, enlists in the army with the intention of fighting on the front lines. Instead he and his regiment first unload a ship, then construct huts in France to house American soldiers.

Eventually some units out of the more than 300,000 black soldiers were assigned to combat duty and became distinguished for their valor. One of the most famous of these fighting units was the Fifteenth Regiment, formed in Harlem. Its formation created a great deal of controversy in the community—some argued that blacks should not fight in a war for the United States, a nation that treated them as inferior people. Others, by contrast, felt that the use of black soldiers in the war would benefit the race by demonstrating its equality to whites. In 1917, the Fifteenth Regiment sailed for France and was assigned to fight alongside the French soldiers. It would be one of the few black regiments that saw combat.

Cited for bravery, the Fifteenth Regiment returned to cheering crowds at the beginning of 1919. By summer this welcoming mood had dampened. More than twenty race riots broke out across the nation in 1919, resulting in the shooting, lynching, and beating of scores of

Claude McKay

blacks. So shaken was Claude McKay that he responded to the violence with a poem: "If we must die, let it not be like hogs . . . / Like men we'll face the murderous, cowardly pack, / Pressed to the wall, dying, but fighting back!" (McKay in Anderson, p. 196).

New militancy. During the early part of the twentieth century, Harlem became the most militant community in black America. Among other movements, it became a center for Marcus Garvey's black nationalism organization. In the 1910s Garvey, who was Jamaican-born like McKay, established the United Negro Improvement Association (UNIA), which advocated black separatism. Garvey argued that blacks should respond to the inequality in the United States by leaving its shores and building their own new republic in Africa. Finding wisdom in Garvey's message, McKay would eventually work for the UNIA and write many articles for its magazine, *Negro World*. He was not alone in his sympathies. After the race riots of 1919 a rising number of black Americans, in fact, agreed with Garvey. Disheartened and seeing little promise of future equality in the United States, scores of blacks joined the UNIA. Garvey went on to organize in 1920 the first International Convention of the Negro Peoples of the World, which further boosted UNIA membership to 4 million worldwide.

Life in Harlem. Nearly two-thirds of the blacks living in New York resided in Harlem by 1920, an area bounded by Eighth Avenue and the East and Harlem Rivers above 106th Street. They settled first in two black areas, one on Seventh Avenue and the other on Lenox Avenue. As their populations grew, the two areas merged to form the black community of Harlem.

Housing was often expensive, because landlords took advantage of the white racism that limited the options where blacks might live. A study released in 1927 showed that nearly 50 percent of black renters spent over twice the amount of their income on housing than whites. To afford the rent, tenants would sometimes throw rent parties, charging partygoers a small amount of money in order to pay what was owed on the apartment. There were other strategies as well. Harlem families would often sublet one of their rooms to single men or women. Some households even operated a "hot bed" policy in which two lodgers with different work shifts shared the same mattress. In *Home to Harlem*, Jake rents a room at the home of a woman named Ma Lawton, along with a number of other tenants.

Black residents labored at various kinds of jobs after settling in Harlem. Its male residents sometimes found work as longshoremen, unloading and loading cargo on the ships, or as railroad porters or waiters.

> You were going all the time. The work was very hard. You know, you got a bale of cotton on a [hand] truck that weighs six or seven hundred pounds and if you didn't know how to handle it, you flew up in the air and lost your load. Somehow, no matter what you did, the son of a bitch boss was always standing there. . . . No free time. As soon as they got to the pier, bam, right to the gate without even taking off their coats.
>
> (Bailey in Kimeldorf, p. 19)

The average employer got away with treating the dock workers poorly because there was such a large supply of them, which also resulted in their salaries being dismally low. In 1915 New York City dock workers earned between $520 and $624 a year, far less than the annual income of $800 that the U.S. government said was necessary to support the average family.

Harlem's women worked as maids, hairdressers, or in some cases as prostitutes, an occupation pursued by Jake's girlfriend, Felice, in *Home to Harlem*. Other women, like Congo Rose,

another character in the novel, worked as dancers in cabarets. Night life bustled along 125th Street and Lenox Avenue, featuring jazz clubs, cabaret shows, and speakeasies, in which alcohol was illegally served.

Jazz clubs. By 1919 Harlem clubs, cabarets and dance halls were playing jazz music. Four-, five-, or six-piece bands played improvised blues. One of the most famous of the Harlem jazz spots was the Lenox Club on Lenox Avenue (a boundary between black and white areas) at 143rd Street:

> Here [at the Lenox Club] the crowd is usually about 90 per cent colored, and the 7 o'clock whistles that call the faithful back to work on Monday morning find the boys and girls of both races drinking briskly.
>
> (Anderson, p. 169)

LONGSHOREMEN OF NEW YORK

In *Home to Harlem*, Jake returns from the war to take a job he had learned during his military service—working as a longshoreman unloading cargo from ships. He quits the job after learning that he was hired as a strikebreaker. In the real world of New York there was actually a dock workers' walkout in 1919, the year in which the novel is set. New York's longshoremen, whatever their ethnic background (many were white Irish or Italian immigrants) suffered miserable working conditions, maintained Bill Bailey, a longshoreman of the day.

People went to clubs like the Lenox to listen to music, dine, drink, and meet with friends. Musicians performed on the dining room floor, close to where the patrons danced. In *Home to Harlem*, Jake dresses up to go out to Lenox Avenue and drink at the bar, and the character Rose dances with her date at the Congo Club in a way described as "an exercise of rhythmical exactness for two" (McKay, *Home to Harlem*, p. 93).

Harlemites also attended theaters such as the Apollo and Lafayette, which presented black stage shows; midnight performances at the Lafayette included comedy, dance, and music. The era featured movie houses too, at which jazz music was sometimes played between screenings.

The Novel in Focus

The plot. *Home to Harlem* tells the story of a black American soldier in World War I named

Jake Brown, who is assigned not to fight but to unload ships. Described as tall and brawny, Jake returns home to Harlem after deserting his post in Europe. At home, he falls in love with a former prostitute named Felice and goes out with her to nightclubs and cabarets each evening, where the two drink and listen to jazz music.

Jake takes a job as a longshoreman, but after learning that he was hired as a strikebreaker, quits and finds a job as a chef on the Pennsylvania Railroad. On the job, Jake meets and befriends a man named Ray, who works as a waiter.

JAZZ IN HARLEM

Jazz emerged at the end of the nineteenth century, growing out of black American musical traditions and characterized by the musicians' use of solos during the course of songs. As many blacks moved northward and settled in Harlem, they brought their knowledge and experience of jazz with them, playing it in theaters along Broadway Avenue as well as in nightclubs and cabarets. Listeners were greatly excited by the long, intense improvisational solos by members of the various bands, which usually featured drums, piano, bass, and horns. In *Home to Harlem*, Jake listens to jazz at all of the clubs that he frequents and mentions specifically the master jazz player James Reese Europe, who led the 369th Division Band in Paris, then returned to play in Harlem.

Nicknamed the "Professor" by his coworkers, Ray is an avid reader. He has come to the United States from Haiti to attend college but cannot pay his tuition. Ray has therefore taken a job on the railroad to earn money for school; he dreams of becoming a writer someday. While working with Jake, Ray teaches his new friend about history, politics, and literature. The two men live in Harlem for a while. Unlike Jake, Ray rarely drinks or visits nightclubs, choosing instead to read newspapers and novels. When Jake is bedridden because of an illness, Ray nurses him back to health.

Eventually both men become restless with Harlem life. Ray decides to take a job as a seaman on a boat headed to Australia and Europe. Jake, too, leaves Harlem and goes to Chicago after being reunited with his girlfriend, Felice.

Black responses to white racism. Jake and Ray portray two opposite approaches not only to life

in general, but also to the more specific problem of being black in white America. While Jake generally acts on instinct and emotion, Ray shows a preference for ideas and the intellect.

Ray feels frustrated with life, and his frustration makes him question things in a way Jake does not:

> Life burned in Ray perhaps more intensely than in Jake. Ray felt more and his range was wider and he could not be satisfied with the easy, simple things that sufficed for Jake. Sometimes he felt like a tree with roots in the soil and sap flowing out and whispering leaves in the air. But he drank in more of life than he could distill into active animal living. Maybe that was why he felt he had to write.
>
> (*Home to Harlem*, p. 265)

The novel ultimately portrays Jake in more positive terms than Ray. Toward the end of his stay in the city, Ray complains that his "little education" hasn't helped him (*Home to Harlem*, p. 274). On the contrary, it has only made him see the futility of his own dreams. Calling himself a "misfit," Ray identifies Jake as happier of the two. "The more I learn," he muses, "the less I understand and love life" (*Home to Harlem*, p. 274).

Toward the end of the novel, Ray feels drawn to Jake's lifestyle and questions the white education that has robbed him of the ability to act freely. Jake dances, drinks, and goes to the nightclubs lining Lenox Avenue, a free spirit, happily at ease among Harlem's vibrant crowds in a way that escapes Ray. While Jake is uneducated (in fact, he had never encountered an educated black until his friendship with Ray), he is nevertheless generous, patriotic, and ethical. His character is balanced in a way that allows him to get on with the business of living despite life's injustices.

In some ways, the contrasts between these two major characters parallel contrasts between two opposing strands in the history of black responses to white racism. In McKay's time, these two approaches were represented on one hand by the accommodationist philosophy of black educator Booker T. Washington, while another strategy was led by the more militant voice of leading black intellectual W. E. B. Du Bois. The two opposing attitudes could be delineated as either a practical, flexible approach of compromise with white society for the sake of overall progress (Washington), or a contrasting insistent, inflexible response that demanded immediate elimination of racist conditions (Du Bois). Related to this second approach but going beyond it to reject not only racism but life in the United States altogether was the tack followed by Marcus Garvey (and for a while by Claude McKay himself). In McKay's novel, Jake, who builds a life for himself without worrying about injustices, represents the first approach. Ray, whose intellectual preoccupations prevent him from reaching such an easy balance, represents the second, going beyond it as Garvey and McKay did.

Sources. Like his character Ray, Claude McKay was an immigrant from the West Indies who came to America for an education and hoped to become a writer. Born and raised in Jamaica, McKay worked as a farmer and constable before moving to Alabama to study agriculture at the Tuskegee Institute in 1912. Feeling drawn to New York City, where he thought he might better pursue his literary ambitions while finding steady work, McKay moved there two years later. He took various menial jobs, including positions as a longshoreman, a porter, and a waiter—all occupations filled by characters in the novel. McKay obviously used his own experiences to help flesh out his characters and to depict their working experiences realistically. Having lived in Harlem during the period in which his novel is set, he also incorporated his own observations of the area in the story.

James Reese Europe

Events in History at the Time the Novel Was Written

Harlem Renaissance. As increasing numbers of African Americans migrated northward, they began to participate in political activities, which, in turn, led to an acceleration in literary and artistic efforts in Harlem. Claude McKay was the first significant writer of an artistic and literary movement known as the Harlem Renaissance. Created by writers in the movement were works that explored black life and culture, showing and helping to stimulate a new sense of confidence and pride in the African American racial heritage. Though the Harlem Renaissance is often described as beginning in the mid-1920s, it was prefigured during the war years by McKay's 1917 poem "The Harlem Dancer," and by his above-mentioned 1919 sonnet "If We Must Die." McKay's poems were some of the first to speak directly and compassionately of the mass experience of blacks in cities. Other emerging African American poets, novelists, dramatists, and nonfiction writers of the Harlem Renaissance include Langston Hughes, Zora Neale Hurston, Countee Cullen, and James Weldon Johnson.

By the mid-1920s the Harlem Renaissance was in full blossom. Black people and customs were, as the journal *Vanity Fair* pointed out, in vogue at the time. Almost everyone was singing black spirituals or blues. Whites from Park Avenue would spend great sums at Harlem's night clubs, learning from blacks how to dance the Charleston and other popular dances.

Meanwhile, a different focus emerged among a segment of writers within the black community at the time. Some of the younger black intellectuals ran up against members of the older generation, as one historian observes:

> In their apparent break with the aesthetic and cultural attitude of their elders, most of the New Negro writers . . . could be said to represent in art what the race militants had represented in politics—not an appeal to compassion and social redress but a bold assertion of self.
>
> (Anderson, p. 197)

In March of 1925, articles and poems from these young, self-described "New Negro" writers were published in a journal and then in *The New Negro,* an anthology often thought to have launched the Harlem Renaissance. McKay's poems are sometimes described as precursors to the genuine movement. The works of the "New Negro" broke with the genteel style of writing that had been prevalent in black American literature until then.

The Harlem Renaissance would continue through the year the novel was published (1928) until the stock market crash of 1929, which signaled the beginning of the Great Depression in the United States. After this disaster, most people's dire economic circumstances diverted much of their attention from literature and art to their own day-to-day survival.

Communism. A number of blacks involved in the Harlem Renaissance aligned themselves politically with the communist movement, as did many white intellectuals of the era. These blacks hoped to integrate their own goal of racial equality with the communist objective of improving economic conditions for the working class. Like other Americans, blacks were struggling to redefine political and economic goals after World War I. In the midst of that war, radical forces in the Russian Empire were able to overthrow the monarchy and begin the world's first communist state. To many around the world, this peasant and workers' revolution that formed Russia's new order seemed glamorous. It helped focus American attention on a possible alternative to capitalism, which seemed not to be working very well for certain groups, such as the poor and the racially isolated. A group of both black and white Americans—Claude McKay among them—began to look upon communism as a viable solution. Meanwhile, panic set in among other Americans who feared a possible threat to democracy. The United States government initiated an effort to root out communist organizations from its midst in 1919, and the 1920s saw an increase in the general antiradical mood in the country. In this environment, McKay grew increasingly disillusioned with prospects in America. In 1922 he left the country to travel in Russia, Western Europe, and North Africa. *Home to Harlem* was published while he lived in this state of self-imposed exile.

Reception. So stridently was McKay's book condemned by black critics that he was hesitant to return to the United States. Though *Home to Harlem* became a bestseller, it was blasted by many prominent members of the black community for its portrayal of life in Harlem. W. E. B. Du Bois, author, teacher, and founder of the National Association for the Advancement of Colored People (NAACP), accused McKay of portraying blacks in a negative light. Du Bois suggested that McKay was appealing to many whites' racist perceptions of blacks by portraying the drinking, promiscu-

ity, fighting, and absence of restraint in Harlem. According to Du Bois, McKay's portrayal did not convey a true picture of African American life anywhere; in fact, it made him feel as if he needed a bath. McKay, objecting to what he felt was the personal tone of this criticism, responded by questioning Du Bois's aesthetic judgment.

Other black critics charged that McKay's novel betrayed their race and showed a hatred of the black middle class. They feared that white readers would take the seaminess portrayed in the novel as representative of the total scope of black life in Harlem. Critics also found fault with McKay's style of writing, arguing that his prose was formless and unpolished even if his content had merit. "Despite the fact that this book is badly written," one reviewer asserted, "it is both interesting and valuable" (Knight, p. 492). Others who objected to the book's gritty, realistic tone shared this condescending acceptance of its value as a social document but not as a work of art.

Yet from other sources McKay received praise for his novel on artistic grounds. The esteemed British critic Cyril Connolly thought that the book must have been a pleasure to write. "It is hard otherwise to explain the easy charm and assurance that glow upon every chapter" (Connolly in Knight, p. 493). A review in the black journal *Opportunity* lauded the novel for its frankness. In later years, such reactions would be more widely endorsed, and the book's stature would grow. Recent critics have found McKay's portrayal of Harlem positive and affirming of black culture during the 1920s. They defend his work as a lively, realistic reflection of the Harlem experience. Among those who expressed this opinion as early as 1928 was Langston Hughes, who shared his enthusiasm for the work in a letter to the black scholar Alain Locke, a respected leader of the Harlem Renaissance. Telling Locke that *Home to Harlem* was the finest low-life novel he had ever read, Hughes said it should be called "Nigger Hell," then went on to describe it as "the flower of the Negro Renaissance, even if it is no lovely lily" (Hughes in Tillery, p. 88).

For More Information

Anderson, Jervin. *This Was Harlem: A Cultural Portrait, 1900-1950.* New York: Farrar Straus Giroux, 1981.

Cooper, Wayne F. *Claude McKay: Rebel Sojourner in*

the *Harlem Renaissance. A Biography.* Baton
Rouge: Louisiana State University Press, 1987.

Huggins, Nathan Irvin. *Harlem Renaissance.* New
York: Oxford University Press, 1971.

Kimeldorf, Howard. *Reds or Rackets? The Making of
Radical and Conservative Unions on the Waterfront.*
Berkeley: University of California Press, 1988.

Knight, Marion A., et al., eds. *Book Review Digest.*
Vol. 24. New York: H. W. Wilson, 1929.

McKay, Claude. *Home to Harlem.* Boston:
Northeastern University Press, 1987.

Tillery, Tyrone. *Claude McKay: A Black Poet's
Struggle for Identity.* Amherst: The University of
Massachusetts Press, 1992.

The House of Mirth

by

Edith Wharton

Born in New York in 1862 to elderly parents, Edith Wharton was raised in a family replete with socially prominent relatives. Wharton traveled abroad and married during a time of transition for women in America. The urban-based Industrial Revolution brought sweeping social changes in her day, some of which altered women's lives. Although traditional standards of femininity continued to be upheld by the upper classes, the role of women was in flux around the turn of the twentieth century. *House of Mirth,* Wharton's second novel, would deal with the changing status of women around this time. A scathing critique of the "marriage market," the novel also depicts the broad spectrum of social tensions that surfaced as a newly rich class of industrial stockholders penetrated New York City's older, traditional monied aristocracy.

Events in History at the Time of the Novel

Economic growth. Following the American Civil War, the country's economy expanded rapidly, spurred by such inventions as the steam engine, the internal combustion engine, and electricity. Europe was debilitated by civil wars and revolutions and its economic edge was blunted, which further encouraged American growth. As the economic balance in the United States shifted from its farms to its industrial cities, so did many of its people; in 1900, 45 percent of Americans lived in urban centers of various sizes, in con-

---

---

trast to the roughly 20 percent of Americans who lived in cities in 1865. Massive immigration from Europe—estimated to have totaled 35 million people in the fifty years following the Civil War—contributed to the rise of urban populations, including that of New York City, where *The House of Mirth* is set.

Before 1890, most of the city's immigrants were from northern and western Europe, predominantly Ireland and Germany; after 1890, however, people began to stream into the city from eastern and southern Europe. Most were escaping political and social strife in countries like Russia. Predictably, the rapid rise in urban populations brought slums that sprang up to accommodate the immigrants and migrants who formed America's new industrial work force. Most were overcrowded, and unsanitary conditions were common. The percentage of the population living in poverty swelled, and the surplus of unskilled and often illiterate workers kept wages very low. With hordes of people eager to take low-paying jobs in the city, business and factory owners could pay exploitative salaries. Immigrants who spoke little or no English, or single women and even children without other means of support were literally recruited off the street and ushered into factories and textile sweatshops, as dramatized in part 2 of *The House of Mirth*. Dark, overcrowded, and poorly ventilated, these workplaces demanded grueling labor for as much as ninety hours a week at miserably low wages. Meanwhile, members of America's upper class (who had also been immigrants to America, but of an older generation) formed the less than one-tenth of the population that wound up controlling over two-thirds of the nation's wealth.

Trust busters. During the era in which Wharton was writing *The House of Mirth,* some of the upper class's financial standing came as a result of its ability to manipulate assets and profits through trusts. Trusts are business monopolies that draw cash from a group of shareholders, thereby providing capital with which to start up major projects that smaller concerns cannot match. Trusts did help to provide the extensive capital required to launch America's industrial growth at the turn of the century, which significantly raised the standard of living for many Americans. But large trusts could also stifle competition and keep prices artificially inflated.

American president Theodore Roosevelt became aware that public opinion blamed the increasing cost of living on major trusts such as Standard Oil (organized in 1899) and the United States Steel Corporation (1901). In 1902, Roosevelt's government targeted the Northern Securities Company, owned by railway magnate J. P. Morgan, charging that the trust was hindering competition in railway transportation. The case went to the U.S. Supreme Court, whose justices decided in 1904 against Northern Securities; the trust was dissolved as a result. Other major trusts dismantled by Roosevelt's government included the oil trust run by the Rockefellers and the Duke tobacco interest. Roosevelt, who protested all along that he was not interested in bringing down the rich and powerful trusts but rather in regulating American business fairly, was dubbed the "trust buster."

The end of the Victorian age. In 1901 Queen Victoria of England died, marking the end of an era not only in Britain but in America as well. During Victorian times—roughly defined by the queen's reign that began in 1837—women were generally considered the moral and spiritual caretakers of their families; they were expected to leave all financial and material responsibilities to men. The home, regarded as the essential unit of society, was elevated in importance to almost religious heights. If the sanctity of the home was in danger, it was believed, so was society as a whole. Consequently, women remained at home to rule a domestic sphere, which included child-rearing, decorating, and entertaining.

FORTUNES MADE ON WALL STREET

In *The House of Mirth,* Edith Wharton describes the select section of society that built on inherited fortunes by trading corporate stocks on Wall Street. Henry Clews refers to this same group in an article of the period from *Cosmopolitan* magazine: "1901 [was] the year of the greatest activity and excitement in this memorable speculative period . . . the stock market had become largely a field of action for certain heavy and reckless speculators, each of whom had suddenly made many millions by the formation of new trusts and railway combinations" (Clews, pp. 408-09).

However, as the Victorian era came to a close, the sharp distinction between male and female spheres of influence relaxed somewhat, and the home became less and less the exclusive domain of women. Doctors and educators (overwhelmingly male), for example, published manuals offering advice on childbirth and childrearing (formerly the domain of female practitioners) that found its way into the home. Meanwhile, some American women of the late Victorian era gradually experienced greater social freedom outside the home than before. With their fathers and husbands at work every day, women of the leisured classes became the custodians and financial backers of culture at large. They traveled, attended plays and concerts, supported new artists and read new authors, and joined service clubs that agitated for social change. It was also becoming more common for women to join in other previously restricted activities outside of the home; in *The House of Mirth,* Wharton depicts smoking and gambling as socially acceptable for women of the upper classes. Another obvious breach of Victorian standards regarding the sacredness of home and hearth is visible in rising divorce rates,

Edith Wharton smoking in 1905, in defiance of standards of the day.

which climbed from about one in twenty marriages in 1880 to one in ten marriages by 1916.

Women, however, were often unprepared for the newly progressive times, and most were unaware as to how to support themselves financially if need be, or how to protect themselves from being taken advantage of sexually. This lack of knowledge left them in a vulnerable position. At the same time, society placed a continuing emphasis on social respectability and began to focus on romantic love as the foundation of marriage. These factors, combined with the vulnerable position of women, made it vital for a woman to make the right marriage—one that preferably would be both a respectable and a love-filled match. By 1900 more than 90 percent of all American women were married. Remaining single, in most cases, relegated a woman to a life of financial hardship and forced her to live on the fringes of socially acceptable society, as Lily does in *The House of Mirth.*

Women and economics. In its scathing criticism of upper-class wealth and morals, including the milieu's attachment of life-or-death importance to marriage for women, Wharton's *The House of Mirth* reflected some new ideas about women as economic players. In 1898 the American feminist scholar Charlotte Perkins Gilman published an influential book entitled *Women and Economics: A Study of the Economic Relation between Men and Women As a Factor in Social Evolution.* In this work, Gilman shows that the traditional dependence of women upon men is not natural nor even beneficial for women. Rather, in her quest to secure for herself a stable means of support—a husband—a woman must spend her energies in becoming a "super-woman," a beautiful breeder of healthy children and a sexual object for the man who will provide for her. There is not much difference between a wife and a prostitute, concludes Gilman—both trade sex for economic stability. The following year, another important book on women's relationship to financial matters appeared; in *The Theory of the Leisure Class: An Economic Study of Institutions*, Thorstein Veblen examined the tedious job performed by the wives of wealthy men. Rather than filling the most enviable position in society, in reality these women seemed to be only the gorgeous servants of their husbands' success, dressed in costly but imprisoning fashions like corsets and high heels. In essence, their sole role in life was to be a sort of advertisement to their husband's wealth and power.

Women working. By the close of the nineteenth century, Victorian attitudes about gender roles had began to change among the general population. Many men had trouble earning enough to provide for their families by themselves. Only upper- and middle-class couples managed even to approximate the ideal of the man as sole household provider. Working-class families were forced to supplement their income by putting their children and wives to work. Earning power had grown shaky for many middle-class wage earners when American businesses suffered depressions in 1884 and again in 1893. The so-called Panic of 1893 led to the collapse of 16,000 firms and a 20 percent unemployment rate. *The House of Mirth* reveals that Lily's father had suddenly lost his fortune and his job shortly before this second depression.

Single women had been flooding the workplace since roughly 1880. Between 1880 and 1910, five years after Wharton published *The House of Mirth,* the number of women working in America nearly doubled, rising from 14.7 percent to 28.8 percent of the labor force. These women found jobs that tended to reinforce domestic roles—teaching, sewing (as Lily does at one point in *The House of Mirth*), nursing, childcare, and office help for male superiors. With the growth of large enterprises, a few jobs became available to middle-class married women, generally clerical jobs or department store positions. Their numbers, however, were small—in 1900, only 5 percent of married women worked. Indeed, many employers refused to employ married women at all, and expected that their female employees would resign their posts upon marriage.

The Novel in Focus

The plot. *The House of Mirth* takes place in 1901, when Lily Bart is twenty-nine years old, dangerously close to becoming an old maid. Every aspect of Lily's life is marked with uncertainty. Born into the upper class, yet not wealthy herself, Lily struggles to maintain a lifestyle comparable to those of her rich friends and relatives, often living from hand-to-mouth, juggling her bills, and stalling her creditors with occasional allowances from her aunt. An unmarried woman without wealthy parents, Lily has no significant income of her own and her social position is hence unstable.

THE WORKING GIRLS OF NEW YORK

Jacob Riis's influential book *How the Other Half Lives,* published in 1890, increased public awareness of the extreme living and working conditions of the urban poor. The following excerpt closely echoes Lily Bart's fate at the end of *The House of Mirth:* ". . . the community was shocked by the story of a gentle and refined woman who, left in direst poverty to earn her own living alone among strangers, threw herself from her attic window, preferring death to dishonor. 'I would have done any honest work, even to scrubbing,' she wrote, drenched and starving, after a vain search for work in a driving storm. She had tramped the streets for weeks on her weary errand, and the only living wages offered her were the wages of sin" (Riis, p. 177).

Although Lily keeps company with the upper class, her interactions with them often resemble servitude—at one point, for example, she acts as a secretary to the rich matron Judy Trenor. Lily knows that the only way to achieve financial and social stability is to marry a rich man. Though her beauty, grace, and charm have brought her several opportunities to do so, she has chosen to remain single, holding out for a man with sufficient wealth whom she can also respect and love.

Part 1 of the novel opens with Lily meeting three eligible bachelors in succession, each of whom she disqualifies because of wealth, ethnicity, or personality. Still in financial distress,

Lily enlists the aid of a married man, Gus Trenor, to invest her money in speculative Wall Street stocks. But Trenor acts improperly, forcing his companionship on her and later attempting to rape her. As a last resort, Lily appeals to her aunt, Mrs. Peniston, for help in repaying Trenor money she owes him, but the aunt proves unsympathetic. Rosedale, one of the bachelors she earlier rejected, offers his assistance if she would marry him, but Lily refuses. She pins her hopes instead on Selden, one of the other bachelors, who seems to reciprocate her affections.

Part 2 of *The House of Mirth* opens in Monte Carlo. Lily has retreated to Europe, hoping that she can escape from the rumors in New York about her involvement with Trenor. In Europe, Lily lives as a guest of Bertha and George Dorset, accompanying them amidst the whirl of society peopled by European aristocrats and American expatriates. Unfortunately, Lily gets involved in yet another scandal when Bertha Dorset accuses her of making advances toward George. Though innocent of the charge, she is unable to defend herself against Bertha Dorset's social power backed by immense wealth. Lily therefore returns to New York, where she again finds herself socially disgraced because of Bertha's insinuations and through no fault of her own.

Shortly before Lily's arrival in New York, her aunt dies, leaving her just enough inheritance to cover her debt to Gus Trenor. However, because of legal technicalities, her aunt's estate cannot be settled for up to another year. In the meantime, Lily has no home nor even any old friends with whom she might stay. She begins socializing and staying with the "nouveaux riches," the next level down in the New York social hierarchy. For a while this works out, but then Bertha Dorset uses her social influence to have Lily cast out of this group as well. Lily encounters Rosedale, who advises her to blackmail Bertha with the evidence she has of Bertha's love for Selden. Uncomfortable with the idea of lowering herself to Bertha's level, Lily maintains her silence.

Reluctant to room with the spinster Gerty Farish, Lily rents a small room of her own and is forced to work for a living. Never having been trained for any occupation other than marriage, Lily hasn't any marketable skills. Now a member of the working class, Lily gets a job sewing hats in a sweatshop. Her poor work performance soon gets her fired, and she finally decides to follow Rosedale's advice about blackmailing Bertha with the evidence of her love for Selden. On the way to Bertha's house, however, Lily decides to drop

in on Selden. During the visit, she loses her nerve and burns the evidence with which she had planned to blackmail Bertha.

On her way home, Lily runs into Nettie Struther, one of Gerty Farish's charity cases who has since married and had a child. Nettie takes Lily to her apartment, and for the first time in her life, Lily witnesses a home, in the truest sense of the word. After leaving Nettie's apartment, Lily returns to her own room and examines her finances. Unexpectedly a messenger arrives with Lily's inheritance check, allowing Lily to write out her payment to Gus Trenor in full. Lily retires for the evening, and in an effort to ensure a good night's sleep, she increases the dose of sleeping drops that she has become addicted to in the past few months, knowing that she risks death by doing so, but believing the risk is small. By the time Gerty and Selden arrive at her apartment the next morning, Lily is dead. Only then, upon examining Lily's checkbook, letters, and other personal items does Selden realize the truth of Lily's innocence and victimization by society.

Anglo-Saxon ideas. *The House of Mirth* was written at a time in which many in Great Britain and America were obsessed with the idea of the primacy of the Anglo-Saxon race. Individuals in both countries were allied in the vision of white superiority, an idea brought about in part by Britain's declining fortunes in her colonies (specifically India) and by America's confrontation with Spain over primacy in Central and South America. Whiteness (a word interchangeable with "Anglo-Saxon") became a virtue that, for many, signified moral uprightness and the right to rule, as well as an ideal standard of beauty. Read in this way, *The House of Mirth* becomes less a novel about the exploitation of a good—though poor—woman than about the stalwart refusal to the death of a 'lily-white' Anglo-Saxon woman to marry a Jewish man. "The terrible fate escaped in this book, finally, is not marriage, but marriage to a Jew: the union of beautiful, pure, upper-class, Anglo-Saxon Lily Bart to the shiny, Semitic invader" (Ammons, p. 79).

Wharton's novel is filled with references to the Jewishness of Rosedale, Lily's erstwhile suitor, that make use of the racial stereotypes prevalent at the time: he is fat, he is mercantile, he is unscrupulous—Wharton's favorite word to describe him is "glossy." She mentions his "race" and his "blood" throughout the novel, turning him into a representative of an entire people. Wharton was not alone in portraying this kind of anti-Semitism; popular literature and private

Stairway in the Ogden Mills house at Staatsburg, New York, reputed to have suggested the one at Bellomont in *The House of Mirth*.

writings of the period frequently stereotyped Jews as unscrupulous moneylenders or sinisterly powerful international bankers. New York City's Jewish community, small at first, had grown significantly by 1900, and as wealthy Jews tried to enter elite society they often met with overt anti-Semitism.

Though these racist ethnic views were very much a part of turn-of-the-century society, there were signs of a change. From the late 1800s to 1905 a series of pogroms, or massacres, in Russia drove thousands of Jewish people to America's shores, and many of them wound up in New York. In an attempt to draw public attention to the plight of these refugees, a group of established and wealthy American Jews decided to celebrate the 250th anniversary of the date that Jews were given the right to remain in the New York area

---

EDITH WHARTON ON WRITING *THE HOUSE OF MIRTH*

There are certain subjects too shallow to yield anything to the most searching gaze.... [N]ow my problem was how to make use of a subject—fashionable New York—which, of all others, seemed most completely to fall within the condemned category.... In what aspect could a society of irresponsible pleasure-seekers be said to have ... any deeper bearing than the people composing such a society guess? The answer was that a frivolous society can acquire dramatic significance only through what its frivolity destroys. Its tragic implication lies in its power of debasing people and ideals. The answer, in short, was my heroine, Lily Bart (Wharton, *Backward Glance*, pp. 206-07).

---

by the Dutch West Indies Company that then governed the territory. On Thanksgiving Day, 1905, the year in which *The House of Mirth* was published, Carnegie Hall hosted the celebrity-filled event. The gathering was addressed by a former president (Grover Cleveland), the governor of the state, the mayor of New York City, and major religious leaders of all denominations. President Theodore Roosevelt sent a congratulatory letter in which he acknowledged that throughout American history, Jewish people have played a key role in the country's success. It would be wrong to say that such commendations did away with American anti-Semitism, but occasions such as this did attempt to honor the Jewish contribution to American society as a whole.

Sources. *The House of Mirth* was Edith Wharton's second full-length work of fiction. Her first novel, *The Valley of Decision,* was set in eighteenth-century Italy. She was encouraged by Henry James (the author of *Daisy Miller* and other works) to "do New York!" (James, introduction to *The House of Mirth,* p. vii). A well-known novelist by then, he finally persuaded her to write a novel on a subject that she knew firsthand, old New York society. But the tale of Lily Bart may perhaps be connected more strongly to Wharton's own life than to New York society in general. Both Wharton's and Lily's mothers were preoccupied with travel as well as fashion, and both fathers were quiet men who died early when their daughters were only nineteen. Wharton's acknowledged childhood goal was to be "the best dressed woman in New York" (Wharton, *Backward Glance,* p. 20). Her mother encouraged her to be fashionable and to develop expensive tastes, just as the fictional Lily Bart was strongly influenced to do by her mother:

> The tradition of elegance was never abandoned, and when we finally returned to live in New York [in 1872] I shared the excitement caused by the annual arrival of the "trunk from Paris," and the enchantment of seeing one resplendent dress after another shaken out of its tissue paper.
>
> (Wharton, *The House of Mirth,* p. 20)

But Wharton eventually disappointed her mother by failing to fit perfectly into the best of social circles. She broke her engagement to a wealthy socialite because his mother did not approve of her; and when she did marry Teddy Wharton in 1885, it was largely due to her mother's initiative rather than her own. Edith's name was even left off the wedding invitation! The idea of being a pawn to larger social forces, then, was not a foreign one to Wharton.

Reviews. *The House of Mirth* was originally published in 1905 in serial format in *Scribner's Monthly Magazine* from January to November. For the most part, Wharton's book was an instant success with critics and readers alike. One reviewer, praising her "integrity of insight and of workmanship," went on to describe the novel as "an achievement of high importance in American life" (Tuttleton, p. 112). "Mrs. Wharton is the most scholarly and distinctive writer of fiction of the day," raved the *New York Times Book Review,* while the English *Times Literary Supplement* commended her "trenchant knowledge of the human spirit and its curious workings" (Tuttleton, p. 117). There were also less enthusiastic reviews. The *Independent,* for example, speculated that "[w]hat she says will not last, because it is simply the fashionable drawing of ephemeral types and still more ephemeral sentiments" (Tuttleton, p. 110); and in a later issue the same journal suggested that the flaw in Wharton's diatribe against upper-crust New York society was that it was too heavy-handed: "People rise quicker to a hope. To offer a warning is like giving a stone when they ask for bread" (Tuttleton, p. 114).

For More Information

Ammons, Elizabeth. "Edith Wharton and the Issue of Race." In *The Cambridge Companion to Wharton.* Edited by Millicent Bell. Cambridge: Cambridge University Press, 1995.

Clews, Henry. "Wall Street's Wild Speculation: 1900-1904." *Cosmopolitan Magazine* 37 (August 1904): 404-10.

Gilman, Charlotte Perkins. *Women and Economics: A Study of the Economic Relation between Men and Women as a Factor in Social Evolution.* 1898. Reprint. New York: Harper, 1966.

Hertzberg, Arthur. *The Jews in America: Four Centuries of an Uneasy Encounter: A History.* New York: Simon & Schuster, 1991.

May, Elaine Tyler. *Great Expectations: Marriage and Divorce in Post-Victorian America.* Chicago: University of Chicago Press, 1980.

Riis, Jacob. *How the Other Half Lives.* New York: Hill & Wang, 1957.

Tuttleton, James W., et al., eds. *Edith Wharton: The Contemporary Reviews.* Cambridge: Cambridge University Press, 1992.

Veblen, Thorstein. *The Theory of the Leisure Class: An Economic Study of Institutions.* 1899. Reprint. New York: Viking, 1965.

Wharton, Edith. *Backward Glance.* New York: D. Appleton-Century, 1934.

Wharton, Edith. *The House of Mirth.* 1905. Reprint. New York: Bantam, 1986.

The Jungle

by
Upton Sinclair

Upton Beall Sinclair Jr. was born in Baltimore, Maryland, in 1878. The stark contrast between his ancestry, made up of distinguished military officers and aristocrats, and the conditions under which he grew up (his father was an alcoholic) made a lasting imprint on the young Sinclair and laid the groundwork for his focus on socioeconomic disparity in later literary works such as *The Jungle*.

Events in History at the Time of the Novel

The birth of American socialism. From the earliest origins of industrialism, there had always been a sector of people who advocated anticapitalistic strategies of some sort to reduce the misery generated by the nature of industrial society. In Europe, the year 1848 saw the publication of the *Communist Manifesto* as well as political turmoil in several countries that resulted in a rise in immigration to the United States. Many of these newcomers held socialist beliefs, and within time political parties based on Marxist ideology began to appear. The first of genuine importance, the Socialist Labor Party, was formed in 1877 and thrived during the depression years of the mid-1890s.

The origin of the American socialist movement lay not in dogma but in a revolt against the social and economic conditions created by the growth of industrialism in America after the Civil War. The period from 1850 to 1900 saw a fundamental shift in the U.S. economy from agri-

THE LITERARY WORK

A novel set in the stockyards of Chicago at the turn of the twentieth century; first published in the socialist journal *The Appeal to Reason* in serial form in 1905.

SYNOPSIS

Jurgis Rudkus and eleven other Lithuanians are lured to the United States in search of wealth and freedom. What they find instead are unendurable hardships in the wretched stockyards of Chicago. Ultimately Rudkus, his body and spirit defeated, finds salvation in socialism.

culture to industry, resulting in a tremendous concentration of financial power in the hands of fewer people. During this time, the number of factory workers increased tenfold. Large corporations grew prosperous, but their wealth failed to trickle down to the worker, whose real wages dropped behind steadily rising prices. Faced with unsafe, unsanitary, and tenuous working conditions, factory workers lacked both economic and emotional security.

The year 1901 saw the formation of the Socialist Party of America. It was comprised of most of the radical groups outside the Socialist Labor Party, which itself consisted of a small and doctrinaire sect of Marxist purists. Members of the Socialist Party of America, while they embraced many of the ideas contained in the *Communist*

Manifesto, rejected its theories of class struggle and demand for revolution. Sinclair, himself a member of the Socialist Party of America, was no exception; he disapproved of calling for mass rebellion. In *The Jungle,* the path to socialism is presented not as a fierce revolution but as a political transformation achieved through established channels such as strikes and elections.

From the turn of the century up until World War I, the socialist movement gained large numbers of adherents in the United States. Its membership, consisting largely of foreign-born members of the urban working class and native-born American farmers in the West, ballooned from 10,000 in 1901 to 117,984 in 1912. And in the 1912 presidential election, the socialist candidate Eugene Debs garnered nearly 900,000 votes, or about 6 percent of the popular vote.

Sinclair himself became a socialist around the turn of the century. He had been writing adventure stories about a West Point cadet and earning a good living before 1900, when he turned to more serious subjects. In 1900 Sinclair married and started a family, proceeding for the next few years to live a life of abject poverty. He began reading *The Appeal to Reason* and, during the summer of 1904, became an official member of the Socialist Party of America. From that point on, he abandoned the romanticism of his earlier novels in favor of a harder, more ideological style.

American meat-packing. From the earliest colonial era, Americans consumed much more beef, pork, mutton, and other animal flesh than their European counterparts. This was due largely to the abundance of land and animals and to the fact that most Americans lived on farms or in small rural communities, close to sources of livestock and wild game. With the growth of industrialism in the 1800s, more people became concentrated in urban areas. Though they were further removed from a ready supply of meat that existed in the countryside, the city-dwellers still desired a diet of fresh meat. Packed meats became the standard method of satisfying this demand.

During the first half of the nineteenth century, meat-packing was a small-scale enterprise. Merchants, not industrialists, dominated the business. In the 1860s, however, a series of technical innovations changed the meat industry forever. A growing network of railway transportation allowed for greater distribution of the packaged products over a wider range of territory; refrigerator railroad cars, combined with cold-storage warehouses, ensured that fresh meat could be kept available for dense urban populations and for export. Other advances included the better mechanization of slaughtering and packing, and the more comprehensive use of animal by-products—for example, knife and toothbrush handles from the shinbones of cattle and violin strings from the entrails of pigs. Together, all these advances helped transform meat-packing from a modest seasonal industry into a highly organized, year-round operation.

LOOKING BACKWARD

The earliest American socialists were probably influenced less by the writings of Karl Marx—his *Manifesto* and *Das Kapital*—than by Edward Bellamy's *Looking Backward.* Bellamy's book begins in the year 1887. Its hero, Julian West, like the hero in *The Jungle,* is about to marry. Unlike *The Jungle*'s hero, West is wealthy. Still he worries about how local labor struggles might affect his wedding. West falls asleep and wakes up in the year 2000 to find himself in a utopia. Replacing the social classes and fierce competition of the 1800s is a humane, classless society whose citizens live in material comfort and contentment. There is one gigantic trust, owned and operated by the national government, that controls business. Citizens from age twenty-one to forty-five make up the industrial work force.

The other great impetus behind the industrialization of meat-packing was the Civil War. The Union army's enormous demand for packed meats gave industrial meat-packing its real economic start. Government contracts provided the money used by country butchers such as Philip Armour, Gustavus Swift, and Nelson Morris so that they could integrate the different phases of slaughter and packaging. In the process, each of these men enjoyed business success. Independent, small-scale production gave way to large-scale industry as packers built enormous plants for slaughtering livestock and packing the meat; there were also areas for the conversion of animal waste into by-products. The large meat-packing enterprises owned and controlled not only the vast stockyards where livestock was held, but the refrigerator cars and cold storage houses as well. In addition, they had interlocking directorships in banking, railroad, and other corporations tied to their industry. Their businesses, in effect, became monopolies.

The muckrakers. In the first decade of the twentieth century, a group of American journalists caused a national stir with their factual accounts of widespread corruption in society by the forces of monopoly and wealth. These writers were given the name "muckrakers" by Teddy Roosevelt after the character in John Bunyan's *Pilgrim's Progress* who is so intent on raking the filth at his feet that he cannot see the celestial crown offered him in exchange for his muck-rake. While the muckrakers did often resort to sensationalism, they nevertheless were serious about exposing corruption, and most were careful to avoid unsubstantiated charges.

Two important factors contributed to the rise of the muckrakers: first, the increased circulation of the cheap magazines in which they wrote (a rise fueled in part by growing literacy rates); second, and more importantly, the unprecedented expansion of the American economy in the second half of the nineteenth century. The value of manufactured goods grew by nearly four times the rate of the population. Yet amid all this wealth, the urban worker gained little, and in most scenarios his condition worsened, as the cost of goods rose and real wages declined. Upton Sinclair, although never a professional journalist, became the best known of the muckrakers because of the reputation that *The Jungle* earned him.

Packinghouse worker gutting a carcass.

THE GROWTH OF LABOR UNIONS

One indication of growing discontent among the masses was the growth of labor union membership from less than half a million in 1897 to slightly over 2 million in 1904. There were also increasing incidents of violent unrest. In 1877 a walkout against wage reduction by workers of the Baltimore and Ohio Railroad set off a series of riots in many cities across the country, while 1892 saw one of the most violent strikes in U.S. history—the Homestead Strike against the Carnegie Steel Company. Then came mining strikes in the western United States, and the great Pullman strike in Chicago, in which Eugene Debs's American Railway Union battled the railroads, the courts, and federal troops.

Chicago's ethnic makeup. At one point in *The Jungle,* Jurgis Rudkus, a Lithuanian immigrant, becomes involved with a corrupt political machine whose agents find him a job in exchange for his getting voters to support its candidate. Chicago, like New York, was controlled by the boss of such a political machine. His power hinged on being able to capture the votes of poor immigrants, whom he repaid with jobs or maybe money for rent or fuel. He headed an unofficial power structure; he was, in effect, the boss of Chicago's elected mayor. Also unofficial was the welfare system he operated for immigrants, and Chicago had its share of such newcomers. The Lithuanians still constituted a relatively small group when *The Jungle* takes place. In 1900 they ranked sixth in the line-up of Chicago's ethnics, after the Germans, Swedes, Russians, Czechs, and Poles.

The Novel in Focus

The plot. The novel begins with the wedding of Jurgis Rudkus and Ona Lukoszaite, who have emigrated with ten other Lithuanians to the United States in search of a better life. The entire wedding party lives and works in Packingtown, a grisly area of Chicago dominated by the meat-packing industry. Although the wedding is a festive event, a dark shadow is cast over the

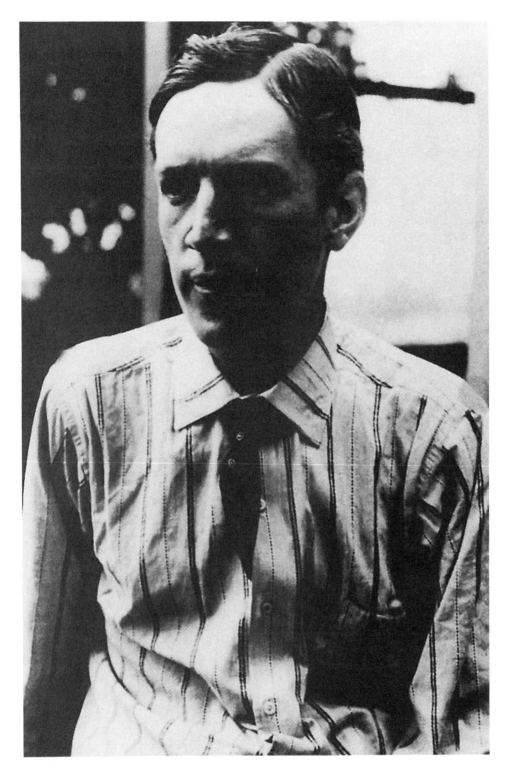

Upton Sinclair

proceedings. According to old-country tradition, the guests are expected to drop a sum of money into a hat to pay for the wedding and to help the newlyweds. Now, instead of contributing their fair share, many of the younger guests slip out without paying, leaving the already poor family with an enormous debt for the liquor bill.

The incident is just one of many misfortunes that befall Jurgis and his group. Their jobs in the meat-packing industry create a situation where their lives are at the mercy of the beef trust. Because he is young and strong, Jurgis finds a job sweeping entrails. Ona sews covers on hams in a similar setting. Their friend Marija paints the cans that will hold the product. Although they at first experience hope for their future and awe at the power of the meat-packing industry, in a short time abusive bosses, wretched working conditions, insufferable winters, and bad luck

---

A CLASS-CONSCIOUS UPBRINGING

Readers of my novels know that I have one favorite theme, the contrast of the social classes; there are characters from both worlds, the rich and the poor, and the plot is contrived to carry you from one to the other. The explanation of this literary phenomenon is that, from the first days I can remember, my life was a series of Cinderella transformations; one night sleeping on a vermin-ridden sofa in a lodging-house, and the next night under silken coverlets in a fashionable home. It was always a question of one thing—whether my father had the money for that week's board.

(Sinclair, *American Outpost*, pp. 12-13)

---

take their toll. Sinclair paints a harrowing picture of the grisly, dangerous, and extremely unsanitary conditions inside the plant. The main characters realize that "nobody rose in Packingtown by doing good work" and that "the great corporation which employed you lied to you, and lied to the whole country; from top to bottom it was nothing but one gigantic lie" (*The Jungle,* pp. 74, 91).

Jurgis finds out that Ona's boss has been forcing himself on her and viciously beats the man. When Jurgis is released from prison for the offense, he discovers that strangers are living in his house and that his family has been evicted. Soon after, Ona, who is terribly ill, dies giving birth to a stillborn child. Jurgis's fortune only worsens; he discovers that he is blacklisted and can no

longer get work in Packingtown. Finally he lands a job at a harvester works plant, but he quickly gets laid off. No sooner does he find another job (this time inside a steel mill) than he comes home to discover that his baby boy Antanas has drowned after falling through the rotting boards that made up the "sidewalk" in front of the home.

The death of Antanas is a turning point for Jurgis. Until now his family has always come first, and for their sake he has made sure to do as told and to abstain from the vices of drink and lechery. But now Jurgis has no family, and he begins to drink. His once-unshakable faith in a hard day's honest work gives way to a new outlook: "he had had enough of them—they had sold him into slavery! Now he was going to be free, to tear off his shackles, to rise up and fight" (*The Jungle,* p. 254). After Jurgis spends the summer wandering around the countryside, winter forces him back to the city. He becomes by turns a beggar, a thief, a political operative, a strikebreaker, and finally a beggar again. One day, while seeking shelter from the cold, he stumbles upon a political rally. Unexpectedly, Jurgis is moved by the speaker's words. The message, he soon learns, has a name: socialism. Jurgis soon joins the party, and it is here that he finds his salvation at last. The novel concludes with a rousing speech by Jurgis, in which he speaks of organizing workers and electing socialist candidates. In conclusion, he voices the battle cry of a generation of exploited workers: "Chicago will be ours!"

Conditions of the workers. As the novel indicates, jobs were extremely difficult to come by in Packingtown around 1900. The unemployed lined up in huge numbers before sunrise in hopes of finding work, especially in the winter, when they were joined by farmhands from rural areas. It helped if a worker had a strong physique like Jurgis, or paid bribe money to her forelady as Ona did. But there was little security in their positions. When Jurgis is injured in *The Jungle,* when Ona finally refuses the sexual advances of her employer, and when Marija's canning factory suddenly closes down, they can only go back to the lineup of would-be workers—or starve.

Workers experienced other kinds of suffering on the job. The work hours were endless. A laborer sometimes had to stay late and do twice the work without receiving a penny more and without voicing any complaint. The alternative was immediate termination. An employer could also "blacklist" a worker by circulating to other business owners his or her name on a list of men or women deemed too troublesome to hire. In any case, the employer had no need to listen to any complaints because for every worker inside there were ten waiting outside to take his or her place. The winter months brought even more suffering. Packing rooms were not heated, and men sometimes had to work all day in animal blood up to their knees.

Sinclair made a special point of enumerating these conditions in *The Jungle*. Through his disclosure of them in the novel, he intended to call the world's attention to the unjust hardships endured by the victims of "wage slavery," a Marxist description for the position of employees who must give up large amounts of their lives just to earn a living wage.

> There were the men in pickle rooms, for instance . . . scarce a one of these that had not some spot of horror on his person. Let a man so much as scrape his finger pushing a truck in the pickle rooms, and he might have a sore that would put him out of the world; all the joints in his fingers might be eaten by the acid, one by one. And as for the . . . men who worked in the tank rooms full of steam, and in some of which there were open vats near the level of the floor, their particular trouble was that they fell into the vats; and when they were fished out, there was never enough of them left to be worth exhibiting—sometimes they would be overlooked for days, till all but the bones of them had gone out to the world as Durham's Pure Beef Lard!
>
> (*The Jungle*, p. 120)

Sources. Sinclair spent seven weeks in the autumn of 1904 researching his novel in the Packingtown district of Chicago, where the stockyard workers had just lost a strike. Although he was an outsider, he interviewed workers, lawyers, doctors, saloonkeepers—anyone who knew anything about the corruption and working conditions in the packing houses. To better collect his evidence, he often toured the meat-packing plants disguised as a worker. In Packingtown he found both his setting and his protagonist, Jurgis Rudkus, who is modeled after a Lithuanian worker he met at a wedding feast.

The meat-packer strike in the novel was based on an actual unsuccessful 1904 strike in Packingtown, and the election that ends the book is a clear reference to socialist candidate Eugene Debs's relative success in the presidential election that same year. Although the paths that led each to socialism differed greatly, Jurgis's victimization and later embrace of socialist ideals give voice to the author's own convictions. *The Appeal to Reason,* the socialist paper that Jurgis

reads, is the very journal in which *The Jungle* was serialized.

The sense of hunger, illness, cold, and fear rendered in the novel, Sinclair later asserted, were parallel to his own experiences of poverty and the bitter cold he and his family had endured one winter. Ona's suffering bears a resemblance to that of Sinclair's wife, who was continually under medical care.

Publication history and response. Three months after conducting his research in the stockyards, Sinclair began serializing his novel in *The Appeal to Reason.* Finally, in February 1906, he succeeded in having it issued in book form by Doubleday, Page, and Company. Before publishing the work, the company sent investigators to Chicago to substantiate Sinclair's portrayal of the beef trust. Macmillan, another publisher, had already rejected the book on the grounds that it was libelous. Doubleday, Page, and Company disagreed.

THE *UNCLE TOM'S CABIN* OF WAGE SLAVERY

In 1905 Jack London, Sinclair's friend and fellow socialist, wrote the following to *The Appeal to Reason:* "Here it is at last! The book we have been waiting for these many years! The 'Uncle Tom's Cabin' of wage slavery! Comrade Sinclair's book, 'The Jungle!' And what 'Uncle Tom's Cabin' did for black slaves, 'The Jungle' has a large chance to do for the wage-slaves of today" (London in Rideout, p. 8).

Sinclair's publisher advertised the novel as an exposé on health violations by the meat-packing industry. This may have subverted Sinclair's original intention, which was to expose the moral outrage of wage slavery, but it also made *The Jungle* a bestseller and its author a world-famous writer. The book can be credited in part for prompting the U.S. Senate to pass the Pure Food and Drug Act of 1906 after, rumor has it, that President Teddy Roosevelt became sickened by reading its account of conditions inside the meat-packing plants.

In the end, the impact of *The Jungle* was as a muckraking novel about unsanitary meat processing rather than a socialist novel about wage slavery. And for Sinclair, whose political convictions ran very deep, this was most certainly a disappointment.

Reviewers acknowledged the powerful effect of *The Jungle,* particularly its description of the horrors of the meat-packing business. A few, however, dismissed it as surely exaggerated and criticized its style. "Mr. Sinclair's indictment of the employing classes would have been more convincing if less hysterical," observed a reviewer for the *Outlook* (Fanning, p. 323). Others complimented the novel for its vividness and anticipated its having a beneficial effect on society. *The Jungle,* predicted one reviewer, "may do some harm; also it will surely do much good" (Fanning, p. 323).

For More Information

Bloodworth, William A. *Upton Sinclair.* Boston: G. K. Hall, 1977.

Chalmers, David Mark. *The Social and Political Ideals of the Muckrakers.* New York: Arno, 1964.

Fanning, Clara Elizabeth. *Book Review Digest.* Vol. 2. Minneapolis: H. W. Wilson, 1906.

Jablonsky, Thomas J. *Pride in the Jungle: Community and Everyday Life in Back of the Yards Chicago.* Baltimore: Johns Hopkins University Press, 1993.

Rideout, Walter B. *The Radical Novel in the United States, 1900-1954: Some Interrelations of Literature and Society.* Cambridge, Mass.: Harvard University Press, 1965.

Shannon, David A. *The Socialist Party of America: A History.* New York: Macmillan, 1955.

Sinclair, Upton. *American Outpost: A Book of Reminiscences.* New York: Farrar & Rinehart, 1932.

Sinclair, Upton. *The Jungle.* New York: Penguin, 1985.

Kim

by
Rudyard Kipling

Born in Bombay, India, of British parents, Rudyard Kipling (1865-1936) spent the first five years of his life with his parents in India before going to England for a proper British education. At seventeen, he returned to India and from 1882 to 1889 pursued a journalistic career in the northern reaches of the country. While working for a British newspaper, Kipling also began to write short works of fiction that were well received. Eventually he departed India for the West, married an American woman, and lived out most of the rest of his life in celebrity in England. The nostalgic novel *Kim* was written while Kipling was recovering from a terrible bout of influenza that nearly killed him and did in fact kill his beloved seven-year-old daughter. Despite its sometimes dark ruminations upon race relations and the charge that it conveys an image of righteous British colonialism, *Kim* is widely considered a masterpiece of children's literature. The novel appeared serially in *McClure's Magazine* (Dec. 1900-Oct. 1901) and in *Cassell's Magazine* (Jan.-Nov. 1901); it was also released in book form in 1901.

Events in History at the Time of the Novel

British India. According to one prominent researcher, there were at one time 225 distinct languages, not including their attendant dialects, in India. Modern counts still put the number at some 212. An ancient crossroads of culture, the Indian subcontinent is home to many different peoples with very different ways of life. These include the Sikhs, the Rajputs, the Bengalis, the Gujaratis, the Marathas, the Brahmins, the

---

THE LITERARY WORK

A novel set in British India around 1900; published in 1901.

SYNOPSIS

A spy thriller as well as a story of a spiritual quest and a coming-of-age tale, *Kim* captures the variety and color of Indian social and political life at the height of the British Empire.

Tamils, the Andhras, the Kannadigas, the Malayalis and the Parsis, among the most prominent groups.

There had been a strong British presence on the Indian subcontinent since the beginning of the seventeenth century, when the East India Company, a British trading conglomerate, set up its first post on India's northwest coast. The Company was to virtually rule India, controlling trade, law and order, and education until 1859, when Queen Victoria proclaimed that India would be governed directly by the British sovereign.

What changed the Company's fortunes in India was the series of events known today as the "Indian Mutiny" or the "First Indian War of Independence." (India would not, in fact, become an independent nation until 1947.) Although the events leading up to the bloodshed were extremely complicated, one of the reasons for the uprising was the suspicion that the British were determined to do away with the most basic Indian social and religious customs and replace them with British ones.

The single event that precipitated the fighting was the arrival from Britain of a new kind of cartridge for the rifles carried by Indian soldiers in the ranks of the East India Company's army. This cartridge demanded a different kind of greasing than the previous model, and the British discovered that a mixture of animal fats worked best. They failed, however, to take into proper account the Hindu taboo against touching any product made from cattle, and the Muslim taboo against pork. While Company officials were careful to specify to British manufacturers of the cartridge-lubricants that only goat or sheep fat was to be used, once subcontractors in India itself began to produce the lubricants, the directions got less precise. A rumor spread that the British purposely used animal fats that would contaminate the Indian soldiers, and the fear of this grew rapidly. A group of eighty-five Indian soldiers at Delhi balked at greasing their rifle cartridges, and were promptly sentenced to ten years in jail for disobedience. Other Indian regiments decried what they saw as an injustice and took up arms against the British. Within days, beginning on May 10, 1857, the British colony at Delhi was butchered in its entirety, including women and children. Soon the violence spread to other parts of the country. The northern city of Lucknow, where the novel's hero, Kim, is sent to a British school, was the scene of a particularly long-drawn-out seige.

> ## THE BENIGHTED OF THE EARTH?
>
> ~
>
> [A]lways in the later nineteenth century an underlying assumption was that the British were a superior nation whose duty was to spread the benefits—material and moral—of trade with them and to propagate their own styles of education, law, and manners to the benighted of the earth, simultaneously making a profit for the imperial metropolis.
>
> (Brown, pp. 103-04)

The Indian uprising was put down within a year, but it was a savage fight, with the British response matching the Indian in terms of atrocities. Sobered by the experience, Britain's Queen Victoria quickly realized how close her empire had come to jeopardizing its significant interests in India and decided she would no longer trust the future of such important trade as spice, tea, cotton, and other natural resources to the management of the East India Company. The Company had significant ties to the British government throughout most of its tenure—for example, the Bank of England had bailed it out of financial troubles, and the Company took pains to institute British law wherever possible in India. But in the aftermath of the mutiny it was relieved of its powers and duties in India, and the government stepped in as the sole official ruler of the subcontinent.

On November 1, 1859, Queen Victoria established the office of the "Viceroy of India," a political appointment subordinate in rank only to the monarch; the creation of this office was intended to demonstrate to the Indian people the high regard and affection of the British Crown for its Indian subjects.

Along with this legislative change came also a certain change in attitude. The events of 1857-1858 had served to increase tension—and racist inclinations—in British-Indian relations. Once, the British had mixed with the Indians around them, often taking Indian wives or mistresses and socializing with the people that they were teaching or commanding. Also the British had filled the ranks of the Company's standing army with Indian men. The new India under the British Crown, in contrast, became much more rigidly segregationist.

The sheer rapidity and scale of the "mutiny" violence had shocked both sides into recognizing that the British presence in India, which had come to dominate the country and people over the past two centuries, resulted in an unnatural, uneasy state of affairs. It was determined by some of the British people living in India that the Indians were a treacherous, untrustworthy, and violent people, a stereotype that gained widespread acceptance in the second half of the nineteenth century. British authorities barred Indians from any real level of power in the administration of India, forbade them to operate artillery in the army until World War I, and strictly regulated their numbers in the army so that there would always be a strong majority of non-Indian soldiers in any area. The British furthermore cloistered themselves in their own communities, staffed by Indian servants who were "kept in their place" by a rigid social code. In *Kim*, for example, an elegant party at a high-ranking British officer's home upon which Kim eavesdrops is attended by only British guests but staffed by Indian cooks, gardeners, and house-attendants.

The Hindu caste system. Indian society in Kipling's day was—and still is to a certain degree—organized by the ancient "caste" system of

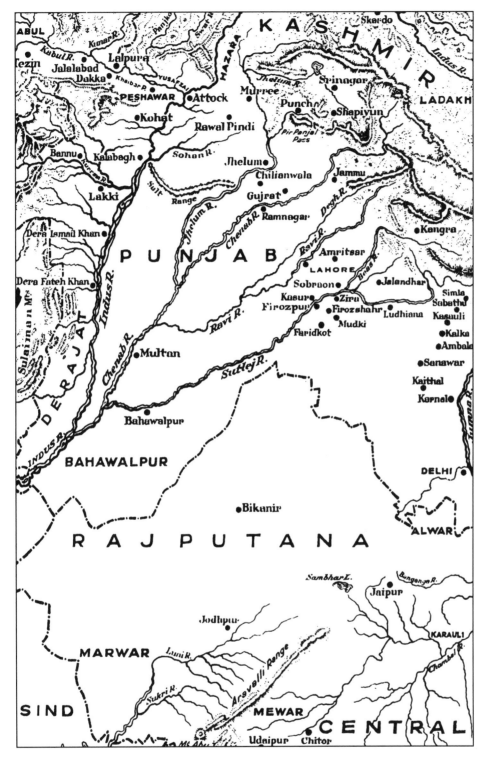

Map of India.

hierarchical, hereditary social classes. People from one caste have little to do with members of other castes; for example, it is forbidden that a person eat food prepared by or touched by a member of a lower caste. Yet caste is actually a component of *Hindu* society, not *Indian* society as such. Hinduism itself is a nebulous concept—it denotes neither a church, nor a religion, but "a body of customs and a body of ideas" (Spear, p. 41) based largely on a sense of shared community; the caste system is one of its distinguishing features. Although the date of Hinduism's origin is unknown, scholars do know that the caste system existed in rudimentary form by 500 B.C.

At the time that Kipling was writing *Kim*, Indian society was still dominated by four classes, or varnas—the priests (*Brahmins*), warriors (*Kshatriyas*), merchants (*Vaishyas*), and the servants or cultivators (*Sudras*, pronounced "shoo'-druhs"). These four groups were then subdivided into an intricate system of caste differentiation. The entire social structure, which endured more or less in its original form until as recently as 150 years ago, can be baffling in its complexity. At various times there have been nearly three thousand different levels of social importance and responsibility that both determined and were determined by one's lineage, occupation, and home. Caste was, of course, passed down through the generations, but there were castes for doctors, writers, leatherworkers, milkmen, and streetcleaners, to name just a few professions. Castes were also formed around geographical location; the Rajput people of the north were traditionally thought of as warriors, for example. A fifth group, known as the "outcasts" or "untouchables," appeared when those outside of the four classes of society, usually members of outlying tribes or conquered peoples, decided to order themselves in the same way as the members of the original four classes. Deprived of any rights, these outcasts were universally despised and abused. The lower one's caste, the fewer one's rights and dignities; even Kim, whose nickname throughout the novel is "Little Friend to all the World," shuns a group of lower-caste travelers that he notices on his journeys in northern India:

> They met a troop of long-haired, strong-scented Sansis with baskets of lizards and other unclean food on their backs, their lean dogs sniffing at their heels. These people kept their own side of the road, moving at a quick, furtive jog-trot, and all other castes gave them ample room; for the Sansi is deep pollution.
>
> (Kipling, *Kim*, p. 86)

The infrastructure. After the opening of the Suez Canal in 1869, the Indian subcontinent was brought into full and rapid contact with the Western world. Meanwhile, within India, the British system of railways and roads was opening the country up to itself. The Grand Trunk Road, for example, along which much of the action of *Kim* takes place, was begun in 1839 and would grow to 1,400 miles in length, linking the northwest frontier to the major cities of Calcutta and Delhi. Before the British arrived, India did not have many roads at all, and those that did exist had been poorly maintained. The British immediately saw that if they were to make full use of India's riches, they were going to have to construct a road system that ensured expedient transportation of raw and manufactured materials from one area to another.

The railway system introduced by the British was even more impressive than the roads and remains a wonder to this day. By 1900, it was carrying 200 million passengers and 46 million tons of freight a year. At the turn of the twentieth century, a combined 25,000 miles of government and private-enterprise tracks crisscrossed the country and employed by far the largest number of laborers in India. These tracks linked the seaports with important inland areas of agricultural production and also forged a link with the outlying, politically significant areas of the country. Neglected by the builders of railroads were southern and central India, while the builders concentrated on the northern reaches of the country. Thanks partly to the perceived threat of Russia's advancing upon India's borders with Afghanistan, the British took greater interest in the northern region. The sheer ingenuity of the engineers who built the tracks that were to crisscross India defies imagination:

> The relatively short run from Bombay to Surat required bridges to be built across eighteen rivers, and some foundations had to be driven 140 feet deep to withstand the torrents of floodwater. When the railway was finally pushed up to Simla, the last 60 miles of track were laid along 103 tunnels blasted through the mountainsides.
>
> (Moorhouse, p. 164)

At the time of their initial development, the railroads were decried as a danger to Indian culture. Critics warned that the railroads would disrupt traditional ways of life and bring different cultures into conflict. As it turned out, the native Indian people took eagerly to the trains, even though the kind of socializing that rail travel necessitated did bring together different castes of people who would never have considered sharing space with one another. "It brought thousands of all castes cheek by jowl in third-class carriages. It did not of course affect the main marriage and other social restrictions, but it encouraged social contact and exchange of ideas" (Spear, pp. 283-84). The train compartment in which Kim and his traveling companion, a Tibetan holy man, ride is filled with people of varying castes, people who would have had no contact with each other outside the railway system.

The Punjab: the final frontier. At the turn of the century, India's northern border with Afghanistan was the most interesting and lucrative part of the country, as far as the British were concerned. This rugged and mountainous region is the geographical area in which *Kim* is set. The educated Indians of the more southern regions, specifically the Hindus from Bengal, were, thanks in part to their excellent Western education, becoming vocal and eloquent opponents of British rule, and were as a result ignored or openly denounced by the British as ungrateful, insurrectionary, or "un-Indian." Because of their education and fluency in English, they were shunned by other Indians who regarded them as quasi-British imperialists. Hurree, the Bengali who in the novel is a British agent, is just such a figure.

In contrast to the southern Bengalis, soldiers from the Punjab, the northwest frontier, had aided the British during the "mutiny," and it was to them that the British now looked with approval—and apprehension. The Russians, whom Kim and his friends encounter at one point in the novel, were also very interested in the province, and were a worrisome threat to the British on two counts. Firstly, the British Crown did not like the idea of another country interfering in its richest and most strategic colony; second, any political success enjoyed by the Russians anywhere in the world at this time was bound to tilt the scales of European power. In the late nineteenth century, the British extended roads, railway lines, and irrigation canals deep into the Punjab, in the hopes of stabilizing their power there. The "Great Game" of spying and counterspying that underlies *Kim* thus had a very real and very high-stakes purpose: British authorities believed that the Russians were plotting an invasion of northern India.

The Indian Civil Service. The Indian Civil Service, or ICS, as it was known, drew the best middle-class British men to it through the promise of adventure, good pay, and perhaps also the idea

that it was a British duty to bring British culture to the Indians. Originally an offshoot of the East India Company, under the British Crown the ICS extended British rule to every corner of India. The Company had established its own British school, Haileybury College in Hertfordshire, England, to train prospective employees in the demanding jobs that the Company required in India. Boys studied a smattering of Oriental languages, as well as more rigorous programs in literature, mathematics, law, history, and politics.

As Britain annexed more and more territory in and around India, the British needed more and more employees to administer the regions, and the numbers soon outdistanced Haileybury's capacity to produce them. The ICS was then thrown open to students at other British universities. Between 1855 and 1859, men from Oxford and Cambridge in England provided the majority of new candidates to the service.

There were three divisions to the ICS: the Executive, the Judicial, and the most desirable and flamboyant of the three, the Indian Political Service, which dealt with external and diplomatic affairs. Attached to this division are many of the characters in *Kim* who ostensibly work for the department of the Indian Survey while actually collecting covert information on people opposed to British rule. For all the excitement and danger of his career as a spy, then, Kim is still a civil servant.

The Novel in Focus

The plot. Young Kimball O'Hara, or Kim, as he is known throughout the novel, is the orphaned son of an Irish sergeant. Kim lives like an Indian street urchin on the streets of Lahore (a city on the northwest frontier of India, just south of Cashmere [Kashmir]). His British blood, however, gives him privilege and self-assurance, and he moves through the city as "Little Friend to all the World," doing exactly as he pleases. His life is forever changed, however, when he meets a strange Tibetan holy man, a Buddhist *lama* or teacher, named Teshoo, with whom he becomes instantly fascinated. Kim vows to accompany the old man in his wanderings throughout India, and the two set out on a great quest for a mystical Indian river in which the old man hopes to rinse away his sins.

Kim's ability to blend with the Indian natives has made him useful to the British Secret Service, for whom he has been an unknowing courier; while the boy intuits that he is transferring secret information to the British from his friend, an Arab horse-trader, he does not realize the extent to which this information is essential to British interests in the area. The "disguise" of being the follower of a holy man allows the boy to slip undetected past enemies of Britain with an incriminating piece of paper that launches a punitive military strike against a potential uprising in the northern part of the country.

Kim envisions a carefree life, traveling with his lama and dabbling occasionally in the low-level espionage that fills him with a sense of self-importance. But a chance encounter with his father's former regiment causes Kim to be handed over to military chaplains in the interests of getting him a British education. Over Kim's horrified protests, the lama concludes that the boy ought to possess the best education that can be found for him and arranges for money to be sent from his Tibetan monastery to achieve this end. News of his "capture" comes to the ears of the high-level British officials who have previously found the boy so useful, and they decide to turn him into one of their operatives. When this is made clear to the lad, Kim grudgingly enters the halls of learning.

Upon his release three years later, Kim resumes his journey with the lama, but also engages in secret spying missions involving political unrest along the northwest frontier. His own quest for self-discovery becomes entangled with the lama's search for enlightenment and with the trade in military secrets that scuttles throughout life in the Punjab. Spiritual enlightenment and political success merge in the novel's famously ambiguous conclusion, in which the lama, who has finally reached his spiritual goal—to leave behind his body and merge with the "Great Soul"—returns to life to help Kim live up to his own spiritual potential.

The Middle Way. Kipling's India was a land of many different belief systems, prominently Hinduism and Islam, but—thanks primarily to the British—Christianity as well. By far the most thoroughly discussed religion in the novel, however, is Buddhism, a belief system that emerged out of Hinduism in the sixth century A.D. The "Middle Way" that Teshoo follows is the spiritual practice of Buddhism. It avoids extremism, aiming to provide a way of life for everyone, not only for priests. The Middle Way counsels moderation in views, resolves, speech, action, living, effort, recollectedness, and meditation. Buddhism declined seriously in India between the first and sixth centuries A.D., although it later gained great popularity abroad in China, Japan, southeast Asia, and Tibet. Although the reason for the Indian decline is uncertain, it may have been related to the preferences of the Indian nobles for Hinduism, which was based on the idea of social hierarchy—a concept Buddhism totally disregarded. Hinduism also did not condemn violence, which Buddhism utterly rejected.

Siddhartha Gautama, the Buddha (which means "enlightened one"), taught that the worldly things that people desired were not real, but an illusion. Attachment to riches, to people, to food or drink, and to all other earthly things, caused human beings to be reborn over and over again into different bodies because they could not give up the world. This chain of reincarnation was expressed in the image of the "Wheel of Life." The drawing that the lama keeps with him and works on throughout the novel is of the Wheel of Life, which plots the six states of man (ranging from gods to demons), the twelve modes of existence (for example, ignorance, sensation, birth, and death) and the three vices of ignorance, anger, and lust. Freedom from the wheel and an end to rebirth comes only with detachment from desires—at this point, one's soul is absorbed into the Great Soul of the universe and one achieves enlightenment or nirvana. Exactly what nirvana is has always been a matter of debate. Scholars dispute whether it means simply final oblivion to the sorrows of life or whether it promises a conscious sense of eternal happiness. Teshoo's transcendent experience, in which, after sitting in contemplation for two days and eating or drinking nothing, he crosses the threshold between life and death, between time and timelessness, suggests the latter:

> [M]y soul went free, and, wheeling like an eagle, saw indeed that there was no Teshoo Lama nor any other soul. As a drop draws to water, so my Soul drew near to the Great Soul which is beyond all things. I saw all Hind [India], from Ceylon in the sea to the Hills. . . . I saw them at one time and in one place; for they were within the Soul. By this I knew the Soul had passed beyond the illusion of Time and Space and of Things. By this I knew that I was free.
> (*Kim*, p. 411)

Because Buddhism taught detachment from the world, it led naturally to monasticism; Teshoo, for example, comes from a monastery in Tibet. Buddhist monasteries, however, are much different from Christian monasteries, in that people can come and go from them as seems proper to them. Teshoo can thus be a Buddhist holy per-

Rudyard Kipling

son without being confined to the space of his monastery, and Buddhist holy people were even expected to wander as he does.

Red bull on a green field. Kim's father was a member of an Irish regiment, the Mavericks, who were on a tour of duty in India as part of the British military exercises there. The standard of this regiment is a red bull on a green background, and the image becomes confusedly entangled with a prophecy about Kim's future. The Indian woman who became Kim's father's mistress after the death of his wife, and who took charge of the boy for a little while, tells him: "[S]ome day . . . there will come for you a great Red Bull on a green field, and the Colonel riding on his tall horse, yes, and . . . nine hundred devils" (*Kim*, p. 3). More than merely a regimental standard, the red bull on the green field also signifies the military presence of the British, whose colonies were always colored red in the green fields of India on maps of the time. But the image is also reminiscent of the Irishness of Kim and his father, of which much is made throughout the novel. Ireland, traditionally associated with the color green, was having its own nationalistic political strife with England at the time Kipling was writing *Kim*; there is almost certainly a pro-Eng-

lish significance to the military image that represents Kim's birthright in the novel. In his introduction to *Kim*, Angus Wilson notes, "It is these two aspects—the wild Irish lad and his taming by working as a British spy that were emphasized by critics and readers in the first forty years after the publication of the novel" (Wilson in *Kipling*, pp. xiv-xv).

Sources. The idea of a novel that featured the secret machinations of the British intelligence network in India first appeared in an unpublished work of Kipling's entitled "Mother Maturin," which concerned the marriage of a poor Irish girl living in Lahore to an upper-class British civil servant and the successful spy ring that they create together. But the most important source for the novel is surely Kipling's own cherished memories of India. *Kim* has been seen by critics as in many ways reflecting Kipling's own childhood, a time that he idealized throughout his life. As a child, the novelist was attended to by an Indian *ayah,* or nanny, and probably spoke an Indian tongue better than English. The story of a little British boy who lives as an Indian native may reflect in certain ways Kipling's own early memories of his first years. The novel opens outside the "Wonder House"—the Lahore Museum, where the holy man goes to meet an English curator who treats him with respect and shows him the impressive collection of Indian artifacts in the museum. The two men recognize each other for lovers of art and knowledge, and through his courteous exchange with the lama, the curator emerges as one of the most honorable characters in the book. The brief sketch of the museum director was modeled after Kipling's father, for a time the curator of the Lahore Museum. He also provided the original illustrations for *Kim's* appearance in book form.

Reviews. When *Kim* first came out, reviewers focused intently on the Irishness of Kim and his father, probably because the turn of the century marked a particularly turbulent time in Irish-English political relations. But, more lastingly, the novel has been studied in terms of its representation of Indian colonialism—the relationships and balance of power between the British ruling class and the Indians in the novel. Perhaps not surprisingly, the reviews have often condemned Kipling's essentially pro-British attitudes. Edmund Wilson, for example, called Kipling a "jingo imperialist" (Wilson in Moorhouse, p. 175). But many critics praise Kipling's sense of adventure, romance and humor, and see in *Kim* both "high literature and . . . perpetual entertainment."

(Bloom, p. 1). Kipling's own opinion of the novel appears in a letter to a friend and editor that announces its completion. "I've done a long leisured asiatic yarn in which there are hardly any Englishmen. It has been a labour of great love and I think it is a bit more temperate and wiser than much of my stuff" (Kipling in Wurgaft, p. 104).

For More Information

Bloom, Harold, ed. *Rudyard Kipling: Modern Critical Views.* New York: Chelsea House, 1987.

Brown, Judith M. *Modern India: The Origins of an Asian Democracy.* The Short Oxford History of the Modern World. 2nd ed. New York: Oxford University Press, 1994.

Kipling, Rudyard. *Kim.* London: Macmillan, 1981.

Moorhouse, Geoffrey. *India Britannica.* New York: Harper & Row, 1983.

Spear, Percival. *India: A Modern History.* Ann Arbor: University of Michigan Press, 1961.

Wurgaft, Lewis D. *The Imperial Imagination: Magic and Myth in Kipling's India.* Middleton, Conn.: Wesleyan University Press, 1983.

The Kitchen God's Wife

by

Amy Tan

Born in Oakland, California, in 1952 to Chinese parents, Amy Tan wrote *The Kitchen God's Wife* to tell the story of her mother, Daisy Tan. The character of Winnie Louie experiences trials and tribulations in pre-Communist China that mirror those suffered by Daisy, who fled to the United States on the last boat from Shanghai in 1949 before the Communist takeover.

THE LITERARY WORK

A novel set predominantly in China from around 1911 to 1949 and set in America around the time of publication; published in 1991.

SYNOPSIS

A mother is forced to reveal the darkest secrets from her past in war-ravaged China to her American daughter.

Events in History at the Time the Novel Takes Place

Dynasties and alien invaders. In the novel the character Winnie Louie presents her daughter with a poignant, richly detailed story of a difficult life in her troubled homeland. She recounts in vivid detail the horrors that her people experienced when the Japanese invaded China. In fact, the Japanese were not the first to try to exploit this vast, lush land with its abundant resources; China's history seems to have been one long struggle against foreign conquerors. Prior to the thirteenth century, China was ruled by a succession of imperialistic dynasties. In 1279 nomadic tribes from the northern land of Mongolia became the first alien invaders to rule the country. In 1368 the Mongols were deposed and native rule was restored by the Ming Dynasty until 1644, when another tribe of foreigners from the north, the Manchus, took over. The Manchus established the last dynasty, the Qing (1644-1912).

Political turmoil (1911-1949). The Revolution of 1911 toppled the Manchu dynasty; in the novel, it causes Winnie Louie's grandfather to commit suicide. Civil War ensued as the Communist Party, formed in 1921 with Mao Zedong (or Tse-Tung) as its leader, jockeyed for power against the nationalist Guomindang (or Kuomintang) rebel group. In 1924 the Guomindang finally aligned itself with the Communist Party during a period of nominal cooperation. Three years later Chiang Kai-shek, who was never very fond of the Communists, assumed leadership of the Guomindang's Central Executive Committee, and the Communist-Guomindang union crumbled. Under the Guomindang's rule, China's doors opened wide to foreign investment and trade, and the merchant class prospered. China's growing wealth sparkled like a jewel across the ocean, enticing the Japanese and adding impetus to their attempt to control the land. The Japanese invaded Manchuria and took over northeast China in 1931. During the ensuing war, the Japanese air campaign showered a blanket of bombs on Shanghai and other major

Chiang Kai-shek

cities that forced citizens to become transients, moving from city to city. Japan formally invaded the rest of China in 1937. By 1942 the Japanese faced certain defeat in China because of the support China was receiving from the U.S. military, so Chiang focused his military resources on battling the Communists. The Liberation War (1946-49) pitted the Guomindang against the Communists and ended with Chiang's—and the Guomindang's—flight to Taiwan, a large island off China's coast then known as Formosa. Fear of a Communist state led many Chinese to desert what did indeed in 1949 become the People's Republic of China. In the novel, Winnie Louie ends up fleeing both the Communists and her abusive husband, Wen Fu.

"The Flying Tigers." A series of violent confrontations had erupted between Japanese citizens of China and Chinese natives well before the Japanese invasion of Manchuria in 1931. The violence sent Chiang Kai-shek to the United States to plead for defensive aid. Wary of becoming embroiled in international conflict, the U.S. government sent an "unofficial" American Air Force mission to China. The American pilots who established the first training school at Hangchow were dismayed to find that success as a

Chinese aviator had depended less on flying skill than on money and political power. In 1937 Chiang coerced Louisiana's legendary pilot Claire Chennault out of retirement to head the "foreign legion," a group of mostly Chinese American men who had little or no experience in military aviation. Chennault had earned his wings in the army in 1918, when aviation was still a new endeavor, and had fought in World War I. At the age of forty-six, having lost much of his hearing, he was forced by the Army Air Corps to retire, after earning a reputation as a tough, chain-smoking, bourbon-drinking fighter with an iron will. Military experts scoffed at the pilots Chennault brought to China to help the Chinese air force, but under Chennault's no-nonsense leadership the American Volunteer Group (AVG) soon emerged as a respectable squadron.

In the novel, Winnie meets Chennault in Hangchow:

> I remember the pilots gave him a good-sounding Chinese name, Shan Nao, which sounded like "Chennault": *shan* as in "lightning," *nao* as in "noisy." Noisy lightning was like the sound of airplanes racing across the sky—zah! And that was why Shan Nao came, to teach the pilots how to fly.
> (Tan, *The Kitchen God's Wife*, p. 165)

The Chinese saw the intimidating image of a shark, complete with sharp, menacing teeth, on the noses of AVG planes and dubbed them "The Flying Tigers." In 1942 the Flying Tigers' destruction of 199 Japanese planes was instrumental in China's victory in its war with Japan.

Superstitions and *daomei* thinking. Many characters in the novel exhibit superstitious thinking called "syncretism"—a form of religion that combines the traditional Eastern philosophies of Taoism, Buddhism, and Confucianism with popular folklore and mythology. The essential aim of syncretism is to master fate; the fundamental belief is that one's actions, even if unintentional, determine whether one is blessed with good luck or cursed with bad. An example is *daomei*—negative thoughts leading to bad events. In the novel, for instance, after Winnie fleetingly imagines Wen Fu dying in the war, he is seriously injured in an accident.

Winnie believes that even the simplest accident, like dropping a pair of scissors, can lead to calamity:

> I remembered what Old Aunt had once said about the bad luck of dropping scissors. I could not remember the reasoning, only the stories: a

woman who lost the sharpness of her mind, a woman whose hair fell out of her head overnight, a woman whose only son poked his eye out with a little twig, and she was so sorry she blinded her own eyes with the same stick. What a terrible thing I had done, dropping my scissors. I called my servant right away and told her to throw those scissors into the lake.

(*The Kitchen God's Wife*, p. 242)

Immediately after dropping her scissors, Winnie gives birth to a stillborn child, which seems to validate her suspicions. Because of Winnie's obsession with *daomei,* her daughter Pearl hesitates to confide in her about a disease; she fears that her mother will somehow blame herself for it.

The Novel in Focus

The plot. *The Kitchen God's Wife* opens in modern-day San Francisco, where Winnie Louie, a Chinese immigrant, runs a small flower shop in Chinatown with her friend Helen. Family obligations—an engagement party and a funeral—bring Winnie's reluctant American daughter, Pearl, to town. At first, the story unfolds through Pearl's narration. Winnie and Pearl have a tense relationship, and Pearl's inner thoughts reveal that Winnie's traditional Chinese superstitions, beliefs, and mannerisms are a source of embarrassment to her American daughter. "Aunt" Helen confronts Pearl at Pearl's cousin's engagement party and drops a bombshell. Convinced that she herself is afflicted with a brain tumor, Helen worries that the weight of Pearl's secret—one that both women have hidden from Winnie for many years—will prevent her from flying to heaven when she dies. If Pearl, who has multiple sclerosis, won't tell Winnie the truth about her condition, Helen will.

The story then shifts to Winnie's narration. Helen blackmails Winnie in the same manner. It becomes clear that Winnie has never told Pearl about the man she married in China decades ago, long before she met Jimmy Louie, Pearl's deceased father. The rest of the novel follows Winnie's story as she tells it to Pearl. She delves deep into the recesses of her dark, troubled past, weaving in rich, occasionally humorous detail her story of a life and country steeped in tradition. Her tale begins in Shanghai in 1911 where Winnie (Jiang Weili), a precocious child, lives what at first appears to be a charmed existence. Her wealthy father, Jiang Sao-yen, owns several factories as well as the large mansion housing Winnie, her doting mother, several servants, and his

other wives. Winnie's luck changes when her beloved mother mysteriously disappears. Her father, wishing to eliminate any reminder of his runaway wife, ships Winnie off to Tsungming Island to live with his brother's family, whose large estate is funded by Winnie's father. No one seems to know what has happened to her mother, but everyone has their theories. Winnie fantasizes that her mother, unhappy in her loveless marriage, has run away with her true love, a Communist revolutionary named Lu, and will someday return to claim her daughter.

Winnie's aunts and uncle, while not outwardly abusive or neglectful, treat her more like a guest than family. Her cousin, Peanut, by contrast, is constantly showered with gifts and praise. Despite the preferential treatment Peanut receives, Winnie doesn't harbor any resentment. Instead, Peanut and Winnie grow into adolescence as two sisters would, sharing everything—even Wen Fu, the man whom Peanut wants to marry.

Winnie and Peanut meet Wen Fu during some New Year's festivities in town, where he performs in a traditional play honoring the "God of the Village." Turning on his actor's charm, Wen Fu playfully flirts with Peanut and buys her presents. Winnie, sensing danger, is not so easily fooled by Wen Fu's charms. After he follows them home and sees their large house and obvious wealth, he begins to court Peanut. When Wen Fu finds out from Auntie Miao, the matchmaker of the village, that Winnie's father subsidizes Peanut's family, the tide of Wen Fu's affections changes course and moves in Winnie's direction.

Winnie's aunts and uncle, eager to marry their niece off, ignore Peanut's expressions of disappointment and gratefully accept the Wen family's proposal of marriage on Winnie's behalf. The family travels to Shanghai to obtain Jiang Sao-yen's blessings. Seeing her father again twelve years after her banishment and exploring her old home stirs a longing in Winnie for family stability. The pending marriage generates more attention for Winnie than she has ever received in her life. Her father treats her as if she has never left and spends a small fortune on treasures, the likes of which Winnie has never known—beautiful hand-carved furniture, silver flatware, dishes, and blankets—for her dowry. Ironically she feels like part of the family just as she is about to leave it.

Swept away by the celebratory rituals, Winnie weds Wen Fu and dreams that she can build a good life with him. In the early years of her marriage, she tries hard to be a good wife, even after Wen Fu starts to physically and verbally abuse her.

Like many other well-to-do young men seeking glory in the fight against the Japanese, Wen Fu joins the air force and moves to Hangchow to be trained by the elite American Volunteer Group. Once in Hangchow, Wen Fu continually criticizes, berates, and even rapes Winnie. Her sole consolation is her friend, Hulan (who later takes the name Helen), whose husband, Jiangao, is Wen Fu's superior.

The two couples end up fleeing across country with the air force base, which keeps moving to evade the Japanese. Wen Fu's abusive behavior escalates with the war, especially after he suffers a head injury in a serious automobile accident. Winnie meets a kind Chinese American man, Jimmy Louie, at a dance. He gives her an American name, and the flicker of attraction between them gives Winnie a taste of the possibility of a better life.

Once the dance is over, however, Winnie goes back to her husband, who hits her for flirting. Wen Fu's flare-ups never abate, even after the birth of his daughter, Yiku, whom he also abuses. Winnie, seven months pregnant with another child, watches Yiku die from a fever when Wen Fu refuses to allow a doctor to treat her. When the new child is born, a son, she names him Danru—"'nonchalance'—a good Buddhist name, as if this baby would never be attached to anything in this life, not even its own mother" (*The Kitchen God's Wife*, p. 268).

After the war, Winnie and Wen Fu move to Shanghai and find out that her father, speechless from a stroke, had pledged allegiance to the Japanese to keep his factories and then, once they were defeated, had lost the bulk of his fortune as punishment for betraying his country. She also discovers that her dowry, intended for Wen Fu and herself to use in their own household, was stolen by Wen Fu's family, who swooped in like vultures and set up camp in her father's house to bilk him of the rest of his money. When Winnie's son dies during an epidemic, her life becomes intolerable. Two chance reunions—with Jimmy Louie and Peanut, who has become a Communist to escape her own terrible marriage—finally give her the courage to change her life.

As Winnie finishes her incredible story, which reveals that she was raped by Wen Fu shortly before leaving China, Pearl reaches the inevitable, disturbing conclusion about who her real father is and gains insight into her strained relationship

Amy Tan

with her mother. Winnie vows to help Pearl fight multiple sclerosis with traditional Chinese medicine, and both women seem to gain a deeper understanding of each other. The surprise ending about Helen's health suggests that a white lie can be a noble gift.

Marriage as a business deal. The traditional Chinese view of marriage had little to do with love or romance.

> You see, Wen Fu decided he really did want to marry Peanut, not because he loved her sincerely—he wanted to marry into her family. And really, he was no different than most men back then. Getting married in those days was like buying real estate.
>
> (*The Kitchen God's Wife*, p. 134)

The importance of the clan, as expressed in Confucian thought, gave rise to the idea of marriage as a business deal that benefits the family, not the individual. Families were tightly knit units in China, and the merging of two families carried far-ranging implications. A rich daughter-in-law was highly prized in traditional Chinese society— the bigger the dowry she brought to her new family, the better. Wives were either "given" by their own family or "taken" by their husband's and, like

Winnie in the novel, had very little choice in the matter. It was the father's duty to approve the match and make sure he was giving his daughter to a good family. As Winnie tells Pearl:

> I found out: My father knew all along the Wen family character was not so good. So by allowing me to marry into the family, he was saying I was not so good either.
>
> (*The Kitchen God's Wife*, p. 150)

Once the woman married into the new family, she assumed the bottom position in the hierarchy. Some men had many wives, and each wife's status in the household depended on how long ago she was married—younger, newer wives had less power than the older ones. The clan operated like a government, with the husband as the chief:

> A lineage community was a society and government unto itself. The rights of family heads over their wives and children—including both the right to punish by banishment or beating and the control of familial property—were recognized by law.
>
> (Lyman, p. 10)

The husband/father had every right in pre-Communist Chinese society to exercise full control over the children and his wives. Before Winnie's marriage, her father advises her, "From now on, you must consider what your husband's opinions are. Yours do not matter so much anymore. Do you understand?" (*The Kitchen God's Wife*, p. 145). Women like Winnie had little recourse when their husbands became abusive. Divorces were difficult to obtain unless both partners willingly agreed to the separation. With the help of a friend who works in a telegram office, Winnie tricks Wen Fu into finally granting her a divorce.

The Kitchen God and his wife. In the beginning of the novel, Winnie presents Pearl with an altar, bequeathed by the recently deceased Auntie Du, dedicated to the Kitchen God. The Kitchen God's origins may go back as far as the eighth century B.C. Also referred to as the "Stove God," the Kitchen God acts as the "policeman" deity. It is believed that he watches the household from his position above the stove and submits a yearly report about each family member's behavior to the supreme deity, who doles out bad luck to anyone who has misbehaved. To ensure a favorable report, the family offers the Kitchen God gifts and burns incense in his honor. When Pearl's husband compares the Kitchen God to Santa Claus, Winnie responds: "He is not like Santa Claus. More like a spy—FBI agent, CIA, Mafia, worse than IRS, that kind of person!" (*The Kitchen God's Wife*, p. 55).

Chinese religion teaches that deities were once mere mortals who became gods only after living virtuous lives on earth. It is thus somewhat unclear why Zhang, the rich farmer who jilted his faithful, dedicated wife Guo, was rewarded with the position of Kitchen God. As Winnie ponders, "Why should I want that kind of person to judge me, a man who cheated his wife? His wife was the good one, not him" (*The Kitchen God's Wife*, p. 55). At the end of the novel, Winnie creates a separate altar for Pearl in honor of the Kitchen God's dedicated wife.

CONFUCIUS: ARCHITECT OF CHINA'S SOCIAL ORDER

Many of China's firm traditions and institutions are rooted in orthodox Confucianism, based on the teachings of Confucius (551–479 b.c.). According to Confucianism, the ideal social structure is a hierarchy in which everyone accepts their designated rights and moral responsibilities according to their position within the hierarchy. The family is regarded as the most important hierarchical unit, because moral and ethical values are passed down from generation to generation. Winnie blames Confucius for the misguided values that led her into a difficult marriage: "I don't know why everyone thought Confucius was so good, so wise. He made everyone look down on someone else, women were the lowest!" (*The Kitchen God's Wife*, p. 103).

Sources. When *The Joy Luck Club* (also covered in *Literature and Its Times*), Amy Tan's first novel, became a huge success, Daisy Tan urged her daughter to write her story. The fictional characters in the *Kitchen God's Wife* thus hark back to real-life counterparts:

Fictional Name	Real-life Source
Winnie Louie	Daisy Tan, Amy Tan's mother
Pearl	Amy Tan
Phil	Amy Tan's husband, Lou DeMattei
Wen Fu	Daisy Tan's abusive husband in China
Jimmy Louie	John Tan, Amy's father
Winnie's mother	Jing-mei, Daisy Tan's mother

The novel diverges from real life, however, in the fate of Winnie's mother. At the beginning of the novel, Winnie's mother takes her daughter to Shanghai for one last day together, then mysteriously disappears. In reality, Amy Tan's actual maternal grandmother Jing-mei was raped and forced to become a concubine. Her life ended tragically—she killed herself by ingesting raw opium that she had placed in her New Year's rice cake.

CHINESE MEDICINE: YIN/YANG IN BALANCE

The fundamental principle of ancient Chinese medicine, the yin/yang doctrine, originated with the Daoist (or Taoist) philosophy as put forth in the *I Jing* (or *I Ching*, or *Book of Changes*). Daoists believe that yin, the female dark element, and yang, the male light element, are complimentary forces present in every being. Unlike Western medicine, with its focus on viruses and bacteria attacking the body from outside of it, the yin/yang doctrine posits that the cause of disease is purely internal. In order to remain healthy, one must possess a balance of yin and yang in every organ; sickness sets in when there is too much of one element. Treatment relies heavily on natural herbs and depends on whether the disease is a "yin condition," such as low blood pressure, or a "yang condition," like high blood pressure.

Events in History at the Time the Novel Was Written

Gaps within the "model minority." According to the U.S. Census, by 1980 Asian Americans had become the nation's best educated and most prosperous minority group, with a median family income that exceeded that of whites. Asian Americans were increasingly referred to as the "Model Minority," a term coined by sociologist William Petersen in his 1966 *New York Times Magazine* article, "Success Story, Japanese American Style." The perception of Asians as more successful, economically and socially, than other minority groups persists to this day and overlooks the fact that within the Asian population wide variations exist.

> The fact is that Chinese Americans are of very different kinds. Chinese Americans themselves draw sharp distinctions: the American-born Chinese (the ABCs) tend to be college-educated, to have middle-class occupations, and to live outside of the inner-city Chinatowns; and the recent immigrants (the FOBs, "fresh off the boat") tend to be poorly educated, deficient in English, to live in Chinatowns, and to ply the low-wage service trades or sweatshop manufacturing enterprises typical of the inner city.
>
> (Daniels, p. 324)

These differences have prompted internal friction, even within the confines of Chinese families, as reflected by Winnie and Pearl's problems in the novel. Winnie is intensely traditional, still clinging to the superstitions and rituals of her homeland, and has trouble accepting her daughter's independent spirit. Pearl barely understands and sometimes scoffs at her mother's ways.

In the end, Winnie gives Pearl a Chinese herbal medication to place on her skin to heal the imbalance she believes is causing Pearl's multiple sclerosis. Pearl's acceptance of this treatment is symbolic—it bridges the cultural and generational gap between herself and her mother.

China today. The Communist leaders of the 1949 revolution, stating their intentions to reform the political system to benefit "the people," implemented massive changes in China's economic and social policies. Under Mao, the government enacted the Marriage Law in 1950, which guarantees everyone the right to choose their own mate. In rural areas, however, the hierarchical familial structure described in *The Kitchen God's Wife* remains virtually untouched by reform. Matchmakers like Auntie Miao in the novel continue to play an important role in arranging marriages, and a woman is still expected to move in with her husband's family rather than setting up a separate household with her husband. Marriage rituals have undergone change in the city, however, where urban dwellers, especially students, are more likely to hold a liberal, western-influenced view of marriage.

Reviews. Tan's best-selling novel *The Joy Luck Club,* published in March of 1989, won high praise from critics. Following up a huge first success is a difficult task for any writer. Some reviewers, such as one in *Newsweek,* argued that Tan failed to show her readers anything new, accusing her of just rehashing the theme of *The Joy Luck Club*—intergenerational tension between Chinese mothers and American daughters (Shapiro, p. 63). Other critics responded well to *The Kitchen God's Wife. The New York Times Book Review* praised Tan's storytelling ability:

> Within the peculiar construction of Amy Tan's second novel is a harrowing, compelling and

at times bitterly humorous tale in which an entire world unfolds in a Tolstoyan tide of event and detail.

(Dew, p. 9)

Paying Tan perhaps the ultimate compliment, a review in *Time* magazine declared that *The Kitchen God's Wife* exceeded the expectations that were raised by her magnificent first novel (Iyer, p. 67).

For More Information

Chen, Jack. *Inside the Cultural Revolution.* New York: Macmillan, 1975.

Ching, Julia. *Chinese Religions.* New York: Orbis, 1993.

Daniels, Roger. *Asian America: Chinese and Japanese in the United States since 1850.* Seattle: University of Washington Press, 1988.

Dew, Robb Forman. "Pangs of an Abandoned Child." Review of *The Kitchen God's Wife,* by Amy Tan. *New York Times Book Review* (June 16, 1991): 9.

Hyatt, Richard. *Chinese Herbal Medicine: An Ancient Art and Modern Healing Science.* New York: Thorsons, 1978.

Iyer, Pico. "The Second Triumph of Amy Tan." Review of *The Kitchen God's Wife,* by Amy Tan. *Time* (June 3, 1991): 67.

Lyman, Stanford. *Chinese Americans.* New York: Random House, 1974.

Shapiro, Laura. "From China with Love." Review of *The Kitchen God's Wife,* by Amy Tan. *Newsweek* (June 14, 1991): 63.

Tan, Amy. *The Kitchen God's Wife.* New York: G.P. Putnam's Sons, 1991.

Whelan, Russell. *The Flying Tigers: The Story of the American Volunteer Group.* New York: Viking, 1943.

Like Water for Chocolate

by

Laura Esquivel

Laura Esquivel grew up in Mexico, where she set her first novel, *Like Water for Chocolate*. Integral to the novel and drawn from her own experience is the relationship between its characters and cooking, a connection that involves the cook, the dishes prepared, and the effect they have on those who consume them. Esquivel explores the ability of cooking and foods to transform people in a story that is intimately connected to the traditional position to which women have been relegated in Mexico and to the technique of magical realism in Latin American writing.

Events in History at the Time the Novel Takes Place

Nineteenth-century women's magazines. The subtitle of *Like Water for Chocolate,* "A Novel in Monthly Installments with Recipes, Romances and Home Remedies," reflects its intent. The novel sets out to parody popular women's magazines of the nineteenth century. Often called "calendars for senoritas," these publications were some of the first literary pieces directed specifically toward women in Mexico. Similar to almanacs, the magazines generally had a moral tone to them, expressing the "proper" role of the female in Mexican society. They consisted of poems, recipes, sewing instructions and household remedies. Many were designed to instruct young girls in the art of becoming a woman.

These magazines also contained serialized fiction, which eventually opened doors for female

authors. Generally the publications did not remain in business very long; two years was an outstanding success.

Some of the magazines were created to further the neglected education of Mexican women. *El Semanario de las Señoritas Mejicanas,* for example, was specifically published as an educational journal, originally divided into sections on the fine arts, physics, literature, and morality. Embroidery patterns soon appeared, however, and the editors eventually added a section on home economics that contained information on household budgeting, hygiene, and articles on the art of cooking. Another successful magazine, *La Semana de las Señoritas Mejicanas,* covered a variety of subjects but carried only a home economics section on a regular basis. Originally filled with translations of French and English works, *La Semana* developed into a magazine that published signed stories, poems, and serialized fiction. It also contained a calendar of historical anniversaries and dispensed advice on almost any subject, including how to keep hands white, how to wash leather gloves, and how to clean pearls and ivory. There were etiquette tips and home remedies, as well as recipes, puzzles, parlor games, and embroidery patterns.

The text of the recipes in these magazines differed from the modern style. The ingredients, for example, were not separated from the cooking instructions. Instead, ingredients and directions were written as a narrative, and sometimes included the author's personal preferences and experiences. Such a style permeates Esquivel's novel, each chapter moving fluidly from recipe directions into the story. Esquivel's novel is also filled with the household hints typical of these nineteenth-century publications, and its romantic, melodramatic plot parallels the type of fiction these magazines produced.

Women in the Mexican Revolution. The Mexican Revolution began in 1910 and lasted for most of the decade. It was a complex struggle that erupted during the rule of Porfirio Díaz. Determined to bring modernity and stability to Mexico, Díaz enacted a series of successful but iron-fisted reforms. He became a dictator who entrenched himself as president by rigging elections, ruling the country from 1877 to 1880 and again from 1884 to 1911. When the moderate candidate Francisco Madero began campaigning for election reform, he attracted enough people to stage an armed uprising, which began in 1910. Unable to quell the insurrection, Díaz fled to Europe in 1911. Madero was elected president but was overthrown in 1913 and replaced by Victoriano Huerta. Four days after being overthrown, Madero was assassinated.

After Madero's fall, rebel armies again sprang up throughout the country in opposition to Huerta. One of the most famous revolutionary leaders was an Indian from southern Mexico named Emiliano Zapata; his followers were known as Zapatistas. In the north, the most famous rebel was the guerrilla fighter Doroteo Arango, better known as Pancho Villa. Villa's forces fought the federal army by staging ambushes, quick strikes and retreats, or sniper-fire volleys. His army became one of the most significant in the revolution.

Women participated in the Mexican Revolution, often accompanying the men to battle sites. The term *soldadera* is sometimes used to describe a woman who followed the army camps. As a matter of policy, the federal army allowed their troops to bring along wives and girlfriends. These women would help the army by roaming the countryside to secure food and supplies such as chicken, beef, and firewood. They would also cook and nurse the wounded. Occasionally, the *soldaderas* even donned a dead soldier's clothing, used his weapon, and joined the fight themselves. Pancho Villa originally had a sizable number of camp followers. Although he eventually determined that they were too burdensome, he accepted them for a time because, as one major put it, "We had to have soldaderas if we wanted to have soldiers" (Fuentes, p. 544).

A NINETEENTH-CENTURY WOMEN'S MAGAZINE

The following excerpt from the preface of an annual called *Calendario de las Senoritas Mejicanas* reveals one male editor's conception regarding the role of women in Mexican society: "And what shall I say of their souls? . . . Here they are not only sentimental, but tender; not only soft, but virtuous. . . . Their passions are seldom tempestuous, and even then they are kindled and extinguished easily; but generally they emit a peaceful light, like the morning star, Venus. Modesty is painted in their eyes, and modesty is the greatest and most irresistible fascination of their souls. In short, the Mexican ladies, by their manifold virtues, are destined to serve as our support whilst we travel through the sad desert of life" (Galván in Calderon de la Barca, p. 16-17).

In the novel, Tita's sister Gertrudis represents another type of woman who fought in the revolution. These female soldiers sometimes dressed in men's garb and carried cartridge belts across the chest, capturing the imagination of the public. They were fewer in number than the *soldaderas,* or camp followers and differed from the followers in several ways. Firstly, most of the female soldiers belonged to a higher social class, and secondly, they set out specifically to fight. They served as spies, messengers, and go-betweens as well as fighters. So directly were these female soldiers involved in the attacks that the army officially recognized them on roster lists, an honor not bestowed on the camp followers.

Many of these women fighters rose through the ranks to become captains. Some, like Gertrudis, even became generals.

Protection in war time. Ranches such as the de la Garzas' in the novel were unsafe during the revolution. Both the federal army and the rebels lived off the land, obtaining food and supplies from the local people. In some instances, the people cooperated. In the south, food was an important link between the Zapatista rebels and some villagers. Women made tortillas, for example, and gave them away as a means of support. In other cases, fighters had to beg, buy, coerce, or steal supplies. Esquivel depicts this dangerous situation when Mama Elena protects her ranch from the revolutionaries. She hides her store of food in the house, and tells the men that they can have what they find outside.

> Laughing, swinging the chicks he was carrying in his hands, the sergeant started toward the door. Mama Elena raised the gun, braced herself against the wall so she wouldn't be knocked to the ground by the kick of the gun, and shot the chickens. Bits of chicken flew in every direction along with the smell of burnt feathers.
> (Esquivel, *Like Water for Chocolate*, p. 90)

Cowed by Mama Elena's deadly aim, the men take only doves for food. As the incident shows, the anarchy of revolution made the times dangerous for women. Some followed the army or became revolutionaries because of their political convictions, but others left home simply because it was safer to be with their menfolk. Unprotected women were often swept away by fighters and returned traumatized the next day to their village. In one instance in a small southern town, more than forty women were carried away in one night. Esquivel's novel portrays such violence against women when the ranch is attacked:

> That night . . . a group of bandits attacked the ranch. They raped Chencha. Mama Elena, trying to defend her honor, suffered a strong blow to her spine and was left a paraplegic, paralyzed from the waist down.
> (*Like Water for Chocolate*, p. 129)

The Novel in Focus

The plot. *Like Water for Chocolate* is narrated by the daughter of Tita's niece. This niece, Esperanza, bequeathed to her daughter Tita's cookbook, the only item to survive in a ranch fire. Her daughter rewrote the cookbook as the story of her great-aunt Tita's love and life. There are

Emiliano Zapata

twelve chapters in *Like Water for Chocolate,* each one bearing the name of a month, from January to December. For every month there is a traditional Mexican recipe, along with how-to and household tips. Each chapter begins with a recipe, telling how to prepare the food; slowly the directions become mingled with the plot.

The story's heroine is Tita, the youngest daughter of the de la Garzas, a middle-class family living in northern Mexico along the Texas border. Tita is very sensitive to onions, a trait she displayed even before she was born. When her mother was pregnant with Tita, she one day began chopping onions in the kitchen. The unborn baby started to cry uncontrollably, and her violent wail brought about an early labor. Tita was born in the kitchen amidst the onions and spices. Mama Elena was unable to nurse her, so instead Nacha, the cook, fed Tita, raising her on nourishing gruels and teaching her the secrets of the kitchen.

The main story begins when Tita is fifteen. She is subject to a family tradition that forbids the youngest daughter to marry. Instead Tita must spend her life caring for her mother, a harsh, stern woman who dominates the family. Thus, when Tita falls madly in love with Pedro, a local youth, and he asks for her hand in marriage, Mama Elena forbids their union. She suggests that Pedro marry Tita's older sister Rosaura, which he agrees to do in order to remain close to Tita.

Mama Elena recognizes Tita's misery but orders her to hide it and never speak to Pedro. In response, Tita expresses her emotions through her cooking, an activity that Mama Elena cannot control. As Tita and Nacha make the cake for Pedro and Rosaura's wedding, Tita cries into the icing. When people eat the wedding cake, they suddenly experience intense longing for lost loves. Nacha dies holding a picture of her own lost fiancé, whom the mother of Mama Elena forbade her to marry. Everybody else vomits on the patio.

Tita's cooking grows more fantastic. A year later, Pedro brings Tita roses to celebrate her first anniversary as the kitchen cook. The roses prick Tita and draw blood. Mama Elena tells Tita to throw them away but Tita cooks them instead. Instructed by the spirit of the dead Nacha, she cooks quails in an exquisite rose petal sauce. Tita's love and passion for Pedro enters him through the food. Struck with burning passion during the meal, Tita's eldest sister Gertrudis takes a shower to cool off. Her body releases so much heat that the water evaporates before it hits her skin, and

the wooden walls of the shower burst into flame. Naked, she runs away from the flames only to be swept up by one of Pancho Villa's captains and carried away on horseback. Gertrudis later becomes a general in the revolutionary army.

Rosaura and Pedro have a baby boy, whom Tita delivers herself. Like Mama Elena, Rosaura is unable to nurse the baby. Tita feeds it, growing to love the baby and feeling like its mother. Since Rosaura spends most of her time in bed, the baby brings Pedro and Tita closer together. Tita is happy and her cooking reflects her mood. For baby Roberto's baptism, she prepares a *mole* (special dish) that leaves the guests feeling euphoric. Suspicious of Tita and Pedro, Mama Elena sends Rosaura, baby Roberto, and Pedro to live with her cousin in San Antonio. Once again, Tita's happiness is dashed. When the baby dies in San Antonio, Tita grows so distraught that she nearly loses her mind.

CURANDEROS

The novel's Morning Light is a *curandera* (masculine *curandero*), the term for a folk or traditional healer in Latino communities. There are many different types of curanderos, and their knowledge and techniques vary. Generally, however, they have a command of traditional medicine that enables them to use herbs and other cures to remedy physical as well as psychological illnesses. Native curanderos were highly esteemed by the Spanish in the early years of their rule of Mexico (1521-1821), and afterward by some of the North Americans who immigrated to the country. In *Like Water for Chocolate* Morning Light, who served as her husband's family doctor, was considered a miracle healer by the North American Anglo community. Her grandson, Dr. Brown, recognizes the efficacy of her cures and wants to prove them scientifically so that they will be generally acceptable to Western society.

Mama Elena sends for Dr. John Brown, ordering him to institutionalize Tita. Instead he takes Tita home and nurses her back to health. Tita refuses to speak and spends many hours staring out the window. She silently passes time with an elderly Indian woman with long braids who resembles Nacha. The woman cooks for Tita and they form a strong bond even though they never exchange words. Tita later discovers that this mysterious woman is the ghost of Dr.

Brown's grandmother, a Kikapu Indian named Morning Light who died years before yet reappears to care for Tita. A traditional curer, Morning Light was the family doctor. She had her own small laboratory in which John Brown spent his boyhood days with her. As a grown doctor, he realizes the value of her knowledge and spends his time trying to scientifically prove her cures. Dr. Brown falls in love with Tita during her stay, and she slowly recovers her sanity with the help of his warmth, security, and positive feeling.

Although Mama Elena and Tita have vowed never to speak to each other, Tita returns to the ranch when Mama Elena falls ill. Convinced that Tita is poisoning her, Mama Elena eventually dies, but her ghost continues to haunt Tita. Rosaura and Pedro return for the funeral and decide to stay at the ranch permanently.

Tita decides to marry Dr. Brown. Furiously jealous, Pedro begs her not to marry. As Rosaura mysteriously grows fat and flatulent, Tita and Pedro begin having an affair. Tita realizes that she cannot marry Dr. Brown even though she cares for him deeply. When Tita thinks she is pregnant, Mama Elena's ghost threatens to curse the child. Only when Tita absolutely rejects her mother's ghost does the apparition disappear. Finally Tita is free.

Rosaura gives birth to a daughter named Esperanza. Despite Pedro and Tita's affair, she refuses to grant Pedro a divorce. She plans to stay married to keep up appearances. Moreover, she intends to follow the oppressive family custom. Esperanza will never marry but will care for Rosaura until she dies. Infuriated, Tita vows to free Esperanza.

Rosaura eventually dies of digestive problems, liberating Esperanza to marry Dr. John Brown's son, Alex. On the day of the wedding, Pedro finally asks Tita for her hand in marriage, twenty-two years after their first romantic exchange. Tita prepares chiles in walnut sauce for the wedding guests, and the dish has an effect similar to the quails in rose petal sauce. The wedding guests soon disperse to more romantic and secluded spots, and Tita and Pedro are finally alone. Together at last, they die from passion and happiness. The flames of their love ignite the ranch, which burns to the ground and continues burning for several weeks. The only thing that survives is Tita's cookbook, which Esperanza later discovers and passes on to her daughter.

Women in Mexico in the early 1900s. Central to the book is the fact that Tita chafes against an oppressive family tradition in which she is for-

Laura Esquivel

bidden to marry but must care for her mother until she dies. In the face of tradition, she is expected to sacrifice her own happiness and well-being for others. Such self-sacrifice was often expected of Mexican women at the time.

According to the dictates of society, becoming a wife and mother was the ultimate expression of a woman's true nature. Her duty was to instill morality and stability into society by establishing a warm, secure, and loving home of her own. But Tita is also subject to a family tradition of the youngest daughter caring for her mother, and therefore cannot establish such a home. Tita finally breaks out of this double bind, but in doing so she behaves contrary to the feminine ideal. Women are supposed to be self-sacrificing, obedient, and modest, but Tita rebels against her mother's wishes and pursues a relationship with the man she loves.

Tita's revolt takes place largely within a traditional female sphere—cooking.

Other females defy gender roles in less traditional ways. The de la Garza ranch lacks a male patriarch; instead Mama Elena runs the place. Domineering, unforgiving, and cold, she displays attributes regarded as decidedly unfeminine. Gertrudis too displays aggressive, masculine-type behavior. She first finds sexual freedom when she rides off with one of Pancho Villa's soldiers, and later not only joins Pancho Villa's revolutionaries but rises to the rank of general. The different female characters suggest that within limits Mexican women of the early 1900s behaved in various ways despite the feminine ideal.

Marianismo. Historians have pointed out that *machismo*—a centuries-old standard of behavior that governs the lives of many Latin American males—has long regulated the way in which families on the continent are organized. According to this ethic, the man is the unchallenged head of the household, with the women—wives, mothers, daughters, and sisters—obedient to his wishes and obligated to maintain absolute decorum in their personal lives. Any suggestion of dishonor on the part of a woman promises to bring shame to her entire family, and can harm the business and social life of the male. The male, on the other hand, is expected to be sexually experienced.

Corresponding to machismo is a code to govern the lives of Latino women. Called *marianismo,* this code is based on the model of Christianity's Virgin Mary, and it prescribes how a woman should behave on a daily basis:

> Among the characteristics of this ideal are semidivinity, moral superiority, and spiritual strength. This spiritual strength engenders . . . an infinite capacity for humility and sacrifice. No self-denial is too great for the Latin American woman.
>
> (Stevens in Yeager, p. 3)

In Esquivel's novel, the long-suffering Tita embodies almost perfectly the behavioral standards of *marianismo.* She cooks the wedding supper for her sister and her own lover, and at the expense of her own happiness she agrees to serve her mother for the duration of the old lady's life. She even nurses her newborn nephew when her sister is too sick to do so. Throughout her life, she sublimates her own sexual desires in the traditional chore of cooking for her family. But Tita also undermines this behavior by investing her cooking with all of the emotions that she is supposed to have suppressed. Desire, bitterness, and love are invisible ingredients in the recipes she prepares at the stove. In the end, when Tita and Pedro consummate their love and set things on fire all around them, the *marianismo* literally explodes.

Sources. The title of the book *Like Water for Chocolate* stems from a Mexican saying. According to Esquivel, early Mexicans drank hot chocolate with water instead of milk. People added chocolate just before the water came to a boil. The expression refers to somebody about to explode or boil, although whether from passion or anger is unclear.

To Esquivel, the book's focus on the art of cooking mirrors her own background. She remembers her grandmother and her mother's kitchens as having specific smells. In the author's kitchen, "mostly what you can smell is garlic, definitely, and onion, of course, also lots of very aromatic herbs and fruit" (Esquivel in Loewenstein, p. 605). The recipes found in the book are actual traditional recipes from all over Mexico.

Other parts of the book also stem from Esquivel's own experience. There were not any *curanderos,* or healers, in Esquivel's family, but she knew a curandera when she was growing up. Many people ask Esquivel whether or not the oppressive de la Garza family tradition of the youngest daughter becoming the mother's caretaker is drawn from real life. In fact, it is not; she made up the tradition when creating the story.

Esquivel describes herself as a vegetarian, gypsy-like hippie who liked to meditate during the 1960s and 1970s. She protested rules that she thought unfair to women. "We weren't allowed to wear pants in school, so we fought to be able to wear them. And we thought that was change. But, I tell you, in all of that I did sometimes forget some essential elements and that's when I had to rediscover all that was happening in the home. . . . [I]t was my own experiences that I wanted to transmit when I wrote *Like Water for Chocolate*" (Esquivel in Loewenstein, p. 603).

Events in History at the Time the Novel Was Written

Changing roles of women in Mexico. The 1910 Mexican Revolution was about government reform and redistribution of land to the masses—and to many men and women in the movement (the large radical left), it was also about a general restructuring of society to more fully include women in the public sphere. One of the main goals of many revolutionaries was the creation of a new constitution. In 1916, seven hundred Mexican women attended the first Feminist Congress. The group wanted reform of the 1884 Civil Code, which denied women the right to act independently of the male leader of a household in almost everything, even in questions of inheritance and child guardianship. The Feminist Congress discussed women's right to vote, education, and the holding of public office, hoping to influence the new constitution. The Congress was successful on limited counts. When the Revolutionary Constitution was drafted in 1917, women were granted (under the law of family relations) the right to draw up contracts, the right to take part in legal suits, and equal authority over children and household finances. In 1953 Mexican women finally gained the right to vote. They went on to break other barriers, becoming active in politics and deeply involved in grassroots causes, though they have not yet been elected to office in significant numbers.

The feminism of Mexican and Chicana women has differed in certain ways from that of women in mainstream America. It is important to note that in the novel Tita does not devalue her domestic work; rather she elevates it above the ordinary, an approach that is in tune with Chicana feminist ideology of the late 1900s. In the United States, feminism has sometimes been perceived as denigrating the traditional role of women within the home, suggesting that real equality and self-worth can be found only in the workplace. In Mexican and Chicana culture, however, feminism has aimed to improve the lives of women without jeopardizing traditional family structures. As one critic observes, the new ideal of womanhood espoused by the Chicana women's movement is one in which the woman "respects men, the family, and the home but combines this with better opportunities for work outside the home and active social and political commitment to the larger Mexicano community" (Melville, p. 106).

Magical realism. The term "magical realism" is difficult to define. First used by the German art critic Franz Roh in 1925, it described a manner of painting that "was not a mixture of reality and fantasy but a way to uncover the mystery hidden in ordinary objects" (Spindler, p. 75). The term soon spread through Latin America and came to describe a variety of fictional techniques.

In the latter half of the twentieth century, magical realism is associated with such noted Latin American authors as Louis Borges, Gabriel García Márquez and Isabel Allende. In their writings, these authors present the supernatural as a part of normal, everyday life. Fantastic, magical elements are an integral aspect of their stories, often accompanied by violence, exaggeration, and other literary devices. *Like Water for Chocolate* incorporates magical realism in its many fantastic plot episodes. Moreover, the magic is presented within a female context: all of the magical characteristics have to do with women and

women's activities. Most obviously, Tita's cooking has the power to ignite lust, euphoria, and a plethora of other emotions in her guests.

Reviews. *Like Water for Chocolate* was an instant success in both Mexico and the United States. It was the third best-selling book in Mexico in 1989, and the English version appeared on the *New York Times* bestseller list in 1993.

There were some critics, such as Antonio Marquet, who found fault with the novel. Marquet stated that the book was immature, adding that a beautiful heroine and large amounts of suffering added up to a recipe for a bestseller, but not a great work. Most reviewers, however, received the book with an enthusiasm that equaled that of the public, as demonstrated by scholar Andrea Lockett's assessment:

> Each mouth-watering traditional recipe is skillfully worked into the intelligent, erotic, and page-turning narrative that is part of the best tradition of magical realism, but with a rare focus on a family of women. The book illustrates the function of food as legacy and communal memory by conveying oral history through fragrance and flavor.
>
> (Lockett, p. 42)

For More Information

Calderon de la Barca, Fanny. [Untitled article.] In *Women in Latin American History: Their Lives and Views.* Edited by June E. Hahnes. Los Angeles: UCLA Latin American Center Publications, 1980.

Esquivel, Laura. *Like Water for Chocolate.* Translated by Carol Christensen and Thomas Christensen. New York: Doubleday, 1992.

Fuentes, Andres Resendez. "Battleground Women: Soldaderas and Female Soldiers in the Mexican Revolution." *The Americas,* 51, no. 4 (1995).

Lockett, Andrea. *Belles Lettres* 8, no. 3 (1993).

Loewenstein, Claudia. "Revolución Interior al Exterior." *Southwest Review* 79, no. 4 (1994).

Macias, Anna. *Against All Odds: The Feminist Movement in Mexico to 1940.* Westport, Conn.: Greenwood, 1982.

Melville, Margarita B., ed. *Twice a Minority: Mexican American Women.* St. Louis: C. V. Mosby, 1980.

Perrone, Bobette, H. Henrietta Stockel, and Victoria Krueger. *Medicine Women, Curanderas, and Women Doctors.* Norman: University of Oklahoma Press, 1989.

Spindler, William. "Magic Realism: A Typology." *Forum for Modern Language Studies* 39, no. 1 (1993).

Yeager, Gertrude M., ed. *Confronting Change, Challenging Tradition: Women in Latin American History.* Wilmington, Del.: Scholarly Resources, 1994.

The Little Foxes

by
Lillian Hellman

A dramatist, screenwriter, and political agitator, Lillian Hellman was born in New Orleans in 1906 and became one of the nation's most prominent playwrights. Her best work engages the political and sociological questions of the time, from strike-breaking to the power of a well-wrought lie. Her most famous work, *The Little Foxes* has sometimes been seen as a socialist drama that offers a scathing critique of American capitalism. Portraying a well-bred Southern family that tears itself apart because of money, Hellman's play delivers an eloquent condemnation of racial and class discrimination, and of the dehumanizing effects of greed.

THE LITERARY WORK

A three-act play, set in the Deep South in the spring of 1900; first produced in New York City on February 15, 1939.

SYNOPSIS

Greed, exploitation, and revenge consume a wealthy Southern family.

Events in History at the Time the Play Takes Place

The New South. *The Little Foxes* takes place in what is often referred to as "the New South"— ideally, an American South that emerged from the Civil War reborn, free of its rural poverty, its racial prejudices, its economic disparities. In the popular imagination, the South as a region was thought of both before and after the war as a culture of "gracious living, leisure, indolence, 'culture', easy, open manners, noblesse oblige" (Smith, *The Rise of Industrial America*, p. 829). But the New South was different than the Old: for one, it had to face the most contentious postwar issue, the status of the newly freed slaves. The specter of the free and equal black person seemed to send racial prejudice to new heights, and, to be fair, not just in the South.

Meanwhile, industrialization increased significantly in the South, particularly in the number of cotton mills that were constructed. Much of the population nevertheless remained desperately poor, and ex-slaves were treated as they always had been, in some cases even more miserably. What had changed in the South, however, was the rise of a new class of Southern businessmen, determined to bring to the South the same level of economic prosperity that the North enjoyed. Of such a class are the main characters of *The Little Foxes,* a wealthy, nonaristocratic family determined to use whatever means necessary—including in this case exploitation of poor laborers as well as of the broken aristocracy—to achieve their goal. And, like many Southern entrepreneurs at the time, the play's Hubbard family allies itself with Northern capital.

Cotton battles. *The Little Foxes* is set in the spring of 1900, a time during which the American North and South were negotiating a truce in their enduring economic and social battle over cotton, a product upon which both economies relied heavily. Both New England and the Southern states produced cotton fabric—the North a rough material, the South a more refined product. The North sold its wares primarily to other Americans, a market it shared with the South, but the South also exported its product, especially to China and Manchuria.

THE IMPACT OF TIME ON THE BLACK CHARACTERS

The Little Foxes was revived in 1967 for a run at the Lincoln Center in Washington, D.C.; while Hellman was generally satisfied with the job that her director, Mike Nichols, did, in a 1968 interview she confessed to having one bone of contention with him:

"We had one minor, and I think rather interesting, problem.... There are two negro servants in *Little Foxes*.... One is a very fine lady who is one of the few so-called good people in the play, the other one's a rather foolish sort of semi-butler.... They were played, as rather conscious present-day negroes, conscious of mocking white people, conscious that white people were their enemies. I did not want this. This seemed to me an historical untruth. He says now that he's sorry he did it. I, in turn, have come to think perhaps it was wise to do it, that it might have added something to the play" (Hellman in Bryer, p. 123).

In the immediate background to *The Little Foxes* lie decades of legislative battles waged over Southern labor practices. The cotton trade caused tensions between North and South both before and after the Civil War because Southern cotton mills were able to take advantage of cheaper labor and relatively little governmental interference in such matters as wages and working hours, and therefore could produce textiles at a low price that the Northern cotton mills could not match. In 1883, a New Hampshire senator by the name of Henry Blair tried to equalize the working conditions throughout the country by sponsoring a bill designed to ensure that Southern workers received the same quality and quantity of education as their Northern counterparts: "The labor of the South is cheap because it is ignorant. Make it intelligent and it will get what it is worth" (Blair in Hearden, p. 95). Inspired more by economics than by a humanitarian impulse to improve the lot of illiterate and exploited Southerners, Blair was one of a number of Northern politicians who did what they could to make Southern labor costs rise.

In 1898, two years before Hellman's play is set, America was emerging from a depression, which had adversely affected industry throughout the nation, but especially weakened Northern manufacturing. The depression had practically killed the domestic demand for cotton, and in the North, wages at cotton mills, as elsewhere, plummeted. The laborers began to agitate for better money and working conditions (something that Hellman alludes to in her play), and Northern business concerns were annoyed that the Southern cotton manufacturers, who were less reliant on domestic cotton sales because of their strong trade ties to the Far East, were managing to stay afloat during the hard times that affected everyone else.

Also in 1898, Massachusetts congressman W. C. Lovering tried to have the U.S. Constitution revised so that the federal government could unilaterally impose legislation upon all states. Lovering's intention was to regulate the number of hours per week that a worker could be kept on the job. In the eyes of employers, there was so much competition in cotton manufacturing and the margin of profit was so slim that a few extra hours of labor in a week meant the difference between a profit and a loss. Many of the Southern employers either used black labor at grossly reduced wages, or threatened their white workers with replacement by a black worker if they should protest their working conditions. Black Americans, it was felt, would work for scant wages and under conditions that white workers might be unwilling to tolerate. Despite the North-South competition in cotton, Lovering's bill was quashed.

By the time that *The Little Foxes* takes place, in the spring of 1900, the competition had quieted. Northern business interests came to realize that it was a waste of time and resources to battle the Southern cotton industry. They decided instead that it was in the national interest to work together in order to compete with European powers. Besides, a successful foreign trade on the part of cotton mills in the South left the domestic market more open to Northern manufacturers. The South's strong economic ties with China and Manchuria were therefore encouraged to an even greater extent than before. New cotton mills sprang up all over the Southern states in expectation of increased trade with Asia, and both Northern and Southern money was poured into these Southern mills, a development captured in *The Little Foxes.*

The Boxer Rebellion. Events in China, however, spoiled American plans for economic expansion in the Far East. At the turn of the twentieth century, European empires—Russia, Germany, and Britain—began to assert themselves more forcefully as trading powers with the Far East, and American mills started to feel the pinch. In 1899, the cloth trade in China brought Americans some $10 million; the following year, the year in which Hellman's play is set, that sum had dwindled by half, to just over $5 million. These figures were also affected dramatically by the outbreak of the Boxer Rebellion (1898-1900), a violent uprising in China instigated by Chinese nationalists at odds with the increasing foreign presence and dominance of their country. In addition to the hundreds of Chinese people killed in this rebellion, at least two hundred foreign nationals and Christian missionaries were murdered. Trade routes used by the British, Japanese, Russians, Americans, and French to ship products to and from China were jeopardized. In response, an eight-nation military force intervened and enforced order. The Chinese insurrectionists capitulated in the fall of 1901, and trade more or less went back to normal for a time. The resumption of Chinese trade, however, occurred after the time period in which the play is set. Thus, just a few short months after they initiated their plans to build a Southern cotton mill, the economic ambitions of the play's Hubbard brothers and their sister Regina might have been thwarted, at least temporarily, by events that took place half a world away.

The Play in Focus

The plot. A play in three acts, *The Little Foxes* is set in the living room of Regina and Horace Giddens. As the curtain rises, the Giddens' black domestic help, Addie and Cal, are putting the finishing touches on an important social and business gathering set for that night to be hosted by Regina and attended by her brothers, Ben and Oscar Hubbard; Oscar's nervous wife, Birdie; their son, Leo; and Regina's young daughter, Alexandra. Their honored guest for the evening is William Marshall, a wealthy businessman from Chicago, with whom Regina and her brothers hope to make a deal concerning the building of a cotton mill in their hometown. The final deal involves a partnership among Ben, Oscar, and Regina's absent husband, Horace,

who is recuperating from a serious illness in a Baltimore hospital.

Together, the Hubbard interest (the two brothers and Regina) will put up $225,000, giving them a controlling 51 percent interest in the new Hubbard Sons and Marshall cotton mill company. Just how that Hubbard quarter of a million dollars is to be parceled out—who will contribute how much—is the central tension in *The Little Foxes,* giving Regina and her family the chance to play for the personal stakes of power and revenge that a lifetime of family conflict has brought about. Regina's share is to come from her husband, the ailing Horace, because she herself has no money; her father left the family fortune to her brothers, Oscar and Ben, and none at all to her.

GOOD STUDENT

While preparing to write *The Little Foxes,* Hellman compiled a research book on Southern culture at the turn of the century, familiarizing herself on everything from typical architecture and interior design to popular music, fashion, even garden layouts. While very little of this specific information made its way into the final version of the play, Hellman confided that the knowledge she gained while compiling her 108-page information project gave her the confidence to undertake the play.

The problem is that Horace and Regina are not exactly the happiest of married couples. His absence in Baltimore—where he is a patient at Johns Hopkins Hospital—seems as much a matter of escaping her as of seeking the finest medical aid for his sickness. Regina's brothers use her uncertainty about Horace's willingness to invest money in the cotton mill to their advantage, suggesting that they might find another partner, and attempting to do her out of an equal opportunity to profit through investment in the deal with Marshall. Regina, however, is their intellectual equal, and manages to bargain her way—using Horace's money—into a position of power, in part by using her daughter, Alexandra, as a bartering chip, offering to marry her to Oscar's son, Leo (whom Alexandra detests), in exchange for greater immediate personal profit.

Her brothers, however, remind Regina that she and Horace are suffering from marital problems and suggest that Horace won't do anything

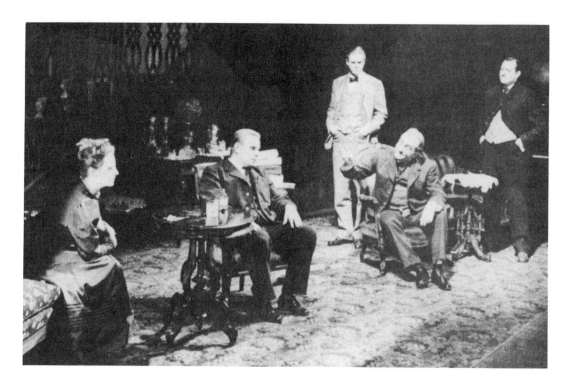

Act II of the 1939 production of *The Little Foxes*: Regina (Tallulah Bankhead), her husband Horace Giddens (Frank Conroy), nephew Leo Hubbard (Dan Duryea), and brothers Ben Hubbard (Charles Dingle) and Oscar Hubbard (Carl Benton Reid).

to help out his wife in her ambitions. Regina attempts to counter this impression, and to keep her brothers from looking for a third partner, by contriving to make Horace return home at once. She dispatches Alexandra to retrieve her father from Baltimore, knowing that Horace is more likely to listen to the pleas of his daughter than to those of his wife. She intimates, however, in her message to her husband, that she, too, desires his return. Her plan works, and Horace returns to the family home, weak and desperately ill. Regina seems to have won the day.

Oscar and Ben, however, with the help of Oscar's weaselly son Leo, discover that Horace has socked away $88,000 in Union Pacific bonds in his security deposit box, which happens to be in a bank at which Leo works. This money would enable the Hubbard boys to completely forgo the need for a third partner; the only catch, of course, is that they have to steal the bonds, at least temporarily. They count on Horace's not looking into his deposit box for several months, by which time they would have returned the bonds, having already made a substantial profit on their initial investment.

Secure in this knowledge, they no longer care what Regina does. But they haven't bargained on

the degree to which Regina and her husband detest each other, and their personal spite undoes the aspirations of the Hubbard brothers. It becomes clear that Horace and Regina have not shared a bed for many years, and that Horace was hoping that her summons to return home from Baltimore meant that her heart had softened toward him. Upon his arrival, however, he learns that she is interested only in his money, not in him. His heart hardens irrevocably.

Horace tells Regina that he knows of the theft of his bonds, having sent for his safe-deposit box several days before, and adds that he has decided, rather than derail the brothers' plans and turn them into the law, to teach Regina a lesson. He informs her that he will tell her brothers, expected shortly, that he intends to look upon the bond theft as a "loan," and that he desires nothing back from them except the bonds themselves when they are done with them—no interest, no profit, no future considerations in the cotton mill deal. He also informs Regina that he is about to rewrite his will, in which he will leave her the $88,000 in bonds, and will leave everything else to Alexandra. In this way, the stolen bonds will become a gift from Regina to her hated brothers, something that she absolutely cannot tolerate.

During the course of a poisonous conversation about their loveless marriage, Horace inadvertently knocks over and breaks the medication he needs to keep himself alive, whereupon a vengeful Regina refuses to get him a replacement. Horace collapses, trying to climb the stairs to the room in which his medication is kept; Regina listens to his struggle, her back turned, and waits until she hears him fall. Only then does she call for Addie and Cal, who help Horace to his room. She then welcomes her brothers, and makes it clear to them that she knows about the stolen bonds. They all know the brothers are safe as long as Horace is alive (he has yet to change his will and to make it official that the bonds are a loan). But a shocked Alexandra soon enters the living room to bring news of Horace's death and to demand of her mother what Horace was doing on the stairs, when he was confined to a wheelchair. Regina just dismisses the question by urging her daughter to go lie down because everyone needs time to get over such a shock. Clearly Regina now holds all the cards. Despite the suspicion that she has somehow been involved in the death of her husband, she manages to negotiate for herself a deal that leaves her with a 75 percent share in the business. As Regina prepares to move to Chicago and into a new, glamorous life of affluence—and possibly to be nearer to William Marshall—the play ends as an idealistic Alexandra tells her mother that she will not go with her, but will fight against such despoilers of goodness as her mother and family.

Social Darwinism. The term "social Darwinism" describes a sociological theory based upon the work of Charles Darwin, a nineteenth-century English scientist who developed the theory of natural selection, or the "survival of the fittest," as the concept is more popularly called. Darwin postulated that nature selected for survival those species that could adapt best to their surroundings; the concept of social Darwinism, which swept America in the second half of the century, extended this theory from biological evolution into sociological success. Its most prominent spokesman was William Sumner, a sociology professor who argued that the poor were poor because they were inferior to those who were able to make themselves rich. To help such failed people would be to encourage the weak among us, which would lower the caliber of the next generation.

The idea of the survival of the fittest runs throughout Hellman's play (with the word "nat-

ural" recurring again and again); according to the philosophy of the Hubbard family, "nature" has selected money as the criteria for social success. "The Southern aristocrat can adapt himself to nothing" (Hellman, *The Little Foxes*, p. 174), declares Ben Hubbard. Ben himself is not an aristocrat, but has married the daughter of a Southern aristocrat, and through this marriage has become the proprietor of the family's extensive cotton fields and plantation home; he therefore represents the triumph of capitalism over established wealth in the economic struggle for dominance in the New South. One critic draws attention to the play's capitalists, saying they represent "the most highly developed social species whose greed, for them, constituted a life force" (Wiles in Estin, p. 101). Hellman herself was a lifelong critic of capitalism; the fact that it is the heinous Hubbards who mouth the philosophy of "survival of the richest" is a telling indictment of the entire social system supported by such an economic stance.

Sources. The Giddens and the Hubbards bear a striking resemblance to members of Hellman's own family; indeed, as she herself once remarked, some of her relatives were thinking about legal action after having seen the play. Hellman described her relatives as "given to breaking the spirit of people for the pleasure of the exercise" (Hellman in Rollyson, p. 18). Hellman's maternal grandmother, Sophie Newhouse, and her great-uncle Jake (who appears in *The Little Foxes* as Ben Hubbard), were powerful and wealthy autocrats who despised Hellman's mother, Julia, for marrying a man with few resources. Family meetings to discuss common economic ventures, over which Sophie and Jake presided with steely precision, also made their way into *The Little Foxes*. Of the autobiographic connection with the play, Hellman once confessed that the closeness she felt toward the characters drove her to the detailed research she conducted before writing the play, and also led to the continual redrafting of the play almost up to the minute it was produced:

> Some of the trouble came because the play has a distant connection to my mother's family and everything . . . had formed a giant tangled time-jungle in which I could find no space to walk without tripping over old roots, hearing old voices speak about histories made long before my day.
>
> (Hellman in Falk, p. 50)

Events in History at the Time the Play Was Written

Crisis of capitalism. On October 29, 1929, prices on the New York Stock Exchange plummeted to a low enough point to cause panic and a rush to sell; within the next few days hundreds of thousands of Americans who had put their savings into stocks became paupers instantly. Banks failed, businesses closed, and suddenly millions were jobless and soon evicted from their houses to wander the country by rail looking for seasonal labor. This dismal situation lasted for most of the 1930s; many historians surmise that it was only with the outbreak of World War II, and the increased demand for the materials of war by Britain and the Allies, that America was able to recover economically. Prior to that were some years of labor unrest during the late 1930s, in which workers struck for higher wages, better working conditions and a reasonable work-week. In the clothing factories in Chicago, for example, the average wage was $2.50 a week; in other parts of the country, women and children worked twelve-hour days, seven days a week in dangerous and unsanitary conditions. Management was forced to pay attention to workers' needs, and it did, particularly in the steel and automobile industries. With the gradual unionization of America's labor forces, employers were forced to improve the conditions under which employees worked. The victory didn't come easily, though; workers were at times killed on the picket line or starved into submission by employers who locked them out. In *The Little Foxes,* Ben Hubbard boasts to William Marshall that the South hadn't ever seen a strike. This did not remain the case, although the South was much more reluctant to accept union agitation tactics than the North. The most prominent Southern union was the STFU, the Southern Tenant Farmers' Union, which was founded in Arkansas in 1934. It sponsored a successful 1935 strike in that state by cotton pickers. Subsequently, when union organizers showed up in Southern towns they risked being driven off by the police (as in Memphis in 1937), beaten severely, jailed, or encountering the Ku Klux Klan.

The red left. In 1952 Lillian Hellman was called to testify before the House Un-American Activities Committee (first set up in 1938) headed by Senator Joseph McCarthy. At issue were her leftist political convictions, and those of her colleagues and acquaintances. The fear was that secrets would be sold or traded to Russians, which would jeopardize American security.

The vehement crusade against American left-leaning intellectuals and artists in the 1940s and 1950s had its roots in the years leading up to World War II. During the 1930s, in the throes of the Great Depression, the failure of capitalism to protect people from the ravages of poverty and exploitation called into question the wisdom of the system, and communist ideas grew more popular, especially among American liberals and leftist intellectuals. Several writers—Richard Wright, John Dos Passos, and Theodore Dreiser, for example—showed communist sympathies (Smith, *Redeeming the Time,* p. 523). Hellman's own political ties remain unclear. In her day, she was never forthcoming about Communist Party membership and probably was merely a liberal activist. The writer herself characterized her political activities before and during the war as "idle lady stuff . . . speeches at rallies for this or that" (Hellman in Falk, p. 15). More subtly, her writing conveyed political viewpoints—the capitalists featured in *The Little Foxes* are unscrupulous business people.

The tendency of Hellman and other intellectuals toward espousing leftist convictions did not go unnoticed in America's corridors of power; the House Un-American Activities Committee (or the "Dies Committee," after its chairman, Martin Dies) was first established in 1938, in response to the growing threat of communism in America. Its founders intended to ferret out foreign spies, and, while they targeted communists, the fear of Nazis was stronger at first. A 1938 Gallup Poll revealed that, by a ratio of nearly 3 to 1, Americans were more concerned that Congress address the problem of Nazi propaganda and activities in the nation rather than those of communist activists.

Senator Joseph McCarthy and Roy Cohn during the House Un-American Activities Committee hearings.

Many American communists believed communism was the traditional and ideological enemy of fascism, especially the right-wing politics of the dictatorships in Germany and Italy at the time. But in August 1939, Soviet leader Josef Stalin sided with Germany's chancellor Adolf Hitler by signing a "nonaggression" pact between the two powers. In response, many American liberals officially left the Communist Party. Russia and Germany soon abandoned their treaty of nonaggression and went to war with one another in 1941. Nonetheless, many on the American left had become disillusioned with Soviet-style communism because of Stalin's brief alliance with Hitler.

HELLMAN'S PURPOSE

The selection of the South as a setting for *The Little Foxes* was purely incidental and fortuitous. I merely wanted, in essence, to say: "Here I am representing for you the sort of person who ruins the world for us."

(Hellman in Bryer, p. 8)

Dashiell Hammett. Hellman had a sporadic romance over thirty years with the writer Dashiell Hammett, one that exerted considerable influence upon her work. *The Little Foxes* in particular bears the mark of his input.

> I'd done the ninth draft of *The Little Foxes* and I finished it and left it in a briefcase in front of his door. Went to bed at about 6 o'clock in the morning and got up about 6 o'clock at night, and he said, "Well, you're on your way. Now start all over again." I never hated anybody so much in my whole life.
>
> (Hellman in Bryer, p. 240)

Hellman met Hammett in 1929, when she and her husband moved to Hollywood, where she read manuscripts for the Metro Goldwyn Mayer studio. Although he was also associated with screenwriting, Hammett was primarily famous for detective fiction such as **The Maltese Falcon** (also covered in *Literature and Its Times*). He encouraged Hellman to take her writing seriously. Hellman, who divorced her husband in 1932, spent much of her subsequent life trying to control her uncontrollable partner, Hammett, who drank too much and often proved unfaithful. Hammett

spent the last years of his life in poverty and ill-health. He was forced to live with friends during this period, including Hellman. Despite these difficulties, Hellman and Hammett remained close until his death from lung cancer in 1961.

Reviews and production. First performed in New York City in the spring of 1939, *The Little Foxes* was a huge success, running for 410 performances. The play was also well received by critics; *Newsweek,* for example, said that "From first to last, 'The Little Foxes' betrays not an inch of compromise, not a sliver of a sop to the comfortable acquiescence of Broadway" (Falk, p. 55). Yet one comment, some ten days after the show closed, linked Hellman's work to radical left-wing politics. In a newspaper column that appeared on Valentine's Day, 1940, *The Little Foxes* was suggested to be an appropriate lover's gift to the American Communist Party.

Whatever its politics, the play has become an American classic. As one critic has noted, *The Little Foxes* looked different to theatergoers when it was reviewed in the late 1960s than it had in 1939: "Then it was regarded as an attack on predatory capitalist morality; now it was an indictment of greed, hate, and the lust for power at any time, in any place" (Moody, p. 342).

For More Information

Bryer, Jackson R., ed. *Conversations with Lillian Hellman.* Jackson: University Press of Mississippi, 1986.

Estin, Mark W., ed. *Critical Essays on Lillian Hellman.* Boston: G. K. Hall, 1989.

Falk, Doris V. *Lillian Hellman.* New York: Frederick Ungar, 1978.

Hearden, Patrick J. *Independence & Empire: The New South's Cotton Mill Campaign, 1865-1901.* DeKalb: Northern Illinois University Press, 1982.

Hellman, Lillian. *The Little Foxes.* In *Six Plays by Lillian Hellman, with an Introduction by the Author.* New York: Modern Library, 1960.

Moody, Richard. *Lillian Hellman: Playwright.* New York: Pegasus, 1972.

Rollyson, Carl. *Lillian Hellman: Her Legend and Her Legacy.* New York: St. Martin's, 1988.

Smith, Page. *Redeeming the Time: A People's History of the 1920s and the New Deal.* New York: McGraw-Hill, 1987.

Smith, Page. *The Rise of Industrial America: A People's History of the Post-Reconstruction Era.* Vol. 6. New York: McGraw-Hill, 1984.

Snyder, Robert E. *Cotton Crisis.* Chapel Hill: University of North Carolina Press, 1984.

The Little Prince

by

Antoine de Saint-Exupéry

A French airman during the "golden age" of aviation, Antoine de Saint-Exupéry flew mail routes in northern Africa throughout the 1920s and 1930s. His experiences piloting the small, open-cockpit planes and brokering peace between the Moors of Africa and the imperial French and Spanish occupiers of the land inspired him to write serious books chronicling his desert adventures during this era. Based on true experiences as well as deeply held beliefs, *The Little Prince* is a fantasy novel that comments on the social ills of Saint-Exupéry's time. With growing emphasis on science and technology in addition to swelling bureaucracy, increased violence and a world war, the first decades of the 1900s were regarded as a time of progress by some and an era of decline by others. *The Little Prince* is Saint-Exupéry's attempt to honor the values he perceives to be important to human existence—the basic concepts of love, integrity, and respect for life—values he felt were being obscured and forgotten by Western society in its dogged pursuit of capital gain, technological advancement, and world domination.

Events in History at the Time of the Novel

The golden age of aviation. The Wright brothers' first successful airplane flight in 1903 launched the aviation industry and inspired a broad interest in flying. From Asia and Europe to the Americas, aircraft was developed and designs refined while pilots strove to master the

---

THE LITERARY WORK

A novel set in the Sahara Desert in the 1940s; published in 1943.

SYNOPSIS

A pilot recalls his encounter with a magical Little Prince whom he meets when stranded in the Sahara Desert and who teaches him the meaning of life.

---

skills of flying and mechanics. Very primitive by today's standards, early airplanes were first used for military purposes and to transport mail and cargo. The speed of the planes was a vast improvement over sea transport and enabled greater communication throughout the world.

Countries such as France that possessed colonies abroad could now more easily exchange goods and information with these territories. The French mail route or "aéropostale" service became vital to the maintenance of the French overseas empire in North Africa. During the 1920s and 1930s, mail planes flew from Toulouse (the seat of aviation in France) to Dakar, the largest French city in Africa, stopping to refuel at points in between. Cape Juby, on the North African coast in present-day Morocco, was one such refueling stop. It doubled as a Spanish military prison—Spain having its own colony in North Africa—and bordered the western Sahara Desert. Antoine de Saint-Exupéry was stationed at Cape

Juby as airfield chief in 1928. At the time he was working for Compagnie Latecoere, an air transportation company. His duties included flying the mail routes and keeping peace among the Moors, the Spanish, and the French.

Flying the French mail routes was a dangerous endeavor for two reasons. First, the Moors were very hostile toward the European presence in North Africa and often shot down the mail planes and demanded ransom for the pilots. In fact, it was one of Saint-Exupéry's duties to arrange payment of ransoms or other appeasements with the Moors when French or Spanish pilots were captured. Equally menacing were the planes themselves because they were ill-equipped and quite unreliable. Since aviation was in its infancy, the planes at this point were to a large degree untested and unfamiliar. The open-cockpit Breguet 14—which most French aéropostale pilots flew—had wood propellers, no radio, no suspension, no instruments, and no brakes. It flew a top speed of 80 miles per hour, traveled just 400 miles per tank, and broke down an average of every 15,500 miles—or every five trips from Toulouse to Dakar. Since the pilots had no radio and went down so frequently—as a result of either mechanical failure or being shot at—the mail planes were outfitted with carrier pigeons, which could carry word to the outside world if the pilot was stranded.

Despite the disadvantages, there was a positive aspect to the simplicity of the planes' design—they could usually be fixed by the pilot with a basic set of tools, which he carried on board. Saint-Exupéry, like his pilot in *The Little Prince*, had many near-death experiences flying in the North African desert. He was downed several times and forced to fix his plane or perish. During one particularly bad episode, the author-aviator crashed in the Libyan desert and nearly died of dehydration. Ultimately these experiences inspired Saint-Exupéry's classic tale of a stranded pilot who encounters a magical Little Prince.

French imperialism in North Africa. In 1667 France began acquiring territory in North Africa and throughout the world during the reign of King Louis XIV. In competition with other European powers—primarily Great Britain—to dominate Europe, Louis XIV expanded the French empire overseas and engaged in six major wars during his quest. As a result of overexpansion and years of warfare, France was forced to give up most overseas holdings to Great Britain in 1763. Economically devastated, France sunk into decline for the next century.

Antoine de Saint-Exupéry as a young man.

In 1871, after Napoleon III had lost the Franco-Prussian War, France re-established a republican form of government and emerged once again as a political and economic force. Colonial expansion once again ensued, especially in Asia and North Africa. Jules Ferry, French premier from 1881 to 1885, led the expansionist movement of this era. Its goal was twofold: to develop potential markets for French business and to "civilize" so-called "backward peoples" (Wright, p. 299). Through expansion, France was also seeking to rebuild her prestige and increase influence in world affairs. Ferry sent out military expeditions to acquire properties throughout Africa and Asia. Backed by business interests, the expeditions established colonies in North Africa and Malaysia.

Though France did not greatly develop her colonies, she did exert her influence on them. Local peoples were Christianized, and had French culture and presence imposed on them. In this age of imperialism, it became commonplace for European powers to acquire colonies and impose their cultures upon indigenous peoples. This often prompted feelings of great hostility from the local peoples toward the Europeans. In North Africa—primarily Algeria—the local Moors were especially adverse to the French and Spanish who had settled there. The Moors often attacked European military forts and hijacked personnel traveling to and from them. Much of the territory outside the forts became extremely hazardous for French and Spanish soldiers or citizens, and few dared to venture far into the desert.

One of the few able to bridge the gap between cultures was Saint-Exupéry. Not holding particular political or religious fervor, the author-aviator lived a life that suited well to his serving as a peacemaker in the region. He occupied a small shack outside the Spanish military prison at Cape Juby. He neither locked his doors nor carried a gun. He paid regular visits to the local Moor kings, and extended an open invitation for all natives to visit him. Saint-Exupéry gained a considerable reputation as a diplomat from his work at Cape Juby, which can be attributed to the fact that his efforts enabled the aéropostale service to safely operate in the hostile region from 1928 to 1935.

Technology and society. The first decades of the 1900s ushered in an era of rapid technological progress. Advancements in all areas of science had a marked impact on society. The automobile, airplane, assembly line, were either developed or perfected during this era, and electricity became more and more common. Born of the Enlightenment movement of the 1700s and scientific revolution of the 1800s, the technological era of the 1900s was described by French intellectual Émile Zola: "The trend of the times is toward science … we are driven in spite of ourselves toward the exact study of facts and things" (Wright, p. 286). The scientific method was applied to all facets of learning, and a cult of reason and science was promoted by most leaders and largely accepted by society. Many people of the age showed a prevailing faith in progress and in technology to solve the world's problems. At the same time, there was a growing skepticism of the metaphysical or anything not based on reason.

"Positivism," a nineteenth-century philosophical movement that rested on faith in science and the progress occurring throughout the Western world, gained a following in France, where it was led by three French intellectuals, Auguste Comte, Hippolyte Taine, and Ernest Renan. The movement emphasized reason over faith, and its members regarded science as a virtual religion. Comte, in particular, modernized the ideas of the Enlightenment and applied them to contemporary life, insisting that scientific advancement indicated progress. Renan and Taine urged skepticism and a rational approach to life. Order, clarity, and logic, according to their view, were the only indicators of truth. For these philosophers, romantic ideas were folly and had no place in modern society. This, moreover, applied to all aspects of life, from science to art. Positivism had a profound impact on French society during this era, encouraging the appearance of renowned French scientists and scientific advancements. Among the notables were Louis Pasteur in medicine, Pierre and Marie Curie in physics, and Henri Poincaré in mathematics.

At the same time, philosopher Henri Bergson attacked the cold reasoning of the scientific method. He argued that intuition and creativity led to truth and produced what was great in human beings. In 1906 he published a treatise called *Creative Evolution* that outlined his views. The piece spoke of man's "élan vital"—that is, the vital urge or creative force that makes men and nations great. Saint-Exupéry clearly agreed with this notion. His *The Little Prince* attacks reason and logic as well as the importance of numbers and technological advancement. The author himself preferred primitive aircraft, despite all its hazards; also his novel argues that it is emotion that gives life meaning, not objectivity.

France in 1940: the Nazi invasion. Weakened after World War I and plagued by an economic recession in the 1930s, France became a prime target for invasion in 1940. The threat posed by German dictator Adolf Hitler had been obvious for some years and was a reflection of the long-standing hostilities between the two nations. Contrary to international agreements, Hitler had retaken the Saarland in 1935, a region bordering France then under international jurisdiction. The following year, he reannexed the Rhineland, a similarly neutral but industrially important region. France failed to respond decisively to these actions. A combination of lack of leadership, uncertain foreign policy, and poor funding for French troops allowed Hitler to acquire more territory and greater resources.

As the situation became more tense in the late 1930s, France looked to several neighboring nations for support. Meanwhile, members of its parliament expressed a fear of communists, fascists, and socialists gaining political control within the country. France tried to ally with Benito Mussolini, the Italian fascist dictator, then sought the aid of the communist leader Joseph Stalin in Russia, but both plans crumbled when each of the leaders signed pacts with Hitler. The news of Stalin's pact with Hitler stunned France into realizing it would have to resist the joint power of Russia and Germany on its own. It could not count on Great Britain for help, since it would be some time before Britain would recover enough from the First World War to rearm properly. Since Great Britain was also a longtime enemy of France—though the two countries had fought together in World War I—there was also some uncertainty about the support France could expect from its neighbor across the English Channel.

After Austria and western Czechoslovakia were taken over by the German armies, Poland became Hitler's next target. Both France and England had mutual assistance treaties with the Polish government, so when German troops invaded Poland on September 1, 1939, France and England declared war on Germany, stepping up World War II. France realized too late that it would be the next target for Nazi invasion. In the midst of modernizing its army and without clear allies or strong leadership, France fell to German invaders in 1940-41.

French political leaders fled the country when it was invaded. Fallen premier Edouard Daladier set up a government-in-exile in North Africa, while General Charles de Gaulle started the Free French Movement in London, England. A fiercely patriotic and charismatic leader, de Gaulle pushed for the restoration of the French socialist republic with himself as its leader. De Gaulle's forceful manner and socialist beliefs caused many to fear he would become a dictator in the mold of those whom France was trying to combat. Among his detractors were American President Franklin Delano Roosevelt and Saint-Exupéry. The alternative to de Gaulle was General Henri Giraud, who, with the help of the Americans, dramatically escaped from a Nazi prison camp in 1942. De Gaulle transferred his headquarters to Algiers in Africa, and Giraud established his headquarters there too. The Americans, now allied with France and England in North Africa, continued to back Giraud until they realized de Gaulle was a force to be reckoned with. Negotiations between the rival generals resulted in their both becoming co-presidents of the French Committee of National Liberation. The goal of the Committee was to attack the Germans from bases in North Africa and retake France with Allied help. By 1943 de Gaulle emerged as the clear leader of the group, leaving Giraud, who had proven weak and unpopular, in the background.

Whether supporters of Giraud or de Gaulle, French men and women volunteered by the thousands to aid the cause of liberation. Some 20,000 had fled France when the Nazis invaded; Saint-Exupéry and others retreated to New York but then later traveled to North Africa to join the fight. From their base in Algeria, the combined French, British, Russian, and American forces bombarded the Germans by air and methodically worked to crush their stronghold in France. For two years the Allies bombed the Nazis from North Africa until the day of August 25, 1944, when Charles de Gaulle led the triumphant Allied troops through the streets of Paris in the official liberation of France.

Deeds, not words. In 1942 Antoine de Saint-Exupéry published an open letter indicating his desire to join the French forces in North Africa. Though forty-two years old and in ill health, Saint-Exupéry desperately wanted to contribute to his country's liberation. Many of his friends considered his letter a "death wish," but he regarded his voluntary service as a debt payment to the 40 million French living under German occupation. After much wrangling he was able to convince authorities to let him fly bombing missions out of North Africa. His last flight took off July 31, 1944, over southern France; he was never seen again. As this deed demonstrates, Saint-Exupéry was a man of action and had little patience for rhetoric. "Words are noises emanating from the mouth," he said. "You must judge people on who they are and what they do" (Saint-Exupéry in Schiff, p. 396).

The Novel in Focus

The plot. The novel opens with the narrator—a French pilot—describing a drawing he made when he was six years old. It featured a boa constrictor swallowing an elephant. He showed it to the adults but they could not see it for what it was; they insisted it was a hat. So he drew it again, this time revealing the contents of the snake's stomach. The grown-ups' response was "to advise me to lay aside my drawings of boa constrictors . . . and devote myself instead to geography, history, arithmetic and grammar" (Saint-Exupéry, *The Little Prince*, p. 4).

The pilot keeps the drawings with him and uses them as a test for determining the character of people whom he encounters. He shares the drawing and if the person recognizes it to be a boa constrictor swallowing an elephant, allows himself to talk to the person about substantive

General De Gaulle inspecting Free French troops in England on Bastille Day (July 14), 1940.

things. If the person sees the drawing as a hat, however, the pilot's tactics change: "I would talk to him about bridge, and golf, and politics, and neckties. And the grown-up would be greatly pleased to have met such a sensible man" (*The Little Prince*, p. 5).

Rarely meeting anyone who recognizes the drawing as a boa constrictor, the pilot has lived most of his life alone. But one day, while stranded in the Sahara Desert because his plane has broken down, he encounters an extraordinary little boy, a little prince. The Little Prince appears seemingly out of nowhere with an urgent request: "Draw me a sheep!" (*The Little Prince*, p. 6). The pilot is dumbfounded. He cannot figure out where this boy has come from and tries to determine who he is and what he is doing there. The boy never responds to his questions, however, and keeps insisting on the drawing of the sheep. The pilot obliges and draws several versions of sheep. But the Little Prince is not happy with any of them, for they all look too much like what sheep are supposed to look like. Exasperated, the pilot draws a box with three holes in it and tells the boy the sheep is in the box. The Little Prince is delighted—that is just what he meant for the man to draw.

Slowly, as they talk, the pilot discovers more about the boy. His home is a tiny planet, Aster-oid B-612. It has three volcanoes, one rose, and is scarcely the size of a house. One can watch the sunset all day simply by moving one's chair.

The Little Prince has left his planet to find out more about life. He has had an argument with his rose, his beautiful companion whom he loves and cares for in addition to his volcanoes. Hitching a ride with a flock of seagulls, he visits six asteroids on his way to Earth. He first encounters Asteroid 325 solely occupied by a king. But the king has no subjects, and the Little Prince thinks it is very odd to be king of nothing and no one.

The Prince next goes to the planet of a conceited man who wants only to hear praise and ignores any questions the boy asks. Quickly growing tired of the conceited man, the Little Prince leaves.

The third planet is occupied by a drinker who explains that he drinks to forget his shame about being a drunk. The boy leaves very confused and concludes yet again that "grown-ups are certainly very, very odd" (*The Little Prince*, p. 52).

The next planet is occupied by a businessman sitting at a desk, frantically adding numbers. He is counting the stars because he owns them and wants an inventory of his possessions. The man says they make him rich and that he has to claim them before anyone else does. The Little Prince asks if he is of any use to the stars, the way the Little Prince is to his rose—the only thing he owns. "The businessman opened his mouth, but he found nothing to say in answer" (*The Little Prince*, p. 57).

The fifth planet is inhabited by a lamplighter who is constantly lighting and extinguishing his lamp because the planet makes an entire revolution every minute. The Little Prince admires the lamplighter for his sense of duty and determines him to be the most respectable of all those encountered so far. But the planet is too small for two people so the Little Prince leaves.

The final planet he visits before Earth is occupied by a geographer. At first the Prince thinks he has finally met someone with a decent profession. But he soon realizes the man knows nothing outside of his maps. Disappointed again and starting to get homesick for his flower, the Little Prince asks if there are any other planets he should visit, whereupon the geographer tells him about Earth.

A PARALLEL ENDING

As if Saint-Exupéry knew he was going to die, the author wrote about a Little Prince who witnesses forty-four sunsets in one day, discovers the truth about life, and then fades from this Earth. Like the Prince, Saint-Exupéry conveyed his message—publishing the novel in 1943—and then disappeared without a trace from North Africa in 1944, the year of his forty-fourth birthday. The Prince returned to his land to tend his flower; Saint Exupéry had returned to France to tend to the needs of his people. For both the commitment is to their nation—they feel responsible for its well-being.

As luck would have it, the Little Prince lands in the middle of the Sahara Desert. He is expecting to see lots of people but instead finds nothing but sand. The first creature he encounters is a deadly snake. The snake explains to the boy that he has landed in Africa and further tells him he can help him return to his own planet if he gets too homesick. The snake feels compassion for the boy and perceives that he is too pure for such a corrupted planet.

The boy next encounters a field of roses, and feels devastated. He thought his rose back home was unique in all the world. He begins crying, and a fox appears. Uplifted by the fox's presence,

the Prince asks it to play. The fox says it cannot play because it is not yet tamed. Explaining that to tame means "to establish ties," the fox begs the boy to tame it. The fox elaborates: "I am nothing more than a fox like a hundred thousand other foxes. But if you tame me, then we shall need each other. To me you will be unique in all the world. To you, I shall be unique in all the world" (*The Little Prince*, p. 80). The Prince then realizes that his rose is special because he has tamed the rose and the rose has tamed him. Upon parting the fox promises to give the boy a present and tells him that "it is only with the heart that one can see rightly; what is essential is invisible to the eye" (*The Little Prince*, p. 87).

The Little Prince journeys on, meeting a railroad switchman, a merchant, and finally the pilot. The pilot is busy trying to fix his broken-down aircraft. Nearly out of water, he is deeply immersed in his work and starting to panic. At first he has no time for the Prince's questions or requests for drawings. But soon the Little Prince captures his heart and the pilot begins to listen to the boy. The Prince then drops off to sleep, and the pilot carries him further into the desert, on a quest to find water. At daybreak they miraculously find a well.

It has been a week and the Prince is now ready to go home, back to his rose, so he talks to the snake. The Prince explains that he cannot bring his own heavy body on the journey for it is too far. He asks the pilot not to watch his encounter with the snake because "You will suffer. I shall look as if I were dead; and that will not be true" (*The Little Prince*, p. 106). He adds that he will simply be leaving behind a shell and "there is nothing sad about shells" (*The Little Prince*, p. 106).

After the boy leaves, the pilot wonders if the boy is with his rose and if the sheep has gotten out of the box and eaten the flower. He concludes his tale with a picture of the spot where he met the Prince and asks readers who visit that same place in the Sahara and encounter a magical, mysterious little being to send word that the Prince is still alive.

Social commentary through fiction. Saint-Exupéry's novel illustrates the modern world as seen through the eyes of an innocent outsider. It embodies the values of Western society in various characters, moving from, for example, conquest and control (the King), to materialism (the businessman), to technological advancement (the geographer). As many critics have noted, the children's story chronicles the social ills of the age (Robinson, p. 129).

The author, Saint-Exupéry, lived in an era of science and mass production. Advancements in agriculture, astronomy, and mathematics enabled crop yields to multiply, stars to be catalogued, and planets to be discovered. Scientific breakthroughs, such as the invention of penicillin and the polio vaccine, produced cures for diseases. But science and technology were also producing weapons of mass destruction, and rather than ushering in an end to all war, the technological era was leading to larger-scale and more violent conflicts. The age of reason was supposed to launch a peaceful era, full of prosperity and growth. Instead, it brought two world wars, the Great Depression, and increased disparity of wealth across the globe.

Written during World War II, the novel includes parallels to Saint-Exupéry's experience with war and displacement. The author was forced to leave France by the Nazis in 1940. The Little Prince was a boy without a planet; Saint-Exupéry became a man without a country. Like the Prince, the author longed to return to his homeland—France.

An optimist at heart and very much a product of his age, Saint-Exupéry ended his tale in a way that ultimately asserts there is good waiting to be discovered amidst the ills of his age. Curiously, after the book was published and only weeks after Saint-Exupéry disappeared in a bombing mission, France was liberated from Nazi occupation and World War II ended.

Sources. Saint-Exupéry wrote *The Little Prince* while recovering from serious illness. Bedridden in New York and displaced from France because of Nazi occupation, he composed the novel as a form of therapy. For years he had scribbled notes and drawings for the book—especially during his time at Cape Juby in the 1930s. Imagery from his life experiences pervades the work: baobabs on the Little Prince's planet he modeled on this tropical plant around Dakar; exotic animals (which he also tried to tame both successfully and unsuccessfully) from the area around Cape Juby; volcanoes from Patagonia; the golden-curled Prince, patterned after himself as a child; the beloved rose, patterned after his wife, Consuela.

For every page he sent to the printer he is said to have torn up a hundred more. Historians argue that the book was his favorite and that he considered it autobiographical. Others speak of the prince as the author's alter-ego or even the son he never had.

Reviews. The author of serious novels about his experiences as an aviator, Saint-Exupéry was not expected to write such a book, and *The Little Prince* took the public by surprise. Later the most translated book in the French language, did not sell well when it was first published in 1943. It spent one week on the *New York Times* bestseller list and two months on the *Herald Tribune* charts, but after four months the book had actually sold just 30,000 copies in English and 7,000 in French. A *Time* magazine reviewer wrote that "this fairy tale for grown-ups challenges man the adult and deplores the loss of the child in man," but many reviewers failed to grasp that the novel was indeed a fairy tale for adults as well as children (Robinson, p. 121). Katherine S. White, a reviewer for the *New Yorker,* insisted that the story was too elaborate and disorganized to be appreciated by either adults or children. Conversely, Anne Carol Moore, writing for *The Horn Book Magazine,* sharply criticized mainstream reviewers such as White. "Is it for adults or children? they [most reviewers] ask. Who shall say? . . . I look upon it as a book so fresh and different, so original yet so infused with wisdom as to take a new place among books in general" (Moore in Cerrito, p. 221).

For More Information

Cerrito, Joann, ed. *Twentieth Century Literary Criticism.* Vol. 56. Detroit: Gale Research, 1995.

Robinson, Joy D. Marie. *Antoine de Saint Exupéry.* Boston: Twayne, 1984.

Saint-Exupéry, Antoine de. *The Little Prince.* San Diego: Harcourt Brace, 1971.

Schiff, Stacy. *Saint-Exupéry: A Biography.* New York: Alfred A. Knopf, 1995.

Wright, Gordon. *France in Modern Times.* New York: W. W. Norton, 1987.

Long Day's Journey into Night

by
Eugene O'Neill

E ugene Gladstone O'Neill was born in a Broadway hotel room in 1888, not far from the theaters that the O'Neill family came to know so well. For decades, his famous father, actor James O'Neill, toured the American theater circuit, his family dutifully in tow. Eugene grew up despising what he perceived as the trite, commercial nature of the industry around him, and when he turned to writing drama in 1912, he resolved to write a very different kind of play for American audiences. The troubles of his Irish-American family inspired many autobiographical portraits in his works, and he was lauded as the finest tragedian the United States had ever produced. When he died in 1953, he left behind among other great plays *Long Day's Journey into Night,* which was so personal that he ordered it not to be published until twenty-five years after his death.

Events in History at the Time the Play Takes Place

Morphine addiction. Blaming the rheumatism in her hands, the aging mother of O'Neill's fictional Tyrone family starts to take morphine again. Like many middle-class women of her generation, she becomes addicted by using medication prescribed for her at a time when the effects of the drug were not fully understood. Doctors valued this derivative of opium as a painkiller and a mood-enhancer, prescribing it for temporary relief of ailments as diverse as insomnia, bronchitis, and syphilis.

THE LITERARY WORK

A play set in the living room of the Tyrones' summer home in New London, Connecticut, on a day in August 1912; written in 1939-1941, published and first performed in 1956.

SYNOPSIS

A family deals with years of accumulated pain and guilt by alternately blaming and trying to forgive one another and themselves.

At age thirteen, Eugene O'Neill happened upon his mother as she was giving herself a morphine injection, and slowly he realized what his father and older brother, Jamie, had already known for years. Mrs. O'Neill felt mortified and accused Eugene of spying on her. She had been able to keep her secret from the family initially, and she fooled her friends by avoiding them or hiding her morphine-brightened eyes behind a veil when she left the house.

Like Mrs. O'Neill, the fictional Mary Tyrone was introduced to morphine after the complicated birth of her last son. In real life, that son was Eugene O'Neill, who later expressed his feelings of guilt in the character Edmund Tyrone. Mrs. O'Neill checked in and out of sanitariums for treatment, with limited success, but ultimately owed her recovery to the help of Carmelite nuns.

By 1912 the medical profession had circulated strong warnings against the indiscriminate use of morphine, and much less of it was being administered. New legislation also made it much harder for people to obtain the drug without a valid prescription, which may in O'Neill's play explain the pharmacist's reluctance to fill an order for Mary Tyrone. In addition, many people were reevaluating their attitude toward morphine addicts because of changes in the addict population. In the late 1800s most of them were middle- and upper-class women, followed by veterans of the Civil War. But by the time of the play, they were being replaced by pleasure-seeking, lower-class addicts, including prostitutes and young urban males.

Tuberculosis. It would not have been comforting to the character Edmund Tyrone, a consumptive, to know that someone in the United States died from tuberculosis, or "consumption" as it was then called, every three minutes during his era. People in the early stages of tuberculosis suffered from weight loss, slight fever in the afternoon, bleeding from the lungs, and a mild cough lasting a month or more. Consumption was already correctly identified as being caused by a living germ in the lungs, but as yet there was no certain cure.

Treatment facilities called sanatoria attempted to deal with the problem by offering patients a good environment for recovery. Fresh air, hearty meals, and plenty of rest were valued as means to check the growth of the germs and strengthen the patient. In addition, an increasing number of physicians were using X-ray technology to detect the fluid that would accumulate in the lungs as a result of the disease. Surgical procedures were sometimes used to drain this fluid or collapse the diseased lung. The medical community disputed the best way to diagnose and treat consumptives, but it agreed with the government, which circulated pamphlets warning that one's chances for recovery depended on early detection and professional care.

Eugene O'Neill himself suffered from tuberculosis in 1912. Unbeknownst to their family and friends, his father first took him to a dilapidated, state-run sanitarium. Two days later Eugene refused to stay, and he transferred to Gaylord Farm, a semiprivate institution, where a doctor punctured his chest with a hollow needle and drained fluid from his right lung. He stayed for six months, and it was there, he said, that he started to write plays.

Alcohol abuse. Around the turn of the century, saloons like those frequented by the Tyrones played an integral part in the social life of American men. Inevitably, heavy drinkers returned regularly to satisfy their thirst, but patrons had many incentives to make visits to the local bar a part of a cherished routine. For a modest price, it offered a place to read the daily newspaper, play cards or billiards, and catch up on sports information and politics. A "free lunch" was usually available at little or no extra cost, and adjacent rooms provided a place for labor unions and lodges to meet.

If men were its primary patrons, however, women were its chief opponents. After all, it was considered their job to maintain a proper home, and to some extent they were blamed if the men in their families sought amusement elsewhere. A housewife had ample reason to express concern about the negative side of her husband's indulgence in saloon life: gambling and intoxication led directly to insolvency and promiscuity, an insult that could bring with it the ugly reality of sexually transmitted diseases like syphilis.

THE ANONYMOUS REMARKS OF ONE WELL-BRED ADDICT

I am the last woman in the world to make excuses for my acts, but you don't know what morphine means to some of us, many of us, modern women without professions, without beliefs. Morphine makes life possible. It adds truth to a dream. What more does religion do? Perhaps I shock you. What I mean is that truth alone is both not enough and too much for us.

(Courtwright, p. 60)

As a result, organizations such as the Woman's Christian Temperance Union fought hard to outlaw the sale and consumption of alcohol. Their radical position eventually won out over efforts aimed merely at regulation and compromise. Many men also supported the temperance movement in the name of improving the health and character of the nation. By 1917 the cause had won so much popular support that Congress passed the Eighteenth Amendment (ratified in 1919), which enacted a ban on the sale of alcohol for almost fourteen years.

Despite the impressive amount of bourbon consumed in the play, no one mentions the growing belief that alcohol dependency was a disease, or that treatment existed for it. By contrast, a double standard is applied to Mary Tyrone's periodic hospitalization and her losing battle against morphine addiction. In real life,

Eugene's brother, Jamie, also checked in and out of sanatoria repeatedly in an effort to curb his alcoholism. Eugene's recollections of his brother's struggle as a substance abuser may account for the fictional Jamie Tyrone's keen disappointment at his mother's failure to break her cycle of dependence. Even Eugene himself was fighting a serious drinking problem.

Irish elements. The tendency to drink heavily is one of several stereotypes about the Irish that finds expression in this play about an Irish American family. Drinkers prized their ability to hold their liquor; James Tyrone's outrage at the idea that alcohol ever interfered with his family life or his work is entirely believable.

The Irish are famous for their storytelling and wit, epitomized in the characters' long monologues and the skillful manipulation of a wealthy American neighbor. The Tyrone family takes pleasure in the prank of their Irish tenant farmer, Shaughnessy, who lets his pigs wallow in the neighbor's ice pond (such a pond supplied ice that would be chopped in the winter and stored in silos for use in warm weather). The incident lays bare a fierce sense of national pride often associated with the Irish.

In the early 1900s, many Irish Americans belonged to the working class, finding employment as domestic servants and factory laborers. After eliminating his thick Irish accent, James O'Neill earned many fans as an actor, but he received a much cooler welcome at the exclusive Thames Club, which accepted very few Irish members. James was careful to be extremely polite to club members, buy them drinks at every opportunity, and limit his own alcohol consumption at the club—reserving true drunkenness for his favorite local bars.

Catholic elements. An Irish background automatically implied belief in the Catholic faith, and immigrants newly arrived from Ireland observed its rituals out of cultural pride as much as religious fervor. The daughters of affluent Catholic families might attend convent schools, which offered the finest education a young woman was likely to receive in the late 1800s, given that most university liberal arts courses were still closed to them.

Eugene O'Neill's mother Ella (born Mary Quinlan) entered the convent of St. Mary at Notre Dame, Indiana, in 1872. Her coursework included classes in philosophy, rhetoric, French, and astronomy, and her talent for the piano drew high praise from an internationally accomplished piano teacher. As a boy, O'Neill venerated his

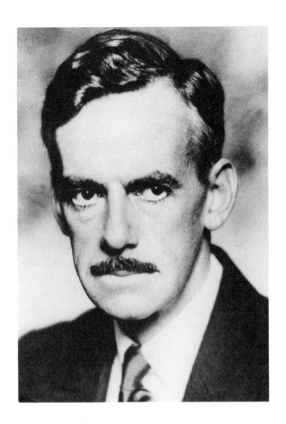

Eugene O'Neill

mother's religious devotion and sought to lose himself, as she did, in the mysteries and the promises of faith. After discovering his mother's addiction to morphine, O'Neill strove to be especially pious for a time, then abandoned his faith at age fifteen.

A life in the theater. The theater milieu was not generally approved of by Catholics, and many of Ella Quinlan's friends dropped her when she married a famous actor. At the time, James O'Neill was widely regarded as one of the most promising stage talents of his day. Skilled in performing classical roles, he was nevertheless unable to pass up the adulation and financial security he found as the hero of a stage melodrama called *The Count of Monte Cristo*. He played the role over three thousand times, and he even hung a sign on the family home in New London, identifying it as "Monte Cristo Cottage."

His two sons, Jamie and Eugene, sometimes joined him onstage reluctantly, and their mother spent many years accompanying her husband on the road. Touring had a dramatic impact on the lives of the O'Neills. Mrs. O'Neill recalled cradling her infant sons in the dresser drawers of hotel rooms, forever wishing for a home more in line with the tastes she had acquired from her upbringing.

Turn-of-the-century theater in the United States was dominated by melodrama, vaudeville skits, and star-driven revivals of the classics, especially Shakespeare's plays. These genres were supported by a profit-oriented theater industry that favored stage gimmicks and matinee idols as means of drawing large audiences regularly. As a result, script quality and artistic integrity often suffered. Eugene O'Neill shared the widespread opinion that his father had sold out his potential as an artist. He rejected the shallow nature of the theater world of his father and strove instead to write serious plays that would challenge the audience.

The Play in Focus

The plot. Sunlight fills the Tyrones' living room one summer morning, as Mary Tyrone flinches under the watchful eyes of her husband, James, and their sons, Jamie and Edmund. They deny scrutinizing her and reassure her with compliments. The family's small talk is punctuated by harsh accusations as the Tyrones address a variety of matters: the antics of an Irish-American tenant farmer; Edmund's failing health; James's tendency to be tightfisted with money; and the poor work ethic of his two sons.

By midday the sunshine outside has given way to haze, and the family starts to gather again for lunch. Jamie and Edmund drink bourbon and worry about how their mother might have passed the morning upstairs. Her recent behavior fits an old pattern that led to the relapse of an unnamed affliction. When she joins them, their worst fears are confirmed, and they and their father are distraught by the new development.

After lunch, the men's dull acceptance of Mary's turn-for-the-worse alternates with a faint hope that she might halt the cycle that has only just begun. Then a local doctor confirms that Edmund has consumption (tuberculosis). The family struggles to absorb the impact of this second crisis in typical Tyrone fashion—each member tries to determine which of them is most responsible for the bad news.

Fog rolls in at dusk, and Mary asks the family's Irish serving girl to keep her company while the men go to town. Although Mary denies it, the indulgence of an old drug habit alters her personality, making her ever more detached. Finally the prescription medicine is named: dope (and later, morphine). After James and Edmund

return for dinner, her addiction and Edmund's poor health are linked in the discussion to an earlier family tragedy, the death of a baby named Eugene.

Around midnight, the living room is lighted by a single, dim lamp as thick fog at the windows hides the world outside. The father James and Edmund show the effects of alcohol and continue to drink as they play cards absent-mindedly, resurrect old arguments, and delve deeper into complicated family problems, both past and present. Thoroughly drunk, son Jamie returns home and has a revealing talk with his brother. Mary joins the men downstairs, and she is now even further withdrawn into her drugged state. She drags her wedding gown on the floor and speaks of her schooldays at a convent, recalling a time before life made her into someone she did not want to become.

THE DISAPPROVAL OF THE YANKEES

We considered the O'Neills shanty Irish, and we associated the Irish, almost automatically, with the servant class. As a matter of fact, I remember being very upset when I first started going to church—my father became a Catholic convert—and I recognized only servants in the church. 'Why do we go to the Irish church?' I remember asking my mother, to her embarrassment. We were among the few Catholic families considered acceptable.—A chagrined appraisal by Mrs. E. Chappell Sheffield, a daughter in the Chappell family, on whom O'Neill modeled the self-important Chatfields in the play.

(Gelb, p. 95)

Shame. The members of the Tyrone family each feel ashamed for a variety of reasons, both in front of one another and in the eyes of society. *Long Day's Journey into Night* examines this shame as an underlying explanation for the ways in which the Tyrones suffer and make each other miserable. They are unable to simply forget their past mistakes because, as Mary explains, "The past is the present, isn't it? It's the future, too. We all try to lie out of that but life won't let us" (O'Neill, *Long Day's Journey into Night,* p. 87).

Mary Tyrone denies and hides her addiction to morphine, a dependence not befitting a wife and mother. Her resentment of her husband's career, her nostalgia, and the dream state caused by the narcotic make her shirk her responsibilities. She feels this inadequacy most painfully when remembering that she placed her husband's desires (and perhaps her own) ahead of caring for an infant son, who died.

James Tyrone recalls his early days as an actor, using the praise he earned then to endure the fact that he chose material security over greatness as an artist. "What the hell was it I wanted to buy," he wonders bitterly, acknowledging that poverty in childhood made him obsessively sensitive about money (*Long Day's Journey into Night*, p. 150). His family blames his miserliness for Edmund's poor health and the failure to provide an adequate home. Whether or not James agrees openly with the family's accusations, their grievances pain him for the truth that is in them.

EUGENE O'NEILL'S PREFERENCE FOR TRAGEDY

To me, the tragic alone has that significant beauty which is truth. It is the meaning of life—and the hope. The noblest is eternally the most tragic. The people who succeed and do not push on to a greater failure are the spiritual middle-classers. Their stopping at success is the proof of their compromising insignificance.

(O'Neill in Gelb, p. 5)

Thoroughly drunk, Jamie Tyrone confesses to Edmund something that his parents have suspected for years: he has jealously and actively tried to ruin his brother. Jamie is also sensitive about having squandered his potential as a good student and depending on his father for work.

Edmund Tyrone feels responsible for his mother's drug addiction and the pain it has caused everyone in the family. It is tempting to consider that Edmund, the character based on O'Neill himself, has the least to feel guilty about, and that the playwright therefore flatters himself. The play itself, however, is an admission, a delayed acceptance of his family and a forgiving of himself and them for the torment they caused one another.

Sources and composition. In many of his earlier plays, the dramatist had already translated the troubled O'Neills into characters modeled on members of his family, including himself. A relationship almost identical to that of Mary and James Tyrone provides the focal point of one such play, *All God's Chillun Got Wings* (1923). Audiences of the time did not relate that play to

O'Neill's own family life since the male protagonist was black. The fact is that like any dramatist who draws on his personal life, O'Neill felt free to change the details in more and less obvious ways. This applies to *Long Day's Journey into Night* as well, although almost each of its details finds a close counterpart in real life. Sometimes, however, the details are manipulated. For example, O'Neill's infant brother, Edmund, died in the manner described in the play, but O'Neill exchanges the names, calling the autobiographical character Edmund and the dead baby Eugene.

By the time O'Neill began work on *Long Day's Journey into Night* early in the summer of 1939, a tremor in his hands made writing almost impossible. O'Neill found dictation and the use of typewriters or recording devices incompatible with his creative process, and the dramatist was stranded. The palsy was the result of a rare degenerative disorder whose victims remain fully competent but intermittently lose control of their limbs and their ability to speak.

Realizing that his productive days as a playwright were numbered, O'Neill discontinued his work on an ambitious cycle of eleven plays and turned instead to the writing of *Long Day's Journey into Night*. His third wife, Carlotta, described the agony her husband endured during the steady work schedule he set himself:

> He would come out of his study looking gaunt, his eyes red from weeping. Sometimes he looked ten years older than when he went in the morning. For a while he tried to have lunch downstairs with me. But it was very bad, because he would sit there and I knew his whole mind was on his play—acts, lines, ideas—and he couldn't talk. I would have to sit there perfectly dumb. I didn't even want to make a sound with the chair that might disturb him. It made me very nervous and it made him nervous seeing me sitting there like that. We decided it would be best for him to have his lunch on a tray, alone.
>
> (Carlotta O'Neill in Gelb, p. 7)

Events in History at the Time the Play Was Written

Changes since 1912. By the time the play was written (1941) and produced (1956), the United States was not the same place it had been in 1912, the year the play takes place. The popular socialism of the early twentieth century—a movement that James Tyrone associates with anarchy—had given way to the patriotism that ostensibly united America during World War II.

In addition, O'Neill's cultural heritage had lost much of its social stigma—so much so that an Irish-Catholic was elected president only five years after *Long Day's Journey into Night* was produced.

Changes in the morphine addict population, hinted at in the play, had become more pronounced. As a result, stricter legislation targeted recreational users and the petty crimes believed to support narcotics habits. Although the war cut off many of the routes used by smugglers of illegal drugs, an underground market survived. In most medications, morphine had long since been replaced by a milder version of the drug, codeine. In other medical news, a professor of microbiology named S. A. Waksman identified streptomycin in 1944 as an antibiotic effective against tuberculosis, and the epidemic waned.

The revival of the alcohol industry after the Eighteenth Amendment was repealed in 1933 promised jobs and precious tax revenue during the Great Depression in America. Wary that the ban might be reimposed, advertisers encouraged drinking in moderation; but within a decade, alcohol consumption matched 1912 figures. O'Neill agreed to professional help for his alcoholism and succeeded in mastering his drinking problem early in 1927, after consultations with a psychoanalyst gave him an explanation for it. The rapid expansion of the support group Alcoholics Anonymous, founded in 1939, the year O'Neill began writing his play, signaled that America's troubles with alcohol abuse were widespread and that they were gaining recognition during this period.

Production, reviews, and honors. Eugene O'Neill wished that *Long Day's Journey into Night* not be published until twenty-five years after his death, citing a request of his eldest son, Eugene, Jr., as the reason. The dramatist took the manuscript to Random House publishers in 1945, where he drew up a document outlining the terms of the play's disappearance. As per O'Neill's wishes, the manuscript was sealed with red sealing wax and deposited in a downstairs safe. Even so, the playwright insisted that it never be produced.

More O'Neill family tragedy followed, however, when Eugene, Jr. committed suicide in 1949. Afterward, his father and Carlotta faced financial hardship and discussed the possibility of publishing the play as a last resort. About two years after her husband's death, Carlotta exercised her legal right to Eugene's works, and the play was retrieved from Random House. Mrs.

O'Neill sent it simultaneously to the Yale University Press and to the director of the Royal Dramatic Theatre in Stockholm.

The Swedish ensemble won acclaim for its production of *Long Day's Journey into Night,* receiving worldwide attention when the play premiered in Stockholm on February 2, 1956. Prominent American producers and directors besieged Carlotta with requests to stage the masterpiece on Broadway in New York. She hesitated for a few months before turning the play over to three young producers who had already succeeded with the revival of another O'Neill play, *The Iceman Cometh.* A four-hour production, *Long Day's Journey into Night,* made its American debut at the Helen Hayes Theater in New York on November 7, 1956, once again earning enthusiastic reviews. Many critics speculated about O'Neill's purpose in writing such a probing, pain-filled analysis of a family in crisis. One wrote:

> That he was damaged by his family is only a fact now, a piece of truth to be put down out of respect for the whole truth; there is no residual rancor. He seems to be asking forgiveness for his own failure to know his father, mother and brother well enough at a time when the need for understanding was like an upstairs cry in the night; and to be reassuring their ghosts wherever they may be that he knows everything awful they have done, and loves them.
>
> (Cronin, p. 16)

Long Day's Journey into Night won O'Neill a fourth Pulitzer Prize and sparked renewed interest in the dramatist and his plays. His popularity had been waning since the early 1930s, despite the fact that, in 1936, O'Neill was the first American dramatist (and only the second American) to receive the Nobel Prize for literature. Even without the overwhelming success of *Long Day's Journey into Night,* Eugene O'Neill's place in the history of the American stage was assured. In an article acknowledging that O'Neill's plays were sometimes hard to like, the famous drama critic Eric Bentley insisted, "He is the leading American playwright; damn him, damn all; and damning all is a big responsibility" (Bentley in Cronin, p. 1).

For More Information

Cronin, Harry. *Eugene O'Neill: Irish and American; A Study in Cultural Context.* New York: Arno, 1976.

Courtwright, David T. *Dark Paradise: Opiate Addiction in America before 1940.* Cambridge, Mass.: Harvard University Press, 1982.

Gelb, Arthur, and Barbara Gelb. *O'Neill*. New York: Harper and Row, 1962.

Keers, R. Y. *Pulmonary Tuberculosis: A Journey Down the Centuries*. London: Ballière Tindall, 1978.

Lender, Mark Edward, and James Kirby Martin. *Drinking in America*. New York: Free Press, 1982.

O'Neill, Eugene. *Long Day's Journey into Night*. New Haven: Yale University Press, 1989.

Raleigh, John Henry. "O'Neill's *Long Day's Journey into Night* and New England Irish-Catholicism." In *O'Neill: A Collection of Critical Essays*. Edited by John Gassner. Englewood Cliffs, N.J.: Prentice-Hall, 1964.

The Maltese Falcon

by
Dashiell Hammett

After a series of unsatisfying jobs, Dashiell Hammett became an agent for Pinkerton's National Detective Agency in 1915. Hammett enjoyed the thrill of the sometimes dangerous job and worked, as his health permitted, on and off as a Pinkerton detective for the next seven years. When poor health forced him to end his employment at Pinkerton's, Hammett began writing detective stories, using his real-life experience as source material. After becoming a leading contributor to the popular magazines of the period, Hammett turned his attention to writing novels. His third novel, *The Maltese Falcon*, remains to this day one of the most widely recognized and respected works of detective fiction.

Events in History at the Time of the Novel

The rise of the private eye. The private investigator in America began with Pinkerton's National Detective Agency, the largest private law enforcement agency in the United States. The agency was founded in 1850 by Allan Pinkerton, who had formerly worked as a Chicago policeman. Pinkerton invented the trademark of his business, the unblinking eye and the motto, "We never sleep," which eventually led to Pinkerton's agents becoming known as "private eyes."

The Pinkerton agents filled a gap between the federal government's Secret Service, a small department at the time, and local police forces. As the nation grew, Pinkerton agents served in-creasingly varied and important functions; the Pinkertons helped to prevent assassinations, systematized crime prevention, and solved difficult cases, especially those which crossed many local jurisdictions. As the organized labor movement spread west, following the railroads into mining camps and new industrial areas, the Pinkertons worked for business leaders and captains of industry to quell labor uprisings. Their principal duties in these incidents included breaking strikes, beating up strikers, burning down union headquarters and the homes of union leaders, and protecting the "scabs" who crossed the picket lines.

During his stint as a Pinkerton employee, Dashiell Hammett investigated union leaders, chased counterfeiters, searched for stolen gold, and even pursued a man suspected of being a foreign spy. It was his experience with the agency that prompted Hammett to try his hand at detective fiction. The numerous stories generated from these experiences launched Hammett toward becoming one of the world's best known writers of detective fiction.

Society, corruption, and criminality in San Francisco. When Dashiell Hammett arrived in San Francisco in 1921, he found himself in the West's greatest metropolis. San Francisco was the focal point of immigration, mining, industry, export, and cultural advances. When the Volstead Act passed, beginning Prohibition, which banned the manufacture and sale of alcohol, it was regarded in San Francisco more as an incentive to commerce than as a law. The city became a major port of entry for illegal liquor. Speakeasies, secret establishments that illegally served alcohol, bought the consent of local authorities, while networks of rumrunners transported liquor inland to cities such as Butte, Denver, and Phoenix. Houses of prostitution flourished during this time. Also the Bay Area around San Francisco attracted German, Italian, and Chinese immigrants during this period. An entire Chinese society complete with criminal gangs, religious institutions, and its own social hierarchy developed in a twenty-square-block area in downtown San Francisco.

San Francisco Chronicle columnist Herb Caen recalls the corrupt and criminal atmosphere of San Francisco in the 1920s, and even makes reference to Sam Spade, the detective hero of Hammett's *Maltese Falcon*:

> The criminal lawyers were young and hungry and knew every shyster trick.... The City Hall, the D.A. and the cops ran the town as though they owned it, and they did. Hookers worked upstairs, not on the street; there were hundreds, maybe thousands, most of them named Sally. The two biggest abortion mills—one on Market, the other on Fillmore—were so well known they might as well have had neon signs. You could play roulette in the Marina, roll craps on O'Farrell, play poker on Mason, get rolled at 4 a.m. in a bar on Eddy, and wake up with a girl whose name you never knew or cared to know.... San Francisco was a Sam Spade city.
> (Caen in Marling, p. 12)

Hammett was fascinated and excited by a metropolis in which law enforcement was minimal and the opportunities for a private eye were so plentiful. Although Hammett's health only permitted him eight months to enjoy the opportunities that San Francisco's rough-and-tumble environment provided, it was enough time to truly absorb the details of the city's seedy underworld, which Hammett would use as the setting for *The Maltese Falcon*. Hammett's depiction of the city's corruption matches Caen's sentiments on the subject. At one point in the novel, Spade tells O'Shaughnessy that he has kept her name from being involved with his partner Archer's murder. When she asks him how he did it, he tells her, "Most things in San Francisco can be bought, or taken" (Hammett, *The Maltese Falcon*, p. 55).

Detective fiction and "pulp" magazines. The earliest roots of detective fiction have been traced back to the gothic novels of Horace Walpole (1717-1797) and Mary Shelley (1797-1851), which featured mystery, death, and revenge. Detective fiction became a more widely recognized genre following the efforts of François-Eugène Vidocq. After serving as a soldier, smuggler, inmate, and secret police spy, Vidocq established his own specialized security department that would eventually form the basis of the French intelligence department. When Vidocq published his memoirs in 1828, the book immediately became popular in France and was translated into English the same year.

Vidocq's memoirs inspired other novelists such as Victor Hugo, Charles Dickens, and Wilkie Collins to create their own versions of the detective novel. In America, Poe read Vidocq's memoirs with great care and went on to write his own detective stories. With these stories, Poe introduced the character of the eccentric detective. He also focused on using inference and observation to solve the crime, elements used by Collins in his stories as well; both elements would serve as models for generations of detective writers to come. The concept of inference and observation was developed even further by Sir Arthur Conan Doyle, whose dauntless sleuth Sherlock Holmes used these tactics to apprehend a slew of treacherous villains.

In the United States, detective stories began to usurp the supremacy of Westerns in the literary market. Henry Nash Smith wrote that the hero of the cowboy novel became "a self-reliant, two-gun man who behaved in almost exactly the same fashion whether he were outlaw or peace officer. Eventually he was transformed into a detective and ceased in any significant sense to be Western" (Smith in Marling, p. 22).

When Hammett became interested in the detective story in 1923, the genre was exploding due to the mass marketing of dime novels. At the time, America's most popular writer of detective stories was Willard Huntington Wright, writing

Humphrey Bogart in the film adaptation of *The Maltese Falcon*.

under the pseudonym of S. S. Van Dine, whose stories centered on the intrepid detective Philo Vance. The Vance stories, at the high end of the detective story market, appeared in *Scribner's,* one of the "slick paper" magazines; others included *Saturday Evening Post, Cosmopolitan,* and *Liberty.* Writers whose stories appeared in these magazines could make up to a dollar a word. At the opposite end of the spectrum were the "pulps," magazines published on cheap newsprint, whose writers garnered only a penny a word. Printed on rough wood-pulp paper to save on production costs, the pulps had been started in 1896 and had grown in popularity since. At the close of World War I, only two dozen pulp magazines were available for readers. By the middle of the 1920s, over two hundred pulp magazines reached 25 million readers.

When Hammett tried to break into the pulps in 1923, the leading author of pulp detective stories was Carroll John Daly, whose most famous hero was Race Williams, a tough-talking, straight-shooting detective. Daly's prime medium was *Black Mask,* a pulp magazine specializing in detective, adventure, and occasionally Western stories. When Hammett began producing salable stories, *Black Mask* became his best market as well. Soon he and Daly would be *Black Mask's* leading contributors.

American disillusionment and the "hard-boiled" detective. Many scholars have suggested that the success of detective writers such as Hammett, Daly, and later Raymond Chandler is due to their use of the "hard-boiled" detective as the heroes of their stories. World War I and its aftermath had seriously challenged Americans' widely held beliefs concerning man's ability to shape his destiny, their ideas regarding the progress of the human race, and their concepts of civilization itself. The grim realities of the war forced many people to realize that the world was not as benevolent or rational as they had once believed. This feeling of disillusionment was heightened by Prohibition in 1920, which suddenly transformed millions of law-abiding citizens into criminals each time they purchased or sold bootleg liquor. Even worse, because of the enormous profits to be made from bootlegging, American cities soon came under the control of gangsters. A declining economy was the final blow to American hopes.

The "hard-boiled" detectives of Daly, Hammett, and Chandler took a hard-fisted approach to detective work, based on a cynical view of the world that matched the conditions and mood in the United States at the time. Gaining immense popularity, detectives such as *The Maltese Falcon*'s Sam Spade suited the tastes of American readers in this era. And the author's touch of gritty realism, gained from his own real-life detective experiences, served to make his stories even more popular with the reading public.

The Novel in Focus

The plot. Sam Spade, a private investigator, meets a Miss Wonderly in his San Francisco office. She asks Spade to rescue her sister from a hoodlum named Floyd Thursby and advances $200 for the job. At this point, Sam's partner, Miles Archer, enters the office, takes half the money and volunteers to do the job.

Early the next morning, Spade receives a call from the police telling him that Archer has been murdered. At the murder scene, Spade elicits curiosity by not wanting to examine the body. Back at his home, Spade is questioned by policemen Tom Polhaus and Lieutenant Dundy, who have discovered that he was having an affair with Archer's wife, which makes him a suspect in the murder. They also tell him that the hoodlum Thursby has been shot and killed.

Spade tracks down Miss Wonderly, who, it turns out, is really Brigid O'Shaughnessy. After a burst of tears and contrived confessions that fail to affect Spade, O'Shaughnessy recruits him to help her recover a valuable object for an additional $500.

The next day, Spade's secretary, Effie Perine, ushers Joel Cairo into his office. Cairo, like O'Shaughnessy, offers Spade a fee if he will help find the object, which he identifies as the Maltese Falcon. He pulls a gun on Spade, who disarms him, but Cairo repeats the trick and searches the offices, though he finds nothing. After his meeting with Cairo, Spade notices that someone is "tailing" him. He arranges a meeting between Cairo and O'Shaughnessy to see if he can get to the bottom of the mystery.

Spade, Cairo, and O'Shaughnessy meet in Sam's office, but are interrupted by officers Polhaus and Dundy, who arrive and threaten to jail all three. Spade finally improvises his way out of the situation, and the police leave, with Cairo following. Spade and O'Shaughnessy spend the night together.

With the help of a clue from the previous night, Spade finds the person shadowing him, a young man named Wilmer, and tells Wilmer he wants to see Wilmer's boss. Back at his office, Spade receives a call from the boss, Casper Gutman. Gutman tells Spade more about the black bird known as the Maltese Falcon, and the people looking for it. Spade pretends to know the bird's whereabouts and gives Gutman a deadline to participate in recovering it.

Afraid that Gutman will kill her, O'Shaughnessy goes into hiding. Spade tries to track her down but finds no clues except for a newspaper clipping about a ship due from Hong Kong called *La Paloma*. Gutman calls, agrees to join with Spade, and tells him the whole story of the bird. It is a priceless jeweled statuette, given to Charles V of Spain as tribute by the Knight Hospitalers of St. John. At the end of the story, Spade passes out; Gutman has drugged him.

Spade wakes up to find Cairo, Wilmer, and Gutman gone. In Cairo's room he discovers another clue about the ship, *La Paloma*. Spade returns to his office, and as he discusses events with Effie, Captain Jacobi of the *La Paloma* enters, carrying the falcon, and he falls dead at their feet.

Spade stashes the falcon in a hiding place and then meets with Gutman, Cairo, Wilmer, and O'Shaughnessy, who turns out to be working with Gutman. He accepts $10,000 from Gutman for the falcon, but insists that someone be turned over to the police to take the rap for the murders. Gutman suggests O'Shaughnessy, but Spade refuses, and then Gutman offers Wilmer, to everyone's satisfaction.

At dawn, Sam orders Effie to retrieve the falcon. It turns out to be a worthless imitation. Gutman leaves with Cairo, and Spade alerts Polhaus and Dundy, but before they can arrest the suspected criminals, Wilmer shoots Gutman. Spade urges O'Shaughnessy to tell him the truth before the police arrive. She admits to conspiring to get the falcon, but denies involvement in Archer's murder. Unfortunately, all of Spade's evidence points to her, and she finally confesses. She tries to secure Spade's loyalty by speaking of their love, but refusing to be her sap, Spade turns her over to the police.

Women in detective fiction. In addition to the drastic political and economic transitions that occurred in the 1920s, many men believed that another threat was emerging that would strike even closer to home. These men, and some women, felt that the changing social ambitions of women threatened to undermine their ideological role as moral figures. Society had long held a belief that women were inherently superior beings as far as morality was concerned. Although women had used this concept of their moral superiority to argue for the ratification of the Nineteenth Amendment, which gave them the vote in 1920, the suffragettes had shown a determination and militancy that raised some eyebrows of disapproval and that was not soon forgotten. Women had also joined the work force in increasing numbers and entered new fields during World War I, all changes that prompted some men to view women as usurpers. During the Progressive Era, women's organizations had pushed for reform, but now with Prohibition adopted, enthusiasm for reform diminished. Meanwhile, women were supposedly enjoying increased personal freedom, including a much-heralded new sexual freedom, that inspired resentment; the increasing attempts of women to fulfill their social, sexual, and intellectual desires were seen as a direct abandonment of their historic status as moral guardians.

In many ways, the hard-boiled detective novel, with *The Maltese Falcon* as an ideal example, reflects the changing status of women in the early twentieth century. Just like the dangerous woman or *femme fatale* characters that appeared so often in nineteenth-century literature, deadly women became a favorite figure for the detective writers of the 1920s. Some scholars have suggested that these dangerous women of detective fiction reflect some of the resentment felt by many men toward the changing women of the era. Hard-boiled detective fiction writers often portrayed women as competitive, devious, wily, and morally degenerate. Women not only compete with men in the novels, but they also prove to be dangerous opponents. Whether or not the changing role of women influenced Hammett in his creation of a deadly female character remains uncertain. But in *The Maltese Falcon,* Brigid O'Shaughnessy proves to be not only competitive but dangerous—she uses her overt sexuality to attract Archer, then kills him to further her own desire for personal gain. Jacobi is also killed when he is persuaded by O'Shaughnessy to help her recover the statue. Against Spade, O'Shaughnessy employs an even more devastating arsenal, using sexuality, love, and sympathy in her attempts to manipulate him. While Spade is victorious, the cost ironically is his return to a lonely life when she is led away to prison.

Sources. The basic source behind Hammett's classic novel was a story he had read regarding an order of knights who had an arrangement with Charles V of Spain during the Crusades of the Middle Ages. The story centers on the religious order, known as the Hospitalers of Saint John, whose members were located on the Isle of Rhodes and charged with providing lodging and care for pilgrims on the way to Jerusalem. Between 1300 and the early 1500s, the order built up tremendous wealth, but its members were eventually displaced by Suleiman the Magnificent and his Turkish armies in 1523. The Hospitalers wandered until 1530, when they gained the patronage of Charles V, who gave them four islands, including Malta. Charles V's only requirement was that they send a live falcon to him yearly as a symbol of tribute. Initially they sent a live bird, but as their wealth grew they substituted jewel-encrusted statuettes. With this as the central device of the story, Hammett simply constructed the typical detective formula around it.

DETECTIVE FICTION FORMULA APPLIED TO *THE MALTESE FALCON*

1. Perfect crime—the murder of Miles Archer and the theft of the Maltese Falcon

2. Wrongly accused suspect—Sam Spade

3. Bungling, dimwitted police—Polhaus and Dundy

4. Greater powers of wit and observation of the detective—Spade realizes that O'Shaughnessy killed Archer

5. Startling denouement—discovery that the falcon is a fake

Many critics have argued that Hammett's detective stories were so engaging because he instilled into them elements from his experience as a Pinkerton detective; *The Maltese Falcon* is no exception. Most of the novel's characters are drawn from Hammett's detective days. Hammett revealed that Gutman was modeled after a man suspected of being a foreign spy, whom Hammett shadowed around Washington, D.C.; Brigid O'Shaughnessy was based on a woman who once hired an operative to fire her housekeeper; Joel Cairo was modeled after a forger Hammett picked up in 1920; the inspiration for Effie was a girl who asked Hammett to join her in a narcotics smuggling operation in San Diego; and the inspiration for Wilmer was a suspect arrested in Stockton, California, known as the "Midget Bandit."

The hero of the novel, Sam Spade, was based on James Wright, the assistant manager of Pinkerton's office in Baltimore, where Hammett got his start. Wright told Hammett that there were three elements to being a good detective: anonymity, morality, and objectivity. Strangely enough, Wright considered morality to be a personal issue and believed that an agent could lie, misrepresent, cheat, steal evidence, break promises, blackmail, and emotionally manipulate people to bring a criminal to justice. Spade thinks in the same way, gradually bringing the criminals in the story together by lying to and manipulating them. When he keeps Brigid's name from being involved, it seems possible that he has stolen evidence to accomplish this.

The critics. After reading *The Maltese Falcon,* Joe Shaw, an editor for *Black Mask,* was stunned by the novel, telling readers, "I have never encountered a story as intense, gripping or as powerful as this one. It is a magnificent piece of writing" (Nolan, *Hammett: A Life at the Edge,* p. 93). Walter Brooks of the *Outlook* and the *Independent* wrote of the novel, "This is not only probably the best detective story we have ever read, it is an exceedingly well-written novel" (Marling, p. 86-7). Will Cuppy wrote in the *New York Herald Tribune* that "it would not surprise us one whit if Mr. Hammett turned out to be the Great American mystery writer" (Marling, p. 87). Finally, the *New Republic* wrote that *The Maltese Falcon* was "not the tawdry gum-shoeing of the ten-cent magazine. It is the genuine presence of the myth" (Marling, p. 87). With *The Maltese Falcon,* Hammett proved himself the top writer of detective stories in the country, and even more than that, showed that the genre could be used to create a legitimate novel, recognized for literary merit in addition to action, suspense, and mystery.

For More Information

Geherin, David. *The American Private Eye: The Image in Fiction.* New York: Frederick Ungar, 1985.

Hallissy, Margaret. *Venomous Woman: Fear of the Female in Literature.* New York: Greenwood, 1987.

Hamilton, Cynthia S. *Western and Hard-Boiled Detective Fiction in America: From High Noon to Midnight.* London: Macmillan, 1987.

Hammett, Dashiell. *The Maltese Falcon.* New York: Random House, 1992.

Marling, William. *Dashiell Hammett.* Boston: Twayne, 1983.

Nolan, William F. *The Black Mask Boys: Masters in the Hard-Boiled School of Detective Fiction.* New York: William Morrow, 1985.

Nolan, William F. *Hammett: A Life at the Edge.* New York: Congdon & Weed, 1983.

"The Most Dangerous Game"

by

Richard Connell

Born in New York in 1893, Richard Connell attended Harvard University, worked as a reporter for the *New York American* newspaper, and served in World War I. Following the war, Connell became a freelance writer. Writing mostly short stories and screenplays, Connell's most famous story, "The Most Dangerous Game," established him as one of the premier writers of fiction in the early 1920s.

Events in History at the Time of the Short Story

American interest in Central America and the Caribbean. When Theodore Roosevelt became president of the United States in 1901, his expansionist attitudes immediately began to affect U.S. foreign policy. One of the first steps of this new foreign policy was intervention in Cuba. American troops had occupied the island since Spain's withdrawal from the country in 1898 after the Spanish-American War. In 1901 the U.S. pushed for and won the Platt Amendment, which provided for American intervention in Cuba in case an unstable new government failed to protect life, liberty, and property. This amendment was written into Cuba's constitution.

With this relationship setting the precedent, American intervention in the internal affairs of unstable Caribbean and Latin American governments soon became common. In relation to its to political interests, the United States also developed economic interests in the area, becoming involved in Latin American banking, invest-

> **THE LITERARY WORK**
>
> A short story set in the Caribbean Sea in the early 1920s; published in 1924.
>
> **SYNOPSIS**
>
> A world-renowned hunter, sailing to the Amazon River to hunt jaguars, falls overboard and swims to a remote island. On the island he meets a wealthy Russian exile who forces him to engage in a deadly hunt in which he is the prey.

ments, and the development of natural resources. This constant intervention in Caribbean and Latin American affairs was officially justified in 1905 by Roosevelt's "Corollary to the Monroe Doctrine." This address to Congress presented Roosevelt's belief that the European nations must stay out of Latin America, leaving the United States as the only authority to step in and restore order or help create policy in the often turbulent nations. This statement was immediately put into practice in Venezuela, where the unstable and corrupt dictatorship refused to honor its debts to Germany. When Germany bombarded Fort San Carlos in an attempt to recoup its outstanding loans, the American government condemned the attack, dissuading the Germans from further action. The policy of American intervention would continue for the next fifty years, with a highlight of this policy being the construction of the

Panama Canal. The strategic passageway was created solely for the strengthening of American shipping and naval power. It is into the turbulent, American-dominated waters of the Caribbean that Rainsford, the central character of "The Most Dangerous Game," falls overboard in the early 1920s. The region was still largely under the influence of its American neighbor.

ROOSEVELT THE HUNTER

Like General Zaroff in "The Most Dangerous Game," Theodore Roosevelt was an insatiable hunter who pursued a wide variety of animals all over the globe. On safari in Africa in 1909, Roosevelt and his son killed 512 animals, including 17 lions, 11 elephants, 20 rhinoceroses, 9 giraffes, 47 gazelles, 8 hippopotamuses, 29 zebras, and 9 hyenas, among their other quarry. In Connell's story, Zaroff describes a similar hunt in Africa during which he was wounded by a charging Cape buffalo. Roosevelt had also hunted the dangerous animal. In the president's mind, though, the American grizzly bear was the most dangerous animal to hunt; Roosevelt had been nearly mauled by one during a hunting trip in Wyoming.

Big game hunting in South America. In Connell's era, big game hunting in South America, like Africa, was done mainly by outfitted safari. The most desired species were jaguar, puma, ocelot, red deer, and buffalo. The jaguar, the most powerful and most feared carnivore in South America, was a highly prized trophy. It attains a length of eight feet and can weigh up to four hundred pounds. The great jungle cat was hunted primarily with hounds in the deep forest areas of Venezuela, Colombia, Peru, Bolivia, Brazil, and Paraguay. In some cases, the jaguar was also hunted with meat bait placed where it came to drink, with hunters waiting in canoes nearby. In "The Most Dangerous Game," Rainsford and his companions are planning to hunt jaguars along the Amazon River in Brazil.

The Russian revolution and its refugees. The final decades of the nineteenth century marked turbulent times for Russia. After the emancipation of the Russian serfs, or peasant laborers, in 1861, the country as a whole began to expect that greater reform was unavoidable. The people would ultimately call for the revolutionary overthrow of the czar (or tsar), the autocratic em-

peror of Russia, but they first took a milder approach. On January 9, 1905, a priest named Georgi Gapon led a march in St. Petersburg to petition Czar Nicholas II for reforms. In response, the czar sent his soldiers, some Cossack troops, against the marchers, and thousands were ruthlessly killed. The incident came to be known as Bloody Sunday, the day on which the czar began to lose the allegiance of his people.

Socialist ideas, particularly the ideas of Karl Marx, were circulating through the nation in the early 1900s, and they gained adherents after 1905. Different Marxist groups appeared, with contrary ideas about the stages Russia must go through before becoming a socialist country. Meanwhile, the educated elite, the intelligentsia, started making a more conscious commitment to remove the czar.

With the outbreak of World War I in 1914, a resurgence of patriotism swept the nation and the revolutionary movement slowed. Russia, however, experienced a string of devastating military defeats, and the economy suffered. Unrest spread rapidly, with the people blaming the czar for the deaths of millions of young Russians in the military disasters and for the abysmal living conditions at home. Workers' strikes and demonstrations were followed by rebellion. Political radicals established a provisional government of their own in Russia in early 1917. The czar and his forces were unable to regain control of the situation. Shortly thereafter, his military leaders recommended that the czar abdicate, and he did.

After the czar abdicated, Russia continued to fight in World War I under the leadership of the country's provisional government. A socialist leader of this government, Alexander Kerensky, sponsored a new offensive in the war, but it failed. There was also little improvement in conditions at home. Food shortages mounted, and the new leaders failed to meet the people's demand for a constitution or for redistribution of land and money in Russia.

The Civil War. Some conservatives attempted to seize power from Kerensky, choosing a Cossack general, Lavrenti Kornilov, to lead their counterrevolutionary movement. To fend them off, Kerensky asked for help from the Bolsheviks, the group of Marxists led by Vladimir I. Lenin. The Bolsheviks were radicals who believed Russia did not have to pass through a capitalist phase before becoming a socialist country, and in the end they prevailed. After helping to defeat Kornilov, they seized control of the government themselves in late 1917.

Malcontents tried to raise armies to oppose these radical rulers, which led to a civil war (1918-1921) between the Bolsheviks (also called the Reds) and their opponents (the Whites). During the Civil War, the Cossacks were divided, some fighting for the anticommunist Whites and others siding with the Bolshevik Reds. The horrors of the struggle were monumental:

> The Civil War was a brutal and destructive bloodletting during which both sides engaged in wanton slaughter and inhumane reprisal. As the armies swept back and forth across the country, millions of people were killed or died of hunger and exposure. Millions more found themselves caught up in the savage carnage . . . killing and looting because someone had previously brutalized them.
>
> (Baradat, p. 67)

This carnage, as well as the gruesome experiences of World War I, no doubt desensitized some participants to the value of human life. Such horrors help explain the cold-heartedness of the Russian emigrant General Zaroff in "The Most Dangerous Game." When his guest objects to his disregard for the value of human life, Zaroff dismisses such concerns by mentioning World War I: "Surely your experiences in the war—" (Connell, "The Most Dangerous Game," p. 81).

The Bolsheviks were victorious in the Civil War in Russia and finally gained full control of the country in 1921. During the war, a pattern of emigration had begun as the enemies of the revolutionaries left the country. The emigration continued when the war ended—numerous conservatives fled possible retribution for their role against the now-legitimate Bolshevik government. Between 1917 and 1921, it is estimated that 2 million Russians left the country. Thirty thousand were Cossacks who had been fighting with the White armies. The greatest wave of them left Russia in early 1920, many wearing small bags of Cossack earth around their necks as a memento of a homeland they never expected to see again; the refugees spread through the world in search of new places to live. In Connell's story, both General Zaroff and his servant Ivan are Cossacks who were forced to flee the country sometime during this period (1917-1921) because of their loyalty to the czar.

Bigotry in America. The early 1920s was a difficult time for immigrants to the United States, who faced not only social and economic problems, but also the prejudiced and often widespread belief that their alien status was "tainting" American society. One of the greatest complaints stemmed from the theory that immigrants were inundating the labor market and lowering the American standard of living. One popular writer of the period, Kenneth Roberts, warned that unrestricted immigration would create "a hybrid race of people as worthless and futile as the good-for-nothing mongrels of Central America and southeastern Europe" (Roberts in Bailyn, p. 334).

With Americans becoming more worried about the possible adverse affects of immigration, public debate in the early twentieth century focused on the best techniques for restricting the entrance of immigrants into the country. The first attempt to better regulate immigration was the Literacy Test of 1917; this attempt failed completely because, contrary to popular belief, most immigrants could read and write. The next attempt was more elaborate, involving set immigration quotas by nationality. In 1921 Congress set strict quotas for each European country. Even more drastic was the National Origins Act of 1924, which initiated even lower immigration quotas. These new regulations assigned higher quotas to English, German, and Scandinavian immigrants while attempting to exclude Italians, Poles, and Slavs almost entirely. The new laws also completely restricted the immigration of Asians, Africans, and Hispanics.

THE COSSACKS

The Cossacks were a group of peoples from the region just north of the Black and Caspian seas. They had a history of independence and received special privileges from the Russian government for their fine military service. During the course of their assistance to various Russian monarchs, the Cossack peoples gradually lost their independence, and by the late eighteenth century, all Cossack males were required to serve in the Russian army for twenty years. Their primary duty in the nineteenth and twentieth centuries was to suppress revolutionary activities within the country.

In "The Most Dangerous Game," Zaroff's comments regarding ethnic types reflect the sentiments of anti-immigrant activists such as Kenneth Roberts. Zaroff describes his hunting of men to Rainsford and justifies it by saying, "I hunt the scum of the earth—sailors from tramp ships—Lascars, blacks, Chinese whites, mongrels—a thoroughbred horse or hound is worth more than

a score of them" ("The Most Dangerous Game,"
p. 81). In the early 1920s, this attitude was not
at all uncommon among white Americans.

The Short Story in Focus

The plot. Sanger Rainsford, a world-renowned
hunter, sails aboard a yacht bound for the Amazon, where he plans to hunt jaguars with several
companions. While passing Man-Trap Island, a
foreboding locale feared by the local sailors,
Rainsford hears shots echoing from the island.
Standing on the rail to get a better look, Rainsford falls overboard and nearly drowns. As the
yacht sails on, Rainsford realizes his only hope
is to swim for the island, where he at least knows
there are other people.

On the island, Rainsford finds evidence of a
hunting expedition: blood on the grass and a
shell casing from a small caliber cartridge. Following the hunter's footprints, he is amazed to
find an opulent chateau built among the island's
dense jungle growth. Rainsford is met at the front
door by an imposing giant of a man who points
a gun at him and shows no comprehension when
Rainsford addresses him. Fortunately, the owner
of the house, General Zaroff, arrives and introduces himself; he turns out to be a fellow hunter
and avid reader of Rainsford's hunting books.
Rainsford is immediately impressed by Zaroff's
elegant sophistication and the refinements he has
maintained even in the midst of his primitive surroundings.

Over a gourmet meal, Zaroff explains that he
is a Cossack nobleman who was forced to flee
Russia when the czar abdicated. His burly servant, Ivan, who is also a Cossack, traveled with
him. After successful hunting expeditions all
over the world, Zaroff had become despondent
when he realized that he no longer felt any challenge in the sport. His greatest disappointment,
he explains to Rainsford, is that animals are unable to reason, and so are easily conquered. Because of this failing in the animal species, Zaroff
has created his own hunting grounds on the islands where he is able to hunt the most dangerous game—prey that is able to reason. Rainsford realizes fearfully that Zaroff hunts men on
his island.

Undaunted by Rainsford's arguments against
his new variety of hunting, Zaroff shows off his
cellar, in which he has several sailors imprisoned.
He tells Rainsford that he gives the men sturdy
clothing and a knife, sets them loose, and then
hunts them. If they can survive for three days in

the jungle, Zaroff promises, he will give them
their freedom. Zaroff laments that the motley
sailors are poor sport and that he misses the excitement of a real challenge. Rainsford compre-
hends that he will be the next target.

The next day Rainsford is given clothing, a
knife, and a three-hour head start into the jungle. After carefully concealing his trail, Rainsford
is disconcerted when he sees Zaroff easily tracking him. Rainsford, understanding that he cannot elude Zaroff, sets a trap for his hunter.
Zaroff's quick reflexes save him from serious injury; nevertheless he is forced to return home to
dress his wound.

During Zaroff's next pursuit, another trap set
by Rainsford kills one of Zaroff's prized hunting
dogs. Though upset over the loss of the dog,
Zaroff commends Rainsford's abilities and is excited by the thrill of the hunt. Rainsford sets yet
another trap, and this time it kills Zaroff's faithful Ivan. As the hounds close in on him, Rainsford leaps off a cliff into the ocean. Zaroff, though
upset at losing both Ivan and Rainsford, still enjoys a luxurious dinner and a leisurely evening.
As he prepares for sleep, Zaroff is startled when
Rainsford steps out from behind a curtain. Rainsford kills Zaroff during the final struggle between
the hunter and the hunted.

Darwinism in the early twentieth century.
When Theodore Roosevelt began his expansionist foreign policies just after the turn of the century, there was a philosophical rationale for such
aggressive foreign policy via certain new ideas
that had come into favor following the Civil War.
These ideas, largely based on Charles Darwin's
treatise *On the Origin of Species,* had generated
great debate and were considered quite revolutionary. Roosevelt and other expansionist-
minded Americans found Darwinian phrases—
such as *natural selection, survival of the fittest,* and
the *law of the jungle*—to be perfectly suited to
their attitudes about foreign policy. Roosevelt
and other proponents of this new wave of "Manifest Destiny" (a term that had been used in the
1840s to describe the inevitability of U.S. expansionism), believed that the United States, as
a result of its emergence as a world power, was
a fit nation, and was furthermore destined to instruct backward countries on how to better manage their affairs.

Attitudes such as these led to assertions that
the United States must gain possessions in the
Caribbean Sea, Pacific Ocean, and Far East. Included in this expansionist doctrine was a belief that the United States must also maintain its

military superiority. Roosevelt warned Americans against a weak stance in foreign affairs. "If we stand idly by, if we seek merely swollen, slothful ease and ignoble peace, if we shrink from the hard contests where men must win at hazard of their lives and the risk of all they hold dear, then the bolder and stronger people will pass us by" (Roosevelt in Bailyn, p. 269). Zaroff's attitudes in "The Most Dangerous Game" follow the same thread of reasoning. Zaroff tells Rainsford, "Life is for the strong, to be lived by the strong, and, if needs be, taken by the strong. The weak of the world were put here to give the strong pleasure. I am strong. Why should I not use my gift?" ("The Most Dangerous Game," p. 81).

Sources. The specific sources that helped inspire "The Most Dangerous Game" are not known. It is, however, possible to draw parallels between events of Connell's period and material in his story, parallels that suggest possible influences in its creation. The attitudes and setting of the story reflect an interest in the major political issues of the early twentieth century, mainly Roosevelt's expansionist policies and the emerging fear of immigration. Roosevelt's hunting exploits were well chronicled in the media, and the story's focus on this activity, especially in the Caribbean, which was a major part of Roosevelt's expansionist politics, may reflect national preoccupations at the time. The fear of communism was another growing concern in Connell's America. His use of a Russian exile as a central character was probably inspired by the recent turmoil in Russia.

Publication and reception. Richard Connell was one of the most prolific short fiction writers of the early twentieth century, writing more than three hundred short stories during his career. Several of Connell's stories were made into films; "The Most Dangerous Game," Connell's best-known work and continually in print since 1924, has inspired several film versions, such as *The Most Dangerous Game* (1932), *A Game of Death* (1945), and *Run for the Sun* (1956). The story was also a success with the critics, winning Connell an O. Henry Award for short fiction in 1924.

For More Information

Acton, Edward. *Rethinking the Russian Revolution.* London: Edward Arnold, 1990.

Bailyn, Bernard, ed. *The Great Republic: A History of the American People.* Lexington: Heath, 1992.

Baradat, Leon P. *Soviet Political Society.* Englewood Cliffs, N.J.: Prentice-Hall, 1986.

Connell, Richard. "The Most Dangerous Game." In *O. Henry Memorial Award Prize Stories of 1924.* Garden City, N.Y.: Doubleday, Page, 1925.

Kunitz, Stanley J. *Twentieth Century Authors: A Biographical Dictionary of Modern Literature.* New York: H. W. Wilson, 1942.

Merli, Frank J. *Makers of American Diplomacy from Benjamin Franklin to Henry Kissinger.* New York: Scribner's, 1974.

Miller, Nathan. *Roosevelt: A Life.* New York: William Morrow, 1992.

Steinbrunner, Chris. *Encyclopedia of Mystery and Detection.* New York: McGraw-Hill, 1976.

Stone, Norman and Michael Glenny. *The Other Russia.* London: Faber & Faber, 1990.

Native Son

by
Richard Wright

Richard Wright, born in 1908 near Natchez, Mississippi, moved to Chicago with his family in 1927. In doing so the Wrights joined a steady stream of black families who left behind Southern poverty and racism to search for a better life in the North, in what came to be known as the "Great Migration." Often, however, they merely ended up trading rural poverty for urban squalor, with only superficial changes in the racism of the surrounding white society. This oppressive urban environment forms the backdrop to *Native Son*, Wright's first full-length novel.

THE LITERARY WORK

A novel set in Chicago in the 1930s; published in 1940.

SYNOPSIS

A young black man accidentally kills a rich white girl, an act that turns out to free him psychologically from the oppressive racism that has shaped his life, even as he is hunted down and imprisoned by white society.

Events in History at the Time of the Novel

The Great Migration. Blacks had begun leaving the South in significant numbers near the end of the nineteenth century, but in the period during and after World War I these numbers jumped dramatically. Between 1915 and 1930, over one million black Americans made the journey north, in what was at that time the largest migratory movement in American history. It would be surpassed only by a second wave of black migration northward, beginning in 1940 and lasting until the 1970s.

Both social and economic factors spurred the Great Migration (this term, originally applied to the first wave, is now often used to include both). During the first wave—that is, from 1915 to 1930—many Southern blacks believed that the racial prejudice to which they were subjected would lessen as they moved north. In Southern

states like Mississippi (where, like Wright himself, Bigger Thomas in *Native Son* was born), rumors spread that whites in the North would welcome black migrants. Even blacks who discounted such rumors made the move, expecting to find less discrimination than in the South. Added to this social incentive was the attraction of industrial jobs in Northern cities, metropolises in which large black populations now appeared for the first time.

The Great Depression. The Great Migration was slowed—but not stopped—by another massive event of the early twentieth century, the Great Depression of the 1930s. Nearly all Americans suffered during this period of economic upheaval as banks collapsed, savings evaporated, and wages fell while unemployment soared. In general, blacks were harder hit than whites, for as their pool of jobs shrank, whites began displacing black workers who had held menial jobs that whites once considered beneath them. The nation's unemployment rate, at 15 percent in 1930, peaked at 25 percent three years later and remained high for the rest of the decade. African American organizations estimated that black unemployment rates during the Depression were at least double the national figures. President Franklin Roosevelt's New Deal programs and the spur to American industry created by the demands of World War II brought some limited relief by the end of the decade, but throughout the 1930s joblessness and extreme poverty created a bleak outlook for urban blacks.

Chicago's South Side. Black populations rose in virtually every major Northern city from 1915 to 1930, but New York City and Chicago had by far the largest. In New York's Upper Manhattan, Harlem became home to the glittering black cultural movement known as the Harlem Renaissance, which flourished during the 1920s. Its Midwestern equivalent was found on Chicago's South Side. A good deal of Chicago's black residents lived on the city's South Side, in a narrow strip of land that whites called the Black Belt. Chicago's black population grew from 44,000 in 1910 to over 100,000 in 1920; by 1930, that figure had shot up to 278,000.

The Black Belt extended for some thirty blocks on either side of South State Street, the major artery running south from the Loop, Chicago's central business district. Unlike white immigrants, blacks were largely restricted to this single area, although there was an enclave located on the West Side. Those lucky enough to find work in a factory or meatpacking plant faced a long commute to and from work. Many, however, had little luck finding a job. "It was hard to get a job, oh real hard," one immigrant from Mississippi later remembered. "And it was double hard, triple hard for a colored to get jobs" (Grossman, pp. 182-83). As *Native Son* opens, Bigger Thomas has received an offer of work that his mother, brother, and sister pressure him to accept. For a young black man such an opportunity would have been rare, which explains his family's concern, for they have no other prospective source of steady income.

Housing in the Black Belt. The Black Belt reached its geographical limitations by about 1920; over the next ten years, as Chicago's black population more than doubled, the area in which blacks were forced to live hardly expanded at all. Housing discrimination prevented middle-class blacks (mostly the Old Settlers) from moving to white areas. Both black and white landlords, tak-

ing advantage of the blacks' inability to live elsewhere, charged high rents for what soon became slum dwellings. Often older run-down apartment buildings were divided up in small units called "kitchenettes," in which an entire family would occupy a single small room. One stove and a rough toilet might be shared among several such families. Bigger's family occupies a single room, whose squalor the opening scene of *Native Son* vividly illustrates as Bigger traps and kills a large, vicious rat.

BLACK INSTITUTIONS ON THE SOUTH SIDE

By the 1930s, the South Side of Chicago was beginning to replace Harlem as the nation's leading black community. Black roots went back further in Chicago than in the more recently settled Harlem, and by the time of the Great Migration older settlers had established a firm civic foundation on which the immigrants could rely. These earlier black immigrants, who had begun arriving in the last decades of the nineteenth century, called themselves "Old Settlers," while they referred to the more recent arrivals from the rural South as "Home People." The Old Settlers established religious institutions, including the African Methodist Episcopal (A.M.E.) Church and the Olivet Baptist Church; the Young Women's Christian Association and Young Men's Christian Association (YWCA and YMCA) also each operated one branch on the South Side. The black newspaper *The Defender*, which vocally attacked antiblack discrimination, had its offices on State Street.

While completing *Native Son*, Wright began work on a book for the Federal Writers' Project (part of Roosevelt's New Deal group of programs) that included a section about the South Side slums. In the book, called *12 Million Black Voices*, Wright describes the slums' economic injustice:

> And the Bosses of the Buildings take these old houses and convert them into "kitchenettes," and then rent them to us at rates so high that they make fabulous fortunes before the houses are too old for habitation. . . . They take, say, a seven-room apartment, which rents for $50 a month to whites, and cut it up into seven small apartments, of one room each. . . . The Bosses of the Buildings rent these kitchenettes to us at the rate of, say, $6 a week. Hence, the same apartment for which white people—who can

get jobs anywhere and who receive higher wages than we—pay $50 a month is rented to us for $42 a week!

(Wright, *12 Million Black Voices,* p. 104)

In *Native Son,* Mr. Dalton, the white man who employs Bigger and whose daughter Bigger accidentally kills, is just such a "Boss of the Buildings," a wealthy man who derives much of his income from renting slum apartments to blacks.

Lynching. The harshest manifestation of white prejudice and hegemony in the South, lynching is the murder without trial, usually by an angry mob, of a person accused of a crime or other transgression. White-on-black lynching mounted in the years after the Civil War, as Southern whites struggled to maintain control over freed blacks. This type of lynching, the most prevalent by far in the postwar years, reached its peak in the 1890s (when more than a hundred blacks were lynched each year), continuing in lesser numbers into the early decades of the twentieth century. Roughly 95 percent of all lynchings occurred in the South.

THE IDA B. WELLS HOMES

Born a slave in 1862, Ida B. Wells moved to Chicago after being driven out of Memphis in the 1890s for her anti-lynching writings in black newspapers there; she died in Chicago in 1930. Chicago's earliest housing project, the Ida B. Wells Homes, was built in the 1930s. The project, which provided housing for over fifteen thousand black families, was finished in 1940, the year that *Native Son* was published. Lauded at first by the black community, such projects were later seen as fostering segregation and helping to create a black ghetto.

Aside from lynching's harsh reality—a Southern reality, remembered if not encountered by black migrants to the North—even blacks in the North faced its constant threat. It is this threat to which Bigger responds when he finds himself, through no fault of his own, about to be discovered with a white girl in her bedroom. For as black antilynching crusader Ida B. Wells pointed out, a common excuse for lynching a black man was that he had raped a white woman. For many Southern white men, "rape" could mean anything from consensual sexual intimacy between a black man and a white woman to their simply holding hands. Or, as all blacks knew, the charge of rape

might simply be a fabricated excuse for whites to get rid of an "uppity" black.

A situation that many black men especially feared was having a white woman make sexual advances toward them. If the man rejected the advances, the woman might accuse him of rape, and he could easily face a lynching. If he accepted them, the couple might be discovered, in which case white men would accuse him of rape, and he would still be lynched. Either way, sexual involvement with a white woman—or even the hint of such involvement—meant mortal danger for black men in the South. In the North, too, the threat of lynching or other white mob violence (as depicted in *Native Son* after Bigger's arrest) remained a very real one in the minds of most blacks. Statistics show there was just cause for this fear. From 1882 to 1968, at least nineteen blacks were lynched in the Northern state of Illinois; they were accused most commonly of murder, assault, or rape.

Black activism in Chicago. If Harlem was African America's cultural capital in the century's opening decades, by the 1930s Chicago was becoming its political center. New York may have been headquarters for major black activist groups, such as the National Association for the Advancement of Colored People (NAACP) and the National Urban League, but the Chicago branches of these organizations were known for their radicalism in championing the rights of African Americans. Also, in the mid-1930s, Chicago became the home of Elijah Muhammad, founder of the Nation of Islam, a black nationalist organization with strong appeal to poor young male migrants from the South. In real life, thousands of potential Biggers changed course by joining the Nation of Islam, also known as the Black Muslims, whose strict dress and behavior codes underlie a strong spirit of community activism.

Native Son, however, explores the predicament of those who lack such antidotes to racism's constant psychological invasions. In keeping with this focus, the novel doesn't mention the Black Muslims. Also in this vein, the novel's references to the NAACP merely stress that organization's inclusion of whites, such as the wealthy Mr. Dalton, who eases his conscience by supporting black organizations while he grows rich charging exorbitant rents from poor blacks.

Communism. Though he would later abandon them, during the 1930s Richard Wright embraced communist ideas, like many American intellectuals at the time. To many writers and

Elijah Muhammad

artists, communism seemed to be a coherent response to democratic capitalism's obvious inequalities and shortcomings. While America and the rest of the capitalist world suffered in the depths of economic depression, communist Russia appeared to be making progress both economically and socially in creating a "classless" society. Wright joined the Communist Party in 1933 and was active in it until 1942.

The party supported black causes, most visibly by providing legal representation for the black defendants in the famous Scottsboro Case of the 1930s. Nine black youths, ages thirteen to twenty, had been arrested in Alabama in 1931, accused of raping two white women. When eight of the nine were sentenced to death by an Alabama court, the Communist Party took up the case, winning on appeal to the United States Supreme Court. Several of the defendants, however, were retried in Alabama and ended up serving long prison sentences, despite one of the alleged victims' having retracted her story. In *Native Son,* Jan Erlone, the communist boyfriend of Mary Dalton (the girl Bigger later kills), brings up the Scottsboro Case in conversation with Bigger, attempting to enlist his sympathies. Bigger, however, remains unresponsive to communist ideas. *Native Son* portrays communism, like black activism, as ultimately inef-

fective in combating racism's social and psychological effects.

The Novel in Focus

The plot. Bigger Thomas, a young black man, lives in poverty in a one-room apartment with his mother, younger brother, and sister. Though Bigger has been in reform school, a local job agency has managed to arrange an interview for him with a wealthy white man, Mr. Dalton, who needs a driver. Bigger grows irritated when his mother and sister pressure him to follow through with the interview, arranged for later that day. While deciding whether to go, Bigger encounters his friends, with whom he shares restlessness and contempt for whites. Prone to sudden acts of violence, Bigger attacks one of his friends at a pool hall where they meet.

Hired by Mr. Dalton, Bigger is given his first task—to drive the Daltons' daughter Mary to the university that evening. Mary, however, instead goes to meet her boyfriend Jan Erlone, a communist. The two whites have been working with the Communist Party to help blacks, and they insist on Bigger's accompanying them to a restaurant frequented by blacks. Later the three of them get drunk and Bigger takes Mary home. The girl is too drunk to make it to her room alone, so

Richard Wright

Bigger helps her to bed. Confused and aroused, Bigger is standing over the unconscious girl when Mrs. Dalton, who is blind, enters the bedroom.

In a panic over the possibility of being caught in a white girl's bedroom, Bigger puts a pillow over Mary's face to keep her from making a noise. As Mrs. Dalton approaches, calling out to see why Mary doesn't answer, Bigger unknowingly pushes down on the pillow, smothering the girl. Mrs. Dalton, meanwhile, having smelt the alcohol and concluded that Mary is drunk, leaves in disgust. Finding than he has killed Mary, Bigger takes the body to the basement and, after cutting the head off to make it fit, stuffs it into the coal furnace.

To avoid discovery, Bigger attempts to frame Jan for Mary's disappearance, lying to investigators and concocting a ransom note that he signs "Red," meaning communist (Wright, *Native Son,* p. 215). His ploy is discovered, however, when the remains of the body cause the furnace to malfunction. The story has by that point gotten heavy press coverage; in fact, a group of reporters are the ones who discover the girl's remains in the furnace after the basement fills with smoke.

Fleeing, Bigger turns to his girlfriend, Bessie, whose aid he had earlier enlisted with the ransom note. Having told her of his crime, he now kills her as well, battering her head with a brick

and dumping her down an air shaft. On the run, Bigger hides in abandoned buildings, venturing out to buy or steal newspapers so that he can keep abreast of the investigation. Finally, after encountering two policemen and knocking one of them out, Bigger is cornered and arrested.

In jail, Bigger turns inward, accepting responsibility for his crime without ever attempting to explain it away by describing the accidental circumstances that led to it. As he told Bessie, he has felt like killing many times before, but never had the opportunity. Now, in accepting his guilt, Bigger has gained a measure of control over his own life for the first time. Jan, who has forgiven Bigger, brings to Bigger's cell Boris Max, a lawyer from the Communist Party who says he will defend Bigger. Aside from the deaths of Mary and Bessie, Bigger is also charged with raping Mary, which most white observers of the case assume him to have done. At first remaining silent, Bigger later strongly denies the rape charge.

The grand jury, presided over by the coroner, opens by questioning the witnesses, including Jan Erlone and the Daltons. Under hostile questioning by the racially prejudiced and anticommunist prosecutor, Jan is accused of advocating, among other things, social equality for blacks. The coroner overrules Boris Max's objections to the questioning. Under Max's examination, Mr. Dalton describes his charitable support of black organizations such as the NAACP, but admits that he charges blacks higher rents than he would charge whites, and that he refuses to rent to blacks in white neighborhoods.

Indicted by the grand jury, Bigger faces a trial that is conducted on similar, racially biased lines. Max's long speech in Bigger's defense outlines the racial prejudice of white society, claiming that society itself has shaped Bigger to an extent that explains—if not excuses—Bigger's crime. Max has had Bigger plead guilty, but argues against a death sentence, asking instead for life imprisonment. After a brief recess, however, the judge sentences Bigger to death.

Having failed to get the governor to commute the sentence, Max visits Bigger, who has shut out the world and struggles to come to terms with his impending execution. In the novel's final scene, Max helps Bigger understand that his white persecutors share, in a fundamental way, the same hate-producing fear that has shaped Bigger's life. Finally freed from hate and fear, Bigger declares that he believes in himself, and that he is ready to face death.

Bigger and the outside world. In Bigger Thomas, Wright was determined to create a character for whom the reader could not feel pity. Only through such a character, Wright believed, could he dramatize the corrosive effects of racism, not only on its perpetrators but also on its victims. Wright thus portrays Bigger in terms that vividly illustrate the alienation that Bigger feels not only from white society, but also from other blacks, even from his own friends and family. Bigger exists as an island of rage and frustration in a world that offers him no rewards save those of violence.

One important way that Bigger interacts with the outside world is through the media—newsreels, magazines, newspapers. In the first half of *Native Son*, Bigger repeatedly feels an urge to retreat from reality into magazines and movie houses, where he views a newsreel featuring Mary Dalton as a glamorous society girl. When he sees news stories of German and Japanese conquests, he identifies with the urge to aggression that they represent. "He was not concerned with whether these acts were right or wrong," the novel tells us, "they simply appealed to him as possible avenues of escape" (*Native Son*, p. 130). Whether of a glamorous yet unreachable white world or of international events, the images he sees offer only momentary escape. Ulti-

mately they merely sharpen his sense of constant frustration.

Only after killing Mary Dalton does Bigger feel that he has somehow taken control of his life. He associates this feeling with the world he has been shown over and over in the media:

> He felt that he had destiny in his grasp. . . . [H]e was moving toward that sense of fulness he had so often but inadequately felt in magazines and movies. The shame and fear and hate which Mary and Jan and Mr. Dalton and that huge rich house had made rise so hot and hard in him had now cooled and softened. His being black and at the bottom of the world was something which he could take with a new-born strength. What his knife and gun had once meant to him, his knowledge of having secretly murdered Mary now meant.
> (*Native Son*, p. 170)

Just as the media exaggerates the glamour of white society, so does it distort Bigger by depicting him as brutishly savage. Describing him as a "beast" and an "ape," newspaper stories about Bigger assume his guilt: "It is easy to imagine how this man, in the grip of a brain-numbing sex passion, overpowered little Mary Dalton, raped her, murdered her, beheaded her" (*Native Son*, p. 323).

FROM A FICTIONAL NEWS STORY IN *NATIVE SON*

An Irish police captain remarked ... "I'm convinced that death is the only cure for the likes of him."... From Jackson, Mississippi, came a report yesterday from Edward Robertson, editor of the *Jackson Daily Star*, regarding Bigger Thomas' boyhood there. The editor wired: "He was raised here and is known to local residents as an irreformable sneak thief and liar."
(*Native Son*, p. 323)

FROM AN ACTUAL NEWS STORY ON ROBERT NIXON

From Tallulah [Louisiana] yesterday came a report on Nixon's boyhood there. Sherif [sic] A. J. D. Sezler of Madison parish wired: "Nixon was raised here and is known as a sneak thief and house prowler.... Nothing but death will cure him."
(*Chicago Daily Tribune*, sec. 1, p. 3)

Sources. Clearly, Wright took much of the material for *Native Son* from his own life experiences as a young migrant to Chicago from Mississippi. In an essay entitled "How 'Bigger' Was

Born," he enumerates no fewer than five "Biggers" he had known at various times in his life. All served as models for the fictional Bigger, though Wright also says that he had met many more Biggers, both black and white. Wright found literary models in the realism of authors such as Sherwood Anderson and Theodore Dreiser. He based the structure of *Native Son* on Dreiser's 1925 novel *An American Tragedy,* in which a young drifter accidentally commits murder, flees, gets caught, and then faces a concluding trial.

Wright also drew on a widely publicized case in which a young black Chicago man, Robert Nixon, was arrested and convicted of killing and raping several women. Wright's friend and biographer Margaret Walker reports that Wright, in New York when he was working on *Native Son,* asked her to send him clippings on the case from the Chicago papers. "The major portion of *Native Son* is built on information and action from those clippings," Walker claims (Walker, p. 123-24). For example, Nixon beat one of the women to death with a brick, and Bigger kills Bessie this same way in the novel. Echoes of the clippings also appear in the news stories that Wright includes in his narrative. Nixon was executed in 1939.

Reception. *Native Son* enjoyed immediate and spectacular success, both commercially and with the critics. Selling 250,000 copies within six weeks, it was chosen by the Book of the Month Club and stayed on the bestseller lists for months. It was reviewed by every major newspaper, making Richard Wright not only a major American literary figure but also a leading spokesman for African Americans.

Critics praised *Native Son* for its honest, unsentimental examination of racism's psychological effects. While most reviews were overwhelmingly favorable, there were a few attacks from both the black and white communities. James Baldwin, a young friend of Wright, dismissed the book in an essay entitled "Everybody's Protest Novel," arguing that its emphasis on social protest detracted from its artistic merit. Wright was also threatened with lynching if he came back to Mississippi. Many, however, agreed with Irving Howe, who wrote that "the day *Native Son* appeared, American culture was changed forever" (Howe in Walker, p. 153).

For More Information

Chicago Daily Tribune. (May 31, 1938): sec. 1, p. 3.

Goodman, James. *Stories of Scottsboro.* New York: Pantheon, 1994.

Grossman, James R. *Land of Hope: Chicago, Black Southerners and the Great Migration.* Chicago: University of Chicago Press, 1989.

Lemann, Nicholas. *The Promised Land: The Great Black Migration and How It Changed America.* New York: Vintage, 1992.

Walker, Margaret. *Richard Wright: Daemonic Genius.* New York: Amistad, 1988.

Wright, Richard. *Native Son.* 1940. Reprint. *Native Son and How "Bigger" Was Born.* New York: Harper, 1993.

Wright, Richard. *12 Million Black Voices: A Folk History of the Negro in the United States.* New York: Viking, 1941.

Noon Wine

by
Katherine Anne Porter

C allie Russell Porter (who later changed her first name to Katherine Anne) was born in a log cabin in Indian Creek, Texas, in 1890. Her travels of the early 1900s took her from revolution-torn Mexico to Berlin, Germany, to Paris, France. It was not until she moved to Paris in 1933 that she began to make use of her Texas past, returning in fiction to the world of her childhood in *Noon Wine*. Several decades later, after receiving high acclaim for her novel *Ship of Fools* (1962), Porter won the National Book Award and the Pulitzer Prize for *The Collected Stories of Katherine Anne Porter* (1965). Along with her latest work, the collection included previously released stories such as *Noon Wine*.

Events in History at the Time the Novel Takes Place

Swedish immigration. Although Swedes had been coming to America as early as 1638, the number of new Swedish immigrants swelled between 1868 and 1873 (103,000) and again between 1880 and 1893 (475,000). The exodus of the late 1800s represented about a fourth of Sweden's total population. The primary motive behind this mass emigration from Sweden was overpopulation. In the early 1800s, a sustained period of peace, the introduction of a vaccine for smallpox and increased production of potatoes in Sweden led to a doubling of the population from the mid-eighteenth to the mid-nineteenth century. The burden of the resulting labor surplus, and the potato famine that followed in the

---

> ### THE LITERARY WORK
>
> A short novel set on a small south Texas farm from 1896 to 1905; published in 1937 in the literary magazine *Story* and in 1939 in the collection *Pale Horse, Pale Rider: Three Short Novels*.
>
> ### SYNOPSIS
>
> Mr. Thompson, who runs a dairy farm with little help from his family, takes on a hired man named Olaf Helton. Industrious and resourceful, Helton soon turns the dilapidated farm into a profitable operation, but his presence there leads unexpectedly to murder.

1860s, hit Sweden's agrarian sector the hardest. By 1870, almost half of the farm population was landless.

Most Swedish immigrants to the United States found work on farms until the 1890s, when the decrease of homesteading and the vanishing of available frontier lands forced roughly a third of them to the cities. Some ambitious individuals had by this time founded colonies of Swedish immigrants in various locations. One instance took place in Texas, where Porter grew up. The rancher S. M. Swenson, an immigrant to Texas, where *Noon Wine* is set, brought over a group of Swedes to work his land in 1848, and his brother continued to bring over Swedes after the Civil War ended in 1865. By 1910, a few years after the story is set, there were as many as 4,000 Swedish Americans living in the vicinity of Austin, Texas. Here, as elsewhere, Swedish immigrants generally had little trouble getting work, for they were regarded as industrious and physically skilled.

LONG HOURS ON THE FARM

The hours of labor on farms were longer than even in the steel mills of Pennsylvania. In the South it was customary to work from sunrise until sunset; work on dairy farms generally started at four or five o'clock in the morning and did not end until seven or eight o'clock at night. Long hours, low pay, and irregular employment were what the immigrant could expect on a farm, so the majority of immigrants eventually found their way to the cities. While the early Swedish immigrants settled largely on farms, later generations would find work in urban centers as, for example machinists, railway laborers, and shipbuilders.

The Texas farmer around 1900. While *Noon Wine* centers around a family whose income depends on dairy farming, the dominant crop in Texas around the turn of the twentieth century was cotton. The year 1900 saw the state produce 2.5 million bales of cotton, and income from farming was on the rise at the time. It had dropped to desperately low levels during most of the 1890s, trapping families into a cycle of having to produce more each year just to keep up with what they had earned the previous year. Most Texas farmers fell increasingly into debt in the 1890s, regardless of how hard they worked. Meanwhile, a depression (1893-1897) crippled industries in the East, so hardship was a nationwide phenomenon during the decade. Conditions brightened by 1900, however, and Texas farmers went on to experience ten prosperous years in which they are said to have earned their fair share of the American income. In *Noon Wine*, the hired hand Helton turns the dairy farm into a moneymaking enterprise. A look at Texas's economic history shows that his efforts to do so roughly coincide with a general upswing in the Texas farm economy. The story, in other words, is set at a time when hard-working farmers were in fact compensated for their industriousness.

Labor shortage in Texas. After the Civil War (1861-1865) Southern capital vanished, bank stocks and deposits lost all value, and plantation owners went bankrupt. In Texas, farm stock decreased 20 percent from 1860 to 1866. In that same period, land values decreased 25 to 90 percent. Frustrated by the presence of recently freed black laborers, Texas planters advocated increased white immigration from other states and from Europe. In *Noon Wine*, Thompson welcomes the prospect of a white hired hand to help work his dairy farm. At one point he employed two black laborers, but, Thompson notes, "what I say is one middlin'-good white man ekals a whole passel of niggers any day of the week" (Porter, *Noon Wine*, p. 224).

The rural Texas economy had begun to recover by 1870, and immigration to Texas continued to increase thereafter. At one time its farmers hoped that the influx of Chinese immigrants would address the rural labor shortage, but the few Chinese who did move to Texas came to work not on the farms but on the railroads instead. The planters had more success promoting immigration from other states. Immigration was encouraged by state legislation designed to foster widespread settlement of the frontier so that pioneers could unite to withstand the constant Indian attacks. A Homestead Act that was passed in 1870 offered the head of a family 160 acres of public land after occupying it for three years, and the state established a Bureau of Immigration to attract not only settlers but also white immigrant labor. Such incentives, combined with unfavorable social and economic conditions in other Southern states, induced many to move west to Texas in hopes of starting anew after suffering through the economic collapse that followed the Civil War.

Insane asylums. In *Noon Wine*, Thompson learns that his hired hand, Helton, was once confined in an insane asylum for committing a murder. Insane asylums grew infamous at the end of the nineteenth century because patients or inmates were often mistreated. Immigrants and criminals formed a large segment of the asylum population, partly the result of states allocating funds to isolate the mentally unstable immigrant and criminal element from the mainstream society. Cases of brutality led to one governmental inquiry after another into the practices of a number of institutions. In 1889 a reporter for the *Chicago Times,* for example, exposed the murder of a patient by three attendants. Raising perhaps the loudest outcry among reformers of the era was the use of mechanical restraints in American insane asylums. In *Noon Wine*, Thompson recalls that they put his Aunt Ida in a straightjacket in the state asylum. She got violent, he said, and they put her in the jacket and tied her to an iron ring in the wall. It made her so wild that she burst a blood vessel. The attendants found her dead. "I'd think one of them things [the restraints] was dangerous," observes Helton (*Noon Wine*, p. 247). This is the type of institution from which Helton has managed to escape.

The Novel in Focus

The plot. Royale Earle Thompson is not a particularly good farmer. Concerned primarily with "his dignity and reputation," he has convinced himself that "running a dairy and chasing after chickens [is] woman's work" (*Noon Wine*, p. 233). His wife Ellie, however, is too weak to assist him, and his sons, Herbert and Arthur, are too young to be of any help. So the lazy and despairing Thompson has let the farm fall into disrepair. The gate is broken and the wagon shed is a receptacle for discarded junk; even his beard is hairy and unkempt.

But everything changes the day a Swede named Olaf Helton arrives from the wheat fields of North Dakota looking for work. Thompson hires him and promptly heads into town for a few drinks, leaving his wife sick in bed. Helton, a tireless worker who always does more than is required of him, quickly ingratiates himself in the Thompson household. Curiously, however, Helton almost never speaks. This disturbs the Thompsons at first, but they soon grow accustomed to it. Each day, when his work is finished, the otherwise inexpressive Helton sits down to play the harmonica—always the same tune. He does not drink, venture into town, or become involved in any sort of trouble. In fact, he does not even go to church. Playing the harmonica is his only diversion. Otherwise he keeps to himself.

Little by little, the once-dilapidated farm begins to look clean and run more efficiently. Before long, Thompson's debts are paid off and he is making a profit. For the first time since his marriage, Thompson has peace of mind. His worries about the cows, the chickens, and the raising of the children gradually fade away. Although secretly a little consternated at Helton's amazing industriousness, Thompson expresses nothing but gratitude and over time raises Helton's pay considerably.

Nine years pass, until one day a man named Homer Hatch arrives looking for Helton. Upon hearing the familiar sound of Helton's harmon-

Katherine Anne Porter

ica, Hatch explains that it is "a kind of Scandahoovian song. . . . It says something about starting out in the morning feeling so good you can't hardly stand it, so you drink up all your likker before noon. All the likker, y' understand, that you was saving for the noon lay-off. . . . It's a kind of drinking song" (*Noon Wine*, p. 246).

Thompson develops an instant dislike for Hatch, a feeling that turns out to be justified when he discovers that Hatch is a bounty hunter intent on taking Helton away. It seems that years ago in North Dakota, Helton killed his own brother with a pitchfork for losing Helton's harmonica, and that instead of being executed for the crime he had been sent to an asylum, from which he later escaped. Two weeks earlier, after nine years of silence, Helton had made his whereabouts known when he sent his mother a letter containing a check for the enormous sum of $850—presumably all of his savings. Hatch pulls out a pair of handcuffs; he wants Thompson's help in apprehending Helton.

But Thompson refuses. He defends Helton's character, claiming that "if he's crazy, why, I think I'll go crazy myself for a change" and ordering Hatch off the farm (*Noon Wine*, p. 247). Hatch draws a blade, and Helton appears from nowhere and intercedes between the two men, only to get stabbed in the stomach. Instinctively, Thompson grabs an ax and brings it down on Hatch's head, inadvertently killing him.

Although the court acquits Thompson of any wrongdoing, his life is never the same. With Helton gone, the farm quickly regresses to its former state of dilapidation. The real damage, however, is to Thompson's reputation and to his soul. Not satisfied with the court's acquittal, he spends his days traveling from house to house, talking to every neighbor about "self-defense" in a campaign to save his good name. Although most nod in agreement, he is convinced they don't believe him.

A FATAL SHOT

Sometime during her childhood, after hearing the sound of a distant shotgun, and shortly thereafter of the fatal shooting of a man named Pink Hodges, Porter watched a man she had never seen before walk through the gate of her family's farm with his wife. Their purpose was to speak to Porter's grandmother: "I swear, it was in self defense! His life or mine! If you don't believe me, ask my wife here. She saw it. My wife won't lie!" (Porter, "*Noon Wine:* The Sources," p. 476). Here was a man who, like Thompson in *Noon Wine,* took pains to declare his innocence in a neighbor-by-neighbor effort to clear his sullied reputation.

Thompson has apocalyptic visions. He is convinced this is the end for him. And one night this proves to be the case when he awakens from a dream about the murder of Hatch to find himself trying to strangle his own wife. When his sons come in, he explains that he did nothing wrong, but they don't believe him. Right then Thompson walks to the kitchen, takes his shotgun, goes to the edge of his property, writes a note to the world swearing his innocence of Hatch's murder, puts his mouth over the barrel of the gun, and pulls the trigger.

The woman's role on the Texas frontier. Thompson is convinced that many of his chores are "woman's work." His wife, Ellie, however, does not share this notion. In any case, Thompson never has the chance to ask her to do the work because she is continually sick in bed. When Thompson leaves for town, she says, "Looks like my head never will get any better."

Later, she wakes: "There she was, thank God, still alive, with supper to cook but no churning on hand" (*Noon Wine,* p. 227). Curiously, Ellie's vague infirmities prevent her from doing any farm work, but when it comes time to fix supper, she miraculously recovers.

Thompson, of course, is sorely disappointed at Ellie's inability to help out on the farm, considering himself "deprived of the main support in life which a man might expect in marriage" (*Noon Wine,* p. 234). And yet it was not Ellie's suitability for work that first attracted Thompson to her. In fact, it was quite the opposite: "He had fallen in love with her delicate waist and lace-trimmed petticoats and big blue eyes" (*Noon Wine,* p. 234). Thompson, it seems, wants both a lady and laborer. But as Ellie's behavior shows, these two roles are irreconcilable in her.

Despite the hardships that inevitably accompanied agrarian life on the frontier, the Anglo-American woman in Texas was nevertheless expected to fulfill the Victorian ideals of the "woman's woman." As Ann Patton Malone points out in *Women on the Texas Frontier,* "The ideal Victorian woman was passive, childlike, unreflective, self-sacrificing, and dependent" (Malone, p. 14). Malone points out that many of these women were not at all used to physical labor and were often bewildered when faced with the untraditional array of tasks that frontier life demanded of them. They had to contend with cooking, spinning, gardening, and frequently with sickness. Outbreaks of cholera and fevers were common, so that women became preoccupied with their health, as Ellie is in *Noon Wine.* Moreover, they suffered an isolated existence since other white settlers tended to situate in a scattered pattern of separate households and women were confined largely to the home.

While many women adapted to these conditions—especially if they had grown up on the Texas frontier—others never quite managed to adjust. Ellie's illness in *Noon Wine* might be legitimate or it could be an escape from or means of rebelling against such conditions. Even the thought of having to discipline her sons for their mischief-making paralyzes her: To get out of trouble, "they might tell her a lie, and she would have to . . . whip them. Or she would have to pretend to believe them, and they would get in the habit of lying. Or they might tell her the truth, and it would be something she would have to whip them for. The very thought of it gave her a headache" (*Noon Wine,* p. 238).

Her husband takes a perverse sort of pride in her delicate condition. Explaining to Hatch that she's been an invalid for fourteen years, Thompson boasts that his wife had four operations that cost him every nickel he made. In his view, a wife as expensive as his was a credit to have.

Sources. *Noon Wine* takes place on a small Texas farm between 1896 and 1905, which corresponds roughly to the time Porter spent in that region. At one point during her childhood, her father left his daughters with his cousin Ellen Skaggs Thompson. The Thompsons ran a chicken, dairy, and cotton farm and had a hired man by the name of Helton. At the time, Ellen Thompson was an invalid, the victim of an undiagnosed illness, much like the fictional Ellie Thompson in *Noon Wine*. It is less probable, however, that her easy-going husband, Gene Thompson, served as the basis for the fictional Royale Earle Thompson. A more likely choice would be Porter's own father, Harrison Porter, who exhibited "exactly the same kind of pride which Porter in the story attributed to Thompson" (Givner, p. 74).

The character of Helton has its roots in another experience from Porter's childhood: "I saw a bony, awkward, tired-looking man, tilted in a kitchen chair against the wall of his comfortless shack.... I was told he was someone's Swedish hired man" ("*Noon Wine:* The Sources," p. 477).

Events in History at the Time the Novel Was Written

Travels abroad. During the 1920s and 1930s, Porter lived in Mexico, Bermuda, Germany, Switzerland, and France. She later wrote that those places were "right" and "timely" for her at this period in her life but confessed that she had not felt at home in any of them. She was continually making notes for stories about Texas. "I was almost instinctively living in a sustained state of mind and feeling, quietly and secretly, comparing one thing with another, always remembering" ("*Noon Wine:* The Sources," p. 470).

Depression era. While Porter was abroad, the Texas economy suffered through the Great Depression that wracked the rest of the nation in the 1930s. Farms in Texas slumped into decline with laborers such as the story's Helton remaining jobless, gathering in cities where they joined unemployed workers. The average income in the Southwest dropped from $334 a year in 1929 to $141 in 1932. So low were prices that farmers left fields of cotton and oranges unharvested. To compound

problems, black blizzards, or "dusters," blighted the Texas Panhandle in 1934 and 1935, along with the drought that crippled farming in nearby states as well. President Franklin Delano Roosevelt responded to the disaster by overseeing the passage of the Farm Relief Act (also called the Agricultural Adjustment Act) that required farmers to limit their production of dairy and other products. In 1937, the year Porter's story appeared, the government set up the Farm Security Administration to enable those who worked hard to become landowners. The generous policy, which provided low-interest loans and a long-term payback period, was reminiscent of the Homestead Acts that had encouraged settlement of Texas in the late 1800s, when Porter's story was set.

A STORY IN SEVEN DAYS

Thirty years after she left her childhood home, the story of the Thompsons and Helton came to Porter in a rush of memory: "I wrote it [the story] as it stands except for a few pen corrections, in just seven days of trancelike absorption in a small room in an inn in rural Pennsylvania, from the early evening of November 14, 1936. Yet I had written the central part, the scene between Hatch and Thompson, which leads up to the murder, in Basel, Switzerland, in the summer of 1932" ("*Noon Wine:* The Sources," p. 487).

Reviews. Upon the publication of *Noon Wine,* the real-life Thompsons did not take kindly to Porter's portrayal of them as hateful and ignorant people, and thought the author should be sued (Givner, p. 76). Few critics agree with the Thompsons' reading; indeed, many have argued that the Thompsons are extremely sympathetic.

Whatever the case, Porter's vivid depictions of farm life were singled out as extraordinary, and critical response to the story as a whole was almost unanimously positive. Robert Penn Warren once said that, "Of the world's best twenty novelettes, she might probably have two of them." He then proceeded to name three: *Old Mortality, Pale Horse, Pale Rider,* and *Noon Wine* (Penn Warren in Stout, p. 256).

For More Information

Givner, Joan. *Katherine Anne Porter: A Life.* Athens: University of Georgia Press, 1991.

Malone, Ann Patton. *Women on the Texas Frontier: A Cross-Cultural Perspective.* El Paso: University of Texas Press, 1983.

Nunn, W. C. *Texas under the Carpetbaggers.* Austin: University of Texas Press, 1962.

Porter, Katherine Anne. *Noon Wine.* In *The Collected Stories of Katherine Anne Porter.* New York: Harcourt, Brace & World, 1965.

Porter, Katherine Anne. "*Noon Wine:* The Sources." In *The Collected Essays and Occasional Writings of Katherine Anne Porter.* New York: Dell, 1970.

Schafer, Joseph. *The Social History of American Agriculture.* New York: Macmillan, 1936.

Stout, James P. *Katherine Anne Porter: A Sense of the Times.* Charlottesville: University Press of Virginia, 1995.

Not without Laughter

by
Langston Hughes

THE LITERARY WORK

A novel set in Kansas in the first decades of the twentieth century; published in 1930.

SYNOPSIS

A young boy, growing up in a poor black family, struggles to understand the conflicts within his own family as well as the conflicts between whites and blacks that divide his community and the nation.

Langston Hughes was born in 1902 in a small town in Missouri, and lived for several years with his grandmother in Kansas before joining his mother in Chicago, Illinois. Moving to New York City, Hughes enrolled at Columbia University in 1921, but was lured away from his studies by the glitter of Broadway and by the flourishing clubs in Harlem. Hughes journeyed to the thriving ports of Africa such as Dakar and Luanda to see what he referred to as the motherland of his people. Then he lived and traveled in Europe before returning to the States, where he became the most famous poet of the Harlem Renaissance. His first novel, *Not without Laughter,* won the Harmon Foundation Gold Award for Literature, a $400 prize awarded to outstanding black artists.

Events in History at the Time the Novel Takes Place

Exodus from the South. After the Civil War, many impoverished blacks felt that they had little choice but to work for their former masters—not as slaves, but as sharecroppers. For the use of a plot of land, tools, seeds, plus clothing and food for his family, the black farmer would surrender to the landowner a share, usually 50 percent, of the harvest. Generally the landowner required that his sharecroppers also buy goods on credit at his store, which often consumed their portion of the income and robbed them of the chance to ever get ahead, or save enough to buy their own plots.

Searching for alternatives, some blacks fled the South. A devastating crop failure in 1878 spurred mass migration westward. Benjamin Singleton, an ex-slave from Tennessee, circulated flyers describing the opportunities in "Sunny Kansas." He established a land company, bought property in Kansas, and led several groups of Southern blacks there to live in separate, all-black towns. Altogether about 100,000 blacks left the South to move westward. Life for the destitute immigrants was scarcely easier in these new homes, and most of the all-black towns eventually dissolved.

The exodus slowed as white Southerners, irritated by the loss of their cheap labor, realized they had to offer better wages or income arrangements to give black workers some incentive to stay. Discouraging news from the new communities in the West dissuaded more migration, on top of which prominent black leaders such as

Frederick Douglass warned blacks against leaving the South, where he contended that they had a virtual monopoly on the labor supply. Nevertheless blacks continued to leave the South, both for Kansas and for even remoter locales like Chicago and even Mexico.

Labor unions. The Emancipation Proclamation added 4 million freed slaves to the United States's labor supply. Although many blacks could do little more than return to plantations as field hands, others competed with skilled white workers for jobs as craftsmen or artisans. To safeguard jobs for their white members, most labor unions denied membership to blacks.

The labor unions in the United States were just beginning to press for reforms, such as a maximum eight-hour workday. But when the white unions organized strikes to force management to heed their demands, management would often replace the strikers with black workers desperate for jobs. This practice forced some unions to change their policy and admit blacks as members.

Other unions, particularly those in the South, continued to deny admission to blacks, even though in doing so the white union members hurt themselves. The Industrial Commission on Relations and Conditions of Capital and Labor established by Congress in 1898 recorded that a unionized white bricklayer demanded $2.50 a day, whereas a black bricklayer could be hired for $1.75. "If a white bricklayer . . . asks for employment," one contractor testified, "and makes known his rate of wages, which is $2.50 a day . . . the employer may say to him in return, I can employ a Negro bricklayer who has as much skill as you, and will do as good service for $1.75. Now, I will put you on at $2.25" (Foner, p. 87).

Booker T. Washington and W. E. B. Du Bois. An ex-slave, Booker T. Washington was asked in 1881 to take charge of an industrial training school for blacks in Tuskegee, Alabama. Washington, by then a teacher, won renown as the Tuskegee Institute's reputation grew. In 1895 Washington delivered his most famous speech, known as the Atlanta Compromise, at the Cotton States and International Exposition in Atlanta. "Keep in mind," Washington warned young blacks, "that we shall prosper in proportion as we learn to dignify and glorify common labor" (Jackson, p. 22). Nothing so calmed the Southern whites as Washington's assertion that for the black people to agitate for social equality at this point would be extreme folly. He advocated a temporary compromise on white practices like segregation.

The year 1895 was also the one in which W. E. B. Du Bois, who would become Washington's most prominent opponent, became the first black man to earn a Ph.D., writing his doctoral thesis at Harvard on the suppression of the African slave trade. Du Bois went on to found the Niagara Movement (1905), which evolved into the National Association for the Advancement of Colored People (NAACP) and dedicated itself to opposing Washington's policy of compromise on practices such as segregation. Du Bois founded and edited *The Crisis* (1910-1934), a magazine that published many of the works of black artists during the Harlem Renaissance as well as his own writings.

Du Bois believed that Washington, by encouraging blacks to seek an industrial education, was limiting their opportunities. In his most famous book, **The Souls of Black Folk,** Du Bois describes Washington's efforts as a program of conciliation to the South, and silence in regard to civil and political rights. Du Bois believed that "the Talented Tenth . . . the best and most capable . . . must be schooled in the colleges and universities," not in a Tuskegee-style industrial training school (Du Bois in Jackson, p. 25). The members of the Talented Tenth would, Du Bois contended, educate and uplift the black people as well as explode myths of racial inferiority.

Blacks and the Christian church. In 1787, after being turned out of the inner sanctuary of the St. George Methodist Episcopal Church in Philadelphia by a white church trustee, two black men, Absalom Jones and Richard Allen, organized the first all-black church. Before this, both in the North and South, free blacks and slaves of all denominations worshipped alongside whites, roped off, however, in a "colored only" section of the church. Inspired by Jones and Allen, blacks founded all-black churches across the nation.

Baptists belong to the Protestant branch of Christianity, their name stemming from their beliefs about the rite of baptism, the symbolic use of water to cleanse a person of original sin. In their view the rite should be administered only to adults when they profess their religious faith, and it should be achieved by total submersion of the person in water. In post-Civil War America, most blacks were Christian, and almost three-fourths of the Christian blacks in the United States were Baptist. The black church served as a center for black social life outside the control of whites. In addition to religious services, churchgoers held suppers, lectures, Sunday schools, and meetings for women's societies or

Langston Hughes

workers. The church also furnished members with money when they were ill and provided funerals for the poor.

At the turn of the century a black middle class composed of white-collar workers and professionals emerged. Many members of this new middle class wished to distance themselves from the poorer blacks, who kept jobs as domestics or agricultural workers. The first step taken by members of this new middle class was to leave the Baptist church in favor of the Presbyterian or Episcopal church. To them, the rite of baptism and the spirituals popular in Baptist congregations seemed crude and primitive. These "cornfield ditties . . . [this] heathenish mode of worship," a Bishop of the African Methodist Episcopal church proclaimed, "[will] drive out all intelligence and refinement" (Meshack, p. 21).

The next step taken by these new members of the middle class was to remove any hint that their churches were all black. The Colored Methodist Episcopal Church became the Christian Methodist Episcopal Church. The middle-class leaders of the African Methodist Episcopal Church substituted *American* for "African." The attempts to compete with white congregations by building equally august and ornate churches left middle-class black congregations virtually bankrupt. Commenting on the demolition of a small church in Virginia to make way for a larger, more expensive building, William Wells Brown—an escaped slave who won fame through his writing after the Civil War—insisted that "the determination of late years to ape the whites in the erection of costly structures to worship in, is very injurious to our people" (Brown in Sernett, p. 242).

Going even further, at the turn of the century, many young black people scorned their parents' faith altogether. Christian piety in a racist nation seemed farcical to them. Commenting on this generation, W. E. B. Du Bois wrote "one type of Negro stands almost ready to curse God and die" (Sernett, p. 317). Harriet, a character in Hughes's novel, repudiates her mother's religion, complaining "the church has made a lot of you old Negroes act like Salvation Army people. . . . Your old Jesus is white. . . . He's white and stiff and don't like niggers!" (Hughes, *Not without Laughter*, p. 55).

Black soldiers in the First World War. When the United States declared war on Germany in 1917, prominent leaders such as Du Bois exhorted African Americans to enlist. The South contributed greatly to the number of blacks who were drafted. There was a tendency among the all-white draft boards in the South to conscript blacks of military-service age rather than take white men from their families. With more than 20,000 blacks already in the regular army and the state national guards, the War Department actually grew reluctant to accept black recruits and issued an order to halt black enlistment.

Brawls erupted between white civilians and black soldiers in training camps. Emboldened by their participation in the war effort, black trainees challenged the "Jim Crow" laws in some communities where they were stationed. When a black sergeant was refused admission to a theater in Manhattanville, Kansas, his regimental mates protested. The white general in charge, C. Ballou, responded by directing the troops to attend quietly to their duties and not venture into places where they were not wanted. When black soldiers tried to board a whites-only tram in Houston, Texas, there was an ensuing fight that claimed the lives of twelve civilians. Fourteen of the soldiers were sentenced to life imprisonment and thirteen were sentenced to death.

In spite of the contemptuous attitudes of white soldiers and officers towards their black comrades, the black combat divisions distinguished themselves as valorous soldiers. One black infantry unit won twenty-one American Distinguished Service Crosses and sixty-eight French War Crosses.

War slogans calling for the self-determination of all peoples and the end of German oppression inspired blacks with the hope that, after an Allied victory, racial justice would prevail in America. In 1919, however, a series of violent race riots which erupted in twenty-six cities across the country shattered these hopes. President Wilson sobered the nation by declaring that most of the outbreaks were started by whites. This injustice, he insisted, was particularly despicable because troops of black Americans had only recently returned from contributing significantly to victory in the war.

The Novel in Focus

The plot. Grandma Hager Williams lives in a dilapidated house in Stanton, Kansas, with Annjee, one of her three daughters, and Sandy, Annjee's son. Annjee works as a maid for a white family, and Grandma Hager, although old, continues to work as a washerwoman, often sending Sandy to fetch white people's clothes, which she then starches and irons. Tempy, Hager's oldest child, has avoided her family ever since she married a

Bessie Smith, "Empress of the Blues."

mail clerk who owns some property. Harriet, Hager's youngest child, has taken a job waiting tables instead of finishing school.

Hager is a loyal Baptist and her children's disinterest in the church worries her. Since she married, Tempy left the Baptist church. "Too many low niggers," she complained. Instead she joined an upper class church "where de best people go" (*Not without Laughter,* p. 37). Annjee is quite infatuated with her husband Jimboy, Sandy's irresponsible father, who is always roaming around the country in search of adventure or a job. She still attends church, where she prays for Jimboy's return. Harriet, who comes and goes at her mother's house, is Hager's greatest concern. Harriet refused to finish high school, insisting "there ain't no use in learnin' books fo' nothin' but to work in white folks' kitchens" (*Not without Laughter,* p. 36). Hager worries because "de chile goes with such a kinder wild crowd o' young folks" (*Not without Laughter,* pp. 38-9).

BLUES MUSICIANS

Opportunities in the music industry lured many blacks to cities like New Orleans, Memphis, St. Louis, and New York. For black women jobs as entertainers were often the sole alternative to tedious work as a domestic. Bessie Smith, for example, left Chattanooga, Tennessee, to pursue a career as a blues singer. She began touring in 1912 and by the 1920s was known as the Empress of the Blues.

Hager erupts with rage when Harriet announces her plans to quit her job as a waitress and work as a chambermaid in a hotel with Maudel, a friend of hers. "You ain't gonna work in no motel," she exclaims. "They's dives o' sin" (*Not without Laughter,* p. 53). She wishes Harriet were more like her sister Tempy. The comparison offends Harriet, who sneers "Tempy? . . . So respectable you can't touch her with a ten-foot pole. . . . When niggers get up in the world, they act just like white folks" (*Not without Laughter,* p. 54).

Jimboy sends a letter announcing his plan to return to Stanton. Scarcely a day after he arrives, the neighborhood echoes with "his rich low baritone voice giving birth to the blues" (*Not without Laughter,* p. 59). When Hager scolds Jimboy for losing his job as a bricklayer, he explains "the white union men started sayin' they couldn't work with me because I wasn't in the union . . . the boss came up and paid me off. 'Good man, too,' he says to me, 'but I can't buck the union.' So I said I'd join, but I knew they wouldn't let me" (*Not without Laughter,* p. 87).

Harriet leaves home and joins a traveling carnival, hoping to begin a career as a blues singer.

Jimboy gets the urge to travel again and leaves without even saying goodbye to Annjee. Once again abandoned by Jimboy, Annjee falls ill and spends her days in bed. Harriet sends a letter from Memphis, Tennessee, asking for enough money to buy her way home to Stanton. Since Annjee has not been able to work, she can only send the money she was saving for Sandy's Christmas present.

Harriet returns to Stanton, but decides to live with her friend Maudel in a seedy part of town rather than with her mother. A letter from Jimboy gives Annjee the resolve to leave Stanton and join him in Detroit, where he hopes to get a job in a car factory. She plans to leave Sandy behind with Hager. "One by one you leaves me," Hager sighs, "But Sandy's gonna stick by me . . . and I's gwine to make a fine man out o' [him]" (*Not without Laughter,* p. 173).

Sandy gets a job sweeping up in a barber shop after school, then soon leaves it to make a little more money cleaning up in a hotel. Harriet is arrested for prostitution and fined $10. Sandy often sees her parading outside the hotel with men in fancy clothes. In the hotel customers recount obscene stories that make Sandy ill. Once, when summoned by a client, he opens the door to see a white woman standing naked in the middle of the room combing her hair. "Come in," the man with her says, "she won't bite." But Sandy flees, thinking "colored boys [get] lynched for looking at white women, even with their clothes on" (*Not without Laughter,* p. 213).

Grandma Hager falls seriously ill. Although she insists she is fine, the doctor says she will soon die. Harriet and Tempy send a letter to Annjee, but Hager dies long before they receive any response. Harriet then disappears, and is rumored to have appeared on stage in Kansas City. Back in Stanton, Sandy moves into Tempy's house, where he must get up early, speak grammatically correct English, and wear outfits from an expensive clothing store.

Sandy gets the mumps, and to amuse himself while he is bedridden, he takes up reading. He leafs through Tempy's copies of *The Crisis,* a monthly publication featuring the writing of W. E. B. Du Bois. "He is a great man," Tempy says. Remembering that Hager had once called

Washington the greatest of men, Sandy asks "Great like Booker T. Washington?" "Teaching Negroes to be servants," Tempy snorts, "that's all Washington did!" (*Not without Laughter*, p. 242).

In spite of Tempy's objections, Sandy starts to spend his evenings at a local pool hall. Here he can shoot dice, play pool, or sit outside with his friends and watch the girls go by. One evening he picks up a newspaper and reads "Actress makes hit . . . Harrietta Williams, sensational young blues-singer, has been packing the Booker Washington Theater" (*Not without Laughter,* p. 253).

World War I has broken out and Tempy is convinced "colored boys are over there fighting . . . white folks will see that the Negro can be trusted in war as well as peace. Times will be better after this for all of us" (*Not without Laughter,* p. 255). A letter from Annjee informs Sandy that his father has enlisted and been sent off to France. Another letter from his mother says that she has found a job for Sandy in Chicago as an elevator attendant. Although he has not yet finished school, Sandy leaves Stanton to join his mother, dreaming of the shiny towers of a metropolitan city.

The dusty slums of Chicago disappoint Sandy, and his work is dull and monotonous. He wants to finish school, but cannot afford to quit his job. When Harriet comes to Chicago to perform, Annjee and Sandy get tickets. The show is a smash. Afterwards Sandy and his mother join Harriet at a restaurant. Harriet is appalled to learn that Sandy has not finished school. "Hager'd turn over in her grave," she exclaims, "the way she wanted to make something out of this kid" (*Not without Laughter,* p. 297). She offers to give Sandy the money he needs to quit his job.

Generational conflicts. Hager's quarrels with her daughters reveal the conflicting attitudes that divided emancipated slaves from their children. When Harriet exclaims:

> Darkies . . . like the church too much, but white folks don't care nothing about it at all. They're too busy getting theirs out of this world, not from God. And I don't blame 'em, except that they're so mean to niggers.
>
> (*Not without Laughter,* p. 82)

Hager scolds her:

> Honey, don't talk that way, it ain't Christian, chile. If you don't like 'em, pray for 'em, but don't feel evil against 'em. I was in slavery, Harrie, an' I been knowin white folks all ma life, an' they's good as far as they can see—but when

it comes to po' niggers, they just can't see far, that's all.
>
> (*Not without Laughter*, p. 82)

But Harriet mistakes her mother's forbearance for resignation. "You can pray for 'em if you want to, mama," she exclaims, "but I hate 'em! . . . I hate white folks!" (*Not without Laughter*, p. 90).

Meanwhile, Tempy's arrogance reflects the haughty disdain many middle-class blacks expressed for poorer blacks. "Tempy," Harriet cries out in disgust, "the highest-class Christian in the family—Episcopal, and so holy she can't even visit her own mother" (*Not without Laughter,* p. 55). Tempy's contempt for Booker T. Washington was another trendy pose for the many middle-class blacks who preferred Du Bois. "Du Bois was a doctor of philosophy and had studied in Europe! . . . That's what Negroes needed to do," Tempy thinks, "get smart, study books, go to Europe" (*Not without Laughter,* p. 242). Hesitant to trust his aunt's judgment, Sandy reads Washington's **Up from Slavery** and decides that both Washington and Du Bois were great men.

Sources. Hughes created his characters based on his own childhood memories. "I wanted to write about a typical Negro family in the Middle West," he explained in his autobiography, "about people like those I had known in Kansas." But he conceded that his "was not a typical Negro family. My grandmother never took in washing or worked in service or went much to church. She had lived in Oberlin and spoke perfect English, without a trace of dialect" (Hughes, *The Big Sea,* p. 303). "For the purposes of the novel," he explains, "I created around myself what seemed to me a family more typical of Negro life in Kansas than my own had been. I gave myself aunts I didn't have, modeled after other children's aunts whom I had known" (Hughes, *The Big Sea,* p. 304).

Although Sandy's family is not like Hughes's family, Sandy resembles Hughes himself. Like Sandy, Hughes worked as a child "cleaning up the lobby and toilets of an old hotel" (Hughes, *The Big Sea,* p. 22). Living in a small town in Kansas, Hughes also dreamt of the seemingly biggest town in the world—Chicago. And Hughes's father, like Jimboy, left Hughes's mother to travel.

Events in History at the Time the Novel Was Written

The novel in Hughes's life. Hughes's parents separated soon after his birth. His father went to

Mexico, hoping to escape discrimination. While his mother traveled in search of a good job, Langston lived in Lawrence, Kansas, with his grandmother. "I was unhappy for a long time, and very lonesome, living with my grandmother," he wrote in his autobiography. "Then it was that books began to happen to me, and I began to believe in books and nothing but books" (Hughes, *The Big Sea*, p. 16). After his grandmother's death in 1914 Hughes lived with an old friend of hers whom he called "Auntie Reed." Auntie Reed, a practicing Christian, made Hughes go to church each Sunday.

Hughes finished high school, and then, after publishing some of his first poems in *The Crisis* in 1921, enrolled at Columbia University. He soon left, however, to take jobs around New York City and later as a cook's helper on a boat to Africa. After traveling in Africa and Europe, Hughes returned to the United States to continue publishing his poetry. In 1926 he enrolled at Lincoln University in Pennsylvania, where he wrote *Not without Laughter*, which was published as he was graduating.

The Harlem Renaissance. The Harlem Renaissance is the term used to describe the creative outpouring of black poets, artists, and musicians in the 1920s centered around this section of Manhattan. In the first decade of the nineteenth century, middle-class blacks had settled in Harlem, then an affluent, predominantly white suburb, to escape the crowded slums of New York. As blacks moved in to the community, many whites moved out. This black community, growing in the center of a city considered the artistic capital of the United States, became a mecca for black artists.

In 1925 Alain Locke, one of the writers of the Harlem Renaissance, captured the spirit of the movement in the title of an anthology of works by young writers, *The New Negro*. Whereas many black artists before the war had sought to imitate European artistic trends, artists of the Harlem Renaissance renounced the goal of assimilation. Confronting, rather than eschewing, racial issues, they forged poetry and music from their experience as an oppressed minority with its own rich cultural traditions.

The surge of interest among whites in black culture during the 1920s coincided with a popular uprising against the restraints of remnants of the Victorian era and Prohibition. While some whites were genuinely interested in the distinc-

tive and innovative black artists, others turned blacks into a symbol of liberation. Many black authors, in sore need of cash prizes offered by white patrons, satisfied this taste, reproducing in their writing the exotic image of the noble savage. "A Negro writer these days is a racket," asserts one of black novelist Wallace Thurman's characters, "and I'm going to make the most of it while it lasts" (Kellner, p. xxiii).

Reception. *Not without Laughter* received mixed reviews. Some critics praised the novel, insisting, "Hughes more than any other author knows and loves the Negro masses" (Dickinson, p. 59). But other reviewers were less enthusiastic. "Hughes would have done well," one critic says, "to treat Sandy at greater length" (Dickinson, p. 58). Some black reviewers considered Sandy's decision to finish his education a triumph of conservative or assimilationist tendencies. "Sandy emerges as a symbol of racial advancement," one critic pointed out, "which is hardly a laughing matter" (Dickinson, p. 59). After listing the "Books We Must Read," the editors of *The Crisis* included *Not without Laughter* in the list of "Books One May Read." This label, however, hardly slowed the sales of Hughes's popular novel, whose publication had been eagerly anticipated; he was by then a prominent poet.

For More Information

Dickinson, Donald. *A Bio-Bibliography of Langston Hughes, 1920-1960.* Ann Arbor, Mich.: University Microfilms, 1964.

Foner, Philip. *Organized Labor and the Black Worker, 1619-1981.* New York: International, 1974.

Hughes, Langston. *Not without Laughter.* New York: Scribner Paperback Fiction, 1969.

Hughes, Langston. *The Big Sea.* New York: Alfred A. Knopf, 1940.

Jackson, Florence. *The Black Man in America, 1877-1905.* New York: Franklin Watts, 1973.

Kellner, Bruce. *The Harlem Renaissance: A Historical Dictionary for the Era.* Westport, Conn.: Greenwood, 1984.

Meshack, B. A., *Is the Baptist Church Relevant to the Black Community?* San Francisco: R. and E. Research Associates, 1976.

Rampersad, Arnold. *The Life of Langston Hughes.* 2 vols. New York: Oxford University Press, 1986-1988.

Sernett, Milton. *Afro-American Religious History.* Durham, N.C.: Duke University Press, 1985.

O Pioneers!

by

Willa Cather

Born in 1873, Willa Cather moved with her family to Webster County, Nebraska, when she was nine years old. Nebraska was an untamed prairie at the time and one inhospitable to settlement. Its dry, hard soil and a lack of trees and greenery made the territory highly unsuitable for farming and living. But encouraged by the federal Homestead Act of 1862, which promised 160 acres to anyone who settled the land, pioneers moved to the region by the thousands and eventually transformed it into the breadbasket of America. Cather wrote *O Pioneers!* based on her experiences as a second-generation immigrant homesteader. In the novel she tells the story of a pioneer family in turn-of-the-century Nebraska, portraying the struggles these early pioneers endured, the hardships they overcame, and physical and cultural transformation they wrought upon the territory in which they lived.

THE LITERARY WORK

A novel set in turn-of-the century Nebraska, written and published in 1913.

SYNOPSIS

Daughter of an original Nebraska homesteader, Alexandra Bergson fulfills her father's dream of transforming the arid, hostile Midwestern territory into fertile farmland.

Events in History at the Time of the Novel

History of Nebraska. An early white explorer traveling in 1806 through the area now known as Nebraska described it as a barren, parched land that would "become in time equally celebrated as the sandy desarts [sic] of Africa" (Creigh, p. 5). Subsequent explorers who mapped the region in 1820 described it as the Great American Desert. Yet despite these foreboding descriptions of the arid climate and wild landscape, American pioneers arrived eagerly to settle the land. At first the area was thought of as

the great highway linking the east and west coasts. The Oregon, California, Overland, and Mormon Trails all passed through what would become Nebraska and from 1841 to 1866 approximately 350,000 settlers traversed the region, most bound for California, Oregon, Utah, and Alaska.

Nebraska did not become a state until 1867. Settlers were lured partly by the promise of land made available through the Homestead Act and also by the building of the transcontinental railroad, which was begun in 1865. They arrived by the thousands, and the population of the state increased dramatically over the next three decades, rising from a few thousand in 1860 to over one million by 1890. In 1863 there were 349 registered claims to land in Nebraska. By 1900 the number of land claims had climbed to 150,000. A number of these claims were located in a region sometimes called the Divide—an expanse of plains situated between the Republican

A late-nineteenth-century frontier homestead.

River and Little Blue River in south central Nebraska.

The Homestead Act. Designed to populate and settle land west of the Mississippi River (for eventual incorporation into the United States), the Homestead Act of 1862 granted 160 acres free of charge to each family head or adult who built a house and settled on the property, then farmed it for five years or paid $1.25 an acre after six months of living on it. Following the Civil War, settlers migrated west in the tens of thousands, many of them lured by the terms of the Homestead Act. Land speculators as well as farmers acquired vast tracts of land thanks to the six-months option. In fact, many took advantage of the six-months option, purchasing the land outright after this time period, then mortgaging it and borrowing against it to make improvements. As illustrated in the novel, many speculators became rich by buying land from destitute early homesteaders who were forced to sell before the land became fruitful.

Most prevalent among the Nebraska pioneers were Civil War veterans and European immigrants who moved to the state with aspirations of becoming prosperous farmers and landowners. However, when the homesteaders arrived, they were greeted with a stark reality. The land was as barren as a desert and the soil seemingly impenetrable. Hostile Native American tribes, including the Mandan and Pawnee, who had been forced from their land through treaties with the American government, provided a second formidable deterrent to settlement. Yet another drawback was that the homesteaders generally settled miles from one another and therefore lived very isolated lives.

Colorful communities. On the Divide, where the novel's fictional Bergson family settles, residents were primarily comprised of northern and eastern European immigrants, primarily German, French, Swedish, Norwegian, Russian, and Bohemian. The Homestead Act coincided with famine and crop failures in Europe in the 1860s, which prompted a flood of European immigration. Religious repression was a second cause of mass immigration to the United States, still a young nation that promised freedom of expression and seemingly limitless economic opportunity.

Most European immigrants who settled in the Midwest were of modest means and had never been landowners. Certainly none had farmed prairie land before and had little knowledge of which crops would thrive and which would fail. The farming of the land was done through trial and error, with each immigrant group trying crops indigenous to their homeland and sharing with neighbors the news of those that failed and those that prospered. For example, the Russians brought with them seeds of winter wheat. This crop turned out to be the most successful of all, and so by 1900 homesteader farmers who remained on the prairie grew winter wheat. Fruit trees, including apricot trees brought by French and Scandinavian settlers, also took root, providing much needed wood and natural barriers to roaming animals, as well as a welcome variation to the bland diet of meat and grains.

Reflected in the novel is the fact that the prairie communities were an eclectic mix. The Norwegian Jansson, German Lutheran, French Catholic, Russian Orthodox, and Bohemian Church were among the religious institutions established on the Divide. It was common for residents to attend a variety of churches and mix socially at each church's functions. Because farms were so far apart and communication so primitive, homesteaders interacted at every opportunity. There was little intermarriage, however, and most ethnic groups preserved their own cultures and languages as long as they could.

Extreme hardship. Loneliness and hardship were familiar parts of homesteaders' lives. From 1872 on, a series of natural disasters occurred in the region annually. Blizzards, tornadoes, dust storms, heavy snowfall, freezes, blistering heat, constant wind, and swarms of grasshoppers numbered among the calamities that befell the Nebraskan settlers. There were no trees with which to build houses and barns, which made settlement very difficult and required innovation. Taking cues from local Mandan and Pawnee Indians, the first homesteaders built sod houses and also carved dugouts into riverbanks. The sod houses, made from a dirt-and-grass mixture, were subject to trampling from buffalo and susceptible to strong wind; the dugouts, cave-like dwellings, were less susceptible to wind and wild animals but remained impractical and far from comfortable. Later dwellings included log houses, such as the one that Alexandra occupies in the novel.

Isolation and women. The isolation of the prairies was especially hard on pioneer women. Though more commonly assigned nondomestic roles than their city-dwelling counterparts, women by and large remained outside of the community of male farmers. Men sometimes worked side by side in the fields, met regularly for business purposes, and gathered in public houses (taverns) in the evenings. Women, on the other hand, rarely worked together outdoors or encountered each other in business settings, and they were not generally allowed in public houses. As one homesteader recollects:

> To me, the greatest credit for the winning of the West should go to the wives and mothers who worked so hard and unendingly to make it possible for their husbands and children to succeed. A man cannot comprehend the torture that many of these women went through, the mental agony they suffered. Deprivations were countless: a sick child . . . dying . . . simply because there was no doctor . . . children crying for food that the family simply didn't have; mothers doing without food in order to keep their children healthy; the ever present loneliness on the prairies, with no other female companionship; homesickness that so overwhelmed them that they would sit alone and cry, cry and cry.
>
> (Youngquist, p. 54)

Leaving behind the culture and comforts of their European homelands was also difficult—especially for Swedish immigrants who had led prosperous lives in thriving communities before the Scandinavian bank failures of the 1870s. Women had to adapt to the absence of community and make do with what few staples existed on the prairie. Cooking and housekeeping in a sod house with dirt floors were highly challenging pursuits. Combined with the desolate landscape and harsh climate, the loneliness of daily life took its toll on many early pioneer women. Suicides by ingestion of lye and hanging were recorded, as were diagnoses of "frontier madness," whose victims were sent to asylums in nearby Iowa until Nebraska built its own in 1869 (Creigh, p. 98). In the novel, Alexandra must constantly battle her loneliness and remedies it by importing Swedish domestic workers. These young women, though not necessary as workers, provided company for Alexandra as well as ties to her Swedish culture.

Swedish immigrants. Between 1851 and 1930, 1.2 million Swedes immigrated to America, settling in states like Minnesota and Nebraska. Crop failures, famine, bank failures, and the thirst for religious freedom were some of their main reasons for emigrating. Swedes tended to be of higher social standing than many other immigrants. By and large most Swedish immigrants arrived in America with some money and had experience as farmers and landowners. Swedes naturally gravitated to the Midwest, where farming and landownership were possible. But the landscape of the Midwest was a stark contrast to that of Sweden, a country of mountains and flat or rolling terrain with large lakes. This meant their previous farming experience proved to be of little value on the Divide. Most who arrived in the 1860s, as Alexandra's father did in the novel, moved elsewhere after ten years.

Hardy, innovative individuals. The harsh living conditions of the Nebraskan settlers produced a unique breed of individual. The extreme ruggedness of the land seemed to require the same traits in those that settled it. The pioneers who stayed and transformed the land are often described as "survivalists" (Steenrod, p. 29). A Nebraskan homesteader recollecting the era says: "What developed was a community of innovative, frugal citizens. Almost overnight they had created a culture [for] which no previous experience could have prepared them. They seemed to be tied to the land" (Steenrod, p. 29). In *O Pioneers!* Carl Linstrum repeatedly insists that Alexandra Bergson is such a rugged individual, able to create fertile farmland under the most adverse of conditions. Cather maintains that "A pioneer should have imagination . . . should be able to enjoy the idea of things more than the things themselves" (Cather in O'Brien, p. 430). This is perhaps the reason why Alexandra is successful when others, including her seemingly dim-witted brothers, are not.

As the novel illustrates, the homesteaders eventually succeeded in turning the hard soil of the prairies into farmable land through innovation and perseverance. After initial corn crops failed, Nebraskan homesteaders began planting more suitable crops, such as wheat, and alfalfa, which adds nutrients to the soil. The fruit trees they planted, in time, provided natural fencing and barriers to roaming cattle and wild animals that threatened to trample crops. After Joseph F. Glidden sold the first piece of barbed wire in 1874, they pioneered the use of barbed-wire fencing to protect fields in the absence of wood for fence-building. They also harnessed the power of the prevalent wind by building windmills, which also gained popularity in the 1870s. Lacking wood for fuel, they burned dried cow manure and through sheer determination and fortitude survived the first years of settlement that produced few gains and much hardship.

By 1913 Nebraska farms were very profitable, producing high yields at good prices (80 cents for a bushel of wheat) and low operating costs. Among the survivors were approximately half of those who originally staked claims in the 1860s. They had withstood the threat of bank foreclo-

Willa Cather

sure on mortgaged land and the frequent natural disasters that ruined so many early harvests, becoming the prosperous farmers and landowners they originally aspired to be. World War I would further bolster profits along the Midwest farm belt, driving demand and prices for wheat up to $1.60 a bushel in 1916. Nebraska truly had become the nation's breadbasket within a matter of decades, a desert literally transformed into a land of "milk and honey."

Victorian era. Turn of the century America—even on the frontier—was strongly influenced by Victorian England. On the surface the Victorian age was characterized by extreme conservatism and prudishness. Sexuality was repressed in public. Books, plays, and publications were censored for sexual content; pregnant women were not to be seen in public; even curved legs on pianos and other furniture would be covered by drapes for fear they might evoke unsavory emotions. Male and female roles were very clearly defined: Men were supposed to be breadwinners and work outside the home; women were relegated to the domestic sphere, in charge of home and child-rearing. Despite these ideals, a survey of American women in the late-nineteenth century showed that in private "a sizeable proportion of educated women enjoyed their sex lives" (Hellerstein et al., p. 126). Also, a growing number of women ventured outside the home to work in schools and, even more daringly, in factories, thereby challenging the limits of their prescribed roles.

The demands of frontier life also challenged many Victorian social conventions and gender roles. Due to the sparse population in the area, pioneers were required to do virtually all jobs pertaining to settlement, regardless of gender. Women planted and harvested crops alongside men when required and even owned land personally (as does Alexandra in the novel), in contrast to conventional standards of the day. The immigrant status of most homesteaders served as a boost for women challenging predefined roles. Not of English ancestry or even born in America, immigrant pioneers were not necessarily bound by Victorian social conventions. But while great strides were made, many Victorian conventions remained firmly in place even on the Divide. As shown in *O Pioneers!*, the concepts of the man being the only acceptable breadwinner, and of repressed sexuality, are conveyed through the relationship between Alexandra and Carl. It is not socially acceptable for Alexandra to be older and more successful than Carl, and she is not allowed to carry on any sort of romantic relationship with him until he becomes the breadwinner. Through the portrayal of Alexandra, Cather shows the positive effects of homesteading on redefining women's roles and on lowering the barriers to equality that remained through the era and beyond.

The Novel in Focus

The plot. *O Pioneers!* opens with a portrait of Hanover, Nebraska, in the 1880s. It is a dusty, windy Midwest town in Nebraska's tableland, sparsely populated by homesteaders. The novel introduces its main characters and exposes the traits that will ultimately determine their fates. Emil Bergson is a five-year-old, fair-haired Swedish boy. Impulsive by nature but intelligent, he is overly reliant on his older sister. Alexandra, a strong, clear-thinking girl in her teens, takes care of her little brother, a role she will obviously play for her entire life. Helpful and able-bodied Carl Linstrum—Alexandra's neighbor—assists Alexandra with her brother and accompanies them back to their homestead from town—a long wagon ride out into the barren prairie. Alexandra is deeply upset because she has just found

out her father will die soon and there is nothing the doctor can do for him.

John Bergson, Alexandra's father, brought his family to the Nebraska Divide eleven years earlier, choosing a spot that overlooked Norway Creek to stake his claim under the Homestead Act. A Swedish immigrant, John hoped to make a better life for his family. Though the land was wild and inhospitable, John believed that one day it would be transformed into valuable, fertile farmland that provided for his family. But like most immigrant homesteaders, he had no previous farming experience in such a climate. He persisted nevertheless, throughout eleven years of labor, trying to turn the hard earth into bountiful soil, producing small returns and encountering grave hardships. Still, his faith never wavered.

GOLD FEVER

In the novel Carl Linstrum spends a year in the Klondike area of the Yukon Territory in Canada near Alaska. A discovery of gold there in 1896 started a rush to the area of 100,000 people by 1898, including hopefuls such as Carl.

Though he has three sons, Lou, Oscar, and Emil, John entrusts his dreams and his property to his daughter, Alexandra. He recognizes that she is as tied to the land as he is, that she will carry on his dreams, and that she has the fortitude and foresight to make them come true. He impresses upon Alexandra his strong desire to keep the homestead intact and implores the brothers to heed her counsel. After he dies, Alexandra takes over the homestead, just as her father had wished.

During the next decades Alexandra struggles to tame the land. She battles against the elements, the fierce and unforgiving climate, the frequent natural disasters, and the constant threat of foreclosure on her holding. She sees most of her neighbors abandon the struggle and move back to the cities in the east, where steady jobs are available. She fights with her brothers to adopt innovative farming techniques and acquire more land at a time when it seems everyone else is fearful of change and ready to leave their homesteads. A visionary and a risk-taker, Alexandra seems through sheer determination to keep the family land intact. Eventually she sees it begin to flourish.

Carl, who is Alexandra's best friend and potential mate, leaves his family's homestead to learn a trade in the cities and seek his fortune in the world. His departure leaves Alexandra virtually alone. Her parents are dead, older brothers married, and younger brother off at college (the first in his family to get a college education). Loneliness is added to the list of hardships that she endures on the prairie.

Emil returns from college and finds that he is deeply attracted to Marie, a married neighbor. Alexandra constantly pairs the two together without realizing the depth of their feelings. It is unthinkable to her that a married woman could be attracted to another man. Tension builds between Marie and Emil. Emil leaves the country, going to Mexico to stave off temptation to be with Marie, but upon his return the old feelings flare up again. Eventually the couple cannot control themselves and meet under a white mulberry tree. Marie's husband, Frank, discovers the two and from a distance fires at them with his rifle. He kills them dead and rushes off to town, where he turns himself in to the authorities.

"PIONEERS, *O PIONEERS!*"

Cather took the title of her novel from a poem of the same name by Walt Whitman that appeared in his masterpiece, *Leaves of Grass*. Written in 1865, the poem pays homage to the courageous and hardy pioneers that settled the West beyond the Mississippi River. An excerpt shows his reverence of and respect for the homesteaders, a reverence that Cather also shared:

O resistless restless race!
O beloved race in all! O my breast aches with tender love for all!
O I mourn and yet exult, I am rapt with love for all,
Pioneers! *O Pioneers!*

(Whitman, p. 203)

Alexandra is devastated by the tragic event. She cannot believe Emil and Marie could commit such an act and blames herself for being party to it (though she clearly had no such intention). Alexandra visits Frank in prison. She informs him that she does not blame him for the murders, and she resolves to help get him pardoned.

Believing that she has let down her brothers, Alexandra now feels utterly alone in the world.

Carl has not been heard from in years, and Alexandra, now close to forty years old, suspects she will be alone forever. Then suddenly she receives a telegram from Carl. He is returning from Alaska, where he has been trying to make his fortune mining gold.

Carl and Alexandra reunite at the old homestead, which Alexandra has transformed into a sprawling, prosperous farm. All the land within view, once a Sahara-like span of barrenness, has turned into rolling fields of green, gold, and red. Carl is impressed by her efforts. Walking across the fields, the two discuss their future together and Alexandra's attachment to the land. Both lonely, they want companionship from each other. Carl asks Alexandra to marry him and she agrees. They will keep her homestead and venture west to fulfill Carl's aspirations as well.

Nurturers or exploiters? In the view of many contemporary analysts, the pioneers exploited the land they settled, driving out native peoples and animals and ruining the natural ecosystem of the area. The settlers' intensive cultivation of the land is believed by many to have partly caused the disastrous "Dust Bowl" erosion that took place in the 1930s. However, Cather's novel shows an attitude among the pioneers that is quite different from that of brazen exploiters. The novel instead depicts pioneers who have tender care for the land; they feel that they are civilizing the area and cultivating the soil. There were, in fact, pioneers like Alexandra and her father, who operated under the belief that they were acting in the image of God or Mother Nature, transforming a barren landscape into a fertile region of milk and honey. Some of the early pioneers felt a deep connection to and responsibility for the terrain, which belies the generalized view of them as self-serving exploiters. It was as if these pioneers were parents entrusted to nurture the land until it grew to be strong and prosperous enough to stand on its own. Cather describes Alexandra's deep connection to her homestead:

That night she had a new consciousness of the country, felt almost a new relation to it. Even her talk with the boys had not taken away the feeling that had overwhelmed her when she drove back to the Divide that afternoon. She had never known before how much the country meant to her. The chirping of the insects down in the long grass had been the sweetest music. She had felt as if her heart were hiding down there, somewhere, with the quail and the plover and the little wild things that crooned or buzzed in the sun. Under the long shaggy ridges, she felt the future stirring.

(Cather, *O Pioneers*, p. 54)

Sources. Cather based the novel on her experience of moving to Webster County, Nebraska, at age nine. According to historians, "the move was a shock, but a shock that was the beginning of love both for the land and the people, and for the rest of her life, Cather was to draw from this experience in creating her fiction" (Magill, p. 474). Daughter of an immigrant homesteader family, she knew well the trials and tribulations the early Nebraska settlers endured. Her first characterization of Alexandra Bergson came in the short story, "Alexandra," which she wrote in 1912. She conceived some of the ideas for the character of Marie in a short story written the same year called "The Bohemian Girl." Though it was her second novel (the first being *Alexander's Bridge* in 1912) Cather considered *O Pioneers!* her first fictional book, convinced that with it she had found her subject matter and her voice as a writer.

Reviews. *O Pioneers!* was one of Cather's most successful and critically acclaimed novels. It established her as a first-rate novelist. After its publication, she was able to quit her career in journalism and concentrate on fiction writing full-time. One early reviewer agreed that Cather had arrived as a novelist in *O Pioneers!:* "She finds the theme most congenial to her interest and to her powers. That theme is the struggle of some elect individual to outgrow the restrictions laid upon him—or more frequently her—by numbing circumstances" (Van Doren in Bryfonski, p. 150). Similarly Bernice Slote contended that Cather "hit the home pasture" with *O Pioneers!*, going on to maintain that "In the change from wilderness to ordered fields, Willa Cather found the most exciting story she had to tell" (Slote, pp. 57, 79).

For More Information

Bryfonski, Dedria, ed. *Twentieth-Century Literary Criticism*. Vol. 1. Detroit: Gale Research, 1978.

Cather, Willa. *O Pioneers!* New York: Signet, 1989.

Creigh, Dorothy Weyer. *Nebraska: A Bicentennial History*. New York: W. W. Norton, 1977.

Hellerstein, Erna Olafson, Leslie Parker Hume, and Karen M. Offen. *Victorian Women*. Stanford, Calif.: Stanford University Press, 1981.

Magill, Frank N. *Critical Survey of Long Fiction*. Vol. 2. Englewood Cliffs, N. J.: Salem, 1983.

O'Brien, Sharon. *Willa Cather: The Emerging Voice*. Oxford: Oxford University Press, 1987.

Slote, Bernice. *Willa Cather: A Pictorial Memoir*. Lincoln: University of Nebraska Press, 1973.

Steenrod, Freida M. *Blowouts, Blizzards and Bunk*. Portland, Ore.: Freida M. Steenrod, 1989.

Whitman, Walt. *Leaves of Grass and Selected Prose*. London: Everyman, 1993.

Youngquist, Erick H. *America Fever: A Swede in the West*. Nashville: Voyageur, 1988.

Of Human Bondage

by
W. Somerset Maugham

THE LITERARY WORK

A novel set in England and Europe from 1885 to 1906; published in 1915.

SYNOPSIS

Philip Carey, orphaned at the age of nine, is sent to live with his aunt and uncle. The alienation he experiences at school and the restrictions placed on him by his guardians leave Philip feeling bitter and restless; at the age of eighteen he strikes out to discover the world—and himself.

William Somerset Maugham, born in 1874, was orphaned at the age of ten and placed under the guardianship of his uncle, the vicar of All Saints' Church in Whitestable. Driven by a restless craving for freedom, Maugham experimented with a host of identities and occupations while growing into manhood. These formative experiences later served as the basis for *Of Human Bondage.*

Events in History at the Time of the Novel

Clubfoot. Also known as *talipes,* clubfoot is a congenital deformity in which the foot is twisted out of shape or position. Although readers of Maugham's novel are never told the details of the main character's clubfoot, there are in fact at least nine different forms of talipes. In Maugham's time doctors still had only partial treatments at their disposal; only in later generations would it become possible to correct clubfoot in infancy by manipulation, braces, and casts, and in severe cases by surgery.

Bildungsroman. A German word, *Bildungsroman* means "novel of education" or "novel of apprenticeship." The term was first used in reference to Johann Wolfgang von Goethe's novel *Wilhelm Meister's Apprenticeship* (1796), which relates Wilhelm's progress from a naive, excitable youth to responsible manhood. The term was later applied to any novel that traced the personal development of a single individual, usually a youth. Susanne Howe elaborates on such stories in the introduction to Maugham's novel. Typically, the adolescent hero of the Bildungsroman "sets out on his way through the world . . . falls in with various guides and counselors, makes many false starts choosing his friends, his wife, and his life work, and finally adjusts himself . . . by finding a sphere of action in which he may work effectively" (Howe in Maurice Maugham, p. xii). The Bildungsroman was an extremely popular literary form during Maugham's time. Other prominent examples of this kind of novel include Charles Dickens's *David Copperfield* (1850), D. H. Lawrence's ***Sons and Lovers*** (1913; also covered in *Literature and Its Times*), James Joyce's ***A Portrait of the Artist as a Young Man*** (1916; also covered in *Literature and Its Times*), and Thomas Mann's *The Magic Mountain* (1924).

Educational reform in nineteenth-century England. Throughout the middle ages, elementary English education was under the complete control of the church (Cruickshank, p. 1). At the secondary level and at England's two universities (Oxford and Cambridge), religion had long been regarded as the basis of all education, and the curriculum remained relatively fixed, with emphasis given to moral philosophy, mathematics, and classical studies. But in the nineteenth century, things began to change. The rise of the age of applied science and industrial expansion resulted in a call for the pursuit of so-called "useful" knowledge.

The push for educational change came from several quarters. Populist movements such as the Chartists, a group dedicated to improving the lot of working men, helped to establish publicly supported "technical" schools for working-class children. These schools emphasized practical subjects such as economics, mechanical drawing, and chemistry.

Another factor contributing to educational change was the growing power of the Noncomformists—dissenters from the Church of England, a motley coalition of various radical groups. In a direct confrontation with clerical rule, these otherwise disparate groups banded together in 1828 to establish London University, the purpose of which was to take a neutral stance toward religious education, offering secular, or nonreligious, courses such as languages, physics, the mental and moral sciences, law, and history. The rise of secularism, which accompanied the Industrial Revolution, and which was punctuated by the publication of Charles Darwin's *Origin of Species* in 1859, only fed the fire of debate between the dissenters and the church. In *Of Human Bondage,* this conflict plays itself out at King's School, where Philip is educated. Though it "prided itself on its antiquity" (Maugham, *Of Human Bondage,* p. 56), the school nevertheless had to confront the inevitability of change embodied in the character of the new headmaster, Mr. Perkins.

Agnosticism. Philip loses religious faith in the novel when he undergoes intellectual indoctrination in Heidelberg. His experience here reflects a widespread nineteenth-century movement called agnosticism, which gained currency not only among the late Victorians in England, but in Europe as a whole. Closely associated with the Industrial Revolution and the rise of the theory of evolution, agnosticism holds that the existence of God cannot be logically proved or disproved. (This is not to be confused with atheism, which asserts that there is no God.) The term *agnostic,*

W. Somerset Maugham

a Greek word meaning "unknowing" or "unknowable," was first coined by the English biologist and educator T. H. Huxley (1825-1895). Heavily influenced by the writings of Charles Darwin, Huxley doubted all things not immediately open to logical analysis and scientific verification. Other prominent popularizers of agnosticism included the English philosopher Herbert Spencer (1820-1903) and German biologist and philosopher Ernst Haeckel (1834-1919). *The Life of Jesus,* a book that Philip Carey reads in *Of Human Bondage,* was published in 1863 by French scholar Ernest Renan, who believed that no one system of religious, scientific, or historical knowledge could claim absolute truth. Interestingly, like both Maugham and the fictional Philip Carey, Renan was a student preparing to enter the clergy when he lost his faith in orthodox religion.

The art scene in Paris. The 1880s and 1890s were vigorous decades for the European artist, and Paris, with its studios, museums, galleries, and patrons, was the undisputed center of all artistic activity, attracting students from as far away as Russia to the east and the United States to the west. In 1886 critic Albert Wolff wrote of Paris as "the Capital of Art" (Milner, p. 25). Yet despite, or perhaps because of, all this activity, fame and wealth were difficult to come by in Paris, and life for the unknown artist could be extremely hard.

There were many studios to accommodate the artists who descended upon Paris, the oldest and most venerable among them being the École des Beaux-Arts, which first opened its doors in 1648. In 1863 the Beaux-Arts set up the *atelier* (studio-teaching) system, which formed the backbone of French art education. The atelier system, in which a celebrated artist taught at his own studio, centered primarily on drawing and painting from a real-life model. The everyday practicalities of the atelier were controlled by the *massiér,* a kind of chief student elected by his or her fellows (in Maugham's novel, the *massiér* is Mrs. Otter). Many renowned artists received their education under the atelier system at the Beaux-Arts, including Georges Seurat and Henri Matisse, to name just two. Other schools, such as Académie Julian (attended by André Derain and Pierre Bonnard), and independent teaching studios like Fernand Cormon's *atelier libre,* or "free studio" (whose students included Toulouse-Lautrec, Émile Bernard, and Vincent Van Gogh), also used the atelier system but were less exclusive than Beaux-Arts and, unlike the École des Beaux-Arts, accepted beginners who were willing to pay. In *Of Human Bondage,* Amitrano's School, which admits Philip, who is a complete novice, more closely resembles these latter institutions than the Beaux-Arts.

THE LOUVRE

First established as *La Musée de la République* in 1793, the Louvre is one of the largest and most spectacular collections of art in the world. Having one's work displayed there has always been regarded as the ultimate recognition of an artist's abilities, and for two centuries, painters and sculptors from all over the world have come to Paris to be challenged and inspired by its vast repository of work.

The Novel in Focus

The plot. The novel opens with the death of Philip Carey's mother. The nine-year-old boy is forced to leave London for the country town of Blackstable to live with his uncle William Carey, an Anglican vicar, and his aunt Louisa Carey. Despite being ostracized by his peers on account of his clubfoot and introverted nature, Philip excels at school, and it is decided for him that he will go to Oxford University and enter the clergy. But Philip yearns to forge his own destiny, and after a protracted fight with his uncle and headmaster he finally gains his freedom.

Philip travels to Germany, where he is boarded and educated in the home of Professor and Frau Erlin. Here he is exposed to the company of young women for the first time and to people from a wide range of backgrounds and points of view. After a year of social and intellectual indoctrination, and many philosophical discussions with his two friends Hayward and Weeks, Philip rejects Christianity and becomes an agnostic.

Upon returning to England, Philip has his first love affair with Miss Wilkinson, a woman at least ten years his senior. At the end of the summer they part tearfully, and Philip heads to London to become an apprentice to an accountant named Herbert Carter. But working in the business world proves miserable for Philip, and in his boredom he turns to drawing. When he is sent to Paris on business, he is so inspired by the artistic activity there that he quits his job. Using his Aunt Louisa's savings, Philip returns to Paris to study art. He encounters a wide range of artistic types, most importantly an English woman named Fanny Price, whom he first sees posing nude for his class at Amitrano's School. Fanny is attracted to Philip, but he has only pity for her. She is a tragic figure—a dedicated artist completely devoid of talent. Later, when Fanny Price commits suicide, Philip calls into question the values of a temperament that would lead a person to kill herself merely on account of mediocrity. Later, Philip is forced to come to grips with his own mediocrity, when his teacher Foinet tells him that his talent is not worth the struggle of an artist's life.

Upon hearing of his Aunt Louisa's death, Philip returns to England, where he decides to pursue medicine at St. Luke's Hospital. It is at this time that Philip meets a woman named Mildred Rogers. Although Mildred is indifferent toward Philip, and he can see that she is shallow and selfish and not particularly beautiful, he nevertheless falls madly in love with her. Everything meaningful in his life diminishes into nothingness in the face of his obsession with Mildred. He spends what little money he has to support her fantasy of a respectable lifestyle. He fails an examination and is nearly dismissed from medical school. Finally, Philip proposes marriage to Mildred, who rejects him because he doesn't have enough money to satisfy her. When he later discovers that she intends to marry a rival suitor, Philip feels crushed. He is, on the positive side, finally released from his enslavement to Mildred—at least for the time being.

With Mildred gone, Philip begins a romance with the pleasant Norah Nesbit, and his life begins to stabilize. But when Mildred returns, dejected and pregnant with another man's child, Philip takes her back. Although Mildred is as selfish and shallow as ever, he continues to support and care for her, and after she has her baby, it is clear that he loves it more than she. Eventually Mildred falls in love with Griffith, Philip's friend from medical school. Although it causes him great suffering, Philip recognizes the great passion Mildred has for Griffith and in an act of martyrdom pays for a weekend trip so that the two of them can be together. Mildred, of course, does not return.

As an outpatient's clerk at the hospital, Philip witnesses new dimensions of human suffering, and discovers that he is a capable and compassionate doctor. He makes friends with Athelny, from whom he learns that humor can do much to soften the blows of life. After earning some money in the stock market, Philip pays for an operation to correct his clubfoot, although the cure is incomplete.

Mildred now enters his life once again. By this time, she is a prostitute. Although Philip takes her in and provides for her and her child, the passion he once felt for her is gone. His indifference is too much for Mildred to bear; in a fit of rage she destroys his apartment and flees. Soon afterward, Philip loses all his money in a stock market speculation. Unable to enlist in the army on account of his foot, he becomes a vagabond, and is saved from starvation by his friend Athelny. He gets a job as a floorwalker, supervising salespeople and assisting customers at a department store, a position that thrusts him into crushing boredom and a life of penury. Soon he begins to pray for the death of his uncle the vicar so that he may receive his inheritance and return to medical school.

Finally, the vicar dies, and Philip inherits the money necessary to finish medical school. Upon receiving his diploma, he goes to work in a small seaport village for Dr. South. Although he proves to be an excellent physician

and Dr. South offers him a partnership, Philip's intention is to go to Spain and then explore the world by ship. His plans change, however, when he gets Athelny's daughter Sally pregnant. He decides to marry her and accept Dr. South's partnership offer. In a final twist, Sally discovers that she is not pregnant after all. Philip is therefore free to embark on his overseas adventures. But he decides to marry Sally anyway, and the two of them settle down to a quiet life on the shore.

The many faces of bondage. As the title implies, *Of Human Bondage* is dominated by the issue of entrapment, of the human soul forever fighting to free itself of preset personal and social limitations. Maugham himself believed that every individual is inherently trapped in his or her own character: "We are the product of our chromosomes. And there's nothing whatever we can do about it. All we can do is try to supplement our own deficiencies" (W. Somerset Maugham in Maurice Maugham, p. 54). This notion holds true in the case of Philip's character, which remains shy and deferential throughout. It is also given concrete form in the novel by Philip's clubfoot, a handicap that neither religious faith nor modern medicine can wholly eradicate.

Philip and the people whom he meets in the novel are forever grappling with various forms of constraints. For example, Philip's Uncle Carey and Headmaster Mr. Perkins want to force Philip into a career in the church. Hedwig, a young girl in Heidelberg, cannot marry the man she loves because he is above her social class. Fanny Price is so committed to the ideal of the self-sacrificing artist that she would rather hang herself than confront her own mediocrity. Perhaps the most tragic case of all is that of Mildred Rogers, whose desperate desire to play the role of a respectable woman leads her to a bitter and tragic end.

Taken together, these examples offer a striking portrait of the narrowness and rigidity of society in nineteenth-century Europe. They suggest that an individual's identity had far more to do with arbitrary external circumstances than the true nature of the self. Philip's progress, however, offers a ray of hope. Although he will always be shy, introverted, and physically handicapped, he nevertheless manages to defy the limitations surrounding him. He proceeds to experiment with many social roles without succumbing to them and relinquishing his identity, until at last he discovers his true desire and lives his life accordingly. Historically speaking, Philip's journey can be viewed as a kind of prototype of classical liberalism. Classical liberalism, which flourished in the nineteenth century and which found expression most notably in the writings of the English philosopher John Stuart Mill, had as its deepest principle the liberty of the individual person. The individual, in this view, was not simply formed by race, class, church, nation, or state but was ultimately independent of all such things (Palmer, p. 603).

Composition and sources. *Of Human Bondage* is an autobiographical novel. Although many details have been altered, the story of Philip's maturation into manhood is essentially Maugham's own. Maugham's mother died when he was eight, and his father's death followed two years later. Though he was not an only child as his character Philip is, with his three older brothers away at boarding school Maugham grew up as if he were one.

Philip's clubfoot is analogous to Maugham's stammer—a handicap that caused him much grief in his youth. Many scholars point out that the writing *Of Human Bondage* was an act of self-liberation: "There is evidence that Maugham began [the novel] in 1911 after the American playwright Edward Sheldon suggested that it might help him overcome the sense of inferiority caused by his stammer" (Calder, p. x).

Like Philip, Maugham left school in England to study and discover the world in Germany. And like Philip, he worked for a brief period as an apprentice to a chartered accountant in London, lived among artists in Paris (although he did not paint), and returned to England and enrolled in medical school. Below are just some of the many places and people in the novel that have counterparts in real life.

Fictional Place	Real-life Source
Blackstable	Whitestable
King's School, Tercanbury	King's School, Canterbury
Oxford	Cambridge
St. Luke's Hospital	St. Thomas Hospital
Chien Noir	Chat Blanc

Fictional Character	Real-life Source
Vicar William Carey	Vicar Henry Maugham
Tom Perkins	Thomas Field
Flanagan	Penryhn Stanlaws
Cronshaw	J. W. Maurice

The source for Mildred Rogers is more complex. There was no corresponding woman in Maugham's life, but many critics speculate that Philip's obsessive relationship with the Cockney waitress in the novel was based on one of Maugham's homosexual affairs.

Reviews. *Of Human Bondage* is now almost unanimously regarded as a classic, though initially it met with a mixed response. The novel was an instant success with the reading public, but the early critical appraisals were not quite so effusive. A review in *The Dial* described the book as "far from being, in the publisher's phrase, 'compellingly great,' but, allowing once for all its inartistic method, it is at least a noteworthy piece of creative composition" (Fanning, p. 321). Theodore Dreiser, however, took a different tack in the *New Republic*: "To me at least it is a gorgeous weave, as interesting and valuable at the beginning as at the end" (Dreiser in Fanning, p. 321).

For More Information

Calder, Robert. Introduction to *Of Human Bondage*, by Somerset Maugham. New York: Penguin Books, 1992.

Cruickshank, Marjorie. *Church and State in English Education: 1870 to the Present Day*. London: MacMillan, 1963.

Fanning, Clara Elizabeth, ed. *Book Review Digest*. Vol 11. White Plains, N.Y.: H. W. Wilson, 1916.

Lawson, John, and Harold Silver. *A Social History of Education in England*. London: Methuen, 1973.

Maugham, Maurice. *Somerset and All the Maughams*. New York: Signet, 1966.

Maugham, W. Somerset. *Of Human Bondage*. New York: Penguin, 1992.

Milner, John. *The Studios of Paris, The Capital of Art in the Late Twentieth Century*. New Haven, Conn.: Yale University Press, 1988.

Palmer, R. R. and Joel Colton. *A History of the Modern World*. 6th ed. New York: Alfred A. Knopf, 1984.

Of Mice and Men

by
John Steinbeck

A young John Steinbeck learned about bindlestiffs—single migrant laborers, generally white men, recruited to work during harvest season—through his own experience on a company-owned ranch. Recognizing the frustration that many such workers felt, Steinbeck's *Of Mice and Men* illuminates the hopes and hopelessness common along California's agricultural belt. Its main characters, George and Lennie, display an uncommon bond that keeps alive their dream of carving their own niche in a society that preys upon laborers like them. The novella portrays a class of previously ignored workers on California ranches of the early 1900s.

Events in History at the Time the Novella Takes Place

California ranches. In the early 1900s central California was producing large supplies of citrus fruits, sugar beets, and cotton. The Salinas Valley, located along California's agricultural belt, featured lettuce as a primary crop; other harvested vegetables included broccoli, carrots, cauliflower, celery, garbanzo beans, and onions. In order to harvest these products, many of which could be picked only during a short period of time, the farms hired laborers on a temporary basis. Some of the larger ranches provided housing and stores for their laborers, who would drift in and out according to the seasons.

Smaller farms not able to afford the expense of hiring a number of temporary workers and providing them with food and shelter were often

---

---

bought out by larger companies. Because the success or failure of a year depended on the harvest of every crop, it was easier for a larger company to survive through many seasons. An individually owned farm could go bankrupt if the season's crop did not meet expectations. Large companies could also afford to conduct widespread searches for temporary employees, sending fliers and messengers out to reach migrant workers at other farms and ranches. Small farms and ranches could not long compete with the financial power of Spreckels and other large companies, and so big business eventually came to control most of the agriculture in California.

Farm labor. Steinbeck himself describes the development of the labor system that came into being in California and provided a work force for the region's farms:

> "Bindlestiffs," single, footloose Caucasian men, made up most of the labor force of the great

wheat farms of the 1870s and 1880s. As California farming shifted its focus to fruits and vegetables, which required more labor during harvests and other intensive work periods, immigrants entered the farm labor market. These workers followed the need for their services up and down the state, creating the nation's first modern migrant agricultural labor force.

(Steinbeck, *The Harvest Gypsies*, p. xi)

California's farms numbered about 88,000 in 1910, of which close to 3,500 were large concerns. California growers were consolidating their efforts at this time, specializing in one type of fruit or vegetable. This benefited the migrant laborers, since the various crops became ready for harvest at different times. Laborers could keep working for as long as thirty-five weeks a year, earning as much as $500 or $600 if they were fortunate. The work was brutal, though. Harvesters would drift from crop to crop, living in crude accommodations, and picking frantically from sunrise to sunset. While these gruesome conditions are clear in retrospect, they were not so apparent then. There were, in fact, reasons for hope on California farms by 1914. The recession of 1912-1913 was fading and the completion of the Panama Canal in 1914 promised to open a new world market for goods.

THE SPRECKELS RANCHES

Large companies controlled the farming industry in California. One of the largest was Spreckels, which owned or leased ranches from below King City in the south to Santa Clara in the north. Ranches typically had a bunkhouse or two, a cook house, and a superintendent's house. Steinbeck worked on several of the Spreckels ranches in different capacities. While these ranches mainly grew beets for producing sugar, they also raised some livestock and produced hay and alfalfa to feed the livestock.

Historically, more than two-thirds of California's agricultural population have been hired hands rather than farm owners, and the majority of laborers have been nonwhite migrant workers. From the late 1800s into the early 1900s, the majority of these nonwhite workers shifted from the Chinese to the Japanese to the Mexicans and,

from India, the Hindustanis. California had at least 54,000 migrant laborers in 1910, and almost half of them were whites.

Of Mice and Men focuses on California's white single migrant laborers before the arrival of white migrant families from the Great Plains during the Depression-era 1930s. The single white laborers moved northward as the crops demanded:

Each ranch had a small semipermanent crew for maintenance and feed operations. They were helped with these chores by the bindlestiffs and hobos who worked their way north every year up the line of Spreckels ranches. They'd get a meal at the southernmost ranch, find out what the work situation was in the valley, and then travel north to where there was work, living on one or more of the company ranches as long as they were needed.

(Benson, *The True Adventures*, pp. 38-9)

The life of a bindlestiff. The word *bindle* is thought to have been taken from the German *Buntel* ("package") and *stiff* was slang for a tramp or hobo. Migrant workers carried their beds in a bundle, so to speak, as they moved from job to job, hence the coining of the word in the late 1890s. In 1900 there were around 125,000 single men circulating along the American and Canadian agricultural belts. The average wage for a migrant worker was $2.50 to $3.00 a day, too little to build up a sizable nest egg of savings. Most workers remained stuck in their low-paying, unproductive positions.

Work took up most of the hours of a bindlestiff. A transient would arrive at a ranch where he would be fed and housed. A week to a few weeks of manual labor would follow, ranging from the heavy lifting of wheat season to the delicate touch needed for picking fruit. The bindlestiffs generally lived in bunkhouses, which they shared with other hired hands. Nights involved homemade entertainment within the confines of the house. Perhaps one night per weekend, or less depending on the harvest, workers would travel to the nearest town, where they frequented bars or brothels.

Debt. Most new arrivals to ranches were broke. Their employers operated stores at which the laborers could purchase food and other necessities on credit. As Steinbeck notes, this virtually enslaved the laborer: "Thus he must work a second day to pay for his first, and so on. He is continually in debt. He must work" (Steinbeck, *The Harvest Gypsies*, p. 35).

In *Of Mice and Men*, despite fearing potential trouble with their supervisor Curley and his wife,

Steinbeck's ranch, Los Gatos, located in the same part of western California in which *Of Mice and Men* is set.

George and Lennie must stay at the ranch and work because they have no money. "For two bits I'd shove out of here," says George, "If we can get jus' a few dollars in the poke we'll shove off and go up the American River and pan gold" (Steinbeck, *Of Mice and Men,* p. 33). This statement, made by George after he anticipates trouble, shows the impossible situation in which he and Lennie are caught. Though staying means trouble, leaving means starvation and hopelessness.

A woman's role. Curley's wife in *Of Mice and Men* enjoys little freedom. She is trapped on her husband's ranch and not even allowed to cultivate friendships. Most of the ranch hands refuse to talk with her for fear of reprisals from Curley. In their eyes, she is his property, and though she may be lonely, that is her husband's business and not theirs.

In the early 1900s men and women were generally restricted to separate spheres of life. Traditionalist values placed women at home in charge of domestic duties, outside of social circles, and men in the workplace, mingling with society at large. While many couples adhered to this traditional division, others in the early twentieth century urged and struggled for new rights for women.

During this period, known as the Progressive Era, women's roles in society and marriage changed dramatically. The most significant development was their gaining the right to vote in 1920. In fact, women's suffrage had already taken place in many states individually, including California, which had granted its female citizens this right as early as 1911.

The workplace became a focal point for the development of women's rights. Career opportunities for women increased from the late 1800s to the early 1900s. In 1900 about 20 percent of women over ten years old worked. This number rose to 25 percent by 1920. The respect women gained by joining the work force, however, did not always translate into respect at home. A common feeling during this time was that married women who were supported by their husbands ought not to take jobs that rightfully belonged to men. Many men believed it was impractical for a woman to juggle motherhood, wifehood, and a career, and equally impractical for a man to share domestic burdens, so most wives did not work.

Though marriage remained a primary goal for most women in the Progressive Era, it in some cases did not leave them feeling fulfilled. There was more emphasis than in previous decades on love and happiness as important ingredients in a marriage—though the old notion that the family's well-being should take priority lingered on for many. Despite the new concern for personal happiness, many people still believed that "The purpose of marriage is the protection of the family idea . . . if the incident of happiness is lost, duty remains!" (Campbell, pp. 74-5). Such contradictory notions must have left many women in inner conflict. Not surprisingly the incidence of divorce increased to a rate of 13 percent around 1920, though society still harshly judged the act of divorce or separation and those who undertook it.

In *Of Mice and Men,* Curley's wife displays a restlessness associated with other women of her situation and status. The attitude matches those of real-life farm wives studied in surveys at the time, which "were filled with complaints of . . . isolation and lack of entertainment" (Banner, p. 59). In the story, instead of providing Curley's wife with the excitement of a new life, her marriage has replaced dreams of being an actress with the reality of a daily life filled with boredom. Though not all women felt so dissatisfied, Curley's wife represents a type of unhappiness that would continue for some married women until their role in society broadened.

The mentally retarded. *Of Mice and Men* concludes with the slow-witted giant Lennie being killed by his companion George. It is an act of mercy executed to spare Lennie from the violent punishment awaiting him for an accidental crime he has committed. Lennie's persistent problem throughout the story is that he can't comprehend the rules that govern society. When it becomes apparent that he never will, he is killed.

By 1915, mental retardation had caught public attention as perhaps the most significant large-scale social problem of the time. People had frightened and often hostile attitudes toward the mentally challenged in the early 1900s. Throughout most of this period, health care specialists, equipped with scientific data from hereditary studies, employed measures such as sterilization of the retarded and segregated them from the larger population by placing them in institutions. Laws disallowing marriage between mentally retarded people were passed by thirty-nine states. Coupled with widespread sterilization, the laws were designed to limit the population of the mentally retarded. California, in fact, was one of the pioneers in adopting a eugenic sterilization measure. This scheme, designed to keep the population genetically superior, was eventually accepted by twenty-three states—and later by Nazi Germany. By 1925, 1,374 sterilization operations had been performed on the mentally retarded, 64 percent of which had taken place in Califor-

nia. Of those who escaped such treatment, most were institutionalized.

In *Of Mice and Men,* Lennie portrays an exception to the rule of institutionalization for mentally disabled people. His freedom until the end of the story shows an attempt by himself and George to integrate with the world of the early 1900s. But society's inability to accept him, as illustrated by his friend's fear that Lennie will be murdered for his accidental crime, demonstrates a refusal of this world to adapt itself to people of varying natures.

The Novella in Focus

The plot. The story begins on a Friday afternoon with two men emerging from their travels into a clearing along the shores of the Salinas River. The two men, Lennie Small and George Milton, appear very different from each other. Lennie is an enormous man, hulking in size but slow-witted. In contrast, George is small in stature but intelligent. They have traveled together in search of work at various ranches along the California agricultural belt, sharing the same dream of someday owning their own farm and controlling their own lives.

The pair make their way to a ranch where they first meet Candy, an old ranch hand; the ranch boss, unnamed; the boss' son Curley; Curley's wife, also unnamed; and the other hired help. The ranch boss, after some questioning about their previous employment, gives them jobs. George befriends Slim, the leader of the ranch hands, and through their conversation, it is revealed that Lennie and George left their last job because of a misunderstanding between Lennie and a lady. They were chased out of town by a lynch mob who thought Lennie guilty of rape. As the discussion progresses, the other hired men enter the bunkhouse.

The ranch hands are relaxing in the bunkhouse on that same evening when Curley bursts in and asks where his wife is. He suspects Slim of eyeing her and storms out in an attempt to find the two. Most of the men follow, anticipating excitement.

Lennie, who has been playing with a puppy Slim gave him, returns from the barn to the bunks and asks George to describe their dream. It involves a ten-acre private farm with some livestock, orchards, and many rabbits for Lennie to tend. Candy overhears the description and desires a piece of the dream. Because he has some money saved, they invite him to share in their dream, making it more realistic.

The rest of the crew returns led by Curley, who is being taunted about his wife and his lack of control over her. Searching for a scapegoat, he lashes into Lennie. After absorbing a few punches, Lennie grabs the smaller man's fist and crushes it. Astonished and broken, Curley is carted out, and the slow-witted Lennie is left whimpering in confusion.

The next night the story's focus turns to Crooks, the black employee who lives apart from the others in the stable, and his encounter with a wandering Lennie after most of the hands have gone to a brothel. Crooks tries to communicate the loneliness he feels as a social outcast, but Lennie is unable to comprehend his meaning. In trying to strike up a conversation, Crooks gets Lennie to spill his dreams of a private farm. Crooks begins dreaming himself of an escape from the sad reality of his life. Candy joins the two in Crooks's room, and the three visualize the future life they can all lead in the romantic ranch of their dreams.

Curley's wife steps into the doorway looking for companionship, and the men's discussion dies down with her appearance. They chastise her for roaming around, and she counters by telling them they are afraid of her friendship. Their argument culminates in her threatening Crooks with a future lynching should he not behave. She leaves, and the dream no longer seems real. George appears and takes Lennie and Candy back to the bunkhouse as Crooks resigns himself to his luckless destiny.

The next day, Sunday, Lennie is alone in the barn. Curley's wife soon appears. She speaks to Lennie of her own loneliness and dreams, letting him know she once had the chance to be an actress. She moves closer to Lennie, who has been obsessed with his own dreams of the rabbits and the farm. He reveals that he likes to touch soft things and she offers him her hair. Eventually, however, she insists he stop, or he will "muss it up." As she raises her voice, Lennie holds on more tightly, telling her to be quiet. He is fearful that George will hear, be displeased, and not let Lennie "tend no rabbits" when they finally have their dream ranch. When she continues to scream, Lennie shakes Curley's wife angrily, attempting to quiet her, and consequently breaks her neck. Upon realizing that he "done a real bad thing," he runs away.

Candy finds the body and notifies the other hands. Curley rages about retribution, and the hired help form a mob to find Lennie. They grab their guns and begin their search.

John Steinbeck

Back at the site of the first scene in the novel, Lennie emerges from the brush. George presently arrives. Instead of chastising Lennie, George calmly comforts him and begins retelling the story of their future plans. As he reaches the part about the rabbits, he shoots Lennie in the back of the head.

Law, order, and vigilante justice. Mob justice is mentioned in *Of Mice and Men* in an exchange between Curley's wife and Crooks. She tells him that she could have him lynched whenever she wanted. This statement, which refers to the illegal killing of a suspect by mob violence, represents a horrifying reality of the era. Mobs exacted vengeance for real or imagined crimes at their own discretion, not waiting for legal justice to take its course, and such lynchings were usually representative of racial tensions in society. Black Americans harbored a legitimate fear of being lynched, since of the 4,312 people lynched in the United States from 1882 to 1920, the vast majority were black. In a few states, however, including California, more whites than blacks were lynched. It is quite plausible, then, that such a fate could have befallen either the black man, Crooks, or the white offender, Lennie, in the story.

All that mattered to lynchers was their own determination of an outsider's guilt. At the beginning of the novel, a conversation reveals that a lynch mob had chased Lennie away from his previous job. And Curley's reaction to the death of his wife again portends Lennie's death at the hands of a mob. When it is determined by Curley and the ranch hands that the misfit has killed the woman, there is no thought of legal justice. This is an accurate portrayal of ranch life at the time. Ranch hands belonged to remote communities· that were comparatively immune to official law enforcement. The isolation and size of the ranches allowed frontier justice to prevail. It was left up to the farm owners themselves to maintain order over the migrant workers who arrived for the harvests. Once a popular—if hasty—decision had been made about a man's supposed guilt, punishment would be extracted by the mob.

Such mobs were capable of atrocious disfigurement of their victims. There were cases, as late as 1930, of mutilation—toes being cut off and the body doused in gasoline and then burned. While such disfigurement was probably less likely for white victims than black, the threat of it certainly makes George's "mercy" killing at the end of the novel more understandable.

In his newspaper articles, Steinbeck himself wrote that farm owners "have found the law inadequate to their uses; and they have become so powerful that such charges as felonious assault, mayhem and inciting to riot, kidnaping [sic] and flogging cannot be brought against them in controlled courts" (Steinbeck, *The Harvest Gypsies*, p. 37). Lynchers as a rule escaped punishment altogether, or in a very few cases were convicted of lesser crimes than murder, such as arson or rioting.

Sources. Beginning in 1919, Steinbeck attended Stanford University in California. He spent summers and lengthy dropout periods from school working for Spreckels ranches that lined the Salinas Valley. One version of the origin of Steinbeck's story ties it to this period in his life. On one of his working periods away from Stanford, claimed Steinbeck, an incident occurred that would prompt him to write *Of Mice and Men*.

> I was a bindlestiff myself for quite a spell. I worked in the same country that the story is laid in. The characters are composites to a certain extent. Lennie was a real person. He's in an insane asylum in California right now. I worked alongside him for many weeks. He

didn't kill a girl. He killed a ranch foreman. Got sore because the boss had fired his pal and stuck a pitchfork right through his stomach.
>
> (Steinbeck in Benson, *The True Adventures*, p. 364)

Originally intended for children, Steinbeck's story changed into a novella for adults written in a style influenced by Ed Rickets. Rickets, a science-minded friend, suggested that Steinbeck adopt a nonteleological style—writing from a completely objective perspective. Steinbeck proceeded to tell the story as it happened, allowing no opinions or biases into the writing; he would simply relay the events that occurred. This effort was manifested in the story's original title, *Something That Happened,* later dropped in favor of a title taken from a line in a Robert Burns poem: "The best laid schemes o' mice an' men / gang aft a-gley / An' lea'e us nought but grief an' pain / For Promis'd Joy" (Burns, p. 59).

Events in History at the Time the Novella Was Written

An influential affair. Steinbeck's relationship with his first wife, Carol, affected where and probably how *Of Mice and Men* was written. Their relationship faltered, and Steinbeck blamed himself as well as his wife for this. Carol strayed from the marriage a few years before Steinbeck wrote *Of Mice and Men*. In 1932 she became involved with Steinbeck's friend, the dashing writer Joseph Campbell. Just how far this affair went remains uncertain, but Steinbeck was certainly aware of it. In the end, Campbell spoke with Steinbeck and then extracted himself from the triangle, leaving the Steinbecks to salvage their marriage. Steinbeck threw himself into his writing, and his wife joined him, typing and retyping his drafts. The marriage, though, had weakened.

In the midst of his writing *Of Mice and Men,* at Carol's urging, the couple moved from Monterey to a thickly forested area about fifty miles to the north. Perhaps, suggests a Steinbeck biographer, she wanted to leave the place because it reminded her of Joseph Campbell and the affair with him was still bothering her (Parini, p. 170). In any case, the marriage improved with the move. In the end, how much Steinbeck's own experience with infidelity affected his portrayal of Curley and his wife in *Of Mice and Men* remains unclear. It should be remembered, though, that "nothing was ever wasted on Steinbeck; he instinctively knew how to milk his experience for what it was worth in imaginative value" (Parini, p. 27).

Migrant families vs. bindlestiffs. "When Steinbeck wrote *Of Mice and Men,* the kind of worker represented by Lennie and George was disappearing, being replaced by whole families migrating in cars, like the people in Steinbeck's next novel, *The Grapes of Wrath*" (Benson, *The Short Novels of John Steinbeck,* p. 40). Though single workers still traveled the circuit, most public consciousness turned to the displaced families who migrated to California from the Dust Bowl, the region of the Great Plains devastated by the dust storms in the 1930s. Steinbeck himself greatly influenced public awareness of their poverty and despair in a series of newspaper articles entitled "Their Blood is Strong" and later in *The Grapes of Wrath.*

Farm laborers found agricultural life difficult as the Great Depression settled in, partly because of the hiring practices of the era. In order to pay the lowest possible wages while still retaining a standard of quality of work accomplished, ranch owners would invite many times the number of employees needed for a job. By the time workers arrived at a ranch, a great overabundance of help existed, creating enormous competition for jobs provided. By greatly oversupplying the number of available workers for a job, management could better control salaries and manipulate their employees. Wages decreased to minimal levels. Workers were forced to accept unfair pay because many other hungry workers waited anxiously for their jobs. Because management would not allow congregations of employees for fear of insurrection and because of the impermanence of migrant laborers, it was difficult for unions to form. For the most part the migrant workers remained individually or family-oriented and so had little recourse when it came to establishing or protecting their rights.

The problem was greater for the migrant families than for the bindlestiffs, who were more mobile, relying only upon themselves for survival. If conditions were too poor at one ranch, they could more easily pack up and travel to another. When migrant families arrived, however, they were locked into a more restrictive cycle of hard work for unfair pay by their responsibilities to their children and other family members. If management on a ranch was paying half what was fair, families often had to accept it or face starvation. They hoped to make enough during one harvest to survive for a trip to the next ranch and the next harvest. Their constant poverty, and the scarcity of and fierce competition for jobs during the Great Depression of the 1930s, allowed no escape to a better life for much of the decade.

Reception. *Of Mice and Men* was guaranteed popularity when it was selected for the Book of the Month Club before it was officially issued. This honor allowed 117,000 copies of the novel to be sold before its official publication date of February 25, 1937.

Most critics responded positively to the novella, expressing great appreciation of its style and compact form. *Of Mice and Men* is often considered the most completely satisfying of Steinbeck's stories, perhaps because by limiting the number of characters and locations, Steinbeck keeps the story simple and direct. The effect was embraced by many critics, one of whom claimed that "Steinbeck places his characters not too close nor too far away [so that] we can see their performances with greatest clarity and fullness" (Hayashi, p. 108).

Critics, however, were not universal in their acclaim. More refined readers occasionally were offended by the gruffness of the characters and their lives. For example, "a journalist had once referred to *Mice's* 'two-syllable language as mean, hard, and sometimes as foul as [the characters'] semi-savage existence'" (Hayashi, p. 119). And the writer F. Scott Fitzgerald faulted Steinbeck's novel for borrowing from another novel— *McTeague* by Frank Norris—the idea of Lennie's dream of escape to a better life and the idea of his being encouraged to repeat the dream again and again in the story. At least one biographer disagrees, however. The "rhythms" of Norris's dialogue "are, as Fitzgerald noted, echoed in *Of Mice and Men* but the similarities stop there" (Parini, p. 173). Others have been overwhelmingly impressed by the book and have offered unqualified praise. "To be technical about it," observed one critic, "*Of Mice and Men* is a perfect work of art" (Hayashi, p. 117).

For More Information

Banner, Lois W. *Women in Modern America: A Brief History.* San Diego, Calif.: Harcourt Brace Jovanovich, 1974.

Benson, Jackson J. *The True Adventures of John Steinbeck, Writer.* New York: Viking, 1984.

Benson, Jackson J. *The Short Novels of John Steinbeck* Durham, N.C.: Duke University Press, 1990.

Burns, Robert. *Burns: Poetry and Prose.* With an

introduction and notes by R. Dewar. London: Oxford University Press, 1929.

Campbell, Barbara Kuhn. *The "Liberated" Woman of 1914*. Ann Arbor, Mich.: UMI Research Press, 1976.

Hayashi, Tetsumaro. *John Steinbeck: The Years of Greatness, 1936-1939*. Tuscaloosa, Ala.: University of Alabama Press, 1993.

Lavender, David. *California: Land of New Beginnings*. Lincoln: University of Nebraska Press, 1972.

Parini, Jay. *John Steinbeck: A Biography*. New York: Henry Holt, 1995.

Steinbeck, John. *The Harvest Gypsies*. San Francisco: San Francisco News, 1936.

Steinbeck, John. *Of Mice and Men*. New York: Viking Penguin, 1937.

The Old Gringo

by

Carlos Fuentes

THE LITERARY WORK

A novel set in Mexico in 1913; published in 1985.

SYNOPSIS

An embittered American (the old gringo of the title) travels to Mexico during the Mexican Revolution, wishing to die by fighting with the revolutionary leader Pancho Villa. While waiting for Villa at an abandoned hacienda, he meets an American teacher and a young revolutionary general.

Born in 1928 in Panama City to a Mexican diplomat, Carlos Fuentes spent much of his youth abroad in Chile, Argentina, and Washington, D.C. He had written more than a dozen novels before completing *The Old Gringo,* combining his career as a writer with government service and teaching. He is a writer who has fused art with politics, focusing in *The Old Gringo* on a subject raised but not yet featured in his previous fiction—the subject of U.S.-Latin American relations.

Events in History at the Time the Novel Takes Place

American expansionism. At the end of the nineteenth century, U.S. leaders urged the expansion of American influence over other countries, primarily through the selling of American goods and the spreading of American culture. Sometimes this expansionism turned into imperialism, or the imposition of political or economic control over other nations. Evidence of the resentment this policy aroused can be seen in *The Old Gringo,* for example, when General Arroyo complains of American and other foreign investment in his country. American investment in Mexico was especially high at the turn of the century. In 1910, Americans controlled almost half of Mexican property and more than half of the country's oil production.

"Big stick" policy. In addition to investing in foreign markets, Americans showed a desire to exert political influence over other countries in hopes that they would follow American democracy and become stable neighbors. This desire was particularly strong in Latin America, where Americans had begun to stake claims as early as 1823, when President James Monroe articulated the famous "Monroe Doctrine." The Monroe Doctrine warned Europe's colonial powers against further expansion in the Western Hemisphere. By the time of the novel, however, American leaders had taken the next step. President Theodore Roosevelt's "big stick" corollary to the Monroe Doctrine (1904) explicitly claimed that the United States had the right to interfere in the internal affairs of nations in the Western Hemisphere. Between 1900 and 1917, American troops intervened in Cuba, Panama, Mexico, and Haiti, as American political leaders attempted to exert influence over those nations' economies and governments.

The Spanish-American War. America's newly powerful role in international politics had grown out of her successful participation in the Spanish-American War (1898). In 1895, the Cuban people revolted against the Spanish colonial government that controlled their island. In attempts to quell the revolution, the Spanish government forced Cubans into "reconcentration" camps to isolate the people from the influence of the revolutionaries in 1895. Cubans were poorly cared for in these camps—food was scarce and disease ran rampant. The United States had close connections to Cuba economically at the time. Not only did American businessmen invest money in Cuba's sugar plantations, but the United States also purchased 90 percent of the sugar produced by Cuba. There were some personal connections, too. Cuban revolutionaries such as José Martí spent time in the United States preparing for their uprising, which contributed to strong sympathy for the rebels among the American public.

In 1898 President William McKinley of the United States ordered the battleship *Maine* to Havana, Cuba, to show support for Americans living in Cuba and for the Cuban rebels. On February 15, in Havana harbor, an explosion ripped through the American ship, killing some 260 of the 354 men on board. Rumors blamed the Spanish for the explosion. American newspapers urged readers to "remember the *Maine*," and the public cried out for action. (It was later suspected that a submarine mine had caused the disaster, but investigators have since concluded that the real cause was probably some internal malfunction such as a broken boiler.)

Following this and other inflammatory incidents, President McKinley sent Spain an ultimatum demanding that it grant Cuba independence, and finally, on April 11, 1898, authorized the use of force against Spain. More than 263,000 men served in the U.S. Army and another 25,000 in the U.S. Navy during the war. In addition to U.S. intervention in Cuba, American troops also entered the Philippines, which was at the time a Spanish colony. The Spanish resistance collapsed before the year's end; in December of 1898 Spain and the United States signed the Treaty of Paris, under which Spain agreed to recognize Cuba's independence and ceded the Philippines, Puerto Rico, and Guam to the United States. In *The Old Gringo*, Captain Winslow, father of the American missionary Harriet Winslow, is portrayed as having fought in this war. Its end signaled America's arrival as a major world power and especially as the dominant power in the Western Hemisphere.

Mexican Revolution. In 1910 Mexican revolutionaries ousted the dictator of Mexico, Porfirio Díaz, who was about to assume the presidency again after his seventh successful election bid. The ensuing revolution, which raged from 1910 to 1920, was largely a response to Díaz's having encouraged American investment in Mexico. By 1910, after several decades of Díaz's rule, American companies owned 186 of the 208 mining companies in the Mexican state of Sonora, for example. Altogether, U.S. investors controlled 38 percent of the total investment in Mexico by 1911. There were, moreover, over 50,000 Americans living and working in Mexico before the revolution, which further aggravated anti-American sentiment. Mexico's revolutionaries sought to reclaim their independence by toppling Díaz's government, ending their economic dependency on the United States, and regaining Mexican land, mineral sites, and water rights held by Americans.

In addition to anti-American feeling, resentment of Mexico's *hacienda* system of landholding spurred the 1910 rebels. Haciendas were large estates owned by the wealthy, for whom peasants worked at low wages. The landowners (*hacendados*) were often accused of treating the peasants (*peónes* or peons) cruelly. To rectify matters, rebel forces seized the haciendas during the revolution, intending to redistribute the land more fairly. Much of the action in *The Old Gringo* occurs at the hacienda of the wealthy Miranda family, whose land has been seized by the revolutionaries.

Immediately after Díaz's overthrow in May of 1911, Francisco Madero assumed power. Madero faced the *Federales*, federal soldiers who still supported former president Díaz, as well as new insurrectionary groups who demanded immediate land reform. The Federales traveled around Mexico harassing revolutionary forces; in *The Old Gringo*, General Arroyo watches out for Federales soldiers while hiding in northern Mexico.

President Wilson opposed the Madero government because of its anti-American stance. Wilson also feared for American investments. When as a precautionary measure Wilson sent American marines to the coast of Mexico, Madero ordered them to leave, insisting that Americans were interfering in Mexican politics. At that same time, America's ambassador to Mexico secretly met with Victoriano Huerta, an anti-Madero revolutionary in Mexico. The United States threw its support behind Huerta, who removed Madero from office and assumed the presidency in 1913.

After taking power, Huerta, too, turned against the United States.

In 1914 the Constitutionalists (rebels led by Venustiana Carranza and Pancho Villa) seized power from Huerta. Carranza assumed power in 1914, but the Constitutionalist Party soon split apart, pitting Carranza and Villa against each other. In *The Old Gringo,* the fictional Villa tells his soldiers that he would make a better leader than the "perfumed old Senator," Carranza (Fuentes, *The Old Gringo,* p. 173).

Pancho Villa. Named Doroteo Arango at birth (June 5, 1878), Pancho Villa grew up at a hacienda on which his parents worked as peons in Sonora, Mexico. The dictator Díaz ruled the nation as Villa matured into adolescence. At age sixteen, he fled to the mountains, living like a hunted animal. While the cause remains uncertain, the most common explanation is that to avenge the rape of his sister he had murdered the son of the patron (landowner). "Hunting, scrounging, stealing, hiding out during the day, traveling at night, Villa managed to survive" (Peterson and Knoles, p. x). He finally joined a band of outlaws, renaming himself Pancho Villa after a famous Mexican outlaw of the 1800s. By 1908 Villa had become the chief bandit across three Mexican states (Durango, Sonora, and Chihuahua). A Robin-Hood-style outlaw, he terrorized the rich and distributed his plunder among the poor, while also gaining a reputation as a great lover of women.

In 1910 Mexican rebels involved Villa in their cause. Francisco Madero had been thrown into prison as a result of his opposition to the dictator Díaz. Madero's supporter Abraham Gonzalez recruited guerrilla leaders to the side of the rebels, explaining to Villa their ideals (including the distribution of land to Mexico's empty-handed peasants). Impressed, Villa mustered a band of outlaws, cowboys, and peons and attacked a small town in Chihuahua, where he scored the first of many victories in the name of the revolution.

After Madero became president, Villa retired briefly to operate a butcher shop in Chihuahua, then took up arms again in support of Madero when the latter's leadership was challenged. Villa now served under General Victoriano Huerta, who at one point was about to have Villa executed for some trumped-up offense when at the last minute, with the help of Madero, Villa was rescued from the firing squad and sent to prison. He escaped to El Paso, Texas, where in 1913 Villa learned that Madero had been murdered. Swear-

Pancho Villa

ing vengeance, Villa raised 10,000 troops and scored a series of stunning victories against Madero's enemies in 1913-1914, close to when the novel is set.

Yellow journalism. At the turn of the century, competition between American newspaper magnates William Randolph Hearst and Joseph Pulitzer led to increased sensationalism in the struggle to win readers. This so-called "yellow journalism" (named for a comic strip, "The Yellow Kid," in Pulitzer's New York *World*) became a nationwide phenomenon, marked by sensational stories focusing on bizarre events or social injustices. The newspapers also offered jingoistic reports on international events, interpretations deliberately calculated to arouse strong public opinion. Ambrose Bierce, the journalist on whose life *The Old Gringo* is based, worked for Hearst's San Francisco *Chronicle*. Fuentes's novel portrays Bierce as a man embittered by his journalistic experience, as the actual Bierce indeed was.

Progressive reforms. Referred to as the Progressive Era, the period 1895 to 1920 was characterized by a nationwide movement toward reform of American society. Woodrow Wilson, like Theodore Roosevelt before him, won the presidency by campaigning on Progressive issues. His "New Freedom" platform, for example, contained pledges to break up corporate monopolies and regulate industries such as banking. In this same spirit of idealism and reform, Wilson wished also to extend democracy to other countries, including Mexico.

Along with political reforms, Progressives often sought to spur social reforms in other lands as well. Missionaries—religious workers who traveled abroad to spread Christianity and Anglo-American values—increased in numbers during this period. Between 1900 and 1915, the number of missionaries sent abroad nearly doubled, from roughly 5,000 to about 9,000. Harriet Winslow, the idealistic young American in *The Old Gringo,* has come to Mexico to teach English to the children of the wealthy *hacendado* Miranda, owner of the hacienda on which most of the novel's action takes place.

PROGRESSIVE REFORMS AND WOMEN

Women played a significant role in the social reform movements of the Progressive Era, particularly in foreign countries. Regarded as the protectors and transmitters of society's morality, they adapted easily to missionary work and teaching. In *The Old Gringo,* Harriet Winslow moves from her home in Washington, D.C., to Mexico to teach English to children at the Miranda hacienda. Along with English lessons, she also teaches the children about Christianity.

The Novel in Focus

The plot. Fuentes based *The Old Gringo* on rumors about the mysterious disappearance and presumed death of the famous American journalist Ambrose Bierce. We are told early in the story that "the old gringo came to Mexico to die," as Bierce was widely reported to have done (*The Old Gringo,* p. 5). Only at the end of the novel, however, is "the old gringo" revealed to be Bierce.

Set during the Mexican Revolution, the story takes place at the Miranda hacienda in Chihuahua, Mexico, in 1914. At the hacienda, the old gringo meets Tomás Arroyo, a young general in Villa's army, and Harriet Winslow, an American schoolteacher working at the hacienda. The family has run away, but Winslow has stayed behind in order to teach Villa's followers how to

read English. The old gringo arrives at the hacienda wishing to join Villa's forces.

At first, Arroyo refuses to accept the old gringo as a revolutionary, but the old gringo impresses him by shooting a hole in a tossed coin. In the meantime, Harriet teaches English at the hacienda while Arroyo waits for his leader, Villa, to arrive. Although Arroyo identifies with the poor peasants, Harriet Winslow learns that his father was the head of the Miranda hacienda. In other words, Arroyo's father was a member of the wealthy upper class in Mexico, the very group against whom Arroyo is fighting as a revolutionary.

Winslow, who becomes physically intimate with Arroyo during the course of the novel, has family ties of her own to Latin America. She tells the story of her father, who was thought to have been killed in Cuba following the Spanish-American War. His grave in Arlington Cemetery remains empty. She has learned that he did not, in fact, die but survived the war and decided to stay in Cuba with his Cuban mistress.

When the old gringo burns some documents that Arroyo believes to be valuable, Arroyo shoots him in the back and has him buried. Villa, however, learns of the killing and demands that the body be exhumed and shot from the front, as in a proper execution. As Arroyo administers the *coup de grace* on the old gringo's dead body, Villa has Arroyo himself shot. Villa will not, says the novel, tolerate his officers engaging in petty disputes with foreigners and creating trouble for him. Harriet Winslow then accompanies the old gringo's body back to the United States, where she arranges for him to take her father's plot in Arlington Cemetery.

Mexican and American identities. *The Old Gringo* uses plot and character to explore Mexico's struggle for identity in the shadow of its powerful northern neighbor. Repeatedly throughout the novel, each country is defined in relation to the other. Near the end of the book, Harriet Winslow's meeting with a Mexican soldier illustrates this two-way process. As she watches the soldier, she knows "that he would always keep his eye on the long northern border of Mexico, because for Mexicans the only reason for war was always the gringos" (*The Old Gringo,* p. 184). The soldier then tells her something that the old gringo used to say: that the United States had no frontiers left, no territory left to conquer in any direction except southward, toward Mexico.

Violence pervades the novel's portrayal of the relationship between Mexico and the United

States. "They're right," the same soldier tells Harriet Winslow, "when they say this isn't a border. It's a scar" (*The Old Gringo,* p. 185). From the time of what American historians call the Mexican War (1846-1848), whose events are repeatedly referred to in the novel, Mexicans have perceived the U.S. as a potential invader. The threat of invasion is more than merely military. There has also been a cultural threat, which is embodied in the novel's two American characters, Harriet Winslow and the old gringo.

On the one hand, progressive elements in American society are shown as possessing an idealistic and naive impulse to "save Mexico for progress and democracy" (*The Old Gringo,* p. 187). Harriet Winslow, who comes to teach English to Mexican children, represents this impulse, which the novel portrays as well-intentioned but condescending and ultimately misguided. The old gringo, on the other hand, through his past as a practitioner of "yellow journalism," recalls a more cynical and overtly selfish aspect of the American attitude toward Mexico, one that uses war and death in Mexico to feed an appetite for sensational stories. It is this past, the novel implies, that the old gringo has come to Mexico to atone for with his death. Both impulses, the idealistic and the cynical, are portrayed as equally destructive.

Just as the two Americans represent opposing national attitudes, so do the novel's two main Mexican characters, Tomás Arroyo and Pancho Villa. Their differences, as in the case of the Americans, are cast in terms of idealism and cynicism. While both are portrayed as forceful, impulsive, sensual men of action, Arroyo possesses a naiveté that in the end proves fatal, for he dies surprised that his beloved leader Villa would have him shot. And even as he draws his final breaths, with his face "the living image of pain and disbelief," he calls out his support for Villa (*The Old Gringo,* p. 178). Villa, by contrast, is portrayed as calculating and manipulative, a man who cleverly evades both his enemies and the cynical questions of the American journalists who follow his troops. At the same time, he exploits the publicity afforded by the journalists' presence to his advantage.

Fuentes also portrays his fictional Villa as fantasizing about invading the United States, as the real Villa would in 1916, three years after the novel takes place. Villa's fantasy in the novel illustrates the resentment created by American attitudes toward Mexico. "The gringos act as if we didn't exist" he tells himself. "Why not invade

Carlos Fuentes

them for once and let them see what it feels like?" (*The Old Gringo,* p. 173).

Sources. Beyond the fact that he disappeared into Mexico in 1913, after stating his intention to join Villa's forces, nothing is known of Ambrose Bierce's actual fate. From this meager background, however, Fuentes weaves a complex narrative in *The Old Gringo* that combines historical people and events with fictional ones. Along with its use of history, the novel also contains references to Bierce's own writings, the most famous of which are *The Devil's Dictionary* and the short story "**An Occurrence at Owl Creek Bridge**" (also covered in *Literature and Its Times*). Both works are repeatedly alluded to in *The Old Gringo.*

For the circumstances under which Fuentes's fictional Bierce is killed, Fuentes drew on actual events. In 1913 Villa's soldiers beat to death a British hacendado named William Benton, who had allegedly threatened Villa's life. When the British government demanded to know the circumstances of Benton's death, Villa claimed that Benton had been tried in court and executed. Villa then ordered the body dug up, shot by a firing squad, and sent home to Britain—just as Bierce's body is treated in *The Old Gringo.* Fuentes perhaps based his portrayal of the Miranda hacienda on descriptions of a famous Mexican hacienda called Terrazas Ranch. In 1913 Villa killed the administrator of the Terrazas hacienda for allegedly treating the peons cruelly. The Terrazas' property was confiscated, like that of the Mirandas, and turned into a base for Villa's soldiers.

Events in History at the Time the Novel Was Written

Late twentieth-century Mexico. Details about social inequalities in Mexico, as well as its relationship with the United States, would change from the 1910s to the 1980s. But many of the same basic concerns would continue to plague the nation. The peasants of the 1910s rebelled at what they had not gained, materially speaking. Conditions would improve little in this sense over the decades. At least half of the population numbered among the unemployed or underemployed in the late 1970s, and the economy was about to worsen. Mexico embraced some recently discovered oil fields within its boundaries as the cure to many of its problems, but a world oil glut in 1981 brought adverse results, including reduced oil prices, and the Mexican economy slumped into a severe crisis.

By then the Mexican government owned or controlled many of the country's industries, from petroleum to railroads and airlines to hotels and banks. In charge of government offices were members of the official political party, Revolutionary Institutional Party (PRI), whose rein on the government of the nation was so tight that by the mid-1980s many spoke of Mexico as being a one-party democracy. Others called it a democratic-style dictatorship, and still others "likened it to the era of Porfirio Díaz" (Miller, p. 354). The country's presidents since the revolution of the 1910s have exercised great power, controlling key appointments to official posts, proposing laws that were enacted, and naming their successors.

Disparities in agriculture remained too. The revolution of Villa's era managed to destroy the feudal-like hacienda system, and redistribute land for the benefit of the poor, but efforts to make farming more equitable were hampered by unclear title to, or ownership of, landholdings and by the fact that Mexico's population was growing faster than its ability to step up food production. After the revolution, about one fourth of all the land became part of a public landholding system. Called *ejidos,* the small plots in

this system were assigned to individuals who did not own their shares but worked them. So small are the plots (30 acres at best, half that size if the land is irrigated) that using machinery to farm the parcels has made little sense. In contrast, a number of large privately owned farms have flourished in late twentieth-century Mexico. Besides crops for export, they produce foodstuff for the nation and provide jobs for some of its people, though not always as in the same capacity as the previous era. Today's laborer on a large farm might as easily work in the farm's packing plant or machine repair shop as in the fields.

Despite efforts of leaders to loosen ties, Mexico has furthermore remained closely connected to the United States. In the mid-1980s the U.S. was still Mexico's primary trading partner, accounting for two-thirds of all Mexican exports and imports. Private American investors sometimes built their factories on the Mexican side of the border, hiring low-paid Mexicans to manufacture products that are then exported to America. By 1980 nearly 600 American-owned plants employed 118,000 Mexican workers along the border. And scores of other Mexicans crossed the border in search of work in the United States. Estimates for the early- to mid-1980s placed the number of illegal Mexican immigrants at more than 100,000 a year. Meanwhile, flowing southward were many U.S. cultural influences that reached Mexico through film, sports, and language expressions. As in the days of *The Old Gringo,* these American influences, both economic and cultural, have inspired resentment in some Mexicans and worry in others.

A difference of opinion. In the 1980s authorities in the United States feared that the Central American country El Salvador would be taken over by communists, who were leading a revolutionary movement there. In order to prevent their victory, U.S. President Ronald Reagan offered military assistance to the Salvadoran government. Reagan also intervened in Nicaragua in the 1980s, supporting the *contra* rebels against the socialist regime of Daniel Ortega and his Sandinista Party. In 1981 the U.S. military began training the Nicaraguan contras. The Mexican president at the time, Lopez Portillo, supported the Sandinistas in Nicaragua, warning the United States against further intervention. In 1982 Portillo visited Nicaragua and stated that the Sandinista Revolution was the continuation of the Mexican Revolution. Reviews of *The Old Gringo* likewise described it as a novel that was, in effect, about Nicaragua's conflict.

Reviews. *The Old Gringo* enjoyed great commercial success and won generally favorable reviews. In contrast with the positive assessments, John Updike called *The Old Gringo* "a very stilted effort, static and wordy" (Updike in Marowski and Matuz, p. 174) and dismissed it as artificial and shallow, if clever in its weaving of history and fiction. An article in *Commentary* spoke of how far the novel ventured from historical accuracy: "Are we really to believe that the old-fashioned and gallant Ambrose Bierce would, in 1914, find himself unable to open his mouth to Miss Winslow without uttering obscenities?" (Eberstadt, p. 39).

On the other hand, Earl Shorris, writing for the *New York Times Book Review,* praised Fuentes's use of "the opposition between nations, the tension of unequals that share a common border, to drive the plot of the novel and to motivate the revelations of history" (Shorris in Marowski and Matuz, p. 174). A number of reviewers found merit in what they saw as the narrative's lyrical, mythic qualities. The American public embraced it, making *The Old Gringo* the first novel by a Mexican to appear on the *New York Times* bestseller list. And the British journal *Punch* explained to its readers that the exceptionally fine novel was not farfetched. British readers, it said, might find it hard to believe that a columnist would "buckle on a six-gun and, out of self-loathing, go and try to get himself killed, but quite a few Americans have" (Pickering, p. 57). The reviewer illustrates his point with an example—a mid-1800s writer named William Walker who with a band called the American Phalanx of Immortals invaded Mexico once and Nicaragua twice, enjoying a brief stint as Nicaragua's president before being ousted for good.

For More Information

Eberstadt, Fernanda. "Montezuma's Literary Revenge." *Commentary* 81, no. 5 (May 1986): 39.

Fuentes, Carlos. *The Old Gringo.* New York: Harper & Row, 1985.

Hill, Patricia R. *The World Their Household: The American Woman's Foreign Mission Movement and Cultural Transformation.* Ann Arbor: University of Michigan Press, 1985.

Knight, Alan. *The Mexican Revolution: Counterrevolution and Reconstruction,* Vol. 2. Cambridge: Cambridge University Press, 1986.

Marowski, Daniel G., and Roger Matuz, *Contemporary Literary Criticism,* Vol. 41. Detroit: Gale Research, 1987.

Miller, Robert Ryal. *Mexico: A History.* Norman: University of Oklahoma Press, 1985.

Peterson, Jessie, and Thelma Cox Knoles, eds. *Pancho Villa: Intimate Recollections by People Who Knew Him.* New York: Hastings House, 1977.

Pickering, Paul. "Down Mexico Way." *Punch* 290 (May 28, 1986): 57.

Vazquez, Josefina Zoraida, and Lorenzo Meyer. *The United States and Mexico.* Chicago: University of Chicago Press, 1985.

Our Town

by
Thornton Wilder

After attending Yale University, Thornton Wilder (1897-1975) became a novelist and a writer of unconventional plays that engage the audience by addressing them directly, by not supplying props or scenery, and by transposing elements from one time period into another. He set his play *Our Town* in Grover's Corners, a fictional rural community that was distant and detached from the growth of industry and commerce occurring in urban New England at the turn of the century. The action takes place before World War I, when there was no apparent threat of global conflict and warfare. The setting allows Wilder's characters to focus on their immediate surroundings without having to contend with all the sociopolitical distractions in urban environments of the time.

Events in History at the Time the Play Takes Place

Invention and growth. Given the rampant progress urban America was undergoing at the turn of the century, the fictional small town in Wilder's play did feel the effects from some of the more dynamic elements of the outside world. The period of time in which *Our Town* takes place, 1901 to 1913, saw an abundance of industrial advancements—the Model T, for example, was introduced by Henry Ford in 1908. The play's Stage Manager refers to future inventions and changes, even referring in Act 3 to the automobile's becoming the basic mode of transportation. As the years pass in the fictional town

of Grover's Corners, the audience learns that the car has begun to replace the horse and buggy.

While small towns remained relatively simplistic in lifestyle in the early twentieth century, they felt the impact of inventions such as the automobile, which saved their inhabitants time and made travel more convenient. On the recreational front, the sport of baseball had its first World Series in 1903 and soon became a popular national pastime. This is reflected in the play by its repeated references to the character George as one of the best baseball players Grover's Corners has ever had. In real life, as baseball became more profitable, scouts would travel to even the most rural areas in search of athletic talent, though none of these scouts appears in the play.

The Progressive movement. In 1901 President William McKinley was assassinated and Theodore Roosevelt became the twenty-sixth president of the United States. A president concerned with reform, Roosevelt's administration

The Stage Manager (Frank Craven) performing George (John Craven) and Emily's (Martha Scott) wedding ceremony in the original production of *Our Town*.

ushered in the Progressive Era in American society. The Progressive movement held that the irresponsible actions of the rich were corrupting both public and private life in the United States; therefore, regulations must be instituted in order to create a more balanced and efficient society. Although the country was experiencing a relatively stable period economically, the social spectrum ranged from the opulently wealthy to the tragically poor. The plight of the American underclass was documented in photographs by Jacob Riis, Lewis Hine, and others. Hine, for example, took haunting pictures of children in factories in an effort to eliminate child labor. Other reformers in the Progressive movement called for legislation to break up the large monopolies ("Trust Busting"), and for the regulation of railroads, provisions for people to vote on laws themselves through referendum, a graduated income tax in which people with higher incomes would pay higher taxes, and greater conservation of natural resources.

The play may be referring to Progressivism in Grover's Corners in Act 1 when an audience member questions Mr. Webb:

> BELLIGERENT MAN: Is there no one in town aware of social injustice and industrial inequality? MR. WEBB: Oh yes, everybody is—

somethin' terrible. Seems like they spend most of their time talking about who's rich and who's poor. BELLIGERENT MAN: Then why don't they do something about it? MR. WEBB: Well, I dunno. I guess we're all hunting like everybody else for a way. . . . Meanwhile, we do all we can to help those who can't help themselves and those that can we leave alone.
>
> (*Our Town*, pp. 24-5)

Childbirth. In Act 3, the play explains that Emily dies in childbirth, a type of death that was very commonplace during this period. Although the play does not give the particulars of Emily's passing, causes of death from childbirth ranged from infection due to the unsanitary conditions of delivery to the transference of disease into the household. "Puerperal fever" was a contagious disease named by Oliver Wendell Holmes Jr., who blamed the condition on germs carried to newborns and mothers by midwives and physicians. In rural communities it was common practice for doctors to care for both people and animals. Louis Pasteur discovered that certain bacteria found in farm animals, particularly cattle and sheep, infected people who had been exposed to a doctor administering to both animals and humans. Holmes's and Pasteur's work was done in the late nineteenth century, but the practice of providing antiseptic environments during medical practices had still not been adopted in all rural areas by the early 1900s.

The Play in Focus

The plot. The narrator of the play is the Stage Manager, who not only provides us with commentary on the action, but even plays a few minor parts himself during the course of the play. Through his introductions, we find out about Grover's Corners and learn about the people, the history of the town, and even what it looks like, though the stage is empty of props. The first act is called "Daily Life," and in it we are introduced to the Webbs and the Gibbses, who live next door to each other. Emily Webb is the teenage daughter of Mr. Webb, editor of the town paper. George Gibbs is the high school baseball star, son of Dr. Gibbs, the town physician. Nurturing and caring figures, Mrs. Webb and Mrs. Gibbs emanate warmth as they mime their way through ordinary household duties like ironing or preparing meals. Act 1 is basically an introduction to the town and its inhabitants, offering up scenes of daily life in each household.

Act 2 is called "Love and Marriage," and it focuses on how George and Emily fall in love as teenagers and then later marry. In Act 3, "Death," the audience learns of Emily's death, observing her funeral and entry into the afterlife. The climax of the play comes in Act 3, when Emily makes a brief visit back in time to relive a day of her life. Though she is warned by the other dead folk, with whom she is now able to communicate, not to "go back," she asks the Stage Manager to take her back to relive her twelfth birthday. The experience is quite frustrating for Emily, who, now dead, understands that the secret to life is to be happy when you are alive and appreciate even the smallest details. She is immensely disappointed to discover how human beings take nearly every simple moment of life for granted:

> I can't. I can't go on. It goes too fast. We don't even have time to look at one another. *She breaks down crying*. . . . I didn't realize. So all that was going on and we never noticed. . . . Good-by, Good-by world. Good-by Grover's Corners . . . and Mama's sunflowers. And food and coffee. And new-ironed dresses and hot baths . . . and sleeping and waking up. Oh, earth, you're too wonderful for anybody to realize you.
>
> (*Our Town*, p. 100)

Grover's Corners. Wilder has stated that capturing life in rural New Hampshire at the turn of the century was not one of his main objectives in writing *Our Town*.

> *Our Town* is not offered as life in a New Hampshire Village; or as a speculation about the conditions of life after death (that element I simply took from Dante's *Purgatory*). It is an attempt to find value above all price for the smaller events in our daily life.
>
> (Wilder, *Our Town*, p. xii)

Wilder's play does, however, step outside the confines of its setting and refer to society at large via the Stage Manager. In Act 1, the Stage Manager conducts a brief question-and-answer period with the audience as well as with Mr. Webb, the town's newspaper editor, about Grover's Corners. Certain characters posing as audience members shout out questions that are addressed. The Stage Manager refers to this session as the "political and social report." Mr. Webb makes the following opening statement:

> MR. WEBB: Well . . . I don't have to tell you that we're run here by a Board of Selectmen. All males vote at the age of twenty-one. Women vote indirect. We're lower middle class: sprinkling of professional men . . . ten percent illiterate laborers. Politically, we're eighty-six percent Republicans; six percent Democrats; four percent Socialists; rest, indifferent.
>
> (*Our Town*, p. 23)

Whether the playwright attempted to portray reality at the time or not, Grover's Corners, New Hampshire, to some degree reflects the political climate of the country in the early twentieth century. The majority of Americans in fact supported the Republicans through the first decade of the century, as indicated by national elections. From 1900 to 1912 the country had three Republican presidents: William McKinley, Theodore Roosevelt, and William Taft. Also, with labor reform on the rise, a small percent of the population declared itself to be Socialist.

Activists of the era included women campaigning for the vote. They mounted a state-by-state campaign as well as a national effort for a constitutional amendment, but theirs was an uphill struggle, and New Hampshire proved to be one of the most recalcitrant states. From 1896 to 1910 the issue of granting women the vote surfaced on the ballot in a number of state elections across the nation, from Oregon and Washington to South Dakota and New Hampshire. And in all these cases the issue went down to defeat. For the time being, New Hampshire's women had to content themselves with bearing indirect pressure on the outcome of elections through the influence they wielded on others, a situation that would continue beyond 1913, the last year in which *Our Town* is set. New Hampshire's women would gain the vote only in 1920 with the adoption of the Nineteenth Amendment to the Constitution, which proclaims that the right to vote shall not be denied to U.S. citizens on account of sex.

The population of Grover's Corners is said to be 2,640, a fairly small community. Meanwhile, urban populations saw significant growth in the United States and abroad at the turn of the century. By 1900 only 35 percent of Americans resided in rural communities.

Sources. It has been noted, based on Wilder's personal journals, in which he unabashedly compliments his mother, that Isabella Niven Wilder is the main role model for female characters in both his plays and novels.

> The feminine ideal was his mother, managing on her own during the absence or illness of a husband. . . . She is in *The Long Christmas Dinner, The Happy Journey to Camden and Trenton* and in Thornton's most popular play . . . *Our Town.*
>
> (Harrison, p. 176)

To some extent, the maternal characters of Mrs. Webb and Mrs. Gibbs certainly take on some characteristics of Isabella Niven Wilder, but most of all it is believed that the character of Emily was modeled after Wilder's mother in respect to her intelligence, her honesty, and her love of the arts.

In his book, *The Enthusiast: The Life of Thornton Wilder*, Gilbert A. Harrison reports that a strained relationship existed between Thornton Wilder and his father, Amos Parker Wilder. This tension is possibly illustrated in Act 2 of *Our Town* during a conversation between Dr. Gibbs and Mrs. Gibbs on the eve of George and Emily's wedding:

> DR. GIBBS: Ye-e-s! I get a shock every time I think of George setting out to be a family man— that great gangling thing!—I tell you Julia, there's nothing so terrifying in the world as a *son.* The relationship of father and son is the darndest, awkwardest—
>
> (*Our Town,* p. 52)

Although his relationships with his children may have been somewhat strained, Amos Wilder provided for his family and tried to teach his sons the value of hard work and ethical behavior. These qualities can be seen both in Mr. Webb and Dr. Gibbs. In Act 1, Dr. Gibbs advises George

to help out his mother with the wood-chopping chore as an act of responsibility and appreciation:

> I suppose she just got tired of asking you. She gave up and decided it was easier to do it herself. And you eat her meals, and put on the clothes she keeps nice for you, and you run off and play baseball. . . . I knew all I had to do was call your attention to it.
>
> (*Our Town,* p. 36)

Events in History at the Time the Play Was Written

A different approach to traditional theater. When *Our Town* was first performed in 1938, Thornton Wilder was better known as the Pulitzer prize-winning novelist for *The Bridge of San Luis Rey* in 1927. Unhappy with most of what he was seeing on the American stage, Wilder decided to introduce a different approach to theater, as he explains in the front matter to the play:

> Toward the end of the twenties I began to lose pleasure in going to the theater. . . . I felt that something had gone wrong with it [the theater] in my time and that it was fulfilling only a small part of its potentialities.
>
> (Wilder, p. vii)

NEW HAMPSHIRE WOMEN'S CLUBS

New Hampshire women exerted influence on politics through their women's clubs, which banded together to form a state federation in 1896. The federation became a civic force, organizing a legislative committee and civil service reform committee, which in 1909, for example, influenced the state to adopt new, humanitarian legislation, such as the Forestry Protection Bill, Industrial School Bill, Work House Bill, and Child Labor Bill.

Our Town was considered an innovative play for its time because of the experimental techniques incorporated by Wilder. The action is narrated by the Stage Manager, a character both inside and outside the play. The Stage Manager comments to the audience on the present, the past, and the future. He is both enclosed in finite time and stands beyond and outside of it. In addition, no props are used, just tables and chairs, and no background scenery occupies the stage. All action that normally involves the use of props is mimed by the actors. This was certainly a risky venture at a time when theater productions were lavish both in costume and scenery. However, Wilder's use of these experimental techniques prompted the audience to focus more on the characters than on where they were located and what they did with respect to the inanimate objects surrounding them. In her book, *Currents in Contemporary Drama,* author Ruby Cohn explains Wilder's theatrical approach:

> The Stage Manager in *Our Town* functions much like an omnipresent author in a novel, but he does not suggest that his characters are actors. . . . On the contrary, the characters are more real than things, because they are present on stage whereas things are not.
>
> (Cohn, p. 209)

Current events and *Our Town*. Because Wilder was drafted just before the end of the First World War, he did not actually enter combat and was able to continue his studies at Yale. He was present in the United States during the stock market crash of 1929 and the Great Depression that followed, but Wilder rarely if ever commented on the social and or political happenings of the day in his writing or his personal journals. In *Our Town* Wilder's Stage Manager does make one brief comment on the subject of war, but the dialogue primarily shows concern for how the war aborted the growth of a promising townsman— that is, for how it impacted the individual rather than for how it affected nations:

> Joe Crowell . . . was awful bright. Graduated high school here head of his class. So he got a scholarship to Massachusetts Tech. Graduated head of his class there too. . . . Goin' to be a great engineer Joe was. But the war broke out and he died in France.— All that education for nothing.
>
> (*Our Town*, p. 10)

Wilder wrote *Our Town* while residing in a small resort in Switzerland in 1937, when Adolf Hitler was in power in nearby Nazi Germany. Though he was living in Europe just two years before the Nazi invasion of Poland in 1939 (which marked the beginning of World War II), Wilder's personal letters and journals suggest that he was focused not on world affairs but on his own creative efforts and his correspondence with other notable writers of the time.

Later, however, Wilder would connect politics to small New England towns such as the one featured in his play. These small towns, Wilder

Thornton Wilder

believed, were full of the kind of spirit needed to restore interest in politics, which waned after the war. "We don't want to think," he said, "and our political apathy is defeating the democratic process. . . . [Writers] must mix the cement for others to build the walls" (Wilder in Simon, p.193). This would entail inflaming the nation with the same sense of responsibility shown in the small town meeting.

Reviews. The first production of *Our Town* was performed in Princeton, New Jersey, on January 22, 1938. The play next opened in Boston, Massachusetts, where it received mixed reviews. The producer felt that if the drama were to succeed it would have to be presented on Broadway in New York. In February of 1938, *Our Town* opened at the Henry Miller Theater in New York. The *New York Times* critiqued the play on several occasions during its run and always gave it an enthusiastic review, complimenting its innovation and social commentary. *Time* magazine, however, did not appreciate the play, implying in its review of February 14, 1938 that Wilder should stick to plays about the living instead of making assumptions about the dead. Though the play attracted some other criticism, it received mostly positive reviews and went on to win the

Pulitzer Prize for drama later in 1938. During the play's original run, Wilder himself took on the role of the Stage Manager for a period of about two weeks because the regular actor fell ill. *The New York Times* noted in a review of the play on September 16, 1938, that although Wilder had a little trouble remembering some of the lines to his own play, he did possess a stage presence:

> Being a lecturer of some renown and having been at one time a schoolmaster, Mr. Wilder has, as they say, stage presence.
>
> (*New York Times Theater Reviews,*
> September 16, 1938)

For More Information

Cohn, Ruby. *Currents in Contemporary Drama.* Bloomington: Indiana University Press, 1969.

Harrison, Gilbert A. *The Enthusiast: A Life of Thornton Wilder.* New Haven, Conn.: Ticknor & Fields, 1983.

Ladewig, Patricia Wieland, Marcia L. London, and Sally B. Olds. *Essentials of Maternal Newborn Nursing.* 3rd ed. Redwood City, Calif.: Benjamin Cummings, 1994.

New York Times Theater Reviews. Vol. 4. New York: New York Times, 1971.

Sellers, Charles, Henry May, and Neil R. McMillen. *A Synopsis of American History, Volume 2: Since the Civil War.* Boston: Houghton Mifflin, 1985.

Simon, Linda. *Thornton Wilder: His World.* Garden City, N.Y.: Doubleday, 1979.

Wilder, Amos Niven. *Thornton Wilder and His Public.* Philadelphia: Fortress, 1980.

Wilder, Thornton. *Three Plays: Our Town, The Skin of Our Teeth, The Matchmaker.* New York: Harper Perennial, 1957.

Out of Africa

by
Isak Dinesen

Karen Christentze Dinesen moved from Denmark to Kenya in 1914, where she married her second cousin, Bror, and became the Baroness von Blixen-Finecke. Despite the title, the Blixens were destined to a hard life as owners of a sprawling farm and coffee plantation that was never a financial success. *Out of Africa,* written under Karen Blixen's pen name Isak Dinesen, chronicles her experiences, harsh and beautiful alike, on the high plateau bordering on the Ngong Hills. The marriage was often an unhappy one, and the couple was divorced seven years after their union. But Dinesen had fallen in love with her new home and remained there quite contentedly, running the farm on her own until 1931, when collapsing finances forced her to return to Denmark. Her story of coping as a European settler in the midst of diverse African cultures captures the rapidly changing social and political landscapes of British East Africa, as well as the decline of the African wilderness in the face of immigration from Europe.

Events in History at the Time of the Autobiography

British East Africa. The land that became Kenya was sparsely populated by small numbers of native peoples until well into the nineteenth century. The first European man to have come there, Joseph Thompson, did not arrive until 1883, and he was on his way to Uganda. It did not take long, however, for European colonizing nations, primarily Britain and Germany, to realize that

THE LITERARY WORK

An autobiography set in Kenya, East Africa, from 1914 to 1931; published in English in 1937.

SYNOPSIS

Dinesen's recollections of life on a coffee farm in British East Africa are set against the backdrop of war, race relations, and colonial expansion.

East Africa was potentially strategic real estate, both economically and politically. Through a deal with the sultan of Zanzibar, who was the nominal ruler over much of the eastern African coast, Germany, in 1885, became the first European nation to make inroads into East Africa. The German East Africa Company emerged on the scene that year, beginning a program of trade and exploration in the area that is now Tanzania.

The British soon followed, concluding an agreement of their own with the sultan. In 1887 he leased the lands that are now Kenya to the Imperial British East Africa Company, a commercial enterprise set up under governmental supervision primarily to establish trade in the area. Eight years later, in 1895, the British government assumed more direct control over the Kenyan lands, setting up what was called the East Africa "Protectorate," a term that designates the relationship between a powerful (generally European) state and an as-yet politically unrecognized territory inhabited mostly by native, non-European people. By 1920 the British had established most of the inland area of Kenya as an official crown colony; the coastal area remained in the control of the sultan of Zanzibar.

The British were intent on constructing a means of transportation, the Uganda Railroad, from the sea westward to the shores of Lake Victoria so that they could control the headwaters of the Nile River and assure their interests in northern Africa. But the railroad, finished in 1901 at the cost of £6 million, turned out to be an expensive proposition. In order to pay for it, the government figured that settling the lands around the railroad would help raise the necessary cash. They planned to sell large tracts of land to European settlers. The settlers didn't have to be British; it was their money the government was interested in, not their nationality. But Africa seemed too far away to many Europeans and too risky. The British government had a difficult time convincing settlers to begin new lives as African landowners.

Britain first offered to help establish a Finnish settlement there, an offer that the Finns rejected in 1902. The British then suggested that citizens of India be persuaded to leave their homes and immigrate to Africa. A certain number complied, leaving India at the height of the British Empire there, but their attempts to establish a community in East Africa were hindered by the intolerant racial attitudes of those Europeans who had previously settled in the area and were determined to keep the Indians an impoverished and marginal population. Later in 1902, there were extensive negotiations between the British government and the leaders of Russian and Polish Jews who were being persecuted in their homelands; the plan to help the Eastern European Jews establish a quasi-independent homeland under British protection also foundered.

All this is not to suggest that East Africa lacked native peoples or that its immense lands failed to attract some settlers. The Europeans to whom the prospect of African resettlement did appeal tended to come from a very specific social class—the upper middle class and the aristocracy. Such people had the money to establish themselves comfortably in Africa, and many of them were wealthy enough to absorb many years of financial failure as the Europeans experimented with what sort of farming was best suited for the unfamiliar African climate. Some of them brought along strong ideas about their privileged class

Isak Dinesen

and culture, which they tried to replicate in their new homes, and which often influenced detrimentally their relationships with the indigenous Africans they encountered. The general attitude toward the Africans tended to be one of scorn and superiority. Unusual in this respect, Dinesen was sometimes despised for her strong pro-native stance. She was extremely sympathetic to the rights and dignity of the African people who worked on her farm. She set up a school for them, which was very uncommon, and inoculated and fed them during a horrible plague and drought that beset the land in 1918.

The number of European settlers in Kenya remained fairly small throughout the early years of the protectorate; in 1905, some eight years before Dinesen's arrival, there were only about six hundred of them. By 1914 that number had reached five thousand. The settlers were not all farmers by any means; as a burgeoning British colony, Kenya warranted a significant number of civil servants to administer its daily affairs. As one source notes, "[W]ithin this European community, in 1911, only 28 percent lived by farming, while 26 percent were connected to government and 16 percent were missionaries" (Clough, p. 31). The slightly more than 1,000 farmers owned 4.5 million acres of Kenyan land.

Kikuyu. Much of *Out of Africa* takes place on what had been the homeland of the Kikuyu people, with whom Dinesen had many of her closest African relationships. By the 1880s, the Kikuyu had moved into the more or less empty lands in the middle of which Dinesen and her husband would later have their farm; occasionally, the Kikuyu encountered the nomadic Dorobo people, with whom they intermarried, fought for occupancy of land, or exchanged land rights.

CHIEF KINANJUI

In *Out of Africa*, the author describes her friend, the great Kikuyu chief Kinanjui, who has come to the coffee farm on official business:

> He had on a large cloak of blue monkey-skins, and on his head a skull-cap of the kind which the Kikuyu make out of sheeps' stomachs. He was always an impressive figure, tall and broad, with no fat on him anywhere; his face too was proud, long and bony, with a slanting forehead like that of a Red Indian. He had a broad nose, so expressive that it looked like the central point of the man, as if the whole stately figure was there only to carry the broad nose about. Like the trunk of an elephant, it was both boldly inquisitive and extremely sensitive and prudent, intensely on the offensive, and on the defensive as well.
>
> (Dinesen, *Out of Africa*, pp. 107-08)

As one historian has observed, the specific geography of Kikuyuland helped to determine the social customs of the Kikuyu people. The land there, which stretches on a high plateau between Mount Kenya to the north and the Ngong Hills to the south, is covered with a pattern of high ridges and deep valleys. "The first pioneers settled the land ridge by ridge—Kikuyu families staking their claims and others moving on to stake theirs—and the ridges, easily defended and dangerous to assault, developed into self-sufficient little communities" (Clough, p. 4). Probably because of this social arrangement, the Kikuyu governed themselves according to family hierarchy and had no social institutions of kingship or larger government, a state of affairs that may have helped the British in their colonizing efforts. In Dinesen's day, one or two of the older Kikuyu men did rise to greater prominence largely through the force of their personalities and their connections with the incoming Euro-

peans. Chief Kinyanjui wa Gathirimu (known in *Out of Africa* as Kinanjui), one of the most prominent and powerful of the Kikuyu after the turn of the century, was a friend to Isak Dinesen.

The "transfer" of land from the Kikuyu to Europeans was due largely to an incredible string of misfortunes that assailed the Kikuyu shortly before the Europeans arrived in large numbers. From 1895 to 1897, the Kikuyu were visited by locusts, rinderpest (which killed domestic animals), drought, famine, and smallpox. The combination of these disasters disabled the Kikuyu. They could not manage the land on which they lived. According to one of their customs, they allowed the new European settlers to take charge of the land—temporarily. This turned out to be a huge mistake on their part, for the Europeans acted as though, and perhaps believed that, the land had now become irreversibly theirs.

World War I. The outbreak of World War I in 1914 affected colonial East Africa almost as soon as it started. It was not just that the British colonists themselves discovered that they were at war with their neighbors—German East Africa was located immediately south of British East Africa—but the war also affected the native Africans, who were suddenly pulled into it. They were drafted into the British army, often unofficially, becoming attached to the impromptu units that their white overlords joined. As one writer observes, "Many Africans went to war, some to fight in the King's African Rifles, but more to serve as caravan porters hauling food and equipment to the front. Their sufferings and the sufferings of Africans at home contributed to a smoldering discontent" (Clough, p. 45). Because there was no one to work the farms or cultivate the land, the people who remained at home suffered not only from the absence of their loved ones, but also from food shortages and economic hardships of all sorts.

Although Europe had been bracing for war for several months, the European settlers in Africa, intent upon the arduous business of scraping out a living from unfamiliar soil, felt somewhat removed from the mounting hostilities so far away. As Europeans, the various groups of colonists doubtless felt a sense of community with one another despite their different nationalities. For example, when Dinesen first sailed to Africa to marry Bror, she met and was befriended by the man who was journeying to German East Africa to take charge of military affairs there. General Paul von Lettow would soon become the most hated man in British East Africa. Her friendship with him would land Dinesen in trouble after war was officially declared; suspected of being a German sympathizer, she was ostracized in British East African society for some time. Not until her younger brother Thomas won a medal fighting in the Canadian army would the stigma of being Germanic—she and Bror were of Swedish and Danish descent—fall away.

On July 29, 1914, the British colonialists were informed via telegrams sent to the African cities of Nairobi and Entebbe that they should be prepared for hostile actions to be taken against them by their German neighbors. Ten days later, on August 8, British warships off the coast of East Africa attacked a radio tower in the German settlement at Dar es Salaam, and war descended upon Africa. With notable exceptions, it was mostly guerrilla warfare, in which raiding parties crossed back and forth over the essentially undefendable border between British and German East Africa to wreak whatever havoc they could. The Uganda Railroad, north of the border, was the most obvious target for the German militia because it was being used as a supply line. Lord Delamere, the leader of the British colonists, immediately organized a border patrol, to which Bror Blixen applied as an intelligence officer.

Postwar Africa was possibly an even more troubled place than it had been during the hostilities. The British government gave 3 million acres of East African farmland to (white) veterans of the war, which increased the economic competition between settlers and decreased the available African manpower. To make matters worse for the farmers, the government was pushing ahead with an ambitious program of railway construction, and for this it required labor that also competed with the manpower requirements of the settlers. Meanwhile, a terrible wave of famine and pestilence had swept the land, killing thousands of Africans. The irate settlers demanded that something be done to guarantee them the native manpower that they had enjoyed before the war. Some of them went so far as to suggest that the government force young native men to work on their farms.

Nairobi. While in Dinesen's time Nairobi was still a frontier town with wooden sidewalks, it had already grown considerably from the disreputable turn-of-the-century shantytown that it had been, despite the fact that Bror Blixen once described it as looking like "a can of anchovies" because most of the roofs were made of tin (Thurman, p. 130). Now that the Uganda Railroad ran through it on the way from Mogamba on the coast to the shores of Lake Victoria,

Nairobi had become the capital of the British colony in East Africa and was an important center for trade and information. Springing up because of the influx of settlers from Europe, the city catered almost exclusively to their needs, housing government offices and commercial concerns, as well as a racetrack and two decent hotels. While the rather large Indian population, as well as the native African communities, were isolated in varying degrees of poverty on the edges of town, the British settlers brought to Nairobi the standards of living that they enjoyed at home. These included the founding of the Muthaiga Club, that, complete with golf course, polo ponies, tennis courts, and a professional chef, became the center of society in Nairobi. Of the town that lay some twelve miles from her farm, Dinesen writes: "During all my time, Nairobi was a medley place, with some fine new stone buildings, and whole quarters of old corrugated iron shops, offices, and bungalows, laid out with long rows of eucalyptus trees along the bare dusty streets. . . . And it was a live place, in movement like running water, and in growth like a young thing, it changed from year to year, and while you were away on a shooting safari" (Out of Africa, p. 20).

Squatters' rights. When Dinesen could no longer afford to run her failing coffee plantation and she made her sad decision to return to Europe, the new owners of her farm would not tolerate the presence of "squatters." The squatters were native Africans who lived in small communities on the land owned by Europeans; many had lived there before the land belonged to the white settlers or had been born on it, and, as Dinesen herself speculated, many looked upon the Europeans as "a sort of superior squatter on their estates" (Out of Africa, p. 19). The new owners demanded that the natives remove themselves within six months to land designated as the Kikuyu reserve; the squatters became alarmed that there would not be enough space for them to all go together and keep intact the community that had grown up on Dinesen's estate. Dinesen records the threat of dissolving into nothingness that befell groups of natives who suddenly found themselves homeless:

> If they were to go away from their land, they must have people round them who had known it, and so could testify to their identity. Then they could still, for some years, talk of the geography and the history of the farm, and what one had forgotten the other would remember.

Isak Dinesen outside her house near Nairobi, Kenya, in 1938.

As it was, they were feeling the shame of extinction falling on them.
(*Out of Africa*, p. 263)

Through a complicated and drawn-out series of negotiations with government officials in Nairobi, Dinesen won for the squatters on her farm the right to live together on a special section of a nearby forest reserve.

The Autobiography in Focus

The plot. *Out of Africa* is a collection of stories, character sketches, and autobiographical observations drawn from the author's life on her African coffee plantation in the first part of the twentieth century. It begins with the observation that the soil on her coffee farm was not, in fact, very good for growing coffee and that times were often hard for her at the foot of the Ngong Hills. The story of the physical and economic hardship exacted by managing the failing enterprise runs through the entire book, with the loss of the farm both opening and concluding the story.

The author tells the story of how she came to know and love the people and the animals who visited or stayed on her farm. Examples range from Kamante, the seriously ill Kikuyu who becomes her faithful houseboy and talented chef, to Lulu, the graceful bushbuck who becomes a house pet

(and provides an important bridge between the domestic and the wild worlds), to the laughing Kikuyu women whom she visits every day.

Dinesen farms, hunts, and acts as both doctor and judge to the natives living on her plantation. She leads a supplies caravan to the British forces encamped on the German East African border during the First World War and entertains Europeans ranging from a mad Swede to the Prince of Wales. In short, her life in Africa seems at times a whirlwind of exotic experiences and adventures. Yet it is out of the dull times that *Out of Africa* first took shape, in the notes and small stories that she wrote at her dining-room table to pass the hours, and in the tales that she would spin for the entertainment of Denys Finch Hatton, her lover, when he returned from safari. A superb hunter and an avid pilot, Finch Hatton was a cultured Englishman who, though fiercely independent, made Dinesen's home his base. Together they flew over East Africa in his small Moth airplane, a joy of which Dinesen often writes. His death in an air crash is the culmination of the series of losses that Dinesen experiences at the end of her stay in Africa, and she returns to Denmark bereft of her home, her friends, and her independence.

Lord Delamere. A marginal character in *Out of Africa*, but one whom Dinesen was more than happy to have as a friend, Hugh Cholmondeley, the third Baron Delamere, was a controversial and important figure in East African politics. Some historians go so far as to credit him personally with the successful founding of a British colony in Africa. Delamere first arrived there in 1897, becoming one of the very first explorers to journey with a caravan down from the north. He settled permanently in the area in 1903 and immediately became the leading voice among the European settlers, pressuring the British government to sponsor the founding of a white colony in East Africa.

In 1902 the British politician Joseph Chamberlain had made an offer to the Jewish communities of Poland and Russia, who were under renewed persecution, of five thousand acres of Britain's East African lands for the establishment of a semiautonomous community there under British protection; Delamere protested at the top of his voice. He organized the settlers already in the area and made it clear to the government that they did not appreciate the offer made to the Jews. His faction of settlers argued that they had had to pay sizeable sums to the government for the right to own land in East Africa, and that they were unwilling to tolerate the encroachment of a "foreign" population into their community. Delamere formally organized the Planters' and Farmers' Association in 1904, which "pressed for the reservation of the Highlands for white settlement" and continued to protest the Jewish settlement (Bennett, p. 12). Their demands caused quite a stir in official circles, until someone noticed that there were, in fact, only thirty-two members in the association. In any case, the Jews themselves decided against moving to East Africa and formally turned down the offer in 1905.

Lord Delamere was a great admirer of the Maasai warrior tribe whose lands bordered the Dinesen farm. Originally from the north of Africa, the Maasai probably moved south into what is now Kenya sometime around the end of the sixteenth century. Before the incursion of the Europeans, the fierce Maasai were the dominant culture in the area. Delamere learned to speak their language and spent a great deal of time among them. In 1904 he solved the already obvious problem of how to guarantee the lands necessary for Africa's game animals to live (and be hunted by rich Europeans on safari) while at the same time opening as much land as possible for agricultural development. His plan was to combine a reserve for the Maasai with a game reserve. The Maasai did not eat game and thus the animals would be safe among them, and new land more suitable for agricultural development would be opened up that might otherwise have been necessary to reserve for animals. In 1904 two large Maasai reserves were created, which extended south to the German East African border. These are the lands on which Dinesen so often rode in solitude, and which lay just across the river from her own property.

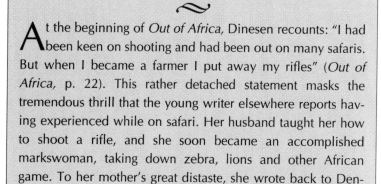

THE HUNT

At the beginning of *Out of Africa*, Dinesen recounts: "I had been keen on shooting and had been out on many safaris. But when I became a farmer I put away my rifles" (*Out of Africa*, p. 22). This rather detached statement masks the tremendous thrill that the young writer elsewhere reports having experienced while on safari. Her husband taught her how to shoot a rifle, and she soon became an accomplished markswoman, taking down zebra, lions and other African game. To her mother's great distaste, she wrote back to Denmark a detailed description of one particular expedition:

> There was bright moonlight, and as you are sitting . . . with your kill not 8 feet away, you can watch the big animals as if you were actually sitting among them. The first to come are the shy, shadowy hyenas, they retreat a couple of times before finally daring to start eating; more and more of them come gliding out of the darkness, you can hear every sound from their teeth. . . . You can see everything quite clearly in the moonlight and could almost touch them with your hand while you sit there as quiet as a mouse with your cocked rifle resting on a branch ready to shoot.
>
> (Dinesen, *Letters from Africa*, p. 22)

Sources. When Dinesen was fifteen years old, she read Olive Schreiner's novel *The Story of an African Farm*, the tale of a European settler in Africa. She would later write "[O]ut in Africa, the book was often in my mind" (Dinesen in Pelensky, p. 141). But the immediate source for *Out of Africa*, it has been suggested, was Dinesen's need, once she was back in Europe, to discover the "dignity of meaning" in her own life (Thurman, p. 313). In chapter 4 of the book, in a sketch called "The Roads of Life," Dinesen tells a story about a man who has a disastrous day—he falls in ditches, loses his way, and is visited by hardship. The next day, he gets up and looks out his window, only to find that the path of his harried scurrying to and fro has traced out the pattern of a stork. His life has a shape and a meaning, even though he couldn't see it at the time. She then reflects: "The tight place, the dark pit in which I am now lying, of what bird is it the talon? When the design of my life is completed, shall I, shall other people, see a stork?" (*Out of Africa*, p. 176).

DINESEN'S ENGLISH

Dinesen's London publishers had to make nearly 8,000 editorial corrections to the manuscript of *Out of Africa*. English was not the first language of the writer, and the English that she had picked up was, in the words of her publisher, "based largely on the King James version of the Bible, and Shakespeare, Shelley and other classic English literature. There is also inevitably a slight foreign flavour which we have not tried to eliminate entirely" (Pelensky, p. 140).

Reviews. Dinesen's London publisher, Constant Huntington, of Putnam's publishing house, considered *Out of Africa* "the most important book I have ever published, and I believe that it will take its place in the permanent great literature of the world" (Pelensky, p. 140). After the book was published, Dinesen heard from Huntington about its fate on the market: "Mr. Huntington writes to me that the intellectual circles in England like it" (Dinesen in Pelensky, p. 141); the rest of the reading public was less enchanted. Possibly this can be explained by the fact that in

the 1930s the British were more interested in such books about Africa as Dinesen's ex-husband, Baron Bror Blixen, wrote; his *African Hunter* was basically a rousing and very masculine account of the dangers and thrills of big-game hunting. In America, however, *Out of Africa* became an instant success. It was chosen as a Book-of-the-Month-Club selection and sold 92,000 copies by mid-April 1938.

For More Information

Bennett, George. *Kenya: A Political History—The Colonial Period.* Oxford: Oxford University Press, 1963.

Bentsen, Cheryl. *Maasai Days.* New York: Summit, 1989.

Clough, Marshall S. *Fighting Two Sides: Kenyan Chiefs and Politicians, 1918-1940.* Niwot: University Press of Colorado, 1990.

Dinesen, Isak. *Letters from Africa.* Chicago: University of Chicago Press, 1978.

Dinesen, Isak. *Out of Africa and Shadows on the Grass.* New York: Penguin Viking, 1985.

Lasson, Franz, ed. *The Life and Destiny of Isak Dinesen.* Chicago: University of Chicago Press, 1970.

Marsh, Z. A. and G. W. Kingsnorth. *An Introduction to the History of East Africa.* 3rd ed. Cambridge: Cambridge University Press, 1965.

Pelensky, Olga A. *Isak Dinesen: The Life and Imagination of a Seducer.* Athens: Ohio University Press, 1991.

Thurman, Judith. *Isak Dinesen: The Life of a Storyteller.* New York: St. Martin's, 1982.

Trzebinski, Errol. *Silence Will Speak: A Study of Denys Finch Hatton and His Relationship with Karen Blixen.* Chicago: University of Chicago Press, 1972.

A Passage to India

by

E. M. Forster

E.M. Forster visited India on two separate occasions, in 1912 and 1922, before the full onset of Indian nationalism that eventually led to the country's independence from England in 1947. In a novel widely regarded as his masterpiece, the author looks at the conflict between East and West, examining how politics and spirituality affected men and women in India. Forster's *A Passage to India* does not deal with the beginning of the expulsion of the English from India until the novel's close. Nonetheless the novel in its entirety offers many insights into the British-Indian clash.

THE LITERARY WORK

A novel set in British India during the early 1920s; published in 1924.

SYNOPSIS

A clash between British and Indian cultures culminates in the courtroom trial of a native Indian.

Events in History at the Time of the Novel

History of the British in India. While the novel opens at a point of high tension between the British and their Indian subjects, such social and political strife was not always so apparent. India's resentment toward its British rulers developed over a long history of oppression. It would prove nearly impossible to understand Forster's plot and characters without some knowledge concerning the history of the British in India.

England's original interest in India dates to 1600. At this time, the South Asian subcontinent offered a variety of spices and silks popular with affluent Europeans. In order to break a Dutch-dominated trade with India, England formed the East India Company. Between the years of 1639 and 1690, the Company acquired territory in three of India's prime trading areas—Madras, Bombay, and Calcutta. On each of these sites, the English erected forts, known as factories, which handled the business of trade and export. The English who ran these forts eventually became involved in local government.

India's last central dynasty, the Moguls, had by this time disintegrated into several camps of feuding princes. With the lack of a centralized governmental organization, India surrendered its power to rule itself without much of a fight. By 1765 England had gained the right to collect land revenues and govern most of India. The areas to which its power did not extend proved too remote to pose much of a threat.

Up to this point, the East India Company had more or less been running the country. Because of growing corruption in the Company, such as private trading, the British government began involving itself in Indian affairs. Under the Regulating Act of 1773, the English Parliament created a Governor General for India. The first man to hold this position was Warren Hastings. During Hastings's term (1773-1785), England consolidated and expanded its territories in India. His successor, Lord Cornwallis, established administrative, legal, and land revenue codes that cemented British authority. Cornwallis's rule (1786-1793), however, also instituted the racial hierarchy that surfaces in the novel.

The governor believed that the East India Company's corruption resulted from interaction with Indians. As such, he excluded Indians from holding high government positions and reinforced a widening socioeconomic gap between British and Indian citizens. Cornwallis's economic cutbacks, such as wage reductions for Indians, came during a population boom. With more mouths to feed and less money to do so, poverty among Indians rose drastically. By the end of Cornwallis's rule, the highest post that an Indian could hope for was either one of subservience to a British official, or one in the shrinking sphere of the independent Indian states.

By 1857 many Indian citizens had begun to feel the sting of British oppression. That year, a group of Indian nationalists led the Indian Mutiny. Because it was a small, poorly organized attempt, the rebellion was quelled in a matter of about four months. It nonetheless presented a pivotal moment in Indian history. For the first time, India showed its resentment toward British insensitivity and attempts at the westernization of its country. The Indian Mutiny (sometimes referred to as the Sepoy Rebellion) proved to be India's first step toward independence.

Indian nationalism. The second chapter of *A Passage to India* finds three Indian men discussing whether or not "it is possible to be friends with an Englishman" (Forster, *A Passage to India,* p. 6). This seemingly minor conversation portends the eventual clash between Forster's British and Indian characters. By the early 1900s, notions of Indian nationalism had certainly found a voice.

Because Forster's novel was written following two separate trips to India, its setting really covers a span of several years. His second trip to the foreign land, in 1921, unveiled a very different India than the author had observed originally in 1912. India was no longer the passive servant to its British master. Forster remarked during his second visit, "It's too late. Indians don't long for social intercourse with Englishmen any longer. They have made a life of their own" (Forster in Lewis, p. 111). Several political events in the early 1900s were responsible for this change.

The first occurred at Amritsar, in the Punjab region of northwest British India. On April 10, 1919, two Indian nationalist leaders, Dr. Kitchlew and Dr. Satyapal, were arrested in Amritsar and deported. Outside the jail, a large crowd formed in protest, and rioting quickly broke out. The rioters entered two banks, murdering the European agents that worked there. A railway guard was also killed, and several other Europeans were attacked. In an effort to quell the unrest, the British army forbade all public meetings. The date of this proclamation, however, fell unluckily on the thirteenth of the month—a day when many country peasants came to town for the horse fair. That evening a prohibited public meeting took place in the Jallianwala Bagh, a large, sunken outdoor bath. When General Reginald Dyer, the commander of the British troops in Amritsar, heard of this, he ordered fifty of his men to fire without warning into the crowd. In total, 379 Indians (87 of whom were country villagers) lost their lives, and the 1,200 wounded received no assistance from their British attackers. By April 15, the British had declared a state of martial law, which lasted until June 9. The events at Amritsar inspired Indian nationalists to new levels in championing their cause. Perhaps no single man rose from this tragedy more powerfully than a local labor leader by the name of Mohandas Karamchand Gandhi.

Educated in London, Gandhi had been admitted to the legal bar in 1891 and had practiced law for several years for an Indian firm in South Africa. After suffering from the discrimination felt by most Indian citizens in South Africa, he began to lead protest campaigns. During these early years he formed his tenets of *satyagraha,* or "steadfastness in truth." A devout Hindu, Gandhi advocated nonviolent protest and passive resistance in order to right political and social wrongs. The massacre at Amritsar inspired him to a career of political protest. By 1920 Gandhi had become the dominant figure in the Indian Nationalist Congress—a group formed in 1885 to help Indians achieve a greater equality with their British rulers. As such he urged other Indians to adopt a policy of noncooperation with British officials. Gandhi and his followers effectively marched against British regulations such as a higher salt tax (1930) and boycotted British goods. For his efforts to release India from British control, Gandhi earned the title of Mahatma, meaning "Great Soul." Gandhi not only worked for social equality in India, but he also advocated religious understanding between feuding Hindu and Muslim groups. His efforts helped India to finally gain its independence

Mohandas Gandhi

from Britain in 1947. Ironically, he was assassinated on January 30, 1948, five months following this political victory.

Religion in India. The tea party thrown by Dr. Fielding in the novel unites not only Eastern and Western cultures, but also the two religious camps of India. Through the characters of Professor Godbole, a devout Hindu, and Dr. Aziz, a reformed Muslim, Forster explores the two religions that dominate the foreign country.

WHITMAN'S "PASSAGE TO INDIA"

E. M. Forster takes the title of his novel from a poem penned by Walt Whitman between 1868 and 1871. Whitman's "Passage to India" discusses the exploration of the East by the West in a literal and spiritual sense. Whitman's poem wonders who "shall justify these restless explorations?" (Whitman, p. 275). In other words, for what purpose was India being explored? Recognizing the great differences between easterners and westerners, the poem ultimately hopes that "[a]ll these separations and gaps shall be taken up and hook'd and link'd together." At such a time, the poem continues, "[t]he whole earth, this cold, impassive, voiceless earth shall be completely justified" (Whitman, p. 275).

Hinduism lays claim to about 85 percent of India's devout. Hindus believe that the soul returns to earth time and again, taking different forms of life depending on the way one has conducted oneself in a past life. This doctrine is called reincarnation, or the transmigration of souls. To achieve a release from this cycle of birth and rebirth, one must follow the pathways of devotion, deeds, and knowledge. The way to these paths is recorded in the *Bhagavad Gita,* Hinduism's most sacred work.

Some of Hinduism's prominent features may seem quite alien to the Western mind. For example, orthodox Hindus believe, among other things, that the lower classes deserve their lot in life because of injustices they committed in past lives. This ideology creates a caste system, a social hierarchy that does not allow for people to move upward in life either financially or socially. While the caste system does not play a major role in Forster's work, other Hindu rules, such as dietary regulations, are apparent. When traveling to the Marabar Caves, Professor Godbole, the

Hindu Brahman or high priest, must have his own cook to prepare dishes that do not violate his spiritual beliefs.

India's other major religious influence comes from Islam. More allied with Judeo-Christian thought, Islam's spiritual focus is centered on the prophet Muhammad. Islam exhibits the same serene faith in God, or Allah, as the Judeo-Christian tradition; other similarities include a revulsion toward a manmade image of God, the concept of a covenant between God and his people, and the idea of a chosen people destined to rule over mankind. When it entered India during the seventh century, Islam did little to shake the foundation of Hinduism. The two religions' vastly differing philosophies, however, constantly conflicted with one another's tenets. For instance, Hindus adore the cow to a point of deification, while Muslims often use this animal in sacrifice. Muslims typically worship in quiet austerity, whereas Hindus lead rambunctious religious processions that often interrupt Muslim mosque (temple) services. In the novel, Aziz repeatedly shows his contempt for Hindus. Of Professor Godbole he states, "Do you know what Deccani Brahmans say? That England conquered India from them—from them, mind, and not from the Moguls [Muslims]. Is not that like their cheek?" (*A Passage to India*, p. 71). Gandhi was, in fact, assassinated by a Hindu fanatic who believed that the spiritual leader was too pro-Muslim in his teachings.

The twentieth-century Islam reform movement, of which Aziz in the novel considers himself a member, has sought to bring the religion more into line with modern society. It has allegorized many of the creation myths in the *Koran,* Islam's holy book, and it has improved the position of women in the Muslim world. In the novel, Aziz comments that he doesn't mind lifting the vow of *purdah,* or segregation of women, for an afternoon outing with Mrs. Moore and Adela Quested; he in fact finds them enchanting companions. Even with such reforms under way, however, twentieth-century India would remain a nation of divided religious loyalties.

The pan-Islamic belief system mandates an allegiance to religion above country. During the late 1920s and early 1930s, India saw a rise in demand for a Muslim state in India, or a "Pakistan" (holy land of the Muslims). Although Forster's novel was published before these years, the tension between its characters foreshadows this turn of events. Under the leadership of Muslim patriot Muhammad Ali Jinnah, India was divided into separate Hindu and Muslim states. On August 14, 1947, Pakistan achieved its independence from the remainder of the country. But despite the separation, tensions between Muslims and Hindus would continue to reverberate throughout this area of the world.

The Novel in Focus

The plot. While visiting her son, the British city magistrate of Chandrapore, Mrs. Moore seeks to discover the country of India that lies beyond the English regime. Dissatisfied with the English activities planned for her sojourn, Mrs. Moore and her traveling companion, Adela Quested, devise their own entertainment. While almost all British citizens living in India shun the company of the native Indians, Mrs. Moore and Adela eagerly seek their friendship. An afternoon tea at a British professor's house provides just this opportunity.

Professor Fielding is the principal of the Government College. Less cynical than the other British officials, he knows several Indians and is quite popular among them. Pleased with the effort that Mrs. Moore and Adela have made to befriend the natives, he invites them to tea along with several Indian guests. The afternoon passes wonderfully. In addition to the two British visitors, Professor Fielding also entertains a young Indian doctor, Dr. Aziz, and a Hindu Brahman, or high priest and scholar, Narayan Godbole. Anxious to impress the visitors, Dr. Aziz promises to lead them on an expedition to the local Marabar Caves. The comfortable conversation and atmosphere ends abruptly with the appearance of Mrs. Moore's son, Ronny Heaslop. Engaged to Adela, Ronny does not approve of the women's association with the Indians and insists on their departure from the party. Nonetheless, the group plans on reuniting for their trip to the caves.

Adela was supposed to have already decided once and for all on her engagement to Ronny. Although she had known him in England, his manner has greatly altered during his time in the foreign land. The departure for the Marabar Caves comes just as she is attempting to sort out her mixed emotions. Because they are late for the train, Mr. Fielding and Professor Godbole cannot join the expedition. Dr. Aziz, along with the help of several servants and a local guide, leads the two English women on his own. No one knows exactly what takes place while at the caves, but at some point during the afternoon, Adela rushes frantically back to Chandrapore. Upon her arrival

E. M. Forster

in the city, she charges that she was assaulted in one of the caves, and names her assailant as none other than Dr. Aziz.

The arrest of Dr. Aziz and his subsequent trial strains the already tenuous relations between the British and Indian citizens living in India. While the English contend that such a violation could only be expected from "those swine" (*A Passage to India,* p. 239), the Indians remain outraged that one of their prominent citizens could so easily suffer accusation and arrest. Perhaps most affected is Mrs. Moore. Torn by her friendship with Aziz, Mrs. Moore refuses to support Adela's claim. Ronny, outraged with his mother's lack of sympathy, sends her home to England. She dies en route.

In the midst of the trial, Adela abruptly drops all charges against Aziz. She then says she had never fully believed that the doctor had attacked her, and when the lawyer insists on her clarity, she recants her original story. This move alienates her not only from the Indians, but from her British countrymen as well. Chandrapore erupts with the news of the mistrial. Indian citizens rush into the streets in celebration of their victory, while British ones flee for safety. Embarrassed by Adela's behavior, Ronny breaks their engagement and turns her out of the house. She takes refuge at Professor Fielding's until her departure for England.

Eventually Fielding returns to England as well. Perceiving this as abandonment, Dr. Aziz renounces him as a friend. This dislike intensifies when Aziz learns that Fielding has married and presumes the bride to be Adela. After the passage of several years, Fielding again visits India. He reunites with Aziz, assuring the doctor that he has married not Adela, but Mrs. Moore's daughter, Stella. Although Fielding and Aziz do settle their differences, there remains a certain distance between the two. Conditions in the nation, which once brought them together, now ironically keep them apart.

The Marabar Caves. Forster recalled that after his first trip to India, he "was clear about the chief characters and the racial tension, had visualized the scenes, and had foreseen that something crucial would happen in the Marabar Caves, but . . . hadn't seen far enough" (Forster in Lewis, p. 85). On his visit to India in 1912, Forster stayed in Bankipore, the British station in Patna. From his diary entries, one immediately recognizes the similarities between this city and the fictional Chandrapore. Like Chandrapore, Bankipore rests on "one street tolerably wide that runs from the eastern to the western gate, but . . . is by no means straight nor regularly built" (Forster in Lewis, p. 32). Bankipore lies in the shadow of the Barabar Hills, which in the novel appear as the Marabar Hills.

While traveling, Forster stayed with two professors in Patna, Charles Russell and V. H. Jackson. At the time, both were pursuing studies of the Buddhist inscriptions found in the Barabar Hills. At their suggestion, the author visited the caves located there. Seven in number, the Barabar Caves are actually rock-cut temples that date back to 252 B.C. Originally used by the followers of the Ajivika sect of Buddhism, they have always been a site of religious worship. Forster himself remarked that "the Malabar [sic] Caves represented an area in which concentration can take place. A cavity. . . . They were something to focus everything up: they were to engender an event like an egg" (Forster in Sahni, p. 99). Early Hindu creation myths tell us that "In the beginning this world was merely non-being. It was existent. It developed. It turned into an egg" (Chandogya Upanishad in Sahni, p. 114). Forster's association of the caves with Hinduism is not accidental. While used initially by Buddhists, the caves were later occupied by Brahman ascetics,

a fact reflected in the Hindu names given to the individual caves.

During the time of Forster's novel, Gandhi, the great Hindu leader who advocated change through nonviolent resistance, was starting to gain a large following. India, struggling for its independence, began to embrace Hinduism in its rejection of the traditionally Western way of thinking. Forster suffered much criticism for making his main Indian character, Aziz, a Muslim. Many saw this as an attempt to make the novel more familiar and therefore more acceptable to a Western readership because of the broad parallels between Islam and Judeo-Christianity. The author nonetheless incorporated many Hindu beliefs in his work, and elsewhere he wrote of his affection for the religion: "Hinduism, unlike Christianity and Buddhism and Islam, does not invite [man] to meet his god congregationally; and this commends it to me" (Forster in Sahni, p. 15). In fact, one scholar argues that *A Passage to India* shows a preference for Hinduism over Islam or Christianity. The novel declares that "Islam's primary belief, 'There is no God but God' does not take us very deep into religious mysteries," and the scene at the caves "refers scornfully to the 'poor talkative Christianity' that had been Mrs. Moore's solace before she entered the Marabar Caves" (McDowell, p. 105). Christianity fails Mrs. Moore at the caves, where she senses a type of cosmic unity and feels disillusioned. She has no desire to communicate with anyone, not even the Christian God.

Mrs. Moore recognizes, despite her disillusionment, that "Nothing evil had been in the cave, but she had not enjoyed herself; no, she had not enjoyed herself" (*A Passage to India*, p. 148). Neither good nor bad is ever tied to the caves. In keeping with this approach, the novel never clearly explains what, if anything, happened to make Adela Quested claim she was assaulted there. It only points out that the primordial caves contain both good and evil, as well as all other polarities. This contemplation of the profound relationship between opposites is in keeping with Hindu philosophy. The nature of good and evil is discussed in the Hindu teachings of the *Upanishads,* which state that good and evil are only relative terms by which the Absolute is not affected. While the plot of the novel is indeed affected by the event at Marabar, the caves themselves remain untouched. Forster writes, "Nothing, nothing attaches to them, and their reputation—for they have one—does not depend upon human speech" (*A Passage to India*, p. 137).

Forster decided very deliberately to leave the incident in the cave an enigma, focusing instead on the Indian-Anglo conflict that was created in its wake. "I tried to show," he said, "that India is an unexplainable muddle by introducing an unexplained muddle—Miss Quested's experience in the cave. When asked what happened there, *I don't know*" (Forster in Beauman, p. 277). In his judgment, if Aziz had definitely touched Miss Quested, India would be less mysterious in the novel, a place more plainly split between forces of good and evil.

Sources. Although E. M. Forster did in fact travel to India, perhaps the primary inspiration for his novel came from an acquaintance made at Oxford University in England. It was there that the author met a very influential friend, Syed Ross Masood. Born and raised in India, Masood hailed from a long line of elite Indian intellectuals. His grandfather, Sir Syed Ahmad Khan, receives credit from many historians for restoring the Muslim community in India during the nineteenth century. In 1906, at the age of seventeen, Masood moved to England in order to receive the kind of education that the Indian universities could not, at that time, provide. In England, Masood had several tutors who prepared him for his studies, and his tutor in Latin was the young E. M. Forster. The friendship that grew from this businesslike arrangement would become the basis for the camaraderie that exists between Forster's characters Dr. Aziz and Professor Fielding. Like Aziz, Masood fostered a passion for poetry in Forster and considered himself an Islamic modernist. Forster's dedication of the novel reads, in fact, "To Syed Ross Masood and to the seventeen years of our friendship" (*A Passage to India*, p. i).

While the author did not, prior to meeting Masood, have any interest in India, his friendship with the young man initiated a curiosity about the foreign land. Forster's financial success from his novel *Howard's End* made possible a visit to India in October of 1912. The journey began on an ocean liner filled with "Anglo-Indians," or British citizens living in India. It was during this trip that Forster first realized the general narrow-mindedness of this society. He observed that they would not associate with a young Indian boy on board who was headed home after years of schooling in Britain. Forster echoes this segregation in his novel when one English woman remarks to an-

other, "You're superior to them, anyway. Don't forget that. You're superior to everyone in India" (*A Passage to India*, p. 42). When Forster eventually met up with Masood in January, he noted that his friend, too, was unhappy with the English presence in India. He, like many educated Indians, continued to suffer grievances under the English and was beginning to question this government's authority.

While on this trip, Forster also noted a distinction between the cultures that social integration could not erase. In Simla, the author attended the wedding of a young Muslim couple. He was disappointed in the families' attempts to bring together traditional Muslim practices and Western rationalism. For instance, during sunset, the traditional time for the Muslim evening prayer, many of the guests danced to a gramophone while the orthodox Muslims prayed. Forster could not reconcile these appositions. He could not see how the Eastern and Western cultures could comfortably coexist.

Two years later, in January of 1914, Forster began *A Passage to India*. Although he initially completed several chapters, he found himself unable to piece together an entire novel. After a second voyage to India in 1921, the author resumed his work. When the book finally was published in 1924, it contained descriptions of people, places, events, and attitudes that Forster had discovered during his two voyages.

Reception of the novel. *A Passage to India* brought Forster both critical and financial success. Because the author had not published a novel since *Howard's End* in 1910, the new book's arrival gave the literary world much to discuss. One early review concluded that "Mr. Forster portrays the super-sensitiveness, the impulsiveness, the charm and the weakness, of Mohammedan and Hindu India, in order to emphasize the honesty, the arrogance . . . and the moral tremors of the governing caste" (Massingham in Gardner, p. 208). Another reviewer of the era announced that *A Passage to India* "has the beauty and pathos which belongs to Mr. Forster's best work" (*Times Literary Supplement* in Gardner, p. 199).

For More Information

Beauman, Nicola. *E. M. Forster: A Biography*. New York: Alfred A. Knopf, 1994.

Forster, E. M. *A Passage to India*. London: Harcourt Brace, 1984.

Gardner, Philip. *E. M. Forster: The Critical Heritage.* London: Routledge and Kegan Paul, 1973.

Lewis, Robin Jared. *E. M. Forster's Passages to India.* New York: Columbia University Press, 1979.

McDowell, Frederick P. W. *E. M. Forster.* New York: Twayne, 1969.

Sahni, Chaman L. *Forster's A Passage to India: The Religious Dimension.* India: Arnold Heinemann, 1981.

Thompson, Edward, and G. T. Garratt. *Rise and Fulfilment of British Rule in India.* New York: AMS, 1971.

Whitman, Walt. "A Passage to India." In *The Portable Walt Whitman.* Edited by Mark Van Doren. New York: Penguin, 1969.

A Portrait of the
Artist as a Young Man

by

James Joyce

Born February 2, 1882, in a Dublin suburb, James Augustine Joyce rocked the literary world with the shocking language, attention to sometimes unsavory detail, and peculiar literary style of *A Portrait of the Artist as a Young Man*. Educated primarily by the Jesuits, at age sixteen the young man considered entering the priesthood but quickly realized that he would be unable to keep a vow of celibacy. Shortly thereafter, he rejected the church entirely, although it was to dominate his imagination for the rest of his life. He rebelled against his Catholic upbringing and against the domestic politics of his native land, leaving Dublin for the European continent in 1904 with Nora Barnacle, his lifelong companion and the mother of his children; they were not actually married until 1931, and then only to give their children and grandchildren legitimacy. *A Portrait of the Artist as a Young Man* critiques middle-class Irish-Catholic society. It questions and condemns such cultural mainstays as marriage, faith, and nationalism, attempting also to give an aesthetic rationale for doing so.

Events in History at the Time of the Novel

Irish Catholics. Even though he early and openly rebelled against the Catholic Church, Joyce continued throughout his career to write about the religion of his youth. This was not merely a self-centered obsession with his own personal doubts and fears, but a tackling of one of the most prominent features of Irish culture.

THE LITERARY WORK

A novel set from the late 1800s to the early 1900s in Dublin; published in serial form in 1914 in *The Egoist*, and as a book in 1916.

SYNOPSIS

The fictional rendition of Joyce's autobiography, *A Portrait of the Artist as a Young Man* chronicles the growing discontent of an aspiring young writer, Stephen Dedalus, within the confines of traditional Irish Catholic culture.

Catholicism was not just a religion in Ireland; it was *the* religion of the indigenous Irish. And because the privileged classes in Dublin were relatively recently arrived British Protestants, Catholicism was strongly related to grassroots Irish cultural and political identity. While the Irish Protestants themselves had major political conflicts with their English counterparts, the Catholic majority in Ireland had been discriminated against for centuries on account of their religion.

The factional strife that set Catholics against Protestants in Joyce's Ireland had its roots in medieval politics and Renaissance religious wars in Europe. Lying so close to England, Ireland almost inevitably became drawn into the political ambitions of its aggressive neighbor. The tight rein kept on the nearby Irish by the powerful

A Portrait of the Artist

James Joyce

English monarchy grew tighter during the Protestant Reformation of the fifteenth and sixteenth centuries, when, for a variety of political reasons having to do with conflict between the king and the pope, England outlawed the Catholic religion. To ensure that its traditionally Catholic neighbor, Ireland, did not ally with its continental Catholic enemies, France and Spain, England initiated a program of land appropriation and resettlement in Ireland. English and Scottish Protestant settlers were sent to Ireland by the English monarchy and were given land and homes taken from the original Irish inhabitants, who wound up as powerless and poor second-class citizens in their own country. The Irish, dispossessed of their lands, were sometimes resettled in inadequate housing. More hardship followed. Through a complicated series of legislative acts, the Irish Catholics at various stages lost the right to vote, own property, hold government positions, and, as late as 1849, even to be educated in Irish history, literature, or language. The Catholic Church was never driven away from Ireland, but its congregation was so poor that it was left without a stable financial base and so powerless that it had minimal political influence.

Union and emancipation. By Joyce's day, Irish Catholic fortunes had improved; the 1829 Catholic Emancipation Bill gave the people back the rights to hold government and military jobs, to practice their religion freely, and to educate their children in the Catholic traditions. But the passage of that bill tarnished the image of the Catholic clergy in the minds of many Irish, as the character Mr. Casey angrily declaims in the first chapter of *A Portrait of the Artist as a Young Man:* "Didn't the bishops and priests sell the aspirations of their country in 1829 in return for catholic emancipation?" (Joyce, *A Portrait of the Artist as a Young Man,* p. 38). In 1800, in exchange for the promised implementation of the emancipation bill (which would take twenty-nine years to occur), the Catholic clergy lobbied for the Act of Union. Passed in 1800, this act dissolved the Irish Parliament in Dublin and merged it with the British Parliament in London. In London the Irish would make up only one-sixth of the members of Parliament, so, in effect, Ireland would be governed by a majority of foreigners.

"Didn't they denounce the fenian movement from the pulpit and in the confessionbox?" continues Mr. Casey's litany of criticisms of the Catholic clergy (*A Portrait of the Artist,* p. 38). The fenians, or "Irish Republican Brotherhood," took their name from the legendary Irish hero, Finn, and were committed to armed rebellion against the British. Whether or not Joyce himself was overly fond of the secretive, militaristic fenians (there is evidence to suggest that he was, at least for a time, sympathetic), Mr. Casey's charge targets a particular sore spot in the relationship between the clergy and their flock. In the eyes of many churchgoers, the Catholic priests bore some responsibility for the religious and cultural oppression suffered by their faithful. Throughout the long years of gradual disenfranchisement suffered by the Irish Catholics, the church had, with a few notable exceptions, counselled acceptance of the situation and avoided entering the political arena itself. One of the catechisms (handbooks of spiritual formation) current in Ireland at the time speaks directly to the problem of how a Catholic believer was to behave politically:

Q. What are the duties of subjects to the temporal powers?

A. The duties of subjects to the temporal powers are, *to be subject to them, and to honour and obey them . . . for conscience' sake. . . .* The Scripture also requires us to show respect to those who rule over us, *to pray for kings, and for all who are in high station, that we may lead a quiet and peaceable life.* (Italics in original.)

(*The Maynooth Catechism*
in Gifford, p. 149)

The nineteenth-century conflict between religion and politics escalated to its most feverish moment in the downfall of Charles Parnell, a collapse to which Joyce returns time and again in his fiction; *A Portrait of the Artist as a Young Man* is no exception.

Parnell. In the first chapter of the novel, a fight breaks out at the Dedalus's Christmas dinner when pro- and anti-Parnell supporters argue the right of the Catholic clergy to "interfere" in politics. At issue is the recent scandal over the private life of Charles Parnell, who was looked upon by many Irish people, both Catholic and Protestant, as the potential political savior of their people.

Parnell, a Protestant landlord, became the leader of the Irish Home Rule (the Irish Parliamentary Party) movement in 1879. The "Home Rulers" aimed for greater powers of self-rule than the 1800 Act of Union permitted Ireland. Specifically, they aimed to restore an independent parliament to Ireland, one that was not merely part of a larger parliament of Great Britain. At the height of his career, and possibly on the brink of success at achieving an independent parliament for Ireland, Parnell was named as co-defendant in the divorce of William and Katherine O'Shea. Though separated, the O'Sheas were still married; in an age when divorce was difficult and usually scandalous, Mrs. O'Shea had for a long time simply been living with Parnell as his wife. In 1889 Captain O'Shea finally sued for divorce, and the revelation that Parnell was an adulterer discredited him so completely that he was ousted from the leadership of the Home Rule party one year later. Parnell died at age forty-five in 1891, probably from the complications of fatigue.

James Joyce first wrote of Parnell, whom he considered to have been betrayed by his fellow Irishmen and by Catholics in particular, when he was nine years old. The Catholic Church, to whom divorce and adultery are sins, became Parnell's worst domestic enemy in the O'Shea scandal, condemning Parnell during the priests' sermons, and rallying for the defeat of his allies in local elections. Joyce clearly regarded Parnell as Ireland's brightest hope for self-rule. In *A Portrait of the Artist as a Young Man*, Stephen's Aunt Dante and Mr. Casey, a family friend, discover themselves at opposite ends of a debate about Parnell. Dante, a staunch Catholic, believes that no man who has committed adultery is fit to run

a political party. Mr. Casey, on the other hand, thinks that religious intolerance has ruined a good man and perhaps even killed Ireland's chances for independence.

—God and religion before everything! Dante cried. God and religion before the world! . . .

·—Very well, then, [Mr. Casey] shouted hoarsely, if it comes to that, no God for Ireland! . . .

—Blasphemer! Devil! screamed Dante, starting to her feet and almost spitting in his face. . . .

At the door Dante turned around violently and shouted down the room, her cheeks flushed and quivering with rage:

—Devil out of hell! We won! We crushed him to death! Fiend!

The door slammed behind her. Mr. Casey . . . suddenly bowed his head on his hands with a sob of pain.

—Poor Parnell! he cried loudly. My dead king! He sobbed loudly and bitterly.

Stephen, raising his terrorstricken face, saw that his father's eyes were full of tears.

(*A Portrait of the Artist*, p. 39)

A Jesuit education. In the novel Stephen, like Joyce himself, is educated by the Jesuits, Catholic priests who belong to the order of the Society of Jesus. The Society, as it is sometimes called, was founded by the Spaniard St. Ignatius Loyola in 1540. As a missionary order, the Jesuits spread over the globe and became involved in teaching. They set very high intellectual standards and called for the taming of the individual will—obedience was of prime importance to them.

The tensions that drive Stephen's religious and cultural rebellion can be fully appreciated only with the realization of the force he was opposing. His teachers, with whom he had more contact than with any other adult presence in his life and who shaped his literary and philosophic tastes and habits, belonged to a society of men who fervently believed in bending one's thoughts and will away from oneself. Its success with even the headstrong Stephen demonstrates aptly the power of such a philosophy: "He had never once disobeyed or allowed turbulent companions to seduce him from his habit of quiet obedience" (*A Portrait of the Artist*, p. 156). In his quest to be an artist and to disclose the workings of his own mind, Stephen's actions are contrary to such a philosophy.

At the head of the Jesuits is a superior general who can make unilateral decisions for the group. Perhaps because of their insistence upon intellectual keenness and precision as well as

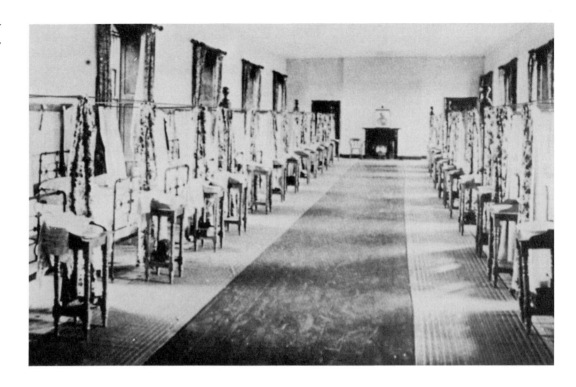

The small boys' dormitory at Clongowes Wood School, which Joyce attended as a boy and which serves as the setting for the first chapter of *A Portrait of the Artist as a Young Man.*

their devotion to their superior general, the Jesuits came to be suspected of subversion and political manipulation. In 1772 the Order was suppressed by the pope, and its members stripped of most of their power and authority. However, they eventually regained the approval of the Vatican and by Joyce's day had reacquired much of their original strength, although the order retained a certain reputation for craftiness.

In *A Portrait of the Artist as a Young Man,* Stephen remembers his experience of the Jesuits more or less kindly:

> Whatever he had heard or read of the craft of jesuits he had put aside frankly as not borne out by his own experience. His masters, even when they had not attracted him, had seemed to him always intelligent and serious priests, athletic and highspirited prefects.
>
> (*A Portrait of the Artist,* p. 156)

The school that young Stephen attends, Clongowes Wood College, was run by the Jesuits and was the best Catholic school in the country. After the real-life Joyce family and the fictional Dedalus family moved to Dublin, it was off to Belvedere College, a Jesuit day-school for boys, for both James Joyce and his character Stephen Dedalus. At such a school, a student would be expected to learn Latin and Greek, literature, phi-

losophy, and other scholarly subjects, and to follow the daily routine of the Jesuits. This entailed daily Mass, regular confessions, instruction in church history, and other religious matters that permeate the novel, such as religious retreats and specific prayers on certain holy days.

Cultural revival. As late as 1849, the Irish National Board of Education taught no Irish history, language, or literature in its school system. Because English-speaking Protestants formed the powerful and privileged class in Ireland, the Irish language and its literature were commonly regarded as the inferior product of an almost barbaric culture. As a result, not a few Irish people felt ashamed about their cultural heritage. To remedy this situation, a group of Irish poets, playwrights, and scholars in the 1890s tried to revive the Irish language as a means of stimulating broader cultural self-respect and creativity. They had a formidable task ahead of them: in 1851 only 25 percent of the population could speak Irish. And, despite their efforts, that figure had dwindled by 1911 to only 12 percent.

Scholars had been debating the problem of Irish cultural decline for a hundred years and to little avail before the 1893 founding of the Gaelic League by a Protestant man by the name of Douglas Hyde. The goals of the Gaelic League included reinstating the Irish language as the national tongue, teaching and publishing Gaelic literature of the past, and encouraging new writers to write in Gaelic. Within ten years some of its goals were, to a modest degree, being met: Irish language and literature were being taught regularly (though not uniformly) at every level, from primary school to the university. The cultural revival took on many forms. Founded in 1884, the Gaelic Athletic Association, for example, strove to boost the popularity of "hurling"—an Irish game something like a hybrid of lacrosse and field hockey—while discouraging such English sports as polo and cricket.

The most famous manifestation of the Gaelic revival is the literary movement referred to as "the Irish literary revival." The literature associated with this movement tends to be characterized by heavy use of Irish mythology, attention to the life of the peasant, and experimentation with an Irish-English linguistic blend. The revival was led by such writers as W. B. Yeats, George Russell, and Lady Gregory. Joyce, too, is often counted among their number, although he would no doubt be less than pleased to be thought so. In the final chapter of *A Portrait of the Artist as a Young Man,* Stephen and his friend, Davin, have a discussion about Irish linguistic nationalism. When questioned as to why he dropped out of the Gaelic League's Irish language class after the first day, Stephen replies, "My ancestors threw off their language and took another. . . . They allowed a handful of foreigners to subject them. Do you fancy I am going to pay in my own life and person debts they made? What for?" (*A Portrait of the Artist,* p. 203).

The Novel in Focus

The plot. Divided into five chapters, *A Portrait of the Artist as a Young Man* opens with the childish impressions of Stephen Dedalus as a very young boy. The description is delivered partly in baby talk: nursery tales, smells, family rituals. Abruptly Stephen is transported from the comforting world of his childhood into the rough-and-tumble world of Clongowes Wood College—a boarding school for boys that is run by Jesuits. Stephen instantly gets cast into the role of outsider; the first thing that happens to him at Clongowes is that he is shoved into a ditch full of brackish water by a bully. He contracts a fever and, in his already fertile imagination, he conjures up pathetic images of his death, conflating his own demise with the much-mourned

death of the nationalist Irish leader Charles Parnell. The themes of being an outcast and of his own potential for heroism recur throughout the novel, as do the political dimensions of being Irish in an age of conflicting nationalism and complacency. A family fight at Christmas, during which Parnell's character becomes the subject of a strident debate, highlights this central concern in the novel. The long process of Stephen Dedalus's alienation from the Catholic faith is also set in motion in the novel's first section, as young Dedalus is punished unjustly by one of the Jesuits for breaking his glasses—intentionally, as the priest supposes.

LIKE THE SKY AND SEA

H. G. Wells once observed of the society portrayed in *A Portrait of the Artist as a Young Man* that "everyone in this Dublin story, every human being, accepts as a matter of course, as a thing in nature like the sky and the sea, that the English are to be hated. . . . I am afraid it is only too true an account of the atmosphere in which a number of brilliant young Irishmen have grown up" (Wells in Anderson, p. 332).

In the novel's second section, Stephen is removed from Clongowes because of declining family fortunes and, for a time, pals around in Dublin and Cork with his uncle Charley and his father. His father's fond reminiscences of his own youthful camaraderies and escapades make Stephen realize how far he himself is alienated from society. Unexpectedly granted entrance to another Jesuit school, Belvedere, Stephen begins to stand apart because of his views on literature and what constitutes "greatness" in the field. Defending the immoral Byron as the greatest of poets, Stephen confronts the possibility of conflict between morality and genius. He acts on this conclusion. Winning a scholarship, Stephen squanders it, albeit with the best of intentions, and ends chapter 2 in the arms of a prostitute.

The struggle between Stephen's lust and his spirituality resumes in chapter 3, in which the main event is a "retreat" sponsored by Stephen's school. In religious terms, a retreat is a structured period of instruction (sometimes as long as a week, but here a weekend), set aside for prayer and religious education. In the novel, two sermons are preached to Stephen and his schoolmates during the retreat. Both concentrate on the torments of hell—the first on the physical torture, the second on the spiritual anguish of eternal damnation. So extreme is the imagery that Stephen is shaken physically and spiritually, imagining himself already in hell.

> Imagine some foul and putrid corpse that has lain rotting and decomposing in the grave, a jellylike mass of liquid corruption. Imagine such a corpse a prey to flames, devoured by the fire of burning brimstone and giving off dense choking fumes of nauseous loathsome decomposition. And then imagine this sickening stench, multiplied a millionfold and a millionfold again from the millions upon millions of fetid carcasses massed together in the reeking darkness, a huge and rotting human fungus.
>
> (*A Portrait of the Artist,* p. 120)

Although the hell described by the Jesuit priest delivering the sermon does not concentrate on the punishment for sexual transgression, Stephen knows this is his own peculiar sin and imagines a hell filled with lechers like himself. In a panic, he flees his rooms at school in search of a church in which to make a confession—to tell his sins to a priest and be forgiven for them. Upon absolution he tries to adhere more closely to his Catholic faith and its rules for pure living. Temporarily he feels peace of mind.

In chapter 4 of the novel, Stephen is offered the chance to become a priest and is tempted to do so. Despite his strong tendency to sin, he also responds deeply to the rituals and the learning of the church. With his mind still not made up, he takes a walk along the seashore, where his decision to reject the church is made for him by his intense emotional and physical reaction to a beautiful girl he sees there. He understands that his real joy will be in celebrating the secular life.

The novel's fifth and final chapter finds Stephen at university trying to work out a theory of art, and secondarily of sociology, that will help him understand himself as an Irish writer. Notoriously puzzling, the novel's ending offers a few brief entries from Stephen's diary, which reveal his decision to leave Ireland behind and seek his fortunes abroad. The novel closes with Stephen packing up to leave Ireland, his self-proclaimed mission—"to forge in the smithy of my soul the uncreated conscience of my race" (*A Portrait of the Artist,* p. 253).

Egoist. To some, it might seem superbly fitting that Joyce's fictional rendition of his own life should make its first appearance in a journal entitled *The Egoist.* The American poet Ezra Pound, to whom Joyce had been mentioned by the great Irish poet W. B. Yeats, was involved with the journal. Pound wrote to Joyce, inviting him to send along a piece of writing for consideration in the journal, adding, "From what [Yeats] says, I imagine we have a hate or two in common" (Pound in Beja, p. 58). Joyce sent him the first three chapters of *A Portrait of the Artist as a Young Man* (the last two were not yet written) and Pound enthusiastically decided to publish the novel serially in *The Egoist.* It did not emerge in quite the form in which Joyce had submitted it, however; printers in those days were legally responsible for whatever came off their presses, and *The Egoist's* presses were reluctant to back Joyce's sometimes bawdy, sometimes sacrilegious, sometimes vulgar tale. Passages referring to bodily functions, and certain anatomical details in particular suffered spontaneous editing. Meanwhile, Joyce was searching for a publisher to produce *A Portrait of the Artist as a Young Man* in book form. It was rejected by at least three European publishing houses before it was accepted by the American firm of Huebsch and Company (now Viking Press) and published in 1916. The American publishers allowed *The Egoist* access to its print sheets to publish the first European edition of Joyce's first novel, which appeared in early 1917.

What's in a name? *A Portrait of the Artist as a Young Man* opens with the Latin words "Et ignotas animum dimittit in artes," which means "And he put his mind to unknown arts." The phrase comes from a work by the Latin poet Ovid, *Metamorphoses* (8.188), and refers to the story of Daedalus and Icarus. Daedalus was an inventor (the name in Greek means "cunning artist/inventor") who worked for Minos, the king of Crete. Minos's wife, Pasiphae, fell in love with a bull, and Daedalus helped her out by creating a false cow for her to hide in while courting the creature's affections. From this affair was born the Minotaur, half-man and half-bull. Daedalus built a giant labyrinth to imprison the Minotaur, but the angry Minos threw Daedalus and his son Icarus into the center of it as punishment for assisting the queen in her deception. In time, Daedalus figured out how to escape, and built wings of wax and feathers for himself and his son to fly away with. Icarus, thrilled with his ability to fly, soared too close to the sun—his wings melted and he plunged into the sea to his death. Daedalus survived and lived the rest of his days in Sicily. Daedalus's "unknown arts," then, gave Icarus his wings but also led to his death. Critics continue to debate the overall relevance of this epigraph to the rest of the novel; some suggest that the pattern of upward flight and downward fall recurs throughout the work; others assert that the art which Stephen pursues not only liberates but also destroys him.

Scholars point out that Joyce's decision to name his hero "Stephen," after the first Christian martyr (who died for his beliefs), may be tied to his understanding of the artist as an outcast from society. Even though his absence from Ireland was entirely of his own choosing, Joyce fancied himself an exile from his homeland. The fact that St. Stephen was a Jew educated in Greek may also have seemed to Joyce to parallel his own linguistic situation, as an Irishman educated in English.

Sources. Work on *A Portrait of the Artist as a Young Man* began on January 7, 1904, when the very youthful James Joyce heard that a new literary journal by the name of *Dana* was being started in Dublin. He wrote a brief autobiographical essay that very day, and soon showed it to one of the journal's editors. It was, after the suggestion of Joyce's younger brother Stanislaus, entitled "A Portrait of the Artist." Despite its lofty title, the piece was judged too obscure for the anticipated tastes of *Dana*'s audience. Joyce, angry over this evaluation, started work on an ambitious novel (which Stanislaus also named), *Stephen Hero,* in which he meant to show that his own life could indeed be of interest as a work of art. *Stephen Hero* would have been a much longer book than *A Portrait of the Artist as a Young Man* eventually turned out to be, but in another angry moment Joyce tossed the manuscript into a fire from which only portions of it were rescued. *A Portrait of the Artist as a Young Man* shares much of the material of *Stephen Hero,* although in the later work the character of Stephen is noticeably less idealized.

Joyce's *Portrait of the Artist as a Young Man* concerns the development of the mind and character of the hero as he passes from childhood into manhood. Formally such a novel is known by the German term *Bildungsroman,* or novel of development. Interested in the Bildungsroman of earlier writers, Joyce was influenced in the creation of his own by at least two other works: George Meredith's *The Ordeal of Richard Feverel* and Walter Pater's *Marius the Epicurean.* The best way, thought Joyce, to study other writers was to copy a few of their paragraphs, a process that undoubtedly led to his picking up some techniques used in developing a style of his own. Since publication, *Portrait of the Artist as a Young Man* has frequently been cited as a prime example of a Bildungsroman itself.

Reviews. *A Portrait of the Artist as a Young Man* drew important reviews—positive and negative—from the American and European press; the negative are remarkable for the strength of their convictions. H. G. Wells, writing in *The New Republic* (March 10, 1917), observed that the novel "is by far the most living and convincing picture that exists of an Irish Catholic upbringing," but also saw fit to draw attention to what he calls Joyce's "cloacal obsession": "He would bring back into the general picture of life aspects which modern drainage and modern decorum have taken out of ordinary intercourse and conversation" (Wells in Anderson, pp. 330-32). This latter sentiment is echoed by the reviewer from *Everyman:* "Garbage. . . . We feel that Mr. Joyce would be at his best in a treatise on drains" (Anderson, p. 336). The *Irish Book Lover* reviewer counsels primly: "No clean-minded person could possibly allow it to remain within reach of his wife, his sons or daughters" (Anderson, p. 337). "[T]he author must revise it and let us see it again," says the Reader's Report from the English publishing firm Duckworth and Co., by way of an explanation for why the book was rejected. "It is too discursive, formless, unrestrained, and ugly things, ugly words, are too prominent; indeed at times they seem to be shoved in one's face, on purpose, unnecessarily" (Anderson, p. 320). The *Manchester Guardian,* on the other hand, was among the book's many admirers: "When one recognizes genius in a book one had perhaps best leave criticism alone" (Anderson, p. 335).

For More Information

Anderson, Chester G., ed. *James Joyce: A Portrait of the Artist as a Young Man. Text, Criticism, and Notes.* New York: Viking, 1968.

Beja, Morris. *James Joyce: A Literary Life.* Columbus: Ohio University Press, 1992.

Bolt, Sydney. *A Preface to James Joyce.* 2nd ed. Burnt Mill, Essex: Longman, 1992.

Bottigheimer, Karl S. *Ireland and the Irish: A Short History.* New York: Columbia University Press, 1982.

Gifford, Don. *Joyce Annotated: Notes for Dubliners and A Portrait of the Artist as a Young Man.* 2nd ed. Berkeley: University of California Press, 1982.

Joyce, James. *A Portrait of the Artist as a Young Man.* Viking Critical Library. New York: Viking, 1964.

Joyce, Stanislaus. *My Brother's Keeper: James Joyce's Early Years.* Edited by Richard Ellmann. New York: Faber, 1958.

Manganiello, Dominic. *Joyce's Politics.* London: Routledge, 1980.

Pygmalion

by

George Bernard Shaw

George Bernard Shaw (1856-1950) was born into a poor family in Dublin, Ireland. Despite childhood neglect and inadequate schooling, he became one of Britain's most articulate and famous writers. His plays, economic and political tracts, journalism, and public speaking appearances were all colored by his socialist views and sparkling wit. He won the Nobel Prize in Literature in 1925, traveled the world, and amassed a considerable fortune before his death. *Pygmalion*, one of his less serious plays, helped secure Shaw's success as a popular playwright.

Events in History at the Time of the Play

Social class and social climbing. In every scene of *Pygmalion*, Shaw juxtaposes different social classes and explores how they relate to one another. Accents, clothing, and manners indicate the degree of wealth and social status of each family. Social climbers in England at the time faced slim odds, while well-to-do families devoted considerable time, energy, and money to the preservation of their status.

The rise of the middle class in nineteenth-century England had fundamentally redefined the class system. As more and more businessmen and their families prospered and imitated the upper classes, subtle distinctions became all-important. Aristocrats tried to maintain their superiority by glorifying attributes that could not be bought easily, such as family history, refined social graces, and old traditions.

The London season. In the play, Eliza's recently refined speech and manners are put to the test one summer day at a garden party, a dinner, and

an embassy reception. Such events filled the London social calendar from May until late July. For the duration of this season, 4,000 of England's richest, most aristocratic families crowded into London to attend events like these. May was replete with social events. The season began with a private gallery exhibition at the Royal Academy. Taking an after-church Sunday stroll in Hyde Park was a fashionable amusement of the month, and the first garden parties of the year were held in May. Also debutantes were presented to English royalty at court receptions, or drawing rooms, during this month. Covent Garden opera season opened in May, and concerts, balls, and theater performances took place.

In the off-season, popular activities included ice skating, horse racing, and the hunting of pheasant, rabbit, stag, partridge, and fox. Throughout Britain, visiting days called "at-homes" also provided entertainment all year long.

The English At-Home. During the Victorian era, members of the upper and upper-middle classes formally visited or "called on" one another several afternoons each week. Eliza gains easy access to Mrs. Higgins, but the average newcomer would have had to earn the chance to visit: she had to have been formally introduced, and in most cases, to have received a card and a visit from the hostess. The would-be social newcomer might then arrive in a carriage and give a card bearing her name to a household servant. The card was taken upstairs and presented to the lady of the house, who decided whether or not to receive the caller. If all went well, the servant returned with the answer that her mistress was "at home," and the relieved visitor proceeded upstairs.

A well-to-do woman made herself available by choosing a day of the week and setting a time between the hours of three and six. The friends she welcomed into her drawing room were almost all women, but men could also attend. Light conversation prevailed as guests sipped tea daintily. If a family had marriageable daughters, it might show them off by having them sing a song or play a piece on the piano. Visits usually lasted fewer than fifteen minutes, especially if one did not know the hostess well. One historian comments on how newcomers would be scrutinized by regular visitors:

> They will listen to her voice (too shrill? too breathy? a trace of undesirable accent?) and pay attention, not just to what she says, but to how she says it. Does she say 'father' rather than the correct 'my father'? Does she gush? Does she wear the right clothes for the occasion, does she move without flurrying, does she keep her gestures to a minimum? Above all, does she carry herself with a poise that declares that she is neither the group's superior nor yet its hopeful probationer but a potential full member as of right?
>
> (Sproule, p. 39)

For better or worse, the at-home gave women a sphere for themselves, to regulate as they pleased. Although it offered them contact with the outside world, the nature of that contact was sometimes considered superficial and unrewarding. Inevitably the at-home cultivated women who were practiced in the arts of flattery and small talk. In the play, Henry Higgins complains about sitting at dinner "with nobody but a damned fool of a fashionable woman to talk to!" (Shaw, *Pygmalion,* p. 71). Ironically, he is the mentor who teaches Eliza to speak and behave like these fashionable women do.

"The Queen's English." Regional differences in pronunciation have always complicated and enriched the communication of British speakers of English. However, Queen Victoria's reign wit-

nessed England's most concerted effort yet to establish a nationwide spoken standard, known as "the Queen's English." The Education Act of 1870 brought together the children (mostly boys) of upper- and middle-class families for education in the English public school system, where accents were smoothed out. By the end of the 1800s, a new term had been coined: Received Pronunciation (RP). This accent was the outward indication that one belonged to the upper or professional middle class or to the Civil Service, and to speak anything "less" denoted a lack of education.

The Doolittles' Cockney intonation provides a striking contrast to the RP spoken by Pickering, the Higginses, and the Eynsford Hills. Higgins, moreover, is so competent in the study of phonetics that he can place anyone he meets within a few miles of his or her birthplace, sometimes even within a few streets. Like Higgins, real phoneticians were working to invent alphabets that could better represent the sounds of spoken English. Sir Isaac Pitman developed and published a shorthand system that became widely

George Bernard Shaw

Victorian era, in which Darwin's *Origin of Species* (1859) was only the most famous of many astonishing scientific theories. Exciting progress in the 1890s, such as the discovery of the x-ray, the electron, and radioactivity, kept these questions current. Shaw himself was fundamentally hopeful about what science could offer society, as he himself noted in a 1909 paper on "Socialism and Medicine":

> I belong to a generation which, I think, began life by hoping more from Science than perhaps any generation ever hoped before, and, possibly, will ever hope again. . . . At the present moment we are passing through a phase of disillusion. Science has not lived up to the hopes we formed of it in the 1860s; but those hopes left a mark on my temperament that I shall never get rid of till I die.
>
> (Shaw in Hynes, p. 132)

The Play in Focus

The plot. Late one rainy night, in the busy Covent Garden section of London, a mother, daughter, and son meet a persistent flower girl who tries to sell them flowers while they look for a taxi. Out of sight, a stranger scribbles notes as the flower girl speaks. She realizes he is writing down her words and soon becomes outraged to discover he can identify where she is from by listening to the way she speaks. A crowd gathers to watch the fun, and the mysterious man shows them the special alphabet he uses to transcribe speech sounds. The stranger, Henry Higgins, boasts that the flower girl could pass for a duchess if he chose to teach her to speak English properly. By chance, the crowd contains another phonetician, Colonel Pickering, who has already heard of Henry Higgins and his alphabet. The two men excitedly schedule time to discuss their interest in the science of speech. In parting, a reluctant Higgins gives the flower girl a few coins, and she treats herself to a ride home in a taxi.

The next morning, the Colonel visits Higgins at home and reviews his colleague's complex phonetic alphabet. The men are surprised by the arrival of the flower girl, Eliza Doolittle, who wishes to hire Higgins as a speech therapist. He rejects the proposal, but the Colonel challenges him to prove his skill and make good his boast, promising to pay the expenses of the work if Eliza succeeds. Higgins accepts the bet and hastily addresses the practical details of the arrangement.

His housekeeper, Mrs. Pearce, admonishes Higgins to mind his own speech and manners while he reforms Eliza's. The girl's inadequate

used. Although Shaw preferred the system of another phonetician, he jotted down the preface to *Pygmalion* in Pitman because it was the only shorthand his secretary could read.

Shaw also had a lifelong interest in the development of a more complete alphabet for everyday use. He advocated simplified spelling and the addition of letters to represent common English sounds for which he felt there were no satisfactory letters. To make his point about simplified spelling, Shaw once wrote the word *Fish* as *Ghoti*, using the *gh* of *rough,* the *o* of *women,* and the *ti* of *nation.* His will provided a substantial amount of money for the reformation of the English language, but a legal ruling held that part of the will to be impractical and directed the money elsewhere.

Science and experimentation. Henry Higgins describes his work with Eliza as "the most absorbing experiment I ever tackled" (*Pygmalion,* p. 58). Insofar as Eliza's ordeal can be considered an experiment, it raises questions that were on the minds of many people in Edwardian England: could science really help to cure society's ills, and how carefully did scientists think out the consequences of their work? These issues tempered the seemingly limitless optimism of the upbringing and impressionable nature have left her ill-equipped to disregard his coarser habits, such as swearing. Higgins promises to be good. He and Pickering are then visited by Eliza's father, Alfred Doolittle. One of the "undeserving poor," Doolittle tries to win their sympathy and coax money out of Higgins. As a parent, he feels entitled to share in Eliza's good fortune. He leaves, satisfied with a five-pound note; Higgins, convinced that they will suffer no more interference, feels ready to start the experiment.

Some months later, Higgins measures Eliza's progress by inviting her to his mother's at-home. Before Eliza is presented, Higgins and his mother are interrupted by the arrival of Pickering, Mrs. Eynsford Hill, her daughter Clara, and her son Freddy. Ironically the Eynsford Hills are the same family Eliza tried to sell flowers to in Act One; Higgins recognizes them, but the others fail to make the connection. Eliza starts off well enough, and she succeeds in charming Freddy. Slowly, her contributions to the conversation become less proper, and she stuns the assembly by using the offensive word "bloody" as she leaves.

Six months after Eliza begins her lessons, Higgins and the Colonel settle their wager by watching people react to her at an ambassador's reception. Eliza has the bearing and speech of a princess, and she fools everyone, including an expert interpreter. Higgins has clearly won the bet.

The three of them arrive at Higgins's house, exhausted after the day's events. Eliza flinches as Higgins expresses relief that the tedious job is over. He and Pickering revel in Eliza's success as if she were not in the room. After the Colonel bids them goodnight, Eliza confronts Higgins in despair, wondering what will become of her. He thoroughly fails to understand her, and the two of them part in anger. Eliza changes into walking clothes and is surprised to meet her admirer, Freddy Eynsford Hill, in the street. She turns to him for consolation, and he is only too happy to comply.

The next day, Higgins and Pickering arrive at Mrs. Higgins's house, desperate to find their lost Eliza, unaware that she has taken refuge upstairs there. Again, Mrs. Higgins points out the flaws in their regard for women, but before she gets very far, Eliza's father pays them a surprise visit. Alfred Doolittle has come into quite a bit of money, and he tells them it is ruining his life. When they discuss what will happen to Eliza, her father makes it clear that he does not want to support her financially. Eliza comes downstairs and thanks Pickering for the courtesy he has consis-

tently shown her, citing his behavior as a turning point in her self-respect. Meanwhile, her composure and pointed comments shock Higgins.

Eliza and Higgins are left alone while the others prepare to attend Alfred Doolittle's wedding that afternoon. The two of them discuss the nature of their acquaintance and Eliza's prospects for the future. Mrs. Higgins returns to collect Eliza, who has made it clear that she intends to marry Freddy and part company with Higgins permanently.

True gentility. Higgins's success in training Eliza calls into question the notion of gentility. The theatergoer is left wondering what, if anything, inherently distinguishes the upper class from their lower-class counterparts. By the end of the play, it is clear that anyone might acquire the riches and superficial refinement often equated with gentility. Alfred Doolittle's fortune and Eliza's chance to join the ranks of high society unexpectedly put the privileges of the upper-middle class within their reach. On the other hand, the well-born Eynsford Hills have come down in the world, and the reduction of their means has caused the daughter, Clara, to become abrasive and unkind. And although Mrs. Higgins is a model of courtesy, her son has turned out to be insensitive to the feelings of others.

The play raises the question of who or what turns Eliza into a lady. Higgins's expertise and Eliza's own talent and motivation are certainly required. But in the end, Eliza gives Pickering the credit, citing his example of unaffected gentility and the self-respect he inspired in her:

> Your calling me Miss Doolittle that day when I first came to Wimpole Street. That was the beginning of self-respect for me. . . . And there

were a hundred little things you never noticed, because they came naturally to you. Things about standing up and taking off your hat and opening doors. . . . You see, really and truly, apart from the things anyone can pick up (the dressing and the proper way of speaking, and so on), the difference between a lady and a flower girl is not how she behaves, but how she's treated.

(*Pygmalion,* p. 90)

Sources. Many scholars have found a close parallel between the story line of *Pygmalion* and an episode in Tobias Smollett's novel *The Adventures of Peregrine Pickle* (1751). Peregrine takes charge of a coarse young woman and transforms her into a fine lady. He compensates her mother with a small sum of money, battles the girl's tendency to swear, and shows her off at a grand ball. Later, the girl elopes with his valet. Peregrine's initial anger cools, and he helps the young couple open a coffee-house and tavern (Eliza and Freddy start a flower shop with Pickering's help, as Shaw explains in the afterword). Other scholars have pointed out the possible influence of a number of plays too, including W. S. Gilbert's *Pygmalion and Galatea* (1871) and Henrik Ibsen's **A Doll's House** (1879; also covered in *Literature and Its Times*). But Shaw denied borrowing the story directly from any of these sources.

Many agree, however, that the play echoes the well-known fairy tale of Cinderella. Like Cinderella, Eliza is a virtuous, hard-working drudge and a victim of circumstance until, by a stroke of luck, she has the chance to mix with elite society. Trademarks of the story—the stepmother, the midnight curfew, and the glass slipper—find counterparts in the play's housekeeper, Mrs. Pearce; the twelve o'clock return home after the reception; and the emphasis on Higgins's slippers. There are also overtones in the play of the ancient Greek myth of Pygmalion, after whom the work is named.

The myth of Pygmalion. "I wish [Mr. Shaw'd] found a better title," observed a flower girl who attended the London premiere. "Who's ter know *Pygmalion* is anything to do wiv flower girls?" (Berst, p. 19). However, Shaw was sure that many regular theatergoers would in fact have recognized the name Pygmalion and remembered the story associated with it. Hoping to surprise the very first audience, he tried to fool it into expecting a classical play. To do this, he produced the play anonymously, chose a leading actress who had never appeared in a low-life part, and trusted that people would, at the very least, link the title with classical mythology.

In Ovid's *Metamorphoses,* Pygmalion is a man disgusted with the behavior of women whom the love goddess, Venus, has turned into whores. He prefers celibacy instead and chooses to carve a beautiful woman out of ivory. The statue seems almost alive, and he runs his hands over it, pays it compliments, and brings it small gifts. Tenderly, he lays it down beside him in his bed, wishing it were real. On a holiday dedicated to Venus, Pygmalion makes a sacrifice to the goddess of love. Not daring to ask that his statue come to life, he prays that his wife be one *like* his ivory girl. Venus understands his true intention, and when he returns to caress the statue in his bed, it comes alive under his hands.

The poets and dramatists of the late Renaissance wondered how the woman must have felt, being born into the world full-grown and waking in the arms of a lover. Similar to this humanized statue, the female creation in Shaw's play expresses how being transformed makes her feel, and she acts in a way that adds a twist to the story: Higgins's masterpiece, Eliza, turns on her "creator" and proceeds to live her life, quite happily, without him.

Production, reviews, and new formats. Shaw chose to produce *Pygmalion* in Vienna and Berlin in 1913 before bringing it to London the next year, citing the fact that "It is the custom of the English press when a play of mine is produced, to inform the world that it is not a play—that it is dull, blasphemous, unpopular, and financially unsuccessful" (Shaw in Weiss, p. 170). When the play did open at His Majesty's Theatre on April 11, 1914, the London critics did not fail to appreciate the acclaim it had won overseas. The success *Pygmalion* enjoyed in London and elsewhere firmly established Shaw's reputation as a popular playwright.

As is so often the case, success was accompanied by controversy, especially regarding Eliza's use of the word *bloody*. Such outrageously offensive language had never before been uttered in a performance at His Majesty's Theatre. Newspapers seized upon the information, and tickets for the premiere sold quickly. Even though they knew what to expect, the audience gasped in unison when the lead actress delivered the line, "Not bloody likely!" (*Pygmalion,* p. 55). A stunned silence and waves of uproarious laughter followed, and the performance ground to a halt briefly. The next day's theater headlines talked of little else: "BERNARD SHAW'S BOLD BAD WORD SPOKEN . . . SENSATION AT HIS MAJESTY'S . . .

Audrey Hepburn as Eliza Doolittle in the film *My Fair Lady,* the musical adaptation of *Pygmalion.*

PROTEST BY DECENCY LEAGUE . . . I SEE NO OBJECTION SAYS PRIME MINISTER" (Berst p. 18). One newspaper, the *Daily Express,* had sent a Charing Cross flower girl named Eliza to review the show:

> I never thought I should be so conspic— conspic—well, yer knows wot I mean! . . . It was all rite, though, wen the curten went up. I reely enjoyed myself then, and wen I 'eard the langwidge, it was quite home-like. I never thought as 'ow they allowed sich langwidge on the stige. . . . I thought it was funny when she got into the taxi wiv her basket. Of course, flower-girls don't make a habit of getting into taxis, but you know, when you've had a good day, you feels sporty. I didn't like the last bit when Eliza's supposed to fall in love with the Prof. He wanted her to go back to him, yet he didn't say he loved her. It wasn't one thing or another.
>
> (Berst, p. 19)

Although she appreciated the familiar Cockney English, the young lady protested that she herself did not speak half as crudely as Eliza. Her dissatisfaction with the ending hinted at a debate that has haunted the play ever since the earliest productions: should there be a romantic ending between Higgins and Eliza or not? Producers and audiences generally favored one, but Shaw insisted that a marriage between the girl of eighteen and the middle-aged bachelor with a mother complex could lead only to misery.

In 1916 he wrote a preface and an afterword, which try to steer the reader away from speculation about a romance between the hero and heroine. Shaw modified the text several times in the years that followed, adding whole scenes for a 1938 film version of *Pygmalion*. Some of them, such as the embassy reception, were then written into the play as optional scenes, creating what is now distributed as the final text. *Pygmalion* was later reworked by others into the musical *My Fair Lady,* which became a motion picture that won several Academy Awards. Many Shaw fans could not bring themselves to applaud the flashy musical, and at least one critic dismissed it as far less intellectually pleasing than the play (Moore in Shaw, p. 48 of insert).

For More Information

Berst, Charles A. *Pygmalion: Shaw's Spin on Myth and Cinderella.* Twayne's Masterworks Series. No. 155. New York: Twayne, 1995.

Ervine, St. John. *Bernard Shaw: His Life, Work and Friends.* New York: William Morrow, 1956.

Himmelfarb, Gertrude. *Poverty and Compassion: The Moral Imagination of the Late Victorians.* New York: Alfred A. Knopf, 1991.

Hynes, Samuel. *The Edwardian Turn of Mind.* Princeton, N.J.: Princeton University Press, 1968.

McCrum, Robert, William Cran, and Robert Mac-Neil. *The Story of English.* New York: Viking, Elizabeth Sifton Books, 1986.

Shaw, George Bernard. *Pygmalion.* New York: Washington Square, 1957.

Sproule, Anna. *The Social Calendar.* Poole, Dorset: Blandford, 1978.

Weiss, Samuel A., ed. *Bernard Shaw's Letters to Siegfried Treditsch.* Stanford, Calif.: Stanford University Press, 1986.

Ragtime

by

E. L. Doctorow

Although E. L. Doctorow sets his novel in an era that preceded his own by some seventy-five years, many of the issues addressed in *Ragtime* remain similar to those faced by members of American society in the mid-1970s. The novel focuses on social change based primarily on two early twentieth century movements—progressivism and radicalism. Through historical and fictional characters alike, Doctorow examines America's reaction to different forms of social evolution.

THE LITERARY WORK

A novel set in the early 1900s in New York; published in 1974.

SYNOPSIS

Several unique turns of events link the lives of a wealthy white family, a poor immigrant Jewish family, and an urban black family together with historical characters like Emma Goldman, Sigmund Freud, and J. P. Morgan.

Events in History at the Time the Novel Takes Place

The Progressive movement. The Progressive movement was a campaign for economic, political, and social reform that swept through the United States at the turn of the twentieth century. From its genesis during a nationwide depression in 1893, the Progressive movement's leaders battled to bring change to American life up until the country's entry into World War I in 1917. With the rise of industrialization in the late 1800s, the United States found itself susceptible to business monopolies, crowded city slums, poor working conditions, and dishonest politicians. The reformers of the late 1890s and early 1900s sought legislation that would right these wrongs. By 1905 they had termed themselves "Progressives."

The majority of the reform leaders came from economically secure, well-educated, upper-middle-class backgrounds. A number of them bore famous family surnames such as du Pont, Spreckels (Claus, "the Sugar King," a German immigrant who had a virtual monopoly on sugar manufac-

turing and sale on the Pacific Coast of the United States, established during the last half of the nineteenth century), and Dodge. Occupationally, most of the male Progressives were successful lawyers or newspaper executives. The motives of this seemingly successful group had taken root in a shared philosophy. Most Progressives held that the advance of mankind into a more enlightened age would not generate spontaneously from the masses, but that it instead would follow from the efforts of a few educated men. President Woodrow Wilson, one of the many Progressive political voices, maintained that government could only come from an educated elite.

However elitist their views, the Progressives did in fact act as a catalyst for reform. They achieved many improvements in the economic, political, and social arenas. In 1903, for example, Progressives in Los Angeles, California, passed the first recall act, allowing voters to literally fire politicians who were suspected of corruption. And the Progressives helped effect a change in the nation's taxation by supporting the

Sixteenth Amendment. Passed in Congress in 1909, the Amendment authorized Congress to impose a federal tax, changing the system from a property-based code to an income-based code. The hope was that under the new law it would no longer be so easy for wealthy landowners to hide their assets from the government. Throughout the early 1900s, writers such as Upton Sinclair (*The Jungle*) and Jacob Riis (*How the Other Half Lives*) exposed the nation's social and political ills in books of the era. Doctorow refers to Riis in the opening chapter of *Ragtime*. Known as muckrakers, these writers took on the responsibility of making the public aware of the need for social reform.

Blacks in America at the turn of the century. The racism faced by the novel's Coalhouse Walker, and the fight that he mounts against it, mirror the struggle of many black Americans in the early 1900s. At the turn of the century, African Americans numbered just over 8.8 million in a total population of 76 million. Only one generation away from the slavery of the past, these emancipated sons and daughters of the Civil War faced the problematic assimilation into a culture that was at best indifferent to them—or at worst openly hostile. Over 90 percent of the black American population lived in the Southern states, where they found themselves denied most of the rights they had expected to enjoy after slavery was abolished by the Thirteenth Amendment in 1865. This marginalized population, however, did not accept its status without a fight.

The late 1800s and early 1900s saw the emergence of a variety of civil rights institutions and organizations. Toward the end of the novel, Coalhouse meets with Booker T. Washington, "the most famous Negro in the country" (Doctorow, *Ragtime*, p. 291). Washington, in fact, was one of two prominent black voices for reform. He focused on economic and occupational progress for blacks, founding the Tuskegee Institute in Alabama, a school that taught agricultural, domestic, and mechanical classes to young black pupils. Washington was willing to temporarily tolerate the political inequities visited upon blacks, which brought him criticism from a new black leader of the era—W. E. B. Du Bois.

Du Bois's 1903 book **The Souls of Black Folk** (also covered in *Literature and Its Times*) openly faulted Washington for his nonthreatening, conservative approach to racism. In 1905 Du Bois helped organize the black Niagara Movement, whose members insisted on total equality for

E. L. Doctorow

blacks immediately. Contrary to Washington's edicts, they would not tolerate, even for the time being, local segregation laws and other such practices. They took legal action to change these practices, supporting blacks who challenged segregation laws in court. In 1909 Du Bois and other Niagara members joined forces with white radicals of the era to form the National Association for the Advancement of Colored People (NAACP).

Washington and Du Bois belonged to a small minority of blacks who exercised some authority in society. Meanwhile, most blacks lived disheartening lives in the North as well as the South. Several thousand blacks lived in New York City at the turn of the twentieth century. Among them were a handful of middle-class blacks—actors, musicians, small businessmen, and clerks. More than 90 percent of the community worked as laborers or servants, filling positions such as porter, waiter, teamster, dressmaker, or janitor. The typical servant or laborer earned from $4 to $6 each back-breaking week, putting in more hours for less money than any other group of wage earners in the city, as reflected by a blues tune of the time: "Now I started at the bottom, and I stays right there, don't seem like I'm gonna get nowhere" (Osofsky, p. 16). Adding to the dismal picture, the health profile of the city's black population was terrible. More died than were born each year, mostly of pneumonia and consumption but also due to violence. There was even discussion among scholars that the black race would, in time, be extinguished—a revival of the idea of social Darwinism that had surfaced a few decades earlier, which held that only the fittest survive.

Meanwhile, blacks poured into New York from other areas of the nation. The population of Manhattan soared from 4,000 or fewer blacks in 1890 to include an additional 25,000 blacks by 1910. Most of them settled in what became the midtown area of Manhattan. They did not form an all-black community but rather lived in handfuls of small, thickly populated one- or two-block stretches that extended from Greenwich Village to Harlem and farther north. The population increase would in the next several years lead to Harlem's becoming the center of black settlement in the city.

As the black population increased, so did racial violence and segregation in the North. Describing a riot that broke out during an August 1900 heat wave in New York, one journalist reported that its blacks "were set upon wherever they could be found and brutally beaten"; another observer reported in a *Harper's Weekly* issue of the time hearing New Yorkers say that they would have felt glad if many of the city's blacks had been killed during the riot (Osofsky, p. 48). The actual extent of the damage and loss of life remains unknown.

Emma Goldman and American radicalism. In this era of change and insistence on reform, it is little wonder that personalities such as Emma Goldman stepped into the American spotlight. Goldman became a prominent voice for reform, and Doctorow refers to her whenever the plot of his novel turns to rebellious movements of the era.

Born to Lithuanian Jewish parents in 1869, Goldman came to the United States in the spring of 1886. She was part of a huge wave of post-1880 immigrants who arrived in the United States from southern and eastern Europe. Their numbers increased as the turn of the twentieth century approached, and 8.8 million of them immigrated from 1900 to 1910, many landing first in New York. At the time, incidents of urban unrest were on the rise. New Yorkers, like residents of other cities in America, blamed the immigrants for the crime, prostitution, poverty, political corruption, and labor disputes that surfaced in the area.

In New York's Lower East Side, where Goldman lived, immigrant communities sometimes held a distinctively European leftist or socialist view of politics. Based upon the teachings of the German philosopher Karl Marx, socialists saw the world as divided into two basic parts: the capitalists who owned the production facilities, and the proletariat, or workers, who earned wages by operating these facilities. Ideally the socialists sought a means of production and distribution of wealth that would prove more egalitarian than existing systems. Unlike the Progressive politicians, socialists felt that such change would arise from the masses. The more aggressive pursuers of socialism referred to themselves as anarchists—advocating the abolition of all government. In the novel, Mother's Younger Brother represents this extreme.

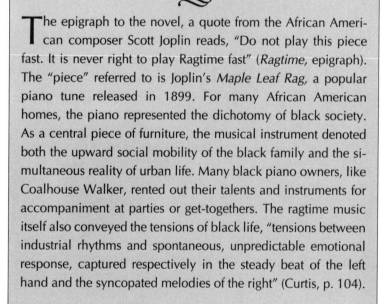

AFRICAN AMERICAN MUSIC

The epigraph to the novel, a quote from the African American composer Scott Joplin reads, "Do not play this piece fast. It is never right to play Ragtime fast" (*Ragtime*, epigraph). The "piece" referred to is Joplin's *Maple Leaf Rag*, a popular piano tune released in 1899. For many African American homes, the piano represented the dichotomy of black society. As a central piece of furniture, the musical instrument denoted both the upward social mobility of the black family and the simultaneous reality of urban life. Many black piano owners, like Coalhouse Walker, rented out their talents and instruments for accompaniment at parties or get-togethers. The ragtime music itself also conveyed the tensions of black life, "tensions between industrial rhythms and spontaneous, unpredictable emotional response, captured respectively in the steady beat of the left hand and the syncopated melodies of the right" (Curtis, p. 104).

Originally Goldman's efforts focused on labor problems. A novice at anarchist theory and public speaking, she nonetheless led rallies for workers' demands such as an eight-hour workday. In 1892 a strike at the Carnegie Steel Company brought Goldman and her companion, Alexander Berkman, to the town of Homestead, Pennsylvania. There they unsuccessfully attempted to assassinate the plant president, Henry Frick. In the novel, Goldman tells Mother's Younger

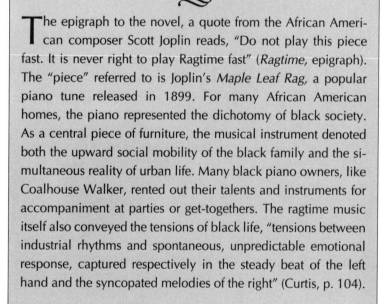
Ragtime

Brother about this very incident. Eventually he joins forces with Goldman and her counterparts. In *Ragtime*, as in real life, Goldman became involved with the Mexican Revolution toward the end of her career. When Mother's Younger Brother flees the United States, it is to join these rebels in Central America.

The Novel in Focus

The plot. Doctorow's novel combines three unique American families with a cast of historical figures ranging from J. P. Morgan to Harry Houdini to Emma Goldman. Although the novel sets up seemingly separate stories for all these people, its ending fuses all of these turn-of-the-century American lives into one grand finale.

Doctorow initially introduces his reader to an upper-middle-class white family from New Rochelle, New York. With such nondescript names as Father, Mother, Mother's Younger Brother, and the Boy, the characters could well be derived from any middle-class American home. Father earns his considerable wealth through his patriotic fireworks and flag business. Although he and Mother's Younger Brother participate together in the venture, clearly Father runs both the business and the family. In its sheltered way, the family maintains a tranquil lifestyle, but its members lack any sort of warmth or loving connection. Mother's Younger Brother feels this emotional void. Through his unrequited love for Evelyn Nesbit, wife of the railway tycoon Harry K. Thaw, he pursues a life separated from the one he maintains with his sister's family. Mother's Younger Brother ventures out into the streets of the "real" New York, following Evelyn to the most unlikely stomping grounds for a young socialite. During a short-lived affair with Evelyn, he becomes entangled with the anarchist movement led by Emma Goldman. While he does not assume a leading role in her political efforts, Mother's Younger Brother does become cognizant of the less fortunate members of American society.

Doctorow juxtaposes this family's material wealth and emotional dearth with the situation in an immigrant family of the era. Two impoverished immigrant Jews, Tateh and his little Girl, lead lives vastly different from those of the upper-middle-class white family introduced before them. They have only each other in the foreign land, but their mutual attachment and affection gives them hope for survival amidst the squalor of New York's tenements. One afternoon, dis-

gusted with the filth to which he and his daughter are subjected, Tateh boards a train with the little Girl and heads north to Lawrence, Massachusetts. While the factory work he manages to get there does not improve his salary or standard of living, Tateh serendipitously discovers fortune. In an effort to entertain his young daughter on a tight budget, he had created a small book with pages that could be flipped rapidly to feature a twirling ice skater. He sells the book to a novelty company, and thus enters the entertainment industry.

Meanwhile, another set of characters is introduced into the wealthy New Rochelle family's life. While gardening one day, Mother hears the muffled cries of a newborn baby. She realizes that the cries come from the earth at her feet. Digging frantically, she uncovers a tiny black child that had been buried alive. Since Father is out of town, she makes her own decision to keep the child. In a short while the police turn up with the mother of the baby. While they wish to prosecute the young black girl, Sarah, for attempted murder, Mother instead offers to act as guardian to the both of them. When Father returns, his initial shock and anger give way to a passive acceptance of the newcomers. Within weeks, the father of the child appears at the home. A well-dressed, articulate black man, Coalhouse Walker charms the entire family. An aspiring jazz pianist, he hopes to earn enough money to take responsibility for his girlfriend and the child. Soon the entire family becomes caught up in the happy fervor of wedding preparations for the couple. Unfortunately, the cheery atmosphere does not last.

While returning to Harlem one evening in his custom-built Model T, Coalhouse is stopped by a group of volunteer firefighters in New Rochelle. They vandalize and steal his car, and threaten him with racial taunts. Afterward, Coalhouse pursues legal avenues of retribution. Both the police and private lawyers laugh at the notion of a black man winning any kind of compensation from the group of white men. This only intensifies Coalhouse's determination. In an effort to help her fiancé, Sarah approaches the Vice President of the United States during one of his campaign stops. Mistaking her for an assassin, the secret police fatally hit Sarah. Coalhouse's pursuit of justice turns violent after her death. He leads a small gang of black youths on a bombing campaign, refusing to stop the violence unless his car is returned and restored to its original condition.

In order to escape the scandal and tension, the white family leaves for the summer, going to the New Jersey shores of Atlantic City. There they make the acquaintance of Tateh and the little Girl. Now a wealthy movie producer, Tateh has vastly improved life for himself and his daughter. The two families spend the summer together as the closest of friends, then return to their separate lives.

Back at home, Father learns that Coalhouse and his men have invaded the library of millionaire banker J. P. Morgan. In a more shocking revelation, he also learns that Mother's Younger Brother has joined forces with Coalhouse's gang. Acting as an intermediary, Father orchestrates the return and repair of Coalhouse's car. In exchange, Coalhouse surrenders his life to the authorities. His followers, including Mother's Younger Brother, disappear.

The event changes the dynamics of the family. Father becomes more involved in his business, while Mother emotionally retreats from her husband. Eventually Father dies, and Mother accepts a marriage proposal from Tateh. It seems that only in the free spirited era of American ragtime could such unlikely friends find their way into each other's lives.

The novelist as historian. A somewhat minor scene in the novel follows the psychiatrist Sigmund Freud throughout his first tour of New York City. Along with his protégé, Carl Jung, Freud visits such landmark sites as Central Park, the Metropolitan Museum, and New York's Chinatown. Despite his whirlwind vacation, the doctor remains unimpressed with America. For the Austrian psychologist, "what oppressed him about the New World was its noise" (*Ragtime,* p. 39). In fact, "the entire population seemed to him over-powered, brash and rude" (*Ragtime,* p. 41). History books, in fact, record a satisfying visit to America made by Freud in 1909. While Doctorow focuses on the famous psychologist's distaste for the United States, Freud actually entertained the notion of immigrating to America when anti-Semitic sentiment began rising in his homeland. Situations like the one described have given rise to great debate concerning the relationship between history and Doctorow's work. While some critics laud the author's ability to turn history into fiction, others contend that *Ragtime* "falsifies history. Freud, Jung, Emma Goldman, Henry Ford, Pierpont Morgan, Stanford White and Harry Houdini simply did not perpetrate the grotesqueries they are made to commit in its pages" (Levy in Harte and Riley, p. 111).

Doctorow answers his critics with an essay entitled "False Documents." He begins with the assertion that "the regime of facts is not from God but man-made, and, as such, infinitely violable" (Doctorow in Trenner, p. 17). He refuses to distinguish between the novelist as a storyteller and the novelist as a historian. He points to other writers, such as Daniel Defoe with his novel *Robinson Crusoe,* who stretch the limits of fact into their own fictitious versions of historical truth. Ultimately Doctorow concludes, "I am thus led to the proposition that there is no fiction or nonfiction as we commonly understand the distinction: there is only narrative" (Doctorow in Trenner, p. 26).

Sources. For sources, Doctorow had to look no further than the pages of American history. As noted, the novel achieves its acclaim through its fusing of the fictional and the historical. Although the author does toy with history in the pages of *Ragtime,* his work is rife with historical allusion. Some, but certainly not all, of Doctorow's references were in fact actual events:

- Teddy Roosevelt's Presidency (p. 3) 1901-1909
- Popularity of Winslow Homer's art (p. 4) 1880s-1890s
- Career of Harry Houdini (p. 9) 1891-1920s
- Theodore Dreiser's *Sister Carrie* (p. 27) 1900
- Sigmund Freud's career (p. 38) 1890s-1939
- Emma Goldman's leftist campaign (p. 55) 1892-1939
- Robert Edwin Peary's discovery of North Pole April 6, 1909 (p. 85)
- William Taft's presidency (p. 86) 1909-1913
- J. P. Morgan's banking success (p. 86) 1871-1901
- Wright Brothers fly first airplane (p. 107) Dec. 17, 1903
- Industrial Workers of the World strike in Lawrence, Mass. (p. 125) 1912
- Henry Ford opens automotive company (p. 144) 1903
- Emiliano Zapata leads Mexican Revolution (p. 173) 1901-1917
- Scott Joplin composes "Maple Leaf Rag" (p. 190) 1899
- Baseball plays its first World Series (p. 234) 1901
- Booker T. Washington becomes black educator (p. 290) 1881-1915

• Archduke Franz Ferdinand I is assassinated, instigating World War I (p. 327) June 28, 1914

Events in History at the Time the Novel Was Written

From the turbulent 1960s to the 1970s. From its inception following the assassination of President John F. Kennedy on November 22, 1963, Lyndon Johnson's presidency witnessed repeated social unrest. During his term as the thirty-sixth President of the United States (1963-69), Johnson oversaw a nation struggling with the civil rights movement and the Vietnam War. In an effort to stabilize the nation, Johnson led a domestic crusade termed the "Great Society" program. His administration fought for social change on three basic fronts—poverty, civil rights, and education. Because of its idealistic reform nature, the Great Society has invited comparison by some historians to the Progressive movement of the early 1900s.

The President's most well-known successes came from his "War on Poverty." Economically, the United States of the 1960s experienced a rise in prosperity. In keeping with this rise, both federal and local governments expanded their spending for social programs like aid to families with dependent children, welfare, and veterans' payments. It was the Office of Economic Opportunity (OEO) that waged the most visible battles in Johnson's War on Poverty. The OEO encompassed a variety of programs, ranging from community action to neighborhood service to legal services, each aiming to improve the quality of life for America's urban and rural poor. During this era, many Americans did see improvement in education, poverty, and civil rights, but at great cost. The government spent billions of additional dollars without raising taxes, which helped create problems in the nation's economy that translated on a personal level into people being unable to purchase as much with a dollar as in the past.

The 1960s also saw a return of the urban violence reminiscent of the early 1900s, with civil disturbances breaking out in several American cities over the two burning issues of the era, civil rights and the Vietnam War. Race riots erupted in New York City in 1964, and Columbia University students staged a demonstration in 1968 that turned violent, with the police pitted against the students. "The construction workers who roamed lower Manhat-

Malcolm X

tan," claims one historian of the period, "beating up long-haired youths were expressing the feelings of innumerable fellow citizens" (Bailyn, p. 837). The target group was different now than it had been in New York's 1900 riot. This time the target was the rebel student, not the average black, but the sentiment smacked of the general rage characteristic of the turn-of-the-century riots. Racial hostility resurfaced in the first half of the 1970s because of court rulings that enforced the busing of students from one part of the city to another to achieve integration. One of the most violent incidents occurred in Boston in 1974, the year *Ragtime* appeared, with whites hurling stones at buses transporting black students.

Radical civil rights. Doctorow's novel offers a portrait of a young black man driven to extremist measures by the injustices he suffers. During the late 1960s, one faction of the civil rights movement moved closer toward this extremist nature under the leadership of Malcolm X.

Like many urban black youths, Malcolm Little had worked several menial jobs in the black communities of New York and Boston. He soon moved into drug dealing and a life of full-time crime as the leader of a burglary ring. Arrested in 1946,

Malcolm converted during his six-year prison term for armed robbery to the Lost-Found Nation of Islam. He emerged reborn as Malcolm X, later becoming a minister of the Black Muslims.

The Black Muslims espoused a separatist doctrine and a belief in racial segregation from whites. Only through such extremes, they believed, would the black community survive. Like the novel's Coalhouse Walker, Black Muslims advocated businesslike attire and articulate speech for their members. Also similar to Coalhouse, the Nation of Islam found that "nonviolence was suicide, and the acceptance of suffering masochistic folly" (Hampton and Fayer, p. 243). Although Malcolm X was assassinated in 1965, his message had by then found a large following, increased by the publication that year of *The Autobiography of Malcolm X,* co-authored with Alex Haley, later of *Roots* fame.

Adopting a similar idea of self-empowerment, the Black Power philosophy emerged during the late 1960s. While Stokely Carmichael, the man who coined the phrase, denied any racial separatism in his ideology, he did profess a belief in self-help that would give black Americans the chance to live with dignity in a multiracial society. He and his followers argued that blacks needed to develop an organized economic and political base from which to assess the needs of their own community. These self-empowerment philosophies differed from the original civil rights movement, whose goals were equality and integration.

Reception of the novel. *Ragtime* proved a huge professional success for Doctorow. The paperback rights to the novel garnered for the author the largest sum in paperback publishing for its time. Not all critics applauded the format of the book, however. While some found it to be "as exhilarating as a deep breath of pure oxygen" (Clemons in Riley and Mendelson, p. 133), others disagreed with its mixture of history and fiction. But the disgruntled critics remained a minority. Most reviewers lauded Doctorow's original prose style and interwoven story lines.

For More Information

Bailyn, Bernard. *The Great Republic: A History of the American People.* Lexington, Mass.: D. C. Heath, 1992.

Curtis, Susan. *Dancing to a Black Man's Tune.* Columbia: University of Missouri Press, 1994.

Doctorow, E. L. *Ragtime.* New York: Fawcett Crest, 1974.

Hampton, Henry, and Steve Fayer. *Voices of Freedom.* New York: Bantam, 1990.

Harte, Barbara, and Carolyn Riley, eds. *Contemporary Authors New Revision Series.* Vol. 33. Detroit: Gale Research, 1991.

Osofsky, Gilbert. *Harlem: The Making of a Ghetto.* New York: Harper Torchbooks, 1963.

Riley, Carolyn, and Phyllis Carmichael Mendelson, eds. *Contemporary Literary Criticism.* Vol. 6. Detroit: Gale Research, 1981.

Trenner, Richard, ed. *E. L. Doctorow: Essays and Conversations.* Princeton: Ontario Review Press, 1983.

Rebecca

by
Daphne du Maurier

THE LITERARY WORK

A novel set primarily in England during the late 1930s; published in 1938.

SYNOPSIS

A young bride lives under the shadow of her husband's former wife and uncovers a mystery surrounding the wife's death.

Married to a man who had previously been engaged to a beautiful socialite, Daphne du Maurier was acquainted with the feelings of jealousy aroused by a mate's former love. Although her own marriage did not include the darker aspects of her novel *Rebecca*'s haunting plot, the author did identify with the psychology of her narrator. She too created in her mind the image of another woman who had shared a past with her husband. And like her narrator, du Maurier often wondered what had kept her husband and his former fiancée from enjoying a blissful wedded life together.

Events in History at the Time of the Novel

Raising women of the social elite. Throughout *Rebecca*, the narrator (the second Mrs. de Winter) comments on the social disparity between her husband, Maxim de Winter, and herself. Not having been brought up for a lifestyle of grandeur, the narrator acts shy and embarrassed when introduced to the friends and family members of her husband's class. She constantly compares herself to Maxim's former wife, the beautiful debutante, Rebecca, who had assuredly socialized with England's gentry. This feeling of awkwardness is understandable in light of the fact that upper-class British women of the 1930s were brought up simply to expect to fulfill a future role as the wife of a wealthy man.

The London *Times* would announce the arrival of children born into well-to-do families. Listed under the Court Circular section, these notices would detail the lineage of the baby, its parents, and its godparents. News of the christen-

ing followed, with references to the christening gown and the quality of lace used. After their heralded arrival into the world, most upper-class children were handed over to the care of nannies. Britishers employed some 250,000 to 500,000 nannies from the years 1921 to 1939.

Once beyond the toddler age, young girls enjoyed the privilege of attending school. The idea of sending daughters away to school became standard practice only during the twentieth century. Prior to this era, most girls had been educated at home by tutors or governesses. Although the more public setting allowed for somewhat greater social and academic freedom, young girls still had to learn and maintain the accomplishments of traditional ladies. In addition to academic subjects, the young women were schooled in activities such as riding, hunting, tennis, and dancing. With this being the type of education common to women of this milieu, it is hardly surprising that most of Maxim's friends cannot believe that his second wife is a novice in all of the mentioned arenas.

Most importantly, all girls from the "right" families underwent the process known as "coming out." In fact, they had little choice about this formal presentation to society. During the Debutante Season, young women, sponsored by their mothers or other female relatives, would attend a whirlwind of parties and dances. The sole purpose for these gatherings was the arrangement of marriages.

With the advent of the industrial society, a new class had emerged in England, the *nouveaux riches*. These families, having acquired their wealth and property through work rather than lineage, did not have the heritage necessary for arranged matches between their daughters and sons and those of the upper classes. Nonetheless, these newcomers did represent a large portion of England's economic wealth. The best manner, therefore, by which to ensure that the nation's money would remain in the hands of its established upper class was to intermarry the new and old monied families. Debutante balls provided the opportunity for young men and women of similar economic backgrounds to socialize with one another. Should the season prove a success, a young woman from the right family might land an outstanding husband.

These matches between old and new monied families helped relax strictures against marriage between members of different classes. Without the aid of an upper-crust upbringing or debutante ball, the second Mrs. de Winter nonetheless manages to marry a man of an elite socioeconomic status. While rigid social standards still held fast throughout England, the interwar period, and especially the 1930s, marked an era of change. The cinema, a popular leisure activity for European youth, provided Hollywood stars to idolize. In response, young factory workers could adopt the guise of wealth by wearing smart clothes and tilting their hats like Greta Garbo, the Swedish-born American actress. This image, however, when put to the test, would not withstand the rigors of the elite's social protocol. In the novel, the presence of the narrator at Maxim's Manderley estate causes quite a stir among the neighboring busybodies. When they learn of her nondescript background, they wonder how Maxim de Winter could have married such a nobody, a girl "so different to Rebecca" (du Maurier, *Rebecca,* p. 121).

Female friendships. For the second Mrs. de Winter, no character proves more of an obstacle to happiness than Manderley's housekeeper, Mrs. Danvers. The housekeeper seems unwilling to accept the new face in the household, and takes no pains to hide her displeasure. Originally the sec-

ond Mrs. de Winter assumes that Mrs. Danvers' attitude derives from a fear of replacement by the new mistress of the estate. She soon learns otherwise. One character informs the second Mrs. de Winter, "She [Mrs. Danvers] resents your being here at all, that's the trouble. . . . She simply adored Rebecca" (*Rebecca,* p. 100). Within time, the narrator learns that the friendship shared by Rebecca and Mrs. Danvers constituted no ordinary bond between master and servant. Rather, the two women were closer to one another than to any other persons in their lives.

Daphne du Maurier had knowledge about this type of relationship. While attending finishing school in Paris, France, she too engaged in an intense friendship with an older woman who occupied a somewhat subservient position. As an adolescent daughter of a socially elite family, Daphne attended a school abroad that cultivated such tastes as art appreciation and knowledge of the French language. There she grew uncommonly close with one teacher, Mademoiselle Fernande Yvon. Upon her initial introduction to the French headmistress, du Maurier wrote to her cousin, stating, "I've quite fallen for that woman I told you about, Mlle. Yvon. She has a fatal attraction . . . she's absolutely kind of lured me on and now I'm coiled in the net" (du Maurier in Forster, p. 28). Her bond with Mlle. Yvon grew rapidly. Originally du Maurier had planned to stay at the school for only one term. Because of her growing affection for and dependence on Mlle. Yvon, she instead remained for three terms. The women treated each other as equals rather than as teacher and student. Just as Rebecca calls Mrs. Danvers "Danny" in the novel, du Maurier gave Mlle. Yvon the affectionate nickname, "Ferdy." This relationship worried du Maurier.

She told her cousin that she feared having "Venetian" (her own term for lesbian) tendencies. Like the fictional Rebecca, du Maurier somewhat resented being a girl. In the novel, Mrs. Danvers tells the narrator, "She [Rebecca] had all the courage and the spirit of a boy. . . . She ought to have been a boy" (*Rebecca,* p. 243). Likewise Daphne envied the greater freedoms and advantages enjoyed by the male population. During puberty, du Maurier convinced herself that, in fact, she *was* a boy. She wore boy's shorts, shirts, and ties at a time when women never wore trousers. She also cultivated the spirit and ambition admired as masculine traits. In a gesture that fostered this attitude, du Maurier's father composed a poem for her that shows an appreciation for her boyish tendencies. Two of the lines read,

Joan Fontaine and Laurence Olivier in the 1940 film adaptation of *Rebecca*.

"And, if I'd had my way, / She would have been, a boy" (Gerald du Maurier in Forster, p. 13).

Although du Maurier decided, at the onset of menstruation, to ignore the boy she saw inside of herself, her friendship with Mlle. Yvon caused her to reconsider. She worried that a woman who loved and was attracted to another woman must be a man at heart. While she struggled with these questions, she never acted on what she feared were her lesbian tendencies. Du Maurier felt that lesbianism was "a feeble substitute for married life, and something to get over in youth" (du Maurier in Shallcross, p. 63). When a critic suggested that the relationship between Rebecca and Mrs. Danvers seemed to have lesbian undertones, the author acknowledged only that "Mrs. Danvers . . . could quite possibly have enjoyed a lesbian relationship with her beloved Rebecca, and that this would have deeply affected her attitude towards the new Mrs. de Winter" (Shallcross, p. 63). In fiction as in her own life, du Maurier neither confirms nor denies the level of intimacy shared between female friends.

Psychology and the crime novel. *Rebecca* belongs to a literary genre known as the "psychological thriller." While the characteristics of the novel seem commonplace by today's standards, at the time they represented a somewhat revolutionary shift in crime and detective fiction. This genre finds its roots in the Gothic novels popular during the eighteenth and nineteenth centuries. With his book *The Castle of Otranto,* Horace Walpole gave birth to the popular Gothic novel in 1764. Later works such as Mary Shelley's *Frankenstein* and Lord Byron's *Vampyre* helped to shape the characteristics of this branch of sinister literature. Within time, common Gothic elements emerged. These included: castle-like settings, supernatural occurrences, elaborate descriptions, heroines in distress, and brooding heroes, all bound together inside a web of mystery. The psychological thriller combines these characteristics with those of the traditional crime novel.

The twentieth century brought with it a heightened interest in crime stories. Amid the clamor of the new scientific age, these works encouraged methodic observation and formulation of conclusions. They also brought readers out of the mundaneness of their own lives and into the world of high adventure. The "thriller" uses, but is not limited to, the characteristics of the crime novel. While it generally presents a mystery, the purpose of the work does not focus so much on a piece-by-piece unraveling of events. Rather, it shrouds the mystery in fear, creating the atmosphere or the psychology of dread. The psychological thriller furthermore attempts to explain, throughout the book, the emotional motivations of the guilty party. This corresponds to a broader attempt by the scientific community of the early 1900s to understand and treat people with psychological or mental problems rather than simply ignoring them or confining them in an institution that isolate them from society.

The world of psychology, during the mid-1900s, promised new and exciting breakthroughs for the mental health profession. For the first time in history, doctors began treating patients with techniques of psychoanalysis. One of the more prominent names in this field was that of Carl Gustav Jung. Born in 1875, Jung made a name for himself early in his career. At the age of thirty-one, he published his first text, *Psychology of Dementia Praecox,* a psychoanalytic study of schizophrenia. In 1907 Jung traveled to Vienna to meet with Sigmund Freud, remaining some six years with the famous psychiatrist. Working with Freud, Jung became one of the first in the mental health profession to apply techniques of psychoanalysis to the study of insanity.

Because of increasing differences of opinion, the two men split in 1913. Shortly before this divergence, Jung published his work *Psychology of the Unconscious,* which revealed his own particular philosophy. The mind, according to this philosophy, was divided into separate parts that people could personify. There was also, according to Jung's philosophy, a collective consciousness that existed in the minds of people, making them common to one another and resulting in the development of mythologies. This personification and mythology, argued the philosophy, provided meaning in peoples' lives.

In any case, along with the focus on psychology in the early to mid-1900s came an explosion of psychological thrillers. The New Zealand writer Ngaio Marsh first combined psychological observation with the crime novel's traditional uncovering of clues and facts. Through her several works in this genre, Marsh introduced elaborate and bizarre methods of murder that the literary world had not yet encountered. In *Overture to Death* (1939), Marsh's victim meets his fate by a handgun cleverly disguised in a piano. Psychology provides the motive for the evil deed. Similarly, *Rebecca* involves a psychologically motivated and rather involved murder. Its focus remains not so much on the solution of the mystery as on the emotional states of the characters involved. Moreover, du Maurier offers no punishment for the crime committed—only the psychological explanation of events.

The advent of the radio and cinema only increased the popularity of the thriller. Its plots provided excellent entertainment for audiences through adaptations into radio plays and film scripts, and many authors began to enjoy unheard-of economic success when they sold their novels to these mediums. *Rebecca* proved no exception. Following the U.S. printing of the novel, Selznick Studios purchased *Rebecca*'s film rights. In 1940 du Maurier's novel came to the silver screen under the direction of Alfred Hitchcock and won an Academy Award that year for best film.

The Novel in Focus

The plot. *Rebecca*'s unnamed narrator relates her first-person tale through an extended flashback. While the opening of the novel finds the narrator and her husband, Maxim de Winter, safely secluded in a hotel room abroad, the chilling events that drove them from home are recalled throughout the book's subsequent pages. Known only to the reader as "the second Mrs. de Winter," the narrator begins her story with her introduction to her future husband.

While acting as a companion to a wealthy but obnoxious American dowager, Mrs. Van Hopper, the narrator mingled with Europe's social elite in the resort regions of southern France. Since she herself hailed from a nondescript, working-class background, the narrator often felt awkward and clumsy as she performed the duties of her occupation. She neither liked her job nor her patron, but with little alternative for earning a living, she showed determination for excelling at her work. During an afternoon lunch, Mrs. Van Hopper noted a fellow diner, stating, "It's Max de Winter . . . the man who owns Manderley. You've heard of it, of course. He looks ill, doesn't he? They say he can't get over his wife's death" (*Rebecca*, p. 11). From that moment on, the narrator's future became intricately woven together with the brooding man and his English country estate, Manderley.

When Mrs. Van Hopper took ill, the narrator had occasion to lunch with Mr. de Winter. Their meetings became routine engagements, and lunches soon stretched into afternoon outings together. By the end of two weeks, the couple had fallen in love. When Mrs. Van Hopper announced that she would soon sail for New York, the narrator and her beau disclosed their affection for each other. Without the blessing of her former employer, the narrator married

Mr. de Winter and embarked on a honeymoon tour of Italy.

After traveling for six weeks, the de Winters returned to England to begin their life together at Manderley. The narrator's initial introduction to the estate, while filled with a bride's nervous trepidation, gave little indication of the events that would later occur on the Manderley grounds. As she grew to know the mansion and its staff, the narrator felt welcome by all the employees, save one. Mrs. Danvers, Manderley's housekeeper, had resided with the de Winters for quite some time, and seemed rather set in her ways. Although others lauded her excellent traits, the housekeeper treated the new Mrs. de Winter with cold disdain. She seemed immediately to resent the new face at Manderley and took no pains to hide her emotions. The narrator nevertheless settled into her role as the mistress of the estate.

Within time she became acquainted with Maxim's friends and family. Though constantly aware of her inferior social upbringing, the narrator strove to improve her social skills for the sake of her new status. Her efforts seemed hampered, however, by the ever-present shadow of Rebecca, Maxim's first wife. Rebecca had accidentally drowned while sailing less than a year earlier, and her presence still permeated Manderley. Mrs. Danvers kept Rebecca's private rooms as they had been on the day of her death. Even her dressing gown lay on the bed, awaiting an owner who would never return. It seemed as though every person with whom the narrator interacted commented on Rebecca's outstanding beauty, grace, charm, and accomplishments. Subject to these comparisons, the second Mrs. de Winter began to feel as though she could never live up to the standards set by her predecessor. Coupled with this, Maxim's mood grew so dark at the mere mention of his former wife that the narrator believed that he had not yet put Rebecca's death behind him.

At the suggestion of several neighbors, the de Winters decided to revive the Manderley fancy dress ball that had been an annual event at the estate. Mrs. Danvers recommended a costume for the narrator so beautiful that she rushed to purchase that exact gown. She kept her attire a secret from her husband, hoping for once to startle him with *her* beauty and grace. When she descended the stairs on the eve of the party, however, his look was not one of affection, but rather of shock and horror. On what would be her last fancy dress ball, Rebecca, his former wife, had worn that exact outfit. Only

then did the narrator realize the extent of Mrs. Danvers' hatred for her.

Unable to clear up the confusion, the narrator and Maxim spent the duration of the party barely speaking to each other. While she had hoped to catch him early the next morning, her apologies had to wait, as a ship had run aground in the bay nearby. The narrator, like many other curious spectators, ran down to the shore to watch the spectacle. No one, it turned out, had suffered injury in the accident, so the excitement of the shipwreck seemed to wane in the late morning. However, when a diver went down to inspect a hole in the ship, he made a startling discovery. On the floor of the ocean he found Rebecca's small sailboat, and peering inside, he discovered a body. Since Maxim had previously identified a different body as that of his former wife, a formal inquest began. The authorities raised the small craft and searched it thoroughly. When they noticed holes driven through the floor of the boat, they began to suspect foul play.

Ironically, these strange events drew the narrator and her husband closer together. Maxim confessed to her that he had killed his former wife. He told her that Rebecca "was vicious, damnable, rotten through and through. We never loved each other. . . . Rebecca was incapable of love, of tenderness, of decency. She was not even normal" (*Rebecca*, p. 271). Tired of her adultery and her lies, and trapped in a loveless marriage, he had shot Rebecca and then sunk her body in the boat. The narrator soothed Maxim, convincing him that their love for each other would see them through whatever lay ahead. Although the authorities did come close to discovering the truth, they ultimately listed suicide as the cause of Rebecca's death. All parties seemed satisfied with this end—everyone, that is, except Mrs. Danvers. While the de Winters were away dealing with the inquest, Mrs. Danvers fled the estate, but not before she had set Manderley on fire.

A psychological novel. Du Maurier's original intent in composing *Rebecca* was to fashion a psychological study whereby the character of the first wife would build in the mind of the second "until wife two is haunted day and night" (du Maurier in Forster, p. 132). Given the novel's first-person perspective, all characters and events had to filter through the interpretation of the narrator. It is the character of Rebecca, however, who most vividly comes to life in the mind of the second Mrs. de Winter. From the moment that she stumbles across a sample of Rebecca's

Judith Anderson and Joan Fontaine in the film adaptation of *Rebecca*.

handwriting, the narrator creates a vision of the person Maxim's first wife must have resembled. She notes, "that bold, slanting hand, stabbing the white paper, the symbol of herself, so certain, so assured" (*Rebecca,* p. 43). By contrast, the narrator sees herself as timid and mild, uncertain at every step. The novel continually contrasts their psychological profiles, creating two women who are not as unequal to each other as the reader originally suspects. By the close of the plot, the second Mrs. de Winter finds the strength to support her husband in his hour of need, while Rebecca diminishes to a faint memory. Most of the contemporary reviews of *Rebecca* overlooked its psychological components, and this neglect came both as a shock and a disappointment to du Maurier.

Du Maurier, later on in her life, became an avid fan of the groundbreaking psychologist Carl Jung. Having wrestled in adolescence with the gender dichotomy inside of herself, she liked Jung's notions of dual personalities in the mind. She did not, as she confessed to a friend, particularly enjoy this duality within herself. "The thing is, why must I always pretend to be someone else . . . it is what Jung calls 'compensation' and 'fantasy'" (du Maurier in Forster, p. 278). However, du Maurier found solace in Jung's explanations that everyone suffered such contrasts within the self. In *Rebecca,* the writer sought to bring these contrasts to light. While many critics saw the second Mrs. de Winter as an autobiographical personification of the author, du Maurier also possessed some of murdered Rebecca's aggressive nature. Because of her psychological interests, du Maurier was disappointed to learn that her work was revered only as a great romance. She had hoped to convey a sense of the frustrations that she herself had sometimes felt. More exactly, du Maurier had hoped her readers would pick up on the battle between the sexes as displayed through the characters of Maxim and the second Mrs. de Winter. Throughout the novel, the narrator acts as a subordinate to her husband, her every action motivated by his wish. Not until the end, when Maxim's precarious legal position comes into play, does the second Mrs. de Winter move onto more equal psychological ground with her husband.

Sources. While the majority of the inspiration for *Rebecca* came from the author's own imagination, du Maurier did draw on autobiographical references for the creation of her novel. The Manderley estate, for instance, closely resembles Menabilly, a home that du Maurier rented and restored over a period of twenty-five years. Located in the Cornwall region of southern England, the home was situated near a holiday retreat owned by du Maurier's parents. As an adolescent, she had spent summers in the region, sailing, swimming, and playing with her sisters and cousins. Although she first fell in love with Menabilly during these early years, she did not actually rent the home until she herself became a wife and mother. With its Tudor-style architecture and isolated location, Menabilly reminds the reader of the de Winters' Manderley. In fact, although du Maurier originally began writing *Rebecca* while traveling with her husband in Egypt, during this period "she found herself fantasizing about Cornwall and in particular about Menabilly" (Forster, p. 133). The author would later return to the area to rent the estate, and at one point would confess how deep her feelings were for it: "It makes me a little ashamed to admit it, but I do believe I love Mena [billy] more than people" (du Maurier in Forster, p. 188).

Du Maurier's life relates to her main character's as well. As mentioned, like the narrator of *Rebecca,* du Maurier also married a man who had experienced a previous love. Tom Browning, or "Boy Browning," immediately captured du Maurier's heart with his good looks and charm. Eleven years her senior, however, Browning had been previously engaged. Although the decision to break off this earlier engagement had been his, du Maurier always harbored a certain jealousy toward her husband's first love. In fact, one afternoon she stumbled upon a bundle of love letters tied together affectionately with a ribbon. Although guilt-ridden at her own brashness, she opened the letters and read each of them. They had been written by Jan Ricardo, the beautiful debutante whom Browning had almost married. The strong handwriting seemed to personify this woman from Browning's past. By contrast, du Maurier herself "looked like a slip of a girl . . . someone who blushed easily and had no authority whatsoever" (Forster, p. 118). Du Maurier borrows this scene for *Rebecca.* Early in the novel, the narrator finds a book of Maxim's with an inscription written by Rebecca. She notes that "the name Rebecca stood out black and strong, the tall and sloping R dwarfing the other letters" (*Rebecca,* p. 33). With this premise in mind, du Maurier began her novel. "Roughly," say her original notes for it, "the book will be about the influence of a first wife on a second" (du Maurier in Forster, p. 132).

Reception of the novel. From the moment that du Maurier sent her novel to her publisher, *Rebecca* enjoyed success. The senior editor at Victor Gollancz announced that the novel "brilliantly creates a sense of atmosphere and suspense" (Collins in Forster, p. 136). Likewise, the critical accounts of *Rebecca* almost unanimously praised du Maurier's achievement. London's *Observer* commented that "the fearlessness with which Miss du Maurier works in material so strange . . . is magnificent" (Swinnerton in Forster, p. 139). Within a month of publication, Rebecca sold 45,000 copies.

For More Information

Ball, John. *The Mystery Story.* Del Mar: University of California, San Diego Press, 1976.

Du Maurier, Daphne. *Rebecca.* New York: Avon, 1938.

Forster, Margaret. *Daphne du Maurier.* New York: Doubleday, 1993.

Johnson, Paul. *20th Century Britain: Economic, Social, and Cultural Change.* New York: Longman, 1994.

Lambert, Angela. *1939: The Last Season of Peace.* New York: Weidenfeld & Nicolson, 1989.

Shallcross, Martyn. *The Private World of Daphne du Maurier.* New York: St. Martin's, 1991.

Storr, Anthony. *C. G. Jung.* New York: Viking, 1973.

The Red Pony

by

John Steinbeck

Like many of John Steinbeck's novels, the four short stories that make up *The Red Pony* take place on a ranch in the Salinas Valley in central California. While Steinbeck himself was raised in the town of Salinas, he was familiar with ranch life, having worked as a young man on beet ranches in the area. Steinbeck has often been praised for his accurate depiction of life in the Salinas Valley as portrayed in *The Red Pony* and his other works of fiction.

Events in History at the Time the Novel Takes Place

The Salinas Valley. Each of the four parts of *The Red Pony* depicts the experiences of Jody Tiflin. Although readers are never told Jody's exact age or in precisely what year his experiences take place, it is believed that Steinbeck drew on his own childhood as a point of reference for the stories. The character of Jody appears to be about eleven or twelve years old. Steinbeck himself was born in Salinas in 1902, and with this in mind, one can most likely place Jody on a small ranch just outside Salinas in approximately 1914.

Like Jody's grandfather in one of the novel's four stories ("The Leader of the People"), Steinbeck's own maternal grandparents migrated from the eastern United States to the Salinas Valley, California, in 1874. His grandfather co-founded the town of Salinas, which grew slowly to include a population of approximately three thousand before 1914. Salinas originally served the cattle ranches that had developed in the Val-

ley and sat between fields that stretched to the Galiban Mountains on the east, and the Santa Lucia Mountains, which bordered the Pacific Ocean, on the west. Although the Salinas Valley did not see as rapid a rise in population as the southern and northern regions of California, the agricultural industry in the central portion of the state was in a constant pattern of growth and flux.

A boom in agriculture. In *The Red Pony*, Steinbeck describes the daily routine of chores on the small ranch where the Tiflin family lived, but does not divulge the types of crops that the ranch yielded or its main source of income. During the early 1900s, the Salinas Valley emerged as a major agricultural center in California and became less involved with livestock ranching. In addition to grain and hay, crops such as sugar beets, dry beans, and peas were cultivated. Bean crops would especially flourish as World War I approached. By 1914 lettuce had also been introduced to the list of new crops being harvested in the Salinas Valley, and it would give rise to a booming industry in the years to follow. In the meantime, smaller ranches, such as the Tiflins' in *The Red Pony*, engaged in just enough crop- and cattle-raising to support themselves. Their meager income is evidenced in the novel by the fact that Billy Buck is the only ranchhand on the Tiflins' property. In "The Great Mountains," Carl Tiflin, Jody's father, also alludes to the constant struggle to keep the ranch afloat when the old man named Gitano shows up one day. "I'm having a hard enough time keeping this ranch out of the Bank of Italy without taking on anybody else to feed" (Steinbeck, *The Red Pony*, p. 49).

Laborers. The laborers employed on the major ranches in the Salinas Valley during the early 1900s consisted largely of Mexican, Japanese, Chinese, and Filipino migrants. These migrant farm laborers would in later years become a major work force in the California agricultural community and pave the way for its unions. The forerunners of these later laborers are represented in the novel by Gitano, whose ethnicity is never specified in Steinbeck's novel. Scholars, however, assume that Gitano is Mexican. He keeps insisting that he was born on or near the Tiflin's ranch, and he has returned home to die there. Steinbeck's term for such workers was "paisano," a name used by the characters Carl Tiflin and Billy Buck when discussing Gitano:

> "This country's full of these old paisanos," Carl said to Billy Buck.
> "They're damn good men," Billy defended them. "They can work older than the white men. I saw one of them a hundred and five years old, and he could still ride a horse. You don't see as many white men as old as Gitano walking twenty or thirty miles."
>
> (*The Red Pony*, p. 49)

The Novel in Focus

The contents. *The Red Pony* consists of four short stories that were published on separate occasions from 1933 to 1937 prior to being collected under one title in 1945. Since the characters and setting are the same in each story, it is considered a short novel with four parts. All four stories center on Jody Tiflin, a boy of about twelve years old whose experiences in each story make the work a coming-of-age tale.

In the first story, "The Gift," Jody receives a new red pony along with the responsibility of

John Steinbeck

caring for and training it, a challenge he meets successfully. One day, however, his feelings are deeply hurt when Billy Buck, the ranchhand whom he looks up to more than his own father, neglects to bring the pony in during a rainstorm. As a result, the pony becomes ill and, despite all his and Billy Buck's efforts, it dies. The young boy undergoes his first experience with death.

The second part, "The Great Mountains," deals with the arrival of an old man, Gitano, at the Tiflin ranch. A bored Jody has been occupying his time torturing small and defenseless animals when Gitano appears seemingly out of nowhere. He claims that he was born there on the ranch and has come home to die. While the old man fascinates Jody, his father, Carl Tiflin, wants little to do with the stranger. He sends Gitano packing, whereupon the old man steals an old horse and rides into the Great Mountains, presumably to die.

Called "The Promise," the third part centers on an offer by Carl Tiflin to breed his mare and give Jody the offspring if Jody will care for the pregnant mare and colt as he did for his first pony. Jody agrees and impatiently sees the mare through the breeding and duration of her pregnancy. Aided by Billy Buck, the birthing requires that the mare be killed so the colt can live—a dilemma that leaves Jody with mixed feelings.

The final part, "The Leader of the People," features Jody's maternal grandfather and his visit to the ranch. While Jody looks forward to the older man's stories about leading a wagon train across the frontier, Carl grows irritated by the repetitive tales and hurts the grandfather's feelings. Jody shows a sense of compassion for the old man that reflects his own developing respect for his grandfather as a man and pioneer.

Billy Buck. Historians consider Billy Buck, the cowhand on the Tiflin ranch, to be an accurate portrayal of a ranch worker during the turn of the twentieth century. Having worked on several ranches and spent time on his own uncle's ranch himself, Steinbeck had firsthand knowledge of a ranchhand's lifestyle and position.

In "The Gift," Jody is always quoting advice or knowledge Billy Buck has given him about ranching: "Jody listened carefully, for he knew and the whole county knew that Billy Buck was a fine hand with horses" (*The Red Pony,* p. 15). Jody's mother makes a remark that indicates Buck's proficiency in more than just the daily chores. "Don't worry about the pony. He'll be all right. Billy's as good as any horse doctor in the county" (*The Red Pony,* p. 24).

An experienced ranchhand had an extensive knowledge about farm animal ailments and cures, as Billy demonstrates when the pony gets sick in "The Gift." He displays this knowledge again in "The Promise" when the mare is pregnant with Jody's colt. He assists in the birthing process and knows that because of the position of the unborn colt in the mare's body, he must kill the mother or both animals will die.

An irony underlying the respect earned for ranchhands such as Billy lay in how they were socially classified. While experienced ranchhands such as Billy Buck were regarded as valued workers on the farm, they were also relegated to a lower social class than those who owned the ranches. In the novel, when Mrs. Tiflin rings the triangle bell for meals, Billy must not sit at the table until a member of the ranch owner's family takes a seat first. He waits on the porch until Jody or Carl sits down, and only then may he come to the table and begin to eat his meal.

Sources. *The Red Pony's* Salinas Valley setting is autobiographical. From an early age John Steinbeck harbored a love of this country that he expresses in the character Jody Tiflin. It is believed that the Tiflin ranch in the novel was modeled after Steinbeck's own uncle's ranch:

> Part of every summer was also spent with Uncle Tom Hamilton at the ranch near King City. . . . There were chores to do among the animals and in the garden, but mostly there was time to blaze trails across the rock . . . and dry grass. The Hamilton ranch was, in part, the model for the Tiflin ranch in *The Red Pony,* and like Jody, John found a special place.
>
> (Benson, p. 9)

Like Jody in "The Gift," Steinbeck received a red pony from his father (John Ernst Steinbeck) on his twelfth birthday. Accounts of Steinbeck's somewhat distant relationship with his father suggest that for the fictional Carl Tiflin the author drew on the personality traits of his own father.

When Steinbeck wrote the first three stories of *The Red Pony* in 1933, he was caring for his dying mother, Olive Hamilton Steinbeck. Some researchers believe that experiencing the death of a loved one motivated Steinbeck to incorporate the life and death cycle in his writing. Included in the first three stories of *The Red Pony* are the death of the red pony; Gitano's return to the ranch to die; and the mare's death while giving birth to the colt. The fourth story, though written later, utilizes the death theme as well in Jody's grandfather's final telling of his westward journey, which marks the end of an era and the closing of the frontier. Jody's struggles with issues of life and death in these stories have been described as a reflection of Steinbeck's own struggles during his mother's fatal illness. In his book, *John Steinbeck,* Warren French traces the genesis of *The Red Pony* to this illness:

> His best works remain those in which self-conscious characters transcend the frustrations of their environments—*The Red Pony, The Grapes of Wrath, Cannery Row*—for these are the only novels in which Steinbeck becomes a timeless artist rather than an American Seer. We must recognize that all three rose from a personal crisis—*The Red Pony,* from his first experience with death in the family.
>
> (French, p. 173)

Events in History at the Time the Novel Was Written

Personal trials. Steinbeck's mother suffered a massive stroke before she died, which left her paralyzed on one side and unable to speak clearly. Her son would sit by her hospital bed day after day, his writing pad in hand as his mother slipped in and out of sleep. It was on such a day that Steinbeck began *The Red Pony*. He began also during this period to muse about stories concerning the life of Mexican migrants, which were told to him by a Monterey high-school teacher, Sue Gregory, who was part Mexican herself. Soon Steinbeck's father's health faltered, too. Collapsing a few months after his wife's stroke, his father suffered from numbness, failing eyesight, and mental instability. Clearly Steinbeck had entered a period of protracted exposure to the death of a loved one and the fragility of human life. His mother would pass away eleven months after the stroke in early 1934, his father in mid-1935.

The Red Pony and the Depression. All four sections of *The Red Pony* first appeared in print in the collection of Steinbeck stories *The Long Valley*. The final story in this 1938 collection, "The Leader of the People," about Jody's grandfather recalling his pioneering days, concerns a subject that preoccupied Steinbeck as well as other novelists of the early 1900s: the relationship of the individual to the group. The Depression years were replete with organizations established by the government (the Emergency Relief Organization, the Works Progress Administration, and the Civilian Conservation Corps, to name a few) that would have only intensified such a preoccupation with the concept of teamwork. At the same time, these years gave rise to a trek westward across the Great Plains by the jobless and the poor migrant families from states blighted by merciless dust storms. Their westward movement brings to mind the wagon train that Jody's grandfather led across the plains to the coast. In contrast to these pioneers, though, the latter-day migrants faced the grim prospects of living in the dismal migrant camps that had sprung up in California during the Depression era.

California farming. John Steinbeck wrote *The Red Pony* while residing at his parents' home in Pacific Grove, California in 1933. The country was still in the midst of the Great Depression, and the agricultural industry in the Salinas Valley also suffered. The large California farms were owned by big operators and banks who employed hundreds of migrant workers. Although the productivity of the farms did not diminish too greatly in the 1930s, low wages for laborers picking and packing fruit and vegetables led to economic unrest. In the 1920s workers were paid 40¢ per hour, a wage that plummeted to a low

of 15¢ per hour in the early years of the Depression. Although public labor camps were subsidized by the government in an effort to alleviate the plight of the agricultural workers, the laborers would eventually strike for better wages and working conditions as times got worse. Steinbeck would depict these times in a novel to follow *The Red Pony, In Dubious Battle*.

Publication and reviews. The first of the novel's stories to be published, "The Gift"—initially titled "The Red Pony"—brought Steinbeck his first taste of critical acclaim. R. S. Hughes comments on the story's impact on the author's success: "'The Gift' originally entitled 'The Red Pony' is the short story that, by some estimates, launched Steinbeck's career . . . it was his first work accepted by a prominent national magazine" (Hughes, p. 92). In fact, the first two sections of the novel were published in issues of the *North American Review* in 1933. A few years later, in 1937, Friede Covici published an edition of *The Red Pony* that contained only the first three stories in the series. Then came the 1938 short story collection, *The Long Valley*, which included all four stories and more. Finally, in 1945, Viking Press published a separate edition of the four short stories under the title *The Red Pony*, producing what was to be the final version of the series. In 1962, the year that Steinbeck won the Nobel Prize in literature, the *New York Times Book Review* featured a piece by Arthur Mizner that singled out the final version of *The Red Pony* for special commendation. His article credited the novel with having "an integrity, a responsibility to experience and a consequent unity of surface and symbol that Steinbeck has never achieved since" (Mizner, p. 43).

For More Information

Benson, Jackson. *The Adventures of John Steinbeck*. New York: Viking, 1984.

French, Warren. *John Steinbeck*. Boston: Twayne, 1975.

Hughes, R. S. *Beyond The Red Pony: A Reader's Companion to Steinbeck's Complete Short Stories*. Metuchen, New Jersey: Scarecrow, 1987.

Mizner, Arthur. "Does a Moral Vision of the Thirties Deserve a Nobel Prize?" *New York Times Book Review* (December 9, 1962): 43-5.

Steinbeck, John. *The Red Pony*. New York: Viking, 1945.

Verado, Jennie Dennis, and Denzil Verado. *The Salinas Valley*. Salinas, Calif.: Windsor, 1989.

The Road from Home

by
David Kherdian

In 1931 Veron Dumehjian Kherdian gave birth to David Kherdian in Racine, Illinois. Her son grew to be a popular author of children's stories and poetry before he resolved to tell the story of his mother's escape from Armenia during World War I. *The Road from Home,* which tells this story, won the resounding acclaim of critics, and was followed in 1981 by *Finding Home,* an account of Veron's life in America.

Events in History at the Time the Novel Takes Place

Pre-World War I prejudice. The modern Republic of Armenia is situated just northeast of Turkey, atop the high plateaus between the Black Sea to the northwest and the Caspian Sea to the northeast. Although Armenians have at various times inhabited land beyond their current holdings (within modern-day Turkey, the Republic of Georgia, Azerbaijan, and Iran), the efforts of the Byzantine Greeks, Islamic Turks, and nomadic Kurds to disperse or destroy the Armenian population have reduced Armenia to its present size.

Lying at the crossroads of Europe, Asia, and Arabia, Armenia was the battleground of the struggles between the Roman and Persian empires, the Mongol invasions, and the European Crusades before falling under the rule of the Ottoman Turks from the 1300s to the 1500s. The Ottoman Turks, followers of the Muslim religion, ruled an empire that at its height stretched from the city of Budapest in the west to Baghdad in the east.

As members of a Christian minority in this empire, Armenians suffered official discrimination under Ottoman rule. They paid outrageous taxes and could neither bear arms nor give legal testimony. Many Armenians reacted by fleeing the Muslim empire for Europe. In the eighteenth and nineteenth centuries, as the Ottoman Empire began to crumble in the face of European threats, Christian victories in other Ottoman territories encouraged an outcry for reform by Armenians who had remained in their homeland.

Instead, the Turks used the Armenians as scapegoats for the fiascoes of Turkish tyranny and misrule. Claims from Europe—like those of Czar Nicholas I, who asserted himself as the guardian of Christians within the Ottoman Empire—excited Turkish paranoia and aggravated the violent repression of vocal Armenian groups. In 1894 an Armenian attempt to defy local au-

The hanging of Armenian doctors.

thority sparked the killings of Armenians in the area. Great Britain, France, and Russia sent a memorandum urging reforms in Turkish Armenia, and Armenians organized a protest in the capital, Constantinople (modern-day Istanbul). Sultan 'Abdul Hamid responded by instituting a reign of terror throughout the Armenian provinces. Armenians were herded into their churches and burned alive, or driven into the sea to drown.

Outraged by the violence, Armenians began to resist. Armenian terrorists threatened to destroy the financial institution of the Ottoman Bank if their demands for reform (in the areas of taxation, protection from abusive authorities, and so on) were ignored. This challenge to his authority infuriated 'Abdul Hamid, who ordered the massacre of the Armenians in Constantinople. Again Turks decimated helpless Armenians, and again the rest of Europe failed to respond effectively. Between 1894 and 1896 an estimated 300,000 Armenians died in the government-organized slaughter.

In 1908 the victorious Young Turk revolution against the despotic sultan awakened hopes for Armenian autonomy within the Ottoman Empire. Both Armenians and Turks had fought to depose the sultan and restore a constitutional government to the land. But between 1908 and 1914 the supposedly egalitarian Young Turks degenerated into extreme nationalists. Their ambitions to create a new Turkish state, stretching beyond the Armenian homeland to include the Turanian peoples living in what is now Turkestan, raised ethnic tensions. In 1909, discussion among Armenians about the creation of an independent state provoked the massacre of 30,000 Armenians in the city of Adana.

World War I. By 1914, three Turkish extremists—Enver, Jemal, and Talaat—jointly ruled the Ottoman Empire. The outbreak of World War I provided an excuse to deport or kill the Armenian people, who lived on both sides of the fragile Turkish-Russian border, on the grounds that they might aid the advancing Russian armies. The executive secretary of the Ottoman Empire maintained:

> We are now at war; there is no more auspicious occasion than this; the intervention of the Great Powers and the protests of the newspapers will not even be considered; and even if they are, the matter will have become an accomplished fact, and thus be closed forever.
>
> (Lang, p. 23)

Another official recommended an easy method of extermination.

We can send those young Armenians who can bear arms to the front lines. There, coupled between fire by the Russians facing them and by special forces in the rear dispatched by us for that purpose, we can trap and annihilate them. In the meantime, we can order our faithful adherents to plunder and to liquidate the old and infirm, women and children, who remain behind.

(Lang, pp. 23-4)

The Armenians had no reason to suspect this Turkish treachery. Although they had resisted assimilation, clinging to their church and language, Armenians themselves had been conscripted to fight in the Turkish armies and had pledged their support to the war effort.

Entire Armenian military units were disarmed and turned into labor groups. At first overworked and starved, they were later simply shot down. The senseless slaughter of useful soldiers and workmen frustrated the Germans, Turkey's strongest allies, who declared "these measures . . . create the impression that the Turkish government itself is intent on losing the war" (Lang, p. 27). For the Young Turk party the extermination of the Armenians seemed to be more important than the war effort.

To save money and ammunition, and to lend their actions some semblance of legality (the argument being that the Armenians were an internal threat), Talaat Pasha, the Minister of the Interior, ordered the deportation of the Armenians to the deserts of Syria and Mesopotamia. Few survived the two- or three-hundred-mile march across the rugged mountains. Many Armenians killed both their children and themselves rather than prolong the torture. Those who survived were herded into concentration camps in the Arabian deserts, where they were beaten, starved, and killed. The most dreadful of these camps was Deir el Zor in Syria, where typhus and cholera ravaged not only the Armenian refugees, but also Arab civilians and Turkish troops. Rotting bodies attracted hyenas from the deserts, and the roads between Turkey and Syria were strewn with the corpses of refugees.

When Turkey surrendered to the Allied powers in 1918, a military tribunal sentenced the leaders of the fallen Ottoman Empire to death. Talaat, who had fled to Germany, was assassinated in Berlin in 1921 by an Armenian student, who was then acquitted by the German courts. Enver, living among Turkish tribes in the Soviet Union, was killed in 1922 leading a revolt against Soviet authorities.

Post-World War I events. The treaty of Sevres, signed by Turkey in 1920, provided for the creation of an Armenian republic, the boundaries of which would be determined by the United States. But the U.S. government showed a reluctance to become involved in international postwar conflicts, and this left a void; meanwhile, Turkish nationalists, enraged by the demands of the Allies, marched into western Armenia. Only an invasion by the Russian Bolsheviks and the establishment in 1920 of a Soviet Republic of Armenia halted the Turkish advance.

The fighting in Turkey was far from over, however. Overeager Greeks, who had gained the coastal city of Smyrna (now called Izmar) from the Turks after World War I, invaded territories stretching far beyond Smyrna into the heart of Turkey. Although at first victorious, they were driven back by Turkish nationalists and eventually expelled from Smyrna itself. Many Armenians were killed in the fighting, but some were able to flee Turkey with the retreating Greek armies.

Before 1914 over 2 million Armenians had lived in Turkey. After the deportations and massacres a scant 100,000 remained. An estimated 1.5 million Armenians were killed between 1914 and 1920. The balance of the survivors fled the country for destinations across the globe.

The Novel in Focus

The plot. Veron Dumehjian, the child of a rich Armenian family in Azizya, Turkey, recounts the pleasures of her childhood between 1907 and 1914, before the disastrous deportations in which most of her family died. A few days after her two uncles were drafted into the Turkish army to fight in World War I, Veron and her family are ordered to gather their belongings and prepare to leave. They are taken to Konya, a Turkish city south of Azizya, under the protection of a Turkish gendarme. Veron overhears him saying to her father:

I have kept my promise to your mother by bringing you safely to Konya . . . but now I must return. . . . We have fallen on evil days. . . . What can I say to lighten your load? May we meet again in Azizya after this present storm has passed.

(Kherdian, *The Road from Home*, p. 40)

He leaves them with the Muslim blessing, "Allah be with you."

In the night Veron overhears her father and grandfather speaking with other men about the deportations. One asserts that only those Armenians with money to spare have managed to survive this long. The men who had not been conscripted to fight have been slaughtered, and the roads to Syria are already littered with the bodies of Armenian refugees. Veron falls asleep.

The next day Veron's father announces that the family is to be deported by the Turks to the Mesopotamian deserts. On their journey, Veron watches in confusion as the old and infirm fall and are left behind. Her uncle pleads to no avail with the Turkish guards to allow Veron's family to take people in their wagon. As the caravan rounds corners, the guards ride back, and rifle shots can be heard; the shots, it is implied, are directed at the old and the infirm.

The refugees arrive at the outskirts of Adana, where the 1909 massacres had taken place. They bathe in the river, and at night Veron's father, who can pass for a Turk, sneaks into town to find food and perhaps news. He returns with sugarcane for the children and hopes that the tide of war has turned. Adana is so overrun by bandits that the Turks can hardly spare troops to continue the deportation. After weeks camped in the outskirts of the city, the Armenians are driven on, first to a cholera-ridden refugee camp in what is now Syria and then farther south, to Meskene, in the Syrian desert. Veron's family's wagon is requisitioned by the Turks, and her father, who speaks Arabic, is sent off to Aleppo and then Baghdad to help the Turks trade with Arabs. In Meskene, all of Veron's siblings die of cholera.

After Veron's father returns from Baghdad, her mother dies. Terrifying rumors about a concentration camp in Deir el Zor, south of Meskene, prompt Veron's father to bribe the gendarmes and secure passage to Birijek, a city north of Meskene, in Turkey. Here he finds lodging for his daughter with other Armenian refugees. He explains, however, that he must leave again to work for the Turkish government in Aleppo, Syria. Returning to Birijek to visit his daughter, he dies of exhaustion.

In Birijek, Veron's "aunties" (as she calls the Armenian women who care for her) find her a job carrying water for two Turkish families. A year passes before Veron receives communication from a relative of hers in Aleppo, who informs her that her grandmother is still alive in Azizya. Eager to rejoin her family, she leaves for Aleppo.

Here Veron meets some of her more distant relatives who had managed to escape the massacres. They are insensitive to her sufferings, and she happily leaves them for an orphanage where she can learn French and English. Here she lives for two years in the company of Armenian girls who, like herself, have lost their families in the deportations.

In 1918 the Turkish surrender convinces Veron and her family that they can return to their homes in Turkey. In Azizya, Veron learns that one of her uncles survived his service in the Turkish army, and that her favorite aunt and cousin are living in Smyrna. She lives in Azizya for two years in relative contentment.

In 1921 the marauding Greeks shatter this peace with their efforts to conquer western Turkey. The Turks in Azizya drive the Armenians to the Turkish parts of town and take refuge in the Armenian quarter. The Greeks, careful not to destroy the Christian dwellings, bomb only the Turkish houses. Veron is injured and taken to a Greek hospital. The Greeks offer safe passage to those Armenians who wish to flee Azizya. Veron's grandmother sends her off with the Greek medics but stays behind herself to guard the family property.

After months in a soldiers' hospital in Afyon, Veron fears that the Turks may soon retake this town. She leaves for Smyrna, where she eventually joins her cousin, Hrpsime, in an orphanage. Hrpsime's mother, Lousapere, lives and works in Smyrna, but is too poor to support her child.

Lousapere finds work for Veron in a tobacco plant, and the two live together, visiting Hrpsime on weekends. But in August 1922, rumors of nearby Turkish victories panic the Armenians in Smyrna. In September the retreating Greek armies flee Smyrna, and Veron takes refuge with the rest of the Armenians in their church. The Turks set fire to the Armenian quarter, and the stone church becomes a prison.

A French-speaking woman passes herself off as a Red Cross worker and wins the support of an American general, who escorts the Armenians from the church to the harbor. Thousands of refugees gather there, hoping to board an outbound ship. From the harbor Veron and her aunt watch as Turkish soldiers trap Armenians in burning buildings and avenues. They remain by the shore all night, packed among the other terrified refugees.

After a few days, a ship from Greece arrives to take the refugees to Athens. Veron lives for two years in Athens before accepting the proposal of an Armenian man (whom she has not yet met) in America. In 1924 she marries Melkon Kherdian in Waukegan, Illinois.

Veron's escape. The Armenian population was tragically unprepared for the wholesale massacres of World War I. After the pogrom of 1909, rather than encourage separatism, Armenian leaders tightened their bonds with the Young Turks. Many Armenians believed that the revolt against a common enemy, the sultan, had forged unity between the Turks and Armenians. Only after the deportations began did they realize the extent of the betrayal. Veron's father exclaims, "Look around you! The Armenians are asleep in their foolish trust, and the Turks believe that two minus one equals three" (*The Road from Home,* p. 38).

The sympathetic Turk who aids the Dumehjian family during their journey to Konya was one of the many Turks who defied government orders by helping the refugees. Especially in the western cities of Turkey, the decrees of the Young Turk party outraged the local authorities. The governor of Angora (modern-day Ankara) flatly refused to deport and kill Armenians. The local police and regional military commander agreed that the Armenians were loyal Ottoman citizens. So the Young Turks replaced these uncooperative, humane authorities with reliable henchmen from Constantinople.

Veron escaped the death camp at Deir el Zor only because her father, once a wealthy man, could bribe the guards. Many of the Turkish soldiers wouldn't have bothered with bribes. An Ottoman Bank president displayed money soaked with blood and torn through with dagger holes. These bills, ripped from the bodies of murdered Armenians, were deposited in Turkish accounts with no questions or objections.

Sources. Kherdian grew up as a bilingual child and learned in his youth many of the Armenian proverbs that he included in his novel. Although he always thought of his mother's childhood as "a hell . . . that I had no intention of entering," he could not forget her request: "Someday you grow up and tell my story" (Kherdian in Sarkissian, p. 275). From fourteen pages, handwritten in Armenian, Kherdian's mother read to him the tale of her persecution and escape. Her son taped his interviews with her and, after a year's work, finished the biographical novel.

Events in History at the Time the Novel Was Written

Retaliation. In 1973 Kourken Yanikian, a man more than seventy-five years old, shot and killed two Turkish diplomats in California. One of the survivors of the Armenian holocaust, Yanikian

David Kherdian

hoped to draw attention to the unacknowledged tragedy of the Armenian genocide.

Armenian terrorist groups have claimed the lives of Turks all over the world. Unlike Yanikian, who saw his family die in the mass deportation, the terrorists are usually younger Armenians, many of whom never lived in Turkey. The two most prominent organizations, the Armenian Secret Army for the Liberation of Armenia (ASALA) and the Justice Commandos of the Armenian Genocide (JCAG), have spoiled the hopes of some Turks that the issue of the Armenian genocide might pass from the world agenda.

The crimes of terrorists have, in fact, drawn more attention to the Armenian massacres than the more patient and less violent reminders of law-abiding Armenians now dispersed throughout the world. The Turkish government has resolutely denied that the massacres took place. As recently as 1981, the Turkish ambassador to America insisted that "the accusations that Ottoman Turks, sixty-five years ago, during World War I, perpetrated systematic massacres of the Armenian population in Turkey . . . are totally baseless" (Koshy, p. 14). Others have acknowledged the massacres but disputed the death count, a statistic recorded not by Armenians but by foreign diplomats and even foreign mercenaries fighting with the Turks.

But regardless of numbers, the intent of the Young Turks to exterminate the Armenians was clear. In 1915, Talaat Pasha assured the governor of Aleppo that his government had decided to exterminate the entire Armenian population of Turkey. No one, Talaat Pasha said, who opposed the order was allowed to hold a position of authority in Turkey; women, children, and invalids would be exterminated as well as men.

The degree of success in reaching the diabolical goal would be remembered even if the individual victims were not. In 1939 the Nazi dictator Adolf Hitler made the following comparison:

> I have given orders to my Death Units to exterminate without mercy or pity men, women, and children belonging to the Polish-speaking race. It is only in this manner that we can acquire the vital territory which we need. After all, who remembers today the extermination of the Armenians?
>
> (Hitler in Kherdian, p. xii)

Present-day Armenia. With the collapse of the former Soviet Union in 1991, Armenia emerged as an independent nation. As Russian troops withdrew, old squabbles erupted between Armenia and the neighboring Republic of Azerbaijan. War broke out over the disputed Nagorny Karabakh territory, an Azerbaijani enclave situated entirely in Armenia. A cease-fire orchestrated by Russia in 1994 has quelled the fighting, but no final settlements have yet been reached.

Reception. Kherdian's novel aroused the scorn of some historians who criticized the description of the Armenian massacres as inadequate. In fact, it was told from the perspective of an innocent child confused by the turmoil of events unfolding around her. Veron's childish musings, contend these critics, understate the horror of her trials.

Other critics responded that the novel in fact succeeds because of Veron's childlike optimism. Rather than dwell on the sufferings of the Armenians, Kherdian convinces us that this is the tale of an uncomprehending girl. This, more than anything else, dramatizes the cruelty of the deportations.

For More Information

Gabrielian, M. C. *Armenia, a Martyr Nation.* New York: Fleming H. Revell, 1918.

Kherdian, David. *The Road from Home.* New York: Greenwillow, 1979.

Koshy, Ninan. *Armenian: The Continuing Tragedy.* Geneva: Commission of the Churches on International Affairs, World Council of Churches, 1984.

Lang, David Marshall. *The Armenians, a People in Exile.* London: Unwin Paperbacks, 1980.

Sarkissian, Adele, ed. *Contemporary Authors Autobiography Series.* Vol. 2. Detroit: Gale Research, 1985.

"The Rocking-Horse Winner"

by

D. H. Lawrence

Born the son of a coal-mine employee in Nottinghamshire, England, in 1885, David Herbert Lawrence is one of English literature's most controversial figures. Several of his novels—most famously, *Lady Chatterley's Lover*—were banned or burned as pornography. His wanderings took him all over the world, from Italy and the south of France to Mexico and New Mexico in the United States, and his work reflects the variety of cultures that he encountered. Throughout his writings, Lawrence focuses on the spiritual problems attendant upon industrial society, castigating people for losing touch with nature and with the wisdom of the body in their drive to accumulate more possessions. Plagued his whole life with respiratory illnesses, Lawrence died in Vence, France, in 1930; his ashes were later taken to Taos, New Mexico, and buried near the ranch where he once lived.

Events in History at the Time of the Short Story

Conspicuous consumption. Money, money, "there must be more money"—this desperate chant echoes throughout the household of the cash-strapped aristocrats in Lawrence's short story (Lawrence, "The Rocking-Horse Winner," p. 790). The tight financial circumstances experienced by the fictional family were shared by many upper-class people in the years following World War I. To understand the seemingly irrational disappointment and disillusionment of the socially ambitious mother in the story, it is necessary to

> ### THE LITERARY WORK
>
> A short story set in London in the 1920s; published in America in *Harper's Bazaar* in July 1926 and in Cynthia Asquith's collection *The Ghost Book* (London) in September 1926.
>
> ### SYNOPSIS
>
> An aristocratic woman's relentless pursuit of wealth ends in her young son's death.

realize the emphasis that was placed on possessions and the appearance of wealth among the privileged classes in early twentieth-century England, and in London in particular. A "perpetual fireworks display," as it has been called, the nonstop social calendar demanded showy clothes, extravagant menus, hordes of servants, trips abroad, and, of course, an impressive automobile (Bédarida, p. 149). This final luxury was regarded as the ultimate status symbol, which probably explains why Hester, the mother in the short story, is so bitter over having to rely on borrowing her brother's car or hiring a taxi. Indeed, it is from her son's innocent question regarding the family's lack of a car that the entire tragic story of "The Rocking-Horse Winner" ensues.

After the end of World War I, many people expected that life would revert to its former status. Perhaps a sense of relief at having emerged victorious and alive from the horrifying trenches in France led some to a frenzied and spendthrift return to prewar ostentation. The "Roaring Twenties," a hedonistic decade of relaxed morals and carefree spending often celebrated in literary works of the time, were not, despite the image, enjoyed by most English people, who remained as poor as they had ever been. In fact, even the very rich soon slipped into hard times because of England's declining economy.

World War I and its aftermath shook England's economy to its foundations. Predominantly a trading nation, England was unable to conduct commerce as usual once the war hit. And war not only disrupted economic life for its duration, it also weakened and destabilized the country in the years following Germany's surrender in 1919. Japan and the United States emerged as the world's new economic giants, and those industries by which England had traditionally prospered—coal, shipping, and textiles—slipped seriously into decline. As one author notes, "Poverty like a leaden cloak enveloped large parts of the country: their inhabitants felt doomed and without hope" (Bédarida, p. 175). It wasn't just the working class and tradesmen who felt the pinch: British landowners lost many of their renters when farmers began to buy land from aristocrats who were anxious for cash and no longer able to maintain the comfortable lifestyles to which they had become accustomed. Where possible, the aristocracy traded its land for money and thus were able in most cases to hold on to their wealth and prestige; but those of the upper and middle classes who were more dependent on earned income were not so lucky. Among these unlucky English are the parents in "The Rocking-Horse Winner."

Racetracks in England. The "sport of kings," horseracing, by which the young hero of Lawrence's story grows rich, was a sport practiced by the most ancient of civilizations; classical Greek, Roman, and Mesopotamian art all attest to its popularity. The sport's English roots extend back to the time of the Crusades of the Middle Ages, when twelfth-century English knights rode off to the Holy Land in an attempt to reassert Christianity's claim to Jerusalem. When they returned, many brought with them spectacular Arabian horses—sleek and fast steeds that they bred with English mares. The English sport branched into two main types—thoroughbred racing, in which horses race for a certain distance on a track, and steeplechase, in which the horses race a course dotted with fences and other barriers of varying heights and difficulties.

D. H. Lawrence

At first, horse races amounted to running two horses against each other to see which was fastest, but during the reign of Queen Anne (1702-1714) this changed; several horses now challenged one another, with the spectators betting on which would win. Queen Anne became the official sponsor of English horseracing, establishing in the Berkshire village of Ascot a racing track that is still in use for some of the nation's most prestigious races—the Ascot Stakes, Coventry Stakes, and Queen Elizabeth Stakes, among others. Racetracks sprang up all over the country, and the money to be won increased to such an extent that it became financially lucrative to raise and breed horses. In 1750 racing enthusiasts formed the Jockey Club to regulate the sport; this organization still exists and controls every aspect of horseracing in England. In 1791 the Club released the first of the many "General Stud" books, which listed the pedigree of every single horse that was racing in England. Thoroughbred horses—those in the General Stud book, and the only horses allowed to compete in races sponsored by the Jockey Club—are so inbred that they all trace their lineage to one of only three horses: the Byerley Turk (born 1679), the Darley Arabian (1700) or the Godolphin Arabian (1724).

The betting system known as "pari-mutuel," which dominates western racetracks, was first invented in the late nineteenth century in France. Of all wagers taken, a certain percentage automatically goes for the purse (the fund to pay owners whose horses win), for track maintenance, and to pay off other race-related expenses. The remaining money is divided by the number of bets laid on each individual horse to determine the payoff for each horse should it win. If a horse is listed as being at 10-1 odds, for example, that means that each $1 wagered will earn $10 in winnings.

THE SACRED NINE

The nine most influential public schools in England were long-established institutions, attended by boys from England's upper classes. Seven of them were boarding schools: Winchester (established 1382), Eton (1440), Shrewsbury (1552), Westminster (1560), Rugby (1567), Harrow (1571), and Charter House (1611). Two day-schools (whose students went home at the end of the day) were also counted among the nine: St. Paul's (1509) and Merchant Taylors (1561).

The British racing season is punctuated by five premier competitions, which, since 1814, have been known as the "classic" races: St. Leger Stakes, Epsom Derby, 2,000 Guineas (these first three races are known together as the English Triple Crown), the Epsom Oaks, and the 1,000 Guineas. The Epsom Derby, the most famous of the British thoroughbred races, covers 1.5 miles. The most famous steeplechase in Britain is the Grand National, which runs 4.5 miles and incorporates thirty jumps, the highest of which is slightly over five feet.

Lawrence and English Schools. In "The Rocking-Horse Winner," the family of the young hero, Paul, takes on the financial burden of the boy's education at Eton, the place of learning his father attended and England's most prestigious secondary school. Eton caters to boys aged twelve to eighteen. Before World War I, two very different schooling systems were in place: the elite and pricey public schools and the free church- or state-sponsored schools for the children of the lower and working classes. In the social atmosphere of the time, precisely where a boy went to secondary school determined the course of his entire future.

It was in the public schools, where the elite classes sent their sons, that the leaders of the country were created (the term *public school* in England is equivalent to the American private school). Children attending the elite schools could expect to study the Latin and Greek classics for the majority of their time, but also other subjects that would prepare them to assume social leadership, such as math, science, and modern languages. Furthermore, most of the best institutions were boarding schools that also taught boys how to conduct themselves socially and how to govern themselves according to age and class.

After World War I, things began to change, though less for the elite than for the children of the working class. The elite schools, even in the late twentieth century, maintain their grip on English social and political life, producing most of the prime ministers—Eton alone asserts to have schooled nineteen—and influential business people in the nation. There were, however, some nationwide changes in the years following the war. In 1918 legislation insisted that no child leave school before age fourteen, and feminist pressure on the government to ensure equal opportunity for girls increased the number of students in government-run classrooms. The curriculum in the schools for the lower classes was decidedly utilitarian, with English, not Latin, becoming the main language of study. Clearly, students in such institutions were viewed as the future's next wave of workers.

Lawrence himself benefited from earlier educational reforms, namely the Education Act of 1870, which aided schools that already existed and created an additional five thousand new ones. Lawrence attended the Beauville boarding school in Eastwood, and while most of his fellow students began their adult lives as coal miners immediately upon graduation, Lawrence won a modest scholarship to attend Nottingham High School. There, he studied English literature, German, French, shorthand, accounting, and the Bible, among other subjects. Eventually, he became a teacher himself, although he was uncertified, or one without university training. He returned to teach in Eastwood, where he came to despise the profession. Nonetheless, upon winning a prestigious scholarship to University College in Nottingham, Lawrence commenced a two-year program that would give him an official teaching credential. His final letter of recommendation reads, in part:

> He would be quite unsuitable for a large class of boys in a rough district. . . . He is em-

phatically a teacher of upper classes. Mr. Lawrence is fastidious in taste, and while working splendidly at anything that interests him, would perhaps easily tire amid the tedium and discouragements of the average classroom.

(Meyers, pp. 39-40)

Unfortunately, Lawrence wound up teaching in a rough London suburb and, true to form, proved "quite unsuitable." By 1912 he had permanently abandoned his teaching career.

The 1920s English family. At the time Lawrence was writing about the alienated relationship between mother and child in "The Rocking-Horse Winner," the English family was undergoing a transformation: married couples were having fewer babies than ever before. Of married couples in 1925, 16 percent had no children, 25 percent only one, 25 percent had two, and 14 percent had three; the three-child family in Lawrence's story is therefore unusually large, which may in part account for the mother's dissatisfaction. While the decline in children had an economic explanation—children have always been expensive—emancipation played at least as important a role in forming the expectations of women, who were looking beyond the home in increasing numbers. In 1918 women over the age of thirty first won the right to vote; in 1928 (two years after Lawrence wrote "The Rocking-Horse Winner"), all women eighteen and older could vote. In 1919 the British Parliament passed the landmark Sex Disqualification Act, allowing females equal access to universities and professions that had previously been closed to them. No longer were women content solely with the traditional roles of wife and mother.

Increasing numbers of them began to seek out intellectual and economic opportunities for themselves. Although she is unsuccessful in her professional ambitions as a fashion designer, Paul's mother attempts to make use of this new economic freedom to save herself and her family from financial ruin.

A further reason for the decline in the birthrate was the specter of overpopulation. Beginning around 1920, the English, battered by war and poverty, began to use contraception more widely. Only the rich were able to afford such scientific methods as condoms and diaphragms; the rest of the British population resorted to biological means—abstention and coitus interruptus. As historians have suggested, "between the end of the nineteenth century—the beginning of contraceptive practices—and the Second World War, when more satisfactory

methods became widespread, English men and women were 'frustrated people'" (Bédarida, p. 229). Such dissatisfaction might account for the aura of chilliness that surrounds the unhappy marriage in Lawrence's story.

The Short Story in Focus

The plot. "The Rocking Horse Winner" recounts the dark tale of young Paul and his cold, socially ambitious mother, a woman whose ruthless pursuit of wealth kills her emotionally, and him literally. Living in a style beyond their means, "in a pleasant house, with a garden, and . . . discreet servants" ("The Rocking-Horse Winner," p. 790), the upper-class parents search desperately for money to keep up appearances, but they only dig themselves deeper into debt. "There must be more money, there must be more money" is the insistent whisper that their preteen-aged son, Paul, imagines he hears everywhere about him ("The Rocking-Horse Winner," p. 790).

HORSE IMAGERY IN LAWRENCE

Horses recur throughout Lawrence's work, most strikingly in his novels *Women in Love, The Rainbow,* and *St. Mawr,* where they often draw attention to man's alienation from nature and to the rival claims of body and intellect. In his critical work, *Apocalypse and the Writings on Revelation,* Lawrence gives an indication of the metaphoric or symbolic associations that he consistently made with the horse: "Far back in our dark soul the horse prances. He is a dominant symbol: he gives us lordship: he links us, the first palpable and throbbing link with the ruddy-glowing Almighty of potency: he is the beginning even of our godhead in the flesh. And as a symbol he roams the dark underworld meadows of the soul. . . . Within the last fifty years man has lost the horse. Now man is lost. Man is lost to life and power—an underling and a wastrel. While horses thrashed the streets of London, London lived" (Lawrence in Sagar, p. 251).

When Paul asks his mother why their family has fewer luxuries (namely, a motor-car) than other family members, she replies, "Because your father has no luck" ("The Rocking-Horse Winner," p. 791). The boy immediately connects luck with money and, further, with his childlike notion of God, who, his mother suggests, may be the only person to know why luck descends on some and not on others. A bizarre ritual develops in which Paul mysteriously seeks "luck" in the frenzied riding of his nursery rocking-horse. "He would sit on his big rocking horse, charging madly into space, with a frenzy that made [his sisters] peer at him uneasily. Wildly the horse careened, the waving dark hair of the boy tossed, his eyes had a strange glare in them. The little girls dared not speak to him" ("The Rocking-Horse Winner," p. 793).

PERSONAL CIRCUMSTANCES

"The Rocking-Horse Winner" was certainly not the only story in which Lawrence treated his friends and acquaintances to fictional representations of their lives and characters. Lady Cynthia Asquith herself makes another appearance in the short story "The Ladybird" under the name "Lady Daphne." Lady Cynthia did not seem to mind her translation into art, but others were not so impressed with the caricatures of themselves that Lawrence sometimes created. Lawrence himself felt that the great art that he was producing more than justified his often mocking description of people he knew, and defended the practice in a letter to a friend: "If I need any woman for my fictional purpose, I shall use her. Why should I let any woman come between me and the flowering of my genius" (Lawrence in Meyers, p. 134). Lawrence also freely borrowed from the personas of his male acquaintances as well in his fiction.

Somehow, inexplicably, magically, the boy hears—from the horse's mouth, as it were—the name of the horse that will win whatever major British horserace is about to take place. With the help of the family gardener, Bassett, Paul starts betting on the races and slowly amasses a small fortune without the knowledge of his parents. His maternal uncle, Oscar, discovers Paul's secret and counsels him to give some money anonymously to the mother. Paul eagerly agrees. That money instantly disappears going to pay off debts and buy more things, notably a place for Paul at Eton.

The pressure to be lucky and to pick the right horse (which involves a combination of frenzied rocking and trusting his own instincts) finally becomes too much for the boy. His last big win lit-

erally costs him his life. He dies of brain fever, incoherently pleading with his mother to acknowledge how lucky he has been. The story closes with the tormented mother being offered small comfort by her brother, Oscar, who observes that the boy is better off dead than seeking so desperately after luck.

With this quotation in mind, "The Rocking-Horse Winner" becomes a sweeping indictment not only of one family's deadly lust for money, but of the spiritual death of England in general.

Batman. The young gardener, Bassett, with whom young Paul plays the horses, is described as the "batman" of Paul's Uncle Oscar. A batman is the military servant of a cavalry officer; given the story's setting in the 1920s, the two men would have served together in World War I. Of the many social ills that plagued England in the years immediately following the war's end—unemployment, poverty, labor unrest—one of the most serious was the sense of betrayal suffered by many of the common soldiers who had risked their lives in the battlefields of France, only to return home to the England for which they had fought to find themselves unappreciated and in the same dismal social plight they had been in when they left. "The ideas of universal brotherhood and prosperity they had cherished in the trenches were, for all their altruism, found to be hopelessly anarchic and at odds with the most elementary political and diplomatic realities" (Bédarida, p. 172).

Sources. "There was a woman who was beautiful, who started with all the advantages, yet she had no luck. She married for love, and the love turned to dust. She had bonny children, yet she felt that they had been thrust upon her, and she could not love them. They looked at her coldly, as if they were finding fault with her" ("The Rocking-Horse Winner," p. 790). Thus begins "The Rocking-Horse Winner"; the model for the dysfunctional family in the story is that of Lawrence's old friend and admirer, Lady Cynthia Asquith, whom he first met in 1913. Lady Cynthia—once described as "the greatest flirt that ever lived" (Feinstein, p. 107)—was the daughter of the Earl of Wemyss and had, on the surface, married well. Her husband, Herbert, was an upper-class barrister whose father was a former prime minister of England. But the Asquiths were beset with troubles: Herbert proved to be an uninspired lawyer and, worse, had suffered severe psychological trauma from his four years as a soldier on the battlefields of France during World War I. The couple was always strapped for cash, and was relegated to a peculiar place as members of the upper classes who were accustomed to wealth but had none of their own.

Cynthia and Herbert Asquith had two sons, Michael and John, both of whom were well known to Lawrence. According to one of Lawrence's biographers, Michael, the younger son, "was critical, even resentful, of the glamorous yet elusive figure who, like many women of her class, neglected her children and was not a good mother" (Meyers, p. 121). Such a sentiment seems to be echoed in the aloof narrator's voice of "The Rocking-Horse Winner." The older Asquith son, John—the model for Paul, the "hero" of the short story—suffered from an undiagnosed mental condition that was probably autism; he could be at times unmanageable, violent, and frenetic. Lawrence took a deep interest in John, speaking of him as the warped product of his parents' marriage, an opinion that the author shared with Cynthia:

> Your own soul is deficient, so it fights for the love of the child . . . he is a direct outcome of repression and falsification of the living spirit, in many generations of the Charterises [Cynthia's family] and Asquiths. He is possessed by an evil spirit that *you* have kept safely inside yourself, cynic and unbelieving. . . . John will come out all right.
>
> (Lawrence in Meyers, p. 122)

John did not, in fact, "come out all right"; like Paul in "The Rocking-Horse Winner," he met an early death. He died in an institution at age twenty-six.

Reviews. "The Rocking-Horse Winner" was singled out in a contemporary review on *The Ghost Book,* in which the story was first collected. "There are two all-but first-raters in the present volume," judged the review, "one by Miss May Sinclair, and one, 'The Rocking-Horse Winner,' by Mr. D. H. Lawrence. The rest reach a praiseworthy rather than an exciting level" (Knight, p. 27). The story has since been praised as one that comes close to reaching literary perfection.

For More Information

Bédarida, François. *A Social History of England, 1851-1990.* Translated by A. S. Forster and J. Hodgkinson. New York: Routledge, 1991.

Feinstein, Elaine. *Lawrence's Women: The Intimate Life of D. H. Lawrence.* London: HarperCollins, 1993.

Knight, Marion A., Mertice M. James, and Matilda L. Berg, eds. *Book Review Digest.* Vol. 23. New York: H. W. Wilson, 1928.

Lawrence, D. H. "The Rocking-Horse Winner." In *The Collected Short Stories of D. H. Lawrence.* Vol. 3. London: Heinemann, 1975.

McElwee, William. *Britain's Locust Years.* London: Faber, 1962.

Meyers, Jeffrey. *D. H. Lawrence: A Biography.* New York: Knopf, 1990.

Sagar, Keith. *D. H. Lawrence: Life into Art.* Athens: University of Georgia Press, 1985.

Roll of Thunder, Hear My Cry

by
Mildred Taylor

M ildred Taylor was born in Mississippi but moved to Ohio with her parents (Wilbert Lee and Deletha M. Taylor) and sister at the age of three weeks. There, she became enthralled by her father's detailed stories of his life in Mississippi and of both the hardships and the good times he had as a boy and an adult. Drawing on these stories to develop the fictional Logan family, she wrote *Roll of Thunder, Hear My Cry*. Her second novel about them, the story portrays what daily life was like for a strong black family during the Depression in the Deep South.

Events in History at the Time the Novel Takes Place

The Great Depression. *Roll of Thunder, Hear My Cry* takes place during the most significant economic depression in United States history. The Great Depression began with the stock market crash of October 29, 1929, in which millions of Americans lost their life savings. At the time, the federal government did not offer insurance to people who deposited money into banks—as it came to do later—so when a bank lost its money, depositors did too. The crash also meant that banks could no longer offer loans or credit to businesses, which in many cases meant the businesses could no longer provide paychecks for employees. By 1932 at least 25 percent of the U.S. adult population was unemployed and left to fend for itself. In desperation many resorted to work that paid meagerly, such as selling apples on the street, while others, primarily young

---

THE LITERARY WORK

A novel set in rural Mississippi during the Great Depression (1932); published in 1976.

SYNOPSIS

A young black girl tells of her life on a farm and of the difficulties her family endured as well as the strong ties they maintained.

---

men, hitched rides on trains in the hopes of escaping their hometowns and finding better opportunities elsewhere. But the Great Depression had taken hold throughout the nation.

Between 1929 and 1932, about one-third of all farmers lost their land because of foreclosure or eviction. This possibility arises in the novel for the Logans, who are among the few black Southerners fortunate enough to own their land. The majority of black farmers during this era labored as tenant farmers or sharecroppers on white-owned land. If they were sharecroppers, as was mostly the case, they used the white landowner's tools and a section of his acreage to raise the crops he wanted them to grow. In return for their labor, the sharecroppers received some supplies and a share of the harvest. More his own boss than the sharecropper, a tenant farmer rented the land, owned his crop, and paid a set amount rather than a share of his harvest.

Both the sharecropper and tenant farmer got tied into a system that had them purchasing on credit necessities that they could not yet afford, accumulating bills that would be paid from the future harvest. While in some areas sharecroppers kept as much as two-thirds of the harvest by the 1930s, the system still made it extremely unlikely that the cropper could escape debt and move into a more lucrative position. The only answer for many was to move to the coal mines, tobacco factories, or cotton mill towns of the South, or head north. Seizing economic opportunities, hundreds of thousands of blacks migrated northward in the beginning of the twentieth century. While this migration declined somewhat during the Great Depression due to a lack of jobs in the North, many Southern blacks continued to move away from the oppressive political and economic conditions in the South during this time.

The Jim Crow era. Along with the severe problems brought on by the Great Depression, blacks in the South also had to contend with the notorious restrictions of the Jim Crow era. From the late nineteenth century until the civil rights movement of the 1950s and 1960s, Jim Crow laws and traditions, which received their name from a popular nineteenth-century song, dictated a policy of extreme segregation and discrimination against blacks. Blacks and whites in the South were required to use different restrooms and drinking fountains, frequent separate theaters and restaurants, and attend separate schools. In 1896 the U.S. Supreme Court ruling in *Plessy v. Ferguson* officially sanctioned the establishment of "separate but equal" facilities for blacks and whites. As was immediately evident to visitors to the South, however, the parallel facilities were anything but equal. The fact that Cassie and her siblings have to walk to school while the white children take a bus provides a clear example of the inferior provisions allocated to blacks.

Blacks faced regular hostility and humiliation from whites. The unwritten social code of the Jim Crow era made it possible for prejudiced whites to exercise appalling control over blacks. The novel's description of Cassie's trip to Strawberry typifies the humiliation blacks encountered. When Lillian Jean demands that Cassie leave the sidewalk and then apologize to "Miz Lillian Jean," she is acting upon the social code that required blacks to defer to whites (Taylor, *Roll of Thunder,* pp. 113-16). Likewise, when Cassie is repeatedly forced to the end of the line in the Barnett Mercantile, she falls victim to the custom that permitted whites to be served before blacks. A sim-

ilar example of the Jim Crow code occurs when the Logan family in Uncle Hammer's new car is expected to pull off the bridge to let a white family's car cross first.

Southern blacks like the Logans had little recourse in the face of such injustice. The Logans are a strong, tight-knit family of individuals who care greatly about their self-esteem and respect, and at one point in the novel they take a brave stand against whites by boycotting the Wallace store. But they know their limits when it comes to confronting whites. After the incident with Lillian Jean in Strawberry, David Logan tells Cassie, "I want you to think real hard on whether or not Lillian Jean's worth taking a stand about" (*Roll of Thunder,* p. 176). Many blacks in this time period chose not to act as boldly as the Logans, instead electing to go along with the Jim Crow rules. Of utmost concern to them was surviving without offending the whites from whom blacks derived their income. The Logans' sharecropper friends who refuse to boycott the Wallace store opt to protect their livelihood at the expense of their independent voice. As is painfully evident when Mrs. Logan loses her teaching job, whites had the power to take away a black's source of income at will, even without good reason.

ORIGINS OF JIM CROW

The label Jim Crow is reported to have come from a song and dance tune set down in writing by white composer Thomas Dartmouth Rice. The tune, which became extremely popular in the 1830s, featured a black man dancing and singing lyrics that revealed his name:

> Come, listen all you gals and boys,
> I'se just from Tucky hoe;
> I'm going to sing a little song,
> My name's Jim Crow.
>
> (Bryson, p. 152)

Politics. The case of Mrs. Logan's firing illustrates the degree of political power held by whites. Since no blacks could serve on the school board, white men such as the story's Mr. Wallace and Mr. Granger could make decisions affecting all-black schools. This lack of black political power stemmed from the Mississippi Constitution of 1890, which circumvented the Fourteenth and Fifteenth Amendments to the

Roll of Thunder, Hear My Cry

United States Constitution. The Mississippi Constitution declared that in order to vote, a citizen must pay a poll tax, must not have committed any crimes of a certain nature, and must pass a reading test that demonstrates his or her understanding of part of the Mississippi Constitution. All of these restrictions made it exceedingly difficult for blacks to qualify for the voting privileges that were supposedly guaranteed by the Fifteenth Amendment to the U.S. Constitution. The high illiteracy level for blacks meant that very few would pass the reading test, which in any case was designed by whites with an interest in making the test so hard for black applicants that they would fail. They had not only to read and write a section of the Constitution but also to give a "reasonable" interpretation of it that satisfied the tester. There was also terrorism to keep black Mississippians away from the polls—white supremacists would ride to the homes of potential black voters at night to beat or even murder them in an attempt to keep them out of the political process. Thus, whites voted whites into office and legally remained in power. This helps to explain why the whites in the novel could easily commit such felonies without fear of punishment—since the police officers, judges, and lawyers were all white, it was unlikely that they would turn in other whites for taking justice into their own hands when the victims were black.

Schools. Rural, and especially rural Southern, schools during the Great Depression had the least adequate educational facilities in the country. This was even more true for rural black schools in the South. By the 1930s, eight years of mandatory education was standard throughout the country except in the rural South. There, only half of the school-aged black children attended school during the Great Depression. Sharecropper families needed their children to help earn income on the land, and the white farm owners didn't object to having the additional workers. Furthermore, many schools at this time ran out of money and simply closed, leaving students with no educational alternatives.

Southern black children received their education in completely separate and unequal facilities from their white counterparts. Generally in deplorable physical condition, black schools were plagued by inadequate supplies and insufficient space in which students could sit. A typical school consisted of one room with benches instead of desks, one stove, and a makeshift blackboard. More than two-thirds of black schools in Mississippi between 1933 and 1935 had no wa-

ter supply, 90 percent had no outhouses, and only 5 percent had a library or supplementary books of any kind. The novel's Cassie and Little Man are indeed fortunate by the standards of the place and time to receive even the dirty, ragged textbooks that have been handed down by the white schools.

Black students of this era also learned from untrained teachers. Anyone who could pass a fourth-grade test was eligible to teach in Mississippi. As late as World War II, more than half the black teachers in the state had not obtained high school diplomas. One visitor to the Dine Hollow School recorded the second-grade teacher's lesson that day, written on the board for the children to complete:

> Write your name ten times,
> Draw an dog, an cat, an rat, an boot.
> Draw an tree, an house, an cow, an goat.
> Draw an book, an apple, an tomato.
> (Tyack et al, p. 142)

The lack of basic grammar skills suggests the low level of education of the teacher. Still, many capable and caring teachers, such as Mrs. Logan, were able to keep students coming to school. Black children were, in fact, extremely interested in learning.

The Novel in Focus

The plot. Cassie Logan tells the story of how she and her family, including her three brothers, go about their daily lives during the era of Jim Crow laws and the Great Depression. Although she does not refer to the Depression or to Jim Crow laws specifically, the experiences she describes attest to the period.

Cassie recounts the growing tension that the Logan family experiences as it tries to keep its land from Harlan Granger, the white neighbor who wants to buy it. Cassie's father, David Logan, works out of town on the railroad throughout much of the story. Her mother raises the family with the help of David's mother, Big Ma. Uncle Hammer, who has moved to the North, comes to visit Cassie's family during the Christmas season.

Despite his absence, Cassie's father, David, earns the children's deepest respect as he encourages them to maintain their dignity even in the face of injustice. Early in the novel, David comes home with Mr. Morrison, a large, imposing man, whom he has hired to stay on the farm and watch for danger. There have been several incidents of arson and other crimes by whites against blacks, and tension is mounting. Since the Logans own their farm, whites in the area resent the black family, whose members face more danger than they would if they were poor tenant farmers. Mr. Granger, a white whose family used to own the Logan's land, continuously plots to purchase the land, but the Logans vow never to give it up.

The Wallaces, who own a store and a good deal of land, are presented as the most sinister of the white families, holding several families as sharecroppers on their land and organizing a white mob that ultimately endangers the lives of a local black family.

During the conflict over the Logans' land, Cassie and her brothers—Stacey, Christopher-John, and Little Man—go to school and have some adventures outside school. On one occasion, having reached their threshold of tolerance for arriving to school wet and muddy from being sprayed by the white kids' school bus, they dig a ditch which fills with water and devours the bus. Although the Logan kids have a great laugh over this triumph, their euphoria is soon replaced by terror as they fear, incorrectly, that the bus driver and other white men are stalking their house at night with plans for revenge.

The climax of the novel occurs as a result of the Barnett Mercantile robbery, when the white mob arrives at the house of T.J., a black boy, to settle the robbery matter outside the law. Mr. Jamison, a white attorney who is sympathetic to blacks, tries to force the mob to bring T.J. to court and proceed lawfully. The mob cannot be stopped, however, until a fire breaks out in the cotton fields. Fearing for their crops, everyone in the area shifts their energy into putting out the fire. In the end we learn that David Logan has set fire to his own fields to distract the mob and prevent harm from befalling any of the black families that night.

Uncle Hammer and David Logan. The two dominant male characters in the Logan family, Uncle Hammer and David Logan ("Papa"), display very different personality traits despite being brothers. Both men react openly to the injustices in their lives. Hammer, who lives in Chicago and is accustomed to the relative equality he enjoys in the North, takes pride in flaunting his material possessions, particularly his new car, in front of whites. This attitude leaves him vulnerable to resentment and acts of aggression, as Mr. Granger implies when he says, "You sure giving folks something to talk 'bout with that car of yours" (*Roll of Thunder*, p. 166). The fiery-tem-

pered Uncle Hammer tends to act on impulse and to handle negative situations by physically confronting his adversaries. For example, when Hammer hears of how Charlie Simms forced Cassie to apologize to Lillian Jean in Strawberry, he immediately heads with his gun to the Simms's house and has to be stopped by Mr. Morrison.

David Logan, on the other hand, remains calm and rational throughout most of the novel. He has lived his entire life in the South and, more than Hammer, remains keenly aware of the ramifications of confrontation with whites. Although he does have a moment in which he longs to react violently, announcing, "Well, a lot of times I feel like doing things Hammer's way" (*Roll of Thunder*, p. 221), he always keeps in mind the consequences of his actions. David's reaction to Cassie's encounter with Charlie Simms is one of inner anger but outer rationality, as he tells her:

> Cassie, there'll be a whole lot of things you ain't gonna wanna do but you'll have to do in this life just so you can survive. Now I don't like the idea of what Charlie Simms did to you no more than your Uncle Hammer, but I had to weigh the hurt of what happened to you to what could've happened if I went after him.
> (*Roll of Thunder*, p. 175)

At the end of the novel in a more desperate situation—that of young T.J.'s fate—David again keeps his family's survival uppermost in his mind but this time takes action on behalf of the victimized black. Refusing to accept the situation, he cleverly sets fire to his own farmland to prevent more violence at the hands of white people.

Sources. In 1973 Mildred Taylor met a little girl named Cassie Logan and decided to create the Logan family for her first novel, *Song of the Trees*. The characters and events in this novel and in *Roll of Thunder, Hear My Cry* closely parallel much of Taylor's family history. Taylor's family in Mississippi had owned their land and had been forced to defend it from whites, as do the Logans. Much like David Logan, Taylor's father emphasized the importance of maintaining self-respect and close family ties in the face of even the most extreme adversity. He served as Taylor's strongest role model and as the impetus for writing the Logans' story. She created Stacey Logan (Cassie's brother in the novel) to resemble her father as a boy and David Logan (Cassie's father) to parallel her father as an adult. Cassie Logan is a mix of several people in Taylor's life, including her aunt. Because of her upbringing, Taylor wanted her novel to reflect the strength of char-

Fanny Lou Hamer

acter in African Americans as well as the solid African American family unit and the support it provided in difficult situations. In school, she had been frustrated with the lack of adequate black role models in lessons and hoped that by writing about a close black family during the Jim Crow era, she would help counter a persistent stereotype of her day that blacks were passive people with weak family ties.

Events in History at the Time the Novel Was Written

Mississippi in the 1970s. The 1970s was the first full decade in which Southern blacks were free from Jim Crow laws. Prejudice and discrimination persisted, but the civil rights movement of the previous two decades had culminated in the Civil Rights Act (1964) and the Voting Rights Act (1965). The first parcel of federal legislation prohibited discrimination in the workplace and public facilities on the basis of race, while the second protected blacks' rights to vote and eliminated quasi-legal obstacles. By the 1970s, Southern blacks were in the process of trying to take advantage of the strides they had made during the civil rights era. Three years after Taylor's novel was published, there were seventeen blacks serving in the Mississippi legislature. But whites

continued to dominate Mississippi politics and business. In any case, the major victory of the civil rights movement concerned the type of terrorism evident in *Roll of Thunder, Hear My Cry*. At the end of the 1960s there began a "substantial reduction in the use of terror to control the state's black population," a result of the growing political power exerted by blacks (Dittmer, p. 426). The state's blacks could finally vote and take other political action without fear of being brutalized for doing so.

Following the lead of the civil rights movement came the women's movement, which gained further momentum in the 1970s. Participation in the women's movement came naturally to black females such as Mississippi civil rights activist Fanny Lou Hamer. Hamer's practicality, her ability to size up existing conditions—whether in civil rights, women's rights, or other causes—and then take rational action echoes the attitude exhibited by Cassie's father, David Logan, in the novel. "Ain't nothing going to be handed to you on a silver platter, nothing," said Hamer in a 1972 interview. "That's not just black people. . . . You've got to fight. Every step of the way, you've got to fight" (Dittmer, p. 434).

Black family life. Other black women felt less comfortable with the women's movement, questioning its de-emphasis on the family, which had been one of the most important focuses of African American society. By 1976 the black family had received much publicity as being in a state of demise. A part of this publicity came from the 1965 Moynihan Report, which received its name from Senator Daniel Moynihan, who headed the study. The report, titled "The Negro Family: The Case for National Action," cited the rising rates of divorce, illegitimacy, and single-parent households among blacks. Its conclusions were later challenged, with one expert pointing out that the black family was not falling apart as the Moynihan Report indicated (Billingsley, p. 199). According to some authorities, the trends Moynihan reported may have affected black families more severely than others, but they were present throughout American society. Furthermore, illegitimacy rates for blacks actually declined between 1960 and 1980, and the vast majority of black families from the 1960s to the 1980s were two-parent households (Hawes and Nybakken, p. 204). As has been shown, Mildred Taylor grew up in a strong, close-knit family in stark contrast to the type of family outlined in the Moynihan Report. When Taylor writes, "if people believe the book to be biographical, it is because I have tried to distill the essence of Black life, so familiar to most Black families" (Taylor in Dussel, p. 602), she expresses her hope that readers of all races will realize that the Logans' family values are also black values.

Reviews. *Roll of Thunder, Hear My Cry* received widespread praise from the literary community. Taylor received the Newbery Award for most distinguished contribution to American children's literature in June 1977, as well as acclaim from several literary critics. Susan Cooper sized up the novel in a review for the *Christian Science Monitor*:

> [A] good straightforward novel about racial prejudice, fierce without being bitter, wholly absorbing. . . . The author brings a controlled power from her own family background to electrify her calm prose toward a wonderfully shaped climax.
>
> (Cooper in Gunton, p. 419)

There was some criticism of the character development in the novel. One reviewer recognized the novel as "burningly honest," then discussed what she deemed a weakness:

> The strength of feeling in the book has been too much for the characters. They remain dim, stiff figures manipulated for the sake of certain key situations, and they are so far based on the author's own family history that they never achieve the independent identity essential to a novel.
>
> (Fisher in Gunton, p. 421)

In contrast, other reviewers spoke of how real the characters seemed. And Taylor was praised for her unusual ability to tell the story of a time and place in which she never lived. Although she visited her extended family in Mississippi on a regular basis, she had never experienced Mississippi life during the Jim Crow era. The stories passed down from her father and other relatives provided enough of a feeling for the setting to enable her to create *Roll of Thunder, Hear My Cry*.

For More Information

Billingsley, Andrew. *Black Families in White America.* Englewood Cliffs, N.J.: Prentice-Hall, 1968.

Bryson, Bill. *Made in America: An Informal History of the English Language in the United States.* New York: Avon, 1994.

Dittmer, John. *Local People: The Struggle for Civil Rights in Mississippi.* Urbana: University of Illinois Press, 1994.

Dussel, Sharon L. "Profile: Mildred D. Taylor." *Language Arts* 58, no. 5 (May 1981): 599-604.

Gunton, Sharon, ed. *Contemporary Literary Criticism.* Vol. 21. Detroit: Gale Research, 1982.

Hawes, Joseph M., and Elizabeth I. Nybakken. *American Families: A Research Guide and Historical Handbook.* New York: Greenwood, 1991.

Taylor, Mildred D. *Roll of Thunder, Hear My Cry.* New York: Dial, 1976.

Tyack, David, Robert Lowe, and Elisabeth Hanson. *Public Schools in Hard Times.* Cambridge, Mass.: Harvard University Press, 1984.

Roll of Thunder, Hear My Cry

A Room of
One's Own

by
Virginia Woolf

Born Adeline Virginia Stephen in 1882, Virginia Woolf is one of the most haunting literary figures of the twentieth century. She was a member of the famed, and sometimes resented, set of artists and intellectuals known as the Bloomsbury Group, whose members strove to free themselves from the moral and intellectual strictures of Victorianism. A respected literary and cultural critic, a prominent essayist and sought-after lecturer, and an avant-garde novelist, Woolf was at the center of England's literary culture until her suicide in 1941. *A Room of One's Own* speaks to those women—and men—on the verge of a new world of gender relations, addressing the uncertainty of how to behave, think, and write at the foreseeable end of the history of female oppression.

Events in History at the Time of the Essay

Woolf's biography. Adeline Virginia Stephen was born on January 25, 1882, the daughter of Sir Leslie Stephen, a renowned Victorian philosopher and writer. Upon their mother's death (May 5, 1895), Virginia and her sister Vanessa assumed the care of their grief-stricken father, entering in many ways into the traditional feminine roles of the Victorian era—those of housekeeper and giver of emotional support. The Stephen girls were educated at home by their father, and it was an education supplemented by their explorations of the family's substantial library.

Their father died in 1904, leaving considerable wealth to his four children. Upon his death,

> **THE LITERARY WORK**
>
> An essay written in England in the late 1920s; published in 1929.
>
> **SYNOPSIS**
>
> One of the milestones of modern British feminist thought, Woolf's essay explores the social and economic factors that determine what—and whether—women will write.

Virginia, Vanessa (a famous painter known by her married name of Vanessa Bell), and their brothers, Thoby (who died shortly thereafter) and Adrian, moved together to the Bloomsbury district of London and began a long association with a group of avant-garde writers, artists, and intellectuals who eventually became known as the Bloomsbury Group. Prominent members of this circle included art critic Clive Bell (who married Vanessa Stephen), painter Duncan Grant, novelist E. M. Forster, writer Lytton Strachey, and philosopher John Maynard Keynes. Together as a group and later separately, these individuals would eventually become a dominant force on the English cultural scene.

In 1912, after some hesitation, Virginia Stephen married Leonard Woolf, who, as the editor of the journal the *Nation*, was to become one of the country's most prominent political journalists. Their marriage, while satisfying to both of them, was blighted by medical advice warn-

Virginia and Leonard Woolf

ing Virginia not to have children, and by their mutual disappointment in their physical relationship. How much of this disappointment was related to Virginia's own bisexual tendencies and the fact that she had been sexually abused in childhood remains uncertain. In any case, in 1917 she and her husband founded Hogarth Press. At the beginning of their publishing enterprise, they did all of the printing work themselves—more as a hobby than anything—and were responsible for making known the work of such eventually famous writers as T. S. Eliot and the aforementioned Forster. Virginia set the type for Eliot's famous poem *The Waste Land* herself, in part to keep her mind off her own writing, which tended to absorb her to the point of exhaustion. Hogarth Press gradually became one of the most powerful presses in England, thanks in part to the Woolfs' decision to spare Virginia the pain and aggravation of dealing with editors by publishing her writing themselves.

Woolf's first novel, *The Voyage Out,* was published in March of 1915, and by the time of her death some twenty-five years later, she had written such masterpieces as *Mrs. Dalloway* (1925), *To the Lighthouse* (1927) and *The Waves* (1931). Her characteristic and highly influential style, sometimes called "stream of consciousness," follows the mental patterns of different characters and of the narrator, with the style of her sentences mimicking the often illogical or nonlinear progression of thought itself. In *A Room of One's Own*, Woolf suggests that the kinds of sentences most commonly to be found in novels written by men are in fact masculine sentences, and that women novelists will, as Jane Austen did, naturally develop a syntax more reflective of their way of thinking. This idea, and the way in which she put it into practice in the writing of her own novels, is perhaps Woolf's most enduring legacy to English literature.

THE BEST THING

In *A Room of One's Own*, Woolf writes movingly of Judith Shakespeare, an imaginary sister to the great poet, who, deprived of the ability and opportunity to develop her gift as a writer, took her own life in despair. During her last struggle with madness, Woolf similarly felt herself incapable of pursuing the reading and writing that sustained her creative life. Her final note to Leonard Woolf reads in part:

> I feel certain that I am going mad again. . . . And I shan't recover this time. I begin to hear voices, and I can't concentrate. So I am doing what seems the best thing to do. . . . You see I can't even write this properly. I can't read. . . . I don't think two people could have been happier than we have been.
>
> (Virginia Woolf in Leonard Woolf, pp. 93-4)

From an early age Virginia Woolf suffered from the ravages of mental illness—prompted, it has been suggested, by the sudden death of her mother or perhaps by having been sexually molested as a child. Her father's death brought on her first full-fledged breakdown; many more would follow. She battled her madness with the help of the always attentive Leonard Woolf. On March 28, 1941, however, tragedy struck. Virginia was feeling distraught by the London air raids and the horrors of World War II in general—Leonard Woolf was Jewish and the couple had a suicide plan in the event that the Germans should conquer Britain. Also feeling worn out

from writing her novel *Between the Acts* and fearful that she was about to descend irrevocably into another period of insanity, Woolf wrote a note of thanks and apology to her husband and disappeared. He found her walking stick by the banks of a nearby river; three weeks later, her body washed ashore.

Bloomsbury. Most Thursday nights in the period after the death of Virginia Woolf's father and before World War I, the Bloomsbury artists and intellectuals would gather for conversation in the home of Virginia and her brother Adrian, or in the nearby house where Virginia's sister Vanessa lived with her husband Clive Bell. They engaged in intellectual, artistic, philosophical, and sexual discussions. Although the people who gathered together had very different interests—ranging from painting, history, and biography to political philosophy, feminism, and fiction—they shared certain common interests. The Bloomsbury circle is said to have cherished above all else aestheticism, or the pursuit and creation of beauty in art. Books written by the Bloomsbury set aimed for a mix or marriage of emotion and intellect. In the religious sphere, many of them were atheists. They worked to dismiss reticence and to speak frankly and openly about sex and the body. They looked to ancient Greek society as a model for the ideal culture. Thanks to the Greeks' use of slaves, ordinary male citizens were free to think and create without being troubled by minor daily hindrances that could distract one from one's artistic and intellectual development. No one in the Bloomsbury Group, of course, believed in reinstituting slavery. On the other hand, its members regarded a paid servant or two as almost essential.

As they grew individually to become the most famous writers, painters, and critics in Britain, the Bloomsbury friends came to practically control the cultural life of London. They decided whose writings were published, whose work was reviewed in the most prestigious journals, and whose paintings were displayed in the finest galleries. Often enough, it tended to be each other's work that commanded the most attention, probably because they shared a common intellectual or aesthetic approach. Naturally, however, this aesthetic camaraderie set them up for all kinds of hostile reactions, and the stereotype of the Bloomsbury Group that endures to the present tends to be quite negative:

> [T]he public legend made them out to be rude busybodies in painting, politics, economics, the novel. They espoused "the new," it was alleged,

more for oddity and sensationalism than anything else. . . . They were bad-mannered egoists. They were self-indulgent. They were homosexuals or lesbians. They practiced free love.

(Edel, p. 255)

Woolf herself, as well as her husband and brother-in-law, protested, denying that there had ever been a "group." It was, they said, only an informal collection of friends and acquaintances interested in some of the same things. The issue remains a matter of debate, but the influence of the people involved on one another and within London was undeniably strong.

Feminism in Britain. *A Room of One's Own* was written in 1928, only a decade after British women over thirty were granted voting rights for the first time. British feminism had been in a sort of holding pattern for over a century after the death in 1797 of its most prominent feminist, the famous Mary Wollstonecraft; scholars cite the eighteenth-century Wollstonecraft as Woolf's most immediate predecessor in the formation of English feminist thought. In an essay published in 1929, the same year that *A Room of One's Own* appeared, Woolf wrote that Wollstonecraft "is alive and active, she argues and experiments, we hear her voice and trace her influence even now among the living" (Woolf, *Women and Writing,* p. 103). The scandal that surrounded the name of Mary Wollstonecraft, who was the mother of an illegitimate child, had kept well-bred women away from the feminist movement in England.

The course of women's suffrage and women's rights in general moved along slowly in England. Not until the Education Act of the 1870s was it made compulsory to educate girls in England, for example. Victorian mores had, at least until the turn of the century, dictated the "proper" female roles of wife and mother, dutiful daughter, and overall gentle angel in the house. In 1903 Emmeline Pankhurst, with her daughters Sylvia and Christabel, founded a radical organization called the Women's Social and Political Union, made up of English women who had the goal of political equality firmly in mind. They were adamant in their tactics. They harassed politicians, incited riots, and went to jail—until the outbreak of World War I turned their attention to the larger issues involved in Britain's struggle against Germany. They were eventually rewarded for this combination of rebellion and support, when in 1918, British women over the age of thirty were permitted to vote for the first time, with wider enfranchisement rights coming eleven years later.

Mary Wollstonecraft

A Room of One's Own, written in 1928, thus speaks to the newly enfranchised, which perhaps accounts for the deep seriousness with which it treats the relationship between material and political success and the production of a literature representative of women's responses to the world:

> Intellectual freedom depends upon material things. Poetry depends upon intellectual freedom, and women have always been poor, not for two hundred years merely, but from the beginning of time. Women have had less intellectual freedom than the sons of Athenian slaves. . . . That is why I have laid so much stress on money and a room of one's own.
>
> (Woolf, *A Room of One's Own,* p. 104)

"Oxbridge." Although she insists that it is an imaginary place, the university that is named "Oxbridge" in *A Room of One's Own* is clearly a combination of Oxford and Cambridge, the two oldest and most prominent universities in England. Cambridge, where the women's colleges of Newnham and Girton are located, dates from the beginning of the thirteenth century; Oxford was founded slightly earlier, sometime in the twelfth century. The universities began as schools for the training of teachers and clergy. Women were first admitted to Cambridge as students in 1869, but were not made full members of the university until 1948. Woolf wrote in *A Room of One's Own* that a university official once shooed her away from the library because a woman required a male chaperon to enter the building. Actually at the time that Woolf wrote *A Room of One's Own*, British university women held a status unequal to that of men at Cambridge, but this was not the case at Oxford. *A Room of One's Own* specifically addresses the female residents of Newnham and Girton at Cambridge University, perhaps for that reason.

The British Museum. "If truth is not to be found on the shelves of the British Museum, where, I asked myself, picking up a notebook and a pencil, is truth?" (*A Room of One's Own*, p. 26). The first place that the narrator of "A Room of One's Own" visits in search of the answer to the essay's central questions, which concern the relationship between gender and the production of texts, is London's massive British Museum. The British Museum was founded in 1753, when the government acquired a large collection of books and artifacts that it decided to combine with an already-existing collection of early manuscripts. Over the centuries the collection was augmented by contributions from the British royal family. In 1973, a few decades after Woolf's essay, the library of the British Museum would be combined with the holdings of other large libraries all over the country to form the British Library. Attached to the museum, this library is located in Bloomsbury, the part of London in which Virginia Woolf lived.

The Essay in Focus

The contents. "A woman must have money and a room of her own if she is to write fiction" (*A Room of One's Own*, p. 6); this is the central contention of "A Room of One's Own." Throughout the six-part essay, which is a reworking of a speech she gave female college students, Woolf calls into question the social forces that keep women financially impoverished, forces that guarantee their daughters will inherit none of the power, prestige, ease, and education that sons inherit from their fathers. The immediate prompt for such ruminations is the experience at "Oxbridge" University of a fictitious "I," a female who is informed that she, like all women, may not enter the library without a letter of introduction or male companion. This fictitious female compares the luxurious, gracious meal she

enjoys as a guest at a men's college with the miserable fare served at the women's college. It becomes clear to her that the women's college is impoverished because women themselves are generally impoverished, and that it is almost impossible for women to come up with the sizeable sums of money required to provide a comfortable atmosphere in which their daughters could study: "At the thought of all those women working year after year and finding it hard to get two thousand pounds together, and as much as they could do to get thirty thousand pounds, we [she and a friend] burst out in scorn at the reprehensible poverty of our sex. What had our mothers been doing then that they had no wealth to leave us? Powdering their noses? Looking in shop windows?" (*A Room of One's Own*, p. 21). Of course, she notes, women are poor not because they do not work or because they are frivolous with their money, but because they are not paid for the work that they do: raising a family and taking care of the home.

The quest for more concrete proof on why women are poorer than men leads Woolf's narrator in the second part of the essay to the British Museum library, where she discovers that there is a staggering number of books about women written by men. In some of these books, Woolf discovers an anger that she attributes to the male need to boost his own sense of power and authority by oppressing and denigrating the female. But instead of despising such men, Woolf's narrator tries to explain their attitude toward women in terms of material considerations of wealth and power; the education of these men, she realizes, has been limited and their experience narrowed by the "rage for acquisition" (*A Room of One's Own*, p. 38) to such an extent that they become objects of pity to those women liberated, by even limited wealth, from their control: "[W]atch in the spring sunshine the stockbroker and the barrister going indoors to make more money and more money and more money when it is a fact that five hundred pounds a year will keep one alive in the sunshine" (*A Room of One's Own*, p. 38).

Having returned from the British Museum without a scientific proof of why women are always poorer than men, Woolf's narrator then decides to look closely at the material conditions of women in the Renaissance, trying to account for the almost complete silence of women writers during that time of bursting creative output in England. To this end she presents the haunting imaginary figure of Shakespeare's sister, Judith, who was as gifted as her brother but who, as a woman, was not permitted to develop her genius. Forced to run away from home because her parents promised her in marriage to someone she did not wish to wed, and hopeful that she might find work on the London stage, Judith Shakespeare ends up impoverished, pregnant, unwed, and dead by her own hand. Such must have been the fate, Woolf speculates, of any talented girl in those days. Even if she had managed to overcome all of the prejudice and danger attached to being a woman living by her own wits in Renaissance London, all that she could have produced would have been "twisted and deformed," born of anger, despair, and frustration (*A Room of One's Own*, p. 49). In order to produce works of enduring worth and beauty, concludes section 3 of the essay, a writer must have peace of mind, something denied women in general throughout history.

In section 4, Woolf looks at the literary efforts of women in the recent past, first focusing on the generally poor writers, such as Aphra Behn. She speculates as to their potential as writers if they had not all had to deal with discouragement and lack of support or education. Then she turns her attention to the masters of nineteenth-century fiction—George Eliot, Jane Austen, Emily Brontë, and Charlotte Brontë—proposing that even they might have written more and produced better had they not suffered from being women in an age when that meant being kept at home and subjected to strict codes of behavior. Also in this section comes perhaps Woolf's most radical idea about the relationship between gender and writing. She proposes that at the sentence level, women write differently than men, and produce their own type of writing, variations that are reflected in the differing bodies of men and women:

> The book has somehow to be adapted to the body, and at a venture one would say that women's books should be shorter, more concentrated, than those of men, and framed so that they do not need long hours of steady and uninterrupted work. For interruptions there will be.
>
> (*A Room of One's Own*, p. 74)

A Room of One's Own turns, in section 5, to the appearance of literary works by women in which they are presented as relating primarily to themselves or to other women, and do not serve as the foils or background for the exploits of men. Such works will allow the recovery of lost (because unspoken) everyday experiences of women. Or at the very least, says the essay, the

historical process of obliteration will be arrested. It also maintains that one should not write strictly as a woman; a person, that is, should not allow gender to dominate the story being told.

The conclusion of *A Room of One's Own* puts forward Woolf's famous idea that the mind of the artist is androgynous, which means that there is a little bit of the masculine in every feminine brain, and vice versa. If this were to be accepted and understood, then it might allow one sex to write insightfully about the other, and perhaps without anger or bitterness. The deliberate shunting of the feminine from the minds of male writers has impoverished their work, she holds, and the same must surely be said of the books written by women too conscious of being women.

Woolf's essay has a final message for the young and educated women of Newnham and Girton Colleges: secure your independence and your leisure, and the stifling bonds of resentment and poverty will fall away from you. Only if this happens will you be able to become great artists.

Aphra Behn. "All women together ought to let flowers fall upon the tomb of Aphra Behn . . . for it was she who earned them the right to speak their minds. It is she—shady and amorous as she was—who makes it not quite fantastic for me to say to you tonight: Earn five hundred a year by your wits" (*A Room of One's Own*, p. 63).

The "shady and amorous" Aphra Behn (1640-89) of whom Woolf speaks is held to be the first woman in England to earn her living by writing. Respectable, aristocratic women, like the Duchess of Winchilsea (whom Woolf mentions in her essay), had put pen to paper before, but they hardly had to support themselves through the sale of their work. Behn, on the other hand, was an adventurer who went to Surinam and other far-flung places, a bit of a rogue with a sharp tongue and scandalous language, a woman not always careful with whom she consorted, and possibly a spy for Charles II during the Anglo-Dutch wars. She wrote novels (the most famous being *Oronooko, or the History of the Royal Slave*) and at least fifteen plays that sold well enough for her to support herself. Woolf's closest friend, Vita Sackville-West, published a biography of Behn in 1928, the year before *A Room of One's Own* appeared, which also asserted that Behn had opened the door for other women, despite the fact that many people accused her of being a low-bred harlot:

> But although she might lay her scenes in brothels and bedrooms, although her language

is not to be recommended to the queasy, and although in her private life she followed the dictates of inclination rather than of conventional morality, Aphra Behn, in the history of English letters, is something much more important than a mere harlot. The fact that she wrote is much more important than the quality of what she wrote.

(Sackville-West, p. 16)

Sources. *A Room of One's Own* was based on two lectures that Woolf gave in October of 1928 at Cambridge's women's colleges, the first to the Arts Society at Newnham College, and the second at Girton College. Throughout her essay, she is careful to emphasize that the experiences written of are not personal, but the universal experiences of any woman faced with the daunting task of establishing herself as a

---

WHAT IS A WOMAN?

In an address given to the National Society for Women's Service (January 21, 1931), two years after the publication of *A Room of One's Own,* Woolf continued the work she began in that essay, alluding to the directive she had given to young women to write. The problem now, says Woolf, is in defining "woman":

> [T]hat young woman [sitting in her room writing] had only to be herself. Ah, but what is "herself"? I mean, what is a woman? I assure you, I do not know. I do not believe that you know. I do not believe that anyone can know until she [i.e., woman] has expressed herself in all the arts and professions open to human skill.
>
> (Woolf, *Women and Writing,* p. 60)

---

writer in a country governed almost exclusively by the desires and dictates of men. But, in a letter dated June 8, 1933, Woolf revealed the autobiographical nature of her work to her friend Ethel Smyth, while giving her some advice about writing as a feminist: "Leave your own case out of it. . . . I didn't write 'A room' without considerable feeling even you will admit; I'm not cool on the subject. And I forced myself to keep my own figure fictitious; legendary. If I had said, Look here am I uneducated, because my brothers used all the family funds which is the fact—Well, they'd have said; she has an axe to grind; and no one would have

taken me seriously" (Woolf, *The Letters of Virginia Woolf,* p. 195).

Reviews. Woolf, generally her own harshest critic, predicted the critical reception of her essay on the eve of its publication by Hogarth Press. "I will here sum up my impressions before publishing *A Room of One's Own.* . . . [I] suspect that there is a shrill feminine tone in it which my intimate friends will dislike. I forecast, then . . . that the press will be kind and talk of its charm and sprightliness; also I shall be attacked for a feminist and hinted at for a Saphhist [a lesbian]. . . . I shall get a good many letters from young women. I am afraid it will not be taken seriously. Mrs Woolf is so accomplished a writer that all she says makes easy reading . . . this very feminine logic . . . a book to be put in the hands of girls" (Woolf, *A Writer's Diary,* p. 148). Her prediction was accurate in some respects, but within four months, by February 14, 1930, *A Room of One's Own* had sold 10,000 copies.

On November 9, 1929, the British journal *Nation and Athenaeum* reviewed *A Room of One's Own;* the reviewer was a woman, Lyn Irvine. As interpreted by Woolf herself, one of Irvine's criticisms of Woolf's reasoning was that, when she writes of the meager diet enjoyed by the women's college in the essay's first section, Woolf does not admit that men would not sit still for such treatment. Woolf responded to the charge: in her "intelligent and generous article" Miss Irvine "infers that men are therefore endowed with some desirable power that women lack" (Woolf, *Women and Writing,* p. 53). However, in Woolf's opinion, the case is actually that the entire British working class, male and female, is too poor to escape such a meager, or bland and repetitive, diet. She thus points her finger more directly at middle-class men than at men in general: "It is the middle-class man to whom we owe our art; but whether he would have enjoyed his very valuable degree of comfort and prosperity had the duty of child-birth been laid upon him in the flower of his youth, and had all the professions been closed to him by his sex, seems to me disputable" (Woolf, *Women and Writing,* pp. 53-4). In this way, Woolf shut the door firmly but politely on the criticism that women were oppressed because they somehow chose to be.

For More Information

Caws, Mary Ann. *Women of Bloomsbury: Virginia, Vanessa and Carrington.* New York: Routledge, 1990.

Edel, Leon. *Bloomsbury: House of Lions.* Philadelphia: Lippincott, 1976.

Sackville-West, Vita. *Aphra Behn.* New York: Viking, 1928.

Woolf, Leonard. *The Journey Not the Arrival Matters: An Autobiography of the Years 1939-1969.* London: Hogarth, 1973.

Woolf, Virginia. *The Letters of Virginia Woolf, Volume 5: 1932-1935.* Edited by Nigel Nicholson and Joanne Trautmann. New York: Harcourt Brace Jovanovich, 1979.

Woolf, Virginia. *A Room of One's Own.* London: Grafton, 1988.

Woolf, Virginia. *Women and Writing.* Introduction by Michele Barrett. London: Women's Press, 1979.

Woolf, Virginia. *A Writer's Diary: Being Extracts from the Diary of Virginia Woolf.* Edited by Leonard Woolf. London: Hogarth, 1954.

"The Secret Life of Walter Mitty"

by

James Thurber

Born in Columbus, Ohio, James Thurber (1894-1961) moved to New York in 1926, where he worked as a reporter, writer, editor, and cartoonist. The unknown Thurber began sending his stories and humorous essays to a new and equally unknown magazine in the city, the *New Yorker*. Like most young authors, he suffered the disappointment of multiple rejections, but eventually his work and tenacity ended with the sale of his short story "An American Romance" to the discriminating magazine in 1927. Following the sale, the *New Yorker*'s founder, Harold Ross, offered Thurber a position on the magazine staff. Thurber left the staff in 1933, remaining a contributor to the magazine, the original publisher of his story "The Secret Life of Walter Mitty." The story comments on the average man's unattainable dreams of grandeur which, when coupled with common stress, can drive him into a world of egotistical fantasy.

Events in History at the Time of the Short Story

The birth of radio entertainment. Before television had captured audiences, entertainment seekers turned to their radios for music, drama, and the news. American radio came into being on November 2, 1920, in a small shack outside of Pittsburgh, Pennsylvania. On this experimental broadcast, radio announcers relayed to listeners the results of the presidential election between Warren G. Harding and James M. Cox. Despite this humble beginning, the owners of sta-

THE LITERARY WORK

A short story set in a suburban Connecticut town during the mid- to late 1930s; published in 1939.

SYNOPSIS

Through his imagination, a man leaves behind his humdrum life for the road to high adventure.

tion KDKA, Westinghouse Electric Company, held fast to their belief in the profitability of the medium. Their faith paid off, for within eighteen months of that initial news program, both the American public and commercial enterprise had turned radio into a national fad. Two years following the inaugural broadcast, 1.5 million homes owned radio sets that could tune in to the 550 stations nationwide.

By the late 1920s, American radio produced a variety of pleasant but insipid shows. Poets like Tony Wons and cheerful hosts like Cheerio (Eugene Fields) mingled their broadcasts with soft music and gentle words. Not until the appearance of *Amos 'n' Andy* in August of 1929 did radio become a format of engaging entertainment. Its two white dialecticians, Freeman Gosden and Charles Correll, posed as black characters whose daily trials and conversations amused the nation. Almost 60 percent of the United States tuned in Monday through Saturday to hear the fifteen-minute program. The show brought success not only to its creators, but to radio programming in general. Both network officials and advertisers jumped on the idea of other serial format shows. By the end of 1929, two other types had come into being. *The Rise of the Goldbergs* introduced drama to the radio waves, while the *Rudy Vallee Show* ushered in the variety-show format.

Originally the motion-picture tycoons of Hollywood resisted involvement with radio. Studios would not allow stars to "cheapen" their box-office appeal by appearing on programs, and most radio stations could not afford the fees demanded by such high-profile personalities. However, with the appearance of *Lux Radio Theater,* a series that dramatized scenes in movies for the radio, the relationship between Hollywood and the airwaves changed. The *Lux* program ran successfully from the mid-1930s through 1955. It featured such stars as William Powell and Myrna Loy in *The Thin Man;* Clark Gable and Claudette Colbert in *It Happened One Night;* Cary Grant, Katharine Hepburn, and James Stewart in *The Philadelphia Story;* and Humphrey Bogart and Walter Huston in *The Treasure of Sierra Madre.*

With such big names appearing over the airwaves, America witnessed the birth of the cult of celebrity. Average listeners not unlike the fictional Walter Mitty could tune into these nightly broadcasts and lose themselves in the fantasy worlds of invented characters whose lives were, of course, much more exciting than their own. Often, fantasy and reality became confused. On October 30, 1938, film director Orson Welles presented a radio adaptation of the H. G. Wells novel **The War of the Worlds** (also covered in *Literature and Its Times*). Enacting the program as if Martians had really invaded America, Orson Welles caused a panic among those listeners who had missed the opening explanation about the nature of the program. From New York City to Seattle, the United States was hit with mass hysteria. This single event demonstrated both the need for programming regulation and the susceptibility of the American public to fictional influences.

Real-life heroes of the 1930s. Most of Thurber's short story takes place in the imagination of Walter Mitty. While the character conjures up several invented roles for himself, the personalities he imagines actually resemble historical figures of the day. James Thurber never acknowledged specific allusions to real-life people in his story. In fact, he felt that "no writer can ever put his finger on the exact inspiration of any character in fiction that is worthwhile" (Thurber in Bern-

Orson Welles on the radio.

stein, p. 311). Nonetheless, Mitty-like daydreamers could turn to some real-life heroes of the 1930s for inspiration.

Medical hero. One of Mitty's first adventures finds him in the shoes of a world-renowned surgeon. Not only is the imaginary Dr. Mitty adept at the operating table, but he also leads his field in research. A colleague remarks, "I've read your book on streptothricosis. . . . A brilliant performance, sir" (Thurber, "The Secret Life of Walter Mitty," pp. 273-74). Within five minutes Dr. Mitty saves a prestigious patient from death's door, and fixes the hospital's anaesthetizer with a common fountain pen. Thurber could have been thinking of Sir Alexander Fleming when he concocted this scenario.

Although no records exist of Fleming reviving hospital equipment, history still remembers him as a brilliant doctor whose work forever altered the course of modern medicine. Born in a rural Scottish community in 1881, Fleming traveled to metropolitan London to begin his medical studies at the age of twenty. Early on, he built his reputation for effortless perfection. Not only did Fleming win the Hospital Entrance Scholarship, the Chemistry Prize, and the Biology Prize within his first year of medical school, but he

Al Capone

also made a name for himself as an expert marksman in the Rifle Club, a member of the water polo team, an active participant in the Dramatic Society, and a member of both the Medical and Debating Societies. He was, in reality, the Renaissance man, or expert at multiple endeavors, that Mitty could only be in his mind. With each year of schooling, Fleming's accolades grew. By the time he completed his exams in 1909, Fleming had become one of the few students to qualify in both the research and the surgical fields.

During the course of his studies, in 1904, Fleming became a member of Almroth Wright's laboratory staff at St. Mary's Medical School in London. For some time Wright had been experimenting with vaccinations as possible cures to bacterial diseases. As a collaborator on many of Wright's research papers, Fleming began to make a name for himself as a bacteriologist. His years of work came to fruition in 1928 when Fleming noticed something peculiar about a petri dish he had saved from the garbage can. It was covered with a bacteria, staphylococci (a bacteria responsible for ailments ranging from strep throat to pneumonia), except in the areas where mold had begun to grow. The mold seemed able to attack the infectious organism. This seemingly

serendipitous discovery eventually led to the development of penicillin. In 1945 Fleming received the Nobel Prize for his work in this field.

Gangster. Walter Mitty's next adventure has him in the role of a notorious killer who claims on the witness stand, "With any known make of gun . . . I could have killed Gregory Fitzhurst at three hundred feet with my left hand" ("The Secret Life of Walter Mitty," p. 275). Although cities like Chicago and New York in the 1920s and 1930s were home to large crime families, perhaps the most well-known mobster was Alphonse Capone. Born in Brooklyn, New York, in 1899, Capone quickly came to dominate the bootleg liquor scene during the era of Prohibition (1920-33). By killing all of his rivals, Capone eliminated any competition during the Chicago gang wars of the 1920s. The single event that earned Capone his true notoriety, however, was the St. Valentine's Day Massacre.

Late in the year of 1928, two brothers in the rival "Bugs" Moran gang received orders to assassinate Capone's chief lieutenant, Jack McGurn. Unfortunately for the brothers, Pete and Frank Gusenberg, and the entire Moran gang, the assassination attempt failed. McGurn, recovering from multiple gunshot wounds, began planning his revenge not only against the two brothers, but against their comrades as well. Al Capone gave his blessing and $10,000 for the counterattack, although he wanted no active role in the killings.

Over a period of weeks, McGurn assembled a team of assassins and closely watched the movements of the Moran gang. He decided to gain access to the gang through the disguise of Chicago policemen on a raid. With the help of an associate, McGurn acquired an authentic police car and uniforms for the assassins to wear. He then arranged for a dummy shipment of whiskey to be sold to Moran at an abandoned garage. Capone kept in constant contact with McGurn during this planning stage, and on the morning of February 14, 1929, the plan went into action.

McGurn's assassins entered the garage, looking like policemen on a routine raid. They ordered the seven Moran gangsters to face the wall with their hands on their head. After disarming the men, the "cops" opened fire with two machine guns, a sawed-off shotgun, and a .45 caliber hand gun. After seeing the seven slaughtered men, a federal detective announced, "Nothing that's ever happened in this town since Prohibition can compare with [this]. . . . Never has there been such a massacre" (Bergreen, p. 312). The "massacre" is how the event quickly came to be known. The fact that the killers had used police uniforms particularly bothered the law and the public, and "Bugs" Moran fingered Capone as the mastermind of the entire affair. With the nationwide headlines, Capone was catapulted into the public eye as the most well-known gangster of the era. Like Walter Mitty's fantasy mobster, however, Capone eventually faced the witness stand. Although authorities could never link him to his bootlegging activities or to the many murders attributed to him, Capone eventually went to prison in October of 1931 on income-tax evasion charges.

Air force pilot. In one of Mitty's final episodes, he assumes the role of an air force pilot. This fantasy perhaps comes closest to resembling one of Thurber's own wishes. Because of blindness in one eye, Thurber could not participate in either of the world wars. He himself regretted this inability to fight. As Captain Mitty, Thurber's character dares to fly alone through enemy territory even though a colleague remarks, "It takes two men to handle that bomber. . . " ("The Secret Life of Walter Mitty," p. 276).

A real-life American who braved what became the most well-known solo flight of the era was Charles Lindbergh. As a young man, Lindbergh ran more toward adventure than academics, and decided to pursue a career in aviation after dropping out of college. While in pilot's training, the young Lindbergh led his class in both talent and intellect. Although he had failed in his university engineering courses, as a pilot he earned the top marks in his class. Lindbergh might have just enjoyed the life of any commercial pilot, however, had it not been for Raymond Orteig. In 1927, this wealthy businessman began a contest which would award $25,000 to the first pilot to fly a solo, nonstop route from New York to Paris, France. Although two men had lost their lives already in pursuit of this goal, Lindbergh felt confident that he could accomplish the feat.

At 7:52 a.m. (New York time) on May 20, 1927, Lindbergh boarded his plane, the *Spirit of St. Louis,* at Roosevelt Field in Long Island. During the ensuing 33 1/2 hours, Lindbergh fought off sleep—and fear of failure—to land his plane safely on the other side of the Atlantic. He arrived at Le Bourget airport in Paris at 10:22 p.m. (French time) on May 21. On arrival, a souvenir hunter grabbed Lindbergh's helmet, and for some time, the crowd thought that the impostor was the real pilot. Eventually the matter was settled, and Lindbergh settled into his hero's welcome. Europe bestowed on him the honorary

keys to various cities, receptions, and parades. Back in the United States, President Calvin Coolidge began planning an even larger celebration. Lindbergh returned home aboard the U.S. Navy cruiser *Memphis.* He was greeted by cheering crowds, ticker-tape parades, and $5 million in endorsement fees, film rights, and record deals. Literally overnight Lindbergh had become one of America's biggest heroes.

Like the character of Mitty's fantasy, Lindbergh served his country in World War II, although in a somewhat different capacity. When fighting broke out across Europe, Lindbergh originally sided with the America First committee, an organization opposed to American involvement in the war. His opposition, however, ended when the Japanese attacked Pearl Harbor on December 7, 1941. Lindbergh afterwards became personally involved. In April of 1944 he joined the war in the Pacific theater as an advisor to the U.S. army and navy forces there. Although technically a civilian, Lindbergh flew in about fifty combat missions. He also helped develop cruise control techniques that aided the accuracy and ability of U.S. fighter planes.

The Short Story in Focus

The plot. Walter Mitty leads the sedate life of any middle-class American. A henpecked husband, the most imposing challenge that Mitty faces during his day involves deciding which brand of puppy biscuit to purchase. This is the reality of Walter Mitty's existence. In his mind, however, Mitty assumes the role of various, vivacious characters.

From a navy hydroplane commander to an accused murderer, the imaginary Walter Mitty appears to be nothing like his realistic counterpart. While Thurber's story does not even total six pages in length, its content is filled with four rich worlds. Mitty the navy commander navigates his men through a hurricane. Dr. Mitty saves the life of a millionaire banker. Defendant Mitty proves that he can shoot a man with a heavy automatic weapon—even with one arm in a sling! Mitty the pilot singlehandedly challenges Germany's air battalion. All the while Mr. Mitty, the good husband, runs errands for his wife. At the close of the story, the imaginary Mitty faces a firing squad just as Walter Mitty faces the reality of his world.

Relationships between men and women. Although she does not have a large speaking role, the character responsible for driving Mitty into the confines of his mind is his wife. The final scene of "The Secret Life of Walter Mitty," in fact, releases the title character from his wife's constant nagging by way of an imaginary firing squad. Thurber writes, "Then, with that faint, fleeting smile playing about his lips, he faced the firing squad; erect and motionless, proud and disdainful, Walter Mitty, the Undefeated, inscrutable to the last" ("The Secret Life of Walter Mitty," p. 277). This theme, a man's imagination conquering an unimaginative woman, surfaces in many of the author's humorous pieces.

In a collection entitled *Fables for Our Time,* Thurber tells the tale of "The Unicorn in the Garden." In the story, an imaginative husband tells his shrewish wife that he has seen a unicorn eating roses in their garden. Naturally she assumes that the man has lost his mind, and telephones for the police and a psychiatrist. The police wind up carting the wife away when she relays her husband's fantasy. The husband then lives happily ever after. Thurber used this type of relationship in several of his other works. While it might appear narrow-minded by today's standards, many of Thurber's readers applauded his notions.

At that time in United States history, divorce was gaining popularity as a viable option in ending a marriage. As more couples sought out the termination of their marriages, the legal requirements grew more relaxed. Couples of the 1930s could file for divorce by proving the breakdown of their marriage on grounds such as alcoholism or nonsupport by either party.

Early in his career, the author had suffered through a miserable divorce from his first wife, Althea. A small-statured, handicapped man himself (he had one glass eye and became almost completely blind in his remaining eye during his later years), Thurber championed the rights of downtrodden men. In *The Middle-Aged Man on the Flying Trapeze,* a work that many consider a masterpiece, he links together a series of short stories using the theme of argument between the sexes. Each of the tales deals with a shrewish woman and her upstanding husband. As the book was assembled during the final stages of Thurber's divorce from Althea, its subject matter is particularly autobiographical. Perhaps the author hoped to ease some of the tabloid gossip by more or less telling his tale on his own. In print, the New York papers cited Thurber's "nonsupport [of his wife] . . . extreme infidelity, desertion, lack of concern for their infant child, and violence" (Bernstein, p. 246). While such stories were for the most part exaggerated, they troubled the author. His tension eased when he met

his second wife, Helen, in 1935. Marriage with Helen proved far more peaceful than it had been with Althea, and the couple remained together until Thurber passed away in 1961. Nonetheless, the wife to whom Thurber owes credit for inspiring his famous Walter Mitty character is the one that he chose to leave.

Sources. Although Thurber created Walter Mitty at the age of forty-five, he drew his character from a lifetime of accumulated inspiration. When graduating from junior high school in 1909, Thurber was selected to write the "Class Prophecy" for the eighth grade. The shy, sensitive boy constructed the following tale:

> One day, as we were sailing easily along, Harold came rushing out of the engine room with disheveled hair and bulging eyes. We asked him what on earth was the matter. For answer he pointed to a piece of rope that had caught in a part of the machinery that was situated on the farthest end of a long beam, which extended far over the side of the Seairoplane. Then he said, "unless that rope is gotten out of the curobater we will all be killed." These awful words astounded us and we all became frightened at once. Suddenly amid all of our lamentations a cry from Harold was heard and we looked up. What was our surprise to see James Thurber walking out on the beam. . . . We were all very joyful that the terrible crisis had been safely passed and afterwards learned that James was a tight rope walker with Barnsells and Ringbaileys circus.
>
> (Thurber in Bernstein, p. 29)

Even as a young boy, Thurber imagined fantastic and captivating roles for himself in his writing.

Although the Mitty character bears no true autobiographical resemblance to Thurber, the author does use the setting of Waterbury, Connecticut, where he lived with his second wife. Beyond that Thurber claims that the "original of Walter Mitty is every other man I have ever known" (Thurber in Bernstein, p. 311). According to his account, six men from across the nation wrote to Thurber following the publication of "The Secret Life of Walter Mitty" to ask if he'd had them in mind while writing his tale.

At least one man, however, seemed certain that Thurber had indeed used him in creating his Mitty character. In 1947 Charles Yale Harrison, author of the novel *Meet Me on the Barricades,* brought James Thurber up on charges of plagiarism. He contended that the Walter Mitty tale might have been inspired by his own book. Indignant, Thurber refused arbitration with a panel of writers, and the case eventually disintegrated. Whether Harrison had a legitimate claim or not, "The Secret Life of Walter Mitty" had simply made Thurber too popular to harm with such an accusation.

Reception of the story. Published in the *New Yorker* magazine on March 18, 1939, "The Secret Life of Walter Mitty" met with immediate success. During World War II, fighter pilots named their planes after the title character and introduced themselves over the radio as "Walter Mitty." Although he could not fight in the war, through his story Thurber felt that he contributed to the overseas effort. Over the years, the story and its character branched out to wider fields of comparison. During a Rams-Raiders football exhibition game on August 19, 1972, an NBC sportscaster announced, "If you want to play Walter Mitty for a moment, put yourself in the place of that guy [a player]" (Bernstein, p. 312). The term "Walter Mitty" appears even in present-day dictionaries, where it has been defined as "a commonplace unadventurous person who seeks escape from reality through daydreaming" (*Merriam Webster's,* s.v. "Walter Mitty").

The story was adapted for several different mediums. Samuel Goldwyn offered Thurber $15,000 for the movie rights to the story in 1944. Charles Hamm created an opera around Walter Mitty, and Broadway even saw the production of a rather unsuccessful Walter Mitty musical. Perhaps the author's favorite rendition of the story, however, was the 1944 radio adaptation starring Robert Benchley.

For More Information

Bergreen, Laurence. *Capone: the Man and the Era.* New York: Simon & Schuster, 1994.

Bernstein, Burton. *Thurber.* New York: Dodd, Mead, 1975.

Lindbergh, Charles. *The Wartime Journals of Charles A. Lindbergh.* New York: Harcourt Brace Jovanovich, 1970.

MacDonald, Fred. *Don't Touch That Dial! Radio Programming in American Life, 1920-1960.* Chicago: Nelson-Hall, 1979.

Macfarlane, Gywn. *Alexander Fleming: the Man and the Myth.* New York: Oxford University Press, 1985.

Merriam Webster's Collegiate Dictionary. 10th ed. Springfield, Mass.: Merriam Webster, 1993.

Thurber, James. "The Secret Life of Walter Mitty." In *21 Great Stories.* Edited by Abraham Lass and Norma L. Tassman. New York: New American Library, 1969.

Sounder

by

William H. Armstrong

Born in 1914 in Lexington, Virginia, white educator William Armstrong worked as a school headmaster and won recognition from the Association of School Administrators. Although he claimed to prefer stone masonry and carpentry to writing, he wrote books expressing his educational philosophy, beginning with *Study is Hard Work* (1956). More informational books followed, with titles like *Peoples of the Ancient World, 87 Ways to Help Your Child in School,* and *Tools of Thinking.* Armstrong then decided to retell a simple story he had heard as a child, scoring an instant success with *Sounder.*

Events in History at the Time the Novel Takes Place

Agriculture in the South. The Southern economy was based on agriculture, particularly cash crops such as tobacco and cotton. Although the Union army destroyed many crops and fields during the Civil War, afterward Southern agriculture rebounded quickly and continued expanding in the early twentieth century. Slavery itself was gone, but Southern landowners continued to rely on black labor. From their own point of view, blacks now faced the problem of earning a living and caring for their families. They knew farming, so most of the freed blacks who stayed in the South ended up hiring themselves out to their old owners or trying their hand at sharecropping—leasing small plots of land to farm for which they paid rent in cash or in a portion of the crops raised.

At the turn of the twentieth century, blacks made up one-third of the Southern population and 40 percent of the farm laborers. However,

few of them earned enough money to buy land for themselves. By 1910, out of 800,000 farms in the South, only 175,000 were owned by blacks. Like most black agricultural families there, the family in *Sounder* worked as sharecroppers.

The sharecropping family. Every member of a black sharecropping family contributed to the family welfare. The father not only worked in the fields but also hunted local game to supplement their food supply. In *Sounder,* the boy's father hunts for possums and raccoons. Because the family needed its children to work and earn money, they helped in the field and with household chores, which left them little time to attend school. In any event, these schools were often located quite far from the sharecroppers' cabins.

The mother took care of the children, worked in the fields, engaged in small money-making activities, and prepared the meals. In some cases, she worked outside the home, as the mother in *Sounder* does, washing the curtains and sheets for the "people in the big houses" (Armstrong, *Sounder,* pp. 39, 55). His mother also cares for the boy and his three siblings, shells walnuts to sell at the store, and prepares the family meals.

Armstrong's novel vividly describes the different foods that the sharecropping family eats, including corn mush, milk gravy and biscuits, sowbelly, possum, and pork. Rural black families generally ate a breakfast of corn mush and took their main meal at noon. To prepare the noontime dinner, the mother collected firewood and water. The meal generally consisted of leftovers from breakfast with some vegetables and meat if available. Most sharecropping families ate a proverbially simple diet of "meat, meal, and molasses" because they could not afford other foods (Jones, p. 89). The family shared a final light meal in the evening.

Sharecropper families lived in cabins on the landowner's acreage. Often these cabins were old, poorly constructed shacks like the one described in *Sounder,* whose "roof sagged from the two rough posts which held it, almost closing the gap between his [the father's] head and the rafters" (*Sounder,* p. 1). The small cabins commonly included only two rooms for the entire family. In *Sounder,* the boy shares a straw bed with his younger brother. Because the cabins were also very dark, often lit only by a small lantern, many sharecropper families went to bed early, shortly after dusk, unable to see well in the poor lighting.

White justice in the South. The prison system of the early twentieth century had one purpose: to punish the convicted criminals. One of the main methods of Southern punishment was hard labor, the punishment that the father receives in *Sounder.* In fact, most Southern felons served time not in prison but on county road gangs or chain gangs. Chain gangs were organized to relieve prison overcrowding and put prisoners to work in public service facilities such as fertilizer factories and stone quarries. The name comes from the fact that the prisoners actually wore leg irons and chains. Their living conditions were poor, characterized by long working hours, little food, and high mortality rates; the father in *Sounder,* for example, is sent to a quarry where a dynamite explosion injures him and kills twelve prisoners.

Southern prison guards were often cruel; prisoners were routinely beaten, and sometimes they simply disappeared in the prison camp system, whose white officers killed nearly half the blacks murdered by whites in the South during the early part of the twentieth century. While blacks in the South made up about 25 percent of the region's total population, they contributed 40 percent of the prison population. This discrepancy grew out of extreme racial inequality before the law, by which blacks were given harsh sentences for even the most minor offenses. *Sounder* clearly reflects these injustices, using as a central event the father's sentence of hard labor for stealing a ham. And when the boy in the novel visits a work camp, the guard hits him with a crowbar, crushing his hand.

SHARECROPPING

Sharecroppers—who were both black and white—worked on the landowner's property and received seed, tools, and housing from him. The landowner assigned each family a portion of land on which to plant and harvest crops such as sugar and cotton. In return, the family would give the owner one-half of the harvested crop. The landowner also often owned the local store, which charged high prices for items like flour. These high prices coupled with the payment to the landowner of as much as half the crop generally put the family in debt and forced them to live on the brink of starvation.

Southern black schools. Education for Southern blacks was generally an abysmal affair until the civil rights era. Southern schools were segregated, with black schools receiving little funding from the state. At the turn of the twentieth century, blacks represented one-third of the school-age population in the South but received only a little more than a tenth of the public-school funds. Until the 1960s, this discrepancy would change little. In 1935, for example, ten Southern states reported spending an average of well under $20 per black student as opposed to about $50 per white student. Black parents in rural areas nevertheless sometimes relied on small schools such as the one depicted in *Sounder,* so that their children could learn and still be available for farm work.

Additionally, libraries were often closed to blacks. Young people hungry for education were forced to look for reading materials in other places—as the boy in *Sounder* does when he searches the trash piles and finds a book.

A family of sharecroppers.

African American religion. The church was one of the most important institutions in the Southern African American community. In *Sounder,* the family attends church services at the nearby meeting house and also encounters other families at the annual church "meeting-house picnic" (*Sounder,* p. 17). Largely poverty-stricken and powerless, blacks turned to the church to hear sermons and sing songs that held out the promise of a better life in the Christian heaven. In *Sounder* the boy's mother often sings a hymn:

> You gotta walk that lonesome valley,
> You gotta walk it by yourself,
> Ain't nobody else gonna walk it for you.
> > (*Sounder,* p. 37)

Hymns like this stressed the contrasts between hardship in this world and spiritual rewards in the next, providing encouragement to a people facing the bleak prospects of poverty and racism.

Another important aspect of the Southern black religious experience was the folk sermon, in which the preacher told a biblical story and the audience spoke with him during certain parts of the story. Such tales were familiar to the congregation, as indeed they are to the boy in *Sounder,* who recalls the stories of David and Lazarus. Black preachers often traveled more frequently than farming laypeople, thereby serving

the double function of minister and agent of communication. In *Sounder* the mother speculates that the traveling preacher may have some information about the father's location during his imprisonment.

The Novel in Focus

The plot. The story of *Sounder* is told in the third person, focusing on a Southern sharecropping family's oldest boy. The boy lives in a run-down cabin on the landowner's property with his father, mother, three younger siblings, and the family's dog, Sounder, named for his loud bark. In order to feed the family, the father often goes hunting with the dog, who helps him by barking in the direction of animals and retrieving the game after the father shoots it. One winter, the possums and raccoons that the father normally hunts do not come out of their dens. Unable to bring back any meat, the father steals a ham and some pork to feed his family. He is caught and arrested by the local sheriff. When Sounder tries to follow his master, the angry sheriff shoots the dog, hitting him in the ear and shoulder. Sounder is badly injured and crawls off into the woods.

The father is taken to jail, and the mother returns the remainder of the stolen meat. Desperately missing both his father and Sounder, the boy visits his father in jail and searches the woods for Sounder. Months after the dog has been shot, he returns to the cabin, limping on three legs, unable to bark, and still healing from the injuries to his ear and shoulder. On Christmas Day, the boy takes his father a cake, which the guard, looking for a file or hacksaw, breaks into small pieces before giving it to the father. The father tells the boy, "I'll be back 'fore long" but is then sent to do work in a labor camp (*Sounder*, p. 63). The boy walks to different work camps in order to look for his father, carrying a book he has found in some trash. At one camp, a prison guard crushes the boy's hand with a crowbar, for no apparent reason other than to punish him for looking through a fence at the convicts. The boy stops at a black school in order to use the water pump to wash the blood from his hand and he meets a male schoolteacher.

The teacher takes the boy to his home and bandages his wound. Impressed with the boy's book, he asks the boy if he would like to attend school. Neither of the boy's parents can read, and—though he desperately wants to attend school—the eight-mile walk is too long for him. The teacher tells the boy that, in exchange for doing chores, he can live in the teacher's cabin so that he may attend the school. The boy discusses the arrangement with his mother, who agrees, providing the boy returns home in the summers to work in the fields.

Years after he is taken away, the father returns to the family's cabin, lame and half-blind from a dynamite blast in the prison quarry. He sets out to go hunting with Sounder one final time. The boy's father dies out in the woods and a few weeks later Sounder dies too.

The family's values. *Sounder* paints a bleak picture of black life in the white South, and one that finds some relief only in the deep values that hold the family together. Chief among these are loyalty, stoicism, and—perhaps most importantly—the boy's hunger for education. Like the hymn that the mother sings, these values stress a deeper value still: self-reliance. Mutual loyalty allows the family to function as a unit that can rely on itself. Similarly, their stoicism allows various family's members to rely on themselves as individuals when away from the family. Finally, the boy's hunger for education holds out promise that he will be able to rely on his own training to make a better life for himself, despite the obstacles of poverty and racism.

By the end of the novel, the boy has learned to read the book that he found in the trash. In it, he has found a message:

> "Only the unwise think that what is changed is dead." He had asked the teacher what it meant, and the teacher had said that if a flower blooms once, it goes on blooming somewhere forever. It blooms on for whoever has seen it blooming. It was not quite clear to the boy then, but it was now.
>
> (*Sounder*, p. 114)

After the boy has grown up, we are told, he will hold memories of the story's events, recalling them over and over. Like the blooming flower, his father and Sounder will go on living as long as he holds the memory of them in his mind. Armstrong's novel thus explicitly links the boy's education—his learning to read—with the chance that he might wring meaning and comfort from the terrible events of his boyhood.

AN ARKANSAS PRISONER FEARS MISTREATMENT

This is a hard place. I am a fread all the time that someone is going to hurt me. The Laws [police] is so hard on the Prison[er] Easpecial the colard [colored] one—they are Beating and lashing all the time . . . some of these Laws outer be in jail themselves.

(Kirby, pp. 221-22)

In the novel's materially desolate world, only spiritual strength allows the boy and his family to persevere. As a white Southerner, Armstrong had a perspective on racism that was unusual for a white author of a story featuring blacks; most stories of Southern blacks have been written by black authors. The emphasis on self-reliance in *Sounder* might be seen as reflecting the belief that blacks in the South needed to rely on themselves for help, because white society was not likely to change.

Sources. William Armstrong grew up in the Green Hill district of Virginia. As he relates in the Author's Note before the novel begins, his father sometimes hired an old black man of the area to do odd jobs. The old man was highly religious, and since preachers rarely visited the area's black church, he "came often to our white man's church and sat alone in the balcony," Armstrong recalls (Author's Note, *Sounder*, p. viii).

Sometimes the minister would call on this eloquent, humble man to lead the congregation

A Georgia chain gang, 1937.

in prayer. He would move quietly to the foot of the balcony steps, pray with the simplicity of the Carpenter of Nazareth, and then return to where he sat alone, for no other black people ever came to join him.

(Author's Note, *Sounder*, p. viii)

The old man, who had grown up in the South after slavery, was also a teacher, and he taught Armstrong how to read. He also told Armstrong stories from the Bible, as well as Greek myths. Armstrong's favorite story was about a loyal coon dog named Sounder. When he began to write books, Armstrong decided to tell the story that his neighbor shared with him, stating "It is the black man's story, not mine. . . . It was history—*his* history" (Author's Note, *Sounder*, p. viii).

At the end of the novel, the boy's possibilities for growth balance the story's sad and tragic events, and we briefly see the boy as a grown man, recalling everything that happened. Armstrong lets his readers suppose that the boy in the story grows up to be much like the old black man who inspired Armstrong as a child. In *Sour Land,* the sequel to *Sounder,* the boy has in fact grown up and plays just such a role for the children of a white farmer.

Events in History at the Time the Novel Was Written

The Moynihan Report. In a report written in 1965, Daniel P. Moynihan, a future U.S. senator, discussed the state of the black family in America. In the report, titled *The Negro Family: The Case for National Action,* he suggested that the black family was disorganized and "deteriorating," citing the high number of black families headed only by the mother (Berry and Blassingame, p. 71). Moynihan also argued that slavery and its effects were the causes of the black family's plight. His report received much criticism, with many critics questioning the validity of his evidence about single-parent black families. Armstrong probably knew of this highly publicized controversy when he set out to write *Sounder*. In his portrayal, he shows the black family as a strong, loyal, nuclear structure in which both parents and children work and sacrifice for each other's welfare. The facts coincided more closely with Armstrong's portrayal than with the impression conveyed by Moynihan's report. Most black families in the 1960s included both a husband and a wife; in 1970, the majority (67 percent) of black children were living with two parents.

Civil rights. The Civil Rights Act of 1964 outlawed racial discrimination against blacks in hotels, restaurants, and other public places. This act changed the legal status of blacks dramatically. "Separate but equal"—the infamous formula by which the Supreme Court had legitimized segregation in its *Plessy v. Ferguson* ruling of 1896—had been overturned in 1954 by *Brown v. Board of Education.* Afterward blacks began to take advantage of new civil rights laws by enrolling in better schools and by exercising the right to vote freely without dealing with the obstacles like literacy tests or poll taxes.

The 1960s movement to integrate public facilities in the South stands in sharp contrast to the days of segregation portrayed in *Sounder*. In the novel, the segregation rules that prevail in the South at the time prohibit the boy from entering the jailhouse through the front door when he visits his father; the boy also attends a segregated school with other black children.

Education in the 1960s. The official attitude in regard to education for blacks had changed greatly by the time *Sounder* was written. In 1964 President Lyndon B. Johnson launched a war on poverty in America that led to the passage of the Elementary and Secondary Education Act a year later. This act allocated money for both remedial education (Title I funds) and preschool education (the Head Start program), measures that greatly affected black youth. The government, by way of the act, was taking responsibility for helping young people compensate for the disadvantages associated with poverty. In the case of poor black people, it was a condition rooted in their history. The government was, in effect, helping their children compensate for disadvantages that harked back to the segregation and slavery suffered by past generations.

Reception. Published in 1969, *Sounder* received positive reviews from most critics, who praised its depiction of the many injustices that blacks encountered in the early part of the twentieth century. A reviewer for the *Christian Science Monitor* likened it to Greek tragedy, saying, "Adults and mature young readers alike will find in the boy's bittersweet memories a parable for our times" (Samudio, p. 43).

A few critics argued that the novel reinforced prejudices by giving no character, other than the dog, a name—thus supposedly denying the individuality of African Americans. Others argued that by leaving the human characters nameless, Armstrong lent his simple tale a timeless and universal quality. Similarly the story was criticized as being too violent for young readers but also praised because of its realistic portrayal of harsh conditions during a certain time and era.

Several critics applauded Armstrong's writing style, particularly his vivid language, citing such passages as the following description of the mother's lips: "When the mother was troubled her lips were rolled inward and drawn long and thin. . . . But when she sang or told stories, her lips were rolled out, big and warm and soft" (*Sounder,* p. 14).

In 1970 *Sounder* won the John Newbery Medal, one of the most prestigious awards in young people's literature.

For More Information

Armstrong, William H. *Sounder.* New York: Harper & Row, 1969.

Berry, Mary Frances and John W. Blassingame. *Long Memory: The Black Experience in America.* New York: Oxford University Press, 1982.

Jaynes, Gerald David and Robin M. Williams, Jr., eds. *Blacks and American Society.* Washington, D.C.: National Academy Press, 1989.

Jones, Jacqueline. *Labor of Love, Labor of Sorrow: Black Women and the Family from Slavery to the Present.* New York: Vintage, 1986.

Kirby, Jack Temple. *Rural Worlds Lost: The American South, 1920-1960.* Baton Rouge: Louisiana State University, 1987.

Levy, Peter B., ed. *Documentary History of the Civil Rights Movement.* New York: Greenwood 1992.

Owens, Charles E. and Bell, Jimmy, eds. *Blacks and Criminal Justice.* Lexington, Ken.: Lexington Press, 1977.

Samudio, Josephine, ed. *Book Review Digest.* Vol. 65. New York: H. W. Wilson, 1970.

Woodward, C. Vann. *Origins of the New South, 1877-1913.* New Orleans: Louisiana State University Press, 1971.

The Strange Case of Dr. Jekyll and Mr. Hyde

by
Robert Louis Stevenson

Born in Edinburgh, Scotland, in 1850, Robert Louis Stevenson came of age during the late Victorian era, a time of widespread scientific, technological, and social change. Stevenson, although Scottish-born, spent most of his life out of the country and married an American. Desperate for money and fighting a fit of depression, he allegedly wrote *The Strange Case of Dr. Jekyll and Mr. Hyde* within ten weeks while residing in Bournemouth, England. The success of the novel cemented Stevenson's writing career.

Events in History at the Time of the Novel

Stevenson and Scottish Calvinism. As a child, Stevenson was raised in an extremely devout Calvinist environment. This Protestant sect taught that humans were innately sinful and could only be saved by the grace of God. Each person's fate was determined before birth; people were predestined for either heavenly salvation or eternal hell. Stevenson's father, a particularly religious man, often told the child tales of destiny and damnation.

Perhaps even more influential in Stevenson's religious upbringing, however, was his nurse Alison Cunningham, known as "Cummy." Cummy was a zealously religious Calvinist as well as an avid storyteller. She had become Stevenson's nurse when he was still an infant. Cummy preached strict Calvinist beliefs to Stevenson and read him Old Testament scrip-

---

THE LITERARY WORK

A novel set in London in the late 1800s; published in 1886.

SYNOPSIS

An eccentric physician named Dr. Jekyll discovers a potion that changes both his physical appearance and personality. This evil alternate identity, known as Mr. Hyde, slowly becomes the dominant portion of his personality.

---

ture. By the time Stevenson was a toddler, she had read the Bible to him several times over. Her religious convictions were combined with a belief in the supernatural. Among the stories she told him were numerous tales of ghosts and body-snatchers.

As a result, young Stevenson had an active imagination and was profoundly religious. He was writing devotional stories by age four and liked to play "church." At night, he wept for Jesus and suffered from nightmares about hell, damnation, and evil. Stevenson was being raised to believe that "there were but two camps in the world; one of the perfectly pious and respectable, one of the perfectly profane, mundane and vicious" (McLynn, p. 19).

Yet as an adult, Stevenson rejected literal Calvinism. The religious background, however, came to permeate his writings. The concept of good and evil locked in combat is, for example, a central theme in *The Strange Case of Dr. Jekyll and Mr. Hyde*. Furthermore, Dr. Jekyll's resignation and acceptance of his progression into vice and evil reflects the Calvinist belief in destiny and predetermination.

A shift in world view. One of the most profound events that affected late Victorian life was the advent of Darwinism. Until the mid-nineteenth century, Western theologians postulated that the animal passions that humans possessed were God's way of testing the human will. Most Christians believed that both humans and animals had been created by God, and that they had not fundamentally changed since the time of Creation. Darwin, in contrast, hypothesized that humans had evolved from lower forms of life. Through a process called adaptation, organisms retained useful characteristics that helped them to survive. Meanwhile, those organisms that could not successfully compete for resources simply died out. Life, in short, constituted a battle in which only the most fit species continued.

The impact of Darwinism was widespread and profound. It shook the very foundations of Victorian philosophy, theology, science, and morality. The universe was now conceptualized as a developing, organic entity, and those who accepted this nonreligious view of life itself began applying the theory of evolution to all facets of life.

Darwinism reinforced the Victorians' belief in the inevitability of progress. Yet it also spurred feelings of pessimism. If life was a struggle for existence, people reasoned, the winners might be the most fit, but not necessarily the best or the most just. If neither man nor God controlled the destiny of humankind, then the strongest, most ruthless and amoral might win, while the good, weak, and humble might lie trampled by the wayside. Furthermore, those who won the struggle for survival supposedly owed their victory to their animal-like qualities rather than to a higher power. Such an idea blurred the distinctions between man and beast. Novels of the era portrayed humans as simply well-developed animals who were endowed with consciousness and intellect but still had much in common with other creatures in the animal kingdom. In the case of Dr. Jekyll, it took only a simple chemical experiment to revert the highly civilized doctor into an animal-like being. The characters in the story often describe Mr. Hyde as a lower form of life, using animal metaphors. Upon meeting Mr. Hyde, for example, Mr. Utterson thinks, "God bless me, the man seems hardly human! Something troglodytic

[from the cave-dwelling age], shall we say?" (Stevenson, *The Strange Case of Dr. Jekyll and Mr. Hyde,* p. 23).

Science and the late Victorians. Until the nineteenth century, the term "science" had been associated with a broad range of intellectual activities that included philosophy and theology. During the first half of the 1800s, however, science came to signify a specialized knowledge of nature. As the century progressed, this field of learning became further subdivided into various branches of scientific study.

Psychology was a discipline that changed drastically during this time, fusing science with the enigmatic and mysterious in its exploration of the human mind. During the latter half of the 1800s, psychology allied itself with biology and physiology in order to better understand human brain structure and the nervous system. Psychologists, starting off from this perspective, went on to explore the more mysterious facets of the human psyche. The founding in 1882 of the Society for Psychical Research brought together philosophers, spiritualists, psychologists, and physicists to scientifically study the occult. Split personalities were a phenomenon of particular interest to psychological researchers. Such cases had been documented for the first time at the beginning of the century and were widely recognized by the end of the 1800s. Pioneers such as the psychologist Sigmund Freud explored the effects of hypnotism on split personalities, which some researchers believed were elements of the conscious mind that had split off from the rest of the inner being.

Meanwhile, in the medical field, new experimental methods helped researchers discover and identify during the 1880s the germs causing typhoid, malaria, tuberculosis, diphtheria, cholera and the bubonic plague. The rabies vaccination was discovered in 1881 and a serum for diphtheria was produced in 1894. All of these discoveries both excited and frightened the Victorians. It seemed that there was nothing that science could not accomplish. Therefore, when Stevenson first published *The Strange Case of Dr. Jekyll and Mr. Hyde,* the story provoked an extreme public reaction, unsettling many because it appeared somewhat plausible. As one scholar notes, "So much excitement did the story cause that sermons were preached about it, and the more timid of the Victorians fervently hoped that the doctors who at that time seemed to be discovering everything would not unearth the mysterious drug which Stevenson made Dr. Jekyll

Robert Louis Stevenson

use to free the unpleasant Mr. Hyde" (Allen in Geduld, p. 8).

Drugs. The character of Dr. Jekyll is one of the first literary figures who experiments with mind- and personality-altering drugs. He accomplishes his amazing transformation with the aid of a chemical compound that he obtains locally. Unfortunately for Dr. Jekyll, the original salt that manages to produce the transformation is impure, and cannot be replicated. In other words, he cannot obtain a similar sample when one is needed to save him from his alter ego, Mr. Hyde.

In England the sale and use of drugs was uncontrolled until 1868. Until that time, people purchased and used potentially harmful drugs like any other product. Drugs could be bought not only from chemists and druggists, but from innumerable other small venues.

Most people used drugs for medicinal rather than recreational purposes. Home remedies were extremely popular, especially among the poor who could not afford doctors. Mind-altering drugs that were widely available during the late 1800s included hashish imported from India, opium and its derivatives from the Far East, and coca. Opium and opium-based products were especially popular medicines. People commonly used opium products to quiet noisy babies and took laudanum, an opium-based potion mixed with alcohol, as a cure for a variety of ailments.

The other drugs, such as hashish, had rather scandalous reputations. It was said that consumption of hashish could lead to insanity, uncontrollable sexual desire, and murderous rage. Potentially dangerous drugs such as coca and cocaine had only recently been introduced; arguments regarding their potential harm or benefit to mankind would continue into the twentieth century.

Only at the very end of the nineteenth century did doctors begin to recognize the addicting properties of some, but not all, narcotics. For example, heroin, first produced in 1898, was promoted as nonaddictive. A movement to control the sale and use of some narcotics had begun by the end of the century, but had not yet achieved much success.

The Novel in Focus

The plot. The story of *The Strange Case of Dr. Jekyll and Mr. Hyde* is told in several different narrative voices, including those of an attorney named Mr. Utterson, as well as Dr. Jekyll and his friend Dr. Lanyon. One day, as Mr. Utterson and his friend Mr. Enfield are walking together, they pass by a strange door. Mr. Enfield tells a story about the door, describing how one day he saw a small, odd-looking man callously trample a small girl. Mr. Enfield and several other adults helped the frightened girl and apprehended the man, whose demeanor struck fear and loathing in their hearts. The odd-looking man agreed to give the girl's family money as compensation. The man entered the door in question and quickly returned with a check drawn on the name of Dr. Jekyll, a well-known, respected doctor and a good friend of Mr. Utterson's. Mr. Enfield tells Mr. Utterson that the stranger's name was Mr. Hyde. "He is not easy to describe. There is something wrong with his appearance; something displeasing, something downright detestable. I never saw a man I so disliked, and yet I scarce know why. He must be deformed somewhere" (*The Strange Case of Dr. Jekyll and Mr. Hyde,* p. 20).

The story disturbs Mr. Utterson, who has himself heard of Mr. Hyde. That night Utterson rereads Dr. Jekyll's will, which is in his possession. The will states that in the case of the death or disappearance of Dr. Jekyll, Mr. Hyde will receive all of Dr. Jekyll's inheritance. The clause disturbs the lawyer and he fears that his friend Jekyll is in trouble. He decides to investigate the matter, and eventually meets Mr. Hyde, who is extremely rude to him. Utterson loathes the man and becomes convinced that Mr. Hyde is blackmailing Dr. Jekyll for some youthful folly.

Nearly a year later, London is shocked by the dreadful murder of Sir Danvers Carew, an elderly, respected gentleman of the community. A maid who witnessed the murder identifies Hyde as the perpetrator. The police ransack Hyde's dwelling and find the murder weapon but cannot locate him. Mr. Utterson hurries to the house of the distraught Dr. Jekyll, who swears that he will never lay eyes on Mr. Hyde again.

For the next few months, Dr. Jekyll seems to have resumed his composure. He once again associates with his old friends, and even throws a dinner party. Only days afterward, however, he locks himself up in his house and refuses to admit anybody. Concerned once again for his friend's well-being, Mr. Utterson visits Dr. Lanyon, another friend of Dr. Jekyll's. Dr. Lanyon is near death, yet secretive about the cause. He says that he has had a shock that will soon kill him and that he never again wants to hear Dr. Jekyll's name. Dr. Lanyon dies soon afterwards, leaving a letter for Utterson with instructions not to read it until the death or disappearance of Dr. Jekyll. Heeding the instructions, Mr. Utterson puts the letter away.

Some time later, Poole, Dr. Jekyll's butler, knocks on Mr. Utterson's door. Visibly terrified, he begs Mr. Utterson to return with him to Dr. Jekyll's house. "I think there's been foul play," says Poole hoarsely (*The Strange Case of Dr. Jekyll and Mr. Hyde,* p. 34).

Poole knocks on the door to Jekyll's chamber and announces that Mr. Utterson has come to visit. A male voice replies that he cannot see anyone. Both Poole and Mr. Utterson agree that the voice does not belong to Dr. Jekyll. They break down the door only to find Mr. Hyde dead on the floor from suicide. Dr. Jekyll is nowhere in sight. They find only a note instructing Utterson to first read Dr. Lanyon's letter and then to read a letter from Dr. Jekyll that lies on the desk.

Dr. Lanyon's letter describes how he saw with his own eyes Mr. Hyde drink a concoction that transformed him back into Dr. Jekyll. Triumphantly, Mr. Hyde held the concoction aloft bragging, "And now you who have so long been bound to the most narrow and material views, you have denied the virtue of transcendental medicine, you who have derided your superiors

—behold!" (*The Strange Case of Dr. Jekyll and Mr. Hyde,* p. 43). Lanyon concludes his letter by stating that his life has been shaken to its roots by the experience, leading to his death.

Mr. Utterson then opens Dr. Jekyll's letter. Jekyll first describes his philosophical reflections upon the duality of his own persona. He tells how one part of him was upright and virtuous, while another part reveled in pleasure and evil. Upon recognizing these two sides of his soul, he searched for, and eventually found, a particular concoction of drugs that released the lower elements of his soul and simultaneously transformed his physical body. When he drank the potion, he changed himself into Mr. Hyde—still a part of Dr. Jekyll, the hedonistic and evil side that had previously been repressed.

At first, Dr. Jekyll liked the alter ego of Mr. Hyde; he was nimble and young. Troubles, however, soon emerged. Mr. Hyde grew stronger and more evil, becoming so depraved that he eventually murdered the aged Carew. As a fugitive, Mr. Hyde purposefully transformed into Dr. Jekyll, who swore never again to change his identity.

But one day shortly thereafter, without the aid of a potion, Dr. Jekyll was transformed into Mr. Hyde while sitting on a park bench. This created a dangerous situation. The drugs he needed to change himself back were in his room. Mr. Hyde was a fugitive and could not enter Dr. Jekyll's house. Hyde decided to employ Dr. Lanyon to get the ingredients for him. The next morning Jekyll was again wracked by the sensations that preceded his transformation into Mr. Hyde. Dr. Jekyll then required a double dose of the serum to maintain himself in that form. From then on, only with great effort could the doctor keep up his own appearance. He always awoke as Mr. Hyde, and was absolutely horrified at his evil self. The body and mind of Dr. Jekyll grew sick and weak, while Mr. Hyde grew stronger.

Dr. Jekyll closed his letter by stating that he had run out of the special salts used to create his potion and was unable to find more. It was under the last dose he composed his suicide letter as Dr. Jekyll: "Here then," explained the tormented doctor, "as I lay down the pen and proceed to seal up my confession, I bring the life of that unhappy Henry Jekyll to an end" (*The Strange Case of Dr. Jekyll and Mr. Hyde,* p. 52).

Victorian morality. Critics relate a variety of elements in *The Strange Case of Dr. Jekyll and Mr. Hyde* to the times in which the story is set. One of the most common interpretations examines the characters of Jekyll and Hyde as metaphors for Victorian social codes. In the story, Dr. Jekyll is a well-respected doctor and upright member of the community. He is, however, reputed to have been rather wild as a youth, and his concerned friend, Mr. Utterson, initially fears that Mr. Hyde is blackmailing Dr. Jekyll for some ancient transgression. He muses, "Poor Harry Jekyll . . . my mind misgives me he is in deep waters! He was wild when he was young; a long while ago to be sure; but in the law of God, there is no statute of limitations" (*The Strange Case of Dr. Jekyll and Mr. Hyde*, p. 24).

Mr. Hyde, however, is not a blackmailer, but an intricate part of Jekyll himself. In his final letter, Jekyll confesses how, in some ways, he had maintained a double identity throughout his life. He describes his internal struggle: on one hand, he set demanding moral standards for himself and desired to maintain a highly acceptable public profile. Yet part of him longed for a life of pleasure and folly. Jekyll had followed the socially correct moral path and hid his secret desires, of which he felt ashamed.

The nature of the young Dr. Jekyll's sins and a complete account of Mr. Hyde's evil deeds are not revealed in the story. In general, however, the Victorian lifestyle was characterized by severity and rigidity. Many of this era strove to adhere strictly to demanding social codes that some found difficult or impossible to meet. The ideal Victorian was virtuous, pious, self-denying, and decorous. "To be an earnest Christian" during this era, one historian notes, "demanded a tremendous effort. One had to hate the world, the flesh, and the devil, to keep all of God's commandments exactly" (Houghton, p. 231).

In an era imbued and prosperous with commercial vigor, people sought affluence, respectability, and success. Wealth was especially desirable because it improved a person's social status, and the era was particularly characterized by the push toward upward mobility. It was possible to enter an upper-class milieu, for example, by buying an estate or a noble title. To be able to afford these trappings usually entailed hard work, which was also valued by the Victorians. Having adopted the Protestant perspective that hard work inherently contained moral worth, the Victorians held work in especially high esteem as a means to commercial success. Idleness was a moral and social sin, and poverty was considered shameful.

Striving to lead pious, respectable lives, the Victorians publicly disdained pastimes that did not lead to self-improvement. In some cases even

popular novels and poetry were considered frivolous. Perhaps this attitude played a part in some critics' originally questioning the "moral intention" of Stevenson's novel.

The struggle for chastity was another aspect of proper Victorian behavior. Surrounded by religiously inspired feelings of shame and fear, the Victorians considered sex particularly sinful and an improper topic for discussion. Boys were taught to worship women as angelic creations, while as adults, many women were taught to view sex as simply a duty they owed their husbands. Sin and sex were inexorably intertwined.

In the face of such rigid social restrictions, some Victorians complied with social conventions despite the fact that they did not believe in them. Others simply discovered that they could not live up to such stringent ideals, which has led some scholars to believe that, in reality, Victorian life was characterized by immense hypocrisy. These scholars note that Victorians often bowed to conformity, concealing their true natures and tastes and pretending to adhere to social norms. Some Victorians passed themselves off as more pious or moral than they really were. But in reality, pornographic literature and prostitution were common phenomena during the late nineteenth century, showing that some Victorians only pretended to lead chaste lives.

After the publication of *The Strange Case of Dr. Jekyll and Mr. Hyde,* Stevenson protested the public's tendency to view Hyde as a sexual deviant. He commented that the Jekyll/Hyde phenomenon was meant to illustrate how desires, when ignored for long periods of time, can become perverted. As an adult, Stevenson himself rebelled against current social mores. He not only rejected his own religious upbringing but also recognized much of the hypocrisy of the era. He lived a Bohemian lifestyle, choosing not to become the engineer his father desired him to be. Instead Stevenson traveled widely, dabbled with socialist politics, and married an older American woman who had left her husband, all of which chafed against British Victorian ideals.

Sources. Stevenson created *The Strange Case of Dr. Jekyll and Mr. Hyde* from a wide variety of sources. He professed to have often been struck by ideas that came to him from dreams inspired by personal muses that he called his "Brownies." In this case, Stevenson was in financial trouble and desperate to write a story. He writes:

> For two days I went racking my brain for a plot
> of any sort; and on the second night I dreamed
> the scene at the window, and a scene afterwards

split in two, in which Hyde, pursued for some crime, took the powder and underwent the change in the presence of his pursuers.

(Stevenson in Abbey, p. 318)

He wrote down the dream and completed the first draft three days later. His wife, Fanny, who often collaborated with Stevenson, disliked the first draft, so he burned it, but then quickly rewrote the story, incorporating the changes she suggested.

Although this story about the birth of *The Strange Case of Dr. Jekyll and Mr. Hyde* has reached near-legendary status, in reality Stevenson had been toying with such a plot for many years. "I had long been trying to write a story on this subject, to find a body, a vehicle, for that strong sense of man's double being which must at times come in upon and overwhelm the mind of every thinking creature" (Stevenson in Abbey, pp. 317-18).

An actual personality of a previous generation, William Brodie, seems to have embodied Stevenson's fascination with the duality of humans. A deacon of the Guild of Wrights in Edinburgh, Brodie was an honest businessman and upright citizen by day. By night, however, he led a gang of cutthroats who engaged in burglary and other crimes. Brodie was hanged for his crimes in Edinburgh in 1788. Stevenson knew of Brodie and was fascinated enough by his life to write a play about him in the early 1880s. While Stevenson himself did not identify Brodie as the inspiration for the character in his 1886 novel, many critics believe that the double life of Dr. Jekyll stems from this colorful historical figure.

Reviews. Initially published as a "shilling shocker"—an inexpensive whole story rather than a serialized work—*The Strange Case of Dr. Jekyll and Mr. Hyde* did not sell well until the London *Times* gave it an excellent review. Thereafter it became popular with the reading public as well as with many critics. Many were horrified at the subject matter, which inspired fear and dread, and some of the reviews reflected this sen-

timent. Most critics acknowledged Stevenson's writing talents, but a number of them questioned the propriety of the subject matter and the novel's intent. There were readers who considered the story absurd or, as the following critic states, too painful to enjoy.

It is indeed a dreadful book, most dreadful because of a certain moral callousness, a want of sympathy, a shutting out of hope. . . . It has left such a deeply painful impression on my heart that I do not know how I am ever to turn to it again.

(Symonds in Abbey, p. 315)

Most critics, however, praised the story. One of Stevenson's most famous reviewers was the novelist Henry James:

Is Dr. Jekyll and Mr. Hyde a work of high philosophic intention, or simply the most ingenious and irresponsible of fictions? . . . It deals with the relation of the baser parts of man to his nobler—of the capacity for evil that exists in the most generous natures, and it expresses these things in a fable which is a wonderfully happy invention.

(James in Abbey, p. 316)

For More Information

Abbey, Cherie, ed. *Nineteenth-Century Literature Criticism.* Vol. 14. Detroit: Gale Research, 1987.

Geduld, Harry M., ed. *The Definitive Dr. Jekyll and Mr. Hyde.* New York: Garland, 1983.

Houghton, Walter E. *The Victorian Frame of Mind, 1830-1870.* New Haven, Conn.: Yale University Press, 1957.

McLynn, Frank. *Robert Louis Stevenson.* London: Hutchinson, 1993.

Stevenson, Robert Louis. *The Strange Case of Dr. Jekyll and Mr. Hyde.* In *The Definitive Dr. Jekyll and Mr. Hyde.* Edited by Harry M. Geduld. New York: Garland, 1983.

Wright, Daniel L. "'The Prisonhouse of My Disposition': A Study of the Psychology of Addiction in 'Dr. Jekyll and Mr. Hyde'." *Studies in the Novel* 26, no. 3 (Fall 1994).

Their Eyes Were Watching God

by
Zora Neale Hurston

Probably born in 1901, Zora Neale Hurston was raised in Florida. She moved to New York in 1925, becoming one of the foremost writers during the Harlem Renaissance, the creative outpouring of works by black artists, thinkers, and musicians of the 1920s. In 1927 Hurston took the first of many trips from Harlem, New York, to the South, where her experiences would inspire her to write an assortment of novels, plays, short stories, essays, and collections of folklore over the next twenty years. Midway through this period, she completed her third novel, the partly autobiographical story for which she is best remembered—*Their Eyes Were Watching God*.

THE LITERARY WORK

A novel set in Florida from about 1900 through the late 1920s; published in 1937.

SYNOPSIS

A young Southern black girl who dreams of romance marries two different oppressive men who demand that she conform to their own conceptions of womanhood. Only when she meets her third and final husband does she discover her own identity and subsequently true love.

Events in History at the Time of the Novel

Race colonies. During the late nineteenth century, ex-slaves occasionally established all-black towns and villages. Sometimes referred to as "race colonies," these communities varied greatly in size and importance. The heaviest concentration of race colonies appeared in the Midwest and the South in rural areas on very poor land. They founded their own schools, churches, and local governments.

The all-black town of Eatonville, Florida, where the novel's main character, Janie, and her second husband live, was established in the tradition of such race colonies. Hurston herself lived in Eatonville until she was thirteen years old. As one biographer notes, "Black Americans had

founded Eatonville because they were denied the opportunity to live as free and equal citizens in white communities" (Witcover, p. 22). The town, incorporated in 1877, went on to become the first black community to win the right of self-government. Unlike other areas of the South, Eatonville did not pass laws to legalize segregation. The widespread Jim Crow laws, which required blacks to use separate schools, hotels, restaurants, theaters, drinking fountains, and other public facilities, did not exist in Eatonville.

Lake Okeechobee. In the novel, a hurricane devastates the Everglades. The incident is based on an actual storm that ravaged the area in September of 1928. Entirely destroyed by this storm was the town of Belle Glade; only six buildings remained standing. The storm's winds blew as strong as 160 miles an hour, causing a tidal wave

The Cotton Club, the famous New York jazz club, as it looked in the 1930s.

that swept great torrents of water onto land. Located only twenty miles from the ocean, Lake Okeechobee filled to capacity, and its dikes collapsed, which led to the flooding of nearby homes. People ran for higher ground, only to place themselves in harm's way near deadly reptiles. Scores of victims perished from snake bites. It is estimated that at least 1,850 died; the majority are thought to have been blacks. Those who escaped drowning or poisonous bites found themselves stranded with no drinking water and impassable roads. In the end, there were so many dead and so few coffins that bodies, often unidentified, had to be piled up and burned.

The Harlem Renaissance. The Harlem Renaissance occurred after a great number of Southern blacks migrated to the North in the early 1900s. By the end of the 1920s, 80 percent of black Americans were still living in the South. But at the same time, often drawn by the Northern industries tooling up to meet the demands of World War I, more than one million blacks had migrated north between 1900 and the end of the 1920s. Many of them settled in the Harlem section of New York City.

When Zora Neale Hurston arrived in New York in 1925 full of hope but with only $1.50 in her pocket, the Harlem Renaissance was in full swing. Lasting from about the end of World War I through the stock market crash, the Renaissance drew together talented black artists, writers, and musicians. In music, jazz and blues dominated the scene, and such noted talents as Duke Ellington and Louis Armstrong eventually reached legendary status. Black actors and actresses such as Paul Robeson and Josephine Baker entered the public consciousness. More books were being published by African Americans than ever before in history. With a cutting wit and a talent as a storyteller, Hurston soon established herself as a significant presence among the Harlem literati.

This cultural revival caught the attention of white audiences, who flocked to Harlem in search of what some saw as exotic, sensual, and primitive artistic works. Many wealthy whites functioned as patrons to black artists, providing them with the money and contacts needed to take their art beyond Harlem's boundaries. Despite their good intentions, however, most patrons usually had specific notions regarding what kind of art their protégés should create. Zora's patron, Mrs. Rufus Osgood Mason, provides one example. Called "godmother" by her clients, Mrs. Mason donated enormous amounts of money to writers and artists of the Harlem movement such as the poet Langston Hughes. She encouraged her artists, including Zora, to express their inner natural selves. "They were to live in Harlem; they were to emphasize in their work what she identified as folk culture or primitivism, and they were to eschew subjects she judged as didactic or smacking of social reform" (Kellner in Kramer, p. 97).

Mrs. Mason paid Zora to collect black Southern folklore, stipulating that anything Zora collected became Mrs. Mason's property. She paid Zora $200 a month for two years, a sum comparable to over $30,000 a year today.

Zora and racial politics. Having grown up in the all-black community of Eatonville, Hurston experienced a community that did not occupy itself with racial politics. Because she lived in such an atypical town—with a black mayor and postmaster, for instance—Hurston did not experience the type of racism and prejudice that confronted most other blacks during this time. Hurston says of her experiences in Eatonville, "I did not have to consider any racial group as a whole. God made them duck by duck and that was the only way I could see them. I learned that skins were no measure of what was inside people" (Hurston in Witcover, p. 14).

As an adult, however, this perspective sometimes clashed with those of her peers. During the 1920s and 1930s, black leaders changed strategy in their fight for racial equality. Early guides like Booker T. Washington had preached a moderate, patient approach. New leaders, such as W. E. B. Du Bois, however, held that the "Talented Tenth," as he labeled educated blacks, should forcefully lead those less fortunate in the demand for immediate integration without compromise. Civil rights leaders fought against lynchings and the virulent Jim Crow laws that permeated many areas. Many artists of the Harlem Renaissance took this message to heart, believing that black writers should portray the harsh conditions of poverty and oppression suffered by their race. This trend continued throughout the 1930s, the decade in which *Their Eyes Were Watching God* was published. Some critics faulted Hurston's writings for their lack of political consciousness. The noted black writer Richard Wright, for example, became one of Hurston's most severe critics. Hurston, however, did not see herself as oppressed and so refused to conform, preferring to emphasize the positive side of life in her writings. She explained her refusal:

> I am not tragically colored. There is no great sorrow dammed up in my soul, nor lurking behind my eyes. . . . I do not mind at all. I do not belong to the sobbing school of Negrohood who hold that nature somehow has given them a lowdown dirty deal and whose feelings are all hurt about it. . . . No, I do not weep at the world—I am too busy sharpening my oyster knife.
>
> (Hurston in Kramer, p. 283)

Furthermore, Hurston's background made her an anomaly among her peers. Although she hid her age throughout her life, she was nearly a decade older than many of the young aspiring Harlem writers, and she had grown up in rural Florida, whereas most of her contemporaries were Northern urbanites. In fact, Hurston's portrayal of black Southern characters and their folklore—the storytelling, jokes, games, and dialect—was taken as an affront by the black literati who knew little of places like Eatonville. Many saw Hurston's writings as frivolous—or worse, as perpetuating black stereotypes. At a time when black artists strove to depict social inequity and suffering, Hurston's writings seemed something of an outrage to politically motivated writers and readers. Many of the black elite criticized the lack of bitterness in her writing, accusing her of dwelling on racial stereotypes in order to amuse white audiences.

PRIMITIVISM

Primitivism was a movement within the art world that began at the turn of the century. Regarding much of Western art as stilted and artificial, some people sought out the creative works of "primitive" societies like those of Africa and the Pacific Islands and encouraged nonwhite artists in the United States to produce such works. The patrons considered these productions free from the influence of modern Western society and therefore more natural and emotional.

The Novel in Focus

The plot. *Their Eyes Were Watching God* details the spiritual and psychological development of an attractive young black woman named Janie. The novel opens when Janie, who lives in West Florida, is sixteen and her thoughts turn to romance. "Oh to be a pear tree—*any* tree in bloom! With kissing bees singing of the beginning of the world! She was sixteen. She had glossy leaves and bursting buds and she wanted to struggle with life but it seemed to elude her. Where were the singing bees for her?" (Hurston, *Their Eyes Were*

Watching God, p. 11). As she struggles with her newfound feelings, Janie experiments by kissing a neighborhood boy. When her grandmother catches them, she decides that Janie must marry Logan Killicks, a young man whom Janie does not love. Logan Killicks has land, however, and Janie's grandmother believes a sound marriage will protect Janie from being abused by men. Janie acquiesces, hoping to eventually love Logan.

A year later, Janie is still unhappy. Logan continually tries to force her to do what he wants, and Janie's romantic hopes have been dashed. One day, Janie meets Joe Starks (Jody), a friendly, stylish, and citified man.

> Joe Starks was the name, yeah Joe Starks from in and through Georgy. Been workin' for white folks all his life. Saved up some money—round three hundred dollars, yes indeed, right here in his pocket. Kept hearin' 'bout them buildin' a new state down heah in Floridy and sort of wanted to come . . . when he heard all about 'em makin' a town all outa colored folks, he knowed dat was de place he wanted to be. . . . He meant to git dere whilst de town wuz yet a baby. He meant to buy in big.
>
> (*Their Eyes Were Watching God,* p. 27)

For Janie, Jody represents an alternative to her present unhappy condition. She runs away from Logan and the marriage, setting out with Jody for Eatonville, the all-black town in which he plans to a build a life for himself.

Once in town, Jody quickly attains wealth and power. A fine talker and a smart investor, he buys the surrounding land to sell to new families in town and calls town meetings to organize the sleepy residents. Under his direction, new roads are built and streets are lighted. Jody opens a general store to supply the town with groceries and runs the post office as well. The townspeople elect him mayor, and the Starkses grow rich.

In his mind, Jody believes a rich man needs a beautiful and submissive wife, and he tries to force Janie to play that role. He does not allow her to articulate her feelings or ideas, but expects her to dress well, mind her manners, and not mix with the poor. Janie longs to participate in the everyday town life but instead keeps to herself, shuttling between the general store and home.

Over the years, Jody becomes more jealous and oppressive. Envious and insecure because of his wife's good looks, he orders Janie to hide her long, thick hair while she works in the store. Janie resists his demands for a while but eventually she hides her feelings and learns to separate her inner life from her outer appearance.

Zora Neale Hurston

Finally, in her late thirties, Janie stands up to Jody. She cuts a customer the wrong size of tobacco, then reacts angrily when her husband publicly berates her intelligence and comments disparagingly about her behind.

> Naw, Ah ain't no young gal no mo' but den Ah ain't no old woman neither. Ah reckon Ah looks mah age too. But Ah'm uh woman every inch of me, and Ah know it. Dat's uh whole lot more'n *you* kin say. You big-bellies round here and put out a lot of brag, but 'tain't nothin' to it but yo' big voice. Humph! Talkin' 'bout *me* lookin' old! When you pull down yo' britches, you look lak de change uh life.
>
> (*Their Eyes Were Watching God,* p. 75)

When Jody dies of kidney failure shortly thereafter, Janie feels a great relief and sense of freedom. She is a wealthy widow just entering middle age.

Nine months later, Janie meets Tea Cake, a dark-skinned migrant worker ten or fifteen years younger than herself. Many men have wooed Janie for her money since Jody's death, but she has ignored them. Tea Cake, however, is different. He teaches Janie to play checkers the first time they meet, and they quickly fall in love. For Janie, Tea Cake brings alive her dreams of love as a young girl. They spend all their time together, fishing in the middle of the night, picnicking, and going to the movies. The townspeople do not approve. Tea Cake is younger and poorer than Janie, certainly not the sort of person with whom a mayor's widow should associate. Janie, however, does not care because Tea Cake makes her soul shine.

Listening to her own heart, Janie sells the store and marries Tea Cake. They move to the Everglades, where Tea Cake earns a living by picking beans and tomatoes and Janie finds her sense of self. The two set up house near Lake Okeechobee and make many friends. Then a terrible hurricane strikes the area. The lake floods, and wind and rain ravage the region. Torrents of water sweep away cars and houses, killing many of the residents. Tea Cake and Janie escape, struggling through raging water to find higher ground. As they flee Janie falls into the torrent. She grabs the tail of a cow which is swimming toward a higher elevation. A rabid dog, standing on the cow's shoulders, attacks Janie. Tea Cake manages to rescue her and kills the dog, but it bites Tea Cake's face during the struggle.

Some time later, they return to the wrecked community. Tea Cake works for a couple of weeks, then falls ill with rabies. The doctor wires for serum but Tea Cake goes mad before it arrives. One day he ferociously attacks Janie, who finally shoots him with a rifle. He bites her as he dies in her arms.

The doctor discovers Janie with Tea Cake's head in her lap and the bite marks on her arm. That same day she is tried and acquitted of the murder. Without Tea Cake, the Everglades is no longer home, so Janie ultimately returns to Eatonville.

Class and color among blacks. Among African Americans, the issue of color and its relationship to the light-skinned upper class was hotly debated during the turn of the century. "Few issues were more emotion-laded in the black community than those relating to the color prejudices and preferences of blacks themselves," maintains one scholar, and evidence of such prejudices can be found within Hurston's novel (Gateworth, p. 151). With her light skin and long, thick hair, the character Janie is considered very beautiful. Characters throughout the novel refer to Janie's beauty; it inspires envy in some of the women and desire in some of the men. One character who wishes to woo her decides not to because, he notes, a man needs to be rich to catch a woman like that.

Janie's first two marriages are indeed to rich men, and for most of the novel she associates with the wealthier segments of society. Her first husband, Logan, is a landowner with the only organ in town. Her second husband, Jody, becomes the richest and most prestigious resident of Eatonville. As his wife, Janie occupies a lofty position in Eatonville society. Yet she is unhappy in this position and continually wishes to associate with the "regular" people, like the men who tell stories on the front porch of the general store.

The stratification of black society after the Civil War was complex. It varied from region to region and changed from the late 1800s to the early 1920s, when an upwardly mobile, black middle class began to emerge. Historians have, nevertheless, drawn some general conclusions about the stratified society. According to one view, it could be traced back to the days of slavery, when social distinctions were made among field hands, house servants, and freemen. After the Civil War, those who had been freemen and favored slaves often obtained more political and economic power than other blacks. The early black elite based its status on factors often associated with such power—wealth, leadership, education, and refinement. Its members are said to have placed a strong emphasis on family heritage, specifying when their family had obtained freedom, what types of slaves their ancestors had been, and how their family had resisted slavery. Moreover, a disproportionate number of the black elite had light skin; many had white ancestors about whom they expressed pride. Some of them "placed a considerable distance between themselves and those [blacks] whom they considered outside of polite society" (Gateworth, p. 345).

On the other hand, historian Joel Williamson points to a closing of the gap between dark-skinned blacks and the often lighter-skinned elite in this era. Williamson takes into account the findings of experts in the 1920s and 1930s that black men, especially the successful ones, preferred light-skinned wives. He grants that this preference existed but questions its importance, pointing out that only a slight majority (56.5 percent) of the couples surveyed in those years fit the profile of a black husband and lighter-skinned wife.

In any case, by the 1920s a new group of economically prosperous blacks had emerged. Its members took to heart Booker T. Washington's avowal that African Americans should concentrate on self-improvement and the acquisition of material wealth, and they attached themselves economically to the larger black community. "The new black economic elite . . . was tied almost exclusively to the black ghetto and less concerned about assimilation into the larger society" (Gateworth, p. 334). Yet the novel's Jody Stark, who is a member of this new elite, shows concern for social distinctions. He marries a light-skinned wife and forbids her to mix with "common" people. When he first meets Janie, he tells her, "A pretty doll-baby lak you is meant to sit on de front porch and rock and fan yo'self and eat p'taters dat other folks plant special just for you" (*Their Eyes Were Watching God,* p 28). His attitude recalls the great variety in black society during this period. Stark's was but one of various social attitudes among successful blacks; his wife's desire to mix with regular people reflects another and apparently newer trend of the times.

After Jody's death, Janie begins an affair with Tea Cake, a man younger, poorer, and considerably darker than herself. The townspeople do not approve of her love for Tea Cake, whom they consider to be beneath her social status. Her friend Pheoby acknowledges that Tea Cake "don't know you'se useter uh more high time crowd than dat. You always did class off." Janie, however, replies, "Jody classed me off. Ah didn't" (*Their Eyes Were Watching God,* p. 107).

When Tea Cake and Janie move, Tea Cake is at first afraid that his society wife will not mix with the poor workers who populate the area. When Tea Cake spontaneously throws a party, he doesn't invite Janie because "Dem wuzn't no high muckty mucks. Dem wuz railroad hands and dey womenfolks. You ain't usetuh folks lak dat and Ah wuz skeered you might git all mad and quit me for takin' you 'mongst 'em" (*Their Eyes Were Watching God,* pp. 118-19). Janie quickly dispels this notion, assuring Tea Cake that she is not a social snob but wishes to experience life to the fullest.

Once established in the Everglades, Janie again encounters people who encourage her to disassociate herself from the general black population. Mrs. Turner, for example, has white features and considers herself to be better than those darker than her. In Hurston's words, "Anyone who looked more white folkish than herself was better than she was in her criteria, therefore it was right that they should be cruel to her at times, just as she was cruel to those more negroid than herself in direct ratio to their negroness" (*Their Eyes Were Watching God,* p. 138). Mrs. Turner seeks Janie for a friend because of her light skin and long hair. Dismayed by her marriage to a man as dark as Tea Cake, Mrs. Turner tells Janie that they ought to "lighten up the race," not mix with darker blacks: "Ah hates tuh see folks lak me and you mixed up wid 'em. Us oughta class off." (*Their Eyes Were Watching God,* p. 135). Characteristically, Janie disagrees.

Though Hurston has been criticized for her refusal to write about racial politics, it is possible to view her treatment of race relations among blacks as a comment on the pervasive nature of prejudice. While other artists concentrated on the relationships between blacks and whites, Hurston's work seemed instead to portray the presence of bigotry within all races and cultures.

Sources. Much of *Their Eyes Were Watching God* stems from local Florida history and folklore. As mentioned, Hurston grew up in an all-black community called Eatonville. One of the founders of Eatonville was Joe Clarke, probably the basis for the character Jody Starks. The source for the general store, a communal gathering place in the story, is Clarke's general store in Eatonville, which Hurston described as "the heart and spring" of the town (Hurston in Witcover, p. 28).

Hurston's educational background may provide in large part the key to understanding her works. She graduated with a Bachelor of Arts degree in anthropology from Varnard College in 1928 and studied for a year at Columbia, pursuing coursework with the famous Franz Boas, one of America's leading anthropologists. As an anthropologist, Hurston actively collected the Southern folklore that appears in her novel. "Playing the dozens," for example, a traditional type of verbal battle between blacks, is referred to in the story when Janie and Jody publicly fight. The talk on the porch of the novel's general store includes storytelling, lying sessions, and plain gossip, which Hurston probably witnessed firsthand in her childhood or in her later travels through the South.

Finally, the heartfelt relationship between Janie and Tea Cake stems from one of Hurston's personal relationships. She fell in love with a man of West Indian heritage, but the relationship turned out to be a stormy one. He insisted Hurston give up her career, but she would not. She later wrote, "The plot was far from the circumstances, but I tried to embalm all the tenderness of my passion for him in *Their Eyes Were Watching God*" (Hurston in Hemenway, p. 231).

Reviews. Zora Neale Hurston allegedly wrote *Their Eyes Were Watching God* in seven weeks. When it was published in 1937, most white reviewers seemed to like it. They noted its occasional rough spots and generally gave it favorable reviews:

> From first to last this is a well-nigh perfect story—a little sententious at the start, but the rest is simple and beautiful and shining with humor. In case there are readers who have a chronic laziness about dialect, it should be added that the dialect here is very easy to follow, and the images it carries are irresistible.
>
> (Tompkins in James and Brown, p. 29)

The black intelligentsia, however, lambasted the novel for its lack of political overtones. Richard Wright even accused Hurston of perpetuating the minstrel tradition in order to appeal to white audiences. Alain Locke, a noted black scholar who was also Hurston's friend, criticized the novel for focusing on black folklore and portraying silly characters.

> When, demanded Locke, would Hurston stop writing about 'these pseudo-primitives who the reading public still loves to laugh with, weep over, and envy,' and start writing, 'motive fiction and social documentation fiction'?
>
> (Witcover, p. 98)

Hurston responded by lashing out at her critics. She held that such remarks were merely condescension to her characters by intellectual snobs who in reality knew nothing of the black communities that she portrayed. It was a battle that was to haunt Hurston for the rest of her writing career.

For More Information

Gateworth, Willard B. *Aristocrats of Color.* Bloomington: Indiana University Press, 1990.

Hemenway, Robert. *Zora Neale Hurston: A Literary Biography.* Urbana: University of Illinois Press, 1977.

Hurston, Zora Neale. *Their Eyes Were Watching God.* 1937. Reprint. New York: Harper & Row, 1990.

Jahoda, Gloria. *Florida: A Bicentennial History.* New York: W. W. Norton, 1976.

James, Mertice M., and Dorothy Brown, eds. *Book Review Digest.* Vol. 33. New York: H. W. Wilson, 1938.

Kramer, Victor A., ed. *The Harlem Renaissance Reexamined.* New York: AMS, 1987.

Wall, Cheryl A. *Women of the Harlem Renaissance.* Bloomington: Indiana University Press, 1995.

Williamson, Joel. *New People: Miscegenation and Mulattoes in the United States.* New York: The Free Press, 1980.

Witcover, Paul. *Zora Neale Hurston.* New York: Chelsea House, 1991.

To Kill a Mockingbird

by

Harper Lee

A descendant of the renowned Southern general Robert E. Lee, (Nelle) Harper Lee was born in 1926 to Frances Finch Lee and Amasa Coleman, a lawyer. She lived with her family in the small Alabama town of Monroeville. Later she studied law at the University of Alabama before pursuing a writing career. Her first and only novel, *To Kill a Mockingbird,* became an instant bestseller and won the Pulitzer Prize in 1961.

THE LITERARY WORK

A novel set in a small town in fictional Maycomb County, Alabama, 1933-35; written in the 1950s, published in 1960.

SYNOPSIS

Two children face discrimination squarely at an early age as their lawyer father defends a black man accused of raping a white woman.

Events in History at the Time the Novel Takes Place

Agricultural and economic background. In *To Kill a Mockingbird,* the Finch family traces its heritage back to an ancestor who owned slaves and set up a modest cotton plantation in Alabama. This realistic if predictable fictional background reminds the reader that cotton had been an important Southern crop for many generations. By the time that the novel takes place, during the Great Depression, the cotton industry had suffered setbacks that affected both black and white residents throughout the South.

Overfarming of single crops, especially cotton, had exhausted the soil in many areas of the South. Widespread tenant farming only worsened the situation as farmers with short-term goals further exploited the land. Additionally, Southerners were reluctant to experiment with new techniques or crops such as rice or sugar cane. When cotton prices fell in 1930 and stayed low for several years, the Southern economy worsened. Adding to this frustration was an exodus of the younger generation of Southerners who had once been a source of farm labor; they were departing the countryside in large numbers now for better educational and job opportunities in the cities.

At the same time, rural blacks started to benefit from practical, hands-on lessons taught by a project called the Movable School. County agents, also black, traveled into their communities and showed them by example how to increase their crop yield and make improvements on their living quarters. Classes taught by men and women gave simple, relevant advice on matters of animal husbandry, mattress-making, canning, and midwifery.

Lastly, President Franklin D. Roosevelt's economic programs, collectively called the New Deal, offered relief to both races during the Depression. The 1933 National Recovery Act (NRA), which is referred to in the novel, provided for codes of fair competition and demanded that minimum wages and maximum hours be set. Also mentioned is the 1935 Works Progress Administration (WPA), which was responsible for putting over 8 million unemployed Americans to work in less than a decade. Aside from hiring workers to build high school stadiums, airports, school buildings, and other such large-scale facilities, the WPA funded artists and ethnic studies projects.

Sexual taboos. Racial relations were complicated by various restrictions in the 1930s. Breaking the taboo against sexual intercourse between a black man and a white woman was considered by most whites and some blacks to be one of the most serious offenses. At the heart of this controversy was the belief that this kind of miscegenation would "taint" racial purity.

Some blacks had an interest in protecting the unity and strength of their own race, which was under constant attack. Others, resentful of the domination that whites continued to exert over them, viewed voluntary sexual relations of blacks with whites as a betrayal of their own people.

Vehement, too, in their opposition to such unions, white supremacists sent a more hate-filled and public message. They asserted that the two races felt a mutual repulsion for one another, which would and should keep them eternally separated. White women, they insisted, could not possibly prefer black men. So if relations did develop, the black man was inevitably accused of using force.

There was in reality a clear double standard when it came to sexual relations between the races. Some white men thought little of forcing themselves on black women, calling their advances "welcome attention" (Hall, p. 156). The children born of these unions were usually not cherished by their fathers, but neither were they loathed the way mixed children born of white mothers often were. Yet even mulatto children from a loving home fared poorly in society. In the novel, Jem Finch points out mixed children who are well cared for by both parents but intimates that they are still subject to rejection by the larger community:

> They're real sad. . . . They don't belong anywhere. Colored folks won't have 'em because they're half white; white folks won't have 'em 'cause they're colored, so they're just in-betweens, don't belong anywhere.
>
> (Lee, *To Kill a Mockingbird,* p. 161)

For these reasons, the mere suggestion in the novel that Tom Robinson, a black man, had re-

lations with Mayella Ewell, a white woman, is enough to prejudice the community against him, even if they later believe that Mayella and her father are lying. With the accusation comes the likelihood that Tom will meet a violent end at the hands of a self-righteous mob, and one gathers outside his jail cell on the night before the trial. It is not only Tom who has something to fear, though: the possibility that this taboo was broken at Mayella's instigation accounts for the savagery with which her own father beats her.

Mob violence. Tom Robinson flees the Ewell house in terror of what might happen if he stays or is caught. In real life, a black man accused of raping a white woman would have cause to fear vigilante retribution. Also, he would have been aware that even if he evaded mob "justice," the lawyer assigned to his case would probably provide an inadequate defense. It should be noted, however, that in the novel the lawyer Atticus expresses optimism about Tom having a decent chance on appeal—this would have been a realistic assumption, since the Alabama Supreme Court tended to be slightly more liberal than the lower state courts.

The hatred of the mobs was displayed in the vicious punishments they exacted. Extremists felt that the suspicion of rape gave them license to be exceptionally cruel. The suspect, if seized, faced such dismal prospects as being beaten, tortured, lynched, or burned alive. In one recorded case, the woman herself was made, against her will, to light the pyre on which the accused stood.

Among the causes of this kind of violence were economic hardship and the wounded pride of whites who saw black laborers and tenant farmers gaining a semblance of financial freedom. When the situation for whites whose livelihood depended on cotton worsened, the number of lynchings mounted. In fact, from about 1930 to 1936, the number of lynchings rose in direct relation to the decrease in the price of cotton.

In 1936, when cotton prices were still low, the number of these killings began to drop. The trend continued downward in the years that followed, due primarily to the effects of two new movements. Roosevelt's New Deal programs were slowly reintegrating poor whites into society by providing them with a job, a bit more money, and a better prognosis for the future. In addition, public support for mob-style justice had begun to erode.

The shift in public opinion could be traced most immediately to the efforts of Southern women who had challenged the idea that mobs

Gregory Peck and Mary Badham in the 1962 film adaptation of *To Kill a Mockingbird.*

were intent only on defending the womenfolk. The strategy of an organization called the Association of Southern Women for the Prevention of Lynching (ASWPL) was twofold. Between violent incidents, they would speak publicly regarding the evils of lynching. And in the event that a mob formed, they hurried to the scene and pleaded on behalf of the victim. Through such tactics the ASWPL slowly began to win public support.

The novel calls attention to Eleanor Roosevelt's visiting Alabama and—to the disapproval of some whites—her interacting with its black citizens. In fact, back in Washington, Eleanor Roosevelt pushed hard for her husband to support the Dyer Antilynching Bill. The president explained his refusal by saying, "If I come out for the antilynching bill, [the Southern politicians] will block every bill I ask Congress to pass to keep America from collapsing. I just can't take that risk" (Roosevelt in Goodwin, p. 163).

A woman's role. Earlier in the century, Alabama had declined to ratify the Nineteenth Amendment, which gave women the right to vote. A majority of other states did ratify it, however, and so it became law for Alabama along with the rest of the country in 1920. Still, the impression persisted that white Southern ladies had no interest or place in the sullying men's world of politics. Many people continued to feel that church clubs

were the venue best suited to women's activities outside the household.

A good portion of the novel focuses on young Jem's first steps toward becoming a man, and his sister Scout's gradual willingness to be made into a lady by the characters Calpurnia, Miss Maudie, and Aunt Alexandra. When her aunt occasionally invites the women in the neighborhood over for coffee, refreshments, and a discussion of church business, Scout starts to unravel the mystery of what is expected socially of a lady in Maycomb, Alabama.

Southern society perpetuated a double standard in its expectations of white women in the private sphere. Historically the region called for these "ladies" to be idle, well-mannered, and skilled in the ways of hospitality. Whatever their family's social standing, this was the ideal to which they were to aspire. Traditionally, the raising of their children had often been left to hardworking black "mammies." The Finch's housekeeper, Calpurnia, is the modern counterpart of her antebellum predecessors. By the 1930s the expectations placed on women had relaxed somewhat, though many continued to live by the more traditional, passive set of values.

Late in the novel, Scout learns from her father Atticus and from Jem about the rights of women in Alabama in regard to rape law. She is surprised to learn that women are not allowed to sit on Alabama juries. At the time, the state did indeed have a mediocre record in the area of women's rights, having been unsupportive of the suffragette movement. The state furthermore gave little encouragement to women to exercise the right to vote once they were accorded that right by federal law.

Small-town life. Small towns were organized socially according to divisions as obvious to most Southerners as skin color or gender. Moving beyond these divisions, however, an observer notes the ingrained Southern emphasis on family history. Especially in a sparsely populated area, it was easy to know everyone else's background, and society ordered itself according to this information.

In the novel, Jem assess the four classes of Maycomb folks:

> There's the ordinary kind like us and the neighbors, there's the kind like the Cunninghams out in the woods, the kind like the Ewells down at the dump, and the Negroes.
> (*To Kill a Mockingbird,* p. 226)

His younger sister fails to see these distinctions, upsetting Jem's neat categories with the mention of other minorities and her conviction that "I think there's just one kind of folks. Folks" (*To Kill a Mockingbird,* p. 227).

Both in small towns and rural areas, Southern society of the early to mid-1900s featured a class structure that was tied to income and achievements. Jem's comment in the novel reflects some small-town distinctions among whites. First come "ordinary" townspeople like Jem, whose father, Atticus Finch, is a hardworking professional, a lawyer whose integrity wins him consistent high regard in the community. Below the Finches are the Cunninghams, hard-working whites who are so poor that they have to pay Atticus with items they can scrounge up, such as stove wood and hickory nuts, rather than cash. Lower still are the Ewells, poor whites with little interest in bettering themselves through school or work. Fourth are the blacks, a class apart that at times suffers brutal treatment, especially at the hands of some poor whites. Rural areas gave rise to a stratified society too, a hierarchy that in part moved up from sharecroppers, who could not even temporarily claim any land as their own, to tenant farmers, who at least rented their own plots, to small farmers, who actually possessed their own parcels. One's achievements also con-

tributed to status in the South. The ability to read and write, the record of having voted in a number of elections, or a family heritage that included one-time ownership of a plantation, for example, were attributes that elevated an individual's position in society.

The Novel in Focus

The plot. As an adult, Jean Louise ("Scout") Finch recalls the experiences she shared with her brother, Jem, in their hometown of Maycomb, Alabama. Her story starts in the summer of 1933, when she is nearly six years old and he is almost ten.

That summer they meet Dill Harris, a spry seven-year-old who suggests they try to make Arthur "Boo" Radley, the town's legendary recluse, come out of his house. The excitement generated by the unsuccessful attempt fades as school starts and Dill returns to his home in Mississippi.

School promises to be a miserable experience for Scout, who is more educated than her first-grade class and wiser in the ways of Maycomb than her teacher is. As the school year progresses, Jem and Scout start to find small objects hidden in a tree on the Radley property. And when Dill reappears the following summer, they turn their attention to the mysterious Radleys again.

A new school year starts, and Scout and Jem find more items in the Radley tree. But when they try to leave a thank-you note for their benefactor, they discover that Boo's older brother, Nathan, has filled the hiding place with cement. That winter, when a house on their street burns down, they encounter the supposedly terrifying Boo Radley without recognizing him.

Slowly, details of an important legal case begin to emerge: the children's father, Atticus, has been appointed to defend Tom Robinson, a respectable black man accused of raping a poor white woman named Mayella Ewell. Jem and Scout's disappointment in their father for being quiet and book-loving turns to whole hearted admiration when he kills a mad dog on their street with one shot.

Later, Atticus tries to show his children courage by exposing them to Mrs. Dubose, a cantankerous old woman struggling to free herself from an addiction to morphine before she dies. In anticipation of the hardship that his own family will soon face, he hopes they will learn from her that real courage is "when you know you're licked before you begin but you begin anyway and you see it through no matter what" (*To Kill a Mockingbird*, p. 112).

The following spring, the children's black housekeeper, Calpurnia, spontaneously takes Jem and Scout with her to church. Their Aunt Alexandra moves in with the family a short time later and expresses disapproval of the liberal manner in which Atticus, a widower, is raising his children. She hopes to instill in Scout and Jem a proper Southern preoccupation with class and family breeding.

Dill returns for the summer and finds the people of Maycomb anticipating the trial of Tom Robinson. As the witnesses give conflicting testimony, the truth becomes clear and vindicates the defendant. Almost everyone who secretly roots for Tom doubts he will be acquitted despite the evidence, given the racist beliefs held by so many people in the town. When Tom is found guilty, his supporters take cold comfort in Atticus's compelling defense. Their other victory lies in the fact that the jury took three-and-a-half hours to convict a man whom they had probably deemed guilty before the trial had begun. Tom is later shot and killed trying to escape a prison camp in desperation.

A BLACK ELDER MUSES ABOUT INTEGRATION IN SOUTHERN SCHOOLS

I wanted to know, "Why do you want the children to go to school together like that?" . . . But since it all happened, I realized that there was so much difference. And I said to myself, I said, "Now I see why white children were so far advanced over the colored, because their books were different. And when they finished they knowed something. And our children, when they finished, they knowed what little they knowed, but it wasn't really much good." —*An Alabama nursing-home worker, looking back at age sixty-two*

(Grundy, pp. 123-24)

After the trial, Maycomb life returns to normal. Atticus discounts the threats made by Mayella's father against Tom's supporters, including the Finch family. On the night of a Halloween pageant, however, the children are attacked by Bob Ewell, but their unseen friend, Boo Radley, watches out for them, as he has done in the past. Out of concern, Boo emerges from his seclusion to be seen for the first time in many years. Satisfied that his young friends will be all

right, and obviously very ill himself, he returns to his house, not to be seen alive again, but never to be forgotten by Jem and Scout.

Black community. With few exceptions, Harper Lee chooses to treat the blacks in the novel primarily as a community. The most notable exceptions are Calpurnia and Tom Robinson, about whom readers learn the most. Tom's wife, Helen, and Reverend Sykes also receive a more than minimal amount of individual attention.

But despite the development of these few characters, no other people in the novel are grouped together in the same way the blacks are. The few times the novel presents the black population, its members are a perfumed presence in the churchyard, or a community struggling to collect coins for the support of Helen and her children. They are invisible within a cluster of snug, well-kept houses past the dump and then expressive as an assembly rising to acknowledge Atticus Finch at the end of the trial. The next morning finds them represented collectively again in the bountiful gifts of food delivered to the lawyer's home out of respect and gratitude.

This focus on the collective group fits with Scout's position as the narrator. For a child-narrator (albeit a sophisticated one), the members of this unfamiliar social group might easily blend together most of the time. On the other hand, the novel repeatedly portrays this supposedly defenseless race as a community bound together by religion, integrity, and patience. As a result, the reader is led to believe that a great deal of justified moral outrage prompts the blacks' subdued show of resentment after the verdict. When Miss Merriweather, a white woman, sees the solemnness in her black servant's eyes, she terms the behavior *sulky* and it makes her so uncomfortable that she nearly fires the woman. Miss Merriweather and those like her in Maycomb may not acknowledge the justifiable outrage that binds the black community together, but the novel's portrayal makes its existence clear to the reader.

Sources. Harper Lee denied that *To Kill a Mockingbird* was autobiographical, and stressed simply that a writer should write truthfully about what she knows.

Lee's rendering of sleepy Maycomb recalls the author's upbringing in the small, quiet Alabama town of Monroeville, where her father was a lawyer. The author herself studied law at the University of Alabama until 1950. The mockingbird is often regarded as a symbol of the South, and it is the state bird of five Southern states. So named for its habit of imitating the songs of other

National Guard troops, called out by Governor Orval Faubus, keep black students from attending Central High School in Little Rock, Arkansas, despite the Supreme Court decision ending school segregation.

birds, it trills year-round. Lee chooses the beloved songbird to represent the devotion, purity of heart, and selflessness of characters like Atticus Finch, Tom Robinson, and Boo Radley.

The central family in the novel shares its name with Lee's mother, whose maiden name was Finch. The name of Maycomb County is fictional. Its closest sounding real-life counterpart is Macon, which lies several counties over from the southwest corner of Alabama, where the story takes place. In her development of characters, Lee has singled out author Truman Capote, one of her childhood companions, as the inspiration for the novel's impish Dill Harris.

When Lee refers to the world beyond Maycomb, she incorporates historical details to suit her purpose. The events are sometimes condensed to fit the timespan of the novel, which covers the summer of 1933 to the fall of 1935. It is improbable, for example, that by 1935, a child in rural Alabama would have heard of Hitler's campaign to imprison the Jews in Europe as occurs in the novel; Hitler's first efforts to round up Jews did not begin to intensify until 1937. Also, the ladies at Aunt Alexandra's missionary circle are four years premature in their disapproval of the First Lady's famous decision to place her chair between the seating areas for whites and blacks in a Birmingham auditorium.

And technically, the National Recovery Act is hailed as dead in the novel a few months before it was formally terminated on January 1, 1936.

Events in History at the Time the Novel Was Written

The civil rights movement. The Association of Southern Women for the Prevention of Lynching was a precursor to the full-fledged civil rights movement that began in the 1950s. Their efforts had perhaps helped open a path for a gradual strengthening of the black voice in public and an eventual mass movement based on civil disobedience.

Humane in its portrayal of many different kinds of Southerners, even the mobs, *To Kill a Mockingbird* appeared at a time when racial tensions were reaching heated proportions in Alabama and the rest of the South. Alabama became famous as a testing ground in the fight against segregation. In the cities of Montgomery, Selma, and Birmingham, protesters evolved a simple but dangerous strategy: they drew the attention of the media to their causes by patiently submitting to beatings, insults, water hoses, and police dogs. The Montgomery bus boycott in 1955-56 was one of the movement's first successes, and its members celebrated the victory cautiously. In fact, white authorities were so resistant to any show of strength by blacks that the National Association for the Advancement of Colored People (NAACP) was banned in Alabama from 1956 to 1965.

Around the same time, rural areas began to feel the effects of a 1954 U.S. Supreme Court decision that ruled segregation in public schools unconstitutional. In small numbers at first, black students of all ages tried to attend previously all-white schools. Often they were escorted to and from school for their own safety. In rural Clay County, Alabama, one family described their experience when their daughter—a junior in high school—was the first to integrate a school in Ashland. The family received death threats, bomb threats, and crank calls, and found a burning cross left for them as a warning—before the girl even attended class. When she started to go to school, in an act that recalls the strength of the black community in the novel, black men in the neighborhood took steps to protect the courageous family. The mother recalls how, "They would come with guns, and they would climb that tree, and watch this house, and take turns all night. Oh, it was terrible" (Grundy, p. 121).

Reception. Harper Lee's first and only novel became an instant bestseller when it was published in 1960. She had written and revised it during the 1950s, and in 1961, the finished version won her the Pulitzer Prize, the Alabama Library Association award, the Brotherhood Award of the National Conference of Christians and Jews, and a year later the *Bestsellers* paperback of the year award.

Critics generally concluded that the story weakens after the verdict, and they debated whether or not a girl less than ten years old was convincing in the role of narrator. But inevitably, they had warm praise for the novel as a whole. One reviewer in the *Chicago Sunday Tribune* highlighted the appeal of both the noble characters and the base ones:

> This is in no way a sociological novel. It underlines no cause. It answers no questions. It offers no solutions. It proposes no programs. It is simply an excellent piece of story telling, which on the way along suggests that there are in Maycomb, Ala., persons of good will in whom love and generous loyalty supersede law, and others in whom meanness—along with envy and fear—breeds lying persecution under law.
> (Sullivan in Bryfonski, p. 340)

For More Information

Bryfonski, Dedria, ed. *Contemporary Literary Criticism.* Vol. 12. Detroit: Gale Research, 1980.

Goodwin, Doris Kearns. *No Ordinary Time: Franklin and Eleanor Roosevelt: The Home Front in World War II.* New York: Simon & Schuster, 1994.

Grundy, Pamela. *You Always Think of Home: A Portrait of Clay County, Alabama.* Athens: University of Georgia Press, 1991.

Hall, Jacquelyn Dowd. *Revolt against Chivalry: Jessie Daniel Ames and the Women's Campaign against Lynching.* New York: Columbia University Press, 1979.

Lee, Harper. *To Kill a Mockingbird.* New York: Warner, 1960.

Wiggins, Sarah Woolfolk, ed. *From Civil War to Civil Rights: Alabama, 1860-1960.* Tuscaloosa: University of Alabama Press, 1987.

A Tree Grows in Brooklyn

by

Betty Smith

Betty Smith, in the first novel of her career, presents a picture of Brooklyn that she knew well. Like her main character, Francie Nolan, Smith lived in the slums of Williamsburg. In a show of courage and hope, however, both Smith and Francie managed to rise above their surroundings to achieve the dream that originally drew foreigners toward the shores of America.

> ## THE LITERARY WORK
>
> A novel set in Brooklyn, New York, about 1900 to 1919; published in 1943.
>
> ## SYNOPSIS
>
> A young girl of an Irish immigrant family comes of age in the Williamsburg slums of Brooklyn.

Events in History at the Time the Novel Takes Place

Brooklyn, New York. In 1898 the New York state legislature expanded the boundaries of New York City, nearly doubling its population overnight. The new area, Greater New York, was divided into five sections known as boroughs. These included Manhattan, Brooklyn, Queens, Richmond, and the Bronx. To some elderly New Yorkers, the new territories seemed so uncharted that they might as well have belonged to a foreign country.

Lying between the East River and the Atlantic Ocean at Coney Island, Brooklyn stretched across an expanse of land three times larger than that of Manhattan Island. Its population, at 2.5 million residents, likewise surpassed the area formerly considered New York City proper. Within its streets, one could travel between merchant wharves and warehouses, skyscrapers, apartment buildings, suburban homes, and slums. Like their counterparts in Manhattan, low-income areas such as Williamsburg,

Brownsville, and Red Hook housed the city's poor in tenements.

In the novel, Francie Nolan and her family make their home in Williamsburg. States one author, "Nothing was more characteristic of New York than the rapid degeneration into slums of areas formerly fashionable" (Morris, p. 274). Some enterprising individual, generally an Irishman, would lease an old mansion, then subdivide it and rent it out to tenants on a weekly basis. Overcrowded, dirty, dank, and full of foul air, such tenements often contained grocery and vegetable shops in their cellars and sometimes grog or liquor shops and dance halls.

More prosperous New Yorkers did not remain entirely insensitive to the plight of the poor. At the turn of the century, philanthropic efforts such as the Henry Street Settlement, begun by Lillian D. Wald and Mary M. Brewster, attracted the attention of socially conscious citizens. The settlement house developed into an organization that provided social services and a forum where members of labor and management could resolve their disputes. Not all of the poorer classes, however, welcomed its existence. Like Mrs. Nolan, many "hated anything that smacked of charity" and rejected such assistance (Smith, *A Tree Grows in Brooklyn,* p. 188). Instead they made their way as best they could and dreamed of one day owning a permanent residence.

In the novel, Mrs. Nolan's mother counsels her on the day of Francie's birth, "Before you die, you must own a bit of land—maybe with a house on it that your child or your children may inherit" (*A Tree Grows in Brooklyn,* p. 78). Although incredulous at the notion, Katie Nolan nonetheless saves a bit of her money every day in hopes of some day owning her own piece of Greater New York.

Irish immigrants in New York. Beginning with a potato crop failure in 1822 and culminating in the Great Famine of 1845-1847, Irish citizens abandoned their nation in droves, searching for more prosperous surroundings. During this period, some 1.5 million Irish immigrants made their way to the United States. Cities like Philadelphia, Boston, Chicago, San Francisco, and New York swelled with new Irish arrivals. According to an 1890 census, the Irish comprised as much as one fourth of the population in the city of New York.

Mostly a young group averaging under thirty-five years of age, the Irish immigrants found jobs, for example, on riverboat and railroad lines. Those who did not work in labor-related industries generally earned their living in domestic-servant positions. Away from work, they tended to focus their lives on the home, the Roman Catholic Church, and the neighborhood saloon.

Irish American drinking. The saloon, along with the church, became a focal point of community life in Irish American neighborhoods. It was intimately connected to three main facets of the Irish immigrant existence—politics, jobs, and individual identity. Cities were divided into wards, each with its own set of street gangs and social clubs controlled by a ward boss, a politician who supplied the people in his ward with jobs, food, and drink. It was common for a ward boss to own and operate saloons himself. Sometimes he would frequent the drinking establishment in person, but usually he dispatched heelers—men who performed his legwork and put pressure on constituents to vote for their candidate.

The relationship between ward boss and constituent was not necessarily as unfriendly as it might sound. A boss, either himself or through his heelers, treated others to a drink to stay in their good graces, meanwhile influencing them with the political talk that followed. "If a barkeeper is given money with which to treat the boys," explained one observer, "even the fairly respectable men who are at the bar, after a round of drinks, look with favor upon the saloon-keeper's candidate. Other things being equal, the man who has the greater number of saloon-keepers on his side will surely be elected" (Stivers, p. 123). Meanwhile, a lot of men frequented these establishments not to become politically informed, but rather in hopes of securing one of the jobs that the ward boss doled out.

The drinking establishment served another function too. It became a place where Irish Americans were welcomed in a society that often shunned them. The help-wanted ad that follows is a realistic example of the prejudice that the Irish encountered at the time: "WOMAN WANTED—To do general housework. . . . English, Scot, Welsh, German, or any country or color except Irish" (Stivers, p. 138).

Irish Americans withstood such prejudice with the help of a tight family unit. Children were usually born at home, and Irish families maintained close ties. As a rule, the family unit worked together to ensure its survival. Fathers frequently died prematurely in their thirties or forties. In fact, the "widow woman" became a classic Irish communal figure. When Francie and Neely's father dies in the novel, the two children take on jobs to help the family. This type of response was typical. If a father passed away, the remaining family members would work to make up for the economic loss.

The Irish in New York politics. In *A Tree Grows in Brooklyn,* Francie's father Johnny Nolan—like many Irish American men—becomes quite involved with the local Democratic Party machine, then known as Tammany Hall, after the name of party headquarters. He takes the family on an all-day boating excursion and picnic hosted by the party leaders and participates actively in election activities. Initially, the Democratic Party had kept the Irish out of its domain as part of its general anti-immigrant stance. On April 24, 1817, however, a group of angry Irishmen stormed Tammany Hall to demand the nomination of the Irishman Thomas Emmet for Congress. A fight broke out and Tammany began to listen to its Irish constituents. By 1821, when the New York State constitutional convention awarded suffrage to every male citizen, Tammany had become a decidedly Irish operation.

Tammany Hall at the turn of the century.

The New York political machine during the early 1900s had its roots in the neighborhood. Children learned songs such as the one Francie sings in the novel:

> Tammany, Tammany,
> Big Chief sits in his teepee,
> Cheering brave to victory,
> Tamma-nee, Tamma-nee.
> (*A Tree Grows in Brooklyn,* p. 156)

Neighborhood politics in New York operated under an unofficial citywide leader who headed a "shadow government," a power structure that was often more responsible for many of the community's aspects and events than its elected governing body. The unofficial leaders collected revenues from local saloonkeepers, gamblers, and contractors. Using these funds, the political party would aid the destitute even if the party was not in office. It might provide legal counsel for those New Yorkers who could not afford it, or help Irish immigrants find their way through a set of confusing governmental regulations so they could become citizens. If the party was in office—that is, when a representative held a New York government post—the political machine could provide more valuable commodities. These included jobs, generally on public works projects.

For most of the time period of the novel, the political boss of Tammany Hall was Charles F. Murphy, under whose administration one company, New York Contracting, won millions of dollars in contracts to construct rail lines. It is unknown whether Murphy profited personally from such deals. Tammany politicians had a reputation for embezzling funds for themselves, but Murphy, in fact, cleaned up the machine during his tenure. He stopped the practice of taking payoffs from saloons, gambling houses, and brothels and instead resolved to get funds from business contracts. There was still corruption in city government, however. Tips were passed on about where the city was about to build a new bridge so that someone could buy the property and then turn around and sell it to the city for a high profit. Such dealings were unethical, but nevertheless more legitimate than in the past. By the end of Murphy's tenure (1902-24), says one historian, Tammany Hall had been turned into "an extraordinarily successful and responsive organization dedicated to the betterment of society" (Allen, p. 231).

The Novel in Focus

The plot. *A Tree Grows in Brooklyn* opens with the image of a tired tree "struggling to reach the sky" (*A Tree Grows in Brooklyn,* p. 7). The author quickly expands this metaphor to encompass not only the setting of the novel, but its characters as well. The story is the struggle of one family to survive in spite of the awesome odds it faces.

Francie Nolan has seen only eleven years of life at the beginning of the novel, yet she displays a wisdom beyond her age. Growing up in the tenements of Brooklyn at the turn of the century, Francie knows hunger and suffering. She watches her mother go to work each morning as a janitress, and she helps her father when he stumbles home drunk every day. Together with her brother Neely, however, Francie finds joy in her world. She never feels shame for her father. She knows him only as the fun and charismatic man that she loves. Francie and Neely help the family however they can—for instance, collecting lead bottle caps to exchange for pennies. Continually dreaming of a better life, Mrs. Nolan and her children contribute weekly to their tin can savings bank.

The novel does not merely focus its energies on the day-to-day hardships of Brooklyn's poorer classes. It maintains, even in its most abysmal moments, an aura of hope. Katie Rommely Nolan, Francie's mother, is a first-generation American, the daughter of Austrian immigrants. Although poor, she and two of her three sisters do read and write. They represent the family's first literate generation. As *her* mother, Mary Rommely, explains, "Don't you see? . . . Already, it is starting—the getting better. . . . This child [Francie] was born of parents who can read and write. . . . To me this is a great wonder" (*A Tree Grows in Brooklyn,* p. 75). This optimistic attitude prevails throughout the novel.

Before Francie graduates from elementary school, her father dies of an alcohol-related illness. He leaves behind not only his widow and two children, but also the unborn baby that Katie carries. Francie postpones her hopes of high school and college to take a job in a factory. When Katie insists that Neely enroll in high school in the fall, Francie becomes the family's primary provider. She also, over this period of time, grows into a young woman. Francie learns not only about her changing body, but also about boys. She discovers that some men will take advantage of women and girls, and she suffers through her first broken heart.

The baby born after the death of Mr. Nolan seems to represent the survival of hope. When Katie eventually remarries a wealthy public official, Francie remarks about the baby, "Annie Laurie McShane! She'll never have the hard times we had, will she?" (*A Tree Grows in Brooklyn,* p. 414). Her brother replies, "No. And she'll never have the fun we had either" (*A Tree Grows in Brooklyn,* p. 414). Although the Nolans did struggle, they faced life's hardships together.

The close of the novel finds Francie headed off to college in anticipation of a brighter future. Coming full circle, Smith again returns to the tree. She states, "this tree in the yard—this tree that men chopped down . . . this tree that they built a bonfire around, trying to burn up its stump—this tree lived!" (*A Tree Grows in Brooklyn,* p. 30). So too does the Nolan family.

The Irish American sense of community. The Irish saloon provided an important focal point for immigrant families, and for the Nolans, this certainly held true. Johnny Nolan, throughout his life, drank heavily and eventually died of alcoholism-related complications. Following his death, however, the saloonkeeper at Johnny's favorite watering hole comes to the aid of the Nolan family. Unable to "get Johnny out of his mind" (*A Tree Grows in Brooklyn,* p. 268), McGarrity calls on the Nolans. He does not feel guilty about his possible role in Johnny's demise, for McGarrity reasons that "if he didn't get it [alcohol] here, he would have got it somewhere else" (*A Tree Grows in Brooklyn,* p. 268). McGarrity simply enjoyed Johnny's company and wants to help out the family. This type of commitment to the community was typical of Irish Americans.

One historian writes, "There were two unwritten rules the rising tradesmen and professional men usually obeyed. One was to live in the neighborhood. . . . The other requirement was a willingness to help the worst off in time of need" (Shannon, p. 37). Neighbors would only patronize the local businessmen whose families they warmly regarded. Everything in the Irish American community came back to the family. Engaged in difficult, physically consuming work, Irish American males typically perished early in life. If a laborer died without insurance, the community would take up door-to-door collections for his remaining family members. No one who hoped to survive in the neighborhood would turn down the collector. From an early age, Irish children were taught the importance of this group survival.

The young boys' gang was a typical sight in an Irish American neighborhood. In the novel, Neely belongs to one of these street fraternities. The gang demanded of its members the qualities of loyalty, cooperation, and obedience, as well as the values of aggressiveness and self-motivation. The raids and street fights that gangs engaged in usually proved who "ran" the block. Within these gangs, however, one's position in the hierarchy usually depended on personal initiative. In this manner, young boys learned the importance of the individual within the community. These ideals, found in childhood, helped the Irish in forming their strong political and communal groups. Community and neighborhood organizations, from an early time, helped to shape Irish American lives.

Sources. While Betty Smith never disclosed any clear sources for her novel, most critics agree that *A Tree Grows in Brooklyn* contains a variety of autobiographical references. Like Francie, Smith grew up in the Williamsburg section of Brooklyn. After leaving school at the age of fourteen, she worked at various jobs ranging from factory laborer to office clerk. Eventually she returned to school and completed her degree at the University of Michigan. Like her main character, Smith found a way to complete the education she so desired.

Events in History at the Time the Novel Was Written

The Prohibition movement. Francie's father was not alone in his struggles with alcoholism. In fact, the lawmakers of the early 1900s so feared the nation's relationship with alcohol that they sought to prohibit it altogether. The close of the novel shows McGarrity preparing for such a reform by stockpiling alcohol in a warehouse just outside of the city. He hoped to become one of the many to earn his fortune during the era of Prohibition.

Prohibition was the result of a long reform movement begun by the Protestant churches during the 1880s and the 1890s. Organizations such as the Women's Christian Temperance Movement and the National Prohibition Party lobbied for the restriction of the sale and consumption of alcohol. During the early 1900s, antisaloon leagues sprang up nationwide. These groups, largely composed of middle-class Americans, sought not only to stifle the sale of alcohol but also to regulate the social habits of the working classes. Urban reform committees became proponents of antisaloonism and Prohibition. Members argued that industrialization, with its expansion of leisure time, had begun a social collapse that only political and legal influences could halt. These organizers viewed al-

cohol as a dangerous drug that disrupted lives and families. They felt it the duty of the government to relieve the temptation of alcohol by banning it altogether.

In January of 1919, the United States Congress ratified the Eighteenth Amendment to the Constitution. This outlawed "the manufacture, sale, or transportation of intoxicating liquors" on a national level. Nine months later, lawmakers passed the Volstead Act, providing the means of enforcing such measures. Much to the dismay of Prohibitionists, however, the act had little effect on the behavior of the American public.

One usually had little trouble obtaining alcohol during the era of Prohibition. Rural distillers manufactured the liquor and "rumrunners" smuggled it into cities for resale in bars like the one that McGarrity planned to open. Eventually the government realized that Prohibition had had little effect on the drinking habits of Americans. In 1933 the Twenty-First Amendment passed Congress, annulling Prohibition altogether. By the time Smith completed her novel, the ban on alcohol had run its entire course.

The evolving Irish American. Whereas the Irish immigrants of the early 1900s struggled against antiforeigner sentiments, latter generation Irish Americans enjoyed the fruits of their ancestors' hard-won battles. With a growing group of respectable merchants, public officials, and civil servants, the Irish changed their image. No longer did the public view them mainly as wild, drunken laborers; as a community, the Irish Americans held too much money, power, and diversity for such a stereotype. That is not to say that they had entirely penetrated the Protestant American inner circles, only that they had achieved a certain elevation over other immigrant cultures. Compared to the newly arrived Italians, Greeks, Poles, and Russian Jews, the Irish were the group closest to wide public acceptance. Ironically, the economic circumstances of the Great Depression helped to boost the Irish American community.

With the virtual collapse of the national economy in 1929, America turned after the Depression to the Democratic Party as the voice of hope. Since this was the political group to which the Irish overwhelmingly belonged, the community stood poised to rise. Coupled with this circumstance was the election of Franklin D. Roosevelt in 1933 into the White House. A more open-minded president than prior Democrats like Grover Cleveland and Woodrow Wilson, Roosevelt welcomed diversity in his cabinet. For the

The liberation of the Dachau concentration camp, 1945.

first time, Irish Americans found themselves in positions of high political power.

In 1933, the Irishman James Aloysius Farley rose as head of the Democratic National Committee. He helped Roosevelt mediate between the administration and the local party organizations through a grassroots campaign. In this manner he built up and solidified the Democratic Party on a national level. A second key player in Roosevelt's administration was Thomas Gardiner Corcoran, or "Tommy the Cork." As an advisor in the Reconstruction Finance Corporation, Corcoran helped to draft legislation, write speeches, and lobby congressmen. Another Irishman, Joseph P. Kennedy, headed the newly formed Securities and Exchange Commission, which policed stock market practices. He eventually became the United States's first Irish American ambassador to England.

A goal of Roosevelt's New Deal administration was to redistribute America's wealth on a more socially conscious level, and Irish Americans—who had long been known to "take care of their own"—seemed natural candidates to help carry out this goal. Their progress in politics was meanwhile accompanied by progress in other areas, beginning in earlier decades and continuing at the time the novel was written. When Francie heads off to college at the close of *A Tree Grows*

in Brooklyn, she achieves a goal that no family member before her had reached. Given that her immigrant grandmother was illiterate, Francie's educational success indicates another type of Irish American advancement.

The Holocaust. One of the novel's opening scenes finds Neely and his gang confronting a young Jewish boy. While playing in the street, they "bedevil" the boy as he makes his way to temple. In a show of neighborhood dominance, Neely and his friends yell, "Don't show your puss on Devoe Street . . . and keep away from Christian girls" (*A Tree Grows in Brooklyn,* p. 20). In the cramped quarters of a Brooklyn neighborhood, people of different nationalities lived only a few streets away from one another. Yet despite this physical proximity, most ethnic groups kept strictly to themselves. Even in the melting pot of immigrant New York, old-world prejudices died hard. A Jewish immigrant of the era, Edward Steiner, recalls being taunted by an Irish lad whose "delight in my suffering made him invent new cruelties, every hour" (Stivers, p. 124).

The novel depicts anti-Semitism in the early 1900s. Overseas it had escalated to deadly proportions by 1943, when the novel was published. Under the leadership of Adolf Hitler, between 1933 and 1938 Nazi Germany boycotted Jewish businesses, forbade marriage between Jews and

Gentiles (under the Nuremberg Laws of 1935), and opened its first concentration camps at Oranienburg, Buchenwald, and Dachau. With the onset of World War II in 1939, Germany moved its campaign of Jewish extermination outside the German borders. Beginning with his invasion of Eastern Europe, Hitler planned to systematically eliminate all peoples of Jewish descent. Tragically, much of this genocide, which eventually took nearly 6 million Jewish lives, occurred without direct protests from those who were aware of the mass murders.

On August 1, 1942, Gerhardt Riegner, the representative of Switzerland in the World Jewish Congress, received a report that he could not ignore. Up until this point, the question of murder had only been grounded in "unconfirmed accounts." On that fateful August day, however, Riegner received word from a German informant that the Nazis had ordered the extermination of all Jews in Europe. The information even related the specific mode of murder, prussic acid administered through communal showers at Germany's various concentration camps. Although reports previous to this one had reached both the United States and Great Britain and had even seen publication in various newspapers, neither government could confirm that a specific order had been issued by Hitler and the Nazis for the complete annihilation of Europe's Jews.

Despite the seemingly overwhelming evidence, the U.S. State Department still suppressed the release of Riegner's information. U.S. officials claimed a need for further documentation. Finally in November of the same year, after much work and frustration, Riegner compiled and documented what the State Department considered to be sufficient evidence for action. On December 8, 1942, President Franklin D. Roosevelt received a twenty-page document entitled *Blue Print for Extermination*.

Soon Britain, the United States, and the Soviet Union moved jointly to both condemn and prosecute the Nazis for their crimes.

Reception of the novel. Smith's novel met with enormous success from among the reading public. The critical reception, however, varied. Orville Prescott wrote in *The Yale Review*, "A Tree Grows in Brooklyn is a first novel of uncommon skill, an almost uncontrollable vitality and zest for life, the work of a fresh, original and highly gifted talent" (Prescott in Gunton, p. 422). A critic for *The Nation*, however, offered this impression: "Miss Smith . . . falls into the common error of forgetting that it takes time to learn the language of literary sensibility: at sixteen, even at eleven, her Francie Nolan thinks with the mind of the mature Betty Smith" (Trilling in Gunton, p. 422). Despite any critical misgivings, Smith's novel found high favor among the general public, and praise as a faithful and almost poetic portrayal of the twentieth-century Brooklyn slums.

For More Information

Allen, Oliver E. *The Tiger: The Rise and Fall of Tammany Hall*. Reading, Mass.: Addison-Wesley, 1993.

Glazer, Nathan, and Daniel Patrick Moynihan. *Beyond the Melting Pot*. Cambridge, Mass.: Harvard University Press, 1963.

Gunton, Sharon R., ed. *Contemporary Literary Criticism*. Vol. 19. Detroit: Gale Research, 1981.

Morris, Lloyd. *Incredible New York*. New York: Random House, 1951.

Shannon, William. *The American Irish*. New York: Macmillan, 1963.

Smith, Betty. *A Tree Grows in Brooklyn*. New York: Harper Collins, 1943.

Stivers, Richard. *A Hair of the Dog: Irish Drinking and American Stereotype*. University Park: Pennsylvania State University Press, 1976.

The War of the Worlds

by
H. G. Wells

H. G. Wells was born in 1866 to a poor family living near London, England. He was apprenticed to menial jobs before beginning his studies at the Normal School of Science in 1884 under the tutelage of Thomas Henry Huxley, a controversial zoologist. Although a promising pupil, Wells considered himself a failure as a student: "[Lacking] the character or the capacity for a proper scientific career, I had convinced myself that I was a remarkable wit and potential writer" (Wells, *Experiment in Autobiography,* p. 238). Wells's exposure to science fostered what he called his prophetic habit of mind, a preoccupation with how things will take shape in the future. His science fiction stories, including *The War of the Worlds,* seem a product of this habit. More fantastic than scientific, they carry evolutionary theory to horrific conclusions.

Events in History at the Time of the Novel

The influence of science on Wells. Although a renowned zoologist in his own right, Thomas Henry Huxley won notoriety through his eloquent defense of Charles Darwin's *Origin of Species.* Darwin's theory that humans were descended from ape-like creatures through a process of mutation lasting countless generations provoked derision from religious authorities. In a famous speech against Darwinian evolution, a zealous bishop turned on Huxley and asked "Is it on your grandfather's or your grandmother's

side that the ape ancestry comes in?" (Taton, p. 478). Huxley replied,

A man has no reason to be ashamed of having an ape for his grandfather. If there were an ancestor whom I should feel shame in recalling it would be a man of restless and versatile intellect who, not content with success in his own sphere of activity, plunges into scientific questions with which he has no real acquaintance, only to obscure them by aimless rhetoric and distract the attention of his hearers from the point at issue by digressions and appeals to religious prejudice.

(Taton, p. 478)

Huxley was an influential mentor of Wells, whose own fascination with evolution is evident in Wells's two most famous novels, *The Time Machine* and *The War of the Worlds.* In one of his first publications, "Man of the Year Million," Wells depicts future humans that have evolved to be much like the marauding *The War of the*

Worlds Martians he later wrote about. In *The War of the Worlds,* Wells imagined that, as the mind grew, it could develop machinery to replace arms and legs. The narrator of the novel maintains, "to me it is quite credible that the Martians may be descended from beings not unlike ourselves, by a gradual development of brain and hands . . . at the expense of the rest of the body" (Wells, *The War of the Worlds,* p. 151).

Wells was not oblivious to the moral or philosophical implications of Darwinian evolution. Indirectly, it held that man's intellect no longer distinguishes him from beast, but seems merely another one of the many Darwinian tools forged not by a divine maker but by biological necessity. The humans in *The War of the Worlds* behave as expected of creatures in a Darwinian fight for survival, trampling each other in flight and squabbling over remaining supplies. An artilleryman's proposal that the weak should die to safeguard the gene pool echoes late nineteenth-century social Darwinism. This extension of Darwin's conclusions suggested that efforts to help the poor merely weakened society by allowing the unfit to survive and reproduce.

Another scientific topic of the day, the second law of thermodynamics, states that the amount of energy in the universe that can be harnessed is always decreasing. This conjured visions of the cosmos as a tremendous clock that at the moment was still ticking but bound eventually to halt. Cosmologists, who realized that the earth's sun has a finite lifespan, were predicting worldly doom. As revealed in the introduction to *The War of the Worlds,* in 1894 Huxley himself warned that "the time will come when . . . all forms of life will die out" (*The War of the Worlds,* p. 28). Wells's novel confronts a topical issue of his day—the prophesied inevitable extinction of humankind. The novel's Martian invasion of Earth furthermore reflects an acceptance of scientific notions of adaptation and change. The Martians have exhausted the resources of their older planet and flee to the fertile young earth.

Wells and religion. Although raised in a religious family, Wells rejected Christianity even before he read the writings of Darwin. A childhood dream of God "basting a poor broken sinner rotating slowly over a fire" (Wells, *Experiment in Autobiography,* p. 46) awoke in him a hatred of God that, as he matured, became a hatred for the church. Wells struggled with his pride when, in order to acquire a teaching position, he was asked to partake in communion, the rite employing bread and wine as a symbol of the Last

H. G. Wells

Supper. He goaded the curate with questions about the influence of Darwinism and geological evidence on biblical history and, after each answer, replied "So that is what I have to believe" (Wells, *Experiment in Autobiography,* p. 150). During the invasion in *The War of the Worlds,* a curate appeals for divine aid but his supplications are futile. The lack of heavenly intervention illustrates Wells's contention that Christ is "a dressed up inconsistent effigy of amiability . . . making vague promises of helpful miracles for the cheating of simple souls, an ever absent help in times of trouble" (Wells, *Experiment in Autobiography,* p. 46).

Despite such cynicism, Wells is the product of a God-fearing society, as is his narrator. The narrator's interpretation of events in the novel bridges religious and scientific views. Although he rejects the curate's hopeless fatalism, he too prays and, when the Martians lie dead and rotting, extends his hands toward the sky and thanks God. By including the narrator's quasi-religious awe as well as the strictly scientific explanation of the Martians' death, the novel shows a respect for both the observable and the unknown.

Late Victorian sentiment. Great Britain flourished during the long reign of Queen Victoria

(1837-1901). Industrialization had secured for many a stable fortune. Louis Pasteur's use of vaccination to treat rabies in 1885 proved that medical science could blunt the menace of disease. Self-righteous colonialists seemed to have tamed what, to the British, were the wildest corners of the globe, and the mighty British navy safeguarded the channel isolating England from the rest of Europe. In 1887 England celebrated the Victorian jubilee, an occasion to demonstrate loyalty to the throne, national patriotism, and imperial pride. It was attended by the ministers of self-governing colonies. A second and larger jubilee in 1897 indicated the continuing prosperity of the empire.

But anxieties rankled beneath this veneer of contentment. The tumult of industrialization and social and philosophical movements in Great Britain had bred an uneasiness about the future. Scientific theories like Darwin's publication of *The Origin of Species* in 1859 had challenged religion. The introduction in England of the German philosopher Friedrich Nietzsche's works announcing the "death of God" helped to undermine conventional ideas of morality. Similarly England's exposure to foreign writers like Henrik Ibsen and George Sand, whose works concerned emancipation from sexual double standards, hinted at future challenges to the institution of marriage. The accelerated pace of change fostered a foreboding uncertainty about the future.

The calamitous wars of the nineteenth century, made devastating by new long-range and semiautomatic weaponry, shaped this unrest into a fear of invasion. In 1871 Sir George Chesney's short story "Battle of Dorking" about a successful German invasion of England alarmed the nation and spawned a new genre of futuristic war stories. "Battle of Dorking" differed from earlier war stories in its suggestion that new, unimagined weapons could play a decisive role in battle. It sparked such anxiety that the prime minister denounced it as alarmist propaganda. Wells took this notion to an extreme in *The War of the Worlds,* suggesting that all of humanity might become the victim of a technology it hardly understood.

This fear of invasion may also have been symptomatic of the guilty conscience of a colonialist power. Throughout the nineteenth century the British had expanded their territories in Canada, Australia, Africa, India, Southeast Asia, and the Middle East. Between 1884 and 1902, 2.5 million square miles of new territory came under British control. The narrator of *The War of the Worlds* likens the Martian invasion to the British conquest of Tasmania, an island south of mainland Australia:

> The Tasmanians, in spite of their human likeness, were entirely swept out of existence in a war of extermination waged by European immigrants. . . . Are we such apostles of mercy as to complain if the Martians warred in the same spirit?
>
> (*War of the Worlds,* p. 52)

In 1804 an unprovoked slaughter of native Tasmanians ignited the Black War, which destroyed over a third of the native Tasmanian population. Wells subjects England to invaders who prove to be as casually brutal as the British colonialist armies were.

Wells contended that much of his writing was a "comment on the false securities and fatuous self-satisfaction of the everyday life" (Wells in Bergonzi, p. 124). He exploited the fear of invasion in order to undermine the complacency of late Victorian society. In an earlier essay entitled "The Extinction of Man," Wells had suggested various ways (disease, vicious land-crabs, predatory ants) the human race might meet its end. Although the tone is ironic and humorous, Wells does pause to point out "man's complacent assumption of the future is too confident. . . . In the case of every other predominant animal . . . the hour of its complete ascendancy has been the eve of its complete overthrow" (Wells in Bergonzi, p. 132).

The outbreak of World War I proved the significance of Wells's prophetic fiction. There is a parallel between the Martian invasion in *The War of the Worlds* and the historical forces born of man's intellect but beyond man's control. Two decades after Wells invented the deadly "black gas" used by the Martians, European powers developed the toxic gases that compounded the misery of trench warfare in World War I. In the end, Wells's attempt "to point out the obvious possibilities of flying, of great guns, of poison gas, and so forth in presently making life uncomfortable if some sort of world peace was not assured" proved futile, for some of his horrific predictions became reality (Wells in Bergonzi, p. 124).

The Novel in Focus

The plot. Before beginning his story, the unnamed narrator points out that never has man entertained the possibility of an alien life form more intelligent than he. "At most," he says, "terrestrial men fancied there might be other men upon Mars, perhaps inferior to themselves and ready to welcome a missionary enterprise" (*The War of the Worlds*, p. 51). He points out the folly of this assumption—since Mars is a much older planet, any being living there would have had longer to evolve.

Beginning his tale, he recounts how he saw through a friend's telescope a succession of bright flashes on the surface of Mars. Days later a metallic cylinder, too hot to be approached, plummets into a pit in the countryside. Noises inside the cylinder cause alarm, and newspapers alert the surrounding towns of the curiosity. When the hideous Martians emerge from their ship, the people first flee in terror, but then regroup at a distance. A team of scientists and police decide to approach the Martians while waving a white flag. As they near the pit, a beam of light shoots from it, turning everything in its path to flame. It sweeps across the fields, killing the nearby people. A distant, hysterical crowd escapes the firestorm, but a few of them are trampled. The narrator flees the massacre weeping.

Before returning to his own home, the narrator meets a group of people who scoff at his warning. Arriving at his house, he warns his wife of the awful creatures but also consoles her, insisting that since the earth's gravity is much stronger than that of Mars, the creatures are confined to their pit.

The next morning, many townspeople are mentioning what a pity it will be to have to destroy the Martians without the chance to learn something about them. They are shocked when, in the evening, the Martian heat ray begins to raze their village. The narrator rents a horse and cart and escapes with his wife to a nearby town, but returns to keep his promise to bring back the cart.

As he approaches his home, a storm breaks out and the lightning allows the narrator to make out tremendous metallic tripods, walking machines that stride across the land, smashing trees and houses as they go. His startled horse slips and breaks its neck. He crawls off, looking desperately for cover, and finds his way back to his own house. An artilleryman seeking shelter comes to the house and explains to the narrator how his division has been destroyed by the Martians in the immense walking machines. The two decide to abandon the house, the artilleryman for London and the narrator for Leatherhead, where he left his wife. Before leaving, they ransack the house for all available food and water.

On their way they encounter scores of troops waiting to intercept the Martians should they head toward London. As they near a town, they halt to help two old women pack a cart to flee. The traffic has been stopped to allow the passage of troops, and people are fighting for spots in the outgoing trains. When shots erupt in the distance, the people look toward them and see five of the terrible Martian machines approaching. Remembering the heat ray, the narrator instructs everyone to dive into the water of a nearby river. As he gasps for air, he sees the artillery hit and destroy one of the tripods, slaying the Martian within. The machine, heat ray still blazing, falls into the river, sending up clouds of steam. The other four Martians approach their fallen comrade, gather its remains, and retreat.

After finding an abandoned boat and journeying alone down river, the narrator reclines in the shadow of a hedge. The mumbling of a curate awakens him. The dull resonance of distant guns worry them both, and they wander away from the sound.

The narrator then interrupts his tale to recount the trials faced by his brother in London. In spite of reports to the contrary, notes the narrator, the citizens of London remained convinced that the Martians were incapacitated by the earth's gravity. But at the news of a deadly black smoke, which decimated the towns just outside the city, the Londoners panicked and fled. To defend themselves from the danger of hidden artillery, the Martians had employed canisters emitting a poisonous gas—the deadly black smoke.

The narrator's brother raids a bicycle shop and escapes. During his flight he notices some ruffians trying to drag two women from their horse-drawn carriage. He fights off the scoundrels and joins the two women. They soon find themselves in a stampede of people fleeing the Martians. Caught up in the frenzy, they make their way to the coast, where they buy passage on a ship to France. Three Martians, striding high in their agile tripods, wade after the many ships heading out to sea. But one of the warships stationed off the coast, in a gallant suicide mission, attacks and destroys two of the Martians before being obliterated by the heat ray.

The narrator and the curate meanwhile have left an empty house where they had taken refuge. The narrator hopes both to make it to Leatherhead and rejoin his wife and to rid himself of the tedious curate, whose futile supplications to a deaf God irritate him. But they soon find themselves surrounded by Martians, who are gathering up the panicked humans and tossing them into a sort of basket on their backs. The two retreat into a nearby house. When another cylinder from Mars crashes into the side of the house, they are trapped inside the ruins.

From a crack in the wall, the narrator can more closely observe the Martians. They have huge round bodies, which seem in fact to be simply large heads. They have two large eyes and a membrane in the back that serves as an ear. Two sets of eight tentacles beneath their fleshy beaks serve as hands. They have lungs and a heart, as later dissection reveals, but no entrails. Rather than eat food that requires digestion, they imbibe the fresh blood of other creatures. Their preference for men is apparent from the humanlike remains of the victims they had brought as provisions from Mars.

MARTIANS IN NEW JERSEY?

Orson Welles adapted *The War of the Worlds* as part of a series of literary works for his radio program "The Mercury Theatre on the Air." Despite Welles's repeated interjections stating that the story was fictitious, the realistic news-broadcast format of Welles's adaptation created panic among thousands of listeners across America, who believed that Martians were invading New Jersey. Following the original broadcast on October 30, 1938, subsequent radio adaptations incited hysterical reactions in other places, such as Ecuador, where several deaths were blamed on a similar program.

From their hiding place the narrator and the curate see men extracted from the baskets to be eaten. The narrator and the curate remain hidden, but they soon begin to quarrel about their remaining supplies, which the curate refuses to conserve. In a fit of madness, the curate declares "the word of the Lord is upon me! . . . I must bear my witness! I go!" (*The War of the Worlds*, p. 159) and proudly stomps off to give himself up. The narrator slugs him with a meat chopper to stop him and knocks him out, but the noise of the scuffle has alerted the Martians. Mechanical limbs stretch through the holes in the wall and drag off the unconscious curate. They do not discover the narrator, who has hidden in the coal cellar.

Eventually thirst draws the narrator forth. The silence from the pit emboldens him, and he peers through the crack in the rubble to see that the

Martians have gone, leaving only piles of human skeletons behind. A strange Martian weed has spread over the surrounding landscape, but is withering in the earth's soil. After rooting up some vegetables from a nearby garden, the narrator heads again for Leatherhead.

He soon encounters the artilleryman from whom he had been separated by the Martian attack. The artilleryman informs him that the Martians have captured London and are building a flying machine in order to command the whole earth. He speculates that these Martians are the pioneers. They will establish themselves and herd humans into breeding colonies for food until the rest of the Martian population arrives. He suggests that the only bearable life left for mankind is to survive as bandits in the sewers and railway tunnels of the ruined cities, attacking the Martians when possible. Cowardice and frailty must not taint the human race, he insists. Weaklings will be abandoned to the Martians.

The narrator is captivated by the artilleryman's prophecy, but soon realizes the difference between this prophet's visions and his abilities. The two begin work on a dugout, but the artilleryman quickly grows weary and suggests they indulge in a few card games. As night falls, the narrator resolves to leave this man and journey toward London with the vague hope of discovering what the Martians, and his fellow men, have been doing.

Wandering the deserted streets of London, the narrator hears a strange distant moan. He notices Martians motionless in their walking machines. The sight of birds circling above the machines emboldens him, and he approaches the Martians. He finds them dead, some rotting in their war machines, others laid in a row, all slain, he later learns, by earthly bacteria, which their immune systems could not tolerate. The diseases that have tormented humans since the beginning of life have also saved the race. The narrator arrives home to discover his wife, still alive, waiting for him.

The humbling of humans. The futile responses to the Martian invasion dramatize the false sense of security enjoyed by many Britishers at the end of the nineteenth century. The majority would have agreed with the artilleryman's boast that England was "the greatest power in the world" (*The War of the Worlds*, p. 171). This contention was bolstered by British conquests, both missionary and military, all over the world. But in the novel the puny guns of the British military and the curate's impassioned pleas to an unre-

H. G. Wells in his study at Hanover Terrace.

sponsive deity prove useless against the Martian invasion.

Before he realizes the extent of the impending doom, the narrator reassures his wife that the Martians are encumbered by the earth's gravity, just as some dodo bird threatened by the arrival of hungry humans on Mauritius Island might have told its mate "We will peck them to death tomorrow my dear" (*The War of the Worlds,* p. 73). He realizes that the Martians have observed humans "as a man with a microscope might scrutinize the transient creatures that swarm and multiply in a drop of water" (*The War of the Worlds,* p. 51). The narrator notes, having watched the Martians devour a human, "the bare idea of this is no doubt horribly repulsive to us, but at the same time I think that we should remember how repulsive our carnivorous habits would seem to an intelligent rabbit" (*The War of the Worlds,* p. 150). The Martians pay no more attention to the frantic strategies of the humans "than a man would [to] the confusion of ants in a nest against which his foot has kicked" (*The War of the Worlds,* pp. 97-8).

Though the triumphs of the nineteenth century suggested to the British that they were lords of the earth, in Wells's novel they are ironically saved from slaughter by the transient microbes that swarm in a drop of water, "the humblest

things that God . . . has put upon this earth" (*The War of the Worlds,* p. 184). The narrator concludes:

> It may be that in the larger design of the universe this invasion from Mars is not without its ultimate benefit for men; it has robbed us of that serene confidence in the future which is the most fruitful source of decadence.
> (*The War of the Worlds,* p. 192)

Sources. Wells first addressed the idea of life on Mars in 1888 at the Debating Society at the Royal College of Science. He concluded "there [is] every reason to suppose that the surface of Mars [is] occupied by living beings" (Wells in Bergonzi, p. 123). In 1896 he modified that statement, adding that Martians could be radically different from terrestrial beings.

As Wells reports, the idea of the British people as the helpless victims of an extraterrestrial invasion stems from a whimsical remark by his brother: "'Suppose some beings from another planet were to drop out of the sky suddenly' [my brother said]. . . . Perhaps we had been talking of the discovery of Tasmania by the Europeans—a very frightful disaster for the native Tasmanians! I forget. But that was the point of departure" (H. G. Wells in Bergonzi, p. 124). The remark inspired H. G. Wells to write the novel, which his brother took an active interest in developing. He passed his time wandering about, marking down places and people that would be suitable for destruction by the novel's Martians.

Reception. Wells was likened by reviewers to both Daniel Defoe and the famous French science fiction writer Jules Verne. These attempts to trace similarities between his fiction and the stories of other artists irritated Wells. Even worse was the criticism of a number of reviewers, who disparaged the novel as an extravagant contrivance. The curate was criticized as a farcical exaggeration, and gory descriptions were considered cheap tricks to attract an audience. The happy ending seemed too improbable to some. Even today, Wells is often thought of as a writer of children's fiction, and the grave implications of his tales are overlooked.

On the positive side, one comparison likened *The War of the Worlds* to **Gulliver's Travels** (also covered in *Literature and Its Times*) in its appeal both to children as a fantasy and adults as an ironic comment on man's arrogance and failures. Wells was praised for the book's criticism of so-cial Darwinism, which held the view that the weak were meant to be sifted out of society and so did not need to be helped by charities or benevolent individuals. Wells's novel carries this to the extreme, threatening all humanity with extinction by more powerful Martians, showing the danger of adopting such an amoral attitude toward the less fortunate. Some readers carried this view of the novel even further, regarding it as an "anti-imperialist fable . . . told from the viewpoint of the oppressed" (Sussman, p. 179).

For More Information

Bergonzi, Bernard. *The Early H. G. Wells.* Manchester: Manchester Press, 1961.

Sussman, Herbert. *Victorians and the Machine.* Cambridge, Mass: Harvard University Press, 1968.

Taton, Rene. *Science in the Nineteenth Century.* New York: Basic, 1961.

Wells, H. G. *Experiment in Autobiography.* New York: Macmillan, 1934.

Wells, H. G. *The War of the Worlds.* Edited by David Hughes and Harry Geduld. Bloomington: Indiana University Press, 1993.

The Waste Land

by

T. S. Eliot

Thomas Stearns Eliot was born in 1888 in St. Louis, Missouri, and died in 1965 in England. Between these two dates, he transformed himself from an American philosophy student to a powerful British man of letters, and in the process also transformed modern English poetry. *The Waste Land* was first published in 1922 in the shadow of World War I and the chaotic, depressed culture of rebuilding and reflection that followed it. The poem became one of the key works of "modernism," an important artistic trend of the early-to-mid 1900s that sought to break with traditional forms and in post-World War I works often reflected a sense of disillusion with the modern world.

Events in History at the Time of the Poem

World War I. On August 3, 1914, Eliot was forced to leave the German town of Marburg, where he was on a travel grant from Harvard University, because the German army had just invaded Belgium in the opening days of the First World War. His displacement turned out not to be too much of an inconvenience for him, since he had already arranged to spend the academic year at Oxford University in England, working on his doctoral thesis in philosophy. Despite, or perhaps because of, his personal detachment from the fighting—as an American whose country would not be at war until April 1917—"he was perfectly placed to watch the Old World go mad" (Marshall in Moody, p. 95). Eliot arrived

---

THE LITERARY WORK

A poem in five parts set in the post-World War I Western world; published in England in October 1922 in the *Criterion*, in America in November 1922 in the *Dial*, and in book form in December 1922.

SYNOPSIS

Through a series of vignettes, *The Waste Land* depicts the social and personal decay and despair of post-World War I Western culture.

---

in England, where the ravages of war had created food and fuel shortages, and headlines daily announced the names and massive numbers of British war dead.

The root causes of World War I were debatable even decades later. Some have described it as a battle of empires for control of worldwide colonies, others as the explosion of tension between nationalism in these colonies and the struggle of the colonizer to maintain its empire, and still others as a gradually worsening disagreement between aristocratic cousins all over Europe. All these conditions existed, and perhaps in combination they thrust the continent of Europe—and the Western world—into the most terrible bloodbath it had ever known.

In Britain the government of Lloyd George seemed anxious to rouse its own complacent nation and make it reassert itself as the dominant

T. S. Eliot

Its officers asked him to resign his job at Lloyd's Bank, and he complied, only to discover that they were not prepared to enlist him at all, at which point he hastened back to the bank to reclaim his old job. By the time the paperwork was all sorted out in 1919, the war was over; Eliot, though he never got to participate, was left almost as ragged and depressed as if he had actually fought in the war.

Aftermath. Wartime life was horrific and draining. But it was the aftermath of World War I that provided the real cultural background for Eliot's poem. As time went on, it became clear that the war had solved little and probably only made things worse. More than 8 million people had died during the four years of war, with another 20 or so million left homeless, wounded, and sick. Europe was faced with large numbers of displaced and ill individuals. The aristocracy, which had seemed the height of European culture and refinement, had mostly been slain, disenfranchised, or impoverished. Unemployment was rampant. And, perhaps most importantly, people began to realize that the ideals of technological "progress" could no longer be trusted—engines of war had nearly destroyed the entire continent, cutting huge swaths through the landscape and killing millions of people. The few changes that had taken place—British women over the age of thirty gained the right to vote, for example, and the working class began to partake somewhat in middle-class standards of living—seemed paltry in the face of the more general decay that was happening all over Europe.

Vivien. On June 26, 1915, Vivien(ne) Haigh-Wood became Mrs. T. S. Eliot. She would be her husband's inspiration, his editor, and eventually his unbearable burden. She came from an upper-middle-class English family and had known the aspiring young American poet for only two months or so by the time they married; their initial unfamiliarity with each other would prove a terrible mistake throughout the years of their tortured union. Bertrand Russell, a former teacher of Eliot's who eventually offered them a room in his flat, met them in July 1915 and recorded his first impressions of them as a couple:

> I expected her to be terrible, from his mysteriousness; but she was not so bad. She is light, a little vulgar, adventurous, full of life. . . . [S]he says she married him to stimulate him, but finds she can't do it. . . . He is ashamed of his marriage, and very grateful if one is kind to her.
>
> (Russell in Cuddy and Hirsch, p. 170)

power in Europe. Lloyd George's government appeared almost eager to battle Germany. This eagerness, however, quickly deteriorated as the fervor of English patriotism contended with the horrors of the Great War: trench warfare, poisonous gasses, killing on the largest scale ever experienced, the destruction of ancient and beautiful cities all over Europe. It seemed as though two thousand years of European culture was in the process of self-destructing. On a personal level for Eliot, one of his closest friends was killed, and his own brother-in-law returned to England with personal tales of the filth and violence of the war. London teemed with foreign refugees and foreign soldiers at the same time that the entire nation was depleted of its young men.

When America entered the war in 1917, Eliot did his best to enlist. The process did not promise to be easy, though. As a married man, he wanted to be sure that he secured a post high-ranking enough to support himself and his wife. His health had never been good and he was particularly underweight and anxious at the time he applied for service. He determined that a post in intelligence would be best for him, and after a time, the United States Naval Intelligence agreed.

Unknown to Eliot, Vivien had suffered throughout her life from a series of "nervous" disorders—migraine headaches, insomnia, cramps, and mood swings—for which she was prescribed a morphine-based medication. The first serious sickness of her married life struck her shortly after the wedding. Some critics suggest that the couple's unsatisfactory sex life might have had something to do with her collapse, but Vivien Eliot's illness was well-established long before she met Eliot.

By 1928 Vivien Eliot had been in and out of sanitoriums all over Europe, often accompanied by her husband, who also complained of nervous disorders of various kinds. *The Waste Land,* in fact, was written, in part, during T. S. Eliot's stay at an asylum in Lausanne, Switzerland, in 1921. Vivien did not accompany him there. It is important to note that asylums and sanitoriums were considered quite fashionable at the time. People thought of them as quiet places of recovery and relaxation rather than as mental hospitals or clinics.

Vivien Eliot's illness would prove to be serious, however. It could not be coaxed into remission by drugs or relaxation, and she began to behave more and more oddly as the years passed. Her persistent ill health became a burden for T. S. Eliot, just as being careful of her husband's delicate constitution and public persona became a burden for Vivien. The strain of her condition showed itself in her habit of picking fights in public—most notably, jealous scenes at parties—and also of claiming that she had a double who was always getting her in trouble.

A decade after *The Waste Land* was published, at the end of his tether because of his wife's complaints and demands, T. S. Eliot accepted a one-year professorship at Harvard University in Massachusetts and left Vivien in Europe. He knew, but did not tell her, that he would never return to the marriage. When he came back to England the following year, he hid from her, having arranged for separation papers to be delivered through solicitors. Vivien never did accept the situation, going so far as to take out an ad in the *London Times:* "Will T. S. Eliot please return to his home 68 Clarence Gate Gardens which he abandoned Sept. 17 1932" (Vivien Eliot in Ackroyd, p. 217). She tried relentlessly to see him—attending multiple performances of plays he had written, going to his office, tracking him in his public appearances. But he eluded her, believing that to meet would be upsetting and dangerous for both of them.

In the summer of 1938, Vivien Eliot would be committed to a mental hospital just outside London. She died there in 1947. Eliot would remarry, to Valerie Fletcher, his long-time secretary, in 1957; he apparently lived the remainder of his life (he died in 1965) in relative stability and peace.

Ezra Pound. In 1914, T. S. Eliot met Ezra Pound in London. Pound (1885-1972), an exuberant and prolific American poet (five volumes of his verse were published while he was still a young man), had placed himself squarely in the center of European cultural life, sponsoring and encouraging young writers, working on literary journals, and vying for financial support of the artists he considered to be reshaping literary history. Besides Eliot, Pound also helped launch the careers of fiction writers Ernest Hemingway and James Joyce.

> ## UNREAL CITIES
>
>
>
> In his notes to the book edition of *The Waste Land,* Eliot mentions that Part V of the poem, entitled "What the Thunder Said," comments, in part, on the decay of postwar Europe. The following passage from the poem expresses something of the disbelief at the unraveling of European culture in cities east and west that permeated the atmosphere of the early 1920s.
>
> > What is the city over the mountains
> > Cracks and reforms and bursts in the violet air
> > Falling towers
> > Jerusalem Athens Alexandria
> > Vienna London
> > Unreal
> >   (Eliot, *The Waste Land,* lines 367-77)

Pound moved to Europe in 1908, and stayed in London from the following year until 1921, when he moved to Paris and then to Italy. He had originally gone abroad because he was interested in the poetry of the Irish writer W. B. Yeats, but he soon became involved in the lives and careers of many other artists, all the while writing his own poetry. Pound is perhaps most famously connected with the very influential literary school of "imagism," which focused on the power of individual images to convey complex meaning. He was also interested in what he called "sequences," the poetic device most characteris-

The Waste Land

tic of *The Waste Land,* in which a chain of apparently distinct images or scenes together combine to create a poem that is not narrative in its development. The American poet Conrad Aiken argues that *The Waste Land* "must be taken . . . as a brilliant and kaleidoscopic confusion; as a series of sharp, discrete, slightly relaxed perceptions and feelings" (Aiken in Cuddy and Hirsch, p. 35). If this is so, then it is perhaps in some part due to Pound's influence.

MY NERVES ARE BAD TO-NIGHT

Part II of *The Waste Land,* "A Game of Chess," seems to recall Vivien Eliot and her insistent sickness,

My nerves are bad to-night. Yes, bad. Stay with me.
Speak to me. Why do you never speak. Speak.
What are you thinking of? What thinking? What?
I never know what you are thinking. Think.
(*The Waste Land,* lines 111-14)

In the margins of the manuscript, in Vivien's handwriting, is the comment "Wonderful."

Some critics will, in fact, claim that *The Waste Land* is as much Pound's poem as it is Eliot's, given the substantial cuts and changes in the original that Pound insisted upon. In 1971 Valerie Eliot, T. S. Eliot's second wife, published the facsimile edition of the original manuscript of *The Waste Land,* complete with Pound's unmistakable editorial marks, and critics dove into the complicated issue of the extent to which Pound recreated or "edited" Eliot's original draft. Opinion varied as to Pound's ultimate role in the poem's production. Some people thought he saw in *The Waste Land* movements and themes that Eliot's words did not adequately express, while others thought that he essentially misunderstood Eliot's spiritual preoccupations.

Ezra Pound was an enthusiastic, if somewhat blunt, editor. In his discussion of the first version of *The Waste Land* (see Cuddy and Hirsch, pp. 167-75), Richard Ellmann points out that Eliot wrote some lines that Pound vetoed:

London, the swarming life you kill and breed,
Huddles between the concrete and the sky,
Responsive to the momentary need,
Vibrates unconscious to its formal destiny.

By these lines in red ink in the margin in Pound's handwriting was the message "B-ll-S"

(Cuddy and Hirsch, p. 174), expressing his opinion that they were full of nonsense. The lines did not make it into the final version of the poem.

The Poem in Focus

The contents. Originally to be entitled "He Do the Police in Different Voices" (Ackroyd, p. 110), *The Waste Land* is divided into five sections: "The Burial of the Dead," "A Game of Chess," "The Fire Sermon," "Death by Water," and "What the Thunder Said." It is impossible to speak of the poem in terms of "plot," for it defies all attempts to follow a narrative thread; this is one of its main contributions to the history of poetry. Many different metaphors have been offered in the hope of adequately describing the poem's method of development, but perhaps the most striking is that of the critic who claims that "*The Waste Land* reveals a web of subcutaneous nerve cells whose synapses fire periodically as we proceed through the poem" (Sigg, p. 195). *The Waste Land* begins with a bleak spring, a rebirth that brings only memories of death:

April is the cruellest month, breeding
Lilacs out of the dead land, mixing
Memory and desire, stirring
Dull roots with spring rain.
Winter kept us warm, covering
Earth in forgetful snow. . . .
(*The Waste Land,* lines 1-6)

These may or may not be the words of "Marie," a German aristocrat who remembers the security and privilege of her childhood. Eliot early on suggests that her world has been forever shattered, alluding to the displacement of thousands during the four years of the Great War and to the virtual disappearance of the aristocracy from much of Europe.

Another major theme of the poem is the grey existence of the ordinary person in postwar society, working at office jobs that steal their energy and joy, as illustrated in the following description of London office workers:

Unreal City
Under the brown fog of a winter dawn,
A crowd flowed over London Bridge, so
    many,
I had not thought death had undone so
    many.
(*The Waste Land,* lines 60-3)

The poem returns again and again to the idea of the pent-up boredom and despair of postwar culture, prominently through the image of a man

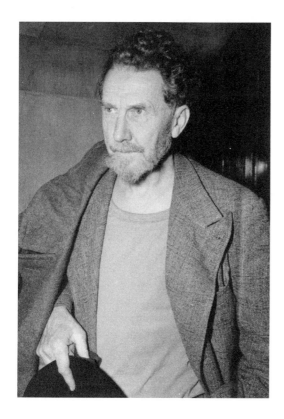

Ezra Pound

and his wife merely going through the motions of married life, the tawdry affair of a typist and a clerk, and an "episode" concerning Lil, a woman whose husband is about to be dismissed from military service. The brown city of London reappears throughout *The Waste Land,* providing a real-life setting for the apocalyptic and strangely fantastical chain of images that composes the poem, and also contributing to the sense of social critique that some readers feel is the main point of the work.

At the same time, there is a certain hope of redemption that runs throughout the poem, expressed most strongly—and most cryptically—in the Sanskrit words that recur at the poem's close: *datta, dayadhvam, damyata* ("give," "sympathize," "control," according to Eliot's notes) and the thrice-repeated word *Shantih,* which forms the last sentence of *The Waste Land. Shantih* is a word that means, basically, "peace," and those critics who would like to claim that Eliot's poem is a sustained cry of despair must contend with this strong evidence to the contrary.

Wild Goose Chase? T. S. Eliot included a set of notes when *The Waste Land* was published in book form, mostly because, as he admitted, the poem just wasn't long enough on its own to war-

rant its own book. In the notes, Eliot mentioned that he had drawn on Jessie Weston's scholarly book, *From Ritual to Romance,* which examined the medieval legends of King Arthur and his knights in some detail. Actually, his note claims that Weston's book could be used to unlock his own poem's meaning:

> Not only the title, but the plan and a good deal of the incidental symbolism of the poem were suggested by Miss Jessie L. Weston's book on the Grail legend. . . . Indeed, so deeply am I indebted, Miss Weston's book will elucidate the difficulties of the poem much better than my notes can do, and I recommend it . . . to any who think such elucidation of the poem worth the trouble.
>
> (*The Waste Land,* p. 47)

These words sent scores of scholars hunting through Weston's book, trying to fit together the puzzle of Eliot's poem based on the highly symbolic and cryptic Grail legends.

As explained by Weston, the "waste land" is a mythical country in which nothing grows any longer—neither human nor animal nor plant. It is ruled over by a wounded king, the "fisher king," who is impotent. The redemption of this land and its king depends upon certain unclearly explained actions that must be taken by a knight entering the country in quest of the Holy Grail, the cup from which Jesus Christ drank at the Last Supper. In the final development of the legend, the cup, held by Joseph of Arimathea, is said to have caught the blood of the crucified Christ. Medieval English, French, and German literature is filled with stories of brave knights who battle monsters and each other, trying to be the man who discovers the sacred object that has remained hidden for centuries.

Weston connects the Grail legends with other early fertility myths, arguing that the Grail itself is actually a symbol of female sexuality and that other elements of the legend are also images of reproduction; the search for the Grail thus becomes a search for general cultural fertility as well as personal power. By Eliot's own admission, then, *The Waste Land* is a poem about personal and cultural impotence and regeneration, based on age-old mythological symbols. Or is it?

Weston's discussion of the fertility myth of the "waste land" that is brought back to life certainly does provide a background of sorts for Eliot's poem, but it by no means unravels the densely packed series of images that the poem contains. Some scholars have even claimed that Eliot's reference to Weston was intended as a huge practical joke on professional scholars. Eliot himself later "confessed" that he had unintentionally led his readers astray:

> It was just, no doubt, that I should pay tribute to the work of Miss Jessie Weston; but I regret having sent so many inquirers off on a wild goose chase after Tarot Cards and the Holy Grail.
>
> (Eliot, *On Poetry and Poets,* p. 110)

I want to die. The Latin and Greek epigraph at the beginning of *The Waste Land* was not Eliot's first choice. He had settled on a few sentences from Joseph Conrad's 1899 novel, *Heart of Darkness:*

> Did he live his life again in every detail of desire, temptation, and surrender during that supreme moment of complete knowledge? He cried in a whisper at some image, at some vision,—he cried out twice, a cry that was no more than a breath—"The horror! the horror!"
>
> (Conrad in Moody, p. 121)

ELIOT'S PURPOSE

Because it first appeared shortly after the end of World War I and because it contains unmistakable references to war-torn London and Europe, *The Waste Land* has been taken to represent the resignation of the entire postwar generation. Whatever his readers might have thought, Eliot himself many years later bluntly rejected the idea that his was the voice of a generation:

> When I wrote a poem called *The Waste Land* some of the more approving critics said that I had expressed the "disillusionment of a generation," which is nonsense. I may have expressed for them their own illusion of being disillusioned, but that did not form part of my intention.
>
> (Eliot in Cuddy and Hirsch, p. 196)

The character referred to in the preceding passage is a European man named Kurtz, who has disappeared into the African jungle and has worked many acts of evil and oppression upon the native people who become his subjects, as well as upon other people who stumble upon his enclave. The scene above occurs at the moment of his death; Eliot seems to have been getting at, among many other things, the personal decay that led Kurtz to his violent actions, as well as the transfixing moment of his terrible self-realization.

Whatever his motives, his choice of the Conrad passage was discouraged by Pound, who felt that it was not weighty enough for Eliot's great poem. Eliot came back with the poem's present part-Latin, part-Greek epigraph, which is drawn from the first century a.d. Roman work, the *Satyricon,* by Petronius Arbiter:

> Nam Sibyllam quidem Cumis ego ipse oculis meis vidi in ampulla pendere, et cum illi pueri dicerent: Sibylla ti theleis; respondebat illa: apothanein thelo.
>
> (Moody, p. 121)

Translated, it means, "For with my own eyes I saw the Cumaean Sibyl hanging in her cage, and when boys asked her, 'Sibyl, what do you want?' she replied, 'I want to die'."

A priestess and prophetess of the Greek god Apollo, the Sybil of Cumae was granted a wish. She asked for eternal life, and it was given to her. However, she had forgotten to specify that what she wanted was actually eternal *youth,* and she was thus doomed to exist forever as an ancient, lonely, and horrible creature, who lived in a cage or a jar suspended between heaven and earth. Her only wish became to die. Critics continue to debate the relevance of this quotation to *The Waste Land* as a whole.

The Latin and Greek quotation is not translated in Eliot's notes, which suggests perhaps that it is the effect of the foreign languages that Eliot is cultivating as much as what those words actually mean; certainly, this fits well with the multilingual allusions—all untranslated—that run throughout the poem; words from Sanskrit, French, Italian, and German are all present.

Sources. At least one contemporary reviewer despised *The Waste Land* on the grounds that it took from so many other works of literature that it could hardly stand on its own. "The borrowed jewels he has set in its head do not make Mr Eliot's toad the more prepossessing," protested the critic, and it is true that *The Waste Land* is filled to overflowing with quotations and snatches of poetry lifted from the history of world poetry (Longenbach in Moody, p. 176). It has become something of a scholarly game to try and trace every allusion that Eliot makes in some 400 lines of poetry. The strange mixture of languages and literatures that make their appearance in *The Waste Land* includes, for example, lines from Dante, St. Augustine, Shakespeare. Milton, Indian vedic poetry, Virgil, Petronius, the Bible, Buddha, Wagner, and the Grail legends.

Reviews. In *The Dial* (December 1922), Edmund Wilson praised *The Waste Land* as a beautiful fusion of personal lament and social criticism:

> Sometimes we feel that he is speaking not only for a personal distress, but for the starvation of a whole civilization—for people grinding at barren office-routine in the cells of gigantic cities, drying up their souls in eternal toil. . . . It is our whole world of strained nerves and shattered institutions.
>
> (Wilson in Cuddy and Hirsch, p. 31)

Wilson did not pretend to understand every word or allusion in the poem, but appreciated its overall effect anyway, much like Virginia Woolf, who liked the *sound* of the poem which Eliot read to her. Not all critics were so generous. On March 3, 1923, *Time,* for example, published an exasperated review: "There is a new kind of literature abroad in the land, whose only obvious fault is that no one can understand it" (*Time* in Cuddy and Hirsch, p. 3).

For More Information

Ackroyd, Peter. *T. S. Eliot: A Life.* New York: Simon & Schuster, 1984.

Cuddy, Lois Q., and David H. Hirsch, eds. *Critical Essays on T. S. Eliot's The Waste Land.* Boston: G. K. Hall, 1991.

Eliot, T. S. *The Waste Land and Other Poems.* New York: Harcourt, Brace and World, 1962.

Eliot, T. S. *On Poetry and Poets.* London: Faber, 1957.

Moody, A. David, ed. *The Cambridge Companion to T. S. Eliot.* Cambridge, England: Cambridge University Press, 1994.

Reeves, Gareth. *T. S. Eliot's The Waste Land.* New York: Harvester Wheatsheaf, 1994.

Sigg, Eric. *The American T. S. Eliot.* Cambridge: Cambridge University Press, 1989.

"A Worn Path"

by
Eudora Welty

Born in Jackson, Mississippi, in 1909, Eudora Welty is deeply immersed in the culture and history of the South. Though raised in an upper-middle-class white family, she traveled extensively throughout the South during the Depression, working for the Works Progress Administration, and learned firsthand the plight of its impoverished black residents. In "A Worn Path" Welty provides a glimpse of the hard life of a poor Southern black woman who must confront both white society and the rapid urban growth and technological advancement of America around the turn of the twentieth century.

THE LITERARY WORK

A short story set in the South sometime between 1890 and 1920; written in the 1930s and published in 1941.

SYNOPSIS

An elderly African American woman travels the hazardous worn path from her rural home to the city to retrieve medicine for her invalid grandchild.

Events in History at the Time the Short Story Takes Place

Rural South. At the turn of the twentieth century, Jackson, Mississippi, was an area rife with divisions. As in other areas of the Deep South, segregation, racism, and poverty continued to dominate African American life, the way they had since the end of the Civil War. Large numbers of blacks moved north to take industrial jobs created by rapid urban growth and technological advancements. Many more, however, remained in the South and continued to farm the land as sharecroppers. Too financially strapped to buy land outright, most African American sharecroppers leased plots from white plantation owners (former slaveowners), for which they paid rent in cash or in a portion of the crops raised, often 50 percent. The landlord dictated what and how much to grow. The soil was generally poor, so farmers could scarcely produce enough to pay their rent, let alone turn a profit. Most owed money to white landlords by the end of each season for items purchased on credit at the landlord's store. It was not until about 1910, when people like the African American scientist George Washington Carver taught farmers how to improve soil conditions and plant more suitable crops, that the lives of sharecroppers began to show some improvement.

Southern black women worked primarily as field hands or in domestic service. Like the sharecroppers, their lives had improved little and in some ways had even worsened since slavery. Many were denied a basic education, and factory jobs or nondomestic positions were all but impossible to secure. The practice of segregation kept blacks in the South out of "white" job sites. And African American women suffered prejudice twofold, since they were both female and black,

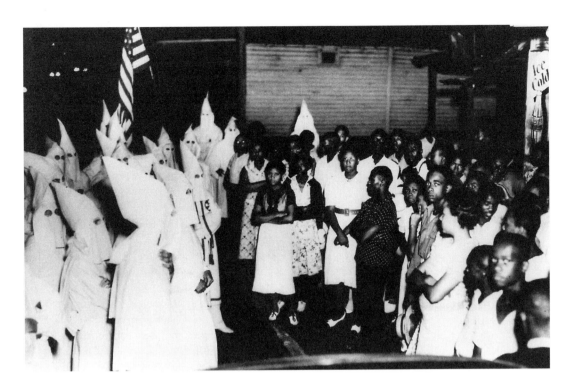

The Ku Klux Klan and African Americans confront each other in the South, 1938.

which limited even further the types of jobs they could hold.

Living conditions for blacks in the rural South were quite impoverished around the turn of the twentieth century. Most Southern towns remained remote outposts, with no indoor plumbing or electricity. The prohibitive cost of new technologies kept modern amenities, such as the automobile, out of the reach of most Southern blacks.

Segregation. In 1896, with the U.S. Supreme Court decision in *Plessy v. Ferguson,* the "separate but equal" doctrine became law. The decision officially sanctioned segregation. Southern restaurants, schools, meeting halls, theaters, and public transportation were all segregated by race. African Americans were expected to drink from separate drinking fountains, ride at the back of trains in separate rail cars, eat in separate sections of restaurants or in specifically "black" restaurants, shop in "black" stores, and attend "black-only" schools. Proponents of the separate-but-equal doctrine claimed it allowed for equality, but most services were anything but equal. For example, black amenities, such as drinking fountains, were generally lower to the ground, tarnished and placed in remote locations—far away from the "white" drinking fountains. More importantly, housing, wages, education, and eco-

nomic opportunities remained vastly inferior to those enjoyed by Southern whites.

A violent era. Rampant violence against African Americans persisted in the South through 1915 and beyond. The Ku Klux Klan and other racist hate groups targeted black Americans in a hate campaign that included lynchings and brutalization. From 1890 to 1896 there was an average of 114 recorded lynchings per year in the United States; an average of 50 per year occurred through 1915. Though emancipated and granted full rights as citizens after the Civil War, African Americans were prevented from exercising those rights by racist Southerners as well as by the law. In 1903 blacks were kept from voting in Alabama when the Supreme Court upheld a clause in the state constitution that restricted voters to "people having an education, employment, property, a war record, good character, and the understanding of the duties of citizenship" (Angel, p. 37). Having been denied most of these opportunities since being brought to America as slaves, most African Americans could not meet these requirements and thus were denied suffrage. The federal government did little to punish or prevent crimes against Southern African Americans. Reluctant to intervene further in Southern affairs after the Reconstruction era, U.S. government authorities let local jurisdictions prosecute lynchings (resulting in very few convictions) and instead urged blacks to rely on their own community for help and support.

Emphasis on education. Black leaders, such as Booker T. Washington and Ida Bell Wells-Barnett, struggled to improve the lot of Southern blacks. Wells-Barnett, a writer for the Memphis, Tennessee, black newspaper *Free Speech and Headlight,* was among the first to publicize lynchings in the 1890s. Her efforts led to the formation of antilynching organizations and raised public awareness of the ongoing injustice. Washington influenced the Southern black community through his promotion of education and vocational training, founding the Tuskegee Institute in Alabama to make possible the achievement of these objectives. Along with the efforts of other pioneering black leaders, Washington's emphasis on education produced positive results. By 1901 the number of African American teachers had risen to 30,000 and the population of black children attending school to 1.5 million. In "A Worn Path" the character Phoenix Jackson is too old to benefit from the educational reforms instituted after the Civil War—something she refers to in the text, hinting that her lack of education has severely limited her opportunities in life.

Progressive age? The first decades of the 1900s were a time of great change and expansion. Cities grew in every direction: skyscrapers were erected, forever altering the American landscape; automobiles replaced horses and carriages in the streets; factories drew immigrants and workers of various ethnic groups into the cities, crowding the streets and polluting the skies and waterways. The expansion of railroads brought mass transit to more parts of the nation, while the inventions of electricity and the assembly line created mass production, standardization of products, and great demand for a low-wage industrial labor force. Thus in some respects the nation flourished—yet great inequalities accompanied such progress, inequalities that most strongly impacted minorities. Low-wage, labor-intensive work was generally performed by blacks, immigrants, women, and children—and while the factory owners (primarily white men) prospered, a growing class of laborers struggled to earn a decent living. In 1910 wages for black men amounted to one-third those of white men, while women and children of any race were paid even less. The average woman or child textile worker earned $6 per week and was required to work twelve hours per day, six days a week. Such glaring inequalities and harsh working conditions

helped the trade union movement gain strength during this era. Aided by President Theodore Roosevelt—the first president to support the concept of organized labor—the government formed Commerce and Labor Departments to regulate business practices, improve working conditions, and control the growth of corporate monopolies.

From 1900 to 1920 reform movements abounded in the United States. Labor laws were passed, educational reforms were implemented (high school and college enrollment among Southern blacks doubled from 1900 to 1920), and women won the right to vote (in 1920 under the Nineteenth Amendment). Social welfare programs emerged as well to aid the urban and rural poor. For the first time in the nation's history, philanthropists and taxes subsidized necessities for the poor such as medical care. But grave inequalities remained—especially in the South. In 1916 the first Federal Bureau of Education study on black education revealed extreme discrepancies between black and white Southern schools. Only 58 percent of black children attended school at all, and high schools for African Americans were nearly nonexistent. The argument among whites for keeping blacks uneducated was that education "spoiled field hands" (Tindall, p. 268). Such an attitude eventually gave way to positive efforts to improve black education in light of this study. Among other measures, roads were built to increase access to rural schools where illiteracy and nonattendance rates were the highest. The plot of "A Worn Path" reveals how difficult progress is when physical, economic, and intellectual access are limited.

Women restricted. At the turn of the century women were restricted in nearly every aspect of their lives. They could not vote, could not enter most professions or attend most colleges, and were physically restricted by their clothing. Heavy long dresses and rib-crushing corsets literally bound women and restrained their movement in the outside world. Fainting was common among women during this era, as corsets cut blood and oxygen flow in the body, and activities such as riding a bicycle were all but impossible. Shoes consisted of lace-up boots, which often required a hook to secure. For many—especially elderly or overweight women—lacing of such shoes proved to be a tremendous chore and was sometimes neglected, as shown by this passage from "A Worn Path":

> She wore a dark striped dress reaching down
> to her shoe tops, and an equally long apron of

bleached sugar sacks, with a full pocket: all neat and tidy, but every time she took a step she might have fallen over her shoelaces, which dragged from her unlaced shoes.

(Welty, "A Worn Path," p. 200)

Harlem Renaissance. By the second decade of 1900, African Americans were having a strong impact on society. In the Harlem section of New York City a cultural revolution was underway (1915-1940) in which African American arts flourished. By 1917 Harlem—in uptown Manhattan—had become home to rising black writers, actors, musicians, dancers, club owners, and other future cultural icons. African and Southern traditions were promoted through theater, literature, music, and dance. Black writers such as Zora Neale Hurston and Langston Hughes related stories of a people and heritage heretofore largely unknown to many white Americans in the North, and these stories had a profound effect on both the black and white communities. The Harlem Renaissance, as this creative outpouring of black artists and thinkers of the time was called, furthered social change by challenging stereotypes and exposing African American strengths and contributions. Black nightclubs featuring jazz, ragtime, and blues thrived, while stories portraying the Southern black experience of poverty and oppression—and of the storytelling and music-making that served as a balm to these circumstances—made their way into print and onto the stage. The promotion of Southern black culture during this era paved the way for writers such as Welty to be published. Though not black, Welty wrote about Southern culture and race relations—subjects that prior to the Harlem Renaissance had been nonexistent in mainstream literature.

Southern storytelling tradition. Welty's realist writing style evolved out of the Southern storytelling tradition. As she explained, "the Southerner is a talker by nature" (Welty, *One Writer's Beginnings*, p. 17). Southerners, by and large an oral society, considered storytelling an important aspect of life. This held true for both its white and its black communities. With literacy rates low and the dispersion of people in remote rural areas, stories were a way to communicate as well as preserve culture and history when one could not easily access outside information. Mark Twain was among the first to capture the sights and sounds of the South—so distinct from any other region of America—on paper. Later writers, such as William Faulkner and Flannery O'Connor, extended the custom of traditional storytelling and ushered in what has been called a Southern renaissance in literature. Eudora Welty was part of this elite group of writers who helped define and contribute to Southern and American literature. In a time when the literary world considered European writers the only true literary masters or innovators of genre, Southern writers added proof that Americans could not only create original works but could produce masterpieces.

The Short Story in Focus

The plot. "A Worn Path" begins with a black woman, Phoenix Jackson, embarking on a familiar journey down the much-trodden path toward town. It is winter. She is walking through the countryside, and the path is frozen and menacing for an old woman such as herself. Her stride, says the story, is like the "pendulum in a grandfather clock" as she makes her way uphill through the woods, past the thorny bushes and "foxes, owls, beetles, jack rabbits, coons and wild animals" ("A Worn Path," p. 200). The journey is much like her life: an uphill struggle filled with obstacles, distractions, and little help.

A thorny bush is the first to attack her. It takes hold of her skirt and threatens to tear it if she pulls away too hard. Clearly unwilling to risk damaging her dress—possibly her only one—Phoenix carefully wrests herself free, all the while understanding that the thorns are only doing their job. Next she negotiates her rickety frame across a creek and stops briefly to rest on the other side. She imagines that a little boy stops to bring her some cake but when she reaches out to take it, awakens from her daydream.

She proceeds under a barbed wire fence and through an old wood, all the while carrying on a dialogue with herself about the perilous journey and sights she sees and recalls from previous trips down the familiar trail. She passes a scarecrow that she mistakes for a ghost, then comes upon a well that has been there since before she was born. She continues on and meets a black dog who startles her. She attempts to tap him with her cane but in doing so falls into a ditch.

It is impossible for Phoenix to get out of the ditch herself and so she lays there contemplating her fate. After a time a white man comes upon her and picks her up out of the ditch. He asks her why she is going to town and urges her not to go because it is so far away. He is completely ignorant as to the urgency and importance of her mission and trivializes it, saying: "I know you old

Eudora Welty

colored people! Wouldn't miss going to see Santa Claus!" ("A Worn Path," p. 203). In reality, Phoenix is on her way to retrieve vital medicine for her invalid grandchild, of whom she is the sole caretaker. But she does not bother to explain herself. She has just seen a nickel fall from the man's pocket and focuses her attention and energy on retrieving it.

At the same time the big black dog reappears and barks ferociously at the white man. Phoenix, admiring the dog's spirit, comments: "Look. . . . He ain't scared of nobody" ("A Worn Path," p. 203). While the man goes after the dog, Phoenix bends down, picks up the nickel and slides it into her apron. She is conscious of God watching her "stealing" and chastises herself a little for doing so. But it is clear that she desperately needs the money and that the man will not even miss it.

When the man comes back from shooting at the dog, he points the barrel of his rifle directly at Phoenix for no apparent reason. She does not even flinch. He asks her why she is not afraid of guns and she replies: "I seen plenty go off closer by, in my day, and for less than what I done" ("A Worn Path," p. 204). The man seems satisfied with her response and tells her that he'd give her

money if he had any—which the reader and Phoenix know is a lie. Then he tells her she should go home and leaves. Phoenix continues on her way toward town.

Phoenix arrives in town and encounters all the people, cars, and shining electric lights of the city. It is a stark contrast to her simple, desolate rural home. She encounters a white woman rushing down the sidewalk, arms full of colorfully wrapped packages. Needing her shoe tied and unable to do it herself, Phoenix stops the woman and asks her to tie it. In a random, unexplained gesture of kindness, the woman obliges, lacing and tying both shoes before continuing on her way.

Phoenix finally reaches her destination. It is a tall building and she climbs several flights of stairs. She enters a doctor's office and encounters a flippant receptionist who eyes her and says immediately: "A charity case, I suppose" ("A Worn Path," p. 205). Whether she refuses to respond to the condescending remark or whether she is overcome by exhaustion or both, Phoenix makes no reply for several minutes. A nurse comes into the room who recognizes her and, knowing how far she has traveled and why, asks her to sit down while she fills her grandson's prescription. The nurse asks how the boy is doing, if his throat is any better. Phoenix sits for a long time and stares blankly. Finally she says that her memory temporarily left her and she forgot why she was there. "I never did go to school," she says in her own defense. "I was too old at the Surrender (of the South, after which she would have been free to attend school) " ("A Worn Path," p. 205). She tells the nurse the boy is just the same, still very ill from swallowing lye two to three years ago. Phoenix has come for the "soothing medicine" that allows him to breathe and swallow, as she always does. The nurse brings out the prescription, hands it to Phoenix, and marks "charity" in her ledger. The nurse then offers Phoenix a nickel because it is Christmas. Phoenix takes the other nickel from her pocket, places the new coin beside it, and stares at her palm. An idea flashes to mind. She taps her cane on the floor and announces she is going to buy her grandson a little paper windmill and march it back to where he is waiting, alone. With that goal set, she turns and walks out the door, back down the long flight of stairs.

The African American family. Welty's short story illustrates, in part, the strength of the extended family in African American society. Conditions in America in the era of slavery had often forced black families to adapt to extremely difficult situations in order to endure. In fact, the majority of slaves lived in mostly stable two-parent households, but the threat of family breakup was constant. Forced into separation in the 1700s and 1800s, black families were torn apart by slavetraders and owners during the pre-Civil War era. Husbands were sometimes taken from their wives and sold to other plantation owners, and children were treated like commodities, regarded not as belonging to their mother or father but rather to the white slaveowner.

The breakup of families only strengthened kinship ties in the black community. Extended kin formed a network, helping slaves adapt to a family breakup. If children were sold to a nearby plantation, blood relatives in the new place—aunts, cousins, or grandparents—took on the role of parents. And if there were no blood relatives, strangers stepped in to care for the children.

Such unconventional families persisted after emancipation, though the two-parent household seems to have been most common then too (Mintz and Kellogg, p. 78). When necessary, black women in the late 1800s and early 1900s worked as a male would, performing farm labor, for example, to support their families. Some couldn't find their husbands after the war, or perhaps their husbands had remarried. Living without spouses, such women often formed community "clusters" in which they would pool resources with other matriarchal families. These clusters became extended families, giving women and their children a greater sense of security, providing emotional and economic support. This type of cooperative measure helped the fragmented black families to maintain a degree of stability and mutual sustenance against the tremendous odds the history of slavery had dealt them.

The number of female-headed households grew. At the turn of the century, when blacks moved en masse to the North, many Southern women were left behind while men took industrial jobs unavailable to black women. By 1940, 17.9 percent of all black families were headed by women in contrast to 10.1 percent of white families. Kinship networks meanwhile remained important, serving to protect children, grandchildren, or other blacks whose families were disrupted by developments like migration to the North.

As many writers assert, "there is no 'the black family'; there are, however, black families" (Low, p. 381). The history of slavery, segregation, prejudice, and economic deprivation has, in other words, produced a variety of family models in the black community. "A Worn Path" illustrates the strength of those families in whatever form they take. Phoenix Jackson, though seemingly 100 years old, is the sole caretaker of her grandson and does whatever is needed to provide for him. Through her example, the story conveys a definition of a family based not on gender and white social conventions but rather on love, responsibility, and support.

Sources. Eudora Welty based "A Worn Path" on a personal observation of an old woman crossing a distant field in rural Mississippi. "I couldn't see her up close," Welty says, "but you could tell it was an old woman going somewhere, and I thought, she is bent on an errand. And I know it isn't for herself. It was just the look of her figure" (Welty in Prenshaw, p. 300). Welty created the story from her imagination but based it on this and other observations. She worked for the federal government's Works Progress Administration (WPA) in the 1930s as a publicity agent and traveled throughout the South. She visited nearly every county in Mississippi, encountering a broad spectrum of people and lifestyles. This experience opened Welty's eyes, she says, to "diversity" and "the great poverty of the state" (Welty in Prenshaw, p. 155). Though she always credits her fertile imagination as the source of her fiction, she is quick to acknowledge "nothing could have been written in the way of a story without such a background, without the knowledge and experience I got from these things [her work for the WPA]" (Welty in Prenshaw, p. 156).

Events in History at the Time the Short Story Was Written

Depression years. In 1929 the stock market crashed and launched the U.S. into the Great Depression. Twelve million people became unemployed and millions found themselves homeless and without food. Franklin Delano Roosevelt was elected President three years after the crash and immediately implemented "New Deal" policies designed to aid the destitute and get the country back on its feet again. Many government agencies were created to put Americans back to work and distribute aid. Among these agencies was the Works Progress Administration, which employed Welty. The WPA hired thousands to perform maintenance on public buildings and also set up programs to aid struggling writers, artists, actors, and musicians. The idea behind the WPA and other New Deal agencies was not to provide charity, but rather to provide opportunity for people to help themselves. Thousands of artists benefited from working for the WPA. Their work, in turn, often addressed the plight of the poorer members of society, which inspired others to aid the disadvantaged. Welty personally interviewed and photographed hundreds of impoverished Southerners in Mississippi for the WPA's guide to Mississippi. While her efforts helped publicize their plight, she also benefited personally by being employed during an era of widespread unemployment.

World War II. The year 1941 marked the start of Roosevelt's third term as President and America's entry into World War II. In December of that year the U.S. naval base at Pearl Harbor was attacked by Japanese bombers, thus bringing an immediate declaration of war against the Axis powers, an alliance of the fascist governments of Japan, Germany, and Italy. The rationing of food and many other commodities became necessary since America was allocating all her resources to aiding the war effort. The cost of living skyrocketed as daily necessities became scarce. Butter jumped from 34.4 cents per pound to 43.5 cents; coffee increased 5 cents per pound, and ham prices increased by 35 percent. On the other hand, the war served to lift the nation out of the Depression by putting the unemployed to work in war-related industries. But for struggling families, such as the one featured in the short story, such drastic price increases would put many commodities and daily necessities out of reach.

One positive effect of the war was that it forced open the doors of the defense industry for minorities. Millions of African Americans found ready work in defense plants across the nation. Though especially slow to accept African Americans, the defense industry and armed services—desperate for personnel—eventually changed hiring practices out of necessity. Among others it was First Lady Eleanor Roosevelt who pushed for the hiring of black men and of women of all races. In her newspaper column, "My Day," she described how "Negro girls are fitted to take training in as many different fields as the white girls, but in New York City and the State [of New York], the greatest number of employment op-

portunities for Negro girls are in domestic service" (Roosevelt, p. 209). She also called attention to the frustration experienced by patriotic African Americans who could not serve their country because they could not enlist. Due in part to her championing the cause, by 1942 one million African Americans were enlisted in all branches of the armed services. The war in this sense furthered the causes of women's rights and civil rights in comparison to their status during the time period in which Welty's story is set.

Reviews. Welty found immediate success when she began writing fiction in 1936. The collection that included "A Worn Path," entitled *A Curtain of Green,* was published in 1941. Her writings—particularly "A Worn Path"—were praised by *New York Times Book Review* editor Robert Van Gelder, who hired her as a literary critic. Among other awards during her career, Welty received four O. Henry awards, the Brandeis Medal of Achievement, the Howells Medal for Fiction, the American Book Award for Fiction, and the Pulitzer Prize in 1972 for her novella, *The Optimist's Daughter.* "A Worn Path" won immediate critical acclaim and has become a standard text in high schools and universities across the nation.

For More Information

Angel, Ann. *America in the 20th Century.* Vol. 1. North Bellmore, N.Y.: Marshall Cavendish, 1995.

Low, Augustus, and Virgil A. Clift. *Encyclopedia of Black America.* New York: McGraw-Hill, 1981.

Mintz, Steven, and Susan Kellogg. *Domestic Revolutions: A Social History of American Family Life.* New York: The Free Press, 1988.

Prenshaw, Peggy Whitman. *Conversations with Eudora Welty.* Jackson: University of Mississippi Press, 1984.

Roosevelt, Eleanor. *My Day.* Edited by Rochelle Chadkoff. New York: Pharos, 1943.

Tindall, George Brown. *The Emergence of the New South.* Lafayette: Louisiana State University Press, 1967.

Welty, Eudora. "A Worn Path." In *A Modern Southern Reader.* Edited by Ben Forkner. Atlanta: Peachtree Publishers Ltd., 1986.

Welty, Eudora. *One Writer's Beginnings.* Cambridge, Mass.: Harvard University Press, 1984.

"Yentl, the Yeshiva Boy"

by

Isaac Bashevis Singer

Isaac Bashevis Singer, the son of Pinchas Mendel Singer and Bathsheba Zylberman, was born in 1904 in the Polish village of Leoncin. His father, an impoverished Hasidic Rabbi, proudly claimed to be a descendant of Rabbi Israel Ben Eliezer, the founder of Eastern European Hasidism. His mother was the offspring of an austere anti-Hasidic rabbi, whose approach to the study of traditional Jewish law and contempt for Hasidic mysticism foredoomed the marriage. The Hasidic's love of folklore, miracles, and marvels clashed with traditional Jewry's faith in the wisdom of painstaking study and scholarship. These two strains of mystical and traditional Judaism appear in "Yentl, the Yeshiva Boy" as well as many other short stories by Singer that dramatize the tension between the rational and the inscrutable.

Events in History at the Time the Short Story Takes Place

A tradition of learning. The primacy of education in Judaism has helped preserve Jewish culture throughout a history of heinous catastrophes. The Jewish scriptures are comprised of the Hebrew Bible, the Talmud, and the rabbinic codes based on the Talmud, which consists of the Mishnah and the Gemara. The Mishnah is the "oral law" said to have been communicated to Moses when he received the ten commandments on Mt. Sinai; the Gemara includes rabbinic interpretations and opinions of the oral law. Traditional education centered largely on interpret-

---

ing the Talmud, which teaches by way of case histories. Jewish law would be extrapolated from these case histories, then applied to new situations in everyday life. The method depended on discussion, a reason for teaming up with another student as the characters Yentl and Avigdor do in Singer's short story. They become study partners in Avigdor's hometown, the *shtetl*, or small town, of Bechev.

Jews in Poland clustered together in *shtetlach* (the plural of shtetl), where they formed a majority of the population of the small towns. Young men of the shtetl won prominence neither through wealth nor through physical prowess, but through their Talmudic studies. Boys embarked on their basic education at age three, focusing on languages, arithmetic, and Jewish subjects. At thirteen those who continued entered the *yeshiva*, an academy where they spent years studying, debating, and reinterpreting the Jewish laws recorded in the Talmud.

A street-scene of Ostrolenko, Poland, a shtetl similar to Bechev.

The ideal boy of Jewish folklore was pale and gaunt, the telltale marks of a child who spent his days in the hermetic isolation of the study room. Mothers longed to see their boys earn distinction in the schools, and wealthy fathers sought out bright young scholars to marry their daughters. Newlyweds sometimes lived with the bride's parents for as long as ten years so the groom could continue his study of the Talmud. The shtetl community even offered an allowance and daily meals in different houses to foster students' scholarly aspirations.

Hasidim and Mitnagdim. Not all religious Jews became preoccupied with the study of religious law. As far back as the 1200s there arose a movement of Jews who concentrated more on the mystical aspects of the religion than on the study of Jewish law. The mystics concerned themselves with attaining an immediate connection with God. Their movement, called Cabala, ultimately faded, but influenced a movement that surfaced in the 1700s among the Jews of Eastern Europe. Founded by Israel Ben Eliezer, or the Baal Shem Tov (which means "master of the good name"), this new movement, called Hasidism, emerged partially as a reaction against the traditional Jewish intelligentsia. Hasidism stressed direct, emotional worship of God through prayer, work, or any physical activity, and initially appealed most to poorer Jews.

This focus nurtured a strong sense of joy and release in worship that contrasted with the sedate prayers of the anti-Hasidic Jews, the Mitnagdim, who opposed the new movement. (*Mitnagdim* is, in fact, the Yiddish word for "opponents.") The Hasidim did not ignore the Talmud, but merely insisted that good actions meant more than strict observance of the law.

The Hasidim created a new charismatic religious leader, the zaddik, or rebbe, who, it was believed, could act as an intermediary and transmit people's supplications to God. It was thought that every generation gave birth to a few gifted individuals, each of whom could help his set of followers communicate with God. The zaddik would win a devoted following and pass on his position of authority to his son.

Clashes between the zaddikim and traditional rabbis erupted. Because the Hasidim accepted a variety of modes of worship and emphasized the mystical aspect of everyday life, the Mitnagdim dismissed them as simple-minded and ignorant. The Mitnagdim ridiculed the assertions of self-proclaimed miracle workers among the Hasidim, but also feared the spreading enthusiasm for Hasidism and so redoubled their emphasis on meticulous study.

The feud subsided in the nineteenth century as the Mitnagdim turned their concern to opposing the Haskalah movement (or Jewish enlightenment movement), which called for the study of worldly subjects more than religious ones. This new movement was perceived as a greater threat to Judaism than Hasidism, whose followers, though unconventional in their manner of prayer, were nevertheless devout. Hasidism ultimately had an impact on mainstream Judaism. The Mitnagdim increasingly adopted the Hasidic belief in the primacy of religious intent over esoteric knowledge.

Meanwhile, the Haskalah movement, which was concerned with worldly enlightenment, gained ground and greatly affected schooling, broadening the curriculum to include such secular subjects as geography, science, and art. Outside the small shtetls, the amount of time devoted to Hebrew studies diminished in the more urban yeshivas. In Warsaw, Poland, some schools began to take steps in this direction as early as 1819, even opening two schools for girls. The story's main character, Yentl, then, was not such an anomaly; though a maverick in the shtetl, she was living in an already changing world.

Jewish women. Traditional Jewish men recited a blessing thanking God, "who did not make me a woman" (Baker, p. 35). A contemporary prayer book adds a footnote alleging:

> [T]here is no degradation of women implied in this blessing. Men thank God for the privilege which is theirs of performing all the precepts of the Torah, many of which are not incumbent upon women.
>
> (*Metsudah siddur*, p. 14)

While apologists insisted that women's roles are different but equal, others have held that women in the nineteenth and earlier centuries were excluded from the two realms most esteemed by the Jewish community: prayer in the synagogue and the study of religious law.

In traditional synagogues women sat separated from men, usually in an upper gallery and sometimes concealed behind a curtain. Women were not allowed to wear the *tallith*, a prayer shawl or to be a part of the *minyan*, the quorum of ten Jews needed to recite public prayers. They could not read aloud from the Torah because their voices were considered sexually provocative. A woman's hair was regarded as so sexually alluring that matrons were expected to shave their heads and wear wigs in order not to attract males other than their own husbands.

Although women were not legally forbidden to study Jewish scripture, learned women were regarded with suspicion. Some Jewish scholars insisted that women, although adroit in the home and marketplace, lacked the acumen necessary for serious study. One rabbi warned "whoever teaches his daughter Torah teaches her *tiflut*", meaning "nonsense" or "useless information"; the word is also sometimes translated as "immorality" (Cantor, p. 103). The fear that grave consequences would attend the admission of women into the yeshiva drove one rabbi to exclaim "let the words of the Torah be burned and not given to women" (Cantor, p. 103).

As in other European households, Jewish women assumed the usual domestic tasks. But Jewish communities could not afford to confine women to only the home. It was necessary for them to work in the marketplace to support their husbands' studies. While the preservation of Jewish law and tradition became the ambition of young men, aside from nurturing the family, the role of women became to facilitate these pursuits.

INFERIOR OR SUPERIOR?

While women were denied certain rights and excused from certain obligations imposed on men in the traditional Jewish community, they nevertheless enjoyed a position of importance. It was a basic tenet of the shtetl that a man without a wife lives a joyless life, that he should love his wife as much as himself, and that he should respect her even more. A woman, many rabbis taught, is capable of deeper faith than a man, has a keener ability to discern truth, and is especially gentle-hearted.

Yet women had no direct influence on the interpretation of the laws that governed them. Even those laws addressing marriage, divorce, and assault were interpreted entirely by men. Wife abuse was not tolerated, since marriage was regarded as sacred and crucial in the preservation of the Jewish people. Divorce laws were strict. If a couple wanted to dissolve the marriage, only the man could petition for divorce. If a man vanished but could not be proven dead, his wife remained anchored (*agunan*) in the status of a "grass widow," and was unable to remarry. In "Yentl, the Yeshiva Boy," Yentl, a girl who impersonates a boy in order to study scripture, is coerced into marrying another girl. By sending divorce papers to her "wife," Yentl prevents the woman from being caught in such a circumstance.

In sum, a Jewish woman in the nineteenth-century shtetl devoted herself to raising children and supporting her husband in his pursuits—she had few outlets for her own intellectual creativity. Women, in fact, suffered exclusion from the studies that were and are a cornerstone of traditional Judaism.

The Short Story in Focus

The plot. After her father's death, a young Jewish girl, Yentl, is compelled to leave her small hometown of Yanev. Rather than rent out her father's house or accept one of many marriage offers, she sells her home and flees Yanev disguised as a man.

As a child Yentl had enjoyed the affection of her father, who during his many bedridden years had studied Torah with her. Proud of his daughter's keen intelligence, he lamented "Yentl, you have the soul of a man" (Singer, "Yentl, the Yeshiva Boy," p. 8). Sometimes while her father slept, Yentl would don his clothes and regard herself in the mirror. Secretly she would even smoke his pipe. After his death, she longed to continue studying Torah at a yeshiva. Rather than resign herself to the dull lot of a housewife, she clips her braids and starts off for the Polish city of Lublin dressed as a man.

On the road to Lublin she meets Avigdor, a yeshiva boy from the town of Bechev. Yentl introduces herself as Anshel, the name of one of her uncles, and says she is looking for a quiet yeshiva. Avigdor suggests she accompany him to Bechev. On the way he tells her the tale of his first engagement.

Avigdor had been engaged to Hadass Vishkower, the daughter of the richest man in Bechev. But her father, Alter Vishkower, forbade the marriage, shattering both his daughter's and Avigdor's dreams. Avigdor's friends suggested other women, but he had no interest.

Arriving in Bechev, Yentl and Avigdor agree to become study partners. Yentl finds lodging and, after a few weeks, becomes a regular guest in Alter Vishkower's home. To Avigdor's persistent questions about Hadass, Yentl replies "two years after she's married, . . . she'll be an old hag" ("Yentl, the Yeshiva Boy," p. 15). Together with

Avigdor, Yentl spends hours musing over the wisdom of the Torah, puffing on cigarettes, and sharing buckwheat cakes. All the while she continues the ruse of portraying herself as a young man.

One day Avigdor astonishes her. Still thinking Yentl is a young man, he requests that she marry Hadass, insisting that it would be "better than [if] a total stranger [married her]" ("Yentl, the Yeshiva Boy," p. 16). He confesses also that his relatives are trying to marry him off to a shrewish widow for fear that no other woman will have him. Yentl tries to discourage him from the idea, but to no avail. Two days later Avigdor becomes engaged to Peshe, a merchant's daughter.

Disturbed by Avigdor's engagement, Yentl dares one evening to ask Hadass why she did not marry Avigdor. Hadass responds, "It wasn't my fault. My father was against it . . . [he] found out a brother of his had hanged himself" ("Yentl, the Yeshiva Boy," p. 19). (Suicide was regarded as a sin more abominable than murder by religious authorities of the era.) Days later, after realizing that she is in love with Avigdor, Yentl proposes to Hadass. Yentl's intentions are neither honorable nor unselfish. She plans to exact a vengeance for Avigdor, while simultaneously drawing him closer, through Hadass, to herself. Hadass's father agrees to the match.

Yentl ponders how she will deceive Hadass. They are both virgins and know little about men. But having read about sex in her studies and heard the coarse swagger of young men, Yentl feels confident she can dupe Hadass. After the wedding night, Hadass's mother and her band invade the couple's chamber. They emerge brandishing bloodstained sheets to prove the consummation.

While Yentl enjoys Hadass's tender care, Avigdor suffers from Peshe's constant nagging. Welcoming a few days respite from his wife, he eagerly accepts an invitation from Yentl to spend a few days in Lublin. Yentl promises to divulge an astonishing secret. In Lublin, she confesses she is a woman. To convince Avigdor, she undresses in front of him.

Yentl explains that even as a child she had read from the Torah with her father. Rather than abandon the joys of study for the tedium of housekeeping, she had assumed the garb of a man and fled her hometown. On the road, continued Yentl, she had met Avigdor, and followed him to Bechev. She had married Hadass only to be closer to him. Avigdor exclaims "You could have married me" ("Yentl, the Yeshiva Boy," p. 49), but Yentl replies that she could never abandon her studies.

Yentl encourages Avigdor to divorce Peshe and marry Hadass. She assures him of Hadass's unflagging love for him and insists that she (Yentl) will leave Bechev and send Hadass the necessary divorce papers. Both Yentl and Avigdor agree that Hadass might not survive the trauma were she to discover she had married a woman. Avigdor is eager to leave Peshe, but hesitant to marry Hadass. He insists that he would rather marry Yentl, but she declines, "No, Avigdor, it wasn't destined to be" ("Yentl, the Yeshiva Boy," p. 52).

Yentl disappears from Bechev and Hadass falls ill of consternation and grief. The town gossips invent a variety of explanations for Yentl's disappearance. They are surprised that even Avigdor, Yentl's best friend, remains silent but even more surprised when he becomes engaged to Hadass. Hadass becomes pregnant soon after the marriage, and the townspeople are again astonished to hear Avigdor name his first son Anshel.

Yentl's liberation. When Yentl's father laments "Yentl, you have the soul of a man" ("Yentl, the Yeshiva Boy", p. 8), he confirms her suspicion that "she had not been created for the noodle board and the pudding dish, for chattering with silly women and pushing for a place at the butcher's block" ("Yentl, the Yeshiva Boy," p. 8). With Avigdor she enters the world of men, studying Torah and tasting cigarettes and strong liquor.

Yet when Avigdor comments "they're trying to talk me into another match, but the girl doesn't appeal to me," Yentl reacts with surprise, "In Bechev, yeshiva boys look at women?" ("Yentl, the Yeshiva Boy," p. 12). Yentl's question reveals her own innocence. Although versed in the lore of the Torah, she remains naive about sex. When her period is late, she fears she "ha[s] conceived merely through desiring a man" ("Yentl, the Yeshiva Boy," p. 22). Yentl manages to deceive Hadass only because Hadass is even more uninformed than she.

Having revealed herself to Avigdor, Yentl forsakes him for her studies. When he insists "you could have married me," she retorts, "I wanted to study the Gemara and Commentaries with you, not darn your socks!" ("Yentl, the Yeshiva Boy," p. 49). In the conservative shtetl she can hardly hope her ambitions will be tolerated. Rather than indulge her love for Avigdor, she must continue the perverse masquerade, a parody that mocks the liberation she seeks by causing her to deny herself another way. She must stifle her romantic desires for Avigdor. In one case or the other, society makes it impossible for Yentl to achieve complete happiness.

HOW YENTL DIVORCED HADASS

There is no other means of obtaining a divorce under Jewish law than by a husband delivering or sending his wife a bill of divorcement called a *get*. To be effective, the get must be freely accepted by the wife. In other words, she cannot be divorced without her consent. The divorce is executed by the husband's act of writing, signing, and delivering the bill to his wife either personally or by a representative. Afterwards the ex-husband and ex-wife are free to remarry and are forbidden to continue occupying their former home.

Sources. Singer's mother, Bathsheba Zylberman, might have provided a model for Yentl. She too was educated by her father, who decried the fact that she hadn't been born a man. In his memoirs, Singer's brother, Joshua, headed the chapter about his parents' ill-fated marriage "A tragedy, due to the fact that fate transposed genders in heaven." He describes his mother as "tall and somewhat stooped, with large, piercing, cold-gray eyes, a sharp nose and a jutting pointed chin like a man's" (Sinclair, p. 13). Singer's sister, Esther, insisted that her mother "looked like a Talmudist who spends his days and nights and years in study, rather than a woman. Even the black dress and velvet jacket she had on scarcely betrayed her" (Sinclair, p. 13).

The sad childhood of Isaac's neglected sister may also have prompted Singer to write Yentl's story. Ignored by her mother, who had hoped for a boy she could train to study Torah, Esther Singer sought love from her less austere father. She "reflected that had she been a boy instead of a girl . . . she would have spent all her time in the study

of the Talmud" (Sinclair, p. 19). But her Hasidic father did not nurture her interests. Hasidism, although welcoming new forms of worship, followed traditional Judaism in encouraging women to "bring . . . happiness into the home by ministering to [their] husband[s] and bearing [them] children" (Sinclair, p. 20). When she overheard her father proudly declare that his son Joshua would one day be a renowned Talmudist, she asked "what am I going to be one day?" He replied "Nothing, of course!" (Sinclair, p. 20). Nevertheless, Esther persevered. She wrote short stories and letters, in which Isaac Bashevis perceived "the first literary spark" in the family (Sinclair, p. 21). Esther escaped to England before World War I. She was sickly all her life and suffered paranoia, perhaps as a result of her parents' disdain.

Events in History at the Time the Short Story Was Written

Yentl and feminism. Singer fled Poland for New York in 1935, where he supervised the translation of his stories from Yiddish into English. A reemergent feminist movement in America was gaining ground when "Yentl, the Yeshiva Boy" was published. It would formally begin in 1963 with the publication of Betty Friedan's book *The Feminine Mystique,* which revealed the emotional misery suffered by women who were unfulfilled by their roles as homemakers. Because Singer's short story articulates some of the frustrations women were suffering in the 1960s, the author's earlier comments about women might seem surprising. Listening to political banter in the writers' haunts in Warsaw, Poland, he had decided he "was an anti-feminist" (Kresh, *The Magician of 86th Street,* p. 105). Singer had been involved in many love affairs in his youth and insisted "I always felt that two girls were better than one and three were better than two" (Kresh, *The Magician of 86th Street,* p. 105). According to Singer, the short story "Yentl, the Yeshiva Boy" has no feminist purpose. It merely showed that "behind all the strict behavior, behind the long skirts and the rules and regulations, human nature was still there. So many things can keep a person captive because of a fear of losing one's reputation, but our passions are still there" (Kresh, *The Magician of 86th Street,* p. 11).

Modern Judaism. After World War II and the Holocaust, in which 6 million Jews were exterminated by the Germans, Jewish women suffered enormous pressure to bear children. The fear that the Jewish population was dying out plagued

Isaac Bashevis Singer

Holocaust survivors, who urged their daughters to marry and begin families.

Women did gain new rights during this period. In the Jewish state of Israel created after the war, the Women's Equal Rights Law of 1951 made women's legal status equal to men's, guaranteeing their rights to own property and serve as a child's guardian. Religious law has been slower to change. It still governs marriage and divorce for the Jews of Israel, a substantial number of whom hail from Poland and other areas of Eastern Europe. There was, moreover, a vestige of discrimination under this law in that it required a divorce to be given by the husband to the wife. In other words, had Yentl's marriage dissolved in 1962, when the story was written, it still would have required the husband supplying the wife with papers to release her from the bond.

Conversely, Holocaust survivors who emigrated to the United States after World War II (as Singer had done in 1935) became subject to civil instead of religious laws in marriage as well as other areas.

The threat of assimilation prompted Jewish leaders to reconsider the question of women's education. Whereas women in the Polish shtetlach had often lived in their fathers' homes, sheltered from corrupting influences, in America most women had some secular education and often lived away from home. Even traditional Jews agreed that to preserve Jewish customs, women should study the Torah. This might prevent women from leaving the Jewish faith while better preparing them to raise their own children as Jews. Not until a decade after Singer wrote his story, though, would even the least conservative branch of American Jewry take a pivotal step on behalf of women. Only in 1972 did Hebrew Union College ordain the first female rabbi in the United States, Sally Priesand.

Reception. "Yentl, the Yeshiva Boy" won acclaim from critics, with one commentator describing it as a tale that "deals with problems confronting Jewish women in the late nineteenth-century Polish shtetlach, problems that have not been resolved" (Cohen, p. 208). The story's popularity encouraged Singer to make it into a play. One critic of the play praised the "resemblances to traditional Yiddish theater . . . ingenious female disguise . . . compelling full length rituals performed in the original Hebrew and quaint shtetl customs" (Cohen, p. 209). Singer wrote a poignant funeral scene for the play, in which Yentl, as a girl, is forbidden to recite a prayer for her father.

The story was later developed into a movie-musical, starring and directed by Barbara Streisand, which was released in 1983. Singer disparaged the film, lamenting,

> I did not find artistic merit neither in the adaptation, nor in the directing [sic]. . . . [T]here was too much singing in this movie, much too much. . . . It did nothing to bring out Yentl's individuality nor to enlighten her conduct. The very opposite.
>
> (Farrell, pp. 224-25)

He decried the happy ending, in which Yentl boards a ship to America, "singing at the top of her lungs" (Farrell, p. 226). "Why would she decide to go to America," Singer asked. "Weren't there enough Yeshivas in Poland or in Lithuania where she could continue to study?" (Farrell, p. 226).

In spite of Singer's widespread popularity, the author had his detractors. Some Yiddish writers criticized him for exposing unsavory features about Polish villages. They insisted that by revealing the sexism of the shtetl he threatened the integrity of the Jewish communities, and called him "The Betrayer of Israel."

Others responded that, by defying conventional stereotypes, Singer's characters challenged common prejudices of his day. In America, for example, Jews were often perceived as a model minority. The average Jew was expected to be a genius, like the scientist Albert Einstein. By deflating these myths, Singer's stories are said to have helped liberate American Jews.

For More Information

Baker, Adrienne. *The Jewish Woman in Contemporary Society.* New York: New York University Press, 1993.

Cantor, Aviva. *Jewish Women/Jewish Men.* San Francisco: Harper, 1995.

Cohen, Sarah Blacher. *From Hester Street to Hollywood: The Jewish-American Stage and Screen.* Bloomington: Indiana University Press, 1983.

Farrell, Grace. *Isaac Bashevis Singer: Conversations.* University: University Press of Mississippi, 1992.

Kresh, Paul. *The Magician of 86th Street.* New York: Dial, 1979.

Kresh, Paul. *The Story of a Storyteller.* New York: Lodestar, 1984.

Metsudah Siddur. New York: Metsudah Publications, 1982.

Sinclair, Clive. *The Brothers Singer.* London, New York: Allison and Busby, 1983.

Singer, Isaac Bashevis. *Yentl, the Yeshiva Boy.* Translated by Marion Magid and Elizabeth Pollet. Toronto: Collins, 1962.

Index

A

Aaron, Hank   **4**:*145, 148*
Abernathy, Ralph   **5**:*89 (illus.)*
Abolitionists/Abolition of slavery
    John Brown's raid on Harper's Ferry   **2**:*188–94*
    changing little for freed slaves   **5**:*19–20*
    controversy and disagreement with, in North
      2:*9, 315, 404*
    as core political issue by mid-19th century
      2:*88, 242*
    early efforts   **2**:*22–24*
    Emancipation Proclamation (1862)   **2**:*59, 60*
      (sidebar), 135, 308, 309
    Liberia   **2**:*404*
    proposals for land for freed slaves   **2**:*41*
    and Underground Railroad   **2**:*16, 60, 62, 189,*
      238, 406–7
    women's role in   **2**:*23–24*
    (*See also* African Americans; Jim Crow laws;
      Reconstruction)
Abortion   **5**:*51, 136*
Abraham Lincoln: The Prairie Years, Sandburg, Carl
    2:*1–7*
Achebe, Chinua, *Things Fall Apart*   **2**:*360–65*
Acheson, Dean   **5**:*101*
Achilles   **1**:*169–70*
Across Five Aprils, Hunt, Irene   **2**:*8–14*
Adam and Eve   **1**:*301–2*
Adams, John   **1**:*29, 72, 94*
Adams, John Quincy   **1**:*209*
Adams, Richard, *Watership Down*   **5**:*346–51*
Addison, Joseph   **1**:*307*
Adoption of children, by African Americans   **4**:*33*
Adultery/infidelity   **5**:*273, 287*
    in *Anna Karenina*   **2**:*34–40*
    in *Ethan Frome*   **2**:*125–29*
    in *Madame Bovary*   **2**:*209–15*
    in *Medea*   **1**:*238–41*
    in *Scarlet Letter*   **1**:*351–57*
Adventures of Don Quixote, The, Cervantes Saavedra,
    Miguel de   **1**:*1–7*
Adventures of Huckleberry Finn, The, Twain, Mark
    2:*15–21*
Advertising
    fostering consumer culture   **3**:*26*
    targeting teenagers   **4**:*392*
    WWII-related ads excluding minorities   **4**:*197*
Advise and Consent   **5**:*4*
Aegean Sea   **1**:*60* (map)
Aeneas. *See Aeneid, The*
Aeneid, The, Virgil   **1**:*8–13*
    parallels to *Beowulf*   **1**:*49*
    parallels to Shakespeare's *The Tempest*   **1**:*383*
Affirmative action   **5**:*181, 183–84, 342*
AFL (American Federation of Labor)   **3**:*44*
Africa and Africans
    in 16th-century England   **1**:*299*
    Algeria   **3**:*212*
    apartheid in South Africa   **1**:*63;* **3**:*86*
    Belgian Congo   **2**:*145–46, 150–51*
    Ethiopia   **4**:*67*
    Gambia   **5**:*298*
    Ghana   **4**:*314*
    impact of WWI   **3**:*292–93*
    independence movements   **4**:*314*
    ivory trade   **2**:*147*
    Kenya   **3**:*290–96*
    Liberia   **2**:*404*
    Maasai   **3**:*295*
    Medea as Egyptian "woman of color"   **1**:*240*
    (sidebar)

Moors   **1**:*297, 299*
natives as "squatters"   **3**:*293–94*
Nigeria   **2**:*360–62, 364–65;* **3**:*84;* **4**:*314*
oral tradition and griots   **5**:*298–300, 301–2*
post-WWI economic problems   **3**:*293*
racism of colonial powers   **2**:*360–65;* **3**:*291*
Rhodesia   **4**:*165–66*
slave trade   **1**:*37, 39, 103, 274, 299, 337–38;*
    2:*361*
Tanzania   **3**:*290*
(*See also* Colonialism, imperialism, and
    interventionism)
African American men
    "humiliations, emasculation" faced by   **4**:*53–54;*
        5:*146, 328–29*
    physicians in Georgia   **3**:*154–55, 156–57*
    relationship of class, race, and manhood
        4:*313–14*
    as soldiers in Vietnam War   **5**:*102–3*
African American women
    accused of black male-bashing   **3**:*87;* **5**:*121*
    African-style clothing and hairdos   **4**:*56;* **5**:*145,*
        300
    and black feminism   **2**:*64;* **3**:*86–87;* **4**:*56*
    cosmetics for   **4**:*50, 56*
    devaluation of   **3**:*80–82;* **4**:*54;* **5**:*115–16*
    differences with white women in civil rights and
        feminist movements   **3**:*354–55;* **5**:*92–93, 117*
    employment in South   **3**:*418–19*
    as heads of families   **3**:*355, 375, 423*
    as "mammies"   **3**:*392*
    race- and gender-based limitations upon
        5:*115–16*
    sexual abuse of   **2**:*49, 60, 169, 406;* **4**:*54;* **5**:*117*
    as single heads of households   **2**:*65;* **3**:*80, 423;*
        4:*2;* **5**:*68, 117, 328–29*
African Americans in 19th century
    churches as cornerstones of community   **5**:*189*
    exodus from South to West   **3**:*249–50*
    gospel songs and black spirituals   **2**:*398, 402,*
        407; **4**:*258*
    mixed race offspring and color prejudice   **5**:*21*
    (*See also* Civil War; Jim Crow laws; Segregation;
        Slavery in America; Slaves)
African Americans in 20th century
    adopting white society's values   **4**:*52*
    adoption of children   **4**:*33*
    in black ghettos. *See* Ghettos
    class/social stratification among   **4**:*2–3, 30*
    communism and   **1**:*398–99;* **3**:*164, 238–39*
    community, kinship, and closeness   **2**:*341–42;*
        3:*383–84, 394;* **4**:*52*
    crime, some turning to   **4**:*145*
    crime, victims of   **4**:*31;* **5**:*340–41*
    during Great Depression   **3**:*154, 236–37*
    education   **4**:*3;* **5**:*342*
    employment opportunities and limitations
        4:*311;* **5**:*341 (sidebar)*
    family life   **3**:*80, 84–86, 353–55, 375, 422–23;*
        4:*33;* **5**:*68, 145–46, 329–30*

Harlem Renaissance   **3**:*159–65, 256, 321,*
    384–85, 421; **4**:*204 (sidebar), 207*
Hollywood's stereotypical images of   **2**:*142;*
    4:*50, 369*
middle class, rise of   **3**:*252, 255, 387–88;* **4**:*2,*
    51
mixed race offspring and color prejudice   **2**:*49;*
    3:*17–18, 81, 83, 387–88;* **4**:*3, 50, 51–52;* **5**:*130*
oral tradition   **5**:*298–300, 301–2*
poverty of many   **3**:*37;* **4**:*5 (sidebar), 145;* **5**:*329*
race colonies   **3**:*383*
religion's importance to   **3**:*372*
riot following assassination of King (1968)
    5:*112 (sidebar)*
riots in central Los Angeles (1992)   **5**:*340*
riots in Watts (1965)   **5**:*340*
(*See also* Great Migration; Jim Crow laws;
    Segregation)
African Americans' civil rights/reform/power
movements
    activism for FEPC (Fair Employment Practices
        Commission)   **3**:*42*
    anti-integrationist   **5**:*15*
    assassinations of leaders   **4**:*54;* **5**:*112 (sidebar)*
    autobiographies as genre   **4**:*205;* **5**:*304*
    Black arts movement   **4**:*207*
    black feminism   **2**:*64;* **3**:*86–87*
    "Black is Beautiful" slogan   **4**:*54, 56*
    Black Muslims and Nation of Islam   **3**:*238, 325;*
        4:*56, 248–50;* **5**:*12–13, 69, 110–11, 302*
    black nationalism, separatism, and Pan-
        Africanism   **3**:*160, 238, 325;* **4**:*56, 211,*
        311–12
    Black Panther Party   **4**:*54, 56, 207*
    Black Power movement   **2**:*97–98;* **3**:*43, 325;*
        4:*56, 207;* **5**:*143–44*
    CORE (Congress of Racial Equality)   **3**:*42;* **4**:*376*
    efforts of 1940s and'50s   **4**:*28–29, 255*
    emphasizing African heritage   **5**:*300–302*
    fostered by Harlem Renaissance   **3**:*163–64, 256*
    King's approach, compared to Malcolm X's
        4:*250;* **5**:*13, 15, 111*
    militancy and Malcolm X   **2**:*98;* **3**:*324–25;* **4**:*54,*
        249–50; **5**:*69–70, 110, 111*
    in Missouri   **4**:*28–29*
    NAACP   **2**:*342, 415;* **3**:*250, 320, 396;* **4**:*195,*
        255, 310; **5**:*88, 120 (sidebar)*
    Niagara Movement (1905)   **3**:*250, 320*
    OAAU (Organization of Afro-American Unity)
        5:*16–17*
    pacifist versus outspoken, sometimes violent
        protest   **4**:*205, 207*
    passive resistance and nonviolence   **5**:*11–12,*
        108, 189, 192
    SCLC (Southern Christian Leadership
        Conference)   **5**:*189*
    seeking African roots   **3**:*86;* **5**:*145*
    self-empowerment philosophies   **3**:*325*
    SNCC (Student Nonviolent Coordinating
        Committee)   **4**:*56;* **5**:*300*

UNIA (United Negro Improvement Association)
  3:*160*; 4:*211*
  urban blacks' involvement in 5:*143*
  WPC (Women's Political Council) 5:*88*
African Americans, literary works concerning
  Adventures of Huckleberry Finn, The 2:*15–21*
  "Ain't I a Woman?" 2:*22–27*
  Almos' a Man 4:*1–6*
  Autobiography of Malcolm X, The 5:*11–18*
  Bear, The 2:*47–53*
  Beloved 2:*59–65*
  Benito Cereno 1:*37–43*
  Betsey Brown 4:*28–34*
  Black Boy 3:*36–43*
  Bluest Eye, The 4:*49–57*
  Color Purple, The 3:*80–87*
  Confessions of Nat Turner, The 2:*93–98*
  Cry, the Beloved Country 4:*94–100*
  Fences 4:*144–50*
  Fire Next Time, The 5:*107–14*
  *for colored girls who have considered suicide / when
    the rainbow is enuf* 5:*115–21*
  Gathering of Old Men, A 5:*129–34*
  Gone with the Wind 2:*137–44*
  Hero Ain't Nothin' but a Sandwich, A 5:*143–48*
  His Own Where 5:*149–55*
  Home to Harlem 3:*159–65*
  "I Have a Dream" 5:*185–93*
  I Know Why the Caged Bird Sings 4:*201–8*
  Incidents in the Life of a Slave Girl 2:*168–73*
  Invisible Man 4:*209–15*
  John Brown's Final Speech 2:*188–94*
  Leaves of Grass 2:*197*
  Manchild in the Promised Land 4:*247–53*
  Member of the Wedding, The 4:*254–59*
  Narrative of the Life of Frederick Douglass
    2:*236–41*
  Native Son 3:*236–42*
  Not without Laughter 3:*249–56*
  Raisin in the Sun, A 4:*309–15*
  Roots 5:*298–305*
  Souls of Black Folk, The 2:*340–46*
  Sounder 3:*370–76*
  Sweet Whispers, Brother Rush 5:*328–32*
  Their Eyes Were Watching God 3:*383–89*
  Tituba of Salem Village 1:*393–99*
  Uncle Remus 2:*397–402*
  Uncle Tom's Cabin 2:*403–9*
  Understand This 5:*339–45*
  Up From Slavery 2:*410–15*
  Worn Path, A 3:*418–24*
African Methodist Episcopal Church 3:*83*
Age of Reason 1:*268–69, 272*
Agee, James, *Death in the Family, A* 3:*100–105*
Agnosticism 3:*265*
AIDS (Acquired Immune Deficiency Syndrome)
  5:*9*
Aiken, Conrad 3:*414*
AIM (American Indian Movement) 2:*79 (sidebar)*;
  5:*246–47*

"Ain't I a Woman?" Truth, Sojourner 2:*22–27*
Air pollution 4:*9*
Alaska 3:*52–56, 261 (sidebar)*
Albania 2:*101*
Albee, Edward, *Zoo Story, The* 4:*397–402*
Alchemy 1:*384, 385 (sidebar)*
Alcohol and alcoholism
  among American Indians 1:*220*; 4:*83, 189
    (sidebar)*; 5:*361*
  among Irish 3:*220, 398, 400*
  among war wives 4:*317*
  among Welsh 3:*65–66*
  Anti-Saloon League and temperance movements
    2:*25 (sidebar), 85–86*; 3:*69, 75, 147, 401*
  Prohibition 3:*22–23*
  saloons as social halls 3:*219, 398, 400*
  as woman's issue 2:*25 (sidebar)*; 3:*219*
  (See also Prohibition)
Alcott, Louisa May, *Little Women* 2:*202–8*
Aldrin, Edwin E. ("Buzz") Jr. 5:*82, 292, 295 (illus.)*
Aleichem, Sholom 3:*123*
Alexander the Great, Czar of Russia 1:*169
  (sidebar)*
Alexander II, Czar of Russia 3:*57, 120*
Alexander III, Czar of Russia 3:*120*
Alger, Horatio, *Ragged Dick* 2:*301–7*
Ali, Muhammad 5:*70 (sidebar), 72 (illus.), 307–8*
Alianza, La 4:*175–76, 321*
Alice's Adventures in Wonderland, Carroll, Lewis
  2:*28–33*
All Creatures Great and Small, Herriott, James
  3:*1–7*
All Quiet on the Western Front, Remarque, Erich
  Maria 3:*8–14*
Allegory, *Animal Farm*, Orwell, George 4:*14–20*
Allen, Ethan 3:*98 (sidebar)*
Allende, Isabel, *House of the Spirits, The* 5:*163–70*
Allende, Salvador 5:*164–65, 166 (illus.), 168–69*
Almanacs, *Poor Richard's Almanac*, Franklin,
  Benjamin 1:*309–15*
Almos' a Man, Wright, Richard 4:*1–6*
Amadis of Gaul 1:*6*
Amazons 1:*58–59, 61–62, 258, 259–60*
America. *See* Colonial America; United States
American Childhood, An, Dillard, Annie 4:*7–13*
American Communist Party
  popularity of, during Great Depression 3:*45*
  standing against racism 3:*40*
  (See also Communism)
American Dream
  achievement as impossible for black men 4:*313*
  achieving through hard work and frugality
    2:*302, 305*; 4:*111*
  achieving through salesmanship in 1950s
    4:*111*
  Ben Franklin as embodiment of 1:*26–27, 309*
  in colonial times 1:*97*
  Dreiser's preoccupation with 2:*331–32*
  merit rather than rank determining success
    1:*72*

American Indians in 16th century, decimated by
  smallpox   **5**:*214*
American Indians in 17th century, displayed in
  Renaissance Europe   **1**:*383*
American Indians in 18th century
  as allies of British in Revolutionary War   **1**:*108*
  as allies of French in French and Indian War
    1:*204–5*
  decimated by smallpox   **1**:*220, 352*
  enslaved   **1**:*103*; **2**:*175*
  French and Indian War (Seven Years' War)
    1:*93, 123, 204–6*
  land/natural resources as considered by   **1**:*220*;
    2:*78, 178*
  legends and Folk, Thelore   **1**:*332*
  Paxton Boys massacre   **1**:*220–21*
  pressure of westward expansion of American
    colonists   **1**:*108, 204, 220–21*
  Puritans' view of   **1**:*102, 422*
  Uncas   **1**:*207 (sidebar), 208*
  "walking purchase" of land from   **1**:*220*
    (sidebar)
American Indians in 19th century
  art   **2**:*348–49, 351–52*
  Battle of Wounded Knee   **2**:*69, 78*
  BIA (Bureau of Indian Affairs)   **5**:*246*
  Black Hills War (1876)   **2**:*67–68, 77*
  buffalo, Great Plains tribes' dependency on
    2:*66–67, 75*
  Crazy Horse   **2**:*348 (illus.)*
  and Dawes Act (1887)   **2**:*68, 179*; **4**:*186*
  decimated by smallpox   **2**:*347*
  defended by Bret Harte   **2**:*287*
  family and family life   **2**:*347*
  Ghost Dance   **2**:*69, 77–78*
  holy men   **2**:*71–72*
  horse culture of Plains tribes   **5**:*364 (sidebar)*
  missions/missionaries and   **2**:*161–62, 392*
    (sidebar)
  national guilt felt by whites   **2**:*79*
  Ongpatonga   **1**:*209 (illus.)*
  parallels to Anglo-Saxons after Norman Conquest
    1:*257*
  peyote religion   **4**:*188*
  religion of   **2**:*71–72, 78*
  Removal Act (1830)   **1**:*208–10*; **2**:*316, 317*
    (sidebar)
  reservations policies of U.S. gov't.   **1**:*224*; **2**:*67,*
    68, 73, 76, 79, 179, 316, 317 (sidebar), 351;
    4:*186–87*
  Sand Creek Massacre   **2**:*77*
  "second parents" among Sioux   **2**:*347*
  spirituality of   **2**:*72, 161*; **5**:*246*
  Sun Dance   **2**:*349 (sidebar)*; **4**:*187–88*
  "Trail of Tears"   **5**:*29–30*
  treaties and U.S. gov't.'s failure to enforce
    2:*75–76, 162*
American Indians in 20th century
  AIM (American Indian Movement)   **2**:*79*
    (sidebar); **5**:*246–47*

alcoholism   **1**:*220*; **4**:*83, 189 (sidebar)*; **5**:*361*
BIA (Bureau of Indian Affairs)   **5**:*246*
Catholic Church   **5**:*244, 361–62*
citizenship status   **4**:*80*
Civil Rights Act of 1964 affecting   **2**:*351*
    (sidebar)
cultural mixture of American Southwest
    4:*320–21*
Indian Reorganization Act (1934)   **2**:*73*; **4**:*186*
matrilineal cultures   **4**:*82 (sidebar)*
military service   **4**:*80, 185–87*; **5**:*362–63*
mission school of Anglican Church   **5**:*195*
Navajo Night Chant   **4**:*188*
poverty of   **5**:*360–61*
prestige factor of Indian ancestry   **5**:*30*
Red Power and rights movements   **2**:*79*
    (sidebar), 179, 351
relocation program (1952)   **4**:*186–87*
self-determination policies (1961 and 1970)
    2:*351*; **4**:*190–91*
storytelling, powers of   **4**:*83 (sidebar), 85, 188,*
    189, 192
and tribal rights (1934)   **2**:*73*
American Indians, literary works concerning
  Bear, The (Chickasaw)   **2**:*47–53*
  Black Elk Speaks (Oglala Sioux)   **2**:*66–73*
  Bury My Heart at Wounded Knee (Western tribes)
    2:*74–80*
  Ceremony (Laguna Pueblo)   **4**:*79–86*
  Drums Along the Mohawk (Iroquois)   **1**:*108*
  House Made of Dawn (Navajo, Jemez Pueblo, and
    WWII veterans)   **4**:*185–92*
  I Heard the Owl Call My Name (Kwakiutl)
    5:*194–200*
  "I Will Fight No More Forever" (Nez Percé)
    2:*160–67*
  Ishi, Last of His Tribe (Yahi)   **2**:*174–80*
  Last of the Mohicans, The (Delaware and Iroquois)
    1:*204–10*
  Leaves of Grass (America's Indian heritage)
    2:*195–201*
  Light in the Forest, The (Delaware)   **1**:*219–24*
  Love Medicine (Chippewa)   **5**:*243–50*
  Story Catcher, The (Oglala Sioux)   **2**:*347–52*
  Tempest, The (Europeans' explorations of New
    World)   **1**:*383*
  Yellow Raft in Blue Water, A (Cree)   **5**:*360–66*
American Indians by tribe
  Arawak (Taino)   **5**:*214*
  Cherokee   **5**:*29–30*
  Cheyenne   **2**:*75, 79*
  Chippewa   **5**:*243–50*
  Chiricahua Apache   **2**:*74–75*
  Cree   **5**:*361 (sidebar), 362 (illus.), 364 (sidebar)*
  Delaware (Lenape)   **1**:*206, 219–20*
  Iroquois   **1**:*108, 110, 205–6*
  Jemez Pueblo   **4**:*187, 189–90, 191*
  Kiowa   **4**:*186, 187–88*
  Kwakiutl (Canada)   **5**:*194–200*
  Laguna Pueblo   **4**:*79–86*

métis   *5:244*
Modoc   *2:79*
Mohegan   *1:352*
Narragansett   *1:352*
Navajo   *2:79*; *4:80, 186, 188*; *5:360*
Nez Percé   *2:75, 79, 160–67*
Pequot   *1:352*
Pueblo   *4:47*
Sioux   *2:66–67, 347–50*; *5:360*
Ute   *2:79*
Yahi   *2:174, 175, 177*
Zuni Pueblo   *4:186*
American Revolution
Continental Congress   *1:125*
Declaration of Independence   *1:93–100*
in *Drums Along the Mohawk*   *1:107–14*
influence of *Common Sense*   *1:71–77, 94*
influence of "Give Me Liberty or Give Me Death"
speech   *1:122–28*
Amistad mutiny   *1:43*
Anaya, Rudolfo A.
Bless Me, Ultima   *4:42–48*
Heart of Aztlán   *4:171–76*
Anderson, Robert, *I Never Sang for My Father*
5:201–7
Anderson, Sherwood, on *Babbitt*   *3:27*
André, Major John   *1:213 (sidebar)*
Angelou, Maya, *I Know Why the Caged Bird Sings*
4:201–8
Angels in America, Kushner, Tony   *5:1–10*
Anglican Church (Church of England)   *1:78, 123,*
129, 232, 233 (sidebar), 306, 351, 393
Dissenters   *1:129, 338, 342, 407, 411*; *3:265*
Anglo-Saxon England   *1:44–45, 153, 181*
Norman Conquest of   *1:181, 250–51, 290*
Animal Farm, Orwell, George   *4:14–20*
politically motivated rejection by publishers
5:252–53
Animals, stories concerning
All Creatures Great and Small   *3:1–7*
Bless the Beasts and Children   *5:34–38*
Call of the Wild, The   *3:51–56*
Day No Pigs Would Die, A   *3:94–99*
Red Pony, The   *3:334–37*
Sounder   *3:370–76*
Watership Down   *5:346–51*
Anna Karenina, Tolstoy, Leo   *2:34–40*
Anne, Queen of England   *1:130–31, 342*
Anne, Queen of France   *1:389*
Annesley, Brian   *1:201*
Anonymous, *Beowulf*   *1:44–50*
Anthropology
comparative   *5:42*
interest in Polynesian peoples' origins   *4:221–27*
researchers' interest in American Indians   *2:72,*
179
Antigone, Sophocles   *1:14–21*
Antinomians   *1:352, 357*
Anti-Semitism
in accusations of fix of 1919 World Series   *4:261*

of African Americans   *4:376–77*
of Argentina's "dirty war"   *5:210*
in Brooklyn   *3:402*
of Charles Lindbergh   *4:373*
contributing to generation gap   *5:203*
diminishing in 1950s and '60s   *5:203*
and Dreyfus affair   *1:91–92, 364 (sidebar)*
in England   *1:182–83*; *2:264–65*
of Father Charles Coughlin   *4:373*
in Germany   *1:370*; *4:157–59*
holocaust denial   *4:40*
in Italy   *1:243–44, 246*
Kristallnacht   *4:159, 162–63*
and moneylending   *1:182–83*; *2:264*
and nationalism   *1:364*
origins of "ghetto"   *1:244, 249*
Pale of Settlement   *3:119–20, 121*
pogroms   *1:364*; *3:120–21*
in Poland   *1:364*
in Russia   *1:364*; *3:119–21*
in Soviet Union   *3:124–25*; *5:122*
in U.S. of 1940s   *4:236–37, 373*
in U.S. military   *4:36–37*
in Wharton's works   *3:170*
(*See also* Holocaust)
Antiwar literature
All Quiet on the Western Front   *3:8–14*
Catch-22   *4:66–72*
Fallen Angels   *5:101–6*
Farewell to Arms, A   *3:112–18*
Red Badge of Courage, The   *2:308–13*
Slaughterhouse Five   *4:343–48*
Waste Land, The   *3:411–17*
Appalachian Trail   *5:278–79*
Arabs, anti-Zionism   *4:107*
Archery   *1:253*
Argentina   *5:208–11, 212–13*
Aristotle
commenting upon *Republic*   *1:328*
influence in 16th century   *1:233*
influence on Jefferson   *1:100*
woodcut of   *1:326 (illus.)*
Armenia   *3:338–43*; *4:199*
Arms control   *4:71*; *5:126, 225, 239, 252 (sidebar)*
prohibiting military use of space   *5:239*
Armstrong, Neil A.   *5:82, 292*
Armstrong, William H., *Sounder*   *3:370–76*
Army. *See* Military
Arnold, Benedict   *1:213 (sidebar)*
Arnold, Thomas   *2:373–74*
Art
African   *4:56*
artists benefitting from New Deal's WPA   *3:391,*
424
as barrier against chaos and loss of faith   *3:117*
Black arts movement   *4:207*
Carnegie Institute of Pittsburgh   *4:9*
first International Exhibition for   *4:8 (sidebar)*
French atelier system of teaching   *3:266*
Modernism   *3:411*; *5:42*

Paris as western capital of   3:265–66
patrons for artists   1:88
Primitivism   3:385 (sidebar)
(See also Literature)
Arthur, King of Celtic England   1:288, 290
in Once and Future King, The   1:288–94
Asians. See Chinese and Chinese Americans;
Japanese and Japanese Americans
Asimov, Isaac, Foundation   5:122–28
Astrology   1:346, 350
ASWPL (Association of Southern Women for the
Prevention of Lynching)   3:391–92
Athena   1:282, 283
Athens. See under Greece in ancient times
Atom bomb
creating "atomic anxiety"   4:255; 5:126
decision to use   4:178–79
Hiroshima and Nagasaki as targets   4:179–82,
180 (illus.), 181 (sidebar)
Manhattan Project   4:71, 81–82, 316; 5:123
Soviets' capability   4:183; 5:96, 126
test site at Bikini atoll   5:124 (illus.)
UN attempts to regulate   5:96
(See also Nuclear weapons)
Atomic energy. See Nuclear energy
Atwood, Margaret, Handmaid's Tale, The   5:135–42
Austen, Jane, Pride and Prejudice   2:295–300
Austria-Hungary   3:11 (sidebar)
Autobiography
American Childhood, An, Dillard, Annie   4:7–13
Autobiography of Benjamin Franklin, The   1:22–29
Autobiography of Malcolm X, The, X, Malcolm and
Haley, Alex   5:11–18
Barrio Boy, Galarza, Ernesto   3:28–35
Black Boy, Wright, Richard   3:36–43
Bound for Glory, Guthrie, Woody   3:44–50
Diary of a Young Girl, The, Frank, Anne
4:116–23
Endless Steppe, The: Growing Up in Siberia,
Hautzig, Esther   4:131–36
Farewell to Manzanar, Houston, Jeanne W. and
James D. Houston   4:137–43
Hiroshima Diary, Hachiya, Michihiko   4:177–84
Hunger of Memory, Rodriguez, Richard
5:178–84
I Know Why the Caged Bird Sings, Angelou, Maya
4:201–8
Incidents in the Life of a Slave Girl, The, Jacobs,
Harriet   2:168–73
Manchild in the Promised Land, Brown, Claude
4:247–53
Narrative of the Life of Frederick Douglass,
Douglass, Frederick   2:16, 236–41
Out of Africa, Dinesen, Isak   3:290–96
So Far from the Bamboo Grove, Watkins, Yoko K.
4:349–55
Up From Slavery, Washington, Booker T.
2:410–15
Woman Warrior, The, Kingston, Maxine Hong
5:352–59

Autobiography of Benjamin Franklin, The, Franklin,
Benjamin   1:22–29
Autobiography of Malcolm X, The, X, Malcolm and
Haley, Alex   5:11–18
Autobiography of Miss Jane Pittman, The (a novel),
Gaines, Ernest J.   5:19–26
Aviation
breaking sound barrier   5:293–94
golden age of   3:211–12
Lindbergh and   3:367
Right Stuff, The   5:291–97
and UFOs (unidentified flying objects)
4:347–48; 5:59 (illus.)
(See also Space Age; War weaponry)
Awakening, The, Chopin, Kate   3:15–20
Azerbaijan   3:343
Aztlán   4:173, 174–75, 176

B

Ba'al Shem Tov   4:87
Babbitt, Lewis, Sinclair   3:21–27
Babe Ruth   4:262, 265
Babi Yar massacre   4:120
Baby boom   1:224; 2:325–26; 4:38, 74, 240
Backswording   2:375
Baer, Dov   4:89
Bakke, Allan   5:181
Baldwin, James, Fire Next Time, The   5:107–14
Baptists   5:19, 188
Baraka, Amiri (Leroi Jones)   4:207
Barbed wire   3:113, 260
Barn Burning, Faulkner, William   2:41–46
Barrio Boy, Galarza, Ernesto   3:28–35
Baseball
Aaron, Hank   4:145, 148
Babe Ruth   4:262, 265
changing strategies of play   4:261–62
creation of two-league system   4:261
growing popularity leading to scouts   3:284
history of scandals   4:260–61, 265
Jackie Robinson   4:146
minor leagues and decrease in college-educated
players   4:261
Negro League   4:145, 148
Pittsburgh Pirates   4:10
segregation in   4:146, 147
White ("Black") Sox fix of 1919 World Series
3:149–50; 4:260–61
(See also Shoeless Joe)
Bay of Pigs fiasco   5:226
Bean Trees, The, Kingsolver, Barbara   5:27–33
Bear, The, Faulkner, William   2:47–53
Beat movement   4:75
(See also Counterculture)
Beauty: A Retelling of the Story of Beauty and the Beast,
McKinley, Robin   1:30–36
Becker, Charles   3:149
Becket, Thomas   1:146
Begin, Menachem   4:103, 105, 107

Behavior modification and conditioning   5:156–57

Behaviorism   **5**:45

Behn, Aphra   3:361–62

Belaúnde, Fernando   5:334

Belgium   2:146–47, 150–51; 3:9; 4:254, 357, 359

Bell, Clive   3:356

Bell Jar, The, Plath, Sylvia   4:21–27

Bellamy, Edward   2:423

Belle of Amherst, The, Luce, William   2:54–58

Belle Glade, Florida   3:383–84

Bellecourt, Clyde   5:247 (*illus.*)

Belleforest, François de   1:139, 141 (*sidebar*)

Beloved, Morrison, Toni   2:59–65

Benito Cereno, Melville, Herman   1:37–43

Beowulf, Anonymous   1:44–50
    influence upon Tolkein   1:153

Bergson, Henri   3:213

Betsey Brown, Shange, Ntozake   4:28–34

Bible, source for Milton's *Paradise Lost*   1:301

Bierce, Ambrose
    as character in *The Old Gringo*   3:279, 280, 281
    Occurrence at Owl Creek Bridge, An   2:255–60

Bilingual education   4:45; 5:172, 179–81, 183, 217

Billy Budd, Melville, Herman   1:51–56

Biloxi Blues, Simon, Neil   4:35–41

Biography (and autobiography)
    Abraham Lincoln: The Prairie Years, Sandburg,
        Carl   2:1–7
    American Childhood, An, Dillard, Annie   4:7–13
    Autobiography of Benjamin Franklin, The, Franklin,
        Benjamin   1:22–29
    Autobiography of Malcolm X, The, Malcolm X as
        told to Alex Haley   5:11–18
    Barrio Boy, Galarza, Ernesto   3:28–35
    Belle of Amherst, The (Emily Dickinson), Luce,
        William   2:54–58
    Black Boy, Wright, Richard   3:36–43
    Black Elk Speaks, Neihardt, John G.   2:66–73
    Bound for Glory, Guthrie, Woody   3:44–50
    Diary of a Young Girl, The, Frank, Anne   4:116–23
    Endless Steppe, The: Growing Up in Siberia,
        Hautzig, Esther   4:131–36
    Farewell to Manzanar, Houston, Jeanne W. and
        James D. Houston   4:137–43
    Hiroshima Diary, Hachiya, Michihiko   4:177–84
    Hunger of Memory, Rodriquez, Richard
        5:178–84
    I Know Why the Caged Bird Sings, Angelou, Maya
        4:201–8
    Incidents in the Life of a Slave Girl, Jacobs, Harriet
        2:168–73
    Manchild in the Promised Land, Brown, Claude
        4:247–53
    Narrative of the Life of Frederick Douglass,
        Douglass, Frederick   2:16, 236–41
    Out of Africa, Dinesen, Isak   3:290–96
    Up From Slavery, Washington, Booker T.
        2:410–15
    Woman Warrior, The, Kingston, Maxine Hong
        5:352–59

Black Boy, Wright, Richard   3:36–43

Black Death. *See* Bubonic plague (Black Death)

Black Elk Speaks, Neihardt, John G.   2:66–73

Black feminism   2:64; 3:86–87

Black Muslims and Nation of Islam   3:238, 325;
    4:56, 248–50; 5:12–13, 69, 110–11, 302

Black Panther Party   4:54, 56, 207

Black Power movement   2:97–98; 3:43, 325; 4:56,
    207; 5:143–44

Blacks. *See* African Americans

Blair, Eric Arthur. *See* Orwell, George

Blake, William   1:410 (*sidebar*), 416; 2:92

Bless the Beasts and Children, Swarthout, Glendon
    5:34–38

Bless Me, Ultima, Anaya, Rudolfo A.   4:42–48

Bligh, Cap't. William   1:273–74, 276–77;
    4:64–65

Blindness. *See* Disabled persons

Blixen, Karen. *See* Dinesen, Isak

Bloomsbury Group   3:356, 358–59

Blue Ridge Mountains   5:278

Blues, the   3:254 (*sidebar*); 4:258

Bluest Eye, The, Morrison, Toni   4:49–57

Boethius   1:344, 345–46, 350

Boleyn, Anne   1:149, 150, 231

Bolt, Robert, *Man for All Seasons, A*   1:231–37

Booth, John Wilkes   2:191

Bosnia   2:37–39

Boston   3:43

Bound for Glory, Guthrie, Woody   3:44–50

Bouquet, Col. Henry   1:221

Bowling   1:335 (*sidebar*)

Boxer Rebellion in China (1900)   3:205; 5:354

Boxing   5:68–69

Bracero Program (1942–1964)   3:34; 4:44

Bradbury, Ray
    Dandelion Wine   3:88–93
    Fahrenheit 451   5:95–100

Braddock, Gen'l. Edward   1:205

Bradford, Richard, *Red Sky at Morning*   4:316–22

Brahmans   1:365, 367 (*sidebar*)

Brave New World, Huxley, Aldous   5:39–45, 141,
    157, 252

Britain. *See* England

Brontë, Charlotte, *Jane Eyre*   1:415 (*sidebar*);
    2:181–87

Brontë, Emily, *Wuthering Heights*   1:413–19

Bronze Age of ancient Greece   1:14, 258, 280, 283
    (*sidebar*)

Brook Farm (utopian community)   1:357; 2:418

Brooke, Arthur   1:347, 349 (*sidebar*)

Brooklyn, New York   3:397–98; 4:88; 5:149–51

Brotherhood of Sleeping Car Porters   3:42

Brown, Claude, *Manchild in the Promised Land*
    4:247–53

Brown, Clifford   4:376

Brown, Dee, *Bury My Heart at Wounded Knee*
    2:74–80

Brown, John   2:89 (*sidebar*), 172
    Final Speech   2:188–94

Brown v. Board of Education 3:375; 4:29–30, 314; 5:90, 108, 180, 181

Brutus (Marcus Junius Brutus) 1:190, 191, 192–93

Bubonic plague (Black Death) 1:159, 160, 344, 345, 350

Buck, Pearl S., *Good Earth, The* 3:131–37

Buckingham, Duke of (George Villiers) 1:388, 389

Buddhism 1:365–69; 3:186–87; 5:48

Buffalo Bill (William F. Cody) 2:68, 177

Buffalo (bison) 2:66, 67, 75; 5:34–35

Bull from the Sea, The, Renault, Mary 1:57–63

Bunche, Ralph 4:255; 5:54

Burial customs
  among Canadian Kwakiutl 5:197
  in ancient Greece 1:18–19
  catacombs in Sicily 2:82
  mourning traditions in Victorian England 1:414–15

Burke, Edmund 1:52–53, 359, 362, 373 (sidebar), 408

Burns, Olive Ann, *Cold Sassy Tree* 3:75–79

Bury My Heart at Wounded Knee, Brown, Dee 2:74–80

Byron, George Gordon Noel (Lord Byron) 1:115, 116, 119, 120; 2:110

C

Caen, Herb 3:226

Caesar, Julius 1:12, 13

Caine Mutiny, The, Wouk, Herman 4:58–65

Cajuns 4:365; 5:21, 130

California
  Clear Lake 4:340–41
  farming and migrant workers 3:29–30, 49, 140–42, 269–71, 275, 335, 337; 4:297 (sidebar)
  gold rushes 2:174–75, 195, 249–50, 281–84
  Sacramento 3:30
  Salinas Valley 3:334–35
  South Central Los Angeles 5:339–42
  Spanish mission system 2:392, 394, 395
  timeline: colonization to independence 2:392 (sidebar)
  (*See also* San Francisco)

Call of the Wild, The, London, Jack 3:51–56

Calvin, John, and Calvinism 2:54, 55; 3:377–78; 4:10, 304

Canada, Kwakiutl of British Columbia 5:194–200

Canals
  Panama 3:231–32, 270
  Suez 3:184; 4:107
  U.S. system of 2:230

Canterbury Tales, The, Chaucer, Geoffrey 1:64–70
  Shakespeare influenced by 1:262

Capital punishment 4:379–80; 5:131

Capitalism
  in America's Gilded Age 2:20, 306, 328
  ethics and regulation, lack of 4:9
  failures of, enhancing appeal of communism 3:208, 210

Hellman's attack on excesses of 3:207, 210
  Steinbeck's warning about 3:144
  versus socialism and Marxism 3:321; 4:18–19
  (*See also* Industrialization)

Capone, Alphonse 3:366

Capote, Truman
  as basis for character in *To Kill a Mockingbird* 3:395
  Christmas Memory, A 3:68–74

Caribbean islands
  Dominican Republic 5:220
  Haiti (formerly Saint-Domingue) 5:116–17
  Puerto Rico 3:277; 4:385–86, 388–89, 401; 5:214–21
  slavery in 1:39
  (*See also* Cuba)

Carlyle, Thomas 1:375; 2:92

Carmichael, Stokely 2:98; 3:325; 4:55 (illus.), 56; 5:145 (illus.)

Carnegie, Andrew 2:306; 4:8, 9

Carranza, Venustiana 3:279

Carrie, King, Stephen 5:46–52

Carroll, Lewis, *Alice's Adventures in Wonderland* 2:28–33

Carson, Rachel, *Silent Spring* 4:337–42

Carthage 1:10, 12

Carver, George Washington 3:418

Cask of Amontillado, The, Poe, Edgar Allan 2:81–86

Castro, Fidel 2:273; 4:279; 5:225

Catch-22, Heller, Joseph 4:66–72; 5:318 (sidebar)

Catcher in the Rye, Salinger, J. D. 4:73–78; 5:318 (sidebar)

Catesby, Robert 1:229 (sidebar)

Cather, Willa, *O Pioneers!* 3:257–63

Catholicism and Catholic Church
  among American Indians 5:244, 361–62, 365–66
  anti-Semitism of 2:264
  comparison to Anglican Church 1:233 (sidebar)
  conflict with English Protestants 1:131, 132, 229, 305–6
  control of education in France 2:210
  criticisms by
    Cervantes 1:6–7
    Chaucer 1:65
    Dante 1:174–75; 3:111
    Joyce 3:111
  Crusades 1:182, 291
  cult of Our Lady of Fatima 5:365–66
  decline in Scotland 4:304–5
  equivocation doctrine 1:230
  Inquisition 1:2, 3
  in Ireland 1:269; 3:107–8, 109–10, 305–7
  Jesuits 3:307–8
  in medieval England and Europe 1:49–50, 65
  Merton, Thomas 5:280–81
  monasticism 3:186–87; 5:280
  opposition to contraception 4:304 (sidebar)
  parochial schools 5:62–63
  Penitentes 4:318 (sidebar)

perpetuation of machismo sentiment 5:173
pilgrimages 1:64–70, 145–46
popes 1:174, 176, 296, 344, 345
Reformation 1:231
Trappist monks 5:280
(See also Protestantism)
Cattle ranching
  on Great Plains 2:321–22
  and leather trade on California missions 2:392
  on reservations 4:79
  (See also Farming)
Celts
  Britons (Gauls) 1:196–97
  Scotland 1:187
Censorship and banning of literary works
  in 14th- and 15th-century Europe 1:349
  Adventures of Don Quixote, The 1:4
  blacklisting by McCarthyites 3:178; 4:72;
    5:96
  Brave New World 5:45
  Catcher in the Rye 4:78; 5:62
  in Communist China 5:98
  Flowers for Algernon 4:156
  Hero Ain't Nothin' but a Sandwich, A 5:148
  His Own Where 5:154
  by Nazis 3:13; 5:99
  One Day in the Life of Ivan Denisovich 4:285
  by Smith Act (1940) 5:97
  by Soviet dictatorship 4:286; 5:96
Central America
  Guatemala and refugees 5:27–29
  Panama Canal 3:231–32, 270
  (See also Mexico)
Central Intelligence Agency (CIA) 4:293
Ceremonies and celebrations
  Chinese New Year 5:75, 76 (illus.)
  Christmas
    A Doll's House 2:111–17
    Child's Christmas in Wales, A 3:63–67
    Christmas Memory, A 3:68–74
    Worn Path, A 3:418–24
  Indian healing ceremonies 4:82–83; 5:249
  Kwakiutl Candlefish 5:196 (sidebar)
  Kwakiutl hamatsa (Cannibal Dance) 5:196–97
  Kwakiutl potlatch 5:198 (illus.), 199
  (See also Burial customs)
Ceremony, Silko, Leslie Marmon 4:79–86
Cervantes Saavedra, Miguel de
  Adventures of Don Quixote, The 1:1–7
  in Battle of Lepanto 1:296 (sidebar)
Chagall, Marc 3:123
Chamberlain, Neville 4:357, 359
Chambers, Whittaker 5:96
Chaplin, Charlie 3:101
Charles I of England 1:299, 303, 304 (illus.), 305,
  306
Charles II of England 1:129, 130, 306, 337, 338
Charles X of France 1:391
Chateaubriand, François René de 1:165
Chaucer, Geoffrey, Canterbury Tales, The 1:64–70

Chávez, César 3:33 (illus.), 34; 4:47, 175, 300–302,
  301 (illus.),409
Chekhov, Anton, Cherry Orchard, The 3:57–62
Chennault, Claire 3:190
Chernobyl disaster 5:286, 287 (illus.)
Cherry Orchard, The, Chekhov, Anton 3:57–62
Chesapeake Bay 4:216–17, 219
Chiang Kai-shek 3:189, 190 (illus.)
Chicago
  in 1920s 3:89–90
  barrios of 5:174
  black activism 3:238
  ethnic makeup 3:176
  and King's northern civil rights campaign
    5:174
  in late 19th century 2:327–28, 330 (illus.)
  meat-packing industry 2:328 (sidebar)
  South Side and Black Belt 3:237–38; 4:309–11
  streetcars 2:328
  suburbs of 5:261–62
Chicanos
  affirmative action programs 5:181, 183–84
  César Chávez 3:33 (illus.), 34; 4:47, 175,
    300–302, 409
  discrimination 5:178
    zoot suit riots of 1940s 4:295–97, 403–10
  education dropout rates and reform efforts
    5:179
  family life 4:45
  folk healing (curanderos) 4:45
  immigration to U.S. from Mexico 3:282;
    4:44–48
  life in New Mexico 4:45
  literary Renaissance of 1960s and '70s
    5:172–73
  Luna (land) and Marez (sea) 4:47
  mestizo (mixed-race) heritage 5:172
  myth of Aztlán 4:174
  origin of term 5:171
  pachuco zoot-suit culture of 1950s 4:173,
    295–97, 403
  post-WWII community 5:178–79
  rights movement 4:47–48, 300–302; 5:171–72,
    179
    Brown Berets 4:176
    Chicanas 3:202; 5:174
    Community Service Organization (CSO)
      4:300
    El Teatro Campesino 4:409; 5:172
    G.I. Forum 4:300
    impact of military service on 4:44
    La Alianza 4:175–76, 321
    La Raza Unida 4:176
    League of United Latin American Citizens
      (LULAC) 4:300
    Mexican American Legal Defense and
      Education Fund (MALDEF) 5:179
    table grape boycott 4:175, 301 (illus.), 409
    United Farm Workers 4:175, 300–302, 409;
      5:171

Richard Rodriguez's autobiography   **5**:*178–84*
Rubén Salazar   **4**:*410*
Vietnam War protesters   **4**:*409–10*
WWII military service   **4**:*44*
(*See also* Latinos)
Child abuse
Fetal Alcohol Syndrome   **5**:*361*
relationship to poverty   **5**:*329 (sidebar)*
and suicide   **5**:*288, 289–90*
Child labor   **2**:*103–4, 335 (sidebar)*; **3**:*76 (sidebar),
77 (illus.), 285*
Childbearing
abortion   **5**:*51, 136*
midwifery   **4**:*218*
by unwed couples   **5**:*267*
in vitro   **5**:*42–43*
(*See also* Family and family life)
Childhood's End, Clarke, Arthur   **5**:*53–60*
Childress, Alice, *Hero Ain't Nothin' but a Sandwich, A*
5:*143–48*
Child's Christmas in Wales, A, Thomas, Dylan
3:*63–67*
Chile   **5**:*163–70*
Chin, Frank, *Donald Duk*   **5**:*74–80*
China
Boxer Rebellion (1900)   **3**:*205*; **5**:*354*
civil strife (1911–49)   **3**:*189–90*; **5**:*229, 254*
communist victory in civil war (1949)   **5**:*254,
354–55*
communists' land reform   **5**:*355*
communists' purge of opponents   **5**:*254–55*
Confucius   **3**:*193 (sidebar)*
divorce in   **2**:*370, 371*; **3**:*132, 193*; **5**:*230*
dynasties and alien invaders   **3**:*189*
footbinding of girls   **3**:*135*; **5**:*230 (sidebar)*
Guomindang   **4**:*126 (sidebar)*; **5**:*230, 254*
Hong Kong conceded to Great Britain   **5**:*354*
Japanese invasion (1930s–40s)   **3**:*189–90*; **4**:*59*;
5:*229–30*
marriages as business deals   **3**:*192–93*
missionaries   **3**:*133*
Nixon's visit (1972)   **5**:*358*
opium addiction   **3**:*134 (sidebar)*
Opium Wars (1839–42 and 1856–60)
5:*354*
peasant farmers   **3**:*131–32*
prostitution in   **3**:*135*
Republican era (1912–49)   **5**:*229–30, 354*
superstition and syncretism   **3**:*133, 190–91*
Taiping Rebellion (1851–64)   **5**:*354*
and Taiwan   **3**:*190*; **5**:*254*
women in   **2**:*366–67, 368 (sidebar), 370–71*;
3:*132–33, 134–35*; **5**:*352, 355*
Chinese and Chinese Americans
assimilation of second generation   **5**:*231–32,
234–35*
Chinese New Year festival   **5**:*75, 76 (illus.)*
defended by Bret Harte   **2**:*287*
immigration in 19th century   **2**:*367–68, 370
(sidebar), 371*; **4**:*124–27*

immigration in 20th century   **2**:*368*; **4**:*125, 127,
129*
as miners in Old West   **2**:*367–68, 369 (illus.)*
as "model minority"   **3**:*194*
in New York's Chinatown   **4**:*126*
racism and prejudice against   **2**:*175, 287,
367–68, 370 (sidebar), 371*; **3**:*30*; **4**:*124–27, 194,
330*; **5**:*230–31*
in San Francisco's Chinatown   **3**:*226*; **5**:*74–75,
77–79*
tongs   **4**:*129*
Chinese and Chinese Americans, literary works
concerning
Donald Duk   **5**:*74–80*
Eat a Bowl of Tea   **4**:*124–30*
Joy Luck Club, The   **5**:*229–35*
Kitchen God's Wife, The   **3**:*189–95*
Thousand Pieces of Gold, McCunn, Ruthanne Lum
2:*366–71*
Woman Warrior, The   **5**:*352–59*
Chivalry   **1**:*2, 66, 291*
Chocolate War, The, Cormier, Robert   **5**:*61–66*
Chopin, Kate, *Awakening, The*   **3**:*15–20*
Chorus in Greek drama   **1**:*10*
Chosen, The, Potok, Chaim   **4**:*87–93*
Christian, Fletcher   **1**:*273, 274*
Christianity
among pioneers of midwest   **3**:*259*
Baldwin on "racist hypocrisy" of   **5**:*112*
clergymen extolling WWI   **3**:*10*
missionaries   **2**:*118–19, 147, 161–62, 361–62*;
3:*133, 280*; **5**:*195*
suicide as sin   **4**:*22*
(*See also* Catholicism and Catholic Church;
Protestantism; Puritanism)
Christmas Memory, A, Capote, Truman   **3**:*68–74*
Chu, Luis, *Eat a Bowl of Tea*   **4**:*124–30*
Churchill, Winston   **1**:*237*; **5**:*53, 95*
Speech on the Evacuation at Dunkirk   **4**:*356–63*
CIA (Central Intelligence Agency)
experiments with drugs   **4**:*293–94*
role in Cuba's Bay of Pigs "invasion"   **5**:*226*
Cicero   **1**:*327*
Cicotte, Eddie   **3**:*149*; **4**:*260*
Ciénaga massacre (Colombia)   **2**:*270*
Cinema. *See* Hollywood and motion picture industry
CIO (Congress of Industrial Organizations)   **3**:*44*
Cisneros, Sandra, *House on Mango Street, The*
5:*171–77*
Citizenship
in ancient Athens   **1**:*241*
for Chinese immigrants   **5**:*231*
for Puerto Ricans   **5**:*215*
City-states
of ancient Greece   **1**:*286, 327–28*
of Italy   **1**:*379–80*
Civil Disobedience, Thoreau, Henry David   **2**:*87–92*
Civil rights movements
affirmative action   **5**:*181, 183–84, 342*
American Indians   **4**:*190–91*; **5**:*246–47*

assassination of King   4:54; 5:112 (sidebar)
Chicano. See Chicanos
Civil Rights Acts of 1957, '64, and '65   2:97;
  3:354, 375; 4:148; 5:91
  FBI & J. Edgar Hoover's theory of communist
    inspiration of   1:399
  focus on South, then North   2:13; 5:25
  fostering literary efforts
    autobiographies   4:205; 5:304
    ethnic and cultural explorations   4:92–93,
      207; 5:15, 62, 145, 217, 300–302
    women's studies programs   5:117
  Freedom Rides   5:88–90
  gay rights movement   4:241
  judicial opposition in 1980s to   5:1–2
  in Louisiana   5:25
  March on Washington (1963)   5:110, 186–88
  origins and growth of   2:97; 3:42–43; 4:28–29,
    155–56, 255, 314–15; 5:185, 192, 300
    Alabama as testing ground   2:220–21; 3:73,
      395–96; 4:314–15; 5:11, 88–90, 185–86
    race riots in "long hot summer" of 1966
      2:97–98; 4:207
  students' free speech movement   5:311
  TV's role in creating public support for   5:108
  women's involvement in   5:92–93
  (See also African Americans' civil
    rights/reform/power movements)
Civil War
  blockade runners   2:138–39
  causes of   2:130–31
  Chancellorsville   2:309
  demise of plantations and wilderness   2:49, 53
  desertion from armies   2:10–11, 312
  draft of mostly poor and lower classes   2:256,
    309
  and Emancipation Proclamation (1862)   2:59,
    60 (sidebar), 135, 308, 309
  families torn by conflicting loyalties   2:10
  in Georgia   2:139, 140 (illus.)
  Gettysburg   2:131–32
  glorification vs. reality of battle   2:257, 258,
    308, 309 (sidebar), 312, 313
  and industrialization of meat-packing   3:175
  John Brown's raid at Harper's Ferry contributing
    to   2:190
  major battles of   2:131 (sidebar)
  Northerners' point of view   2:11, 22
  overview of   2:308–10
  railroads' importance   2:255, 256 (illus.)
  Shiloh   2:257
  in southern Illinois   2:9–10
  Southerners' point of view   2:11, 22
  spies   2:255–56
  Union Army leadership troubles and poor morale
    2:308–10
  Vicksburg   2:217
  western migration and Mexican War contributing
    to   2:88, 89, 395, 405
  Walt Whitman, impact on   2:195–96

(See also Reconstruction)
Clairvoyance   5:239
Clark, Walter Van Tilburg, Ox-Bow Incident, The
  2:288–94
Clarke, Arthur, Childhood's End   5:53–60
Clay, Cassius. See Ali, Muhammad
Clemens, Samuel. See Twain, Mark
Cleopatra   1:190
Clipper ships   2:391
Clothing
  for slaves   2:237
  (See also Fashions)
Coal mining   3:63, 64
Cody, William F. (Buffalo Bill)   2:68, 177
Cohn, Roy   5:2–4
Cold Sassy Tree, Burns, Olive Ann   3:75–79
Cold War
  arms race   5:252 (sidebar)
  Berlin Wall   5:238, 293
  Cuban missile crisis and Bay of Pigs   4:135;
    5:225, 226, 238–39, 293
  and "domino" theory   2:13–14
  FBI investigations   4:129; 5:127
  fear of Communist China and Chinese
    immigrants   4:129
  fear of nuclear war   4:12, 13 (illus.); 5:53, 59,
    225
  fear of "radicalism"   1:399; 4:236
  fear of "socialized" medicine   4:12
  fear of Soviet strength   4:110; 5:225, 292
  fostering American interventions in third world
    1:223
  as indirect, hostile competition of ideologies
    5:225, 254, 292
  iron curtain for Eastern Europe   5:95–96
  Kennedy's olive branch with militancy
    5:224–26
  and McCarthyism   1:84, 398; 3:208, 209 (illus.);
    4:71, 110, 398; 5:2, 3 (illus.), 96, 97, 127
  NATO (North Atlantic Treaty Organization)
    5:124, 224, 292
  and "Red Scare"   1:84–86; 3:105; 4:71–72; 5:2,
    127
  reflected in United Nations   5:254
  trade as weapon in   5:126
  Truman Doctrine (1947–49)   4:110; 5:123–24
  Truman's loyalty program for federal employees
    4:72, 236
  U.S. support for oppressive Latin American
    military dictatorships   5:27–28
  U.S.-Soviet competition for global influence
    5:95–96
  U.S.-Soviet competition in space   5:53
  (See also Communism)
Coleridge, Samuel Taylor   1:116, 416
Colombia, South America   2:268–70, 272–73
Colonial America
  American Revolution   1:122–27
  Boston Tea Party   1:125
  class and economic stratification   1:97, 102, 108

democracy and revolutionary fervor   1:*71–72,*
74, 76–77, 93–94, 96–97, 108
Dutch in New Netherland (New York)   1:*211,*
212, 330–32, 333 (illus.), 335 (sidebar), 336
French and Indian War (Seven Years' War)
1:*93, 123, 204–6*
indentured servants   1:*394*
materialism   1:*102, 105, 311*
militias and Continental Army   1:*110 (sidebar)*
money, credit, and inflation   1:*103–4*
New England area   1:*78–80*
New York area   1:*107–8, 110, 112 (illus.)*
population and economic growth   1:*310*
reactions to
Stamp/Tea/Townshend/Intolerable/Molasses
Acts   1:*93, 94 (sidebar), 102, 123–25*
regional conflicts   1:*211–12*
rhetoric in   1:*123*
smuggling   1:*102–3*
towns and cities   1:*102*
westward expansion   1:*102, 103, 107, 204*
Yankee stereotype   1:*217*
(*See also* American Indians; American Revolution;
Slavery in America; United States)
Colonialism, imperialism, and interventionism
American
bolstered by social Darwinism   3:*234–35*
Chile   5:*164–65*
Cuba   3:*231, 278;* 4:*135;* 5:*225, 226,*
238–39, 293
Domican Republic   5:*220*
El Salvador   3:*282*
Guam   3:*277*
Guatemala   5:*27–28*
Latin America   3:*231, 277–78, 280–81*
Liberia   2:*404*
Monroe Doctrine (1823) and "big stick"
corollary (1904)   3:*277*
Nicaragua   3:*282*
Panama Canal   3:*231–32*
Philippines   3:*101, 278*
Puerto Rico   3:*277;* 4:*385–86;* 5:*215*
Spanish-American War (1898)   3:*101, 278*
Belgian   2:*145–46, 150–51*
British   2:*118–19*
in America. *See* Colonial America
bolstered by overseas commerce   1:*337*
criticized by H. G. Wells   3:*406, 410*
and decolonization of late 1940s   4:*165*
East Africa   3:*290–91*
end of   5:*107*
fostering sense of superiority   2:*154*
India   2:*182–84, 276–77;* 3:*181–82, 297–98*
Ireland. *See* Ireland
Nigeria and Igbo people   2:*362, 364;* 3:*84*
Palestine   4:*102–5*
Rhodesia   4:*165–66*
Tasmania   3:*406*
viewed as "bettering" and "civilizing" native
peoples   1:*118;* 2:*146;* 3:*84*

Wales   1:*149*
West Indies   2:*183–84*
in China   3:*205*
Dutch   1:*338*
French
Algeria   3:*211–13*
Indochina (Vietnam)   5:*101, 306*
Saint-Domingue (Haiti)   5:*116–17*
German   3:*290*
Italian   4:*67*
Japanese   4:*58–59, 92, 177–78, 349–54*
missionaries   2:*118–19, 147, 161–62, 183,*
361–62; 3:*133, 280*
segregation of rulers and ruled   3:*182*
Spanish
Colombia   2:*268*
Mexico   5:*172*
Puerto Rico   5:*214–15*
Color Purple, The, Walker, Alice   3:*80–87*
Comiskey, Charles   3:*149;* 5:*314, 316*
Common Sense, Paine, Thomas   1:*71–77*
effectiveness of   1:*94*
Communal movements
Communards and Paris Commune   1:*363*
Shakerism   3:*95, 99*
Twin Oaks colony   5:*279*
Communism
and anti-Bolshevik reactions of 1920s   3:*21–22,*
44
appeal of, to blacks   3:*164, 238–39*
in China   3:*136, 194*
communists as targets of Holocaust   4:*160,*
267
contrast with capitalism   4:*166*
global disillusion with, following revelations of
Stalin's purges   4:*166*
Great Depression enhancing appeal of   3:*39–40,*
45, 129, 208–10
influence on Jack London   3:*52*
labor organizers accused of   3:*144*
landowners as "capitalist" enemies of   4:*282*
and Marxism   3:*59, 179, 321;* 4:*18–19*
opposition to racism and prejudice   3:*40;* 4:*211*
as theory   4:*166*
use of folksongs   3:*47, 50*
(*See also* Cold War; Soviet Union)
Communist Manifesto   1:*376*
Computers   5:*97, 127*
Comstock Lode (Nevada silver mines)   2:*288–89,*
290 (sidebar)
Comte, Auguste   3:*213*
Confessions of Nat Turner, The, Styron, William
2:*93–98*
Confucius   3:*193 (sidebar)*
Congregationalists   1:*357, 424–25*
Connell, Richard, *Most Dangerous Game, The*
3:*231–35*
Conrad, Joseph, *Heart of Darkness*   2:*145–51*
Conroy, Pat, *Prince of Tides, The*   5:*285–90*
Conservatism

fundamentalism and New/Religious Right
  5:*137–39*
Contender, The, Lipsyte, Robert   **5**:*67–73*
Copernicus, Nicolaus   **1**:*24, 94, 305*
Corcoran, Thomas "Tommy the Cork" Gardiner
  3:*402*
CORE (Congress of Racial Equality)   **3**:*42*; **4**:*376*
Corey, Giles   **1**:*83 (sidebar), 395*
Corinth   **1**:*238, 241*
Cormier, Robert, *Chocolate War, The*   **5**:*61–66*
Cossacks   **3**:*233*
Cotton
  causing soil exhaustion   **3**:*390*
  crop failures from boll weevil   **4**:*2*
  as "King" Cotton   **2**:*15, 22, 44 (illus.), 168, 403*
  North-South contention over trade in   **3**:*203–4*
  plummeting of prices for farmers in 1920s and
    '30s   **3**:*153, 390, 391*
  for typhus prevention, advantages of clothing and
    bedding of   **1**:*115*
Cotton, John   **1**:*352*
Coughlin, Father Charles   **4**:*373*
Count of Monte-Cristo, The, Dumas, Alexandre
  2:*99–104*
Counterculture (beatniks, hippies, and protesters)
  in 1950s   **4**:*75, 289, 293, 399–400*
  in 1960s   **5**:*37, 64 (sidebar), 83, 158, 237, 272,*
    279, 308–10, 323–25
Coxey, Jacob S. and Coxey's Army   **3**:*51–52*
Crane, Stephen, *Red Badge of Courage, The*
  2:*308–13*
Craven, Margaret, *I Heard the Owl Call My Name*
  5:*194–200*
Creationism   **2**:*30*
Creoles   **3**:*15–18*; **4**:*365*; **5**:*21, 130*
Creon   **1**:*15, 17, 18, 19*
Crime
  blacks and Latinos as victims of   **4**:*31*;
    5:*340–41*
  blacks turning to   **4**:*145*
  and capital punishment   **4**:*379–80*; **5**:*131*
  by Chinese American tongs   **4**:*129*
  and creation of police detectives   **2**:*153–54*
  drug-related   **4**:*250–51*
  during Reconstruction, violence and unequal
    justice for freed slaves   **5**:*20–21*
  gang truce in Los Angeles   **5**:*341*
  by gangs, juvenile delinquents   **4**:*251, 386,*
    387–89
  gangsters (*tsotsi*) of South Africa   **4**:*97*
  outlaws on American western frontier
    1:*256–57*
  outlaws in medieval England   **1**:*252–53*
  and Pinkerton's National Detective Agency
    3:*225–26*
  Prohibition fostering corruption, bootlegging, and
    gangsterism   **3**:*69, 147–48, 366–67, 401*
  in slums, ghettos   **5**:*13, 67–68, 112, 146, 150,*
    339–42
(*See also* Law enforcement; Lynching)
Cromwell, Oliver   **1**:*299, 306*
Crucible, The, Miller, Arthur   **1**:*78–86*
Crusades   **1**:*182, 291*
Cry, the Beloved Country, Paton, Alan   **4**:*94–100*
Cuba
  American interventions of 1898 and 1901
    3:*231, 278*
  Bay of Pigs and missile crisis   **4**:*135*; **5**:*225,*
    226, 238–39, 293
  personalismo   **4**:*275*
  religion   **4**:*274–75*
  Revolution of 1950s   **2**:*273*
  role of luck   **4**:*275–76*
Cultural conflict. *See* Ethnic and cultural conflicts
Cyprus   **1**:*296*
Cyrano de Bergerac, Rostand, Edmond   **1**:*87–92*
Cyrano de Bergerac, Savinien de   **1**:*87, 88*
  (*sidebar*), *89–90*

D

Daisy Miller, James, Henry   **2**:*105–10*
Daly, Carroll John   **3**:*227*
Damnation. *See* Sin and damnation
Dana, Richard Henry, Jr., *Two Years before the Mast*
  2:*391–96*
Dance   **4**:*387*
Dandelion Wine, Bradbury, Ray   **3**:*88–93*
Dante Alighieri
  Divine Comedy   **1**:*175 (sidebar), 178*
  Inferno   **1**:*174–80*
  influence on Joyce   **3**:*111*
Daoism (also Taoism)   **5**:*237*
D'Artagnan (Charles-Ogier de Batz de Castelmore)
  1:*387*
Darwin, Charles   **2**:*29, 119*
Darwin, Erasmus   **1**:*116*
Darwinism. *See* Evolution
Dawes Act (1887)   **2**:*68, 179*; **4**:*186*
Dawn, Wiesel, Elie   **4**:*101–8*
Day No Pigs Would Die, A, Peck, Robert Newton
  3:*94–99*
DDT   **4**:*338–39*
De Beauvoir, Simone   **4**:*167*
De Gaulle, Charles   **3**:*214*
De Tocqueville, Alexis   **2**:*106*
Deafness. *See* Disabled persons
Dean, James   **4**:*392, 400*
Dean, John   **5**:*159 (illus.)*
Death in the Family, A, Agee, James   **3**:*100–105*
Death of a Salesman, Miller, Arthur   **4**:*109–15*
Debs, Eugene V.   **3**:*54, 175*
Declaration of Independence, The, Jefferson, Thomas
  1:*93–100*
  comparison to language in *Common Sense*   **1**:*76*
  evoked in King's "I Have Dream" speech   **5**:*191*
  evoked in Lincoln's Gettysburg Address
    2:*134–35*

Declaration of the Rights of Man (French Revolution) 1:372

Declaration of Sentiments (for women's rights)   2:24, 55, 204; 3:16

Dee, John   1:385 (sidebar)

Defoe, Daniel   1:131, 268, 342

    Robinson Crusoe   1:337–43

Delamere, Hugh Cholmondeley, Baron   3:295

Delaware (Lenape) Indians   1:206, 219–20

Democracy

    in 19th-century America   2:87–88, 89–91

    in ancient Greece   1:18, 321, 322

    before and after publication of *Common Sense* 1:74

    individualism and egalitarianism contributing to 2:302

    influence of Declaration of Independence upon 1:100

    Kennedy's call for defense of freedom 5:226–27

    at King Arthur's round table   1:292

    rise of common people as political force in France   1:164, 165

    role of printing press in promoting   1:162 (sidebar)

    Whitman as poet of   2:196

    (*See also* Suffrage)

Denmark   1:136–38, 141

Depression, The Great   2:45

Detective fiction. *See* Mystery and detective stories

Developmental disabilities. *See* Disabled persons

Devil (Satan)

    comparative conceptions of   5:57 (sidebar)

    in Dante's *Inferno*   1:177, 179 (illus.)

    Lucifer in Milton's *Paradise Lost*   1:301–3, 305

    Puritans' belief in   1:79–81, 102, 393, 394

Devil and Tom Walker, The, Irving, Washington 1:101–6

DeWitt, John   4:138

Diary of a Young Girl, The, Frank, Anne   4:116–23

Diaspora   4:101

Díaz, Porfirio   3:28, 29, 197, 278

Dickens, Charles   2:92, 375

    Oliver Twist   2:261–67

    Tale of Two Cities, A   1:371–78

Dickinson, Emily   2:54–58

Dictatorship

    of Argentina's military rulers   5:208–11, 212–13

    of Chile's military junta   5:169

    in Communist China   5:254–55

    and "divine right" of Charles I of England 1:303

    of Japan's prewar military   4:178, 183

    opposition to, in *Twenty-Thousand Leagues under the Sea*   2:387

    Orwell's attacks upon   5:254 (sidebar)

    of Peru's military junta   5:333–34

    warnings against   1:18

    (*See also* Fascism; Hitler, Adolf; Soviet Union; Stalin, Josef)

Diem, Ngo Dinh   5:102

Diet

    of concentration camp inmates   4:268

    of poor farmers   3:371

    of Siberian work camp inmates   4:283–84

    of slaves   2:237

Dillard, Annie

    American Childhood, An   4:7–13

    Pilgrim at Tinker Creek   5:278–84

Dinesen, Isak, *Out of Africa*   3:290–96

Disabled persons

    in almshouses in 18th-century America   2:216, 219 (sidebar)

    Clubfooted   3:264

    education for   2:216–17, 221–22

    Independent Living movement   2:123

    overcoming pity   2:218–19

    views of, in 1970s   2:123

    views of, in Victorian Age   2:119–20

    (*See also* Mental and emotional disabilities)

Diseases

    AIDS   5:9

    atomic radiation sickness   4:181

    bronchitis   2:335

    bubonic plague (Black Death)   1:159, 160, 344, 345, 350

    cancer   2:335; 4:340

    cholera   2:103

    "fainting"   3:420

    "hysteria"   2:425

    leprosy   2:362

    measles   1:220

    "nerves" (stress, depression)   2:278–79

    neurofibromatosis   2:122

    polio   4:9–10

    postcombat syndrome   4:80 (sidebar)

    postpartum depression   2:425

    Proteus syndrome   2:122

    puerperal fever   3:285

    rabies   3:387, 406

    radioactive poisoning   4:85

    respiratory   2:335; 3:2, 76, 219, 223

    resulting from depression   5:273

    scarlet fever   2:206 (sidebar)

    sickle cell anemia   2:362 (sidebar)

    smallpox   1:220, 352; 2:347; 5:214

    trench foot and trench fever   3:9, 115 (sidebar)

    tuberculosis   2:335; 3:2, 219, 223

    typhoid, typhus   2:185 (sidebar); 3:2

    venereal   4:37

    (*See also* Alcohol and alcoholism; Drug/substance abuse; Medicine; Mental and emotional disabilities)

Dissenters. *See* Anglican Church

Divine Comedy. *See* Inferno

Divorce

    in 1800s   2:126, 127, 158, 212, 355–56

    among Issei couples   4:332

    in China   2:370, 371; 3:132, 193; 5:230

    in czarist Russia   2:37, 39

Doyle's support for reform   2:158
    in early 20th-century America   3:167–68, 272, 368
    for Jews   3:427, 429 (sidebar)
    legalization spurred by Protestantism   2:113
    and remarriage   4:242
    soaring rate of, in late 20th century   2:65;
        4:241–42; 5:36, 138, 267, 273, 286–88
Dix, Dorothy   3:17
Doctorow, E. L., Ragtime   3:319–25
Doctors. See Diseases; Medicine
Documents
    Declaration of Independence (American Revolution)
        1:93–100
    Declaration of the Rights of Man (French
        Revolution)   1:372
    Declaration of Sentiments (for women's rights in
        America)   2:24, 55, 204; 3:16
    (See also Essays; Narratives; Speeches)
Dodgson, Charles Lutwidge. See Carroll, Lewis
Doll's House, A, Ibsen, Henrik   2:111–17
Dominican Republic   5:220
Don Quixote. See Adventures of Don Quixote, The
Donald Duk, Chin, Frank   5:74–80
Doolittle, James "Jimmy"   4:68
Dorris, Michael, Yellow Raft in Blue Water, A
    5:360–66
Douglas, Stephen A.   2:2, 242
Douglass, Frederick
    influence upon Toni Morrison   2:63
    Narrative of the Life of Frederick Douglass
        2:236–41
    on Uncle Tom's Cabin   2:409
Doyle, Arthur Conan, Hound of the Baskervilles
    2:152–59
Drama. See Plays; Theater
Dreiser, Theodore, Sister Carrie   2:327–33
Dreyfus, Alfred   1:91–92, 364 (sidebar)
Drug/substance abuse
    among African Americans   4:250–51
    among American Indians   4:83
    attitudes of 1950s   5:99 (sidebar)
    among beatniks   4:75
    dealers' self-concept as respectable and superior
        5:341–42
    experiments by CIA   4:293–94
    fines and prison required by Boggs Act (1951)
        5:99 (sidebar)
    LSD   4:288, 289, 292, 293–94; 5:82–83, 324–25
    morphine addiction   3:218–19, 223
    Narcotics Control Act (1956)   4:250
    opium addiction in China   3:134 (sidebar)
    opium products   3:379
    in prep schools   4:74
    psychedelic   5:82–83
    by Puerto Ricans   5:217
    risk of AIDS   5:342
    suspicions of conspiracy by white officials to
        allow in ghettos   5:144
    unequal, unjust penalties for dealing   5:342

aomng youth of 1950s   4:173
    (See also Alcohol and alcoholism)
Drums Along the Mohawk, Edmonds, Walter D.
    1:107–14
Drury, Allen   5:4
Du Bois, W. E. B.
    advocating education for "talented tenth"
        3:250, 385
    advocating no toleration of segregation or
        inequality   3:320
    compared to Booker T. Washington   2:345
        (sidebar); 3:250, 320, 385
    criticism of Up from Slavery   2:415
    Souls of Black Folk, The   2:340–46; 3:162–63
Du Maurier, Daphne, Rebecca   3:326–33
Dubliners, Joyce, James   3:106–11
Dueling   1:389 (sidebar)
Dumas, Alexandre
    Count of Monte-Cristo, The   2:99–104
    Three Musketeers, The   1:386–92
Duncan, King of Scotland   1:225
Dune, Herbert, Frank   5:81–87
Dunkirk evacuation   4:356, 359–63
Dust Bowl, The   3:34, 46, 138–40; 4:297
Dutch in New Netherland (New York)   1:211, 212,
    330–32, 333 (illus.), 335 (sidebar), 336
Dutch Reformed Church   1:331, 425
Dystopian literature
    Brave New World as   5:141, 252
    described   5:100, 141, 252
    Handmaid's Tale, The as   5:141
    Nineteen Eighty-Four as   5:100, 141

E

Earthquakes, in Chile   5:168 (sidebar)
Eat a Bowl of Tea, Chu, Luis   4:124–30
Eatonville, Florida   3:383
Edmonds, Walter D., Drums Along the Mohawk
    1:107–14
Education
    in 19th-century America   2:42–43, 204–5
    for African Americans
        in blacks-only schools   2:413; 3:371, 375
        and Brown v. Board of Education   3:375;
            4:29–30, 314; 5:90, 108, 180, 181
        demand for more control by   5:144
        dropout rates of   5:342
        forbidden use of libraries   3:40, 371
        freed slaves   2:411–12, 413, 414
        improvements in   3:375, 420
        integrated   3:43, 396; 4:29–30, 31 (illus.),
            314; 5:116, 131–32, 181
        in "Movable School"   3:380
        negative effects of segregation on   4:33
    of American Indian children   5:244, 246,
        361–62
    bilingual   4:45; 5:172, 179–81, 183, 217
    of black South Africans   4:97
    creating generation gap   5:182, 198, 244, 246

criticality for Jews   3:425

for disabled persons   2:216–17, 221–22;
4:151–52

by governesses in Victorian Age   2:182, 183
(sidebar), 378–80

increases in school attendance during Depression
3:153–54

in Japanese schools in 1930s California   4:333

and *Lau v. Nichols*   5:180

of migrant farm workers' children   3:144
(sidebar)

minority studies programs
African American history   5:147–48
in Black English or Ebonics   5:145, 154, 342
increasing college enrollments   5:217
Puerto Rican history and culture   5:217
women's studies   5:117

at prep schools   4:74

promoted by G.I. Bill   3:92; 4:73

schools handling contentious issues   5:311–12

in small communities   4:217

in Southern mill towns   3:78; 4:256

in Southern rural towns during Depression
3:352

textbook content reviewed by Religious Right
5:138

through Americorps program   5:340

University of California v. Bakke   5:181

Education, of men
apprenticeship system   2:262
in boarding schools   4:240
boys' street gangs   3:400–401
in colonial America   1:23, 123
in czarist Russia   3:58
English schools   2:372–77; 3:346
fagging   2:375
G.I. Bill (1944)   3:92; 4:73
hunting as rite of passage   2:48
importance for achieving middle-class status
2:303
in New Netherland   1:212–13
in private/prep schools   4:325–27; 5:62–63
reforms in 19th-century England   3:265
scientific, in France   2:386
in skills of knighthood   1:182 (sidebar), 290–91
in traditional Jewish communities of Eastern
Europe   3:425–26
Wollstonecraft on   1:410

Education, of women
in 17th-century England (Tudor era)   1:232–33,
236
in 17th-century France   1:30
in 18th-century France   1:32
in 18th-century New Netherland   1:212–13
in 19th-century America vs. Europe   2:106
in 19th-century England   1:412; 2:30, 181–82,
297, 422–23
in 19th-century France   1:408; 2:210, 245
in 19th-century New England   2:55, 56
(sidebar), 203

in 19th-century South   2:42
in 20th-century America   1:35
in 20th-century Scotland   4:303–4
Ben Franklin on   1:24 (sidebar)
blacks on athletic scholarships   4:149
college and increased opportunities for   5:174
Jewish   3:427, 430
skepticism for   1:236
in Victorian Age   1:412; 2:30, 181–82, 422–23
Wollstonecraft on   1:409–10; 2:297

Edward I of England   1:244, 291

Egypt, Six-Day War with Israel   4:107

Eichmann, Adolf   4:107 (sidebar), 269, 270, 272,
273; 5:210

Eisenhower, Dwight D.   4:398; 5:53, 91

Eleanor of Aquitaine   1:250

Elephant Man, The, Pomerance, Bernard   2:118–24

Eliezer, Israel Ben   4:87

Eliot, T.S.   5:42
Waste Land, The   3:411–17

Elizabeth I of England
bolstering national pride   1:349
Catholic faction's opposition to   1:149, 349
conspiracy of Earl of Essex   1:194, 349
courtiers   1:263
proving effectiveness of female monarch   1:233,
236
rivalry with, execution of Mary, Queen of Scots
1:141, 149, 150, 349
succession of crown to James of Scotland
1:201
unification and commercial strengthening of
England   1:150, 201, 263
as virgin queen   1:201, 261, 262–63, 350

Elizabethan Age
belief in supernatural   1:4, 141, 142 (sidebar),
194–95, 227–28, 262, 346, 350
bubonic plague   1:344, 350
concepts of sin and damnation   1:143
education of women in Tudor era   1:232–33,
236
family life and obligations   1:203
foreign influence/corruption   1:150
growth of American colonies   1:149
kinship ties   1:141, 145
popularity of history plays   1:150
popularity of revenge tragedies   1:142
popularity of satire and puns   1:349
treatment of insane   1:203
wars with Spain   1:1–2

Ellison, Ralph, *Invisible Man*   4:209–15

Emancipation
Emancipation Proclamation (1862)   2:59, 60
(sidebar), 135, 308, 309
life little changed for freed slaves   5:19–20
(*See also* Abolitionists/Abolition of slavery)

Embrey, Sue Kunitomi   4:143

Emerson, Ralph Waldo
influence on Dickinson   2:57
on John Brown   2:193

as model for Prof. Bhaer in *Little Women*   2:*207*
opposition to war with Mexico   2:*89*
Self-Reliance   2:*314–20*
support for abolition   2:*315, 316*
support for American Indians   2:*316, 317*
support for Thoreau   2:*417*
as transcendentalist   1:*356*; 2:*92, 314*
on *Two Years before the Mast*   2:*396*
Endless Steppe, The: Growing Up in Siberia, Hautzig,
   Esther   4:*131–36*
Engels, Friedrich   1:*376*
England in medieval times
   Anglo-Saxons   1:*44–45, 153, 181*
   Celts, Britons, and Arthurian legends   1:*196–97,
      288, 289 (illus.), 290*
   expulsion of Jews   1:*244, 246, 248*
   feudalism   1:*65–66, 153*
   Magna Carta   1:*255*
   Norman Conquest   1:*181, 251–53*
   relations with Scotland   1:*145, 149–50*
   Romans   1:*288*
   royal forests   1:*251–52*
   Saxon invaders and Wales   1:*288*
   wars with France   1:*159, 160*
England in 16th century
   Henry VIII   1:*149, 150, 231, 232, 234 (illus.)*
   (*See also* Elizabeth I; Elizabethan Age)
England in 17th century
   civil war, execution of King Charles I, and
      Restoration   1:*129, 303, 305–6*
   class consciousness   1:*338*
   foreign influences upon   1:*150*
   Glorious Revolution and William of Orange
      1:*130, 338–39, 342–43*
   growth of tolerance   1:*299–300*
   Gunpowder Plot   1:*229*
   slave trading by   1:*337–38*; 2:*361*
   wars with France   1:*130–31, 305*
   wars with Spain   1:*87, 201*
England in 18th century
   British Royal Navy   1:*273–79*
   class consciousness   1:*342*
   Dissenters and Test Act   1:*129, 338, 342, 407,
      411*
   French and Indian War   1:*93, 123*
   historic rivalry with France   1:*391–92*
   London vs. country living   2:*296–97*
   as power in foreign trade   1:*400, 401*
   publishing industry's growth   1:*342*
   reactions to French Revolution   1:*359–60,
      372–73, 373 (sidebar), 376, 408*
   Tories vs. Whigs   1:*129–31, 305–6, 311, 337, 342*
   wars with France   1:*51–52, 93, 123, 204–6,
      220–21*
   wars with Spain   1:*130–31*
England in 19th century
   apprenticeship system   2:*262*
   British Royal Navy   1:*51–56, 404–5*
   class consciousness   1:*376, 413–14*; 2:*152–53,
      157, 277–78, 296–97*

and *nouveaux riches*   3:*327*
War of 1812   1:*53*
(*See also* Victorian Age; Victorian women)
England in 20th century
   birthrate/population decline   3:*347*; 5:*348*
   British Library   3:*360*
   British Royal Navy   4:*229*
   classes, and fading of social hierarchies   3:*312,
      315–16, 326–27*; 5:*347–48*
   consumerism, materialism, conspciuous
      consumption   1:*237*; 3:*344–45, 348*
   as cultural superpower in 1950s   4:*307*
      (sidebar)
   despair, decay, and decline   2:*275–76*;
      3:*344–45, 348*; 5:*39–40*
   fascism in 1930s   4:*304*
   General Strike of 1926   5:*40*
   London "season"   3:*312*
   nationalism and socialism   4:*231*
   post-WWII decline and recovery   3:*66*; 4:*229,
      231*; 5:*256–57*
   Scotland   4:*305*
   Wales   3:*63–64, 66*
   in WWI   3:*9, 11 (sidebar)*
   Yorkshire   3:*1–3*
Enlightenment, The (Age of Reason)
   American   2:*416*
   and American "moral sense"   1:*94, 96*
   backlash as Romantic movement   1:*106*
   as belief in reason, science, and "progress":
      perfectibility of humankind and its institutions
      1:*24–25, 268*; 2:*416*
   decline of religious influence and increase of
      materialism   1:*102, 311*
   early scientific discoveries fostering   1:*24–25,
      94, 96*
   failures of, fostering fierce satires   1:*272*
   Franklin's common sense approach to
      experimentation   1:*25–26*
   influence on Patrick Henry   1:*123*
   Jewish (*Haskalah*)   3:*120, 426*; 4:*88*
   "natural rights" theories of John Locke   1:*100*
   treatment of disabled persons   2:*119–20*
Entailment   2:*296 (sidebar)*
Entertainment
   carnival season of Italy and France   2:*81–82*
   circuses and freak shows   2:*33, 120, 329*
   dancing   3:*23*
   drive-in restaurants of 1950s   4:*392*
      (sidebar)
   illicit wartime amusements   4:*37, 38*
   as industry   2:*329*
   jazz clubs   3:*161*
   lotteries   4:*235–36*
   minstrel shows   2:*16–17, 21, 398*
   ouija board   5:*56*
   practical jokes   1:*212*
   pubs in England   3:*3*
   radio   3:*154, 364–65*; 4:*386, 391*
   standardization of, in 1920s   3:*101*

tale-telling and storytelling   1:*49, 66–68, 70*;
  2:*397*; 3:*421*; 4:*83 (sidebar), 85*
taverns   1:*331*; 3:*219, 398, 400*
theaters and concert halls   2:*329*
for troops of WWII   4:*38, 68–69*
of working and middle classes   2:*303–4*
(*See also* Games and sports; Hollywood and
  motion picture industry; Television)
Environment
  air pollution   4:*9*
  Chernobyl disaster   5:*286, 287 (illus.)*
  concerns reflected in *Dune*   5:*85–86*
  conservation of buffalo   5:*34–35*
  destruction of wilderness   2:*49, 53*
  first Earth Day (April 22, 1970)   5:*279 (sidebar)*
  nuclear waste disposal   5:*286*
  pesticides ("biocides") and DDT   4:*337–42*;
    5:*347, 351*
  rabbit population in England   5:*347*
  Walden movement and Twin Oaks colony
    5:*279*
Epic poems   1:*49, 153, 172, 173, 282 (sidebar), 285*
  (*See also* Poetry)
Equal Rights Amendment (ERA)   3:*79*; 5:*51, 136,
  358–59*
"Equality" in America
  Emancipation Proclamation (1862)   2:*59, 60
    (sidebar), 135, 308, 309*
  on eve of Revolution   1:*99*
  individualism and egalitarian ideals of late 19th
    century   2:*302*
  (*See also* African Americans' civil
    rights/reform/power movements; Civil rights
    movements; Segregation; Women's rights
    movement)
Equivocation doctrine   1:*230*
Erasmus, Desiderius   1:*2, 6*
Erdrich, Louise, *Love Medicine*   5:*243–50*
Escapism
  fantasies of African American youths   4:*4
    (sidebar)*
  as response to despair   5:*40*
  and Thurber's Walter Mitty   3:*364, 369*
Espionage
  Civil War spies   2:*255–56*
  Cold War spies   4:*71–72*
  Rosenbergs executed for   4:*72, 380, 381 (illus.)*;
    5:*2, 127*
Esquivel, Laura, *Like Water for Chocolate*
  3:*196–202*
Essays
  Civil Disobedience, Thoreau, Henry David
    2:*87–92*
  Common Sense, Paine, Thomas   1:*71–77, 94*
  Fire Next Time, The, Baldwin, James   5:*107–14*
  Modest Proposal, A, Swift, Jonathan   1:*266–72*
  Pilgrim at Tinker Creek, Dillard, Annie
    5:*278–84*
  Prince, The, Machiavelli, Niccolò   1:*316–20*
  Republic, Plato   1:*321–29*

Room of One's Own, A, Woolf, Virginia
  3:*356–63*
Self-Reliance, Emerson, Ralph Waldo   2:*314–20*
Silent Spring, Carson, Rachel   4:*337–42*
Souls of Black Folk, The, Du Bois, W. E. B.
  2:*340–46*
Vindication of the Rights of Woman, A,
  Wollstonecraft, Mary   1:*406–12*
Walden, Thoreau, Henry David   2:*416–21*
Essex (Robert Devereaux, Earl of Essex)   1:*194,
248, 349*
Ethan Frome, Wharton, Edith   2:*125–29*
Ethiopia   4:*67*
Ethnicities. *See* African Americans; American
  Indians; Chinese and Chinese Americans; Japanese
  and Japanese Americans; Jews; Latinos; Puerto Rico
  and Puerto Ricans)
Ethnic and cultural conflicts
  American Indian versus white. *See* American
    Indians
  Anglo-Saxon English versus Norman   1:*181*
  Asian versus white. *See under* Racism and
    prejudice
  Christian versus modern-day secular in U.S.
    3:*102*; 5:*138*
  Christian versus warrior, in England   1:*49–50*
  Dutch versus English in New Netherland
    1:*330–32, 334–35*
  Eastern (Muslim, Hindu) versus Western
    3:*303*
  Latino versus white. *See* Chicanos; Latinos
  male-dominated versus ancient matriarchal
    1:*61–62*
  rural versus urban in U.S.   3:*101–2, 140–41*
  Scottish Highlanders versus English   1:*187*
  Southern versus Southwestern U.S.   4:*320–21*
  Southern versus Yankee in U.S.   2:*217–18*
  (*See also* Multiculturalism; Racism and prejudice)
Ethnology   2:*232–33*
Eugenics   3:*272*; 4:*152*; 5:*41–42*
Euripides, *Medea*   1:*238–41*
Europe, appeal of, to American upper class
  2:*105–6*
Europe, James Reese   3:*162 (sidebar), 163 (illus.)*
Everything That Rises Must Converge, O'Connor,
  Flannery   5:*88–94*
Evolution
  as Darwin's theory of (Darwinism)   1:*293*; 2:*29,
    121*
  fostering belief in progress and man's capacity to
    reform   2:*195*; 3:*378*
  fostering doubt of man's divine nature   3:*378*
  interest of H. G. Wells in   3:*404–5*
  opposed by religious-minded   3:*102, 404*; 5:*138*
  and Scopes Trial   3:*102 (sidebar)*
  as social Darwinism ("survival of the fittest")
    contributing to racism   2:*341*
    impact on views of poor and disabled
      2:*217, 306, 312*; 3:*207, 410*
    H. G. Wells' criticism of   3:*410*

white superiority, Manifest Destiny, and
   "white man's burden"   2:*119, 147, 341*;
   3:*170, 172, 182 (sidebar)*
Extrasensory perception (ESP)   5:*47, 239*

F

Fabre, Jean Henri Casimer   5:*282*
Facism
   depression of 1930s enhancing appeal of   3:*129*
   (*See also* Nazis)
Fahrenheit 451, Bradbury, Ray   5:*95–100*
Fairfield, John   2:*189*
Fallen Angels, Myers, Walter Dean   5:*101–6*
Falwell, Jerry   5:*137–38, 140 (illus.)*
Family and family life
   in 19th-century New England   2:*54, 126–27*
   in 20th-century England   3:*347*
   of African Americans   3:*80, 84–86, 353–55,*
      375, 422–23; 4:*33*; 5:*68, 145–46, 329–30*
   for Truman Capote   3:*72*
   in Celtic society   1:*197*
   changing roles within   5:*139*
   Chicano   4:*45*
   in China   3:*131–32, 192–93*
   in colonial America   1:*207–8, 217, 221, 334*
   in Elizabethan/Jacobean England   1:*141, 150,*
      203
   of gang members, and gangs as substitutes for
      5:*266–67*
   intergenerational conflicts
      among African Americans   3:*255*; 4:*252*
      among American Indians   5:*244, 246*
      among Canadian Kwakiutl   5:*198*
      among Chicanos   5:*182*
      among Chinese Americans   5:*358*
      over marriage to person of differing ethnicity
         5:*203–4, 232*
      over WWII   4:*327*
   of Mexican Americans   4:*172–73*
   pro-family movement of religious right
      5:*138–39*
   role of black female servants in   4:*257–58*
   in sharecropper families   3:*370–71, 373, 375*
   single-female heads of households   2:*65*; 3:*80,*
      423; 4:*2*; 5:*68, 117, 136, 138, 267, 328–29*
   in slave families   2:*60, 169, 237–38, 405, 406,*
      410; 4:*204–5*
   in South   3:*78, 80*
   in stepfamilies   5:*36*
   in Dylan Thomas's work   3:*65*
   (*See also* Divorce; Love and marriage)
Family and family life: literary works depicting
   Beloved   2:*59–65*
   Betsey Brown   4:*28–34*
   Bless Me, Ultima   4:*42–48*
   Bluest Eye, The   4:*49–57*
   Cold Sassy Tree   3:*75–79*
   Color Purple, The   3:*80–87*
   Dandelion Wine   3:*88–93*

Death in the Family, A   3:*100–105*
Death of a Salesman   4:*109–15*
Doll's House, A   2:*111–17*
Ethan Frome   2:*125–29*
Fences   4:*144–50*
Fiddler on the Roof   3:*119–24*
Gone with the Wind   2:*137–44*
Good Earth, The   3:*131–37*
Hamlet   1:*136–43*
Heart of Aztlán   4:*171–76*
Hero Ain't Nothin' but a Sandwich, A   5:*143–48*
His Own Where   5:*149–55*
Human Comedy, The   4:*193–200*
I Never Sang for My Father   5:*201–7*
In Nueva York   5:*214–21*
Jacob Have I Loved   4:*216–20*
King Lear   1:*196–203*
Like Water for Chocolate   3:*196–202*
Little Foxes, The   3:*203–10*
Little Women   2:*202–8*
Long Day's Journey into Night   3:*218–24*
Love Medicine   5:*243–50*
Man without a Face, The   4:*240–46*
Member of the Wedding, The   4:*254–59*
Not without Laughter   3:*249–56*
Ordinary People   5:*259–64*
Pocho   4:*295–302*
Prince of Tides, The   5:*285–90*
Raisin in the Sun, A   4:*309–15*
Red Sky at Morning   4:*316–22*
Roll of Thunder, Hear My Cry   3:*350–55*
Runner, The   5:*306–13*
Seventeen Syllables   4:*330–36*
Sons and Lovers   2:*334–39*
Sounder   3:*370–76*
Sweet Whispers, Brother Rush   5:*328–32*
Tree Grows in Brooklyn, A   3:*397–403*
Yellow Raft in Blue Water, A   5:*360–66*
(*See also* Autobiography)
Fantasy
   Alice's Adventures in Wonderland   2:*28–33*
   *Beauty: A Retelling of the Story of Beauty and the
      Beast*   1:*30–36*
   Devil and Tom Walker, The   1:*101–6*
   Handmaid's Tale, The   5:*135–42*
   Hobbit, The   1:*152–58*
   Rip Van Winkle   1:*330–36*
   Secret Life of Walter Mitty, The   3:*364–69*
   (*See also* Folklore and fairy tales; Science fiction)
Fard, W. D.   5:*12–13, 110*
Farewell to Arms, A, Hemingway, Ernest   3:*112–18*
Farewell to Manzanar, Houston, Jeanne W. and
   James D. Houston   4:*137–43*
Farley, James Aloysius   3:*402*
Farming
   Bracero Program (1942–1964)   3:*34*; 4:*44*
   in California   3:*269–71, 275, 334–35*
   chemicalization of, in 1950s   4:*203*
   by Cherokee   5:*29*
   in Chile   5:*163–64, 165*

Dust Bowl of 1930s   *3:34, 46, 138–40*; *4:297*
in England   *2:353–54, 358*; *3:2, 5–6*
families displaced by large corporations   *3:92, 269*
hard times in 1920s   *3:25, 94–95*
Homestead Act (1870)   *2:322–23*; *3:244, 257*
mechanization of, in 1930s and '40s   *4:203 (sidebar)*
in Mexico's *ejidos* system   *3:282*
in Mexico's hacienda system   *3:29, 278, 282*
migrant workers and discrimination   *3:29–30, 49, 140–42, 269–71, 275, 335, 337*; *4:297 (sidebar)*
in New England   *1:102, 217*; *2:125*
nurture versus exploitation debate   *3:262*
racism against Japanese farmers   *4:331*
skyrocketing production and surpluses of 1960s   *4:338*
social stratification of owners versus workers   *3:336*
in South Africa   *4:94*
Spreckels sugar interests   *3:269, 270 (sidebar), 319*
tenant farming and sharecropping   *2:42, 411*; *3:80, 249, 370–71*
in Texas of 1900s   *3:244*
training in, of and by blacks in "Movable School"   *3:380*
under Soviet Five-Year Plans   *4:132*
unions for farm workers   *3:34, 49–50, 141, 275*; *4:175–76*
United Farm Workers   *4:175, 300–302, 409*
and use of pesticides ("biocides")   *4:337–42*
working conditions, long hours   *3:244 (sidebar)*
(See also Cattle ranching; Cotton)
Fascism
characteristics of   *4:304, 306–7*
described   *1:293–94*
neo-fascists   *4:40*
origins in Italy   *4:66*
and *Ox-Bow Incident*   *2:293*
Fashions
African-style clothing and hairdos   *4:56*; *5:145, 300*
American Indian style   *5:247*
cosmetics for African American women   *4:50, 56*
global popularity of American   *1:223*
as symbols of generational conflict   *5:271–72*
women's
daring styles of 1920s   *3:23*
"New Look" of 1940s and '50s   *4:22*
restrictiveness in Victorian era   *3:420*
as status symbol   *2:246, 247 (sidebar)*
in youth culture of 1950s   *4:172, 392*
"zoot suits"   *4:173, 403, 404–5, 408–9*
(See also Clothing)
Fate
in ancient Greece   *1:169*
in Middle Ages   *1:160*

portents in Elizabethan era   *1:194–95*
Faulkner, William
Barn Burning   *2:41–46*
Bear, The   *2:47–53*
FDR. *See* Roosevelt, Franklin Delano
Federal Writers' Project   *3:237*
Felsch, Oscar "Happy"   *3:149*
Feltre, Fra Bernardino de   *1:244*
Feminine Mystique, The, and Betty Friedan   *1:62*; *2:58*; *3:430*; *4:11 (sidebar), 167, 241, 394*; *5:51 (illus.), 136*
Feminism. *See* Women's rights movement (and feminism)
Fences, Wilson, August   *4:144–50*
Fencing   *1:141*
FEPC (Fair Employment Practices Commission)   *3:42*
Feudalism   *1:65–66, 159–61, 187, 290*
Fiddler on the Roof, Stein, Joseph   *3:119–24*
Film. *See* Hollywood and motion picture industry
Fire Next Time, The, Baldwin, James   *5:107–14*
First Inaugural Address, Roosevelt, Franklin D.   *3:125–30*
Fishing
aquaculture   *5:285–86*
crabs and oysters   *4:216–17, 219*
game fish   *4:274, 275 (sidebar), 279 (sidebar)*
by Kwakiutl of British Columbia   *5:195*
shrimping   *5:285–86*
Fitzgerald, F. Scott, *Great Gatsby, The*   *3:146–52*
Flaubert, Gustave, *Madame Bovary*   *2:209–15*
Fleming, Alexander   *3:365–66*
Florence, Italy   *1:174–76, 316–18*
Florida
Belle Glade   *3:383–84*
Eatonville   *3:383*
Flowers for Algernon, Keyes, Daniel   *4:151–56*
Folklore and fairy tales   *1:31–32, 36, 106*
adapted to American themes   *1:335*
African   *2:63, 64*
American Indian   *1:332*
of American South   *2:48–49*
Beauty: A Retelling of the Story of Beauty and the Beast, McKinley, Robin   *1:30–36*
Dutch   *1:332*
efforts to collect in late 19th century   *2:397*
Germanic   *1:105, 106*
impact of Disney fairy tales on socialization of girls   *1:36*
Merry Adventures of Robin Hood, The, Pyle, Howard   *1:250–57*
mixed with Judeo-Christian beliefs   *1:50, 138*
origins of *Beowulf* in   *1:49*
as social commentary and criticism   *1:31–32, 36*
Uncle Remus, Harris, Joel Chandler   *2:397–402*
in Yorkshire, England   *1:418–19*
(See also Myth)
Football   *4:145–46, 147*; *5:63*
for colored girls who have considered suicide / when the rainbow is enuf, Shange, Ntozake   *5:115–21*

Ford, Henry and Ford Motor Company   3:23, 77, 88, 101; 5:43 (illus.), 44–45
Fordism   5:46
Forster, E. M.   3:356
   Passage to India, A   3:297–304
Fort William Henry Massacre   1:205
Foundation, Asimov, Isaac   5:122–28
France in 15th century   1:159–61
France in 16th century, invasion of Italy   1:317
France in 17th century
   dueling   1:389 (sidebar)
   Gascons   1:386, 391
   musketeers   1:386, 387
   wars and civil turmoil   1:87–89, 305, 386–89
   women's position in   1:30
France in 18th century
   class hatred   1:358–60, 361, 371–72
   love and marriage   1:31
   wars with England   1:51–52, 93, 123, 130–31, 204–6, 220–21, 360
   women's position in   1:408, 409
France in 18th century: French Revolution
   American Revolution's contributions to 2:223–24
   echoes in *Frankenstein*   1:116
   emigrés fleeing   1:360–61, 372
   English reactions to   1:359–60, 372–73, 373 (sidebar), 376, 408
   guillotine   1:360 (sidebar), 373
   Jacobins   1:372
   origins of   1:51, 358–60, 371–72; 2:223–24, 295
   Paris Commune and Communards   1:363
   Reign of Terror   1:372; 2:102, 224
   storming of Bastille   1:358, 362 (illus.), 372; 2:224
   women ignored in proposals for education reform   1:408
France in 19th century
   bourgeoisie   2:209–10
   censorship in   2:383
   class hatred   2:224
   Dreyfus affair   1:91–92, 364 (sidebar)
   historic rivalry with England   1:391–92
   Industrial Age in   2:103–4
   landmark historical dates   1:160 (sidebar)
   Louis Napoleon and end of republic (1848) 2:228–29
   Napoleonic era and wars   2:99–100, 224, 227 (sidebar), 245, 295–96
   Paris as capital of Western art   3:265–66
   Republican government of 1870s   1:91
   Restoration of monarchy after Napoleon (1816) 2:100–101, 224
   Revolution of 1830   1:163–65, 391; 2:100
   Revolution of 1832   2:224–25
   wars with England   1:123, 130–31, 159, 160, 204–6, 220–21, 305, 360
   White Terror (1815)   2:102
   women, education and rights   1:32; 2:210, 245
France in 20th century

African colonies   3:211–13
   as nonracist haven for Richard Wright   4:4
   in WWI   3:9, 11 (sidebar)
Franco, Francisco   4:67
Frank, Anne, *Diary of a Young Girl, The*   4:116–23
Frankenstein, Shelley, Mary   1:115–21
Franklin, Benjamin
   Autobiography of Benjamin Franklin, The 1:22–29
   as embodiment of American Dream   1:26–27, 309
   Poor Richard's Almanac   1:309–15
Freedom Rides   5:88–90
Freemasons (Masons)   2:82
French and Indian War (Seven Years' War)   1:93, 123, 204–6, 220–21
Freud, Sigmund   2:336; 5:260, 261
   and psychoanalysis   4:168 (sidebar); 5:42, 260–61, 263
Frick, Henry Clay   4:8
Friedan, Betty   1:62; 2:58; 3:430; 4:11 (sidebar), 167, 241, 394; 5:51 (illus.), 136
Friedrich, Richter, Hans Peter   4:157–64
Fuchs, Klaus   4:72
Fuentes, Carlos, *Old Gringo, The*   3:277–83
Fugitive Slave Acts (1793 and 1850)   1:42; 2:16, 62, 170, 189, 410
Fujimori, Alberto   5:334
Fuller, Edward   3:149
Fuller, Margaret   1:356, 357
Fundamentalism and New/Religious Right 5:137–39

G

G.I. Bill (1944)   3:92; 4:73
Gaelic League   3:109, 308–9
Gaines, Ernest J.
   Autobiography of Miss Jane Pittman, The   5:19–26
   Gathering of Old Men, A   5:129–34
Galarza, Ernesto, *Barrio Boy*   3:28–35
Galileo   1:305
Games and sports
   archery and quarterstaff fencing   1:253
   backswording   2:375
   bowling   1:335 (sidebar)
   boxing   5:68–69
   "chicken"   4:172
   fencing   1:141
   football   4:145–46, 147; 5:63
   frog-jumping contests   2:251–52
   gambling in mining camps   2:250, 282–83
   hero-worship of players   4:262
   horseracing in England   3:345–46
   hunting   2:47–48; 3:232
   hurling   3:109, 309
   involving animals   1:212
   jingling matches   2:375
   mahjong   5:232 (sidebar)
   racism continuing into 1980s   4:149

rodeo   5:*362, 364 (sidebar)*
rugby in England   2:*374–75*
running feats of Jemez Pueblo   4:*191*
tournaments of knights' skills   1:*291*
values inculcated in students   5:*63*
(*See also* Baseball; Entertainment)
Gandhi, (Mahatma) Mohandas Karamchand   2:*92*;
  3:*298–300, 302*; 5:*192*
Gandil, Arnold "Chick"   3:*149*; 4:*260*; 5:*314, 315*
García Márquez, Gabriel, *One Hundred Years of*
  Solitude   2:*268–74*
Garden of Eden   1:*301–2*
Garnet, Father Henry   1:*230*
Garrison, William Lloyd   2:*23, 89 (sidebar), 242*
Garvey, Marcus   3:*160, 163*; 4:*211, 312*
Gathering of Old Men, A, Gaines, Ernest J.
  5:*129–34*
Gay rights movement   4:*241*
Geller, Uri   5:*48*
Gematriya   4:*89*
General literature, *Poor Richard's Almanac*, Franklin,
  Benjamin   1:*309–15*
Geoffrey of Monmouth   1:*290*
George I of England   1:*131, 266, 342*
George II of England   1:*130, 269, 270 (illus.)*
George III of England   1:*93, 95 (illus.), 97*
Germany
  Berlin Wall   5:*238, 293*
  early 20th century   1:*370*
  education in post-WWII period ignoring Third
    Reich   4:*163*
  fascism in   1:*293–94*
  Tripartite Pact (Japan, Germany, Italy; 1940)
    4:*59*
  WWI   1:*277–78*; 3:*8, 11 (sidebar)*
  (*See also* Hitler; Nazis)
Gettysburg Address, Lincoln, Abraham   2:*130–36*
  influence on white South Africans of 20th
    century   4:*99*
Ghana   4:*314*
Ghettos
  black   4:*30–31*; 5:*71–72, 143, 149–51*
    Bedford-Stuyvesant   5:*149–51*
    crime in   5:*13, 67–68, 112, 146, 150,*
      339–42
      drugs, suspicions of conspiracy by white
        officials to allow   5:*144*
    South Central Los Angeles   5:*339–42*
  Brooklyn   3:*397–98*; 4:*88*
  Jewish   1:*244, 249*; 4:*118*
  schools in, as overcrowded and inadequate
    5:*151–52*
Ghibellines   1:*174, 175, 345*
Ghosts. *See* Supernatural
Gibson, William, *Miracle Worker, The*   2:*216–22*
Gilded Age (late 19th-century America)   2:*20, 306,*
  328, 331
Gilman, Charlotte Perkins   3:*168–69*
  Yellow Wallpaper, The   2:*422–28*

Ginsberg, Allen   4:*75*; 5:*83, 84 (illus.), 324*
"Give Me Liberty or Give Me Death," Henry, Patrick
  1:*122–28*
Glenn, John   5:*292, 296*
Glover, Goodwife (Goody)   1:*79*
Goddard, Robert   5:*54*
Godwin, William   1:*115, 119, 407, 411 (illus.),*
  411–12
Gold rushes and silver strikes
  in Black Hills of Dakota   2:*67–68*
  boom towns   2:*289*
  in California   2:*174–75, 195, 249–50, 281–84*
  on Cherokee land in Oklahoma   5:*29*
  Chinese immigration for   4:*124*; 5:*74, 352*
  Klondike   3:*52–56, 261 (sidebar)*
  miners subject to robbers   1:*256*
  in Nevada   2:*288–89, 290 (sidebar)*
  in Nez Percé territory   2:*162*
  (*See also* Mining industry)
Golden Notebook, The, Lessing, Doris   4:*165–70*
Golding, William, *Lord of the Flies*   4:*228–34*
Goldman, Emma   3:*321*
Gone with the Wind, Mitchell, Margaret   2:*137–44*
Good Earth, The, Buck, Pearl S.   3:*131–37*
Good, Sarah   1:*79, 395, 396*
Good versus evil. *See* Sin and damnation
Gorbachev, Mikhail   5:*8*
Gothic horror stories and romances   2:*81, 85, 185*;
  3:*338*
  Jane Eyre   1:*415 (sidebar), 419*; 2:*181–87*
  Rebecca   3:*326–33*
Gouzenko, Igor   4:*72*
Governesses in Victorian Age   2:*182, 183 (sidebar),*
  378–80
Gowrie Conspiracy   1:*229*
Grady, Henry   2:*399*
Graetz, Heinrich   4:*89*
Grant, Duncan   3:*356*
Grant, Ulysses S.   2:*217*
Grapes of Wrath, The, Steinbeck, John   3:*138–45*
"Graying" of America   5:*202–4*
Great Awakenings
  in American colonies   1:*73, 106, 122*
  in early 19th-century America   1:*424–25*
Great Britain. *See* England
"Great Chain of Being"   1:*201, 203*
Great Depression, The (1930s)
  in agriculture   3:*32, 34, 138–40, 153, 247,*
    350–51
  causes of   3:*125, 138*
  comparisons to hard times of Reconstruction
    2:*143–44*
  Coxey's Army   3:*51–52*
  Dust Bowl   3:*34, 46, 138–40*; 4:*297*
  in England   5:*39–40*
  enhancing appeal of communism   3:*39–40, 45,*
    129, 208–10
  hobo tradition   3:*46, 270*
  homelessness   3:*126, 140, 142*

impact on African Americans   3:*154, 236–37*
impact on South   3:*68–69*
New Deal programs
    Farm Relief Act (Agricultural Adjustment Act)
      (1933)   3:*247*
    Federal Writers' Project   3:*237*
    FERA (Federal Emergency Relief
      Administration)   1:*113*
    FLSA (Fair Labor Standards Act) (1938)
      3:*49*
    FSA (Farm Security Administration) (1937)
      3:*142*
    NLRA (National Labor Relations Act) (1933)
      3:*128*
    NRA (National Recovery Act) (1933)
      3:*390–91*
    purposes of   3:*45, 142*
    questionable effectiveness   3:*69, 128*
    Social Security System   3:*49, 128*
    WPA (Works Progress Administration)
      3:*128, 391, 423–24;* 4:*44*
Okies   3:*140*
plight of sharecroppers and tenant farmers
    3:*105, 350–51*
rural Southern education   3:*352*
soup kitchens   3:*45 (illus.)*
stock market crash and bank failures
    3:*125–26, 208*
teamwork, as preoccupation of Steinbeck
    3:*337*
widespread unemployment and poverty   3:*68,
126, 350*
WWII helping to end   2:*45;* 3:*424*
Great Gatsby, The, Fitzgerald, F. Scott   3:*146–52*
Great Goddess (ancient Greece)   1:*59, 61–62*
Great Migration (1915–1960)
affecting Harlem Renaissance   3:*159–65, 256,
321, 384, 421*
blacks and issue of union membership   3:*39;*
    4:*210*
causing increase of single female-headed families
    3:*80, 423;* 4:*2*
estimates of numbers of   4:*2, 50, 203*
exacerbating racial tensions in Northern cities
    2:*6*
housing discrimination in North   3:*39, 159;*
    4:*30–31*
increasing with WWI   3:*236, 384*
increasing with WWII   4:*51*
making race a national question   4:*209–10*
offering hope, then disillusion   3:*39, 80, 159,
236;* 4:*50–51*
to Pittsburgh's steel and coal industries   4:*144*
reasons for   4:*202–3*
sharecroppers fleeing economic and racial
    oppression   3:*351*
targeting Chicago and New York City   4:*309*
transforming African Americans' sense of identity
    4:*210*

two phases of   4:*309*
Great War, The. *See* World War I
Greece, invasion of Turkey (1920)   3:*340*
Greece in ancient times
Athens
    citizenship law   1:*241*
    Parthenon   1:*240*
    Pericles   1:*17, 18, 240, 241, 322*
    Plato   1:*321–22, 328*
    Socrates   1:*240, 322, 323 (illus.), 324, 327*
    Sophists   1:*19, 240*
    Theseus   1:*57, 61 (sidebar), 258, 259*
Bronze Age   1:*14, 258, 280, 283 (sidebar)*
burial rites   1:*18–19*
civic/human laws versus divine   1:*17, 20*
and concept of barbarians   1:*173*
Corinth   1:*238, 241*
"Dark Ages"   1:*167, 172, 283 (sidebar), 286*
Mycenaean Age   1:*57–59, 167, 258, 281–82,
283 (sidebar)*
Peloponnesian War   1:*241, 324, 328*
position of women in   1:*17, 20, 58–59, 230–40,
259*
ritual sacrifice   1:*283*
Sparta   1:*324–25, 328*
suicide as honorable   4:*22*
Thebes   1:*14*
Thirty Tyrants   1:*322, 324, 325 (sidebar)*
Trojan War   1:*8, 14, 166–69, 281, 283 (sidebar)*
Greek myths
basis of *Aeneid* in   1:*9*
basis of *Antigone* in   1:*14*
basis of *Medea* in   1:*238*
basis of *Midsummer Night's Dream* in   1:*259
(sidebar)*
Great Goddess and Amazons   1:*58–59, 61–62,
258, 259–60*
Ovid's *Metamorphoses* as source of   1:*262*
as sources of ideas for humanists   1:*380*
as sources for Milton's *Paradise Lost*   1:*301*
Zeus   1:*9, 59, 61, 170, 282, 283, 301*
Green Mountain Boys   3:*98 (sidebar)*
Greene, Bette, *Summer of My German Soldier*
    4:*371–77*
Griffes   3:*18*
Grissom, Gus   5:*296*
Guatemala and refugees   5:*27–29*
Guelphs   1:*174, 175, 345*
Guest, Judith, *Ordinary People*   5:*259–64*
Guillotine   1:*360 (sidebar), 373*
Guillotine, Dr. Joseph Ignace   1:*360*
Gulliver's Travels
    Swift, Jonathan   1:*129–35*
    War of the Worlds compared to   3:*410*
Gunpowder Plot   1:*229*
Guthrie, Woody
    Bound for Glory   3:*44–50*
    on songs of New Deal era   3:*128 (sidebar)*
Gypsies

in England   3:3
as victims of holocaust   4:119, 160, 267

H

Hachiya, Michihiko, *Hiroshima Diary*   4:177–84
Hades   1:283, 285
Haiti (formerly Saint-Domingue)   5:116–17
Haley, Alex
    Autobiography of Malcolm X, The (with Malcolm
       X)   5:11–18
    Roots   5:298–305
Hall, James Norman, *Mutiny on the Bounty*
    1:273–79
Hamer, Fanny Lou   3:354
Hamilton, Virginia, *Sweet Whispers, Brother Rush*
    5:328–32
Hamlet, Shakespeare, William   1:136–43
Hammett, Dashiell
    influence upon Hellman   3:210
    Maltese Falcon, The   3:225–30
Handmaid's Tale, The, Atwood, Margaret   5:135–42
Hansberry, Lorraine, *Raisin in the Sun, A*   4:309–15
Harding, Warren G.   3:22 (illus.)
Hardy, Thomas, *Tess of the D'Urbervilles*   2:353–59
Harlem, New York   4:247–48; 5:67–68
Harlem Renaissance   3:159–65, 256, 321, 384–85,
    421; 4:204 (sidebar), 207
Harrington, Michael   5:266 (sidebar)
Harris, Joel Chandler, *Uncle Remus*   2:397–402
Hart, Leo   3:144 (sidebar)
Harte, Bret, *Outcasts of Poker Flat, The*   2:281–87
Harwood, Richard   4:40
Hasidim   3:425, 426; 4:87–90
Hate groups
    Knights of the White Camellia   5:21 (sidebar)
    (*See also* Ku Klux Klan)
Hathorne, John   1:83 (sidebar), 396, 420, 422, 424
    (sidebar), 425 (sidebar)
Hathorne, William   1:420, 424 (sidebar)
Hautzig, Esther, *Endless Steppe, The: Growing Up in
    Siberia*   4:131–36
Hawthorne, Nathaniel
    Scarlet Letter, The   1:351–57
    Young Goodman Brown   1:420–26
Haya de la Torre, Raul   5:333, 334
Hays, Mary   1:412
Health issues
    Medicaid   5:68
    overcrowding of hospitals in ghettos   5:150
    scientific improvements in Victorian Age
       1:115; 2:119
    (*See also* Disabled persons; Diseases;
       Drug/substance abuse; Mental and emotional
       disabilities)
Heart of Aztlán, Anaya, Rudolfo A.   4:171–76
Heart of Darkness, Conrad, Joseph   2:145–51
Heart Is a Lonely Hunter, The, McCullers, Carson
    3:153–58
Hebrides   1:226

Hector   1:170
Heinlein, Robert A., *Stranger in a Strange Land*
    5:321–27
Heinz, Henry   4:8
Heisenberg, Werner   5:283
Helen of Troy   1:8, 166, 168 (illus.), 281
Hell. *See* Devil (Satan); *Inferno*; *Paradise Lost*; Sin
   and damnation
Heller, Joseph, *Catch-22*   4:66–72
Hellman, Lillian, *Little Foxes, The*   3:203–10
Hemingway, Ernest
    Farewell to Arms, A   3:112–18
    Old Man and the Sea, The   4:274–80
Henry II of England   1:250, 251, 254–55
Henry IV of England   1:144
Henry IV, Part I, Shakespeare, William   1:144–51
Henry, Patrick
    as "American, not Virginian"   1:96–97
    "Give Me Liberty or Give Me Death" speech
       1:122–28
Henry V of England   1:146
Henry VIII of England   1:149, 150, 231, 232, 234
    (illus.)
Herbert, Frank, *Dune*   5:81–87
Hero Ain't Nothin' but a Sandwich, A, Childress, Alice
    5:143–48
Herodotus   1:286
Herriott, James, *All Creatures Great and Small*
    3:1–7
Herzl, Theodore   4:102
Hesse, Hermann, *Siddhartha*   1:365–70
Heyerdahl, Thor, *Kon-Tiki*   4:221–27
Hidalgos   1:2–3
Highlanders of Scotland   1:187
Hinduism   3:300, 302
Hine, Lewis   3:285
Hinton, S. E., *Outsiders, The*   5:265–70
Hippies. *See* Counterculture
Hippolyta and Amazons   1:58–59, 61–62, 258,
    259–60
Hirohito, Emperor of Japan   4:178, 183
Hiroshima Diary, Hachiya, Michihiko   4:177–84
Hirsch, Samson Raphael   4:90 (sidebar)
His Own Where, Jordan, June   5:149–55
Hispanics. *See* Chicanos; Latinos
Hiss, Alger   4:110; 5:96
Histories
    Bury My Heart at Wounded Knee, Brown, Dee
       2:74–80
    Two Years before the Mast, Dana, Richard Henry,
       Jr.   2:391–96
Hitler, Adolf   1:113–14, 294; 3:210; 4:157–58, 305
    (illus.), 356–57; 5:122–23
Hobbit, The, Tolkien, J.R.R.   1:152–58
Holinshed, Raphael   1:148, 227
Holland   4:116–19
Holland, Isabelle, *Man without a Face, The*
    4:240–46
Hollywood and motion picture industry
    Caucasian ideal of beauty reinforced by   4:50

development of   3:3, *89, 101*
end of golden age of (1920s–45)   4:*75–76*
ethnic stereotypes used by   2:*142*; 4:*50, 369*
female as sex object   4:*393*
late 1940s attempts to address real issues
  4:*75–76*
patriotic films for WWII   4:*325*
reflecting and influencing teenagers and
  generation gap   4:*392, 394*
as target of witch hunts for "Reds"   4:*236*
"thrillers" as new genre   3:*329*
(See also Television)
Holocaust
  adding to urgency of Zionist appeal   4:*102*
  beginnings within Germany (1933–38)
    3:*401–3*; 4:*267*
  collusion of some Jews in   4:*269–70, 272–73*
  concentration camps   4:*160–61, 194, 267–73*
  delayed U.S. acceptance of proof   3:*403*
  denial by anti-Semites and neo-fascists   4:*40*
  described   4:*119–20*
  estimates of number of victims   4:*194*
  extension outside German borders (1939)
    3:*403*; 4:*267*
  as "final solution"   4:*267*
  Israel exacting justice for atrocities   4:*107*
    (sidebar)
  Jews in Siberia "spared"   4:*134*
  Kristallnacht   4:*159, 162–63*
  liberation of Buchenwald   4:*269, 272*
  made easier by Nazis' deceptions and some Jews'
    willingness to be deceived   4:*272, 273*
  Nazi "scapegoating" of Jews (1933–39)
    4:*159–60*
  in occupied Holland   4:*117–18*
  reactions of Germans to   4:*194*
  subsequent pressure upon Jewish women to bear
    children   3:*430*
  Vrba-Wetzler report and warnings to Hungarian
    Jews   4:*269, 272*
  war crimes trials   4:*272–73*
  (See also Diary of a Young Girl, The; Friedrich;
    Night)
Holy Grail legends   4:*264–65*
Holy League   1:*296*
Holy Roman Empire   1:*87, 174, 176, 344, 345*
Home to Harlem, McKay, Claude   3:*159–65*
Homelessness
  of deinstitutionalized mental patients   4:*289*
  during The Great Depression of 1930s   3:*126,
    140, 142*
  in South Africa   4:*97*
  of Vietnam veterans   5:*106*
Homer
  Iliad   1:*166–73*
  Odyssey   1:*280–87*
Homosexuality
  in Angels in America   5:*1–10*
  in Biloxi Blues   4:*38*
  in Catcher in the Rye   4:*74*

growth of gay subculture   4:*241, 245–46*
and lesbianism   3:*327–28, 357, 362*
in Man without a Face, The   4:*244*
in military   4:*38, 39–40*
and Mormonism   5:*4–5*
as reported by Kinsey   4:*398 (sidebar)*; 5:*324*
seen as pathological deviance   4:*77*
targeted by Nazis in Holocaust   4:*119, 160*
targeted by New/Religious Right   5:*136, 137–38*
Hood, Robin   1:*188, 255 (sidebar)*
  (See also Merry Adventures of Robin Hood)
Hoover, Herbert   3:*126–27*
Hoover, J. Edgar   1:*84 (sidebar), 399*
Horror fiction
  Carrie   5:*46–52*
  Frankenstein   1:*115–21*
  Psycho   5:*46–47*
Hound of the Baskervilles, Doyle, Arthur Conan
  2:*152–59*
House Made of Dawn, Momaday, N. Scott
  4:*185–92*
House of Mirth, The, Wharton, Edith   3:*166–73*
House of Stairs, Sleator, William   5:*156–62*
House of the Spirits, The, Allende, Isabel   5:*163–70*
House on Mango Street, The, Cisneros, Sandra
  5:*171–77*
Housing
  adobes   4:*318*
  in barrios   5:*174*
  in black ghettos. See Ghettos
  discrimination against African Americans   2:*13*;
    3:*39, 237*; 4:*30–31, 310*; 5:*13*
  in middle-class suburbs   5:*261–62*
  postwar prosperity, G.I. Bill, and home
    ownership   4:*73*
  and racial violence   4:*310 (sidebar)*
  racist restrictions ruled illegal   4:*201*
  rent control ordinances   4:*384, 400*
  rent supplements   5:*68*
  shacks of sharecropper families   3:*371*
  in slum tenements of New York   3:*397–98*;
    4:*384–85, 401*; 5:*67–68, 149–50*
  in South Africa   4:*95, 96–97*
  streetcars' impact on   4:*366*
  "white flight" to suburbs   4:*384, 385*
Houston, Jeanne W. and James D. Houston, Farewell
  to Manzanar   4:*137–43*
Howe, Samuel Gridley   2:*217*
Huerta, Dolores   4:*47*
Huerta, Victoriano   3:*278–79*
Hughes, Langston   3:*164*
  Not without Laughter   3:*249–56*
Hughes, Thomas, Tom Brown's Schooldays
  2:*372–77*
Hugo, Victor
  Hunchback of Notre Dame, The   1:*159–65*
  on John Brown   2:*193*
  Les Misérables   2:*223–29*
Human Comedy, The, Saroyan, William   4:*193–200*
Humanism   1:*2, 142, 233, 380, 381*

Hunchback of Notre Dame, The, Hugo, Victor
  1:*159–65*
Hundred Years' War   **1**:*159, 160*
Hungary   **4**:*166*
Hunger of Memory, Rodriguez, Richard   **5**:*178–84*
Hunt, Irene, *Across Five Aprils*   **2**:*8–14*
Hurston, Zora Neale, *Their Eyes Were Watching God*
  3:*383–89*
Hutchinson, Anne   **1**:*352 (sidebar), 352–53*
Huxley, Aldous, *Brave New World*   **5**:*39–45*
Huxley, Thomas Henry   **3**:*265, 404*; **5**:*324–25*
Hydrogen bomb   **4**:*183*

I

"I Have a Dream," King, Martin Luther, Jr.
  5:*185–93*
I Heard the Owl Call My Name, Craven, Margaret
  5:*194–200*
I Know Why the Caged Bird Sings, Angelou, Maya
  4:*201–8*
I Never Sang for My Father, Anderson, Robert
  5:*201–7*
"I Will Fight No More Forever," Chief Joseph
  2:*160–67*
Ibsen, Henrik   **3**:*406*
  Doll's House, A   **2**:*111–17*
Idaho   **2**:*367*
Igbo of Africa, late 19th century   **2**:*360–62*
Iliad, Homer   **1**:*9, 166–73*
Illinois. *See* Chicago
Imagining Argentina, Thornton, Laurence   **5**:*208–13*
Imagism   **3**:*413–14*
Imlay, Gilbert   **1**:*410*
Immigration in 19th century
  Chinese   **2**:*367–68, 370 (sidebar), 371*;
    4:*124–27*; **5**:*74*
  Chinese Exclusion Acts (1882 and 1902)
    2:*368*; **4**:*125*; **5**:*74, 231*
  Geary Act (1892)   **2**:*368*; **4**:*125*
  Irish   **3**:*107, 398–99*
  Jewish   **3**:*121*
  to steel mills   **4**:*8*
  Swedish   **3**:*243–44, 259–60*
  urbanization with   **2**:*302, 327*; **3**:*166*
  to Western homesteads   **3**:*258–61*
Immigration in 20th century
  America as "salad bowl" rather than melting pot
    5:*176*
  anti-immigrant bigotry and fears   **3**:*233, 402*;
    4:*330–31*; **5**:*180*
  Armenian   **4**:*199*
  California Alien Land Act (1913)   **4**:*331*
  Chinese   **2**:*368*; **4**:*125, 127, 129*; **5**:*229, 352–54*
  Chinese Exclusion Act and Geary Acts (1904,
    1922, 1924)   **2**:*368*; **5**:*231*
  feelings of shame and inferiority among children
    of   **5**:*78–79*
  generational conflicts between children and
    parents   **4**:*385*; **5**:*78–79, 182, 358*

Guatemalan political refugees   **5**:*28–29*
Immigration Acts (1924, 1965, 1980)   **4**:*331*;
    5:*28, 75 (sidebar)*
  Irish   **3**:*401–2*
  Japanese   **3**:*30*; **4**:*137, 143, 330–31*
  Japanese "picture brides"   **4**:*331–32*
  Jewish   **3**:*121*; **4**:*92, 102–3, 104 (illus.), 106*
  Literacy Test (1917)   **3**:*233*
  Mexican   **3**:*29–30*; **4**:*44–48*
  National Origins Act (1924)   **3**:*233*
  of Puerto Ricans   **4**:*385*; **5**:*215–16*
  restrictions of 1920s enhancing opportunity for
    blacks   **4**:*203*
  Russian   **3**:*233*
  Sanctuary Movement   **5**:*29*
  urbanization with   **3**:*101, 102*
  War Brides Act (1945)   **4**:*124, 127*; **5**:*231*
Imperialism. *See* Colonialism, imperialism, and
  interventionism
Impressment of sailors by Royal Navy   **1**:*52*
In medias res   **2**:*62*
In Nueva York, Mohr, Nicholasa   **5**:*214–21*
Inaugural Address
  Kennedy, John F.   **5**:*222–28*
  Roosevelt, Franklin D.   **3**:*125–30*
Incest   **4**:*52*
Incidents in the Life of a Slave Girl, Jacobs, Harriet
  2:*168–73*
  influence upon Toni Morrison   **2**:*63*
Independent Living Movement   **2**:*123*
Indeterminacy, principle of   **5**:*283*
India
  500s to 300s b.c.   **1**:*365*
  Amritsar massacre   **3**:*298*
  Buddhism   **1**:*365–69*; **3**:*186–87*; **5**:*48*
  caste system   **1**:*366*; **3**:*182, 184*
  civil service   **3**:*185*
  infrastructure   **3**:*184–85*
  map of   **3**:*183 (illus.)*
  nationalism   **3**:*298–300*
  religions   **1**:*366*; **3**:*300–301, 302*
  under British rule   **2**:*182–84, 276–77*; **3**:*181–82,
    297–98*
Indians. *See* American Indians
Individualism
  and classical liberalism   **3**:*268*
  criticism of "cult" of   **5**:*2 (sidebar)*
  decline in, during 1950s era of conformity
    4:*382*; **5**:*323–24*
  and egalitarian ideals in 19th-century America
    2:*302*
  machine age as debasing   **5**:*41, 46*
  Teddy Roosevelt popularizing "Old West" myth
    of   **5**:*206*
  of Thoreau   **2**:*88–89*
Industrialization
  allowing growth of middle class   **2**:*118, 153*
  democracy and capitalism, shift toward
    2:*334–35*
  in France   **2**:*103–4, 245–46*

leading to Romantic movement   1:106, 115–16

leading to worker/owner class distinctions
    2:303

reaction of Luddites   1:119–20, 120 (illus.)

social and economic improvement and upheaval
    1:106; 2:417

stimulants of   1:115, 336, 417

women's increasing opportunities for jobs
    2:423

working conditions and attempts to improve
    3:174–75, 178–79

working conditions and worker's revolts   1:363;
    2:328, 329, 404

(See also Capitalism; Labor unions; Urbanization)

Inferno, Dante Alighieri   1:174–80

Inheritance, by entailment   2:296 (sidebar)

Integration

Baldwin on moral standards of   5:113

Brown v. Board of Education   3:375; 4:29–30,
    314; 5:90, 108, 180, 181

opposition of Malcolm X to   5:15

of schools   3:43, 396; 4:29–30, 31 (illus.), 314;
    5:116, 131–32, 181

slow pace of   4:33–34

of University of Mississippi   5:19

Internment of Japanese Americans (1942–44)
    4:138–43, 195, 335–36

Interventionism. See Colonialism, imperialism, and
    interventionism

Invisible Man, Ellison, Ralph   4:209–15

Ionesco, Eugène   4:400

Ireland

Absentees   1:266, 269 (sidebar), 269

Catholicism in   1:269; 3:107–8, 109–10, 305–7

concessions by James I   1:131

cultural revival   3:108–9, 308–9

English subjugation of   1:131–32, 267; 3:106–7,
    305–6

famine and emigration in mid-19th century
    2:302

Home Rule movement   3:109, 307

Irishness as depicted in Kim   3:187

misgovernment and economic decline in 18th
    century   1:266–69

Parnell, Charles   3:109–10

Potato Famine of 1845   3:107

Protestants and Patriots   1:267

(See also England)

Irish Americans

growing acceptance of   3:401–2

sense of community   3:400–401

stereotypes of heavy drinking   3:220, 398, 400

Irving, Washington

Devil and Tom Walker, The   1:101–6

Legend of Sleepy Hollow, The   1:211–18

Rip Van Winkle   1:330–36

The Sketch Book   1:335–36

on slavery   1:103

Ishi, Last of His Tribe, Kroeber, Theodora   2:174–80

Islam   1:296; 3:300

and Nation of Islam   3:238, 325; 4:56, 248–50;
    5:12–13, 69, 110–11, 302

Israel

Biblical history of   4:101

as British mandate of Palestine   4:102–3, 105

conflicts with Arabs   4:106–8

Hasidic opposition to   4:88

immigration to

denied by Soviet government   3:124

from Europe of 1880s   3:121

Six-Day War (1967)   4:93

War of Independence (1948–49)   4:106

Women's Equal Rights Law (1951)   3:430

Italy

in 16th century   1:316

in ancient times   1:9

fascism in   1:293–94

Florence   1:174–76, 316–18

Jews in   1:246, 248–49

map of   1:345 (illus.)

Milan   1:379–80

Mussolini, Benito   2:293–94

Venice   1:242–46, 295–97

Verona   1:344–45

in and after WWI   3:11 (sidebar), 113–14; 4:66

in WWII   4:66–67

Ithaca   1:281

Ivanhoe, Scott, Sir Walter   1:181–88

J

Jackson, Andrew   1:209–10

Jackson, Shirley, Lottery, The   4:235–39

Jackson, "Shoeless" Joe   3:149; 4:265; 5:314, 316

Jacob Have I Loved, Paterson, Katherine   4:216–20

Jacobs, Harriet, Incidents in the Life of a Slave Girl
    2:168–73

James, Henry

Daisy Miller   2:105–10

on Dr Jekyll and Mr. Hyde   3:382

Turn of the Screw, The   2:378–83

James I of England (James IV of Scotland)

belief in supernatural and witchcraft   1:228,
    384, 385

concessions to Irish   1:131

daughter's marriage subject to her own approval
    1:385

increase of political and religious factions
    1:299

parallels to life of Hamlet   1:141

subject of regicidal conspiracies   1:229, 230

succession to throne of England   1:141, 149,
    150, 201

support for theater and arts   1:299

James II of England   1:130

Jamestown, Virginia   1:379, 384, 394

Jane Eyre, Brontë, Charlotte   1:415 (sidebar), 419;
    2:181–87

Japan

in 19th century   4:177

countries conquered during WWII 5:*123*
(*sidebar*)
dictatorship of prewar military 4:*178, 183*
Emperor Hirohito 4:*178, 183*
frosty relations with Korea 4:*353–54*
furor over textbooks' coverage of WWII 4:*354*
Hiroshima as first atom bomb target 4:*179–82*
imperialism of 4:*58–59*
invasion of China (1930s and '40s) 3:*189–90;*
5:*229–30*
invasion and occupation of Korea (1894-95,
1904-05, 1910-45) 4:*59, 177, 349–54*
Korean laborers in 4:*353*
Nagasaki as second atom bomb target 4:*180*
(*illus.*), *181* (*sidebar*)
rapprochement with South Korea 4:*354*
Russo-Japanese War (1904–05) 4:*59*
WWII 4:*58–61*
Japanese and Japanese Americans
as farm workers 3:*30*
immigration 3:*30;* 4:*137, 143, 330–31*
Issei and Nisei 4:*137*
Japanese and Japanese Americans, works concerning
Farewell to Manzanar 4:*137–43*
Hiroshima Diary 4:*177–84*
Seventeen Syllables 4:*330–36*
So Far from the Bamboo Grove 4:*349–55*
Jara, Victor 5:*164, 168*
Jason 1:*238–39*
Jazz 3:*162* (*sidebar*); 4:*258*
Jefferson, Thomas
Declaration of Independence, The 1:*93–100*
on Patrick Henry 1:*127*
Jerusalem 1:*182*
Jesuits 3:*307–8*
Jews
in America 3:*430*
assimilation, threat of 3:*120, 123, 430;* 4:*88, 90*
(*sidebar*), *91*
British offer of homeland in Africa 3:*291*
criticality of education for 3:*425*
Diaspora 4:*101*
divorce 3:*427, 429* (*sidebar*)
education of women 3:*427, 430*
in England 1:*182–83, 185;* 2:*264–65*
expulsion or conversion to Christianity 1:*244,
246;* 2:*264*
Gematriya 4:*89*
in ghettos 1:*244, 249;* 4:*118*
Hasidim 3:*425, 426;* 4:*87–90;* 5:*283* (*sidebar*)
immigrating to America and Israel 3:*121*
immigration in 20th century 3:*121;* 4:*92,
102–4, 106*
in Italy 1:*243, 246, 248–49*
Jewish Enlightenment (*Haskalah*) 3:*120, 426;*
4:*88*
Levantines 1:*248*
Marranos 1:*248, 249*
marriage-bed custom 3:*428* (*sidebar*)
Mitnagdim 3:*426*

and moneylending 1:*182–83;* 2:*264*
Orthodox 4:*93*
of Poland 4:*131–32*
revival of American 4:*91–92, 93*
role and rights of women 3:*427–30*
suicide and 3:*428;* 4:*22*
traditional marriage 3:*119*
Zionism 3:*121;* 4:*88, 101–2*
(*See also* Anti-Semitism; Holocaust)
Jews, literary works concerning
Biloxi Blues 4:*35–41*
Chosen, The 4:*87–93*
Dawn 4:*101–8*
Diary of a Young Girl, The 4:*116–23*
Endless Steppe, The: Growing Up in Siberia
4:*131–36*
Fiddler on the Roof 3:*119–24*
Friedrich 4:*157–64*
Night 4:*267–73*
Summer of My German Soldier 4:*371–77*
A Tree Grows in Brooklyn 3:*402*
Yentl, the Yeshiva Boy 3:*425–31*
Jim Crow laws
African American responses to 2:*413*
challenges to, by black soldiers of WWI 3:*252*
coming under fire in 1930s and '40s 2:*53*
described 3:*81, 351;* 5:*90*
federal authorities ignoring 4:*1*
origins of term 2:*21, 341;* 3:*351*
upheld by *Plessy v. Ferguson* 2:*21, 341,
399–400, 413;* 3:*351, 375, 419;* 4:*1;* 5:*90, 107–8*
John Brown's Final Speech, Brown, John 2:*188–94*
John I of England 1:*251*
Johnson, Lyndon Baines 3:*324;* 4:*347, 375,* 5:*68,
102*
Johnson, Samuel 1:*307*
Jolly Roger (pirates' flag) 1:*401*
Jones, Leroi (Amiri Baraka) 4:*207*
Jonson, Ben 1:*150, 300*
Jordan, June, *His Own Where* 5:*149–55*
Joseph, Chief of Wallowa Nez Percé, "I Will Fight
No More Forever" 2:*160–67*
Joy Luck Club, The, Tan, Amy 5:*229–35*
Joyce, James 5:*42*
Dubliners 3:*106–11*
Portrait of the Artist as a Young Man, A
3:*305–11*
Julius Caesar 1:*169* (*sidebar*), *189–91*
Julius Caesar, Shakespeare, William 1:*189–95*
Jung, Carl Gustav 3:*329*
Jungle, The, Sinclair, Upton 3:*174–80*
Jupiter 1:*191*

K

Kansas-Nebraska Act (1854) 1:*42;* 2:*5* (*sidebar*),
172, 193
Karma 1:*367*
Kasztner, Rezso 4:*269–70, 272–73*
Katherine of Aragon 1:*231*

Keats, John   1:406
Keller, Helen   2:220 (illus.)
   (See also Miracle Worker, The)
Kelly, Charles T. and Kelly's Army   3:51–52
Kennedy, John F.
   appeal to, by King for civil rights   5:186
   Bay of Pigs and Cuban Missile Crisis   4:135;
      5:225, 226, 238–39, 293
   environmental concerns   4:338, 341 (sidebar)
   expanding U.S. role in Vietnam   4:375
   Inaugural Address   5:222–28
   intervention on behalf of civil rights protesters in
      Alabama   5:12
   moon walk goal launching space race   5:81,
      292, 293 (sidebar), 321–22
   opposing Nixon for president   5:321–22
   President's Panel on Mental Retardation   4:152
   sending "advisors" to Vietnam   5:158, 307
Kennedy, Joseph P.   3:402
Kennedy, Robert   5:90
Kentucky
   in Civil War   2:60 (sidebar)
   slavery in   2:59–60
Kenya   3:290–96
Kerensky, Alexander   3:232
Kerouac, Jack   4:75
Kesey, Ken, One Flew over the Cuckoo's Nest
   4:288–94
Keyes, Daniel, Flowers for Algernon   4:151–56
Keynes, John Maynard   3:356
Kherdian, David, Road from Home, The   3:338–43
Khrushchev, Nikita   4:135, 166, 286, 398, 399
   (illus.); 5:225
Kim, Kipling, Rudyard   3:181–88
King, Dr. Martin Luther, Jr.   5:14 (illus.), 89 (illus.),
   109 (illus.)
   appeal to Kennedy for help in civil rights
      movement   5:12, 186
   assassination of   4:54; 5:112 (sidebar)
   criticism of, by Malcolm X   4:250; 5:13, 15, 111
   education and pastorate   5:108
   influenced by Ghandi and passive resistance
      2:92; 5:108, 189, 192
   influenced by Thoreau   2:92
   organization of Montgomery bus boycott   5:11,
      88, 108
   protesting residential segregation   2:12 (illus.),
      13, 97
   speech: "I Have a Dream"   5:185–93
King Lear, Shakespeare, William   1:196–203
King, Rodney   5:340
King, Stephen, Carrie   5:46–52
Kingsolver, Barbara, Bean Trees, The   5:27–33
Kingston, Maxine Hong, Woman Warrior, The
   5:352–59
Kinsella, W. P., Shoeless Joe   5:314–20
Kinsey, Alfred Charles and Kinsey Report   4:75,
   241, 398–99 (sidebar); 5:324
Kipling, Rudyard, Kim   3:181–88
Kitchen God's Wife, The, Tan, Amy   3:189–95

Klondike   3:52–56, 261 (sidebar)
Knights and knighthood   1:182 (sidebar), 290–91
Knights of the White Camellia   5:21 (sidebar)
Knowles, John, Separate Peace, A   4:323–29
Knox, John   4:304
Kon-Tiki, Heyerdahl, Thor   4:221–27
Korea
   frosty relations with Japan   4:353–54
   invasion by Japan (1894–95 and 1904–05)
      4:59, 177
   occupation by Japan (1910–45)   4:349–50
   reprisals against fleeing Japanese (1944–45)
      4:350, 352 (sidebar)
Korean War   1:223; 3:73; 4:92
Kristallnacht   4:159, 162–63
Kroeber, Theodora, Ishi, Last of His Tribe   2:174–80
Ku Klux Klan
   birth of, in 1865–66   2:141 (sidebar), 412;
      3:102; 5:21
   law enforcement officers enlisting in   4:4, 202
   lynchings and violence against blacks   2:141
      (sidebar), 143 (sidebar), 412; 3:419; 5:25, 130
   re-emergence during
      1920s xenophobic, anti-Bolshevik era   2:143
         (sidebar); 3:22; 4:201–2
      1940s   4:201–2
      1960s civil rights era   5:21 (sidebar), 25
Kushner, Tony, Angels in America   5:1–10

L

Labor unions
   accused of being "red" (communist or socialist)
      3:144
   AFL (American Federation of Labor)   3:44
   African Americans excluded, then included
      2:341; 3:250; 4:210–11
   Agricultural Labor Relations Act (1975)   4:48
   anti-labor and anti-Bolshevik reactions of 1920s
      3:21–22
   attempts to limit power of, Taft-Hartley Act
      (1947)   4:172, 173 (sidebar)
   Brotherhoood of Sleeping Car Porters   3:42
   Carnegie Steel and Homestead Strike (1892)
      3:321
   CIO (Congress of Industrial Organizations)
      3:44
   "closed" and "union" shops   4:173 (sidebar)
   conflicts with management   2:328, 336 (sidebar)
   and Debs, Eugene V.   3:54
   for farm workers   3:34, 49–50, 141, 275
   growth of   2:328, 336 (sidebar), 341; 3:176
      (sidebar)
   leaders cooperating with business owners
      4:172
   leaders' corruption   4:145
   and Mexican Americans   4:172, 175–76
   National Labor Relations Act (1933)   3:128
   opposition to   3:44, 141, 155 (sidebar), 208
   Pinkerton's detectives hired to thwart   3:225

STFU (Southern Tenant Farmers' Union)   3:*208*
strikes and violence   3:*176 (sidebar)*, *179*; 4:*109*
table grape boycott   4:*175*
Language. *See* Linguistic considerations
Lasch, Christopher   4:*111*
Last of the Mohicans, The, Cooper, James Fenimore
  1:*204–10*
Latinos
  Chicanos. *See* Chicanos
  concepts of *machismo* and *marianismo*   3:*201*;
    4:*278–79, 299*; 5:*167, 173–74, 337*
  curanderos   3:*199*; 4:*45*
  decline of paternal authority   4:*172–73*
  enlisting in military for WWII   4:*44*
  help to Dust Bowl migrants   4:*297 (sidebar)*
  life in barrios   4:*172 (sidebar)*
  men admired for adultery   5:*337*
  mestizo or mixed-race heritage   5:*172, 334*
  Puerto Rico and Puerto Ricans   3:*277*;
    4:*385–86, 388–89, 401*; 5:*214–21*
  the Virgin de Guadalupe and La Malinche
    5:*173*
  women's roles   4:*299*; 5:*167–68, 173–74*
  in WWII   4:*295, 406*
  (*See also* Cuba; Mexico)
Latinos, literary works concerning
  Barrio Boy   3:*28–35*
  Bless Me, Ultima   4:*42–48*
  Heart of Aztlán   4:*171–76*
  House of the Spirits, The   5:*163–70*
  House on Mango Street, The   5:*171–77*
  Hunger of Memory   5:*178–84*
  Imagining Argentina   5:*208–13*
  In Nueva York   5:*214–21*
  Like Water for Chocolate   3:*196–202*
  Old Gringo, The   3:*277–83*
  Old Man and the Sea, The   4:*274–80*
  One Hundred Years of Solitude   2:*268–74*
  Pocho   4:*295–302*
  Time of the Hero, The   5:*333–38*
Laudanum   3:*379*
Laurents, Arthur, *et al.*, *West Side Story*   4:*384–90*
Law
  American jury system   4:*378–79*
  capital punishment   4:*379–80*; 5:*131*
  conviction, then successful appeal in Sleepy
    Lagoon murder case   4:*405*
  judicial opposition in 1980s to civil rights
    legislation   5:*1–2*
  Jury Selection and Service Act   4:*379*
  lawyers' apprenticeships and circuit riding   2:*1–2*
  legal challenges to internment of Japanese
    4:*140–41*
  legal challenges to restrictive housing covenants
    4:*310*
  as legislation. *See under individual topics, e. g.* Civil
    rights movements; Great Depression; Labor
    unions; Segregation
  weakness of Prohibition as legislation   3:*22–23,
    69*

Law enforcement
  absence on American frontier   2:*323*
  absence on rural California farms   3:*274*
  attacking civil rights protesters   5:*23 (illus.)*
  at Democratic National Convention of 1968
    5:*271*
  officers enlisting in Ku Klux Klan   4:*4, 202*
  prisons   3:*371, 374 (illus.)*
  slave patrols   2:*190 (sidebar)*
  (*See also* Crime; Vigilantism)
Lawrence, D. H.
  Rocking-Horse Winner, The   3:*344–49*
  Sons and Lovers   2:*334–39*
Leary, Timothy   5:*82–83, 324*
Leaves of Grass, Whitman, Walt   2:*195–201*
Lee, Ann   3:*95*
Lee, Harper, *To Kill a Mockingbird*   3:*390–96*
Left Hand of Darkness, The, LeGuin, Ursula
  5:*236–42*
Legend of Sleepy Hollow, The, Irving, Washington
  1:*211–18*
Legends. *See* Myth
Legislation. *See under individual topics, e. g.* Civil
  rights movements; Great Depression; Labor unions;
  Segregation
LeGuin, Ursula, *Left Hand of Darkness, The*
  5:*236–42*
Lenape (Delaware) Indians   1:*206, 219–20*
Lenin, Vladimir   4:*14, 15 (illus.)*
Leopold, King of Belgium   2:*146–47, 150–51*
Lepanto, Battle of   1:*296*
Lesbianism
  and bisexuality of Woolf   3:*357*
  hints in *Rebecca* and concern for du Maurier
    3:*327–28*
Lessing, Doris, *Golden Notebook, The*   4:*165–70*
Leuchter, Fred. A.   4:*40*
Levantine Jews   1:*248*
Levellers   1:*359*
Lewis, C. S.   1:*158*
Lewis, John L.   3:*155 (sidebar)*
Lewis, Oscar   5:*266*
Lewis, Sinclair, *Babbitt*   3:*21–27*
Liberalism, classical
  and individualism   3:*268*
  targeted by New Right   5:*136*
Liberia   2:*404*
Liddell, Alice   2:*29 (illus.)*
Light in the Forest, The, Richter, Conrad   1:*219–24*
Like Water for Chocolate, Esquivel, Laura
  3:*196–202*
Lincoln, Abraham
  biography of   2:*1–7*
  Emancipation Proclamation (1862)   2:*59, 60
    (sidebar), 135, 308, 309*
  Gettysburg Address   2:*130–36*
  influence on white South Africans of 20th
    century   4:*99*
  quote from *Declaration of Independence*   1:*99*
  on race   2:*3, 5*

Walt Whitman on   **2**:196 (sidebar)
Lindbergh, Charles   **3**:367; **4**:373
Lindner, Robert   **4**:77–78
Linguistic considerations
   alliteration   **5**:223
   Black English, or Ebonics   **5**:145, 154, 342
   Churchill's rhetoric   **4**:361–62
   colloquial prose of Lardner   **4**:262 (sidebar)
   Dutch place-names in New York   **1**:331
    (sidebar)
   English accents   **3**:4–5, 313–14
   English as melding of French and Old English
    1:183 (sidebar)
   ethnic idioms, street slang, and group
    identification   **4**:249 (sidebar), 386
   ethnic/racist slurs   **4**:32, 386
   fading/loss of native or immigrants' languages
    4:85, 142
   Gaelic League   **3**:109, 308–9
   ghetto street slang   **5**:17
   Kennedy's rhetoric   **5**:186
   King's rhetoric   **5**:223–24
   metaphor   **5**:186
   Mycenaean alphabet   **1**:172 (sidebar)
   "naming", power of   **5**:176
   non-Greek-speakers as barbarians   **1**:173
    (sidebar)
   oratory, rhetoric of speeches   **5**:186, 223
   Phoenician alphabet   **1**:286–87
   plain, simple language of common men
    1:72–73, 76, 163, 342
   pronouns, inclusive   **5**:186
   puns in Shakespeare   **1**:348–49
   puns in Victorian Age   **2**:30
   repetition   **5**:186
   rhyme   **5**:223
   rhythm   **5**:223
   Roman names   **1**:190
   Roosevelt's (Franklin Delano) rhetoric   **3**:127
   Southern dialect
    in *Cold Sassy Tree*   **3**:79
    in *Color Purple, The*   **3**:87
    in *Gathering of Old Men, A*   **5**:133
    in *Huckleberry Finn*   **2**:17
    in *Uncle Remus*   **2**:397, 398–99
   Southwestern dialects   **4**:321 (sidebar)
   suppression of native languages by colonialists
    4:350
   Western dialect in *Notorious Jumping Frog*   **2**:252
   Yiddish   **3**:120
Linguistic considerations: etymological
   "acid and acid heads"   **5**:83
   barrios   **4**:44
   "bindlestiffs"   **3**:269–70, 275
   "blackamoor"   **4**:54
   "blacklisting"   **3**:178; **4**:72
   "Catch-22"   **4**:70 (sidebar)
   "Chinaman's chance"   **2**:368
   "colored", "Negro", "African American" and
    "black"   **5**:120 (sidebar)

   "coolies"   **4**:124
   "democracy", Paine's redefinition of   **1**:74
   "dry" years and "Drys"   **3**:69, 75
   "Dust Bowl"   **3**:46
   "flappers"   **3**:147
   "flipping" trains   **3**:46
   "freaking out"   **5**:83
   "gas him"   **5**:37 (sidebar)
   "ghetto"   **1**:244
   "greasers"   **5**:266
   "Hoovervilles"   **3**:126
   "Jim Crow"   **2**:21, 341
   "lost generation" (post-WWI)   **3**:13, 112,
    116–17
   "mashers"   **2**:331
   "moonshine"   **3**:69
   "no man's land"   **3**:9, 113
   "octoroons"   **3**:18
   "Okies"   **3**:46
   "*pachuco*"   **4**:173, 296
   "quadroons"   **3**:17–18
   "revolution," Paine's redefinition of   **1**:74
   "runrummers"   **3**:147
   "Say it ain't so, Joe"   **3**:150
   "Simon Legree"   **2**:409
   "skid row"   **3**:46
   "speakeasies"   **3**:69, 147
   "Tenderloin"   **4**:37
   "trench foot"   **3**:9
   "trips and bad trips"   **5**:83
   "Uncle Tom"   **2**:409
   "wage slavery"   **3**:179
   "Walter Mitty"   **3**:369
Lipsyte, Robert, *Contender, The*   **5**:67–73
Literature
   for adolescents and young adults, as genre
    5:61–62, 265–66, 268–70, 331
   allegory and fable   **4**:16 (sidebar), 19
   almanacs (*Poor Richard's Almanac*)   **1**:309–15
   bildungsroman   **3**:264, 311; **4**:47
   calendarios de las señoritas (Mexican magazines for
    women)   **3**:196–97
   choreopoems   **5**:117–18
   crime stories and "Newgate Novels"   **2**:83, 267
   detective fiction   **2**:325; **3**:226–27
   development in 17th-century French salons
    1:88
   "dime" novels with romance, adventure, and
    violence   **2**:306; **3**:226–27
   dystopian   **5**:100, 141, 252
   of Enlightenment   **2**:211 (sidebar)
   for ethnic groups, minorities   **5**:62
   future history   **5**:127
   Gothic horror stories and romances   **2**:81, 85,
    185; **3**:338
   horror fiction   **5**:46–47
   Imagism   **3**:413–14
   Latin American   **2**:273
   "magical" realism   **2**:271, 273; **3**:196, 202; **4**:48;
    5:169, 213, 330

novels, birth of   1:*341–42*
pornographic   3:*381*
printing and publishing, impact of advances in
   1:*160, 162 (sidebar);* 2:*234, 306, 419*
pulp magazines   2:*325;* 3:*226–27*
realism. *See* Realism
repetition as literary device   4:*70*
romance novels of 1980s   5:*331*
romances   2:*210*
of Romantic era. *See* Romantic movement
satirical. *See* Satire
science fiction. *See* Science fiction
slave narratives. *See* Slave narratives
Southern renaissance in   3:*421*
stream of consciousness technique   3:*111, 358*
thrillers, psychological   3:*328–29*
utopian   5:*251–52*
westerns   2:*321, 325*
Wilder's view of importance of   3:*288*
writers
   benefitting from New Deal's Federal Writers'
      Project   3:*237*
   patrons for   1:*88*
   prejudice against women as   2:*186, 203,
      212, 424–25;* 5:*282 (sidebar)*
   (*See also* Biography (and autobiography);
      Censorship and banning of literary works;
      Documents; Essays; Narratives; Novels; Plays;
      Short stories; Speeches)
Little Foxes, The, Hellman, Lillian   3:*203–10*
Little Prince, The, Saint-Exupéry, Antoine de
   3:*210–17*
Little Women, Alcott, Louisa May   2:*202–8*
Locke, Alain   3:*256, 389*
Locke, John   1:*100*
London, England   1:*417*
London, Jack, *Call of the Wild, The*   3:*51–56*
Long Day's Journey into Night, O'Neill, Eugene
   3:*218–24*
López, Dr. Roderigo   1:*248*
Lord of the Flies, Golding, William   4:*228–34*
"Lost generation" (post-WWI)   3:*13, 112, 116–17*
Lotteries   4:*235–36*
Lottery, The, Jackson, Shirley   4:*235–39*
Louis Napoleon   2:*228–29*
Louis Phillippe of France   1:*164*
Louis XI of France   1:*160*
Louis XIII of France   1:*386, 387, 388*
Louis XIV of France   1:*31, 87, 88, 130, 386, 387;*
   3:*212*
Louis XVI of France   1:*51, 358, 359, 372*
Louis XVIII of France   1:*391*
Louisiana   3:*15–18;* 4:*365–66;* 5:*21, 22, 25, 130,
   131–32*
L'Ouverture, Toussaint   5:*116–17*
Love and marriage
   in 18th-century France   1:*31*
   according to Thurber   3:*367–68*
   adultery/infidelity   5:*273, 287*
   in ancient Greece   1:*285*

children of immigrants marrying Caucasians
   5:*232*
   in China and Chinese culture   3:*132, 192–93,
      194;* 4:*128*
   in colonial America   1:*24*
   debutantes' "coming out"   3:*326–27*
   in early 17th-century England   1:*263–64, 385*
   for Emily Dickinson   2:*55–56, 57*
   for England's landed gentry   1:*414;* 2:*296,
      354–55;* 3:*326–27*
   happiness versus duty in   3:*271–72*
   Japanese "picture brides"   4:*331–32*
   polygamy   5:*4*
   problems of adjustment to retirement   5:*203,
      273*
   sexual dimension of, in 19th century   2:*212,
      423*
   or spinsterhood   2:*297*
   for traditional Jews   3:*119, 123*
   for underage teens   5:*151*
   in Victorian Age   2:*116, 336*
   War Brides Act (1945)   4:*124, 127;* 5:*231*
   Wollstonecraft on   1:*410–11*
   for women of 1970s   2:*58*
   (*See also* Divorce; Family and family life)
Love and marriage, works emphasizing
   Anna Karenina   2:*34–40*
   *Beauty: A Retelling of the Story of Beauty and the
      Beast*   1:*30–36*
   Color Purple, The   3:*80–87*
   Daisy Miller   2:*105–10*
   Doll's House, A   2:*111–17*
   Ethan Frome   2:*125–29*
   Farewell to Arms, A   3:*112–18*
   Gone with the Wind   2:*137–44*
   Handmaid's Tale, The   5:*135–42*
   His Own Where   5:*149–55*
   House of Mirth, The   3:*166–73*
   Jane Eyre   2:*181–87*
   Kitchen God's Wife, The   3:*189–95*
   Like Water for Chocolate   3:*196–202*
   Love Medicine   5:*243–50*
   Madame Bovary   2:*209–15*
   Merchant of Venice, The   1:*247*
   Othello   1:*297*
   Pride and Prejudice   2:*295–300*
   Romeo and Juliet   1:*346*
   Scarlet Letter   1:*351–57*
   Seventeen Syllables   4:*330–36*
   Sons and Lovers   2:*334–39*
   Tess of the D'Urbervilles   2:*353–59*
   Wuthering Heights   1:*413–19*
Love Medicine, Erdrich, Louise   5:*243–50*
Lower classes   1:*363, 366 (sidebar), 366*
LSD (lysergic acid diethylamide)   4:*288, 289, 292,
   293–94;* 5:*82–83, 324–25*
Luce, William, *Belle of Amherst, The*   2:*54–58*
Lucifer. *See* Devil (Satan)
Luddite movement   1:*119–20, 120 (illus.)*
Luther, Martin   1:*231–32, 232 (illus.);* 2:*113*

Luxembourg   4:254–55

Lynching

advocation of, by racist propaganda   2:400

anti-lynching crusader Ida B. Wells-Barnett
3:83, 238

ASWPL (Association of Southern Women for the
Prevention of Lynching)   3:391–92; 5:133

of black soldiers during WWII   4:197

"defense of white womanhood" excuse   5:133

Dyer Antilynching Bill   3:392

economic aspect of excuses for   3:83, 391

estimates of deaths from   2:341; 3:37, 83, 238,
419; 4:202; 5:131

FDR's reason for refusal to sign Dyer
Antilynching Bill   3:154, 392; 4:202

horrific cruelties of   2:412; 3:274, 391

increasing with desperation of Great Depression
(1930s)   3:45

by Ku Klux Klan   2:141 (sidebar), 143 (sidebar),
412; 3:419; 5:130–31

in Northern states   3:238

perpetrators generally escaping punishment
3:274

police joining mobs   4:4, 202

to prevent exercise of voting rights   2:412; 3:419

sexual aspect of excuses for   3:83, 238, 273

as Southern phenomenon   3:238

of whites   3:273–74

M

MacArthur, Douglas   4:80–81, 350

Macbeth, Shakespeare, William   1:225–30

McCarthy, Joseph and McCarthyism   1:84, 398;
3:208, 209 (illus.); 4:71, 110, 398; 5:2, 3 (illus.), 96,
97, 127

McCullers, Carson

Heart Is a Lonely Hunter, The   3:153–58

Member of the Wedding, The   4:254–59

McCunn, Ruthanne Lum, Thousand Pieces of Gold
2:366–71

Machiavelli, Niccolò, Prince, The   1:316–20

McKay, Claude, Home to Harlem   3:159–65

McKinley, Robin, Beauty: A Retelling of the Story of
Beauty and the Beast   1:30–36

McMullin, Fred   3:149

Madame Bovary, Flaubert, Gustave   2:209–15

Madero, Francisco   3:29, 197, 278

"Magical" realism   2:271, 273; 3:196, 202; 4:48;
5:169, 213, 330

Magna Carta   1:255

Maimon, Solomon   4:88

Malamud, Bernard, Natural, The   4:260–66

Malcolm II of Scotland   1:225

Malcolm III of Scotland   1:226

Mallory, Thomas   1:290, 293

Maltese Falcon, The, Hammett, Dashiell   3:225–30

Man for All Seasons, A, Bolt, Robert   1:231–37

Man without a Face, The, Holland, Isabelle
4:240–46

Manchild in the Promised Land, Brown, Claude
4:247–53

Manchuria   4:59, 178, 350; 5:230

Manhattan Project   4:71, 81–82, 316

Manifest Destiny   2:76 (sidebar); 3:234

Manorial system   1:251

Mao Zedong   3:136, 189; 5:254

Mark Antony   1:13, 189, 191

Marooning   1:401–2

Marranos   1:248, 249

Marsh, Ngaio   3:329

Marshall Plan   5:123–24, 224, 292

Martinez, Vilma   5:179

Marx, Karl   1:376; 3:232

Marxism

concept of capitalists versus proletariat   3:321

concepts of "wage slavery" and "estranged labor"
3:179; 4:18–19

in Czarist Russia   3:59

(See also Communism)

Mary Stuart, Queen of Scots   1:141, 149–50, 349

Masons (Freemasons)   2:82

Mather, Cotton

associated with Puritan excess   1:213

comparison to J. Edgar Hoover   1:84 (sidebar)

excerpt from Bonifacius   1:28

impact of Memorable Providences   1:79, 80, 396

impact of The Wonders of the Invisible World
1:80 (illus.), 80, 422, 424

Mather, Increase   1:424

Matlovich, Leonard Jr.   4:39

Maugham, W. Somerset, Of Human Bondage
3:264–68

Maupassant, Guy de, Necklace, The   2:244–48

Meat-packing industry   3:175

Medea, Euripides   1:238–41

Media

black press airing grievances of black soldiers in
WWII   4:195

contributing to anti-Japanese hysteria of WWII
4:138, 140, 141, 194

creating crime-ridden image of Central Park
4:401

decrying racial violence   4:310 (sidebar)

fanning 1940s hysteria over zoot suiters and
"Mexican goon squads"   4:296, 404, 405

FDR's popularity with and concealment of
disability   3:127

misrepresentation of "black power"   4:56

misrepresentation of Malcolm X   5:16

muckraking journalists   3:176, 320

"New Journalism"   5:293

overlooking violence against minorities and
homeless   4:401

patriotic emphasis during WWII   4:371

role in consolidation of Japanese culture in
California   4:332

use of, for propaganda   4:66–67

and "yellow journalism"   3:279

(See also Television)

Medici, House of   1:*316, 317, 318*
Medici, Marie de'   1:*387*
Medicine
   ambulances of WWI   3:*114*
   Chinese   3:*194 (sidebar)*
   Chippewa "love medicine"   5:*249*
   homeopathy   3:*68–69*
   Indian remedies   3:*68–69*; 5:*249*
   Latino *curanderos*   3:*199*; 4:*45*
   as male dominated   4:*218*
   midwifery   4:*218*
   Navajo Night Chant   4:*188*
   opium products   3:*379*
   penicillin   3:*366*
   polio vaccines   4:*10*
   "socialized", 1950s fear of   4:*12*
   (*See also* Diseases)
Mediterranean
   Albania   2:*101*
   in ancient times   1:*9*
   Egypt   4:*107*
   Ethiopia   4:*67*
   Palestine   4:*102–3, 105*; 5:*54*
   Peloponnesian War   1:*241, 324, 328*
   Sicily   4:*67*
   Suez Canal   3:*184*; 4:*107*
   (*See also* Greece in ancient times; Israel; Italy;
     Turkey)
Melanesia   4:*222*
Melville, Herman   2:*92*
   Benito Cereno   1:*37–43*
   Billy Budd   1:*51–56*
   Moby Dick   2:*230–35*
   praise for *Young Goodman Brown*   1:*425*
Member of the Wedding, The, McCullers, Carson
   4:*254–59*
Mencken, H. L.
   on *Babbitt*   3:*25, 27*
   influence on Sinclair Lewis   3:*26–27*
   on Scopes Trial   3:*102 (sidebar)*
   on Southern culture   3:*40 (sidebar)*
Mendel, Gregor   2:*217*
Mendelssohn, Moses   4:*88*
Menelaus   1:*281*
Mental and emotional disabilities
   association with pressure to conform   4:*74*
   asylums/institutions
      abuses in   3:*244–45*
      and deinstitutionalization   4:*289*
      as fashionable "resorts"   3:*413*
      hospitalization in   3:*272*; 4:*77*
   changing attitudes in 1950s and '60s   4:*151–56*
   connectedness of mental health and human
     relationships   4:*153*
   developments in psychology   3:*329, 378*; 4:*77*
   education for children   4:*151–52*
   effects of childhood abuse   5:*289–90*
   eugenic sterilization of retarded   3:*272*; 4:*152*;
     5:*41, 42*
   Fetal Alcohol Syndrome   5:*361*

   "frontier madness"   3:*259*
   history of   4:*288–89*
   National Association for Retarded Children
     (NARC)   4:*151*
   in Shakespeare's time   1:*139 (sidebar), 203*
   stigma of   5:*262–63*
   targeted by Nazis in Holocaust   4:*119*
   treatments for
     electroconvulsive therapy (ECT)   4:*24*
      (sidebar), *289–90*
     lobotomy   4:*290*
     methods of 1940s and '50s   4:*289–90*
     pyschosurgery   4:*290*
     "rest cure"   2:*425–26*
     tranquilizing drugs   4:*289*
   in Victorian Age   2:*119–20, 184, 185–86,*
     278–79
   writers suffering from
     T. S. Eliot's wife   3:*412–13*
     Gilman   2:*427*
     Plath   4:*21–26*
     Woolf   3:*358*
   of WWII veterans   4:*80 (sidebar), 325*
Merchant of Venice, Shakespeare, William
   1:*242–49*
   parallels to *Ivanhoe*   1:*187*
Meredith, James   5:*19*
Merry Adventures of Robin Hood, The, Pyle, Howard
   1:*250–57*
Merton, Thomas   5:*280–81*
Metamorphoses, Ovid   1:*262*
Methodism   2:*357–58*
Mexican Americans. *See* Chicanos; Latinos
Mexican War   2:*88, 89, 242*; 5:*172*
Mexico
   Bracero Program (1942–1964)   3:*34*; 4:*44*
   close ties to U.S.   3:*282*
   dictatorship of Díaz (1876–1910)   3:*28–30*
   ejidos system   3:*282*
   hacienda system   3:*29, 278, 282*
   immigration to U.S. from   3:*282*; 4:*44–48*
   mining industry   3:*28*
   PRI and one-party democracy   3:*282*
   Revolution (1910–20)   3:*29, 278–79*; 4:*295,*
     296 (sidebar)
   women in   3:*197–98, 200–202*
Micronesia   4:*222*
Middle Ages
   as depicted in *Beowulf*   1:*44–50*
   as depicted in Chaucer   1:*64–70*
   importance of kings and kinship   1:*153*
Middle class, rise of
   African Americans in 20th century   3:*252, 255,*
     387–88; 4:*2, 51*
   in American East   2:*303, 306*
   bourgeoisie of France   2:*209–10, 245–46*
   in England   1:*66, 72, 338, 342, 371*; 2:*118, 153,*
     354; 3:*312*
   importance of proper manners   2:*297*
   moving to suburbs   4:*73*

Index

replacing aristocray of Old South   4:364–65
Midsummer Night's Dream, A, Shakespeare, William
    1:258–65
Midwifery   4:218
Migrant farm workers   3:29–30, 34, 49, 140–42,
    143 (sidebar), 269–71, 275, 335, 337; 4:297
    (sidebar)
    braceros   3:34; 4:44
Milan, Italy   1:379–80
Military
    African Americans in   3:160, 424
    American Indians in   4:80, 185–87; 5:362–63
    anti-Semitism in   4:36–37
    Army training camps   4:36
    authority and mutiny   4:63–64
    British "batmen"   3:348
    Claire Chennault and American Volunteer Group
        3:190
    desertion during Civil War   2:10–11, 312
    desertion in Vietnam   2:13 (sidebar)
    and "Flying Tigers"   3:190
    homosexuals in   4:38, 39–40
    illicit wartime amusements   4:37, 38
    Latinos in   4:44
    racial discrimination in   3:41–42; 4:195, 197,
        212
    reservists and regulars   4:63 (sidebar)
    United Service Organizations (USO)   4:38
    (See also War)
Military draft
    of American Indians for WWII   4:80
    of blacks for Vietnam   5:102–3
    of Chicanos for Vietnam   4:176
    of Chinese Americans for WWII   4:127
    of disadvantaged for Vietnam (Project 100,000)
        5:102–3, 158, 307
    dodging and avoiding   2:256, 309; 4:324, 327
    induction process   4:35–36
    of Nisei for WWII   4:140 (sidebar)
    of poor/lower classes for Civil War   2:256, 309
    of Puerto Ricans for WWI   5:215
    as target of blacks' protest   4:213
    for WWII in 1940   4:35, 324–25
Mill, John Stuart   2:182 (sidebar)
Miller, Arthur
    Crucible, The   1:78–86
    Death of a Salesman   4:109–15
    importance in American theater   1:85
Mills, C. Wright   4:74
Milton, John, *Paradise Lost*   1:301–8
Minh, Ho Chi   5:101
Mining industry
    accidents and disease   2:335
    child labor   2:335 (sidebar)
    in Chile   5:163, 164
    Chinese in   2:367; 5:352
    coal   3:63, 64; 4:9; 5:39–40
    in Mexico   3:28
    (See also Gold rushes and silver strikes; *Thousand
        Pieces of Gold*)

Minotaur   1:259
Minstrel shows   2:16–17, 21
Miracle Worker, The, Gibson, William   2:216–22
Les Misérables, Hugo, Victor   2:223–29
Missionaries   2:118–19, 147, 161–62, 361–62;
    3:133, 280; 5:195
Mississippi River   2:16, 17
Missouri Compromise (1820)   2:5 (sidebar), 15–16,
    22
Mitchell, Margaret, *Gone with the Wind*   2:137–44
Mitnagdim   3:426
Moby Dick, Melville, Herman   2:230–35
Modernism   3:411; 5:42
Modest Proposal, A, Swift, Jonathan   1:266–72
Mohammed, Sufi Abdul   4:211
Mohr, Nicholasa, *In Nueva York*   5:214–21
Momaday, N. Scott, *House Made of Dawn*
    4:185–92
Monasticism   3:186–87
    Trappist monks   5:280
Money
    in colonial America   1:103–4, 310
    "Wood's Coins" in Ireland   1:268
Moneylending (usury)   1:103–4, 182–83, 243
    (sidebar), 243, 247
Monro, Lt. Col. George   1:205
Monroe, James   1:209
Moors   1:297, 299; 3:212, 213
More, Sir Thomas   1:232, 233, 237
Mormonism   5:4
Morrison, Toni
    Beloved   2:59–65
    Bluest Eye, The   4:49–57
Mortimer family   1:144, 145
Most Dangerous Game, The, Connell, Richard
    3:231–35
Motion pictures. *See* Hollywood and motion picture
    industry
Mott, Lucretia Coffin   2:24, 55; 3:16
Moynihan, Daniel
    Moynihan Report (1965)   3:355, 375
    on Project 100,000   5:103
Muhammad, Elijah   3:239 (illus.); 4:249; 5:13, 69,
    110–11
Mulattos   3:18
Multiculturalism
    America as "salad bowl" rather than melting pot
        5:176
    encouraging autobiographies   3:32, 34
    ethnic studies programs
        African American history   5:147–48
        in Black English, or Ebonics   5:145, 154,
            342
        increasing college enrollments   5:217
        Puerto Rican history and culture   5:217
    and women's studies   5:117
    (See also African Americans; American Indians;
        Chinese and Chinese Americans; Japanese and
        Japanese Americans; Jews; Latinos; Puerto Rico
        and Puerto Ricans)

Murphy, Charles F.   3:*148*, *399*

Music
   blues   3:*254* (sidebar); 4:*258*
   Chinese opera   5:*75*
   and dance   4:*387*
   effectiveness in theatrical productions   4:*258*
   folksongs of 1930s and 1940s   3:*47*, *128*
   gospel songs and black spirituals   2:*398*, *402*,
     407; 4:*258*
   importance to slaves   2:*398*
   jazz   3:*162* (sidebar); 4:*258*
   New Chilean Song   5:*164*
   ragtime   3:*321* (sidebar)
   reflecting generation gap   4:*386*
   rock 'n' roll   4:*172*, *386*, *391–92*
   Smith, Bessie   3:*253* (illus.)
   Welsh regard for   3:*65*

Musicals
   *for colored girls who have considered suicide / when
     the rainbow is enuf*, Shange, Ntozake
     5:*115–21*
   golden age on Broadway   4:*387*
   West Side Story, Laurents, Arthur, *et al.*
     4:*384–90*

Musketeers   1:*386*, *387*

Muslim Turks   1:*296*

Mussolini, Benito   2:*293–94*; 4:*66–67*, *305* (illus.)

Mutiny
   aboard *Amistad*   1:*43*
   aboard HMS *Bounty*   1:*273–79*, *276* (illus.)
   aboard USS *Somers*   1:*56*
   in *Benito Cereno*   1:*37–43*
   in *Billy Budd*   1:*51–56*
   in *Caine Mutiny, The*   4:*58–65*
   at Spithead and Nore   1:*53*

Mutiny on the Bounty, Nordhoff, Charles and James
   Norman Hall   1:*273–79*

Mycenaean Age of ancient Greece   1:*57–59*, *167*,
   258, *281–82*, *283* (sidebar)

Myers, Walter Dean, *Fallen Angels*   5:*101–6*

Mystery and detective stories
   Hound of the Baskervilles   2:*152–59*
   Jane Eyre   1:*415* (sidebar), *419*; 2:*181–87*
   Maltese Falcon, The   3:*225–30*
   rise of   2:*325*; 3:*226–27*

Mysticism   1:*416*
   Hasidic Jews   3:*425*, *426*

Myth
   Arthurian   1:*288*, *290*
   Chinese   5:*77* (sidebar), *358*
   and comparative anthropology   5:*42*
   creation of   1:*152*
   disguising contemporary social criticism   1:*15*,
     63
   founding of Rome   1:*10* (sidebar)
   Holy Grail legends   4:*264–65*
   Irish   3:*109*
   Mexican and Aztlán   4:*173*, *174–75*, *176*
   Norse   1:*50*, *152*, *153*, *156*
   (*See also* Folklore and fairy tales; Greek myth)

N

NAACP (National Association for the Advancement
   of Colored People)   2:*342*, *415*; 3:*250*, *320*, *396*;
   4:*195*, *255*, *310*; 5:*88*, *120* (sidebar)

Nairobi   3:*293*

"Naming", power of   5:*176*

Napoleon Bonaparte   1:*163*, *391*; 2:*99–100*, *224*,
   225 (sidebar), *295–96*

Napoleonic code   4:*365*

Narrative of the Life of Frederick Douglass, Douglass,
   Frederick   2:*236–41*
   inspiring resistance on part of slaves   2:*16*

Narratives
   Black Elk Speaks, Neihardt, John G.   2:*66–73*
   Bury My Heart at Wounded Knee, Brown, Dee
     2:*74–80*
   Kon-Tiki, Heyerdahl, Thor   4:*221–27*
   Two Years before the Mast, Dana, Richard Henry,
     Jr.   2:*391–96*
   (*See also* Slave narratives)

NASA (National Aeronautics and Space
   Administration)   5:*81*, *291*

Nation of Islam   3:*238*, *325*; 4:*56*, *248–50*;
   5:*12–13*, *69*, *110–11*, *302*

National Labor Relations Act (1933)   3:*128*

National Organization of Women (NOW)   1:*62*;
   4:*22*, *394*; 5:*136*, *237*

Nationalism
   and anti-Semitism   1:*364*
   as aspect of fascism   4:*304*
   of Black Muslims and Nation of Islam   3:*238*,
     325; 4:*56*, *248–50*; 5:*12–13*, *69*, *110–11*, *302*
   of black separatists   3:*160*
   caused by economic hardship   1:*113*
   ethnic movements   1:*363–64*
   extremes of   1:*292*, *293–94*
   in *Hound of the Baskervilles*   2:*157*
   under Young Turks   3:*339*

Native Americans. *See* American Indians

Native Son, Wright, Richard   3:*236–42*

NATO (North Atlantic Treaty Organization)
   5:*124*, *224*, *292*

Natural, The, Malamud, Bernard   4:*260–66*

Naturalism   1:*293*

Nature
   celebration of   1:*413*, *416*
   (*See also* Romantic movement)

Nazis
   achieving dictatorship   4:*158*
   anti-Semitism fostering emigration of Jews
     4:*102*
   condemnation of *All Quiet on the Western Front*
     3:*13*
   countries conquered by   5:*123* (sidebar)
   escaping to Argentina   5:*210*
   execution of Remarque's sister   3:*14*
   Great Depression enhancing appeal of facism
     3:*129*
   nationalism of   1:*294*

neo-nazis   4:163–64
   plans for extermination of Jews and
      "undesirables"   3:124
   rabid racism and belief in Aryan superiority
      4:158, 193; 5:42
   remilitarization of Germany   4:356–57
   rise of and consolidation of power   4:157, 158,
      356–57
   (See also Holocaust; World War II)
Nebraska   3:257–58, 260
Necklace, The, Maupassant, Guy de   2:244–48
Neihardt, John G., Black Elk Speaks   2:66–73
Neruda, Pablo   5:164, 168
New Deal. See under Great Depression, The
New England
   agricultural decline   2:125–26
   Boston   3:43
   Boston Tea Party   1:125
   Massachusetts   1:78–80, 355, 395–97
"New Journalism"   5:293
New Mexico
   Chicano life in   4:45, 171
   Gallup   4:83
   Laguna Pueblo   4:79–80, 85
   Los Alamos   4:81, 316–17
   Manhattan Project   4:71, 81–82, 316–17
   Sagrado   4:318
   Tierra Amarilla   4:174
   Trinity Site detonation of atom bomb   4:81–82
   Walatowa (Jemez Pueblo)   4:187
   WWII village life   4:318–21
New Netherland (New York)   1:211, 212
New Orleans   3:15
New York
   Brooklyn   3:397–98; 4:88; 5:149–51
   Chinatown   4:126
   Dutch in (New Netherland)   1:211, 212,
      330–32, 333 (illus.), 335 (sidebar), 336
   Hudson Valley   1:330–32, 333 (illus.), 334–35,
      336
   in late 18th century   1:107–8, 110
   Mohawk Valley   1:108, 110, 112 (illus.)
   New York City   2:301–7, 313; 3:146–47
      Central Park   4:401
      "garbage riots" (1969)   5:220 (sidebar)
      Harlem   4:247–48; 5:67–68
      Harlem and Harlem Renaissance   3:159–65,
         256, 321, 384–85, 421; 4:204 (sidebar), 207
      Harlem Renaissance   3:159–65, 256, 384–85,
         421
      Manhattan's West Side   4:384–89, 400–401
      Puerto Ricans   4:385–86, 388–89, 401;
         5:214–21
      Spanish Harlem (El Barrio)   5:214, 216–17
      Tweed Ring   2:306–7
      Tammany Hall   3:148–49, 398–99
Newspapers
   origins of   1:268
   "yellow journalism"   3:279
Newton, Huey P.   4:54

Newton, Sir Isaac   1:24, 94
Niagara Movement (1905)   3:250, 320
Nicholas II, Czar of Russia   3:121, 232
Nietzsche, Friedrich   3:54
Nigeria   2:360–62, 364–65; 3:84; 4:314
Night, Wiesel, Elie   4:267–73
Nineteen Eighty-Four, Orwell, George   5:251–58
   as dystopian   5:100
Nirvana   1:366, 367
Nixon, Richard
   "kitchen debate" with Khrushchev   4:398, 399
      (illus.); 5:321–22
   loss to Kennedy attributed to poor appearance on
      TV   5:223
   use of anti-communism for campaign   5:96
   visit to Communist China   5:358
   Watergate scandal   3:99; 5:158–59, 263, 317
Nonfiction
   almanacs (Poor Richard's Almanac)   1:309–15
   Kon-Tiki, Heyerdahl, Thor
   Right Stuff, The, Wolfe, Tom   5:291–97
   Two Years before the Mast, Dana, Richard Henry,
      Jr.   2:391–96
   (See also Biography (and autobiography);
      Documents; Essays; Slave narratives; Speeches)
Noon Wine, Porter, Katherine Anne   3:243–48
Nordhoff, Charles, Mutiny on the Bounty   1:273–79
Norman Conquest of Anglo-Saxon England   1:181,
   250–51, 290
Norse myths   1:50, 152, 153, 156
North Carolina   2:168
North Dakota   5:244
Norway   1:137–38; 2:111–13
Not without Laughter, Hughes, Langston   3:249–56
Notorious Jumping Frog of Calaveras County, The,
   Twain, Mark   2:249–54
Notre Dame cathedral   1:161, 162 (illus.), 163, 164
   (sidebar)
Novellas
   Awakening, The, Chopin, Kate   3:15–20
   Daisy Miller, James, Henry   2:105–10
   Heart of Darkness, The, Conrad, Joseph
      2:145–51
   Of Mice and Men, Steinbeck, John   3:269–76
   Turn of the Screw, The, James, Henry   2:378–83
Novels
   birth of   1:341–42
   Across Five Aprils, Hunt, Irene   2:8–14
   Adventures of Don Quixote, The, Cervantes
      Saavedra, Miguel de   1:1–7
   Adventures of Huckleberry Finn, The, Twain, Mark
      2:15–21
   Alice's Adventures in Wonderland, Carroll, Lewis
      2:28–33
   All Creatures Great and Small, Herriott, James
      3:1–7
   All Quiet on the Western Front, Remarque, Erich
      Maria   3:8–14
   Animal Farm, Orwell, George   4:14–20
   Anna Karenina, Tolstoy, Leo   2:34–40

Autobiography of Miss Jane Pittman, The, Gaines, Ernest J.   **5**:*19–26*

Babbitt, Lewis, Sinclair   **3**:*21–27*

Bean Trees, The, Kingsolver, Barbara   **5**:*27–33*

Beauty: A Retelling of the Story of Beauty and the Beast, McKinley, Robin   **1**:*30–36*

Bell Jar, The, Plath, Sylvia   **4**:*21–27*

Beloved, Morrison, Toni   **2**:*59–65*

Benito Cereno, Melville, Herman   **1**:*37–43*

Betsey Brown, Shange, Ntozake   **4**:*28–34*

Billy Budd, Melville, Herman   **1**:*51–56*

Bless the Beasts and Children, Swarthout, Glendon   **5**:*34–38*

Bless Me, Ultima, Anaya, Rudolfo A.   **4**:*42–48*

Bluest Eye, The, Morrison, Toni   **4**:*49–57*

Brave New World, Huxley, Aldous   **5**:*39–45*

Bull from the Sea, The, Renault, Mary   **1**:*57–63*

Caine Mutiny, The, Wouk, Herman   **4**:*58–65*

Call of the Wild, The, London, Jack   **3**:*51–56*

Carrie, King, Stephen   **5**:*46–52*

Catch-22, Heller, Joseph   **4**:*66-72*

Catcher in the Rye, Salinger, J. D.   **4**:*73–78*

Ceremony, Silko, Leslie Marmon   **4**:*79–86*

Childhood's End, Clarke, Arthur   **5**:*53–60*

Chocolate War, The, Cormier, Robert   **5**:*61–66*

Chosen, The, Potok, Chaim   **4**:*87–93*

Cold Sassy Tree, Burns, Olive Ann   **3**:*75–79*

Color Purple, The, Walker, Alice   **3**:*80–87*

Confessions of Nat Turner, The, Styron, William   **2**:*93–98*

Contender, The, Lipsyte, Robert   **5**:*67–73*

Count of Monte-Cristo, The, Dumas, Alexandre   **2**:*99–104*

Cry, the Beloved Country, Paton, Alan   **4**:*94–100*

Dandelion Wine, Bradbury, Ray   **3**:*88–93*

Dawn, Wiesel, Elie   **4**:*101–8*

Day No Pigs Would Die, A, Peck, Robert Newton   **3**:*94–99*

Death in the Family, A, Agee, James   **3**:*100–105*

Donald Duk, Chin, Frank   **5**:*74–80*

Drums Along the Mohawk, Edmonds, Walter D.   **1**:*107–14*

Dune, Herbert, Frank   **5**:*81–87*

Eat a Bowl of Tea, Chu, Luis   **4**:*124–30*

Ethan Frome, Wharton, Edith   **2**:*125–29*

Fahrenheit 451, Bradbury, Ray   **5**:*95–100*

Fallen Angels, Myers, Walter Dean   **5**:*101–6*

Farewell to Arms, A, Hemingway, Ernest   **3**:*112–18*

Flowers for Algernon, Keyes, Daniel   **4**:*151–56*

Foundation, Asimov, Isaac   **5**:*122–28*

Frankenstein, Shelley, Mary   **1**:*115–21*

Friedrich, Richter, Hans Peter   **4**:*157–64*

Gathering of Old Men, A, Gaines, Ernest J.   **5**:*129–34*

Golden Notebook, The, Lessing, Doris   **4**:*165–70*

Gone with the Wind, Mitchell, Margaret   **2**:*137–44*

Good Earth, The, Buck, Pearl S.   **3**:*131–37*

Grapes of Wrath, The, Steinbeck, John   **3**:*138–45*

Great Gatsby, The, Fitzgerald, F. Scott   **3**:*146–52*

Gulliver's Travels, Swift, Jonathan   **1**:*129–35*

Handmaid's Tale, The, Atwood, Margaret   **5**:*135–42*

Heart of Aztlán, Anaya, Rudolfo A.   **4**:*171–76*

Heart Is a Lonely Hunter, The, McCullers, Carson   **3**:*153–58*

Hero Ain't Nothin' but a Sandwich, A, Childress, Alice   **5**:*143–48*

His Own Where, Jordan, June   **5**:*149–55*

Hobbit, The, Tolkien, J.R.R.   **1**:*152–58*

Home to Harlem, McKay, Claude   **3**:*159–65*

Hound of the Baskervilles, Doyle, Arthur Conan   **2**:*152–59*

House Made of Dawn, Momaday, N. Scott   **4**:*185–92*

House of Mirth, The, Wharton, Edith   **3**:*166–73*

House of Stairs, Sleator, William   **5**:*156–62*

House of the Spirits, The, Allende, Isabel   **5**:*163–70*

House on Mango Street, The, Cisneros, Sandra   **5**:*171–77*

Human Comedy, The, Saroyan, William   **4**:*193–200*

Hunchback of Notre Dame, The, Hugo, Victor   **1**:*159–65*

I Heard the Owl Call My Name, Craven, Margaret   **5**:*194–200*

Imagining Argentina, Thornton, Laurence   **5**:*208–13*

In Nueva York, Mohr, Nicholasa   **5**:*214–21*

Invisible Man, Ellison, Ralph   **4**:*209–15*

Ishi, Last of His Tribe, Kroeber, Theodora   **2**:*174–80*

Ivanhoe, Scott, Sir Walter   **1**:*181–88*

Jacob Have I Loved, Paterson, Katherine   **4**:*216–20*

Jane Eyre, Brontë, Charlotte   **2**:*181–87*

Joy Luck Club, The, Tan, Amy   **5**:*229–35*

Jungle, The, Sinclair, Upton   **3**:*174–80*

Kim, Kipling, Rudyard   **3**:*181–88*

Kitchen God's Wife, The, Tan, Amy   **3**:*189–95*

Last of the Mohicans, The, Cooper, James Fenimore   **1**:*204–10*

Left Hand of Darkness, The, LeGuin, Ursula   **5**:*236–42*

Light in the Forest, The, Richter, Conrad   **1**:*219–24*

Like Water for Chocolate, Esquivel, Laura   **3**:*196–202*

Little Prince, The, Saint-Exupéry, Antoine de   **3**:*210–17*

Little Women, Alcott, Louisa May   **2**:*202–8*

Lord of the Flies, Golding, William   **4**:*228–34*

Love Medicine, Erdrich, Louise   **5**:*243–50*

Madame Bovary, Flaubert, Gustave   **2**:*209–15*

Maltese Falcon, The, Hammett, Dashiell   **3**:*225–30*

Man without a Face, The, Holland, Isabelle   **4**:*240–46*

Merry Adventures of Robin Hood, The, Pyle, Howard   **1**:*250–57*

Les Misérables, Hugo, Victor   **2**:*223–29*

Moby Dick, Melville, Herman   **2**:*230–35*

Mutiny on the Bounty, Nordhoff, Charles and James Norman Hall   **1**:*273–79*

Native Son, Wright, Richard   **3**:*236–42*

Natural, The, Malamud, Bernard   **4**:*260–66*

Night, Wiesel, Elie   **4**:*267–73*

Nineteen Eighty-Four, Orwell, George   **5**:*251–58*

Not without Laughter, Hughes, Langston   **3**:*249–56*

O Pioneers!, Cather, Willa   **3**:*257–63*

Of Human Bondage, Maugham, W. Somerset   **3**:*264–68*

Old Gringo, The, Fuentes, Carlos   **3**:*277–83*

Old Man and the Sea, The, Hemingway, Ernest   **4**:*274–80*

Oliver Twist, Dickens, Charles   **2**:*261–67*

One Day in the Life of Ivan Denisovich, Solzhenitsyn, Alexander   **4**:*281–87*

One Flew over the Cuckoo's Nest, Kesey, Ken   **4**:*288–94*

One Hundred Years of Solitude, García Márquez, Gabriel   **2**:*268–74*

Ordinary People, Guest, Judith   **5**:*259–64*

Outsiders, The, Hinton, S. E.   **5**:*265–70*

Ox-Bow Incident, The, Clark, Walter Van Tilburg   **2**:*288–94*

Passage to India, A, Forster, E.M.   **3**:*297–304*

Pigman, The, Zindel, Paul   **5**:*271–77*

Pocho, Villarreal, José Antonio   **4**:*295–302*

Portrait of the Artist as a Young Man, A, Joyce, James   **3**:*305–11*

Pride and Prejudice, Austen, Jane   **2**:*295–300*

Prime of Miss Jean Brodie, The, Spark, Muriel   **4**:*303–8*

Prince of Tides, The, Conroy, Pat   **5**:*285–90*

Ragged Dick, Alger, Horatio   **2**:*301–7*

Ragtime, Doctorow, E. L.   **3**:*319–25*

Rebecca, du Maurier, Daphne   **3**:*326–33*

Red Badge of Courage, The, Crane, Stephen   **2**:*308–13*

Red Pony, The, Steinbeck, John   **3**:*334–37*

Red Sky at Morning, Bradford, Richard   **4**:*316–22*

Road from Home, The, Kherdian, David   **3**:*338–43*

Robinson Crusoe, Defoe, Daniel   **1**:*337–43*

Roll of Thunder, Hear My Cry, Taylor, Mildred   **3**:*350–55*

Roots, Haley, Alex   **5**:*298–305*

Runner, The, Voigt, Cynthia   **5**:*306–13*

Scarlet Letter, The, Hawthorne, Nathaniel   **1**:*351–57*

Scarlet Pimpernel, The, Orczy, Baroness Emmuska   **1**:*358–64*

Separate Peace, A, Knowles, John   **4**:*323–29*

Shane, Schaefer, Jack   **2**:*321–26*

Shoeless Joe, Kinsella, W. P.   **5**:*314–20*

Siddhartha, Hesse, Hermann   **1**:*365–70*

Sister Carrie, Dreiser, Theodore   **2**:*327–33*

Slaughterhouse Five, Vonnegut, Kurt, Jr.   **4**:*343–48*

Sons and Lovers, Lawrence, D. H.   **2**:*334–39*

Sounder, Armstrong, William H.   **3**:*370–76*

Story Catcher, The, Sandoz, Mari   **2**:*347–52*

Strange Case of Dr. Jekyll and Mr. Hyde, The, Stevenson, Robert Louis   **3**:*377–82*

Stranger in a Strange Land, Heinlein, Robert A.   **5**:*321–27*

Summer of My German Soldier, Greene, Bette   **4**:*371–77*

Sweet Whispers, Brother Rush, Hamilton, Virginia   **5**:*328–32*

Tale of Two Cities, A, Dickens, Charles   **1**:*371–78*

Tess of the D'Urbervilles, Hardy, Thomas   **2**:*353–59*

Their Eyes Were Watching God, Hurston, Zora Neale   **3**:*383–89*

Things Fall Apart, Achebe, Chinua   **2**:*360–65*

Thousand Pieces of Gold, McCunn, Ruthanne Lum   **2**:*366–71*

Three Musketeers, The, Dumas, Alexandre   **1**:*386–92*

Time of the Hero, The, Vargas Llosa, Mario   **5**:*333–38*

Tituba of Salem Village, Petry, Ann   **1**:*393–99*

To Kill a Mockingbird, Lee, Harper   **3**:*390–96*

Tom Brown's Schooldays, Hughes, Thomas   **2**:*372–77*

Treasure Island, Stevenson, Robert Louis   **1**:*400–405*

Tree Grows in Brooklyn, A, Smith, Betty   **3**:*397–403*

Twenty-Thousand Leagues under the Sea, Verne, Jules   **2**:*384–90*

Uncle Tom's Cabin, Stowe, Harriet Beecher   **2**:*403–9*

Understand This, Tervalon, Jervey   **5**:*339–45*

War of the Worlds, The, Wells, H.G.   **3**:*404–10*

Watership Down, Adams, Richard   **5**:*346–51*

Wuthering Heights, Brontë, Emily   **1**:*413–19*

Yellow Raft in Blue Water, A, Dorris, Michael   **5**:*360–66*

NOW (National Organization of Women)   **1**:*62;* **4**:*22, 394,* **5**:*136, 237*

Nuclear energy   **5**:*124, 127, 286*
    Chernobyl disaster   **5**:*286, 287 (illus.)*

Nuclear weapons
    and arms control   **4**:*71;* **5**:*126, 225, 239, 252 (sidebar)*
    arms race   **5**:*252 (sidebar)*
    hydrogen bomb   **4**:*183*
    (*See also* Atom bomb)

O

O Pioneers!, Cather, Willa   **3**:*257–63*

Oates, Joyce Carol, *Where Are You Going, Where*

Have You Been? 4:391–96
Occurrence at Owl Creek Bridge, An, Bierce, Ambrose 2:255–60; 3:281
O'Connor, Flannery, *Everything That Rises Must Converge* 5:88–94
Octavian (Octavius Caesar) 1:12 *(sidebar)*, 13
Octoroons 3:18
Odria, Manuel 5:333–34
Odyssey, Homer 1:280–87
  Odysseus and the Sirens 1:284 *(illus.)*
  parallels to *Ivanhoe* 1:187
Oedipus complex (Freud) 2:336–37
Of Human Bondage, Maugham, W. Somerset 3:264–68
Of Mice and Men, Steinbeck, John 3:269–76
Ohio River, and Underground Railroad 2:16, 60
Oil booms of 1920s 3:45–46
"Okies" 3:46, 47, 49
Oklahoma 5:29, 269
Old age. *See* Senior citizens
Old Gringo, The, Fuentes, Carlos 3:277–83
Old Man and the Sea, The, Hemingway, Ernest 4:274–80
Oliver Twist, Dickens, Charles 2:261–67
Olympians 1:301
Once and Future King, The, White, T.H. 1:288–94
One Day in the Life of Ivan Denisovich, Solzhenitsyn, Alexander 4:281–87
One Flew over the Cuckoo's Nest, Kesey, Ken 4:288–94; 5:318 *(sidebar)*
One Hundred Years of Solitude, García Márquez, Gabriel 2:268–74
O'Neill, Eugene, *Long Day's Journey into Night* 3:218–24
Ongpatonga 1:209 *(illus.)*
Open Window, The, Saki 2:275–80
Oppenheimer, Robert 4:316
Orczy, Baroness Emmuska, *Scarlet Pimpernel, The* 1:358–64
Ordinary People, Guest, Judith 5:259–64
Orwell, George
  Animal Farm 4:14–20
  Nineteen Eighty-Four 5:251–58
Osborne, Sarah 1:79, 395, 396
Othello, Shakespeare, William 1:295–300
Ottoman Turks 1:295–96; 3:338–40
Our Town, Wilder, Thornton 3:284–89
Out of Africa, Dinesen, Isak 3:290–96
Outcasts of Poker Flat, The, Harte, Bret 2:281–87
Outsiders, The, Hinton, S. E. 5:265–70
Ovid, *Metamorphoses* 1:262
Ox-Bow Incident, The, Clark, Walter Van Tilburg 2:288–94

P

Pabel, Reinhold 4:373 *(sidebar)*
Pacificism 1:23 *(sidebar)*, 142, 365, 369, 370
Paine, Thomas
  Common Sense 1:71–77, 94

  opposition to slavery 1:72 *(sidebar)*
  The Rights of Man 1:52
Pakistan 3:300, 301
Palestine 4:102–3, 105; 5:54
  (See also Israel)
Pamphlets
  Common Sense, Paine, Thomas 1:71–77
  Modest Proposal, A, Swift, Jonathan 1:266–72
  popularity in England 1:268
  popularity and limitations in colonies 1:72–73, 122
  by Swift 1:132
Panama Canal 3:231–32, 270
Pankhurst, Emmeline 2:335–36; 3:359
Paradise Lost, Milton, John 1:301–8
  influence on Herman Melville 1:54
  popularity in America 1:307
Paranormal phenomena 2:383 *(sidebar)*; 5:47–48, 56, 239
Paredes, Américo 5:172
Paris, France
  as capital of western art 3:265–66
  Notre Dame cathedral 1:161, 162 *(illus.)*, 163, 164 *(sidebar)*
Paris (Trojan prince) 1:8, 166, 281
Parks, Rosa 3:73; 5:11, 88, 185
Parnell, Charles 3:109–10
Parody 1:4
Parris, Rev. Samuel 1:79, 83 *(sidebar)*, 394, 395, 421
Parthenon 1:240
Passage to India, A, Forster, E.M. 3:297–304
Pastoral novels 1:6
Paterson, Katherine, *Jacob Have I Loved* 4:216–20
Paton, Alan, *Cry, the Beloved Country* 4:94–100
Paxton Boys massacre 1:220–21
Peck, Robert Newton, *Day No Pigs Would Die, A* 3:94–99
Peloponnesian War 1:241, 324, 328
Pennsylvania 1:22, 71–72, 310
  Pittsburgh 4:7–9, 144, 149
Percy family 1:144–45, 149
Pericles of ancient Athens 1:17, 18, 240, 241, 322
Perón, Juan and Eva 5:208–9, 210
Persephone 1:283
Peru 4:221, 222; 5:333–38
Pesticides ("biocides") 4:337–42; 5:347, 351
Petrarch 1:345, 348
Petry, Ann, *Tituba of Salem Village* 1:393–99
Philadelphia, Pennsylvania 1:71–72, 310
Philippines 3:101
  Bataan Death March 4:81
Phillips, Wendell 2:89 *(sidebar)*
Phoenician alphabet 1:286–87
"Phrenology" 2:211
Pigman, The, Zindel, Paul 5:271–77
Pilgrim at Tinker Creek, Dillard, Annie 5:278–84
Pilgrimages 1:64–70, 145–46, 182
Pinkerton's National Detective Agency 3:225–26
Pinochet, August 5:169 *(illus.)*

Piracy   **1**:*400–402, 405*
Pittsburgh, Pennsylvania   **4**:*7–9*
Plath, Sylvia, *Bell Jar, The*   **4**:*21–27*
Plato
   Academy   **1**:*328*
   complaining of Homer   **1**:*285, 286 (sidebar)*
   Republic   **1**:*321–29*
Plays
   Angels in America, Kushner, Tony   **5**:*1–10*
   Antigone, Sophocles   **1**:*14–21*
   Belle of Amherst, The, Luce, William   **2**:*54–58*
   Biloxi Blues, Simon, Neil   **4**:*35–41*
   Cherry Orchard, The, Chekhov, Anton   **3**:*57–62*
   Crucible, The, Miller, Arthur   **1**:*78–86*
   Cyrano de Bergerac, Rostand, Edmond   **1**:*87–92*
   Death of a Salesman, Miller, Arthur   **4**:*109–15*
   Doll's House, A, Ibsen, Henrik   **2**:*111–17*
   Elephant Man, The, Pomerance, Bernard
     2:*118–24*
   Fences, Wilson, August   **4**:*144–50*
   Fiddler on the Roof, Stein, Joseph   **3**:*119–24*
   *for colored girls who have considered suicide / when
     the rainbow is enuf*, Shange, Ntozake   **5**:*115–21*
   Hamlet, Shakespeare, William   **1**:*136–43*
   Henry IV, Part I, Shakespeare, William   **1**:*144–51*
   I Never Sang for My Father, Anderson, Robert
     5:*201–7*
   Julius Caesar, Shakespeare, William   **1**:*189–95*
   King Lear, Shakespeare, William   **1**:*196–203*
   Little Foxes, The, Hellman, Lillian   **3**:*203–10*
   Long Day's Journey into Night, O'Neill, Eugene
     3:*218–24*
   Macbeth, Shakespeare, William   **1**:*225–30*
   Man for All Seasons, A, Bolt, Robert   **1**:*231–37*
   Medea, Euripides   **1**:*238–41*
   Member of the Wedding, The, McCullers, Carson
     4:*254–59*
   Merchant of Venice, The Shakespeare, William
     1:*242–49*
   Midsummer Night's Dream, A, Shakespeare,
     William   **1**:*258–65*
   Miracle Worker, The, Gibson, William   **2**:*216–22*
   Othello, Shakespeare, William   **1**:*295–300*
   Our Town, Wilder, Thornton   **3**:*284–89*
   Pygmalion, Shaw, George Bernard   **3**:*312–18*
   Raisin in the Sun, A, Hansberry, Lorraine
     4:*309–15*
   Romeo and Juliet, Shakespeare, William
     1:*344–50*
   Streetcar Named Desire, A, Williams, Tennesse
     4:*364–70*
   Tempest, The, Shakespeare, William   **1**:*379–85*
   Twelve Angry Men, Rose, Reginald (screenplay)
     4:*378–83*
   West Side Story, Laurents, Arthur, *et al.*
     4:*384–90*
   Zoo Story, The, Albee, Edward   **4**:*397–402*
   Zoot Suit, Valdez, Luis   **4**:*403–10*
Plays, descriptions by type
   choreopoems   **5**:*115, 117–18, 120–21*

histories   **1**:*150*
   morality plays   **1**:*148*
   revenge tragedies   **1**:*142*
Plessy v. Ferguson (Supreme Court ruling allowing
   segregation)   **2**:*21, 399–400, 413*; **3**:*351, 375,
   419*; **4**:*1*; **5**:*90, 107–8*
Plutarch   **1**:*193–94*
Pocho, Villarreal, José Antonio   **4**:*295–302*
Poe, Edgar Allan, *Cask of Amontillado, The*   **2**:*81–86*
Poetry
   Welsh regard for   **3**:*64*
   Aeneid, The, Virgil   **1**:*8–13*
   Beowulf, Anonymous   **1**:*44–50*
   Canterbury Tales, The, Chaucer, Geoffrey
     1:*64–70*
   haiku   **4**:*333, 334*
   Iliad, Homer   **1**:*166–73*
   Inferno, Dante Alighieri   **1**:*174–80*
   Leaves of Grass, Whitman, Walt   **2**:*195–201*
   Odyssey, Homer   **1**:*280–87*
   Paradise Lost, Milton, John   **1**:*301–8*
   Waste Land, The, Eliot, T.S.   **3**:*411–17*
Poetry, types of
   blank verse   **1**:*303 (sidebar)*
   choreopoems   **5**:*117–18*
   epic poems   **1**:*49, 153, 172, 173, 282 (sidebar),
     285*
Pogroms
   against Armenians   **3**:*342*
   against Jews   **1**:*364*
Poland
   of 1800s   **2**:*384–85*
   "capitalists" deported from, by Soviets
     4:*131–32*
   Nazi invasion of   **3**:*214*; **4**:*193*
   Stalin/Hitler partition agreement   **4**:*17, 131*
"Polis" or Greek city-state   **1**:*286, 327–28*
Political parties in America
   American Communist Party   **3**:*40*
   Democratic, as party of Irish Americans
     3:*401–2*
   Democratic South becoming Republican   **3**:*79*
   Republicans of Progressive era   **3**:*286*
   Socialist Labor Party   **3**:*174–75*
   ward bosses   **3**:*398*
   Whigs, Democrats, and Republicans   **2**:*2, 87*
Politics in America
   campaigning in mid-19th century   **2**:*2*
   Chinese American influence on   **4**:*126–27*
   during Reconstruction, African Americans in
     2:*412*
   enactment of income tax   **3**:*285, 320*
   enactment of referenda provisions   **3**:*285*
   first recall act   **3**:*319*
   Irish American neighborhoods   **3**:*398–99*
   New York's Tammany Hall   **3**:*148–49, 398–99*
   politicians' invocation of Lincoln   **2**:*7*
   Teapot Dome scandal   **3**:*25*
   televised debates costing Nixon 1960 presidential
     election   **5**:*223*

Polynesia   4:222

Pomerance, Bernard, *Elephant Man, The*   2:118–24

Poor Richard's Almanac, Franklin, Benjamin
    1:309–15

Poorhouses, almshouses in 18th-century America
    2:216, 219 (sidebar)

Pope, Alexander   1:343

Pope Boniface VIII   1:176, 177

Popes
    competing for control of Tuscany   1:174
    conflicts with Holy Roman Emperors   1:174,
        176, 344, 345
    fathering children   1:296

Pornography, prevalence in Victorian Age   3:381

Porter, Katherine Anne, *Noon Wine*   3:243–48

Portrait of the Artist as a Young Man, A, Joyce, James
    3:305–11
    as example of bildungsroman   3:264, 311

"Positivism"   3:213

Post-traumatic stress disorder   5:106

Potlatch ceremony of Kwakiutl   5:198 (illus.), 199

Potok, Chaim, *Chosen, The*   4:87–93

Pound, Ezra   3:413–14, 416; 5:42

Poverty
    of African American families   3:37; 4:5
        (sidebar), 145; 5:329
    of American Indians   5:360–61
    and child abuse   5:329 (sidebar)
    as deserved, in Hinduism   3:300
    of Great Depression years   3:68, 126, 350
    and Johnson's War on Poverty   3:324; 5:68,
        150, 266
    linked to emotional depression and pessimism
        5:266 (sidebar)
    of Puerto Ricans   5:215–16
    and Reagan's welfare cuts   5:1, 329
    in South Central Los Angeles   5:339–42
    studies of, in 1960s   5:266

Poynings Law   1:267

*Prairie Years, The. See Abraham Lincoln: The Prairie
    Years*

Predestination   4:304

Prejudice. *See* Racism and prejudice

Premarital sex   5:324

Presbyterianism   4:10, 304

Presley, Elvis   4:172, 386

Pride and Prejudice, Austen, Jane   2:295–300

Prime of Miss Jean Brodie, The, Spark, Muriel
    4:303–8

Primitivism   3:385 (sidebar)

Prince, The, Machiavelli, Niccolò   1:316–20
    influence in early 16th century   1:233
    influence upon Shakespeare   1:200, 380

Prince of Tides, The, Conroy, Pat   5:285–90

Printing and publishing
    advances in   1:160, 162 (sidebar); 2:234, 306,
        419
    muckraking magazines   3:176
    paperback books   2:325
    pulp magazines   2:325; 3:226–27

Prisons   3:371, 374 (illus.)

Privateers   1:400

Proctor, John   1:81 (sidebar), 83 (sidebar)

Progress, belief in
    Stephen Crane's objections to   2:313
    destroyed by WWI   3:412
    fostered by Enlightenment (Age of Reason)
        1:24–25, 268; 2:416
    reality belying   3:217, 227
    science and technology ("positivism") as 19th
        century's evidence for   2:416; 3:213
    Second Great Awakening contributing to
        2:417–18
    tempered by Victorians' doubt   3:314
    and utopian philosophies of 19th century
        2:195
    H. G. Wells's objections to   3:409
    (*See also* Evolution; Science/technology)

Prohibition
    disillusionment with   3:69, 227, 401
    fostering corruption, bootlegging, and
        gangsterism   3:69, 147–48, 366–67, 401
    restrictions retained in South   4:207 (sidebar)
    in San Francisco   3:226
    support by Anti-Saloon League and temperance
        movements   2:25 (sidebar), 85–86; 3:69, 75,
        147, 401
    support from rural, anti-urban areas   3:69–70
    Volstead Act   3:147, 151, 401
    weaknesses of, as legislation   3:22–23, 69
    (*See also* Alcohol and alcoholism)

Project 100,000, draft of disadvantaged for Vietnam
    5:102–3, 158, 307

Propaganda
    as aspect of fascism   4:304; 5:253
    pro-war, from Hollywood   4:325
    use by British   5:252, 257
    use of media for   4:66–67
    use by Soviets   5:252

Prosser, Gabriel   1:39, 42; 2:94

Prostitution
    in China   3:135
    of female Chinese immigrants   2:366–67
    near military installations   4:37
    serving gold miners of California   2:283–84
    women driven to, by lack of work
        America of 1880s   2:328–29
        France of 1800s   2:228
        Victorian England   2:264, 355
    women kept as, for repayment of debts
        (Victorian London)   2:264

Protest movements. *See* Civil rights movements;
    Counterculture

Protestantism
    African Methodist Episcopal Church   3:83
    all-black churches   3:250, 252
    Anglican Church (Church of England)   1:78,
        123, 129, 232, 233 (sidebar), 306, 351, 393
    and anti-Catholic prejudice and policies   1:74,
        132, 230, 269

Baptists   5:*19*, *188*
Christian Socialist movement   **2**:*377*
clergymen denouncing women's rights activists
   2:25
creationism   **2**:*30*
decline of influence in late 18th century   **1**:*102*
decline of influence in late 19th century   **2**:*329*
Dutch Reformed Church   **1**:*331, 425*
establishment of distinct denominations in
   colonial America   **1**:*106*
fundamentalists and New/Religious Right
   5:*137–39*
Great Awakening in American colonies   **1**:*73,
   106, 122, 424–25*
in Ireland   **1**:*267, 269*
Methodism   **2**:*357–58*
Presbyterianism   **4**:*10, 304*
as protest against abuses of Catholic Church
   1:*231*
Quakerism   **1**:*23*; **2**:*22, 25, 88–89*
as Reformation of Catholic Church   **1**:*231*;
   2:*113*
revival meetings   **1**:*425*; **2**:*315–16*
Second Great Awakening in America   **1**:*424–25*;
   2:*23, 315–16, 404, 417–18*
segregation of churches   **5**:*189*
Shakerism   **3**:*95–99*
spread of, spurring legalization of divorce   **2**:*113*
television evangelists   **5**:*31–32*
Unitarianism   **2**:*54, 315*
(*See also* Puritanism)
Psychology
   behavior modification and conditioning
      5:*156–57*
   changing views of mental illness   **4**:*289*
   conceptions of intelligence   **4**:*152–53*
   conflicting theories of nature of mankind
      4:*233–34*
   connectedness of mental health and human
      relationships   **4**:*153*
   development of   **3**:*329, 378*; **4**:*77*
   ethical considerations of experimentation   **4**:*153*
   insistence on domesticity and dependence for
      women   **4**:*167*
   as means of rehabilitation of nonconformists
      4:*399*
   and paranormal phenomena   **2**:*383* (*sidebar*);
      5:*47–48, 56, 239*
   psychiatry   **4**:*289* (*sidebar*)
   psychoanalysis   **4**:*168* (*sidebar*); **5**:*42, 260–61,
      262*
   PTSD (post-traumatic stress disorder)   **5**:*106*
   theories of absent father   **4**:*244–45*
   theories of community collusion in evil   **4**:*238*
   twins and struggle for identity   **4**:*219*
   (*See also* Mental and emotional disabilities;
      Suicide)
Ptolemy   **1**:*305*
Puerto Rico and Puerto Ricans   **3**:*277*; **4**:*385–86,
   388–89, 401*; **5**:*214–21*

Punishments
   in 19th-century America   **2**:*17*
   in 19th-century France   **2**:*225, 228*
   aboard ships of Royal Navy   **1**:*273–74, 275* (*illus.*)
   branding   **1**:*420*
   capital   **4**:*379–80*; **5**:*131*
   collective, in British colonies   **2**:*362*
   of drug users, racial inequality of   **4**:*250*
   dueling   **1**:*389* (*sidebar*)
   in Elizabethan England   **1**:*198* (*sidebar*)
   of English schoolboys   **2**:*373–74*
   feuds   **2**:*17* (*sidebar*)
   flogging   **2**:*394, 395*
   guillotining   **1**:*373*
   hazing on ship   **2**:*394*
   inequality of, for blacks   **5**:*16*
   marooning   **1**:*401–2*
   prisons   **3**:*371, 374* (*illus.*)
   public hanging   **1**:*374*
   quartering   **1**:*373–74*
   of seamen   **2**:*394, 395*
   in Southern prisons and road/chain gangs
      3:*371, 374* (*illus.*)
   in Soviet Union, Siberian exile and forced labor
      4:*132, 282*
   tarring and feathering   **2**:*17* (*sidebar*)
Puns
   in Shakespeare   **1**:*348–49*
   in Victorian Age   **2**:*30*
Puritanism
   and Antinomians   **1**:*352, 357*
   austerity and discipline   **1**:*78, 101, 393–94*
   belief in witchcraft and Satan   **1**:*79–81, 394,
      395–96, 421–23*
   Calvinism   **2**:*54, 55*; **3**:*377–78*; **4**:*304*
   concept of conversion   **2**:*55* (*sidebar*)
   and Congregationalists   **1**:*357, 424–25*
   Defoe influenced by   **1**:*338*
   doctrines of   **1**:*23, 101–2, 352, 393–94*
   Franklin influenced by   **1**:*311*
   good works and redemption   **1**:*23, 101–2, 352*
   Half-Way Covenant   **1**:*421*
   hardships faced by colonists in New England
      1:*351*
   immigration to New England   **1**:*421*
   intolerance   **1**:*102, 394*
   Milton influenced by   **1**:*307*
   as "purifiers" of Church of England   **1**:*299, 420*
Putnam, Ann   **1**:*79, 83* (*sidebar*), *396*
Pygmalion, Shaw, George Bernard   **3**:*312–18*
Pyle, Howard, *Merry Adventures of Robin Hood, The*
   1:*250–57*
Pyramus and Thisbe   **1**:*259* (*sidebar*)

Q

Quadroons   **3**:*17–18*
Quakerism   **1**:*23*; **2**:*22, 25, 88–89*
Quarterstaff fencing   **1**:*253*
Quixote. *See Adventures of Don Quixote, The*

Rabbits   5:*336–37, 348 (illus.)*

Racism and prejudice

American Communist Party's stand against
3:*40;* 4:*211*

in American jury system before 1969   4:*379*
(sidebar)

of Aryans, neo-Nazis, and neo-fascists   4:*40, 50;*
5:*42*

in concept of "white man's burden"   2:*147;*
3:*170, 172, 182 (sidebar)*

eliminating through claiming of identity   5:*176*

of eugenics movement   5:*42*

FEPC (Fair Employment Practices Commission)
to investigate   3:*42*

(*See also* Holocaust)

Racism and prejudice, against

African Americans

among immigrants   4:*52*

antiblack propaganda   2:*400*

Baldwin's condemnation of   5:*111, 113*

in Caucasian standards of beauty   4:*49–50*

combated by Du Bois   2:*343–46*

covert   4:*314*

creating self-hatred   4:*53–54;* 5:*116*

economic   4:*30–31, 33*

exacerbated by economic competition   2:*43*

housing discrimination   2:*13;* 3:*39, 237;*
4:*30–31*

by Ku Klux Klan   2:*141 (sidebar), 143*
(sidebar), 412; 3:*419;* 5:*25, 130*

by labor unions   2:*341*

in legal and prison systems   3:*371*

Lincoln on   2:*3, 5*

in minstrel shows   2:*16–17, 21, 398*

in New South   2:*399–400;* 3:*36–37, 41, 203,
320*

in professional sports   4:*149*

race riots of early 19th century   2:*6, 404;*
3:*160, 252, 321;* 4:*310*

race riots of 1940s   4:*197, 201, 213, 247,
248 (illus.)*

"science" of ethnology contributing to
2:*232–33*

Scottsboro case   3:*39, 239*

sexual taboos   3:*391*

social Darwinism contributing to   2:*341*

soldiers in WWII   4:*212–13*

stereotyping justifying slavery   1:*39, 41, 42,
394;* 2:*403, 404*

as viewed by Styron   2:*97*

by white supremacists   3:*352*

(*See also* Lynching; Segregation; Slavery)

African blacks   1:*63;* 2:*360–65;* 3:*291;* 4:*94–100*

American Indians. *See* American Indians

Anglos   4:*320*

Armenians   4:*200*

Chinese   2:*175, 287, 367–68, 370 (sidebar), 371;*
3:*30;* 4:*124–27, 194, 330;* 5:*230–31*

Germans during WWII   4:*375*

immigrants in general   4:*194*

Irish   3:*220, 221 (sidebar)*

Japanese   3:*30;* 4:*137, 138–43, 194, 195,
330–31*

Jews. *See* Anti-Semitism

Latinos

deportations of braceros in 1930s   4:*44*

mestizos or *criollos*   5:*334–36*

in Southwest   4:*320*

zoot suit riots of 1940s   4:*295–97, 403–10*

lower castes in India   1:*366;* 2:*183;* 3:*182, 184,
300*

migrant farm workers   3:*29–30, 34, 49, 140–42,
143 (sidebar), 269–71, 275, 335, 337;* 4:*297
(sidebar)*

Moors   1:*297, 299, 300*

Poles   4:*369*

users of sign language   2:*217*

Radio

Dylan Thomas's broadcasts   3:*66–67*

FDR taking advantage of   3:*127*

new teenage audience of 1950s   4:*386, 391*

popularity of   3:*3, 45*

"thrillers" produced on   3:*329*

Ragged Dick, Alger, Horatio   2:*301–7*

Ragtime, Doctorow, E. L.   3:*319–25*

Railroads

in England   2:*353, 354, 358*

in France   2:*209–10*

in India   3:*184–85*

Railroads in U.S.

California population boom and   2:*175, 195*

Chinese workers on   4:*124, 125;* 5:*75–77, 78
(illus.)*

contributing to western migration   2:*327*

federal and state funding for expansion of
2:*230*

hobo tradition of 1930s   3:*46*

importance in Civil War   2:*255, 256 (illus.)*

importance to travelers   2:*175*

luxury travel in Pullman cars   2:*306*

raising farm incomes   2:*417*

refrigerated cars for transport of perishables
2:*328;* 3:*175*

Thoreau's disapproval of   2:*416*

Raisin in the Sun, A, Hansberry, Lorraine   4:*309–15*

Randolph, A. Philip   3:*42, 159–60;* 4:*255;* 5:*186,
188*

Realism

Bierce on   2:*259–60*

of Crane   2:*312*

described   2:*259*

of Dreiser   2:*327, 331*

of Joyce, as "slice of life"   3:*111*

levels of   1:*4, 6 (sidebar)*

in literature for young adults   5:*265–66, 276*

"magical"   2:*271, 273;* 3:*196, 202;* 4:*48;* 5:*169,
213, 330*

of *Les Misérables*   2:*229*

versus stereotypes   **1**:*42*
Whitman's impact on   **2**:*200*
Rebecca, du Maurier, Daphne   **3**:*326–33*
Reconnaissance planes   **5**:*96*
Reconstruction
    African Americans in politics   **2**:*412*
    Black Codes   **2**:*412*; **5**:*21*
    carpetbaggers and scalawags   **2**:*141*
    civil rights granted, then ignored   **2**:*21, 340–41,
        412*
    demise of plantations and wilderness   **2**:*49, 53*
    economy of South   **2**:*41–42*
    education of freed slaves   **2**:*411–12, 413, 414*
    end of   **2**:*412–13*
    Force Acts (1871 and 1872)   **2**:*412*
    Freedman's Bureau   **2**:*411*
    in Georgia   **2**:*139–40*
    Ku Klux Klan   **2**:*141* (sidebar), *143* (sidebar),
        412
    lack of training or means of survival for freed
        slaves   **2**:*59, 411*
    sharecropping and tenant farming   **2**:*42, 411*
    violence and unequal justice for freed slaves
        5:*20–21*
    white backlash following   **2**:*340–41, 412–13*
    (*See also* Jim Crow laws; Segregation)
Red Badge of Courage, The, Crane, Stephen
    2:*308–13*
Red Pony, The, Steinbeck, John   **3**:*334–37*
Red Power movement   **2**:*79* (sidebar)
"Red Scare"   **1**:*84–86*; **3**:*105*; **4**:*71–72*; **5**:*2, 127*
    (*See also* Cold War)
Red Sky at Morning, Bradford, Richard   **4**:*316–22*
Reform movements of 19th century
    child labor laws   **2**:*103–4*
    encouraged by belief in progress   **2**:*195, 196*
    multifaceted nature of   **2**:*23*
    as response to rapid change of Industrial
        Revolution   **2**:*417*
    settlement houses   **3**:*397–98*
    strengthened by Romantic movement   **2**:*316*
    temperance movement   **2**:*25* (sidebar), *85*; **3**:*147*
    utopian societies of 1840s   **2**:*418*
    women's involvement in   **2**:*423*
Reform movements of 20th century
    against child labor   **3**:*76* (sidebar), *77* (illus.)
    during Progressive Era   **3**:*75–76*
    Independent Living Movement   **2**:*123*
    Pure Food and Drug Act (1906)   **3**:*179*
    temperance movement   **3**:*69, 75, 147*
    (*See also* Civil rights movements; Prohibition)
Reformation   **1**:*231*; **2**:*113*
Refugees   **5**:*28–29*
Reincarnation   **3**:*300*
Reisman, David   **4**:*75, 111, 382*
Religion
    and agnosticism   **3**:*265*
    of American Indians   **2**:*71–72, 78, 178*; **4**:*188*
        healing ceremonies for returning war veterans
            5:*363*

in ancient Greece   **1**:*15–16, 169*
ancient sacrificial rites   **4**:*238*
Buddhism   **1**:*365–69*; **3**:*186–87*; **5**:*48*
in China   **3**:*133, 190, 193*
Chippewa *manitou*   **5**:*246, 249* (sidebar)
comparative conceptions of   **5**:*57* (sidebar)
conflicts with Darwinists   **3**:*102, 404*
conflicts with non-believers in 20th century
    3:*102*
cults   **5**:*83–84*
Daoism (also Taoism)   **5**:*237*
Eastern, in America   **5**:*237*
freedom of, in America   **1**:*73–74*
"Great Chain of Being"   **1**:*201, 203*
Hinduism   **3**:*300, 302*
in India   **1**:*366*; **3**:*300–301*
Islam   **1**:*296*; **3**:*300*
miracles and paranormal phenomena   **5**:*48*
monasticism   **3**:*186–87*
moral sense directed toward political issues
    1:*96*
Mormonism   **5**:*4*
Nation of Islam   **3**:*238, 325*; **4**:*56, 248–50*;
    5:*12–13, 69, 110–11, 302*
of Nez Percé   **2**:*161*
People's Temple and Jim Jones   **5**:*84*
pilgrimages   **1**:*64*
of Pueblo Indians   **4**:*79*
rationalistic versus mystical/emotional   **1**:*425*;
    3:*426*
reincarnation   **3**:*300*
vs. science in Victorian Age   **2**:*29–30, 121–22*
syncretism   **3**:*190–91*; **4**:*44* (sidebar)
transcendentalism   **1**:*356–57*; **2**:*54, 92, 314,
    316–19, 416, 418–19*
Unification Church   **5**:*83*
Zen Buddhism   **4**:*334*
(*See also* Christianity; Greek myth; Jews; Sin and
    damnation)
Remarque, Erich Maria, *All Quiet on the Western
    Front*   **3**:*8–14*
Renaissance   **1**:*2, 380*
Renan, Ernest   **3**:*213*
Renault, Mary, *Bull from the Sea, The*   **1**:*57–63*
Republic, Plato   **1**:*321–29*
Republican Party of 1830s   **2**:*2*
"Resurrection men"   **1**:*120–21*
Retirement, problems of adjustment to   **5**:*203, 273*
Revival meetings   **1**:*425*
Revolution, French. *See* France in 18th century:
    French Revolution
Revolutions of 1848   **1**:*376*
Rhetoric
    of Churchill's speeches   **4**:*361–62*
    in colonial America   **1**:*123*
    of Kennedy's speeches   **5**:*223*
    of King's oratory   **5**:*186*
Rhodesia   **4**:*165–66*
Richard I of England (the Lion-Hearted)
    1:*181–82, 184* (illus.), *188, 251*

Richard II of England   1:*144*
Richelieu, Cardinal Duc de   1:*387–89*
Richter, Conrad, *Light in the Forest, The*   1:*219–24*
Richter, Hans Peter, *Friedrich*   4:*157–64*
Riegner, Gerhardt,   3:*403*
Right Stuff, The, Wolfe, Tom   5:*291–97*
Riis, Jacob   3:*169 (sidebar), 285, 320*
Rip Van Winkle, Irving, Washington   1:*330–36*
Risberg, Charles "Swede"   3:*149*
Road from Home, The, Kherdian, David   3:*338–43*
Roberts, Oral   5:*31–32*
Robeson, Paul   1:*389–90*
Robespierre, Maximilien   1:*359 (illus.), 372*
Robinson Crusoe, Defoe, Daniel   1:*337–43*
Rock 'n' roll   4:*172, 386, 391–92*
Rockefeller, John D.   2:*306*
Rocking-Horse Winner, The, Lawrence, D.H.
   3:*344–49*
Rodeo   5:*362, 364 (sidebar)*
Rodriguez, Richard, *Hunger of Memory*   5:*178–84*
Roll of Thunder, Hear My Cry, Taylor, Mildred
   3:*350–55*
Romantic movement
   Darwin's influence on   1:*116*
   disapproval of Industrial Revolution   1:*115–16,
      120*
   emphasizing emotion, imagination, mystery,
      individuality, and nationalism   1:*106, 115,
      118–19, 217, 406*
   favoring plain speech of common people   1:*163*
   influence on Dumas   2:*104*
   influence on Emerson   2:*316–17, 319*
   influence of French Revolution   1:*116*
   influence on Hermann Hesse   1:*365, 370*
   interest in medieval romance   1:*413*
   interest in past   2:*104*
   as reaction against rationality of Enlightenment
      1:*106, 217, 406*
   reflections in Emily Brontë's works   1:*413*
   reflections in Jane Austen's works   2:*300*
   and transcendentalism   1:*356–57;* 2:*54, 92, 314,
      316–19, 416, 418–19*
Rome, Italy
   in ancient times   1:*9, 12–13, 189–92*
   civil war, republic, and dictatorship   1:*190*
   mythical founding of   1:*10 (sidebar)*
   religious holidays   1:*191–92*
Romeo and Juliet, Shakespeare, William   1:*344–50*
   as model for *West Side Story*   4:*384*
Room of One's Own, A, Woolf, Virginia   3:*356–63*
Roosevelt, Eleanor   3:*154, 392, 395, 424;* 4:*297*
Roosevelt, Franklin Delano
   authorizing internment of Japanese Americans
      4:*138*
   First Inaugural Address   3:*125–30*
   invocation of Lincoln   2:*7*
   New Deal   1:*113;* 3:*45, 69, 128, 141*
   political appointments of Irish Americans
      3:*401–2*
   political support from Sandburg   2:*7*
   reason for refusal to sign Dyer Antilynching Bill
      3:*154, 392*
   support for equal rights   4:*255*
Roosevelt, Theodore
   as big game hunter   3:*232 (sidebar)*
   "big stick" corollary to Monroe Doctrine   3:*277*
   coining term "muckrakers"   3:*176*
   expansionism of   3:*101, 231*
   popularizing "Old West" myth of individualism
      5:*206*
   as Progressive reformer   3:*284–85*
   support for preservation of buffalo   5:*34*
   support for trade union movement   3:*420*
   as trust buster   3:*167*
Roots, Haley, Alex   5:*298–305*
Rose, Reginald, *Twelve Angry Men* (screenplay)
   4:*378–83*
Rosenberg, Julius and Ethel   4:*72, 380, 381 (illus.);*
   5:*2, 127*
Rostand, Edmond, *Cyrano de Bergerac*   1:*87–92*
Rotarians   5:*202*
Rothstein, Arnold   3:*149–50;* 4:*261;* 5:*315, 316
   (illus.)*
Rousseau, Jean-Jacques   1:*409 (sidebar)*
Runner, The, Voigt, Cynthia   5:*306–13*
Rush, Benjamin   4:*289*
Russia, czarist
   anti-Semitism and pogroms   1:*364;* 3:*119–21*
   Bolshevik Revolution   4:*14, 16*
   Bolsheviks and Mensheviks   4:*14*
   Cossacks   3:*233*
   decline of nobility   2:*35–36;* 3:*57*
   education reform   3:*58*
   emancipation of serfs   2:*34*
   industrialization   4:*14*
   intelligentsia   3:*58*
   land ownership   3:*57–58, 60*
   local government   2:*35*
   marriage and divorce   2:*37, 39*
   oppression of Poland   2:*384–85*
   peasants and intelligentsia   4:*14*
   revolution of 1905   1:*363;* 3:*59, 232*
   Russo-Japanese War (1904–05)   4:*59*
   Russo-Turkish war   2:*37–39*
   as threat to British-controlled Punjab   3:*184,
      185*
   women's rights movement   2:*37, 39*
   WWI   3:*8, 11 (sidebar)*
   (See also Soviet Union)
Rustin, Bayard   5:*188*

S

Sacatras   3:*18*
Sackville-West, Vita   3:*361–62*
Sailboats   2:*395*
Saint-Domingue (Haiti)   5:*116–17*
Saint-Exupéry, Antoine de, *Little Prince, The*
   3:*210–17*
Saki, *Open Window, The*   2:*275–80*

Salazar, Rubén   4:47, 410
Salem, Massachusetts   1:78–80, 355, 395–97
Salinas Valley, California   3:334–35
Salinger, J. D.
    Catcher in the Rye   4:73–78
    as reclusive   5:319
Salk, Jonas Edward   4:10
San Francisco
    in 1920s   3:226
    Chinatown   3:226; 5:74–75, 77–79
    prejudice against Chinese   2:367–68
    vigilantes   2:286–87
Sand, George (Amantine-Aurore-Lucile Dupin)
    2:212; 3:406
Sandburg, Carl
    Abraham Lincoln: The Prairie Years   2:1–7
    on Call of the Wild   3:56
Sandoz, Mari, Story Catcher, The   2:347–52
Saroyan, William, Human Comedy, The   4:193–200
Satan. See Devil (Satan)
Satire
    Adventures of Don Quixote, The   1:4, 6–7
    Devil and Tom Walker, The   1:101–6
    Gulliver's Travels   1:129–35
    Modest Proposal, A   1:266–72
    use in Shakespeare's time   1:349
Saxo Grammaticus   1:136, 139, 141 (sidebar)
Scarlet Letter, The, Hawthorne, Nathaniel   1:351–57
Scarlet Pimpernel, The, Orczy, Baroness Emmuska
    1:358–64
Schaefer, Jack, Shane   2:321–26
Schlafly, Phyllis   5:136–37, 138 (illus.)
Schooners   1:401
Science fiction   2:388–89; 4:347; 5:54–56, 126
    (sidebar)
    Brave New World   5:39–45
    Childhood's End   5:53–60
    Dune   5:81–87
    episodes in Slaughterhouse Five   4:347
    Fahrenheit 451   5:95–100
    Foundation   5:122–28
    House of Stairs   5:156–62
    Left Hand of Darkness, The   5:236–42
    Nineteen Eighty-Four   5:251–58
    and purported UFOs   4:347–48; 5:59 (illus.)
    as "speculative fiction"   5:141
    Stranger in a Strange Land   5:321–27
    Jules Verne as father of   2:388–89
    War of the Worlds, The   3:404–10
    H. G. Wells as father of   2:389
    women writers of   5:239
    (See also Fantasy)
Science/technology
    American Enlightenment   2:416
    anthropology   2:72, 179; 4:221–27; 5:42
    assembly line production and mass production
        3:89, 100–101, 102
    automobile   2:128 (sidebar); 3:23, 77, 88–89,
        94, 101; 5:40 (illus.)
    aviation   3:211–12, 367; 5:96, 293–94

behaviorism   5:45
civilian applications of war technology   4:236
computers   5:97, 127
contraceptives   2:211; 5:272, 324
cotton gin   2:403
drugs and pharmaceuticals   3:379
electricity   3:89
in Elizabethan Age   1:142 (sidebar), 200
in Enlightenment   1:24–26, 268–69, 272
"ethnology"   2:232–33
eugenics   3:272; 4:152; 5:41–42
explorations   1:118 (sidebar)
explosives   5:76
extrasensory perception (ESP)   5:47, 239
on farms   3:5–6
in Franklin's day   1:24–26
Galileo, Copernicus, and Newton   1:24, 94, 305
indoor plumbing   3:77
Industrial Revolution   1:115, 336; 2:119
influence on H. G. Wells   3:404–5
innoculations against disease   3:378, 406
jet engine   4:71
motion pictures   3:3, 89, 101
nuclear energy   5:124, 127, 286
Pasteur's discoveries   3:285, 406
penicillin   3:366
pesticides ("biocides") and DDT   4:337–42
"phrenology"   2:211
physics and principle of indeterminacy   5:283
printing and publishing   1:160, 162 (sidebar);
    2:234, 306, 419
professionalization and specialization of   2:119
psychiatry   4:289 (sidebar)
psychoanalysis   4:168 (sidebar); 5:42, 260–61,
    263
psychokinesis and telekinesis   5:47–48
radio   3:3, 45, 89
religion and   2:29–30, 121–22
and "resurrection men"   1:120–21
in Romantic period   1:116
satellites in space   5:54
space exploration   5:53, 54, 81–82
steam threshing machine   2:354
steamships   2:391, 394–95
submarines   2:385–86
telecommunications   5:54
telephone   2:128 (sidebar); 3:77
tractors   3:6, 92
(See also Evolution; Progress, belief in;
    Psychology; Railroads; Television; War
    weaponry)
Scopes Trial   3:102 (sidebar)
Scotland
    Calvinism in   3:377; 4:304
    education of women in 1930s   4:303–4
    Gowrie Conspiracy   1:229
    Hebrides   1:226
    Highlanders   1:187
    as Presbyterians   4:10, 304
    status of women in 11th century   1:226

in time of *Macbeth* (11th century)   1:225–26
troubled relations with England   1:145, 150,
    181, 187, 201
Scott, Sir Walter
    emulated by Cooper   1:208
    friend of Washington Irving   1:105
    influencing Hugo   1:165
    Ivanhoe   1:181–88
Scottsboro case   3:39, 239
Seale, Bobby   4:54
Second Great Awakening   1:424–25; 2:23, 404,
    417–18
Secret Life of Walter Mitty, The, Thurber, James
    3:364–69
Secular humanism   5:138
Segregation
    acceptance for time being by Booker T.
        Washington   2:341, 342, 343, 344, 345, 410,
        413, 414; 3:162, 250, 320, 385
    of churches   5:189
    documentation of negative effects   4:32–33
    in New Orleans   3:17–18; 5:22
    protest by (multiracial) high school football team
        4:29
    in public facilities   3:38 (illus.), 42 (illus.); 4:29
        (illus.)
    in public transportation   5:88–90, 185–86
    in schools for disabled   2:221 (sidebar)
    in South   1:399; 2:97; 3:419; 4:28–29, 373–74;
        5:22
    in Supreme Court rulings
        overturned for residential housing, interstate
            bus travel   4:201
        overturned for schools in *Brown v. Board of
            Education*   3:375; 4:29–30, 314; 5:90, 108,
            180, 181
        sanctioned by *Plessy v. Ferguson*   2:21,
            399–400, 413; 3:351, 375, 419; 4:1; 5:90,
            107–8
    of U.S. military during WWII   3:41–42; 4:195,
        197, 374 (sidebar)
    (*See also* African Americans' civil
        rights/reform/power movements; Integration;
        Jim Crow laws)
Self-Reliance, Emerson, Ralph Waldo   2:314–20
Senior citizens
    loneliness, depression, serious illness, and suicide
        5:273, 275 (illus.)
    problems of adjustment to retirement   5:203,
        273
Separate Peace, A, Knowles, John   4:323–29
Serbia   3:8, 11 (sidebar)
Serling, Rod   4:379
Seventeen Syllables, Yamamoto, Hisaye   4:330–36
Sex education
    for mentally handicapped   4:152
    programs of 1960s   5:153 (sidebar)
    social purity movement of late 19th century
        2:423
Sexual dimension of life

in 19th century   2:212, 423
abuse of African American women   4:54
abuse of female slaves   2:49, 60, 169, 406
adultery/infidelity   5:273, 287
AIDS   5:9
Catholic and Presbyterian views on   4:304
    (sidebar)
changing mores   5:272–73
contraceptives   2:211; 5:272, 324
effects of childhood abuse   5:289–90
"free love" movement of 1960s   5:272
Freud's arguments against repression   3:23
harassment of women in workplace   1:35
hypocrisy of public attitudes   4:75
impotence   4:128
incest   4:52
interracial taboos, miscegenation   3:391
Kinsey Report   4:75, 241, 398–99 (sidebar);
    5:324
rape   4:395; 5:117, 136, 141
sexual revolution of 1960s and '70s   5:151
treatment in literature as shocking   4:74
Victorians' repression of   2:334, 336, 338–39,
    355; 3:18, 380–81
(*See also* Homosexuality; Love and marriage;
    Prostitution)
Shakerism   3:95–99
Shakespeare, William
    Hamlet   1:136–43
    Henry IV, Part I   1:144–51
    Julius Caesar   1:189–95
    King Lear   1:196–203
    Macbeth   1:225–30
    Merchant of Venice, The   1:242–49
    Midsummer Night's Dream, A   1:258–65
    Othello   1:295–300
    Romeo and Juliet   1:344–50
    Tempest, The   1:379–85
Shane, Schaefer, Jack   2:321–26
Shange, Ntozake
    Betsey Brown   4:28–34
    *for colored girls who have considered suicide / when
        the rainbow is enuf*   5:115–21
Sharecropping and tenant farming   2:42, 411; 3:80,
    104, 105, 249, 350–51, 370–71, 418; 4:2
    STFU (Southern Tenant Farmers' Union)   3:208
Shaw, George Bernard, *Pygmalion*   3:312–18
Shelley, Mary
    daughter of Mary Wollstonecraft   1:115, 116,
        407
    Frankenstein   1:115–21
Shelley, Percy Bysshe   1:115, 116, 119
Shepard, Alan   5:292, 296
Sherman, William Tecumseh   2:139, 140 (illus.),
    165 (sidebar)
Shipping industry
    of early 19th century   2:391–92, 393, 394–95
    longshoremen   3:161 (sidebar)
Ships
    privateers   1:400

sailboats 2:395

schooners 1:401

steam-powered 1:404 (sidebar); 2:394–95

Shoeless Joe, Kinsella, W. P. 5:314–20

Short stories

    Almos' a Man, Wright, Richard 4:1–6

    Barn Burning, Faulkner, William 2:41–46

    Bear, The, Faulkner, William 2:47–53

    Cask of Amontillado, The, Poe, Edgar Allan
      2:81–86

    Child's Christmas in Wales, A, Thomas, Dylan
      3:63–67

    Christmas Memory, A, Capote, Truman 3:68–74

    Devil and Tom Walker, The, Irving, Washington
      1:101–6

    Dubliners, Joyce, James 3:106–11

    Everything That Rises Must Converge, O'Connor,
      Flannery 5:88–94

    Legend of Sleepy Hollow, The, Irving, Washington
      1:211–18

    Lottery, The, Jackson, Shirley 4:235–39

    Most Dangerous Game, The, Connell, Richard
      3:231–35

    Necklace, The, Maupassant, Guy de 2:244–48

    Noon Wine, Porter, Katherine Anne 3:243–48

    Notorious Jumping Frog of Calaveras County, The,
      Twain, Mark 2:249–54

    Occurrence at Owl Creek Bridge, An, Bierce,
      Ambrose 2:255–60

    Open Window, The, Saki 2:275–80

    Outcasts of Poker Flat, The, Harte, Bret
      2:281–87

    Rip Van Winkle, Irving, Washington 1:330–36

    Rocking-Horse Winner, The, Lawrence, D.H.
      3:344–49

    Secret Life of Walter Mitty, The, Thurber, James
      3:364–69

    Seventeen Syllables, Yamamoto, Hisaye
      4:330–36

    Where Are You Going, Where Have You Been?,
      Oates, Joyce Carol 4:391–96

    Worn Path, A, Welty, Eudora 3:418–24

    Yellow Wallpaper, The, Gilman, Charlotte Perkins
      2:422–28

    Yentl, the Yeshiva Boy, Singer, Isaac Bashevis
      3:425–31

    Young Goodman Brown, Hawthorne, Nathaniel
      1:420–26

Siberia 4:133–35

Sicily 4:67

Siddartha Gautama 1:365–68

Siddhartha, Hesse, Hermann 1:365–70

Silent Spring, Carson, Rachel 4:337–42; 5:35

Silko, Leslie Marmon, *Ceremony* 4:79–86

Silver. *See* Gold rushes and silver strikes

Simon, Neil, *Biloxi Blues* 4:35–41

Sin and damnation

    beliefs of Calvinists 3:377; 4:304

    beliefs of Puritans 1:23, 393, 421

    beliefs in Shakespeare's time 1:143

    depictions in morality plays 1:148

    and guilt in *The Scarlet Letter* 1:351, 355–56

    in *Paradise Lost* 1:301, 306

    and predestination 4:304

    in *Young Goodman Brown* 1:420–26

Sinclair, Upton, *Jungle, The* 3:174–80, 320

Singer, Isaac Bashevis, *Yentl, the Yeshiva Boy*
    3:425–31

Sister Carrie, Dreiser, Theodore 2:327–33

Skinner, B. F. 5:156, 279

Slaughterhouse Five, Vonnegut, Kurt, Jr. 4:343–48

Slave narratives

    described 2:171; 4:205

    Douglass, Frederick (*Narrative of the Life of
      Frederick Douglass*) 2:236–41

    Jacobs, Harriet (*Incidents in the Life of a Slave Girl*)
      2:168–73

    by Northrup, Solomon 2:410

    Roots as 5:305

Slave trade

    auction block 1:40 (illus.)

    diagram of slave ship 1:38 (illus.)

    English involvement in/prohibition of
      1:274–75, 299, 337–38; 2:361

    impelled by need for labor 1:103

    missionaries' attempts to atone for 2:361–62

    overview 1:37, 103

    traders despised 1:103

Slavery in America

    of American Indians by forced indenture
      2:175

    causing rift between North and South 2:88,
      172, 188, 403–4

    of Chinese prostitutes 2:366–67

    in colonial America 1:394; 2:93, 175

    Compromise of 1850 2:404–5

    as depicted in *Tituba of Salem Village* 1:397–98

    extent of, in Old South 2:188, 405, 410

    Fugitive Slave Acts (1793 and 1850) 1:42;
      2:16, 62, 170, 189, 404–5, 410

    Kansas-Nebraska Act (1854) 1:42; 2:5
      (sidebar), 172, 193

    in Kentucky 2:59–60

    Kongo kingdom and 2:145

    legacy of, in late 20th century 2:65

    in Maryland 2:236–37

    Missouri Compromise (1820) 2:5 (sidebar),
      15–16, 22

    Nat Turner's Rebellion 2:169–70

    in North Carolina 2:168

    opposition of

      Patrick Henry 1:126 (sidebar)

      Thomas Paine 1:72 (sidebar)

      Henry David Thoreau 1:88, 89 (sidebar)

    racist justifications of 1:39, 41, 42, 394; 2:403,
      404

    references to, deleted from Declaration of
      Independence 1:98

    reliance upon, for harvesting of cotton 2:15,
      22, 44 (illus.), 59, 168, 403

slave codes and patrols   1:*103*; 2:*189, 190* (sidebar)

as soul-corrupting for whites   2:*52, 408*

Southern states avoiding mention in state constitutions   1:*99* (sidebar)

and Underground Railroad   2:*16, 60, 62, 189, 238, 406–7*

whites' feelings of guilt at   2:*52, 53*

(See also Abolitionists/Abolition of slavery; African Americans)

Slavery in North America

among Canadian Kwakiutl   5:*194–95*

brought by Spaniards to Puerto Rico   5:*214*

Slaves

Amistad mutiny   1:*43*

arson by   2:*189*

cimaroons   1:*401–2*

communities and culture   2:*407*

escapes, rebellions, and resistance   1:*39, 43, 401–2*; 2:*60, 93, 94–95, 169–70, 188–89, 406–7*

family life   2:*60, 169, 237–38, 405, 406, 410*; 3:*423*; 4:*204–5*

female, sexual abuse of   2:*49, 60, 169, 406*

food and clothing   2:*237*

freed before Emancipation Proclamation   2:*93–94, 168–69, 238*

ill-prepared for freedom   2:*411*

literacy   2:*16, 24–25*

living and working conditions   2:*189* (sidebar), *237, 405, 410*

loyalty of some to white masters during Civil War   2:*410–11*

music   2:*398, 407*

punishment   2:*240–42, 405, 410*

religion   2:*407*; 3:*83*

social distinctions between   3:*387*

use of cunning and manipulative behavior   2:*401*

Sleator, William, *House of Stairs*   5:*156–62*

Smith, Bessie   3:*253* (illus.)

Smith, Betty, *Tree Grows in Brooklyn, A*   3:*397–403*

Smith, Henry Nash   3:*226*

Smith, Joseph Jr.   5:*4*

Smoking. See Tobacco

So Far from the Bamboo Grove, Watkins, Yoko K.   4:*349–55*

Social Darwinism. See under Evolution

Social Security System   3:*128*

Socialism

American, birth of   3:*174–75*

labor unions accused of   3:*144*

opposed by fascism   4:*66*

popular among European immigrants   3:*321*

utopian   5:*251–52*

Socrates   1:*240, 322–24, 327*

Solzhenitsyn, Alexander, *One Day in the Life of Ivan Denisovich*   4:*281–87*

Sons and Lovers, Lawrence, D. H.   2:*334–39*

as example of bildungsroman   3:*264*

Sophists   1:*19, 240*

Sophocles, *Antigone*   1:*14–21*

Souls of Black Folk, The, Du Bois, W. E. B.   2:*340–46*; 3:*320*

Sounder, Armstrong, William H.   3:*370–76*

South, The

of 1980s   3:*78–79*

anti-Yankee bias   3:*76*

Christmas traditions   3:*69*

folklore in   2:*48–49*

homeopathy and Indian remedies   3:*68–69*

hunting in   2:*47–48*

Illinois' ties to   2:*8–9*

industrialization/decline of agriculture and aristocracy   3:*76, 203*; 4:*364–65, 368*; 5:*91, 129–30*

and "King" Cotton   2:*15, 22, 44* (illus.), *168, 403*

mixed race offspring   2:*49*; 3:*17–18, 81, 83*

"New"   3:*72–73, 203*

plantation life   2:*137–38*

religious influences   3:*76–77*

segregation in   1:*399*; 2:*97*; 3:*419*; 4:*28–29, 373–74*; 5:*22*

social stratification in rural areas and small towns   3:*393*

storytelling tradition   3:*421*

textile mills and mill towns   3:*76, 153, 203–4*; 4:*256*

womanhood, ideal of   3:*19, 392–93*; 4:*366–67*

(See also Civil War; Jim Crow laws; Reconstruction)

South Africa, racism and apartheid   1:*63*; 3:*86*; 4:*94–100*

South America

Argentina   5:*208–11, 212–13*

Chile   5:*163–70*

Colombia   2:*268–70, 272–73*

Peru   4:*221, 222*; 5:*333–38*

South Carolina   5:*285–86*

South Pacific

climate   4:*231* (sidebar)

island fighting and major sea battles (1942–45)   4:*60–61*

island peoples' origins   4:*221–22*

Japanese conquests in WWII   4:*178*

Philippines   3:*101*; 4:*81*

Southey, Robert   1:*121*

Soviet Union

anti-Semitism   3:*124–25*; 5:*122*

anti-Zionism   4:*107–8*

atomic bomb capability   4:*183*; 5:*96, 126*

centralized planning and control of means of production   5:*124*

de-Stalinization   4:*285–86*

European conquests and sphere of influence   5:*123* (sidebar), *224, 253–54*

Five-Year Plans and forced labor   4:*16, 132*

forced collectivization of agriculture   4:*281–85*

Gorbachev and "perestroika"   5:*8*

gulag system of labor camp prisons   4:*282–85*; 5:*239* (sidebar) invasion of Armenia   3:*340*

invasion of Poland   3:*340*; 4:*131*

propaganda   5:*252*

reprisals against Japanese in Korea and
Manchuria   4:*350*

seen as "controlling" international communism
4:*166*

Siberia   4:*133–35*

Sputniks and space program   5:*81, 291, 292,
293, 294, 321*

Stalin/Hitler non-aggression pact (1939)   3:*210,
214*; 4:*17*

Stalin's reign of terror and purges   4:*16–17, 166*

suppression of Hungarian uprising (1956)
4:*166*

totalitarianism   4:*16*

Ukraine, Babi Yar massacre   4:*120*

(*See also* Russia)

Space Age

Dillard's musings   5:*279–80, 281* (sidebar)

manned space flight highlights   5:*294* (sidebar)

moon landing   5:*81–82*

NASA (National Aeronautics and Space
Administration)   5:*81, 291*

Right Stuff, The   5:*291–97*

satellites for communications   5:*54*

treaty prohibiting military use of space   5:*239*

U.S.-Soviet competition in space race   5:*53, 81,
321–22*

(*See also* Aviation; War weaponry)

Spain

Civil War   4:*67*

decline of empire   1:*1–3*

fascism in   1:*293–94*; 4:*67*

Inquisition   1:*2–3*

invasion of Italy   1:*317*

wars with England and France   1:*1–2, 87, 88,
130–31, 201, 305*

Spanish-American War (1898)   3:*101, 278*

Spark, Muriel, *Prime of Miss Jean Brodie, The*
4:*303–8*

Sparta   1:*324–25, 328*

Speech on the Evacuation at Dunkirk, Churchill,
Winston   4:*356–63*

Speeches

"Ain't I a Woman?", Truth, Sojourner   2:*22–27*

John Brown's Final Speech, Brown, John
2:*188–94*

First Inaugural Address, Roosevelt, Franklin D.
3:*125–30*

Gettysburg Address, Lincoln, Abraham   2:*130–36*

"Give Me Liberty or Give Me Death", Henry,
Patrick   1:*122–28*

"I Have a Dream", King, Martin Luther, Jr.
5:*185–93*

"I Will Fight No More Forever", Joseph, Chief
2:*160–67*

Inaugural Address, Kennedy, John F.   5:*222–28*

On the Evacuation at Dunkirk, Churchill,
Winston   4:*356–63*

Spencer, Herbert   2:*341*

Spinsterhood, in early 19th-century England
2:*297*

Spock, Benjamin   4:*21–22*

Sports. *See* Entertainment; Games and sports

Spreckels, Claus and sugar interests   3:*269, 270*
(sidebar), *319*

Sputnik   5:*81, 291, 292, 293, 294, 321*

Stalin, Josef

banning books depicting life in West   5:*96*

British outrage at   4:*17*

Five-Year Plans for economic development
4:*16, 282*

forced collectivization of agriculture   4:*281–82*;
5:*122*

as Marxist Party member   4:*14, 15* (illus.)

non-aggression pact with Hitler   3:*210, 213–14*;
4:*17*

oppression or extermination of Jews   3:*123–24*

political prisoners exiled to Siberian gulags
4:*282–85*; 5:*239* (sidebar)

purges of opponents   4:*16–17*; 5:*122, 254*

(*See also* Soviet Union)

Stanley, Henry Morton   2:*146*

Stanton, Elizabeth Cady   2:*24, 55*; 3:*16*

Steamships   1:*404* (sidebar); 2:*391, 394–95*

Stein, Joseph, *Fiddler on the Roof*   3:*119–24*

Steinbeck, John

Grapes of Wrath, The   3:*138–45*

Of Mice and Men   3:*269–76*

Red Pony, The   3:*334–37*

Stevenson, Robert Louis

on *Pride and Prejudice*   2:*300*

Strange Case of Dr. Jekyll and Mr. Hyde, The
3:*377–82*

on *Tess of the D'Urbervilles*   2:*359*

Treasure Island   1:*400–405*

STFU (Southern Tenant Farmers' Union)   3:*208*

Stock market

1929 crash and bank failures   3:*125–26, 208*

speculation fever of 1920s   3:*146*

speculations in trusts and railroads of 1900
3:*167* (sidebar)

(*See also* Great Depression)

Stoicism   1:*192–93*

Stoneham, C. A.   3:*149*

Story Catcher, The, Sandoz, Mari   2:*347–52*

Stowe, Harriet Beecher

relationship with Harriet Jacobs   2:*172*

Uncle Tom's Cabin   2:*403–9*

Strachey, Lytton   3:*356*

Strange Case of Dr. Jekyll and Mr. Hyde, The,
Stevenson, Robert Louis   3:*377–82*

Stranger in a Strange Land, Heinlein, Robert A.
5:*321–27*

"Stream of consciousness" writing   3:*111, 358*

Streetcar Named Desire, A, Williams, Tennessee
4:*364–70*

Streetcars   2:*328*; 3:*25*; 4:*366*

Stuyvesant, Peter   1:*331*

Styron, William, *Confessions of Nat Turner, The*
    2:93–98
Submarines   2:385–86
Suburbia   4:73
Suez Canal   3:184; 4:107
Suffrage (right to vote)
    for African Americans   4:148
        granted by 14th and 15th Amendments
            5:21
        Jim Crow laws restricting   3:37, 352, 419;
            4:1; 5:22
        Mississippi Plan (1890) preventing   5:22
        protected by Civil Rights and Voting Rights
            Acts (1957 and 1965)   5:22, 186
    for American Indians   4:80
    expansion by elimination of property
        qualifications   2:302
    hindered for freed blacks   2:341
    Nationality Act (1940)   4:80
    for women. *See* Women's suffrage
Suicide
    by American Indians   4:83
    attempts by Shange   5:120
    effects of childhood abuse   5:288, 289–90
    of interned Japanese Americans   4:140
    of Japanese girls in Korea (1944–45)   4:350,
        353
    of Jim Jones and 911 members of People's
        Temple   5:84
    by kamikazi pilots   4:61 (sidebar), 62 (illus.)
    in *Madame Bovary*   2:211–12
    by men   4:23, 114 (sidebar)
    of prep school students   4:74
    as response to depression   5:259–60
    of Sylvia Plath   4:22–26
    of teenagers   5:259–60, 261
    by Vietnam War veterans   5:106
    by white males   5:273
Sullivan, Joseph   3:149
Summer of My German Soldier, Greene, Bette
    4:371–77
Sumner, William   3:207
Sun Yat-Sen, Dr.   4:126; 5:229
Supernatural
    alchemy   1:384, 385 (sidebar)
    astrology   1:346, 350
    belief in, by American Indians   4:83
    belief in *curanderismo*   4:45
    belief in, in China   3:133
    belief in, in Elizabethan/Jacobean era   1:194–95,
        227–28, 262, 346, 350
    belief in, in Victorian England   1:418–19;
        2:185, 383
    in *Beloved*   2:63
    in *Beowulf*   1:46–48, 49
    brujas (witches)   4:46
    dreams related to   1:424
    in *Hamlet*   1:138, 141, 142 (sidebar)
    in *The Hobbit*   1:153
    in *Julius Caesar*   1:195

in *Legend of Sleepy Hollow, The*   1:213, 215, 217
    and "mysteriousness" of African and African
        American culture   5:330
    and mysticism   1:416
    and paranormal phenomena   2:383 (sidebar);
        5:47–48, 56, 239
    in *Romeo and Juliet*   1:346, 350
    superstitions associated with Chinese New Year
        5:75, 76 (illus.)
    in *Tempest, The*   1:381, 383
    in *Turn of the Screw, The*   2:381
    (*See also* Witchcraft)
Swarthout, Glendon, *Bless the Beasts and Children*
    5:34–38
Sweden, immigration to U.S.   3:243–44, 259–60
Sweet Whispers, Brother Rush, Hamilton, Virginia
    5:328–32
Swift, Jonathan
    criticism of *Robinson Crusoe*   1:343
    Gulliver's Travels   1:129–35
    Modest Proposal, A   1:266–72
Syncretism   3:190–91; 4:44 (sidebar)

T

Tahiti,   1:274, 278, 392
Taine, Hippolyte   3:213
Taiwan   3:190; 5:254
Tale of Two Cities, A, Dickens, Charles   1:371–78
Tammany Hall, New York   3:148–49, 398–99
Tan, Amy
    Joy Luck Club, The   5:229–35
    Kitchen God's Wife, The   3:189–95
Tasmania   3:406
Taverns   1:331
Taylor, Mildred, *Roll of Thunder, Hear My Cry*
    3:350–55
Teapot Dome scandal   3:25
Technology. *See* Science/technology
Teilhard de Chardin, Pierre   5:93
Telecommunications   5:54
Telekinesis   5:47–48
Telepathy   5:239
Television
    as babysitter   5:36–37
    Bonanza creating sense of family security   5:203
        (sidebar)
    debates costing Nixon 1960 presidential election
        5:223
    development of   3:92; 5:96–97
    golden age of TV drama   4:379
    impact on conduct of Vietnam War and antiwar
        sentiment   5:37
    impact on public support for civil rights
        protesters   5:108
    interconnectedness versus loneliness of viewers
        4:398
    spreading conformity   4:236
    violent content of programming   5:62

westerns   5:201–2
(See also Media)
Television evangelists   5:31–32, 137–38, 140 (illus.)
Temperance movement   2:25 (sidebar), 85–86;
   3:69, 75, 147
Tempest, The, Shakespeare, William   1:379–85
Templars   1:182, 185 (sidebar)
Tenant farming and sharecropping   2:42, 411;
   3:80, 104, 105, 249, 350–51, 370–71, 418; 4:2
Terrorism
   Arab against Israel   4:106
   by Argentine military junta   5:209–10, 212–13
   by Chilean military junta   5:169
   by Guatemalan military   5:28
   of Herut Party in Israel   4:107
   of Irgun in British Mandatory Palestine   4:103
   (See also Ku Klux Klan)
Tervalon, Jervey, Understand This   5:339–45
Tess of the D'Urbervilles, Hardy, Thomas   2:353–59
Theater
   Chinese opera   5:75
   in early 1900s in America   3:220–21
   El Teatro Campesino   4:409; 5:172
   Elizabethan   1:261–62, 263
   golden age of television drama   3:92; 4:236,
      379
   importance in ancient Greece   1:19–20, 240
   innovations of Wilder   3:287–88
   musicals   4:387
   in postmodern era   2:123
   realism in   1:92
   supported by James I   1:299
   Teatro Rodante Puertorriqueño   5:216
   and Theater of the Absurd   4:400
   (See also Plays)
Thebes (in ancient Greece)   1:14
Their Eyes Were Watching God, Hurston, Zora Neale
   3:383–89
Theseus   1:57, 61 (sidebar), 258, 259
Things Fall Apart, Achebe, Chinua   2:360–65
Thirty Years War   1:87, 88, 388 (sidebar), 388
Thisbe   1:259 (sidebar)
Thomas, Dylan, Child's Christmas in Wales, A
   3:63–67
Thoreau, Henry David
   Civil Disobedience   2:87–92
   influence on Dickinson   2:57
   influence on King   5:192
   on John Brown   2:193
   as transcendentalist   1:356; 2:92, 416
   Walden   2:416–21
Thornton, Laurence, Imagining Argentina   5:208–13
Thousand Pieces of Gold, McCunn, Ruthanne Lum
   2:366–71
Three Musketeers, The, Dumas, Alexandre
   1:386–92
Thucydides   1:14
Thurber, James, Secret Life of Walter Mitty, The
   3:364–69
Tijerina, Lopez Reies   4:175, 176, 321

Time of the Hero, The, Vargas Llosa, Mario
   5:333–38
Titans   1:301
Tituba (in real life)   1:79, 83 (sidebar), 394–96,
   422–23
Tituba of Salem Village, Petry, Ann   1:393–99
To Kill a Mockingbird, Lee, Harper   3:390–96
Tobacco
   cigars   3:65
   rise during 1920s in popularity of smoking
      3:89
   snuff   3:71 (sidebar)
   for women   3:19, 23, 167, 168 (illus.)
Tolkien, J.R.R., Hobbit, The   1:152–58
Tolstoy, Leo
   Anna Karenina   2:34–40
   on Uncle Tom's Cabin   2:409
Tom Brown's Schooldays, Hughes, Thomas
   2:372–77
Totalitarianism. See Dictatorship
Tournaments   1:291
Towns and cities, growth of. See Urbanization
Transcendentalism   1:356–57; 2:54, 92, 314,
   316–19, 416, 418–19
Transportation
   Appalachian Trail   5:278–79
   automobiles   2:128 (sidebar); 3:23, 77, 88–89,
      94, 101; 5:40 (illus.)
   aviation   3:211–12
   canals   2:230; 3:184, 231–32, 270; 4:107
   public, segregation of   5:88–90, 185–86
   roads and highways   3:77, 91
      Blue Ridge Parkway   5:278
      creating suburbs   5:262
      National System of Interstate and Defense
         Highways (1956)   3:73
      Route 66   3:140
   sled dogs   3:52–56
   streetcars   2:328; 3:25; 4:366
   (See also Railroads in U.S.)
Treasure Island, Stevenson, Robert Louis
   1:400–405
Tree Grows in Brooklyn, A, Smith, Betty   3:397–403
Trojan War   1:8, 14, 166–69, 281, 283 (sidebar)
Trotsky, Leon   4:16; 5:254
Truman Doctrine (1947–49)   4:110; 5:123–24
Truman, Harry S   4:72, 173 (sidebar); 5:96, 123
Truth, Sojourner, "Ain't I a Woman?"   2:22–27
Tubman, Harriet   2:189
Turkey
   Ali Pasha   2:101
   genocide of Armenians   3:338–43; 4:199
   "guest" workers from, in Europe   4:163–64
   under Ottoman Turks   1:295–96; 3:338–40
   WWI and British occupation of former holdings
      4:102
   and Young Turks   3:339, 340, 342
Turn of the Screw, The, James, Henry   2:378–83
Turner, Nat   2:93–94, 95, 169–70, 188
   (See also Confessions of Nat Turner, The)

Tuskegee Institute   2:*413, 414*
Twain, Mark
    Adventures of Huckleberry Finn, The   2:*15–21*
    Notorious Jumping Frog of Calaveras County, The
        2:*249–54*
Twelve Angry Men, Rose, Reginald (screenplay)
    4:*378–83*
Twenty-Thousand Leagues under the Sea, Verne, Jules
    2:*384–90*
Twinship   4:*219*
Two Years before the Mast, Dana, Richard Henry, Jr.
    2:*391–96*
Tyler, Wat (Peasant's Revolt of 1381)   1:*65*

U

UFOs (unidentified flying objects)   4:*347–48*; 5:*59*
    (*illus.*)
Ukraine, Babi Yar massacre   4:*120*
Uncas   1:*207* (*sidebar*), *208*
Uncle Remus, Harris, Joel Chandler   2:*397–402*
Uncle Tom's Cabin, Stowe, Harriet Beecher   2:*403–9*
    aggravating North-South rift over slavery   2:*172*
Underground Railroad   2:*16, 60, 62, 189, 238,*
    406–7
Understand This, Tervalon, Jervey   5:*339–45*
UNIA (United Negro Improvement Association)
    3:*160*; 4:*211*
Unions. *See* Labor unions
Unitarianism   2:*54, 315*
United Nations   4:*103, 107–8*
    birth of   5:*53–54*
    Cold War reflected in   5:*254*
    "Convention Relating to Status of Refugees"
        5:*28–29*
    and Declaration of Women's Rights (1967)
        5:*174*
United Service Organizations (USO)   4:*38*
United States in 19th century
    American Enlightenment   2:*416*
    American literature, birth of   1:*210, 211, 217,*
        218, 335–36; 2:*419*
    American literature, maturation of   2:*109,*
        234–35
    appeal of European travel to middle- to upper-
        class Americans   2:*105–6*
    belief in progress   2:*195, 196, 313, 416*
    canal system   2:*230*
    conservatism and commerce   2:*199, 306, 312,*
        328, 331
    democracy, growth of   2:*87–88, 89–91*
    depressions in later years   3:*51, 169*
    dissent, protest, and civil disobedience   2:*87,*
        89, 90, 312
    economic growth   2:*195, 230, 416*
    Gilded Age   2:*20, 199, 306, 312, 328, 331*
    Jackson administration   2:*314–15*
    Mexican War   2:*88, 89, 242*
    rural New England   2:*125–26*
    War of 1812   1:*53*; 2:*416*

whaling industry   2:*230, 232–34*
    (*See also* Civil War; Railroads in U.S.;
        Reconstruction; Slavery in America; West, The;
        Western migration)
United States in 20th century: Progressive Era
    (1900–1919)
    as era of reform   3:*75–76, 284–85*
    labor unions, support for   3:*420*
    muckraking journalists   3:*176, 320*
    multifaceted agenda of   3:*285, 319–20*
    postwar return to (probusiness) normalcy
        3:*21*
    reformers as elitist   3:*319*
    reforming zeal carried to other countries   3:*280*
    trust busters and Teddy Roosevelt   3:*167*
    women's roles changing   3:*271–72, 280*
        (*sidebar*)
    Woodrow Wilson   3:*279–80, 319*
    World War I (1917–18). *See* World War I
United States in 20th century: Roaring Twenties
    (1920–1929)
    assembly line/mass production   3:*89, 100–101,*
        102
    boomtowns   3:*25*
    buying on credit   3:*89*
    car culture   3:*23*
    consumer/mass culture, advertising   3:*26, 89,*
        100–101, 102
    gangsters and St. Valentine's Day Massacre
        3:*366–67*
    hard times for farmers   3:*94–95, 138–40*
    machine age as degrading individualism and
        culture   5:*41*
    modern morals and changing status of women
        3:*23, 228–29*
    postwar economic boom   3:*146*
    Prohibition. *See* Prohibition
    race riots (1919)   2:*6, 404*; 3:*160, 252, 321*;
        4:*310*
    San Francisco's corruption   3:*226*
    stock market speculation fever   3:*146*
    Teapot Dome scandal   3:*25*
    and United Fruit Company in South America
        2:*269–70*
United States in 20th century: Thirties (1930–1940).
    See Great Depression, The
United States in 20th century: World War II
    (1941–45). *See* World War II
United States in 20th century: 1946–1959
    age of big government   4:*110*
    baby boom   1:*224*; 2:*325–26*; 4:*38, 74, 240*
    beatniks, counterculture, hippies, and protesters
        4:*75, 289, 293, 399–400*
    Cold War. *See* Cold War
    consumerism, credit buying, and conformity
        3:*2, 91*; 4:*73–74, 110–11, 236, 328, 397–401*;
        5:*322–23*
    disillusion, dehumanization, and dystopian
        literature   5:*252*
    divorce rate increase   4:*38*

global commercial and cultural influence
1:223; 3:92

"heroes" as powerful and nonconformist   4:262,
292, 381–82

inflation and anxiety   4:109–10

mass culture and influence of television   4:111,
379, 398

postwar boom, prosperity   4:109–10, 328

teenage culture   4:391–93, 394–95

War Brides Act   4:124, 127; 5:231

white male economic dominance   4:397

women and cult of domesticity   4:237, 240–41

women as sex objects   4:393

United States in 20th century: 1960s

appeal of Eastern religions   5:237, 281

civil rights protests. *See* Civil rights movements

counterculture, hippies, and protesters   5:37,
64 (sidebar), 83, 158, 237, 272, 279, 308–10,
323–25

cults, iconoclasm, rebels as heros   5:83–84, 318
(sidebar), 323–24

decade of tumult   5:309 (sidebar)

environment, concern for   4:337–42; 5:85–86,
279

feminism. *See* Women's rights movement (and
feminism)

"free love" movement   5:272

"graying" of America   5:202–4

Johnson's Great Society and War on Poverty
3:324; 5:68, 150, 266

riots   2:97–98; 3:324; 4:207; 5:112 (sidebar),
340

self-fulfillment and human potential movement
5:204, 287–88

(*See also* Vietnam War)

United States in 20th century: 1970s–1980s

antibusing incidents   3:324

disillusion with government after Nixon and
Watergate   3:99; 5:158–59, 263, 317

environment, concern for   5:279 (sidebar)

feminism. *See* Women's rights movement (and
feminism)

judicial opposition to civil rights legislation
5:1–2

"me" generation and self-help movements
5:263, 287–88

official apology and monetary compensation to
Japanese Americans for WWII internment
4:143, 195

probusiness conservatism (Reagan presidency)
5:1

recession, unemployment, and welfare cuts
5:1, 329

rise of New Right and religious fundamentalists
5:136–39

sexual revolution   5:151

(*See also* Vietnam War)

U.S. Army. *See* Military

United States Military. *See* Military

U.S.S.R. *See* Soviet Union

Up From Slavery, Washington, Booker T.   2:410–15

Urbanization

in 19th-century America   2:125, 195, 301–4

of 19th-century England   1:106, 217, 417;
2:118, 353, 354, 358

in 19th-century France   2:103–4, 209

in 20th-century America   3:25, 73, 88–89;
4:171–72

in 20th-century South   5:91

in 20th-century South Africa   4:95

by American Indians in 20th century   4:186

in Chile   5:164

cities viewed as hotbeds of sin   3:69

of colonial America   1:102

department stores made possible by   2:303

with immigration   2:302, 327; 3:101, 102, 166

and Mexican Americans   4:171

promoting individualism   2:302

replacing rural, agrarian society   2:312, 327;
5:91

rise of crime and police detectives   2:153–54

(*See also* Ghettos; Housing)

USS *Somers*   1:56

Usury (moneylending)   1:103–4, 182–83, 243, 247

Utopian societies

depicted in literature   5:251–52

in novel *Looking Backward* (1888)   2:423

of 1840s   2:418

Shakers   3:95–99

Twin Oaks colony   5:279

Walden movement   5:279

V

Valdez, Luis   5:172

Zoot Suit   4:403–10

Van Dine, S. S.   3:227

Vargas Llosa, Mario   5:211 (sidebar)

Time of the Hero, The   5:333–38

Veblen, Thorstein   3:169

Venice, Italy   1:242–46, 295–97

Verne, Jules

Twenty-Thousand Leagues under the Sea
2:384–90

H. G. Wells compared to   3:410

Verona, Italy   1:344–45

Verrall, Richard   4:40

Vesey, Denmark   2:94–95

Veterinarians   3:1

Victor Emmanuel III, King of Italy   4:66, 67

Victoria, Queen of England   2:28, 335

Victorian Age

agricultural depression   2:353

charity   2:264

circuses and freak shows   2:33, 120, 329

class divisions and social stratification
2:152–53, 157, 358

crime in London   2:262–64

debt, bankruptcy, and poorhouses   2:211–12,
261–62, 266

divorce   2:*158, 355–56*
education, progress in   1:*412;* 2:*334*
England as world's leading economic power
   2:*334*
foreign competition and economic depression
   2:*152*
humor and puns   2:*30*
hypocrisy of   3:*381*
imperialism   2:*118–19*
landed gentry's decline   2:*354–55*
London as center of   1:*417;* 2:*20, 196*
love and marriage in   2:*106, 116, 336*
men's roles in   2:*107–8, 336*
mining industry   2:*335*
mourning traditions   1:*414–15*
police, reorganization of   2:*153–54*
pride plus anxiety   3:*405–6, 408–9*
public school system   2:*372–77*
science vs. religion   2:*29–30;* 3:*404*
sexual repression   2:*334, 336, 338–39, 355;*
   3:*18, 380–81*
urbanization with industrialization   1:*417;*
   2:*118, 353, 354, 358*
work ethic and circumscribed codes of
   behavior/decorum   2:*20, 108, 196, 378–79;*
   3:*381*
Yorkshire   1:*417–18*
(*See also* Colonialism, imperialism, and
   interventionism)
Victorian women
   American stereotype of   2:*107*
   divorce   2:*158, 355–56*
   dowries for   2:*246*
   education of   1:*412;* 2:*30, 181–82, 422–23*
   emancipation of, opponents and proponents
      1:*356;* 3:*167*
   employment
      denial of meaningful work   2:*426, 427*
      as governesses   2:*182, 183 (sidebar), 378–80*
      limited opportunities for   2:*203, 355*
      need to supplement husband's income
         3:*168–69*
      in prostitution   2:*228, 264, 328–29, 355*
   evolution and the "Woman Question"
      2:*423–24*
   fashion and home furnishings for status   2:*246,*
      247 (sidebar); 3:*420*
   fashionable clothing as restricting   3:*420*
   as "feminine"   2:*204, 206–7*
   as "helpless"   3:*19*
   as "hysterical"   2:*425*
   ignorant preferred to educated, by men   2:*380*
   as innocent and chaste   2:*422–25*
   lack of rights   2:*356*
   marriage and domestic roles for   2:*106–7, 108,*
      116, 202, 303, 336; 3:*167*
   as "maternal"   2:*212, 404*
   prejudice against as writers   1:*415 (sidebar);*
      2:*56, 186, 203, 212, 424–25*
   shopping and department stores   2:*303*

social calls   3:*321–23*
as spinsters in England   2:*297*
supposed moral superiority of   2:*106;* 3:*16, 18,*
   167, 228
view of themselves as "interesting"   2:*106*
Vidocq, François-Eugène   3:*226*
Vietnam War
   American Indian soldiers in   5:*362–63*
   anti-Vietnam war movements   3:*98, 324*
   arising from Cold War's "domino theory"
      4:*347, 375;* 5:*101–2, 158*
   arising from French hopes to recolonize
      Indochina   5:*306–7*
   atrocities, compared to those inflicted upon
      American Indians   2:*79*
   black soldiers in   5:*102–3*
   combat against jungle guerillas   5:*103*
   draft of disadvantaged for (Project 100,000)
      5:*102–3, 158, 307*
   fall of South Vietnam to communist North
      5:*307*
   Johnson's escalation of involvement   5:*158, 307*
   Kennedy's sending of "advisors"   5:*158, 307*
   protested by
      antiwar forces in U.S.   2:*13–14;* 4:*347;*
         5:*105–6, 158, 307–8*
      blacks   4:*207;* 5:*103 (sidebar)*
      Chicanos   4:*409–10*
      students at Kent State University   5:*158*
      women and mothers   5:*308*
      young men subject to draft   5:*307–8*
      young people   5:*271*
   return of POWs   4:*376*
   seen as West's failure to contain communism
      4:*135*
   U.S. forces withdrawn from   4:*375–76*
   U.S. soldiers questioning purposes of   5:*104–5*
   U.S. soldiers' reasons for enlisting   5:*307*
      (*sidebar*)
   veterans' postwar experience   5:*105–6*
   Vietnam Memorial   5:*105 (illus.), 106, 312*
   as world's first "television" war   5:*3–7, 37*
Vigilantism
   in frontier West   1:*256–57;* 2:*323–24*
   in rural California   3:*273–74*
   in San Francisco of 1850s   2:*286–87*
   tarring and feathering by mobs   2:*17 (sidebar)*
   (*See also* Ku Klux Klan; Lynching)
Vikings   1:*49, 138, 226*
Villa, Pancho (Doroteo Arango)   3:*197, 279*
Villarreal, José Antonio   5:*172*
   Pocho   4:*295–302*
Vindication of the Rights of Woman, A, Wollstonecraft,
   Mary   1:*406–12;* 2:*297*
Viracocha people   4:*221, 222*
Virgil
   Aeneid, The   1:*8–13*
   as character in Dante's *Inferno*   1:*176–77,*
      178–79
Virginia   1:*379, 384, 394;* 5:*278–84*

Voigt, Cynthia, *Runner, The*   5:306–13
Vonnegut, Kurt, Jr., *Slaughterhouse Five*   4:343–48

W

Walden, Thoreau, Henry David   2:416–21
Wales   1:288; 3:63–64, 66
Walker, Alice, *Color Purple, The*   3:80–87
Walpole, Robert   1:266, 269
War
   and antiwar sentiment. *See* Antiwar literature
   Arab-Israeli Six-Day War (1967)   4:93
   Cold War   1:84, 223, 388–89
   England's civil war   1:303, 305–6
   England's wars with France   1:51–52, 93, 123,
      130–31, 159, 160, 204–6, 220–21, 305
   England's wars with Spain   1:1–2, 87, 88,
      130–31, 201, 306
   French and Indian War (Seven Years' War)
      1:93, 123, 204–6, 220–21
   glorification vs. reality of battle   2:257, 258,
      308, 309 (sidebar), 312, 313; 3:9–11, 12–13;
      4:69–70
   Korean   1:223; 3:73; 4:92
   Mexican   2:88, 89, 242; 5:172
   Napoleonic   2:99–100, 295–96
   Peloponnesian   1:241, 324, 328
   Revolutions of 1848   1:376
   Russo-Turkish   2:37–39
   Spanish-American (1898)   3:101, 278
   Thirty Years   1:87, 88, 388 (sidebar), 388
   Trojan   1:8, 14, 166–69, 281 (illus.), 281, 283
      (sidebar)
   Vietnam. *See* Vietnam War
   War of 1812   1:53; 2:416
   (*See also* American Revolution; Antiwar literature;
      Civil War; France in 18th century: French
      Revolution; Military; World War I; World War
      II)
War on Poverty   3:324; 5:68, 150, 266
War weaponry
   aircraft
      bombers   4:67–68
      dive-bombers   4:359
      fighter bombers   4:67
      fighters   4:361
      helicopters   4:71
      jets   4:71
   aircraft carriers   4:59
   atomic/nuclear   4:71
      arms control proposals   4:71; 5:126, 225,
         239, 252 (sidebar)
      hydrogen bomb   4:183; 5:126
      Manhattan Project   4:71, 81–82, 316
      missiles   5:124
      (*See also* Atom bomb)
   barbed wire used as   3:113
   in *Beowulf*   1:46 (illus.)
   field artillery   3:113
   incendiary bombs   4:179

landing craft   4:60
machine gun   3:9, 113
minesweepers   4:61
rockets   5:54, 96
submarines   1:277–78
technological enhancements during WWI
   3:113
technology causing anxiety   3:406; 4:255
War of the Worlds, The, Wells, H.G.   3:404–10
   Orson Welles' October 1938 broadcast of
      3:154, 365, 408 (sidebar)
Warren, Mary   1:81 (sidebar), 83 (sidebar)
Washington, Booker T.
   advocating (temporary) acceptance of segregation
      2:341, 342, 343, 344, 345, 410, 413, 414; 3:162,
      250, 320, 385
   autobiography: *Up From Slavery*   2:410–15
   compared to Du Bois   2:345 (sidebar); 3:162,
      250, 320, 385
Waste Land, The, Eliot, T.S.   3:357, 411–17
Watergate scandal   3:99; 5:158–59, 263, 317
Watership Down, Adams, Richard   5:346–51
Watkins, Yoko K., *So Far from the Bamboo Grove*
   4:349–55
Watson, John Boradus   5:45
Weaver, George "Buck"   3:149
Weizmann, Chaim   4:102, 103
Weld, Theodore D.   2:242
Welles, Orson   3:365, 408
Wells Fargo   2:293
Wells, H. G.
   influenced by science and Darwinism   3:404–5
   on *Portrait of the Artist as a Young Man*   3:309
      (sidebar), 311
   rejection of Christianity   3:404
   War of the Worlds, The   3:404–10
Wells-Barnett, Ida B.   3:83, 420
Welty, Eudora, *Worn Path, A*   3:418–24
West, The
   California gold rush   2:174–75, 195, 249–50,
      281–84
   Chinese prostitutes   2:366–67
   gunfighters   2:323–24
   homesteaders   2:127 (sidebar), 128, 322–23;
      3:244, 257, 259, 260–61
   humor, practical jokes, and tall tales   2:250–51
   Nebraska   3:257–58, 260
   racism against Chinese   2:175, 287, 367–68,
      370 (sidebar), 371
   ranching and cattle barons on Great Plains
      2:321–22
   Teddy Roosevelt popularizing "Old West" myth
      of individualism   5:206
   settling and demise of frontier   2:312
   Wells Fargo   2:293
   women on frontier   2:323
West Side Story, Laurents, Arthur, *et al.*   4:384–90
Western migration
   beginning in colonial times   1:102, 103, 107
   California gold rush   2:174–75, 195, 249–50

Donner Party   2:282 (sidebar)
encouraged by Homestead Act (1870)
   2:322–23; 3:244, 257
encouraged by U.S. gov't.   2:314
end of western frontier   2:68
hardship and survivalism   3:259–60
increasing job opportunities for women in East
   2:423
land speculators   3:258
and Manifest Destiny   2:76 (sidebar); 3:234
and Mexican War   2:88, 395
to Nebraska   3:257–58
Nevada silver strikes   2:288–89, 290 (sidebar)
pressures upon American Indians   2:67, 74
railroads   2:175, 195
single women absent from   2:56, 250
(See also Gold rushes and silver strikes)
Weston, Jessie L.   3:415
Wet-nurses   2:211
Whaling industry   2:230, 232–34
Wharton, Edith
   Ethan Frome   2:125–29
   House of Mirth, The   3:166–73
Where Are You Going, Where Have You Been?, Oates,
   Joyce Carol   4:391–96
"White man's burden" and white supremacy
   2:119, 147, 341; 3:170, 172, 182 (sidebar)
Whitman, Walt
   on imperialism   3:300 (sidebar)
   Leaves of Grass   2:195–201
Whyte, William   4:75, 382
Wiesel, Elie
   Dawn   4:101–8
   Night   4:267–73
Wiesenthal, Simon   4:273
Wight, James Alfred. See Herriott, James
Wilder, Thornton, Our Town   3:284–89
Wilhelm II, Kaiser (Germany)   3:8
Wilkins, Roy   5:186, 188
William the Conqueror   1:250, 290
William of Orange   1:130
Williams, Claude "Lefty"   3:149; 4:260, 261; 5:316
Williams, Paulette Linda. See Shange, Ntozake
Williams, Tennesse, Streetcar Named Desire, A
   4:364–70
Williamson, Joel   3:387
Wilson, August, Fences   4:144–50
Wilson, Edmund
   praise for Animal Farm   4:19–20
   praise for The Waste Land   3:417
Wilson, Woodrow   3:279–80, 319
Winthrop, Gov. John   1:78, 352 (sidebar)
Witchcraft
   belief in, in medieval Scotland   1:227–28
   belief in, by Latinos (brujas)   4:46
   belief in, by Puritans   1:79–81, 102, 393, 394
   in The Crucible   1:78–86
   in The Devil and Tom Walker   1:101–6
   interest of James I in   1:228
   in Macbeth   1:227–28

spectral evidence of   1:421–22
   in Tituba of Salem Village   1:394–97
   witch trials   1:79, 83, 85 (illus.), 355, 395–96,
      397 (illus.), 423 (illus.)
   in Young Goodman Brown   1:420–26
   (See also Supernatural)
Wolfe, Tom, Right Stuff, The   5:291–97
Wollstonecraft, Mary
   as first English feminist   3:359
   mother of Mary Shelley   1:115, 116, 407
   similarities to, in Elizabeth Bennet   2:297
   tribute by William Blake   1:410 (sidebar)
   Vindication of the Rights of Woman, A   1:406–12
Woman Warrior, The, Kingston, Maxine Hong
   5:352–59
Women, (See also Education of women; Love and
   marriage)
Women in ancient times
   as "Great Goddesses" and Amazons   1:58–59,
      61–62, 258, 259–60
   in Greece   1:17, 20, 58–59, 259, 327
   names in Rome   1:190 (sidebar)
   Plato on leadership roles for   1:325, 327
   as rulers in Celtic England   1:197
   as spoils of war   1:8, 169, 170–71
Women in medieval times
   as depicted by Chaucer   1:69
   in Scotland   1:226
Women in 15th century, in salons of Paris   1:31,
   88–89
Women in 16th century
   prejudice against, as leaders   1:236
   in Tudor and Elizabethan England   1:232–33,
      236, 263–64
Women in 17th century, targeted in witchhunts
   1:80
Women in 18th century
   on colonial farms   1:334
   defiance of convention   1:406, 407, 409
   urging education and rights for   1:406, 408–11
   as wet-nurses   2:211
Women in 19th century
   American Southern ideal of, 2.138, 3.19m
      3:392–93
   Chinese   2:366–67, 368 (sidebar), 370–71
   in France   2:212, 244, 247
   involvement in abolition of slavery   2:23–24
   involvement in reform movements   2:423
   isolation of farms and homesteads   2:127
      (sidebar), 128; 3:259, 260–61
   in prostitution   2:228, 264, 283–84, 328–29,
      355; 4:37
   teaching freed slaves   2:411–12
   as wet-nurses   2:211
   (See also Victorian women)
Women in 20th century
   Chinese   3:132–33, 134–35, 191–93; 4:128
   dangers of childbirth   3:285–86
   as domestic, passive, and "feminine"   1:33–34,
      35–36; 2:326; 4:22, 74, 167, 237, 240–41

emancipation of
  negative portrayals in detective fiction of 1920s   3:228–29
  new freedoms of 1920s   3:147
  opponents and proponents   3:167
  single mothers of 1950s as "irrational"   4:169 (sidebar)
employment for   2:326; 3:271; 5:138
  as chorus girls   2:329
  as midwives   4:218
  as repugnant to Religious Right   5:137
  in wartime and afterwards   4:21–22, 74, 166–67, 196 (illus.), 197–98
fashions for. See Fashions
importance of marriage   3:168
Jewish   3:427–30
in Maoist thought   3:136
Mexican   3:197–98, 200–202
participation in Progressive Era's reform movements   3:75, 76
protesting Vietnam War   5:308
rural life
  isolation of   3:271
  for sharecropper families   3:370–71
  on Texas frontier   3:246
as sexual goddesses, sex objects   4:74, 393
as single heads of households   2:65; 3:80, 423; 4:2; 5:68, 117, 136, 138, 267, 328–29
subject to sexual double standard   4:38, 74, 395
and suicide   4:22–26
(See also African American women)
Women's rights movement (and feminism)
  abortion and Roe v. Wade   5:51, 136
  advocating self-determination   5:138–39
  antifeminist backlash   5:136
  authors active in
    Gilman   2:424
    Le Guin's take on   5:237–38
    Morrison   2:64
    Renault's sympathy with   1:62
    Woolf   3:330–32
  battered wives shelters   5:136
  and black feminism   2:64; 3:86–87, 354–55; 5:92–93, 117
  in Britain   3:359
  Chicana women's movement   3:202
  in czarist Russia   2:37, 39
  educated women at core of   5:135
  hiatus between 1918 and 1960s   5:135–36
  legislation affecting
    Civil Rights Act (1964), Title VII   1:35; 5:136
    Equal Pay Act (1963)   1:35; 5:237
    Equal Rights Amendment (ERA)   3:79; 5:51 (illus.), 136, 358–59
    Higher Education Act (1972), Title IX   5:136
  in Mexico   3:201–2
  National Organization of Women (NOW)   1:62; 4:22, 394; 5:136, 237

in Norway   2:112–13
origins in
  19th century   2:22, 24, 25, 27, 55, 204, 423; 3:16
  abolitionist movement   2:24, 204
  civil rights movement of 20th century   1:35; 2:58
  discontent of women in 1950s   4:167–70; 5:136
  EEOC's refusal to enforce Title VII   5:237
  Friedan's Feminine Mystique   1:62; 2:58; 3:430; 4:11 (sidebar), 167, 241, 394; 5: 136
  gender discrimination in workplace   1:35; 5:136
  myths of women's selfless inclination to serve and nurture   5:136, 288
  objections to sexual double standard   4:38, 74, 395
  oppression and discrimination   2:23–24, 355–56, 380, 422, 423–26
  sexual harassment in workplace   1:35
  women's subordination to men   4:169, 170
rape crisis centers   5:136
role of women's clubs   2:336; 3:16–17, 287 (sidebar)
in Victorian England   2:335
women's studies programs resulting   5:117
Women's rights and roles, discussion pertaining to
  Antigone   1:14–21
  Canterbury Tales, The   1:68–69
  Ethan Frome   2:126–27, 128–29
  Left Hand of Darkness, The   5:237–38, 239–40, 242
  Lottery, The   4:237
  Macbeth   1:226
  Maltese Falcon, The   3:228–29
  Midsummer Night's Dream, A   1:259–60, 261–64
  Noon Wine   3:246–47
  Odyssey   1:282, 285
  Of Mice and Men   3:271–72
  Passage to India, A   3:301–2
  Sweet Whispers, Brother Rush   5:329
  Turn of the Screw, The   2:378–83
  Worn Path, A   3:420–21
Women's rights and roles, literary works emphasizing
  "Ain't I a Woman?"   2:22–27
  Anna Karenina   2:34–40
  Awakening, The   3:15–20
  Beauty: A Retelling of the Story of Beauty and the Beast   1:30–36
  Bell Jar, The   4:21–27
  Belle of Amherst, The   2:54–58
  Beloved   2:59–65
  Bluest Eye, The   4:49–57
  Carrie   5:46–52
  Color Purple, The   3:80–87
  Daisy Miller   2:105–10
  Doll's House, A   2:111–17

For Colored Girls Who Have Considered Suicide When the Rainbow Is Enuf 5:115–21
Golden Notebook, The 4:165–70
Gone with the Wind 2:137–44
Handmaid's Tale, The 5:135–42
House of Mirth, The 3:166–73
House of the Spirits, The 5:163–70
House on Mango Street, The 5:171–77
I Know Why the Caged Bird Sings 4:201–8
Incidents in the Life of a Slave Girl 2:168–73
Jacob Have I Loved 4:216–20
Jane Eyre 1:415; 2:181–87
Joy Luck Club, The 5:229–35
Kitchen God's Wife, The 3:189–95
Like Water for Chocolate 3:196–202
Little Women 2:202–8
Madame Bovary 2:209–15
Medea 1:238–41
Member of the Wedding, The 4:254–59
O Pioneers! 3:257–63
Out of Africa 3:290–96
Pride and Prejudice 2:295–300
Prime of Miss Jean Brodie, The 4:303–8
Pygmalion 3:312–18
Rebecca 3:326–33
Room of One's Own, A 3:356–63
Scarlet Letter, The 1:351–57
Seventeen Syllables 4:330–36
Sister Carrie 2:327–33
Streetcar Named Desire, A 4:364–70
Sweet Whispers, Brother Rush (portions of) 5:329
Tess of the D'Urbervilles 2:353–59
Their Eyes Were Watching God 3:383–89
Thousand Pieces of Gold 2:366–71
Turn of the Screw, The 2:378–83
Vindication of the Rights of Woman, A 1:406–12; 2:297
Where Are You Going, Where Have You Been? 4:391–96
Woman Warrior, The 5:352–59
Wuthering Heights 1:413–19
Yellow Raft in Blue Water, A 5:360–66
Yellow Wallpaper, The 2:422–28
Yentl, the Yeshiva Boy 3:425–31
Women's suffrage
    achieved in 1919 and 1930 in Britain 3:359
    achieved in 1920 in U.S. 3:76, 287
    agitation for change 2:335–36; 3:16
    in California by 1911 3:271
    in Chile in 1952 5:167
    defeated in many states of U.S. 3:286–87
    denounced in Victorian Age 2:335
    expanding by 1890 2:424
    in Kansas (1861), although limited 2:424
    ratification denied in Alabama 3:392
    in Wyoming in 1869 2:323
Woodstock Music and Art Fair (1969) 5:65 (illus.), 324
Woolf, Virginia 5:42

Room of One's Own, A 3:356–63
Wordsworth, William 1:416
World War I
    Africa, impact on 3:292–93
    ambulance service 3:114
    British occupation of former Ottoman Empire 4:102
    casualties of 3:11 (sidebar)
    causes and outbreak 1:157–58; 3:8–9, 112–13, 411
    Italy's role in 3:113–14
    losses, destruction 1:157–58; 3:11 (sidebar), 411–12
    "lost generation" 3:13, 112, 116–17
    navies' roles in 1:277–78
    older generations supporting 3:9–11, 12–13
    Ottoman slaughter of Armenians 3:339–40
    postwar issues
        disillusionment and despair 3:227, 412
        German reparations, inflation, and unemployment 4:157
        global expansion 1:223; 3:21, 88
    proving H. G. Wells's fiction as prophetic 3:406
    racial issues
        African Americans as employees and soldiers 3:160, 252; 4:144, 145, 212–13
        segregation of U.S. military 4:212–13
    reasons for joining 1:278
    Russian defeats, civil war, revolution (1917) 3:232–33
    sacrifices on German home front 3:11
    technological enhancements of weaponry 3:113
    Treaty of Berlin (1921) 3:88
    trench warfare 3:9, 113, 115 (sidebar)
World War II
    American mobilization for 2:45; 3:424; 4:325
    America's prewar isolationism 4:323, 362
    aviation
        bomber crews 4:68–70
        Lindbergh's contributions to 3:367
    causes of 1:113–14; 4:157, 356–57
    chronology
        Nazi precursor conquests in Europe (1935–366) 1:113–14; 3:213, 214; 4:357
        British "appeasements" of Hitler (1936–39) 4:356, 357, 362
        Rome-Berlin Axis (1936) 4:67
        Stalin/Hitler nonaggression pact (1939) 3:210, 214; 4:357
        Poland partitioned by Germany and Soviet Union (1939) 4:131
        France and England declare war on Germany (1939) 3:214
        French unpreparedness (1939) 3:213–14
        Tripartite Pact (Japan, Germany, Italy; 1940) 4:59
        standoff at Maginot Line 4:357
        "blitzkrieg"; Germany invades Belgium, Luxembourg, and France 4:254–55, 357, 359

first American peacetime draft (1940)   **4**:*35,
    324–25*
Italy helps Nazis (1940)   **4**:*67*
German occupation of Holland (1940)
    4:*116–19*
Dunkirk, evacuation of (May 1940)   **4**:*356,
    359–63*
German invasion of Russia, (1941)   **3**:*124;*
    4:*131*
Pearl Harbor (1941)   **4**:*59, 178, 323*
Lend-Lease (1941–45)   **4**:*228–29, 363*
Pacific theater (1942–45)   **4**:*60–61, 80–81,
    178*
Philippines' Bataan Death March   **4**:*81*
Aleutian islands, battles for (1942–43)
    4:*254*
Allies establish North African base (1942–44)
    3:*214*
emergence of De Gaulle (1943)   **3**:*214*
Allied invasion of Sicily (1943)   **4**:*67*
Italy declares war on Germany (1943)   **4**:*67*
kamikazi missions (1944)   **4**:*61 (sidebar), 62
    (illus.)*
liberation of France (1944)   **3**:*214*
Battle of the Bulge (Dec. '44)   **4**:*343*
Yalta Conference (Feb. '45)   **4**:*344*
Dresden, firebombing by Allies (Feb. '45)
    4:*343–44*
founding of United Nations   **5**:*54*
atomic bombing of Japan (Aug. '45)
    4:*178–82, 180 (illus.), 181 (sidebar)*
Nuremberg war crimes trials of former Nazis
    4:*272–73*
conquests by dictatorships   **5**:*123 (sidebar), 224,
    253–54*
on home front
    for American South, industrialization and
        economic recovery from Depression   **2**:*53;*
        3:*72–73*
    cynicism and opportunism   **4**:*371*
    families of servicemen   **4**:*317–18*
    German prisoners of war   **4**:*371–73*
    intergenerational conflict   **4**:*327*
    media's partiotic emphasis on war issues
        4:*371*
    persecution and internment of Japanese
        Americans (1942–44)   **4**:*137–43, 194–95,
        335–36*
    race riots of 1940s   **4**:*197, 201, 213, 247,
        248 (illus.), 295–97, 403–10*
    racism   **4**:*199, 200*
    rationing and inflation   **3**:*424;* **5**:*256–57*
    women at work   **4**:*21–22, 74, 166–67, 196
        (illus.), 197–98*
importance of Churchill's rhetoric and
    determination   **4**:*361–62*
Palestine   **4**:*102–5*
postwar issues
    baby boom   **1**:*224;* **2**:*325–26;* **4**:*38, 74, 240*
    Britain   **4**:*229, 231;* **5**:*256–57*

emphasis on home and materialism
    2:*325–26*
Marshall Plan   **5**:*123–24, 224, 292*
(*See also* Cold War)
psychological casualties and postcombat
    syndrome   **4**:*80 (sidebar), 325*
racial issues
    African Americans as employees and soldiers
        3:*424*
    American Indians in   **4**:*80–81*
    Chicano rights movement watershed   **4**:*44*
    Latinos in   **4**:*295, 406*
    segregation of U.S. military   **3**:*41–42;* **4**:*195,
        197, 374 (sidebar)*
    (*See also* Holocaust)
reservists and regulars   **4**:*63 (sidebar)*
(*See also* Nazis)
Worn Path, A, Welty, Eudora   **3**:*418–24*
Wouk, Herman, *Caine Mutiny, The*   **4**:*58–65*
WPA (Works Progress Administration)   **3**:*128, 391,
    423–24;* **4**:*44*
Wright, Richard
    Almos' a Man   **4**:*1–6*
    on anti-Semitism of his youth   **4**:*376*
    Black Boy   **3**:*36–43*
    as critic of Hurston   **3**:*385, 389*
    Native Son   **3**:*236–42*
    on *The Heart Is a Lonely Hunter*   **3**:*157*
Wuthering Heights, Brontë, Emily   **1**:*413–19*
Wyoming, women's suffrage in 1869   **2**:*323*

X

X, Malcolm   **2**:*98;* **3**:*324–25;* **4**:*54, 249–50;*
    5:*69–70, 111*
    with Alex Haley, *Autobiography of Malcolm X, The*
        5:*11–18*

Y

Yamamoto, Hisaye, *Seventeen Syllables*   **4**:*330–36*
Yankees   **1**:*217, 332, 334, 335;* **2**:*8–9, 137*
Yeager, Chuck   **5**:*293*
Yellow Raft in Blue Water, A, Dorris, Michael
    5:*360–66*
Yellow Wallpaper, The, Gilman, Charlotte Perkins
    2:*422–28*
Yentl, the Yeshiva Boy, Singer, Isaac Bashevis
    3:*425–31*
Yorkshire, England   **1**:*417–18;* **3**:*1–3, 5–6*
Young Goodman Brown, Hawthorne, Nathaniel
    1:*420–26*
Young Turks   **3**:*339, 340, 342*
Youth
    adolescence in hiding from Holocaust   **4**:*121–22*
    antiestablishment rebellion   **5**:*272*
    and dance   **4**:*387*
    distinctive *pachuco* culture of 1950s   **4**:*173, 296*
    distinctive teenage culture of 1950s   **4**:*172,
        391–93, 394–95*

facing conflict and violence   **5**:*268–69*
gang membership   **4**:*251, 386, 387–89*; **5**:*216*
gang truce in Los Angeles   **5**:*341*
and generation gap   **4**:*386, 394*; **5**:*198*
juvenile delinquency   **4**:*251, 386, 387–89*; **5**:*37*
literature for adolescents, as genre   **5**:*61–62, 265–66, 268–70*
moral laxity of war years   **4**:*37*
peer pressure and negativity   **5**:*65–66, 71–72, 217*
protesting against Vietnam War   **5**:*271*
psychotherapy for   **5**:*260–61*
students' free speech movement   **5**:*311*
suicide by teenagers   **5**:*259–60, 261*
television as babysitter   **5**:*36–37*
television as too violent   **5**:*62*

Yukon territory and Klondike River   **3**:*52–56, 261 (sidebar)*

Z

Zapata, Emiliano   **3**:*197, 198 (illus.)*
Zen Buddhism   **4**:*334*
Zeus   **1**:*9, 59, 61, 170, 282, 283, 301*
Zindel, Paul, *Pigman, The*   **5**:*271–77*
Zionism   **3**:*121*; **4**:*88, 101–2*
    and Arabic anti-Zionism   **4**:*107*
    and Soviet anti-Zionism   **4**:*107–8*
Zoo Story, The, Albee, Edward   **4**:*397–402*
Zoot Suit, Valdez, Luis   **4**:*403–10*
Zundel, Ernst   **4**:*40*